D0838484

# BACKWARD GLANCES

# BACKWARD GLANCES

## PEOPLE AND EVENTS FROM INSIDE AND OUT

# CONRAD BLACK

SIGNAL

McCLELLAND
& STEWART

Hardcover edition published 2016

Signal is an imprint of McClelland & Stewart,
a division of Penguin Random House Canada Limited,
a Penguin Random House Company

Signal and colophon are registered trademarks of McClelland & Stewart

Library and Archives Canada Cataloguing in Publication is available upon request

Published simultaneously in the United States of America by Signal,
an imprint of McClelland & Stewart, a division of Penguin Random House Canada

Library of Congress Control Number is available upon request

ISBN: 978-0-7710-0920-4
ebook ISBN: 978-0-7710-0921-1

Typeset in Electra by M&S, Toronto
Cover and text design by Andrew Roberts

Printed and bound in USA

Published by Signal,
an imprint of McClelland & Stewart,
a division of Penguin Random House Canada Limited,
a Penguin Random House Company

www.penguinrandomhouse.ca

1   2   3   4   5     20   19   18   17   16

TO MY GOOD FRIENDS OVER MANY DECADES:
MONIQUE BENOÎT, ODETTE BEAUDOIN, JONATHAN
BIRKS, JACK COCKWELL, DAN COLSON, JUNE DOULL,
IVAN FECAN, ROBERT FRANCIS, JOHN FRASER, NAOMI
GRIFFITHS, HAL JACKMAN, LINDA RADCLIFFE, ANDREW
ROBERTS, JONATHAN ROBINSON, MURRAY SINCLAIR,
JR., MARC SOLE, BRIAN STEWART, LYN WESTWOOD,
PETER WHITE, KEN WHYTE, AND THE LATE MORTON
BERG, BERTHE BUREAU-DUFRESNE, SIR DAVID FROST,
ERIC JOHNSON, IGOR KAPLAN, CLIFFORD SCOTT, AND
MURRAY SINCLAIR, SR.

# CONTENTS

# ACKNOWLEDGEMENTS

As this is a collection of columns and essays already written, the efforts of fewer people were engaged than in previous books requiring a lot of research and organization. Once again, for the seventh time, I thank the always resourceful Joan Maida, my collaborator for twenty-seven years, as well as Danella Connors and Adam Daifallah, for their invaluable help in rounding up material. And again also, I thank my publisher and editor, Doug Pepper and Jenny Bradshaw, for their support and encouragement. My wife Barbara has shown her usual patience, even though she has been preoccupied with writing a real book, and had every reason to be less philosophical than she has been.

# FOREWORD

by Mark Steyn

In 2012, a fortnight or so before Conrad Black was released from jail, I chanced to have tea in Toronto with his wife, Barbara Amiel. Over the Darjeeling and finger sandwiches (we were at the King Edward), I observed that, say what you will about U.S. federal prison, it appeared to have had a remarkably invigorating impact on Conrad's writing. "Oh, please," sighed Barbara. "Do you know what it's like to marry a corporate titan and watch him slowly turn into a freelance writer?"

As the ensuing seven hundred pages demonstrate, Conrad has been working on this grim metamorphosis for some years. As a fellow grubbing hack, I'm heartened to see that he's managed to salvage a few essays spiked by fainthearted editors and publishers over the decades. I'm also glad to see some of the unspiked ones enjoy a wider circulation. The earliest piece in this collection goes back half a century, a paean to Lyndon Johnson written for the Sherbrooke *Record* in Quebec, then the flagship of Conrad's media empire (he also owned the *Eastern Townships Advertiser*). I have no idea what the good burghers of the Townships made of what was, for a small Québécois newspaper, an unusually in-depth analysis of foreign affairs, but south of the border, J.J. Pickle, Democrat of Texas, liked it enough to have it read into the *Congressional Record* (no relation to the Sherbrooke *Record*).

I have a vague memory of this article featuring in Conrad's trial in Chicago four decades later, when counsel for the defence brought it up during cross-examination of Black's turncoat business partner, whose name escapes me, as I trust it does Conrad. The former Number Two of the company had, as is customary in U.S. federal prosecutions, been prevailed upon to "cooperate" with the authorities in return for a perfunctory sentence. Conrad's lawyer put it to the stoolie that getting a piece from the Sherbrooke *Record* read into the *Congressional Record* surely testified to what a splendid job Black was doing as publisher. His disloyal deputy demurred. If memory serves, he said something to the effect that what mattered in newspapers was how much you could charge the proprietor of Bud's Discount Furniture Warehouse per display ad for his massive storewide clearances.

This has always been the creative tension in the newspaper trade, and in that respect Conrad Black has always been a publisher on the side of writers. Even those lefties who disagree with his politics (and I have to confess, as a bona fide right-wing madman myself, I find him a bit of a squish on some of the ground covered herein) should surely admit that his too-brief reign in Canadian newspapering was the last good time for the Dominion's journalism. Elsewhere around the world, in the rubble of the Hollinger empire, his successors have managed to render some of the great marquee names in newspapers feeble and irrelevant. Not long before he went to prison in Florida, I heard Conrad expound upon the secret of newspapering: "You have to have a feel for it," he said, and he did that thing he does whereby he cups and rotates his hand like a man either tuning a radio or tweaking a passing nipple. These days, very few people have a feel for it. And even when they do, few proprietors seek the company of writers except when they need someone to write them a speech for a conference on digital synergization and figure they might as well use someone already on the payroll.

By contrast, Black read his newspapers voraciously and enjoyed the company of selected writers, at least those who could write reasonably well while not being excessively "malodorous" (as he described certain of the less hygiene-conscious Fleet Street types attending his trial). It's something of an occupational hazard, I'm afraid.

The late songwriter Sammy Cahn liked to conclude assessments of Frank Sinatra's fine acting with the words: "And that's not even what he does!" And so it was for most of Black the businessman's adult life: writing is not even what he does, but he does it awfully well. Reading of some or other newly discovered great Canadian painter, I almost always recall a long-ago aside from Conrad that Canadian art mysteriously loses 90 per cent of its value whenever it leaves the country – which is cruel, but not untrue. And I recall this defining insight amidst the usual effusions in a sycophantic Festschrift on Pierre Trudeau: "I always found him a delightful conversationalist and a gracious host, though perhaps slow to reach for the bill in a restaurant, even when we were there on his invitation."

Very true. M. Trudeau left us with the bill, in every sense.

Whenever I'm asked about the modest craft of opinion journalism, I generally offer two tips: a column should try to include one fascinating fact with which readers can impress their friends at cocktail parties; and, more generally, it always benefits from historical perspective. Unlike so many of us in the pundit class, Conrad does not live in the endless whirring din of the present tense and is absolutely brimming with cocktail-party fascinating facts. Any writer will tell you that the hardest columns of all are the ones that through the vagaries of the calendar fall on Valentine's Day or Christmas Eve and one is obliged to say something about the occasion that hasn't been said a million times before. In these pages, Conrad's observance of Victoria Day is a masterpiece of the form, moving from fireworks and childhood reminiscence to the late Queen-Empress's critical role in the birth of Canadian self-government – and including such details as the fact that the wreath Her Majesty sent for Sir John A. Macdonald's funeral was placed on his coffin by the great-great grandfather of the CBC's Peter Gzowski, Sir Casimir. You can't really look up that kind of stuff as you're writing – well, you can, but it's time-consuming and, at Canadian freelance rates, it's not economically viable. Fortunately, Conrad doesn't need to: it all seems to be up there, jostling around in his head. During his trial, we were glimpsed one night at Spiaggia, which happens to be both President Obama's and Lord Black's favourite Chicago restaurant. A reporter asked me what aspect of the case we had been in such lively discussion over, and I replied that we'd been talking about John C. Breckinridge, the only vice-president who subsequently fled the United States to live in Canada (at least until Joe Biden escapes the Trump Terror for a retirement condo in Elliot Lake). I was mostly bluffing my way through the topic, but Conrad knew chapter and verse.

He was not to everyone's taste as a boss. There were many writers, comfortable in the bland, genteel decline of the Southam group under previous management, who objected to Conrad's takeover of the chain because supposedly he would be interfering with their journalistic integrity on weighty affairs of state. In fact, during all my years of labour in the Black salt mines, I can recall only two examples of proprietorial interference with what passes for my integrity. The *Sunday Telegraph* in London asked me to do a profile of Elton John, and the editor alerted me to the fact that Elt was a close pal of Conrad's and so it might be prudent to ease up on the fat-old-queen gags. The other occasion was over his fellow proprietor the *Washington Post*'s Katharine Graham, also a friend of the Blacks. On the latter, I ignored the editor's advice and trashed her mercilessly, which Conrad seemed to enjoy, if only for the low comedy. With Sir Elton, I blush to say that I did indeed mothball my integrity and dial back the shtick, which I'm rather glad I did, as he has proved a fast friend to Conrad during a decade of torment, as so many smaller men on both sides of the Atlantic have not. Elton's plea for clemency entered during the sentencing phase of Black's trial provoked the shrill twerp of a deputy U.S. attorney to roar in court the faintly surreal line "Does Elton John know the real Conrad Black?"

I think Elton does, and so will you by the end of this collection. He wrote his autobiography young, a third of a century ago, and, while it is small consolation, he has a much better story to tell today – of rise, and fall, and a kind of grace and redemption of which his writing is surely a part. That dramatic arc carries this book from the grand sweep of world affairs through the more personal reflections on the vicissitudes of life. Conrad Black is one of those writers whose work I can never read without hearing in it his distinctive voice. I used to spend time on the Lower North Shore of the St. Lawrence, where the only receivable television was francophone, and one would occasionally glimpse Conrad giving an interview *en français*. Like the Queen, he speaks near flawless French but in the same unmistakable measured cadences of his English, and it was always a pleasure to see him respond to some Radio-Canada popinjay with a magisterial *"mais c'est absolument ridicule!"* or some such.

There are those, both anglophone and francophone, who find this voice pompous. Certainly, the dime-store Javerts who hounded him down south found him so. And north of the border he made too unsympathetic a victim for the usual touchy maple-boosterists to care about the U.S. "justice" system's infringements of Canadian sovereignty. He went to prison for a "crime" that does not exist in any other Western nation, and which not even those who put him there can explain in a way that anybody comprehends. Indeed, its very impenetrability caused too many distinguished friends, including William F. Buckley and Henry Kissinger, to defer to his tormentors. As the most pro-American Canadian of his generation, Conrad was hopelessly naive about a United States Department of "Justice" that wins 97 per cent of its prosecutions, which success rate would make pikers like Saddam Hussein and Kim Jong-un blush. Sensing what was about to happen, I suggested he climb in the bed of my pickup and let me throw a tarp over him and spirit him across the Canadian border, where we would drive through the night to Newfoundland, hop a ferry to St. Pierre and Miquelon, and on the latter's small landing strip procure an aircraft to fly him beyond the grasp of the U.S. attorney. He was having none of it: he believed in America, and he believed that this great Republic's justice system would vindicate him. He was accused of a bazillion separate crimes, some of which fell away before the trial, others during jury deliberations. Of the small number of which he was convicted, almost all were vacated by a unanimous verdict of the U.S. Supreme Court. The trial judge was ordered to reconsider the remaining charge, and Conrad was released from jail, albeit only temporarily. I urge you to read his statement to the court at his "resentencing hearing" (page 683):

"The Prosecutors have never ceased to accuse me of being defiant of the law, of disrespecting the courts, and of being an antagonistic critic of the American justice system. Nothing could be further from the truth. . . . What I have done is exercise my absolute right to legal self-defence, a right guaranteed to everyone who is drawn into the court system of this and every other civilized country."

How pitiful that it requires a foreigner to say such things to an American judge. Conrad did not seem to understand that it's not about guilt or innocence; it's about "settling." A businessman is supposed to recognize that it's just business, just another deal: You don't want to exercise your right to a fair trial, pally, because we've got unlimited resources and we can buy as many witnesses as we need. The "co-operative" business partner's negotiated settlement permitted him to serve eighteen months, and in a Canadian "penitentiary" off the coast of British Columbia, a prison regime so gruelling and punitive that its brochure advertises in-house activities such as horseback riding and amateur theatre. So Black's deputy departed for a slightly longer than usual summer camp of gymkhanas and playing third gambler on the left in Cell Block E's acclaimed production of *Guys and Dolls*. As for Conrad, one of the many intriguing aspects of the fine print in U.S. justice is that, unlike other white-collar criminals, he was not eligible for minimum security prison – whether because he was Canadian or a member of the House of Lords I forget, but presumably both are high-risk categories. So he was imprisoned with rapists and drug dealers and whatnot and became, as he put it, "one more unjustly imprisoned Black man."

Every aspect of federal prison is designed to crush the human spirit. I confess that I thought it would crush Conrad's. Instead, swapping the company of the very highest in the land for that of the very lowest did indeed in some strange way deepen and enrich his writing. He liked his jail mates, and they liked him. Through it all, he has eschewed self-pity, not least in his dignified reaction to the Canadian state's pathetic catch-up me-tooism, culminating in his disgraceful expulsion from the Order of Canada and the Privy Council. In a passing reference while noting the death of the great Václav Havel, Black acknowledges "the consciousness-raising experience of being sent to prison." He shouldn't have had to have his consciousness raised by the Federal Bureau of

Prisons, and he shouldn't have had to suffer the petty indignity of being stripped of his post-nominals. But in the end a writer needs only his name. No longer chairman or chief executive, CC or PC, he stands on the quality of his writing and the authority of his byline: Conrad Black.

Mark Steyn

# AUTHOR'S NOTE

Collections of past writings are a lazy and often dubious excuse for writing a book, and I can only plead that the relaunch of my commercial career has afforded me less time to write an original non-fiction book than I had when I was chiefly preoccupied by the antics of the American justice system and its Canadian emulators. I have tried to deal with a wide variety of issues and people and events over forty-five years of writing. I ask readers to remember that most important subjects require the attention of a columnist on a number of different occasions and that many columns are to some extent old wine in new bottles. The complete elimination of repetition would have required more extreme editorial surgery on a few pieces than seemed to me to be appropriate. I beg a greater degree of indulgence of repetition to reset the stage for two or three opinions expressed on evolving subjects than I would normally have any right to ask.

Conrad Black
Toronto, June 2016

| BACKWARD GLANCES

# CANADA

## THE MENACE POSED BY A YUPPIE-RIDDEN LUMPENPROLETARIAT

*Report on Business Magazine*, v.3, #4, October 1986

The desultory roundel about free and freer trade is a great deal more important than the absurd character of much of the discussion would, at first, incline one to believe. Most adult Canadians were raised believing in the imperishable prosperity of our country because of limitless natural resources.

At a time when base and precious metals and forest products appeared to be in short supply and wars were erupting ostensibly in the pursuit of resources, *Lebensraum*, and "co-prosperity," Canada's benign destiny appeared to have been clearly disclosed. Postwar waves of European immigration confirmed us in our confident belief that the world would beat a path to our door. Our dollar was at a premium to the U.S. dollar, it was widely believed by Canadians, because Canadians were, if not exactly more industrious, at least more reliable than Americans.

Forty years ago, the United States was the only other large developed country that had not been economically devastated by war. Japan was burned out, presided over by General MacArthur, and not expected to have industrial ambitions much beyond the production of paper fans, *Mikado* stage sets, and plastic flowers for the balance of this century. We have watched with a passivity that has rarely roused itself from an indolent torpor as virtually all these bygone assumptions were rendered obsolete.

Countries which in those times were thought to be inhabited by peasant denizens of mud or thatched or corrugated-steel huts, raising sinew-lean arms to the heavens in frustration at their primitiveness, have risen to great manufacturing prowess. In the process, the Japanese and others have exploited the greed and short-sightedness of many other nationalities to promote an oversupply of almost everything that was bountiful in Canada. Gluttonous companies like Inco so abused their market domination that they made economical the development of vast alternate sources all around the world, transforming themselves into marginal and often money-losing producers.

Canada's performance in secondary industry has been, on balance, mediocre. There have been some uplifting exceptions such as Spar, Bombardier, and Magna, but generally Canadian manufacturing is concentrated between Windsor and Oshawa and around the City of Montreal, and is largely auto-related, branch-plant, heavily protected, or very marginal.

We have adjusted to the emergence of powerful and highly motivated economic rivals by debasing our currency, pampering and over-unionizing our workforce, harassing our local capitalists with fatuous hectoring about "concentration," a unique Canadian self-flagellation applied to the successful, and by a steady descent into overregulation, excessive taxation, protectionism, and Orwellian newspeak.

This is especially pronounced in Ontario, where the Liberals are in office and the NDP in power. While Bill Davis was not easily recognizable as a Conservative, the present regime, despite the saner instincts of many ministers and Premier David Peterson's own moderation, is busily trying to turn the province into a yuppie-ridden lumpen-proletariat. Teeming locust-swarms of NDP leader Bob Rae lookalikes will decree comparative pay levels, categorizing jobs without regard to merit, means, or utility (and calling it "pay equity"). The (aptly defined) provincial state will interpose itself between employer and employee; doctor and patients (who now may not give presents to their physicians, even at Christmas or birthdays); testator and beneficiary; landlord and tenant; spouse and spouse. All is "reform"; complacency is "quality of life"; fiscal profligacy is "compassion"; protectionism is decontamination, if not "cultural sovereignty"; confiscation is fairness; authoritarianism is progressive enlightenment. It is not even *Animal Farm*; it is just Ontario NDP pigsty. "High Marx for the nanny state," as columnist Barbara Amiel, [who, I am very happy and proud to mention, became my wife in 1992] used to say (though it is now almost equal measures of Groucho and Karl).

The only obvious alternative to circling and then penetrating the socialist drain is greater competition. The Americans, from a much more exalted position of self-serving mythology and postwar world dominance, have responded differently than Canada to the challenges both countries have faced. Uncompetitive industries have gone to the wall; people have moved to resources instead of the other way round; unionization levels have fallen steeply; strikes are rare and unpopular; taxes lower and simpler. The only society in the history of the world to have an extensive social-security system, an enormous defence establishment, and a predominant private sector has now had fourteen consecutive quarters of rising prosperity. During this period, the Reagan administration has tolerated foreigners dumping an extraordinary amount of finished goods and raw materials in the United States in order to accelerate the rationalization and modernization of U.S. production and render it competitive. Now the gates are closing on the one era in American history when the United States has favoured free trade.

The People's Republic of Ontario has been built on the Auto Pact and the economic collapse of Quebec and Alberta. There is no alternative to increased access to the U.S. market, except, as Allan Gotlieb recently told Barbara Frum, "the slippery slope and the hangman's rope." The only durable tenet of Pierre Trudeau's foreign policy was the Third Option (North-South and the Third Track being, mercifully, short-lived infatuations). Trudeau laboured mightily from 1973 to 1984 to increase trade with Western Europe, but, in that period, exports to Western Europe as a proportion of total Canadian trade were cut in half. It is fraud to suggest that there is any path to Canadian prosperity except increased competitive access, especially for manufacturers, to the U.S. market.

Admission to the monetary Group of Seven will make it difficult for us to go on falsifying competition by devaluing our currency.

Driving straight into the socialist abyss and enjoying the conversion of Humpty Dumpty is the only other way to wean Canada away from its smug insularity and artificial support programs. It would be a national, as well as a joint personal, tragedy if Brian Mulroney lost or John Turner won for the wrong reasons. Much freer continental trade is an idea whose time has come, and an opportunity which could quickly fly away.

# CANADA'S CONTINUING IDENTITY CRISIS

*Foreign Affairs*, Summer 1995

## THE PROBLEM THAT WON'T GO AWAY

F oreign observers are often incredulous that Canada, with a long history of domestic tranquility, heroism in war, and solidarity in the Western Alliance, is again threatened by the secession of Quebec after 128 years of Confederation. Astonishingly, a land that is almost as immaculate as Scandinavia and is almost the only serious country in the world whose general level of real prosperity approaches that of the United States now faces the possibility of constitutional dissolution.

Almost none of Canada's twenty-eight million people live in what would qualify in the United States as a slum-dwelling. The population is 88 per cent of European origin. Polls consistently indicate that more than 90 per cent of English-speaking Canadians and almost as great a percentage of French Canadians believe they live in the world's most pleasantly habitable country, and the United Nations has recognized Canada's quality of life as the highest of any country in the world for the last two years.

Yet in the autumn of 1994, Quebec, which is over 80 per cent French-speaking and has about a quarter of the country's whole population, narrowly elected a government pledged to achieve its independence, though this was a secondary election issue to be dealt with in a subsequent refer-endum. The new premier, Jacques Parizeau, served in the only previous avowedly separatist government of Quebec, which held office from 1976 to 1985 and was defeated 60 to 40 per cent when it asked the voters of Quebec in 1980 to authorize negotiation of Quebec's independence.

The issue of Quebec's continued participation in Canada has been bandied about in influential Quebec circles since shortly after the British conquest in the Seven Years War, and Quebec's indepen-dence has been an explicit political option endorsed by one or another of the province's political parties for more than thirty years. Parizeau himself, a jovial and florid sixty-four-year-old former *haut fonctionnaire* and university professor, seems less the torch-bearing awakener of a new nation than the ultimate Molièresque bourgeois. He scrupulously avoids the word *independence* and has pledged instead to have the provincial parliament (which has called itself the National Assembly of Quebec for twenty-five years) declare that Quebec is a sovereign state and to ask the voters' approval of this step this year, probably by the summer.

Parizeau's definition of sovereignty is extremely fuzzy and includes retention of Canadian passports, Canadian money, membership in NAFTA and the WTO, and even the British Commonwealth. The federal government's participation in this constitutional minuet is so far con-fined to the humbug that it has no legitimate authority to negotiate the secession of a province.

Parizeau and his separatist predecessors have generally tried to sell a version of sovereignty that essentially combines all the advantages of Canadian Confederation with the exaltation of soul sought in indepen-dent statehood. Though he is studiously vague on the point, he would presumably seek to issue Quebec passports and currency after a decent interval of adjustment. Polls at year-end 1994 continue to show a mod-est majority against sovereignty, but it remains to be seen whether the attempt to sugar-coat such a drastic step in gradualism and ambiguity will sedate or alarm the province.

## WHAT IS A CANADIAN?

Historically, Canada was a collection of people who weren't Americans: French Canadians abandoned by France in 1763 after the British military victory; Empire Loyalists who fled the American Revolution; immigrants and fugitives from Europe and recently other places, including the United States but also including many who couldn't gain entry to the United States; Newfoundlanders, who narrowly elected to become a Canadian province in 1949 after going bankrupt as an autonomous dominion. Though Canada has by most criteria been very successful, it has not thus far succeeded as a politically coherent entity whose institutional permanence or even durability could be assumed. Until the last twenty years or so, there persisted a self-conscious aura of the secondary and the derivative and a spirit of envy and insecurity, especially vis-à-vis the United States.

For most of its history, the rationale for the country was provided by the British connection and the French fact – francophones made up a third, though more recently only about a quarter, of the population – as well as a diffuse but not normally antagonistic fear of the United States. As the British connection slackened under the weight of years, immigration from central and southern Europe, and the pervasive American influence, the French population flirted evermore explicitly with outright independence as the Holy Grail waiting at the end of nearly four hundred years of their history.

Over the last twenty years or so, the federal government, through grants to many cultural institutions and strong influence on public broadcasting and the National Film Board and a strenuous emphasis of national symbols and festivals, has successfully promoted, at least among the English-speaking population, a more self-confident view of Canada. Great folkloric stress has been placed on the physical grandeur of the country, on the one million lakes, rivers, and streams of Canada which provide 30 per cent of the world's fresh water. What was once less solemnly described as "the cry of the loon and the dip of the paddle" has assumed considerable mythic proportions. Parallel to the awakening of Quebec, the rest of Canada has undoubtedly become less self-conscious about its status as an entity distinct, if not always easily distinguishable, from the United States. This effort has not been notably successful in rallying Quebec to a pan-Canadian view but it has elevated English-speaking Canada's view of itself.

Like medieval theologians in arcane dogmatic debate, Canadians have constantly redefined the national mission, to distinguish the country from the United States. The identity problem is accentuated by the ease with which Canadians can integrate in the United States. Canada is surpassed only by the British Isles, Germany, Italy, and Mexico as a source of immigrants to the United States.

Among the 4.4 million Canadians who have made this easy trek are Zbigniew Brzezinski, Alexander Graham Bell, Saul Bellow, John Kenneth Galbraith, Peter Jennings, Dean Acheson's father, and many screen personalities, including one of America's principal images of Abraham Lincoln, Raymond Massey, and "America's sweetheart," Mary Pickford. Apart from the habitual pronunciation of a handful of words, English-speaking Canadians are almost impossible to distinguish from people of the neighbouring American states.

Thus any definition of Canada's purposes as an independent country must be based on advantages that could not be found in a union with the United States. In these circumstances, Canada's political, academic, journalistic, and bureaucratic elites, which tend to be rather pallid and unoriginal beside their American counterparts with whom proximity invites comparison, spontaneously devised the new national mission of being "more caring and compassionate" than the Americans. The comparison between elites may be rather unfair, as the United States has nine times Canada's population and thirteen times English Canada's, but unlike Europe, where there are groups of principal and secondary countries, in North America, on a daily basis, Canada has only the United States as a point of comparison. In absolute terms it is bound to be a difficult yardstick.

This endeavour to promote Canada as a more generous and peaceable country began innocuously enough with universal medical care, rigorous gun control, and a larger public-sector share of GNP than the United States. But the notion of government as friend was central to the British colonization of central and western Canada. In the statute establishing Canada's autonomy in 1867, "peace, order and good government" are the stated objectives which roughly correspond to "life, liberty and the pursuit of happiness" in Jefferson's Declaration of Independence.

British and succeeding Canadian authorities had generally less difficulty with North American Indians than the United Sates did, and Canada's less complex sociology and strict gun control rules, on the British model, have undoubtedly made Canada a more peaceable country than its neighbour. (Sociology has surely had more to do with it than the gun laws, which almost amount to a constitutional prohibition against bearing arms.) American per capita murder rates are four times Canada's, and the United States has seven times as many imprisoned people per capita as Canada. [Little did I imagine that I would add to the American numbers.] Successive generations of Canadians have been fascinated but horrified by the U.S. Civil War, southern lynchings, American gangland struggles, race riots, and more recent variants of U.S. urban violence, none of which has had easily discernible Canadian counterparts.

With this comparative gentleness, Canada's unsuccessful receive a good deal more from the state, and the most accomplished are less appreciated and more highly taxed than in the United States. Not coincidentally, significant numbers of successful Canadians steadily move to the United Sates, with little flow of people in reverse, though the gap is made up, to some degree, by immigration to Canada from abroad.

Canada has spontaneously adopted a protective notion of public policy more like the Scandinavian model of climatically and ethnically more comparable countries than the individualism of the more temperate and diverse United States, a country founded by revolution and built essentially by individual initiative. The Canadian social safety net has become a hammock relative to the American one (other than for the elderly: the U.S. social-security system is more generous to the aged than its Canadian counterpart), while Canadian tax levels have gone as far above American levels as they can without causing a human wave of economic refugees to cross the famously unguarded U.S. frontier. Prior to recent reductions in tobacco sales taxes and the most recent decline in the relative value of the Canadian dollar, there were tremendous binges of cross-border shopping and smuggling by Canadians.

In order to sustain its chosen national vocation as an ambitious redistributor of wealth, Canada has massaged an inordinate proportion of national resources from the most to the less wealthy regions, especially to Quebec, which has happily accepted tens of billions of dollars of "equalization payments" and other preferments and now threatens to secede without being altogether convincing about shouldering its per capita share of the national debt. Western Canada, which has long felt underrepresented in a central government it has considered obsessed with placating Quebec, has become almost as disenchanted with that government as Quebec and in the 1993 federal election voted almost as regionally as Quebec did in electing mainly the western-based Reform Party. This new movement wants to revisit many of the bilingual and redistributive assumptions of modern Canadian federalism. The whole process of taking money from those regions and individuals who have earned it and redistributing it to those who haven't has saddled a fundamentally rich country with a back-breaking amount of debt.

A conservative definition of public-sector debt (excluding unfunded pension liabilities and the debt of state-owned companies) yields a total about equal to the GNP (around C$700 billion). The federal government elected in 1993, unable to dodge altogether the implications of elemental arithmetic, has made purposeful noises about reducing the federal deficit from its recent 13 per cent rate of compound growth to about 3 per cent, so the ratio between public-sector debt and GNP would cease to deteriorate. At time of writing, the seriousness of its commitment to this goal was still unclear and currently rising interest rates aggravate the problem. Most of the ten provinces, including Quebec, also have chronic debt problems, and no influence over monetary policy.

With public-sector wage settlements showing the way, the wage component of primary and secondary industries' production costs have almost steadily increased over more than thirty years compared to those in the United States and elsewhere. "Competitiveness" has been maintained despite declining relative productivity, by devaluing the Canadian dollar by about 30 per cent in the same period relative to the U.S. dollar (and by over 5 per cent in 1994 alone). Wage settlements have belatedly responded to recessionary conditions, and the latest economic growth and productivity figures are favourable, but a slow erosion of the relative value of the currency has remained the principal contributor to the current trade surplus.

Ontario, which provides half of Canada's GNP, added to the country's problems in 1990 by electing a camp socialist provincial government. This regime has raised taxes, institutionalized political correctness, and delivered the commanding heights of the economy over to the Luddites of local organized labour (who yet have the effrontery to profess that the provincial government's concessions have been insufficient).

All indications are that the electors will liberate Ontario's governing legislators to spend more time with their families after the provincial election later this year. That government has made a deathbed effort to conform to economic realities as perceived by most others, including the principal bond rating agencies. (It has added $33 million per day to the province's debt for four and a half years.) In the provincial public sector, salary caps have been imposed in exchange for job security, and encouraging noises have finally been made to the long-suffering private sector. This remedial course correction came, however, after Ontario had already become the unwitting author of one of the Unites States' greatest job creation programs since the New Deal. Approximately half a million Ontario jobs were lost from 1991 to 1993. Many were lost due to the recession and about a third have now been recovered, but a very large number permanently decamped to more employer-friendly jurisdictions in the United States.

## THE KINDNESS OF NEIGHBOURS

The theory of Canada's superior generosity as a society (which in practice means more socialistic and less violent) conveniently encompasses the system of inter-regional transfers designed to keep Quebec in the country as Canada wrestles with its identity crisis. Canada has had the very questionable distinction since 1982 of being the only country in the history of the world to establish regional economic equality as a constitutional raison d'être. In order to give the Danegeld paid to Quebec as equalization payments some intellectual uniformity, while

emphasizing the tangible virtues of federalism, a formula for transferring money from "have" to "have-not" provinces was established in
the 1950s. In 1982 this quest for regional economic equality was elevated
to a constitutionally entrenched national objective, although there is
no successful precedent for transferring resources to people rather than
the other way round. (The only way for Newfoundlanders to achieve a
standard of living comparable to Alberta's is for large numbers of them
to move to Alberta.)

Quebec's most successful political leader, Maurice Duplessis – who
by persuading conservatives and nationalists to vote together (for him)
governed Quebec almost uninterruptedly from 1936 until his death
in 1959 – used to say that the Quebec nationalists were like a "ten
pound fish on a five pound line. They have to be reeled in and let
out with great care." His successors have generally lacked Duplessis's
dexterity. English Canada has responded to Quebec's relentless jurisdictional demands with good will, and Canada undoubtedly possesses,
whatever the future may hold, a considerable natural talent at endless good faith negotiations producing occasional minor agreements.
(Canada's inter-regional discussions may have contributed to its flair for
international peacekeeping; it has provided about 10 per cent of United
Nations peacekeepers.) A well-known Canadian historian described
the country, in light of Canada's profound ambiguities, as "strong only
in moderation and governable only by compromise."

In the 1950s, the regional economic equalization program was promulgated by the federal government of Louis St. Laurent. In the 1960s,
full concurrence of Quebec in direct taxation was conceded by Lester
Pearson's government. In the 1970s, official bilingualism was promoted
throughout the country by Pierre Trudeau, in packaging, broadcasting, access of individuals to the federal government, and organization
of the federal civil service. In the 1980s and early 1990s, unsuccessful
attempts at constitutional devolution which would have enhanced the
authority of all the provinces were made by the Mulroney government.
Canada was already the most decentralized advanced country in the
world except for Switzerland. The provinces controlled property, civil
rights, education, almost all welfare programs except unemployment

insurance, most natural resources, and much of taxes. Under Mulroney's plans, they would also effectively have taken over the nomination of Supreme Court justices, of directors of the central bank, and of members of a strengthened federal upper house of Parliament, and at least concurrent jurisdiction in matters of immigration and radio and television licensing.

Despite the fact that the last of Mulroney's schemes was supported by all three federal political parties and all ten provincial governments, who tried prodigiously to mobilize support for it in a national referendum in October 1992, 54 per cent of Canadians voted against it. There was an apparent majority of both English- and French-speaking voters against the accord, though for different reasons. English Canada effectively said to Quebec that it would not countenance any further jurisdictional dismemberment of the federal state.

Quebec apparently rejected the second arrangement out of pique at the failure of the first arrangement, which some of the other provinces failed to ratify because Quebec had exercised the provincial right to overturn Supreme Court rulings in matters of civil rights and legislated that commercial signs could only be unilingually French. Bilingual signs were banned. For a country that is 75 per cent English-speaking, which deluges billions of dollars of federal largesse annually on its French-speaking compatriots, and has a long and admirable commitment to freedom of expression including original subscription to Roosevelt and Churchill's Atlantic Charter (composed by them in Newfoundland in 1941), this was an unacceptable provocation. The constitutional dialogue broke down in 1992 and has not resumed.

Quebec was clearly not rejected or treated disrespectfully in the referendum of October 1992, but the English-speaking federalist majority of Canada was unwilling to strip its government any more to appease the sovereigntist appetite of Quebec – abetted, as is the Canadian pattern, by the premiers of the other provinces. If constitutional powers are being dispensed, they all happily join the queue behind Quebec.

On the heels of this remarkable repudiation of the political class, Canadians eliminated two of the country's three national historic political parties in the general election of 1993. The governing Progressive

Conservative Party emerged with just two MPs and the left-wing New
Democrats were whittled down to 6 per cent of the vote from their
normal position in the 20s, partly in response to the inanities of their
colleagues in the government of Ontario.

Not since the collapse of the British and American Whigs in the
mid-nineteenth century has an advanced country with a history of
strong and continuous party affiliations eliminated an established political party. For so placid an electorate as Canada's has traditionally been,
to banish two-thirds of its parties to the dustbin of history was a seismic
change.* Canada has no history of referendary revolts, taxpayers' strikes,
or electoral recall of high public-office holders in midterm unlike the
United States and some other countries. The Western world's most successful party of government, the Liberal Party of Canada, which has
been in power for nearly seventy of the last hundred years, won a strong
mandate in 1993, with the opposition fragmented between the Quebec
separatists, running implausibly in a federal election, and the western
conservatives of the Reform Party.

The Progressive Conservatives had been a coalition of regionally
discontented elements, but Mulroney's well-intentioned gamble on
constitutional reform provoked the desertion of the West on perceived
excessive concessions to Quebec and the alienation of Quebec over the
Conservative government's inability to secure western approval of those
concessions.

In the gentlest, most quintessentially Canadian way, English
Canadians have invited Quebec to adhere to Canada or go from it,
but to stop implicitly threatening secession in the absence of further concessions. It is neither an ultimatum nor a rejection, but a
fatigued statement in a spirit many Quebeckers share. What Duplessis
described nearly fifty years ago as the federal–provincial *circonférences*
can not continue. Thus Canada has now reached the point where
neither of its two distinctive missions – socialistic welfare statism and
coddling Quebec – is tenable. Tax levels are excessive, debt levels are

---

* Two of them regrouped to form the Conservative Party government and official opposition to come, and the NDP regrouped, temporarily to surpass, and then to resume, its
traditional status.

unsustainable, the brain drain to the United States has not abated, and Quebec has again elected an avowedly separatist government, albeit with a paper-thin plurality and absolutely no mandate to secede.

## CAN THE CENTRE HOLD?

Canadians and, for once, the world are curious to know whether the country will make itself whole, sunder, or muddle through as it has so often before. Always before when the Quebec nationalists contested with the sober bourgeois spirit of Quebec's Breton- and Norman-descended people for the province's destiny, prudence has prevailed. Few Quebeckers have any real interest in Canada other than as a matter of economic convenience, and Quebec demonstrated during the free trade (with the United States) debate of 1988 that it considers English Canada's attempts to distinguish itself from the Americans to be completely spurious. (This judgment may be a little harsh, but such distinctions are at least as subtle as those that separate Texans from Oregonians or Californians from New Englanders.)

While Quebec was pushing on an open door and accepting pre-emptive concessions from an English Canada whose elites, at least, attached considerable credence to Quebec's well-rehearsed grievances about having been treated as the second-class descendants of a conquered people, secession seemed logical enough. Yet the federal government has been led from Quebec for all but eleven of the past forty-seven years. (Under prime ministers Louis St. Laurent, 1948–1957; Pierre Trudeau, 1968–1979, 1980–1984; Brian Mulroney, 1984–1993; and Jean Chrétien, since 1993). English Canadians have lately made a huge effort to accommodate and promote the French language, filling French-immersion schools across western Canada. Despite pervasive efforts by Quebec's nationalist demagogues to unearth francophobic incidents in English Canada, such as one school where French- and English-speaking children were supposedly (but improbably) assigned different lavatories, there is minimal French–English social friction. Such discrimination as exists is now more often practised by Québécois on the English-speaking minority in that province, as in the banning of bilingual commercial signs – even sidewalk chalkboards describing the daily specials of restaurants in French *and* English. This parochial imbecility has attracted the disapproval even of the United Nations but has probably helped to satisfy bloodlessly French Canada's long-repressed lust for self-assertion. (Perhaps the late Northrop Frye, one of Canada's most distinguished academics, was right when he said of Quebec, in 1990: "The more separatist its policies, the more inevitably provincial their characteristics.")

Yet this sort of authoritarian retribution has its limits, and has probably reached them, even in a country where almost everyone is endowed with an officially recognized grievance by virtue of geography, ethnicity, gender, sexual proclivity, or physical or psychological challenges. (In Canada, governmentally designated victims outnumber the entire population because of the possibility of accumulating conditions of victimization like food stamps.) Canada is doubtless outgrowing the victim culture, as a recent ground-breaking refusal to apologize to Ukrainian and Chinese Canadians for the treatment of their ancestors prior to and during the First World War indicates. For a time at least, Canada's febrile search for victims of every conceivable abuse, from ethnic disparagement to sexual harassment, provided the coruscation of the efforts of the misguided architects of official "care and compassion." Canada became, in some respects, the most politically correct country in the world.

English Canada has done a full and costly penance for two centuries of ignoring and perhaps slightly condescending to the French. The French Canadians have an unbroken record of canny political attention to their self-interest. By any reckoning, Quebec's independence would be complicated, costly, and at best an exhilarating and frightening voyage into the unknown.

There is a powerful body of opinion, in English- and French-speaking Canada, that wishes to bring the long-standing uncertainty over Quebec's future to an end. Most Canadians agree that the process of having a plebiscite on the future of Canada conducted in Quebec alone every ten to fifteen years must stop.

Because the rest of Canada is no longer prepared to make concessions of authority to appease Quebec, Quebec will finally have to

decide whether it really wishes to participate in Canada or not. I pre-
dict that Parizeau's attempt to back into independence via a fraudulent
referendum on sovereignty within Canadian Confederation will be
rejected as a scam, probably by the Québécois but if necessary by the
countries with which he would seek to exchange embassies.

A narrow plurality for his version of sovereignty, while it would
aggravate existing instability in Canada, would not be believable to
anyone as the birth of a nation. The English-speaking majority in
western Quebec and the native people of the vast northern regions
of the province (to which Canada would have a serious legal claim)
would immediately announce their continued adherence to Canada.
The fledgling state of Quebec would be resistless against these developments, no matter how much sovereignty it had purported to confer
upon itself.

Parizeau and the other separatist leaders are unwilling to present
independence otherwise than as a painless and almost imperceptible
conclusion of an inexorable process of nature. In fact most Québécois
should know that a sovereigntist majority is more likely to lead to an
economic and political shambles, at least temporarily, than to a brave
new world, and I doubt that the sophisticated Quebec voters, who have
played their hand so astutely for all of Canada's democratic history of
155 years, will give the separatists more than the 40 per cent they won in
the 1980 referendum. Since almost all parties are determined to resolve
this issue once and for all and the federalists will make no more concessions, such a defeat for the separatists should mean that the option
has been finally rejected and is closed.

If this prognosis is correct, the political insecurity that has so
tortured Canada throughout its history could swiftly recede, leaving
Canada a far more vigorous and self-possessed nation than it has been.
If by some confluence of circumstances the separatists were to prevail,
however, their victory would also open interesting possibilities for the
rest of the continent.

Deprived of the principal source of its distinctiveness opposite
the United States, post-Quebec English Canada would doubtless profess a determination to carry on without its reluctant and gangrenous
French partner, like Churchillian Britain in 1940. In fact, truncated,

debt-ridden, demoralized, mired in the Ozymandian constitutional wreckage of a binational country, defining itself in large part through (overrated) social programs, and prone to regional centrifugation only slightly less jarring than Quebec's, Canada would finally put its original differences with the United States to the supreme test.

The only real difference between English Canada and the United States is political and ideological. The Empire Loyalist forebears of English Canada believed in the hierarchical imposition of peace and order by legitimate authority. They fled the democratic republic where all unallocated powers reside with the citizens, and their descendants are still frightened and enthralled by the fermentation of the American political process. The loyalty of the original English-speaking Canadians was to the sovereign. They were, by definition, "statists" and so, relatively, have their descendants remained. The founders of the United States were individualists and the nation that has just elevated congressmen Gingrich and Armey has remained essentially faithful to that concept also.

Without Quebec, the four Atlantic provinces and the far west would have occasion to reappraise their membership in what would have become an incoherent confederation. The continuing provinces and territories would almost still qualify as a G7 economy with about twenty-one million homogenous well-trained, rather law-abiding people living in a narrow ribbon along the American border of a vast, rich land. Finally, Canada would have to learn whether the identity it has been trying to define for nearly two hundred years has any substance or not. In these circumstances, the secession of Quebec and the retrenchment of Canada, I suspect the unabated might of the United States, the world's only superpower, would be more magnetic at least to its kindred and intimate neighbour than ever (assuming crime rates continued to decline and America appeared to be solving some of its gravest urban problems). Especially in a world where the principal alternate civilizations might eventually be Oriental and Islamic militancies, the assembling of English-speaking, North American, liberal democratic capitalism in one country instead of two would have considerable appeal to both countries.

Mere annexation would not be acceptable to Canadians, as too demeaning. But an American proposal of federal union, promising debt and tax reduction for Canada, and at least a transitional retention of control of residential immigration so all America's chronic welfare cases didn't descend overnight on the comparatively generous Canadian social-security system, might be acceptable.

For the United States, it would mean twenty-one million industrious people, easily assimilable, and a colossal accretion of almost every natural resource. For Canada, after the painful collapse of the long bicultural experiment, adherence to the world's foremost nationality would mean security and identity at last while retaining regional individuality. In the abstract, English-speaking Canadians could undoubtedly make a more advantageous arrangement with the United States than they have had with Quebec. The United States would have the ability, and presumably also the inclination, to make an attractive offer, even if different Canadian provinces, on a staggered and unpredictable timetable, responded with varying and evolving levels of enthusiasm.

Despite the best efforts of the "caring and compassionate" school of Canadian nationalism, the only believable rationale for a Canada separate from the United States has been the principle of a distinctive bicultural nationalism – that is if English- and French-speaking Canadians feel they are fortunate to share a country with each other. Be it ever so hackneyed and abused, I believe *bonne entente* was the only formula that was ever going to work, and that, despite all the vicissitudes, it will work. Only the French Canadians, not hosts of social workers and tax collectors, really distinguish Canada from its neighbour. Only the English Canadians can prevent Quebec from being an insignificant French postage stamp on the northern marches of the United States; a large, cold, resource-rich Puerto Rico.

The Empire Loyalists founded English Canada to preserve part of North America for the British Empire and to demarcate spheres of influence with the American republic in the New World. Their descendants tried to make a country with the French Canadians. If that endeavour finally fails, the whole original enterprise will ultimately probably fail. That new republic, which in less than two hundred years became the greatest economic, military, and cultural force in the history of the world and is likely to remain so for some time, would eventually embrace a fragmented Canada, either by satellization, partial absorption, or outright fusion, whichever the Canadians wished. And, un-Canadian though this opinion might be now, no amount of spontaneous or orchestrated histrionics about compassion and the caring state would have much impact on the timetable, however enviable the perceived quality of life or keen the patriotic fervour in what would then be left of Canada. That denouement would be a more important geopolitical phenomenon than the reunification of Germany has been.

Even without Quebec, Canada has more people and infinitely more resources than East Germany had. It would be at least fifty years before there was any more wishful talk, even in the most rabidly anti-American circles, about the decline of the United States. There would be an immediate 5 per cent increase in the U.S. GNP, a virtual doubling of territory, and the instant replenishment of all the resources Americans have consumed or wasted in this century. Geopolitically, America would almost be born again.

The likelihood, to be arbitrary, is about two to one that the secession of Quebec will not occur. However, under either scenario, as an unambiguously united and sensibly bicultural country, or as an important component or adjunct of a greatly reinforced United States of America, Canada will play a role in the world considerably more important than any it has enjoyed in its two centuries as, in the famous words of a British colonial official in the 1830s, "two nations warring in the bosom of single state."

A Canada no longer subject to Quebec's endless threats of secession, where Quebec's permanent adherence had been effectively exchanged for an entrenched official status from sea to sea (as Trudeau originally proposed in the 1970s), would be a steadily more important G7 country. It would fully occupy the political role available to one of the world's ten or twelve most important countries.

If English-speaking Canada coalesced with the United States, the impact on America would be immensely positive and reassuring and Canadians would be a stabilizing influence in America's complicated demography.

The first, more likely, and most desired scenario is the fulfilment of Canada's dreams. If it becomes impossible because of Quebec's antics, the second is not a completely unpalatable fate; one great country or, eventually, a number of important states in or affiliated with the world's principal country. Perpetuation of the ancient and present uncertainties is an unpalatable fate and is seen to be so by almost all Canadians, English and French.

# AIRBUS

*Financial Post*, February 23, 1996

There must be many who are discouraged, as I am, by the Airbus affair. Like most Canadians, I was brought up to believe in the relative superiority of our judicial and police systems and in the fairness of most Canadians. These beliefs have survived, with difficulty, some disillusioning personal experiences.

The Canadian spirit of envy rises up against almost anyone who actually achieves anything in or for this country. Only the skilful few who manage to seem impenetrably benign or who win a ceasefire after a long lifetime of attrition with the compulsive levellers escape altogether the national passion to humble the visible minority of the successful. The desire of most of the Canadian media to avoid anything that disturbs the Pablum of their self-righteous complacency and soft-left biases is notorious but, in this extreme case, surprising.

The relevant facts are that an official of the federal justice department wrote to the Swiss government requesting information about certain bank accounts. She asserted as an unqualified fact that access was necessary because of criminal wrongdoing by the former prime minister, Brian Mulroney, and others in accepting from $11 million to $20 million in bribes to promote Air Canada's purchase of $1.8 billion worth of Airbuses. It was claimed that 25 per cent of the bribes were taken by Brian Mulroney himself. The author of this astonishing allegation purported to be relying on a CBC documentary which did not in fact mention Mr. Mulroney, even implicitly, and on a report in the scurrilous left-wing German magazine *Der Spiegel*, and on an unnamed reliable source. This source is almost certainly a rather dubious multiple criminal indictee and civil fraud respondent. This individual (who also deserves to be presumed innocent, but is hardly a credible accuser against a former prime minister of Canada) was advised by a lawyer who was convicted of fraud and disbarred. In any case, this "reliable" individual has denied that he furnished evidence inculpating Mr. Mulroney. The author of the letter of the Justice Department of Canada had every reason to believe that her letter would eventually go to more than twenty directors of Swiss Bank Corporation and that public disclosure would be almost inevitable.

The justice department refused to interview Mr. Mulroney to hear his side of these events even when he requested it after learning of the existence and contents of this infamous letter. The highest authorities at Air Canada have denied there was ever any political pressure to buy the Airbus. The main bank account in question has been shown to have been opened for a person other than Mr. Mulroney and to have been almost completely inactive.

Without laying a charge or apparently having any more grounds to do so than a malicious aside in a muckraking German magazine that no one with an IQ above single figures would take seriously, the government of Canada has effectively accused the twice-chosen head of this country of stealing millions of dollars from the Canadian taxpayers.

A flimsier, more contemptible basis for the official written assertion to a foreign government of a civilized jurisdiction, of a "persisting plot/conspiracy by Mr. Mulroney" and others "who defrauded the Canadian government in the amount of millions of dollars during the time Mr. Mulroney was in office," could not have been imagined by Kafka, Koestler, and Orwell in the piping days of Stalin's show trials.

Precisely because Canada is generally thought to be a civil society governed by decent people, Brian Mulroney, with no history of serious legal difficulties, as he reconstructs his career in the private sector, is widely assumed, in Canada and elsewhere, to be the author of wrongdoing on a scale rarely associated with advanced countries and unprecedented in this one.

Allan Rock, the federal justice minister, an able lawyer and a principled man, unctuously declared that "politicians should not be involved in police investigations." Of course they should not, and no serious person would suggest otherwise, but they should restrain federal officials from needless defamations of those who have every right to the presumption of innocence. Where necessary, the justice minister should take appropriate corrective action when he finds his officials have been engaged in the furtherance of injustice. Nothing could have been easier, once this outrage started to surface, than to have retransmitted the letter to the Swiss removing unsubstantiated criminal accusations but explaining the (by then) increased need for clarification.

Mr. Rock showed astonishing energy last year in the persecution of innocuous gun-collectors and those who require firearms to protect their livestock from predators. On this issue, however, he and the solicitor general, Herb Gray, whom I also know to be normally a fair-minded man and who is officially responsible for the hare-brained palookas in the RCMP who first comprised this lynch mob, have been as silent and inert as suet puddings. So, with a few honourable exceptions, such as William Thorsell, George Bain, and Douglas Fisher, have been the self-nominated public defenders in the media. All of them who are silent are complicit in this monstrous travesty, in which a Canadian citizen has been extra-judicially accused by his own government of grand larceny and extortion on no apparent evidence at all. His accusers have slunk away and hidden behind a glazed pall of official prevarication. Most of our crusading press has been struck dumb like Zachariah in the temple (but without his excuse of supernatural intervention).

I have had my ups and downs with Brian Mulroney, though we have been friends for over thirty years, but I have never supported him as fervently as I do now. He and his young family are entitled to no less and seek no more than is the right, the birthright, of all Canadians, not to be defamed by libels insolently masquerading as essential official business. It is all Canadians who are shamed, diminished, and ultimately threatened by this evil and totalitarian proceeding.

# TIRED LEFTIES
# ON PARADE

*National Post*, July 4, 2009

There fell solemnly from a recent Saturday edition of a Canadian newspaper a well-printed, stapled booklet of fifty pages, on magazine stock, called *Corporate Knights*. Wishing to know more about contemporary Canadian business leaders, I started leafing through it, and shortly came across a peppy message from the publisher – with an accompanying photo that showed her to be a pleasant and purposeful-seeming youngish woman. Beside her was a declaration that any contributor whose writing was found to be influenced by an advertiser would be dismissed.

The magazine is a quarterly and has a staff of twenty-five named people, including interns, and didn't have much advertising. I am quite familiar with the commercial economics of publishing periodicals, and this one would require heavy subsidization. I surmised this was partly accounted for by the advice that some research and reporting received "the financial support of Industry Canada."

Persevering determinedly through my edition, I quickly discovered an article entitled "A Roundtable, a Feast, and a Chivalrous Scientist." The gracious man of science being profiled was none other than James Lovelock, "world-renowned scientist and originator of the Gaia hypothesis."

It was at this point that I began to suffer glottal stops. Gaia is billed by its author as "a complex entity involving the Earth's biosphere, atmosphere, oceans and soil; the totality constituting a feedback or cybernetic system, which seeks an optimal physical and chemical environment for life on this planet." This isn't a scientific formulation at all; it's just a cargo-cult-level platitude counselling against excessive spoliation of resources.

Lovelock's new book, which he was promoting in Canada, is billed as his last, to the relief of the many eco-skeptics who have tired of the man's decades of flogging eco-terror. In it, he effectively abandons the theory that the world is on suicide watch but says that people may perish from their own wastefulness, extinguishing themselves but leaving our planet in habitable condition.

Thankfully, eco-terrorists such as Lovelock are now being severely challenged. The public in most advanced countries were never sold on the more exotic notions of climate change and imperative remedial action to begin with. And now the politicians are having second thoughts, as well.

But don't tell that to Lovelock. According to *Corporate Knights*, he told a Canadian audience that teeming masses of fugitives from hot countries will shortly be pressing against the Canada–U.S. border, and that the best antidote to global warming is to turn huge quantities of cow and pig ordure into charcoal and drop it in immense volume onto the world's ocean beds.

I looked for more indications that the article was a send-up, unsuccessfully. Has the ecology industry really come to this; to this unlikely tocsin to uplift and frighten the susceptible?

That overindulged industry will have to do better than that to deal with the rising tide of doubts about human-caused global warming. Australia and New Zealand have rescinded their carbon-emission legislation. The Polish Academy of Sciences has renounced its previous faith in the Al Gore/UN conventional wisdom about climate change. Hundreds of scientists have apostacized, including Nobel Prize winner (Physics) Ivar Giaever; the world's first female Ph.D. in meteorology, Dr. Joanne Simpson; and the Japanese environmental chemist Dr. Kiminori Itoh, who participated in the UN climate reports of recent years but now regards the theory of man-made climate warming as "the worst scientific scandal in history."

The Earth's temperatures generally have not changed in the last eight years, and the polar ice cap, rising oceans, and the health and weather horror stories that have been used to frighten the world into mad self-inflicted economic wounds and nostrums have been scientifically debunked. (This includes the aptly named Obama/Pelosi "cap-and-trade bill"; if passed into U.S. law in its present form, it will earn its authors dunce caps, and trade economic growth for the national poor house.)

The fact is that the world has almost been railroaded by scammers like Al Gore, he who inflicted famine on millions with his nonsense about the potential of corn as a fuel, which priced it as food beyond the reach of much of the developing world.

After the hallelujah chorus for James Lovelock, *Corporate Knights* presented a photograph from the World Economic Forum at Davos of the director of *Corporate Knights* with some of the more inevitable habitués of that world's fair of trendiness. I was on that circuit for many years, including as a session chairman and plenary panellist (most memorably when Rupert Murdoch and I tried to explain to Yehudi Menuhin what the dot-com era would do for the Third World – the answer, which we both tried to put diplomatically, was that those countries weren't prosperous enough to lose too much when the bubble burst, as many in the auditorium would).

Others in the Davos photograph included Lord Stern, George Soros, and Joseph Stiglitz, all such pillars of the chic left that they are almost part of the furniture in the awful hotels of Davos. Nicholas Stern is the British Labour Party's official dissembler of justifications for mad environmental radicalism, which, as noted above, would be colossally "unsustainable" and bring down economic misery on a large share of the population of any country that took it seriously.

George Soros is as sharp and avaricious a speculator as there is in the world, but he has been a champion of every left-wing cause within reach, including the Nicaraguan Sandinistas, and opposition to Ronald Reagan's Strategic Defence Initiative, which won the last round of the Cold War and is now all that gives any comfort of missile defence to the neighbours of Iran and North Korea. Soros hears the same drummer as

Cyrus Eaton and Armand Hammer, a bridge between ideologies, while also stuffing his pockets with profits from the former communist world.

Joseph Stiglitz is a Nobel Prize economist who is another desperate partisan, leading the Greek chorus that the current economic problems debunk the achievements of Reagan and Thatcher; he is one of the Democratic Party's noisiest economic junkyard dogs.

As I was wondering what possessed Industry Canada, and, I presume, some of the "sustainable" corporations which are not allowed to influence content in the magazine I was reading, to bankroll this hobnobbing with the most clichéd roués of the chronic conferencing left, there came a startling revelation: a *Corporate Knights* dinner with Gwynne Dyer.

Gwynne Dyer! From what dank catacomb did the *Knights* exhume that bedraggled old ringtail?

The most unrelievedly gloomy, implacably alarmist, Americophobic, Israel-baiting heirloom of Cold War defeatism, so dyspeptic he made Admiral Gene La Rocque seem like Douglas MacArthur, Gwynne Dyer devised a new scenario every fortnight for twenty years for how the United States would destroy the world.

The suspense was thick and pungent as I read on: what new grotesqueries had this Paleolithic Cassandra in mind for his *Knight*-errant hosts?

He did not disappoint: we are on the knife-edge of global war over climate and famine, and a possible American invasion of Canada to steal Canada's fresh water.

I put down the magazine after this, at page 15; I could not go on. It was strangely nostalgic to read Dyer's fatuities again, but we are being railroaded by a mob of charlatans and poseurs. When George Soros, James Lovelock, Nicholas Stern, Joseph Stiglitz, and Gwynne Dyer are singing off the same song sheet, it's time to change the music.

The backers of the *Corporate Knights* should invite them to generate a serious debate and to give equal time to the larger and more rigorous group that dissents from the climate change industry's fearmongering. Nigel (Lord) Lawson, a brilliant former chancellor and authority on environmental policy, has written a much better book on the subject than Lovelock and is coming to Canada soon. Let the

*Knights* have him to dinner; they will get a lot more for their supporters' money than Gwynne Dyer's call to the battlements to defend Canadian water from the U.S. Marines, much less James Lovelock's war trumpet to cover the ocean floors with transmogrified barnyard animal excrement.

# THE SENSIBLE GRANDEUR
# OF CANADA

*National Post*, April 24, 2010

---

Since Confederation 143 years ago, there have been only two political murders (D'Arcy McGee and Pierre Laporte), a maximum of five riots resulting in several fatalities (one over a grossly mistreated hockey star), and a few weeks of martial law in one province, with no resulting injuries or property damage.

We have had no revolts, because we did not provoke them, no pogroms or race riots, because no one wished or would submit to them. We fought only just wars, only voluntarily, always bravely, always on the good and winning side, and never with each other.

The *Wall Street Journal* recently editorialized that of all the nine advanced countries that have imposed a value-added tax (the GST), only Canada has reduced its rate since it was introduced.

Of course, this is desperately mundane, but it is important, and an astounding achievement. And it is part of a pattern: this is the relatively sensible country.

The strength of Canada is that it is a huge treasure chest of natural resources inhabited by fewer people than Greater Tokyo (which has thirty-four million people), who have flourished under adapted British political traditions and a benign American military umbrella. When our parents and grandparents sought inspiring eloquence from leaders, they got it from Churchill and Roosevelt, not Mackenzie King, who actually told the country in 1940 that the menace of "Nazism towers above us like an avalanche." Thus there have benignly failed to appear the sources of the wrenching dramas of civil war, invasion, terror, and popular revolt that have made up so much of the historical excitement and importance of other countries. That is why we don't have a Warsaw Ghetto, Katyn Forest, Battle of Verdun (or Vimy), Gettysburg Address, or Valley of the Fallen (Spain). They are all inspiring, but they represent millions of the violently dead.

Yet we have more and better history than most countries, and are one of the world's senior democracies (after only the Anglo-Americans and a smattering of Swiss, Scandinavians, and Dutch). We should know our history better, such as the unrecognized likelihood that we owe our first forty-five years of independence, opposite the United States, to John A. Macdonald's and Wilfrid Laurier's status as the greatest statesmen in North America, a good deal more adept than the eight men who followed Abraham Lincoln to the White House in their time as prime minister.

Canada has tried to make the best of its peacekeeping role, but it is a bit of a political free lunch, as the casualties are light, the costs are low, and to those unaware of what a corrupt shambles much of UN peacekeeping is, it is unsurpassably altruistic. We've wrung what we can from the explorers, of whom only a few, such as d'Iberville, La Vérendrye, and Jolliet, were born in what is now Canada. More could be done with the War of 1812, although in a ringing expression of the values of old Toronto, we tore down the house of John Graves Simcoe (who prepared Ontario for the war) to build a public school. We have driven the last spike on the railway builders.

No Canadian scandal has ever amounted to much. The South African government just made a straight, barefaced kickback worth $1 billion, via the Japanese company Hitachi, to which it awarded a huge hydroelectric contract, to the governing party, Nelson Mandela's sainted African National Congress. That is a scandal.

Face it, Canada, and live with it: at scandals, as at most bad things, we're flops. What we are good at isn't much celebrated, because few other countries are good at it. So we shall have to celebrate it ourselves.

We have no reason to be self-righteous or self-conscious, and there have been national tendencies to both. But we must learn some of our neighbour's genius for showmanship. It's all packaging, as Americans from Jefferson to Ann Coulter have realized.

We have been approaching this problem, of getting comfortable with ourselves, from the wrong angle. In the full realization that I am writing for Canadian readers, I suggest something radical. Canada must be seen as what it can be and largely is already – as having the elegance, and not just the utility, of simplicity and non-pretension: what George Orwell was to English prose and Ferdinand Porsche and Walter Gropius were to modern design, and Le Corbusier to modern residential architecture ("a machine for living in"). This is the naturally beautiful, relatively civil, modern, rich, tasteful, uncluttered country that works, and tries to act justly and usually does.

Public policy should reflect this. Our principal cities all need plans for increased architectural distinction, using the world's greatest architects, as Berlin and Beijing have done, and Toronto did with its city hall. We should invest heavily in our academic and cultural and scientific institutions, and try to beef up the ranks of our intellectual and research leadership, and try to attract back some of those millions of enterprising Canadians who have left, most to the United States. We should incentivize the leading writers and filmmakers of the world to set their stories in Canada.

Stephen Harper grasps, as Disraeli, Churchill, Thatcher, de Gaulle, Theodore Roosevelt, and Ronald Reagan (and even Duplessis) did, that a successful Conservative Party has to be the intelligent nationalist party. Harper showed what could be done with the Olympic Games. He returned to his senses about Afghanistan, where we have as much right as anyone but the United States to be present at the victory, if there is one. In our highest military tradition, Canada wasn't under threat – civilization was – and we fought.

We need an ambitious outline of a successor to Sir John A. Macdonald's ambitious National Policy of 1878. This was the program that propelled him back into government for the rest of his life. (He died in 1891, aged seventy-six, after an unequalled six elections as prime minister, and one term as opposition leader, following a decade before that as the co-leading figure of the so-called United Province of Canada.)

The 1878 program was essentially one of high tariffs to assist Canadian manufacturing, as opposed to Liberal support for freer trade with the United States. But Macdonald's spin team and his own polemical flourishes sketched out a comprehensive policy of a transcontinental railroad and fast steamship service off each end of the railway, to Europe and the Far East; accelerated immigration and development of the underpopulated West; and extensive development of harbours and other elements of what would today be called infrastructure. It was an ambitious plan, was endorsed by the voters and enacted, and did, with the *bonne entente* with federalist French Canadians, assure the survival and progress of the country.

As the distinguished recent biographer of Macdonald, Richard Gwyn, has pointed out, little confidence was expressed in Britain or the United States in the viability of Canadian Confederation when it was launched in 1867, and Macdonald deserves more credit than anyone else for the fact that it did prove to be a successful country.

Between Abraham Lincoln and Theodore Roosevelt, the United States had no need of leaders who would do more than welcome immigration and allow the laissez-faire economic system to produce astounding rates of growth and productivity increases, though punctuated, as unfettered capitalism is, by severe downturns.

Of course, the condition of Canada now is incomparably stronger, as a G7 country that has never participated in a losing or objectively unjust war, has admirably pulled more than its weight in the great wars and contests with totalitarianism of the last century, has made biculturalism work tolerably well, been usefully present at the creation of almost all respectable international organizations, and been a relatively just and peaceable society, where wealth is spread more evenly yet freely than in many prosperous countries.

It is familiar and frequently galling to Canadians, including me on occasion, that Canada has what the French call the fault of our qualities: the relative absence of violence and conflict and drama makes it a less spontaneously interesting country, to itself and to foreigners, than more tumultuous and eventful and exceptional places that are more prone to extremes of heroism and depravity, or are generally more flamboyant or stylish. Most of the world's traditionally premier nationalities would qualify in one of those categories.

Since no sane Canadian would wish to make the country more exciting by rending its social fabric or squandering its human, or natural, resources, Canada can only be competitively interesting, as opposed to the rarer and more desirable quality of being very congenial to live in, compared to some other great nations, by being exceptionally and imaginatively creative as a place to live. In pursuit of this, what we should expect from our political class is a plan of action to build out on the country's advantages. We need a program of policy excellence that transcends ghastly clichés such as a "just" or "great" society.

We should start by getting rid, once and for all, of this bunk about secession. A number of readers made the points that the recognized territories of native people should not be dragged out of Canada against the will of their own majorities; and that a seceding province should assume more than half of its per capita federal debt. I agree. On debt assumption, I think 75 per cent is a reasonable number. And if a seceding province (i.e., a province that has voted by a margin of over 60 per cent to secede on a clear referendum question) contains a recognized territory that has voted not to secede (the Cree areas of Quebec, for instance), then that territory secedes from the province and not the country.

After establishing the pre-eminent indivisibility of the country over that of any province, the next priority is to give the country a military capability capable of ensuring the nation's writ runs throughout the land, and making Canada an appropriately well-known and benignly helpful presence throughout the world.

Defence technology is the most efficient form of economic stimulus, and Bombardier's jetliner project cannot be allowed to fail as A.V. Roe's was more than fifty years ago. We had an aircraft carrier from the Second World War to the Trudeau era, and they are ideal projection platforms. We should retrieve that capability, which we possessed when we had barely a third of our present population. Apart from its ability to deploy military capability and strengthen Canada within the deteriorating Western Alliance, it would hugely increase our ability to assist in coping with overseas disasters such as earthquakes and tsunamis.

Showing the flag is easy to mock, but not by people who lament the underrecognition of the country in the world. As a matter of the pursuit of sane arms control and the upholding of international law, Canada should privately advocate a military assault on the Iranian military nuclear program if it is not halted and subject to inspection, and should contribute escorting aircraft to such a mission by the Americans or Israelis.

Then, we must innovate in social policy. The contemporary world is a public-policy wasteland. The world is waiting for some imaginative leadership.

In this national interest, I modestly offer the government some suggestions. In fiscal and tax policy, it should reduce personal and corporate income taxes further, especially on modest incomes, and raise the HST on non-essential spending (essential spending could be largely defined as food and other normal domestic products bought in stores rather than at restaurants and luxury goods dealers, clothing of average cost, up-to average residential expenses, and energy required for comfort at home and in gaining an income).

Canada is a naturally rich country that has been fiscally responsible for decades under both major parties and should lead the world back to hard and reliable currencies. The gold standard would be unwisely confining, but no currencies today have any value other than relatively to each other. Canada would be quickly followed if it adopted a mixed gold-oil-consumer basket yardstick of value and held to it.

As I have written here before, but not for a couple of years, I doubt if poverty can be dealt with further by extending traditional methods of taxing and spending. I suggest a modest wealth tax on high-net-worth people that would not be collected but would be applied by the taxpayer to approved innovations designed by the taxpayer to reduce poverty. The tax would be reduced as defined poverty was reduced, and the ablest financial minds in the country would have a powerful incentive to assist in eliminating poverty. And instead of raising interest rates in inflationary times, there should be standby tax changes that would eliminate taxes on the proceeds of savings and investment and would raise taxes on the non-essential ingredients in calculation of the consumer price index. Every 1 per cent rise in the interest rate raises inflation by 0.5 per cent. It pours gasoline on the fire until a bone-cracking recession is induced, a cure often worse than the ailment.

Our armed forces should be doubled in size; defence spending is (as economist Martin Feldstein and others – readers have inquired – have pointed out) the best form of economic stimulus. The Canadian fashion industry should design more elegant uniforms for our men and women in the forces. Canada must develop some self-defence and alliance-projection capacity and take the pride in our armed forces that they deserve and that a country requires to be taken seriously in the world.

We should get over our aversion to joint public–private sector activities. These contributed indispensably to the growth of Canada, from Jean Talon in the seventeenth century through Macdonald's Canadian Pacific Railway, the Laurier–Sifton immigration policies, and C.D. Howe's Trans-Canada Pipeline. Canada doesn't have the capital markets to sustain an entirely private-sector approach to full economic maturation, and this is the fast-track out of an excessively branch-plant or subsidiary economy, and we should start with a serious ownership interest in the automobile industry and an enhanced presence in aerospace and defence production.

We have the executives and the capital, but it requires non-controlling but facilitating government participation. Our aviation industry still has not recovered altogether from the cancellation of the Avro Arrow and our entire jet engine industry by John Diefenbaker in 1959.

# CANADA'S INHUMANE
# PRISON PLAN

*National Post*, May 29, 2010, and March 12, 2011

---

I n the past two years, as regular readers in this space would know, thanks to my gracious hosts in the U.S. government, I have had what could be called extensive hands-on experience of the American correctional system. I have been tutoring and teaching fellow prisoners in English and in U.S. history. And some of them have taught me how to read music, play the piano, keep fit, diet sensibly, and assimilate some local folkways, while I have been fighting my way through the courts toward a just disposition of the few remaining (unfounded) charges that bedevil me. The fact that all my life any definition of Canada's virtue and distinctiveness has prominently included references to civility and decency explains my alarm and outrage at finally reading the three-year-old report on the Correctional Service of Canada, misleadingly titled "A Roadmap to Strengthening Public Safety."

As so often in other fields, this document seeks to import to Canada much of the worst of American practice, and none of the best, unless Canada now idealizes gratuitous official severity.

I have not succumbed to an inverse Stockholm Syndrome and become an apologist for the convicted community. But I disbelieve even more fervently than I did before my sojourn among them in the

Manichaean process of baiting, dehumanization, and stigmatization promoted by the roadmap and similarly inspired correctional nostrums.

In my present abode, I have met many rather dodgy people, but none whose ethics I consider inferior to some prosecutors and judges I have encountered in the last few years. And I have met many fine as well as some mediocre and poor correctional officers, but few who rise above the level of benign non-skilled labour, profoundly underqualified to practise untrammelled social engineering on those entrusted to them.

I believe, civilly and theologically, in the confession and repentance of wrongdoing, in the prosecution and punishment of crime, and in a maximum reasonable effort by the state to protect the public, especially from threats to person and property. But I also believe that everyone has rights, including the unborn, demented, incurably ill, military adversaries, and the criminal, and that the rights of those whose entitlements are for any reason circumscribed are not inferior for being narrower and should be as great as they practically can be, without violating the rights of others.

This roadmap – which was released in 2007, and which the Harper government began officially responding to in its budget in 2008, setting out a five-year plan – turns the humane traditions of Canada upside down. It implicitly assumes that all who are convicted are guilty and have no remaining claim to decency from the state, and that treating confinees accordingly is in the interest of the legally unexceptionable majority.

The roadmap does not mention prisoners' rights, beyond basic food, shelter, clothing, and medical care, and assumes that they are probably not recoverable for society and that the longer they are imprisoned the better it is for society. Almost no distinction is made between violent and non-violent offenders.

Of course, great caution must be shown in the reintegration into society of violent criminals. But the objective of the penal system must be to return those capable of functioning licitly in society as quickly as practical, allowing also for straight punitive or retributive penalties but not for mindless vengeance. The whole system must be guided by the fact that the treatment of the accused and confined has been recognized by ethicists and cultural historians for centuries as one of the hallmarks of civilized society.

The roadmap holds that anything beyond the necessities for physical survival must be "earned." Traditionally, the punishment is supposed to be the imprisonment itself, not the additional oppressions of that regime, and the proverbial debt to society is paid when the sentence has been served; it does not continue as a permanent Sisyphean burden. In the interests of eliminating illegal drugs in prison, the authors of the roadmap want all visits to be glass-segregated, no physical contact. This is just a pretext to assist in the destruction of families and friendships.

The importation of contraband by prisoners' visitors can be stopped by strip-searching the prisoners before they leave the visitors' centre, as happens to us here, unless the prison staff, who have the unfathomable delight of inspecting us *au naturel*, are on the take, which is, of course, the problem, as correctional officers in many prisons are frequently caught smuggling and aren't well enough trained to command higher salaries to make them more resistant to temptation. It is a problem, but it will not be solved by targeting unoffending relatives of inmates. The roadmap also has naively exaggerated confidence in certain types of scanning devices.

It also recommends unspecified concentration on generating employment skills, which is sensible, except that it is specifically foreseen that they will replace other programs of more general education, substance abuse avoidance, and behavioural adaptation.

I am no hemophiliac bleeding heart, but non-violent people can sometimes be helped to abandon illicit practices by some of these programs. No useful purposes will be served by cranking back into the world unreconstructed sociopaths who can fix an air conditioner or unclog a drain. The roadmap even asks for research to be undertaken that will support this recommendation, an inversion of the usual sequence in which research determines policy and not the other way around.

There is a demand for investment of over $1 billion in new and larger prisons (an insane extravagance) and for sharply longer sentences, mandatory minimum sentences, and "earned parole" in place of supervised release after two-thirds of the sentence in the absence of misconduct that would militate against such comparative liberality. In practice, this means imprisonment at the pleasure of the carceral establishment for the maximum time possible. (Prisoners cost $40,000 per year to keep.) All of these draconian measures have been tried and have failed in the United States.

As Michael Jackson and Graham Stewart point out in their excellent essay in the current *Literary Review of Canada*, "Fear-Driven Policy," this plan would fall especially heavily on native people, who already comprise nearly seven times greater a percentage of imprisoned Canadians than they represent in the whole population.

The roadmap is the self-serving work of reactionary, authoritarian palookas, what we might have expected forty years ago from a committee of Southern U.S. police chiefs. It is counterintuitive and contrahistorical: the crime rate has been declining for years, and there is no evidence cited to support any of the repression that is requested. It appears to defy a number of Supreme Court decisions and is an affront at least to the spirit of the Charter of Rights.

The Canada I remember and look forward to returning to should do exactly the opposite. Prison is an antiquarian and absurd treatment of non-violent lawbreakers. It only continues because it has.

The whole concept of prison should be terminated, except for violent criminals and chronic non-violent recidivists, and replaced by closely supervised pro bono or subsistence-paid work by bonded convicts in the fields of their specialty. Swindlers and embezzlers, hackers and sleazy telemarketers are capable people and they should serve their sentences by contributing honest work to government-insured employers.

Canada would save $1 billion annually in prison costs and the employers of the penitent-workers would save $2 billion annually, a tremendous shot in the arm to national productivity. Many of the prisons could be reconfigured as assisted housing for the homeless and slum-dwellers. Canada would again be a model of the innovative public-policy pursuit of institutionalized decency and social reform.

The principle that the rape of the rights of the least is an assault on the rights of all is attributed to Jesus Christ and is at the core of Judeo-Christian civilization and the rule of law in both common- and civil-law jurisdictions. And it is not just a tradition; there are several million Canadians in families that have bitter memories of personal or close relatives' encounters with the vagaries of justice. They aren't a visible bloc, but this is not a political free lunch.

It is painful for me to write that with this garrote of a blueprint, the government I generally support is flirting with moral and political catastrophe. My respect for the prime minister prevents me from being any more explicit here about the implications of failure to reconsider the government's course on this issue.

The roadmap is a bad plan to take Canada to a destination it should not wish to reach.

## A RESPONSE TO A COLUMN SIMILAR TO THE ONE ABOVE

*National Post*, March 12, 2011

---

A friendly acquaintance recently was moved to publish a reply to a *National Post* column I wrote about crime and punishment several weeks ago. He showed me a draft of his article, which led to a sharpish and entertaining, but not very enlightening, exchange, as he defended the Conservative government's "A Roadmap to Strengthening Public Safety," a collection of harsh policies that I had attacked in this space as "bad, unjust, and expensive."

His draft – which, though argued in good faith, misconstrued my opinions on the subject – persuaded me that I owe readers greater clarity regarding what I object to in current government policy, and what reforms I suggest.

My greatest objections to the so-called roadmap are that it proposes to tighten the regime governing visits to prisons and would narrow the discretion available to judges in order to make prison sentences automatically longer. I further object to the overuse of imprisonment, having been confined to a prison in the United States for twenty-nine months, as inappropriate for many of the criminals who are sentenced to it (quite apart from the very many in the United States, and significant number in Canada, who are not actually criminals yet have been convicted nonetheless after being bulldozed by the unequal correlation of forces in favour of prosecutors).

I believe in the exercise of liberty by apparently responsible people up to the limit that their exercise of liberty does not compromise the right of others to the same liberty. In a statutory framework, such a principle argues that judges must have reasonable discretion to assess guilt and balance punishment with the desire to encourage, where practical, the swiftest possible successful return to normal life of convicted people who are judged to be a threat neither to society nor the physical safety of anyone else.

In the case of all but the most dangerous, repulsive, and sociopathic criminal acts, places of detention should aspire, if they are not just transitory holding tanks, to be repair shops and not garbage dumps. Accused people must genuinely be presumed to be innocent, and convicted people who have served their sentences must genuinely be presumed to have paid for their misconduct.

I oppose the death penalty, because mistakes inevitably will be made, and because the spectacle of the state ceremoniously taking a life is barbarous and disgusting, and demeans everyone in the society that approves the practice. I am not unlimitedly sympathetic to lawbreakers, but nor am I one of the "hang 'em, jail 'em, flog 'em" set. The roadmap takes no account of the special circumstances of First Nations people, who would be its chief victims, nor of the steady decline in most categories of crime as the population ages and law enforcement techniques become more sophisticated.

It should never be the objective of the state to shatter the family and personal life of prisoners. Even those thought to be probably incorrigible are entitled to the retention of some connection to people not similarly situated who want to see them; and it is indisputable that normal family, romantic, and friendly relations with law-abiding people are a stabilizing influence on people. I well know this from my own experience and observations as a prisoner; and there is absolutely no excuse, apart from primal vindictiveness, to apply the restraints on prison visitors proposed by the roadmap.

The proposal to have glass barriers between visitors and inmates at all times, in particular, is sadistic and dehumanizing. And the excuse given – to eliminate smuggling of contraband – can be accomplished in other ways. Ninety per cent of such traffic is conducted by suborned correctional officers anyway.

The roadmap's ambition to take sentencing latitude away from judges (which already has been partly enacted) is a usurpation by the legislators of the judicial function. The judge administers the evidence and monitors the case and knows the facts.

Of course, the intelligence and fair-mindedness of judges vary widely, and some are hopelessly miscast (I know something about that, too, in both the United States and Canada). But they are virtually all better qualified to try a case and bring down a sentence than uninvolved legislators shooting arbitrarily from the hip before the fact.

Legislators may establish a range of sentencing that faithfully reflects an enlightened public level of concern at certain offences, and these fluctuate over time. But it is not the role of the legislator to impose an ironclad prejudgment of penalty on every convicted person, regardless of the detailed facts and of considerations of tempering justice with mercy.

The underlying suspicion of Stephen Harper's government – which is that the bench is infested with softies and that it is right to punish crimes more severely than they have been in the past – is a reactionary and brutish reflex that is presumably aimed at a political constituency unlikely to stray into the arms of this government's opponents anyway. Handcuffing the judges merely makes justice more unlikely. And simply raising the sentences for everyone, which is essentially what is recommended, is not justified by the recidivism rates in many categories of offence. It also would legitimize the repugnant concept that criminal penalties should exceed that which is necessary to expiate the past and discourage a return to crime.

I recommend many further reforms that diverge radically from the spirit of the government's roadmap, and there is not space here to explore them all adequately. But I will summarize some of them.

Ontario Justice Marc Rosenberg's recent criticism of the plea-bargain system (made in the context of a Toronto man induced to make a dubious confession) is absolutely correct. People are entitled to a day in court, and the plea bargain is based on intimidation.

The act of determining whether there is sufficient evidence to charge must, as in Germany, be put in independent hands that are distinct from the police and prosecutors. There should not be more ex-prosecutors than ex-defence counsel on the bench; the legal-aid system should provide legicare for those who need it; poverty should not deprive people of their right to trial, any more than of their right to medical care. And a day in court should be a trial, not a rubber stamp of an extorted plea that shafts the accused and reduces the judge to the status of clerk. These changes would cost much less than the government's proposed orgy of prison-building, and the public would be better served by them.

Prison should not be a place of languishing; its purpose should be punishment, reparable stigmatization other than for extreme offenders, and largely regimented time to be spent in activity sensibly designed to make the returning prisoner less likely to reoffend. This would include therapy, skills training, and reorientation. It should be authoritarian enough to incite non-return, but not so heavy-handed that it over-penalizes and breaks the will of inmates to resume life with a promising likelihood of success.

I believe that many sentences would be better finished, or even entirely served, in pro bono outside work, whereby bonded employers would monitor performance, and the length of this form of service would depend on performance.

Obviously, such a program would have to be very carefully introduced, applied, and administered, but prisons are more inflexible and nasty environments than is appropriate for many offenders. The idea of making them nastier and less remitting is uncivilized and unsuitable to this principled but generous country.

# CANADA DESERVES
# A UN SEAT, EVEN IF THE UN
# DOES NOT DESERVE US

*National Post*, October 9, 2010, and June 30, 2012

---

There is a classically Canadian half-hearted campaign for Canada to become a permanent Security Council member at the United Nations. It reminds me of the late Mitchell Sharp, the Canadian head of the Trilateral Commission (after having been minister of finance and of external affairs), telling me that when he set out to secure approval for Canadian continuation in the Trilateral Commission, he could find no enthusiasm for it. This is an organization of fairly eminent people from Western Europe, the United States, Canada, and Japan that meets every year and goes over a wide range of contemporary issues. Finally, Mitchell won agreement that if every other country was renewing its participation, Canada should also. Canadians tend to be diffident and rather inept self-promoters. The Germans, Japanese, Indians, and Brazilians are campaigning feverishly all around the world, seeking to become permanent members of the Security Council, joining the founding members, the United States, Russia, the United Kingdom, China, and France.

The Canadian effort is a very low-key affair, hobbled by internal foreign ministry reservations and some editorial comment to the effect that this would not be appropriate because Stephen Harper's heart isn't in it; Canada has been too pro-Israel; Canada has been insufficiently generous with development aid; and the UN is passé and we shouldn't waste our time (meaning we have no chance so let's not try). Since Canada is in the G7; is one of the most strategic storehouses of accessible resources in the world; has one of the ten or eleven largest economies in the world, depending on fluctuating exchange rates; has a stable political system; has a good history in rights and cultural tolerance; and is coming well through the economic downturn, it is worthy of natural consideration as one of the twelve or fewer most important countries. Politically it is one of the very most enlightened and reliable. Naturally, Canadian modesty is here competing with Brazilian and Italian panache, German and Japanese muscle, Indonesia as the largest Muslim country and large oil exporter, and India's unfailing ability to represent itself as the font of all human wisdom, as well as a bulky demographic with an impressive future.

The reasons raised against seeking membership are nonsense, in the fine tradition of Canadian diffidence in the presence of countries traditionally intimate with and senior to it (the United States, United Kingdom, and France). Stephen Harper is a perfectly presentable government leader in United Nations terms. He has an impeccable record in supporting disinterested ("untied") development aid and peacekeeping, and has been a more solid supporter of the Afghan effort than the Americans. And his strong support of Israel is a triumph of principle over the cowardice and the hypocrisy of the relativists. While even the United States acquiesced in Israel's non-election to the Middle Eastern section of the United Nations Human Rights Council, Canada maintained its support for Israel's right to be present, even as, perversely, Libya took the chair of the group. (This was a typical mockery of any serious standards, as the politically primitive countries continue to use the United Nations as a playpen from which to throw their toys at the wealthy and overindulgent benefactors of the organization.)

The fact is that last week, when he spoke at the UN's General Assembly, Benjamin Netanyahu established himself as one of the West's leaders, in the classical sense of expressing and incarnating the highest values of the West. He referred to the UN commission on the Gaza

War as a blood libel on Israel and reflected on the fact that after Israel withdrew from Gaza and forcibly removed eight thousand Israeli settlers from Gaza, the Gaza Palestinians fired over ten thousand rockets at civilian targets in Israel, killing hundreds of Israelis, without this terrorist aggression eliciting one vote of censure at the United Nations. He referred to the response of the Western Allies the last time a democratic country, Great Britain, was subjected to sustained rocket attack against civilian populated areas, in the v-1 and v-2 attacks by Germany in 1944 and 1945: the Allied air forces escalated their aerial war against Germany to include the massive devastation and firebombing of many cities, including Dresden. It was perfectly logical for Netanyahu to tell the United Nations, as he did, that by this reasoning Winston Churchill and Franklin D. Roosevelt, the founders of the United Nations, instead of being revered as the giants of civilized statesmanship that they rightly are, would be arraigned as war criminals before the world, as Israel was by the UN's unspeakable Gaza War Report.

At the founding meeting of the United Nations at San Francisco in 1945, future external affairs minister Pearson urged "a symphony orchestra" rather than a "string quartet" (France had just been elevated to the status of a founder). Canada has been consistent in advocating collegiality among responsible states in UN matters. It has been one of the most frequent contributors of peacekeeping contingents (partly because that has been a cheap way of making a well-publicized contribution to international stability that was neither manpower-intensive nor overly costly in lives or money).

The one argument against Canada pursuing a permanent Security Council seat that holds any water is that the UN has become a farce. But that is precisely why the status of Canada should be augmented. If the UN is to be rescued from utter degradation and mockery, the serious countries will have to prevent any further degeneration and reform the organization, after sixty-five years. Notoriously, the peacekeeping missions are more often than not the hired factional reinforcement of warring groups within countries, mercenaries that are informally rented out to the warlords to generate hard currency for the participating states. United Nations peacekeeping forces are often completely undisciplined and just as barbarous as the elements they are supposed to be restraining and do more escalation of war than maintenance of peace. This is especially true of the large UN presence in the Congo.

The United Nations is corrupt and overinfluenced by countries which are not morally or politically qualified even to sit in it. It has become a source of payola windfalls for corrupt agency officials as well as a substitute for theatre and psychiatry for many of the world's most disreputable regimes. Muammar Gaddafi's Libya was elected to the chair of the Human Rights Commission (precursor of the present Human Rights Council), and the whole hierarchy of the UN was implicated in the misappropriation of many millions of oil dollars supposedly destined for humanitarian purposes in Iraq. The chief humanitarian beneficiaries were Saddam Hussein and crooked UN officials.

Unfortunately, Canada was, for most of the UN's history, far too indulgent of it. First, as a victorious ally and charter member, it was part of the Anglo-American governing consensus. Then, after Lodge gave Pearson the Suez peacekeeper idea (and Pearson forgot that it wasn't his originally), the foreign policy establishment in Ottawa began to view the UN as a way for Canada to distinguish itself from the United States at little cost, and to allow itself, with a modest foreign aid budget, to pander to Third World countries without seriously annoying our traditional allies. This gradually developed into the Chrétien government's endorsement of "soft power," a phrase originated by former U.S. president Bill Clinton's national security adviser Joe Nye, which was a soft alternative to the use of American military might. It is a concept that has any validity only when there is a hard-power option, which Canada did not possess. As practised by this country, soft power was a fraud, it was just more softness.

Despite Canada's long championship of the United Nations, the UN high commissioner for human rights, Navi Pillay (a Tamil South African from Durban and notorious anti-Western racist), still saw fit to criticize the absence of human rights in Quebec last week, lumping Canada in with Syria, Mali, Eritrea, and North Korea. (The first three of those countries have been wracked by civil wars, replete with tortured political prisoners and executions; and the fourth is the most severe totalitarian state in the world.) Pillay was the chief author of the Durban declaration against racism in 2001, itself a militantly racist document, and she has disputed the legality of killing Osama bin Laden and ostentatiously supported Iran's lunatic president Mahmoud Ahmadinejad. In her recent comments, she praised the Arab Charter on Human Rights, which makes all rights subject to the law of sharia. She did not recognize that the Quebec law on the right to assemble and demonstrate has not led to general violence, is not violently imposed, and is subject to review by an independent judiciary and to revocation of the government by voters in free elections.

At the Human Rights Council meeting in Geneva on June 22, there was a parallel meeting held by Hamas and other radical Palestinian organizations, with the blessing and publicity of the United Nations, in which Israel was subjected to the customary flood of blood libels. More than 40 per cent of the council's own resolutions are devoted to the pathological Jew-baiting and anti-Zionism of radical Islam and its secular espousers.

All of the countries most actively seeking permanent Security Council membership – Canada and the six mentioned, plus Italy and Indonesia – should hold hands and require admission together and at once. And a reinvigorated Security Council should undertake a comprehensive reform of the United Nations to convert it from the riotous unsupervised daycare centre it is now to the serious forum of promotion of responsible international law and cooperation it was intended to be. To start, countries completely in default of the Universal Declaration on Human Rights, which could be defined as all with less personal freedom than China, and would be about fifty of them, should be suspended from voting until they achieve that status.

Canada has every right and reason to play a primary role in trying to make something useful out of the United Nations. This would be a much more appropriate stance for Canada, now that it has been so unjustly pilloried by the anthill of bigotry of a Human Rights Council, than continued reverence for this citadel of hypocrisy. The United Nations is both a mad cow and a sacred cow; it is in desperate need of radical reform.

# THE STRANGE DEATH OF LIBERAL CANADA

*Standpoint*, June 2011

Michael Ignatieff always appeared to be the predestined man, scion of a noble Russian family, including one of the last czar's ministers, and of a prominent Anglo-Canadian family of academics and business leaders. He was a star in one of Canada's most exclusive schools, and an alumnus of the University of Toronto, Oxford, and Harvard. He became a well-regarded university lecturer and a prize-winning author, and not only in the suspiciously log-rolling and back-scratching world of Can(adian) Lit(erature). He was shortlisted for the Booker and endorsed by Isaiah Berlin, a professor and mentor at Oxford, as his biographer.

He acquired a reputation as an expert on human rights and gained credibility by being independent-minded and not just another cipher of Amnesty International and Human Rights Watch attacking every foreign policy initiative of the United States. He was rewarded with a prominent civil rights chair at Harvard. There were problems of abrupt changes of position, including his very public and rigorous endorsement of the Iraq War followed by his eventual complete recantation when WMD were not discovered, as if that were the only reason for disposing of Saddam Hussein, or the principal one given by the U.S. government, or even by Ignatieff himself.

His father, George Ignatieff, was a very respected diplomat and public servant, and prominent member of the Liberal establishment that staffed the senior civil and diplomatic service from 1896 to 2006 and governed Canada for eighty of those years. The Canadian Liberals were the most successful party in the democratic world throughout this time, basically because they were the only pan-Canadian party that alternated English- and French-Canadian leaders; because they were not the party that imposed conscription on an unconvinced French Canada in 1917; and because they sold themselves in Quebec as the party that would make Canada work for Quebec, and in the rest of the country as the party that would keep Quebec in Canada, by whatever combination of *bonne entente* and *force majeure* was required.

Part of the genius of the Canadian Liberals was the habit of selecting leaders in an unpredictable and exotic manner that was rivalled only by the Holy See for mystery and surprise. The Commonwealth's longest serving prime minister, W.L. Mackenzie King (twenty-two years), was a Harvard alumnus, a defeated former junior minister, and long resident in the United States when he was elected to a twenty-nine-year stint as Liberal leader, following the death of Sir Wilfrid Laurier, who had been Liberal leader for thirty-two years. King's successor, Louis St. Laurent, had never dreamed of entering public life in his sixty years until King tapped him for the succession. Lester Pearson, a mentor of George Ignatieff, was a career foreign service officer when he got the call, and Pierre Trudeau was an underemployed academic with inherited wealth, who had never even supported the Liberals, when he was recruited by Pearson. Between them these five men led their party for ninety-seven consecutive years, sixty-six of those as prime minister.

No party that has ever had to fight a real election has had as serene and durable a conviction that it was the natural party of government as the Canadian Liberals. From 1896 to 1984 the Liberals won fifteen full terms to four for the Conservatives. Through the years since the death in 1891 of Sir John Macdonald, the founder of the country as an autonomous confederation in 1867, and of the Conservative Party, that party was essentially a catchment for disparate elements who happened not to be Liberals, in particular grumpy prairie farmers and the Toronto financial community, who could not agree on anything except their dislike of the Liberals. From 1891 to 2006, the Liberals had eight leaders, seven elected to full terms as prime minister, and the Conservatives had nineteen leaders, only four of whom were elected to full terms as prime minister.

The Liberal fortress was first sacked when the Conservatives finally chose a leader who spoke French and knew Quebec intimately, Brian Mulroney; and in 1984 he shattered the Liberal stranglehold on Quebec. The status of the Liberals as Canada's indispensable guarantor of the integrity of the country evaporated. Mulroney produced a constitutional resolution plan that ultimately foundered on objections from Newfoundland and native people (Plains Indians), while his Quebec support defected to the separatists and his western support to a regional grouping; Mulroney retired, still a master of parliamentary majority. But his successor presided over the reduction of a Conservative majority in a Parliament of over three hundred to a total of two Conservative MPs (not including Mulroney's successor as prime minister, Kim Campbell, whose next post was consul general in Los Angeles).

The next three Liberal leaders, John Turner, Jean Chrétien, and Paul Martin, only had twenty-two years as leader and thirteen as prime minister, as the great Liberal mystique had gone and all that was left was a severely fragmented opposition. That enabled Chrétien, a stout-hearted federalist veteran of a whole generation of Quebec political battles, but a rough man who was not always comprehensible in either official language, and who almost lost the 1995 independence referendum in Quebec with a wail of appeal on its eve not to "break up the country," to remain in office for ten years. He became the only elected prime minister in Canadian history to be evicted from that office by his own party.

His successor and finance minister, Paul Martin (it was a little like Paul Keating pulling the rug out from under Bob Hawke in Australia in 1991, though the Australians, as usual, were more colourful personalities), was handed a grenade with the pin pulled by Chrétien in a scandal involving Liberal largesse to supporters in the 1995 referendum. By this time Stephen Harper, former head of a conservative taxpayers' activist group, had united the old Conservative Party with the western renegade conservative party of which he, an Albertan, had been a founder. Harper brought down the Liberal government in 2006 and defeated Martin at the polls.

The next Liberal leader, Stéphane Dion, was the first in 119 years not to be prime minister. Dion only won the leadership after Martin was defeated at the polls. Michael Ignatieff, who had been parachuted into a safe constituency to the very audible disgruntlement of the incumbent Liberal, blew his campaign for the leadership, having started as the favourite. This was where the Ignatieff predestination script started to go horribly wrong. Two years later, after Dion had committed the Liberals to a mad adherence to the Kyoto Accords that would have impoverished Canada, Harper was re-elected with an enlarged minority government.

After his rout at the polls, Dion attempted a hare-brained coalition with the unofficial opposition parties, the comparatively socialist New Democrats and the federal representatives of Quebec separatism, who had replaced the Liberals as the principal beneficiary of the large tribal vote from Quebec. Ignatieff had abstained from this insanity and was anointed leader by the party elders.

He began as the idol of the Canadian national media, which almost unanimously assumed that he could force and win an election at will. He was the Liberal leader and Dion, it was felt, had been aberrant. Ignatieff would restore power to its natural holders.

But that status was irretrievable; neither Quebec nor the rest of Canada believed a word of it. The separatists had most of the Quebec MPs; Quebec's ability to blackmail Canada had been reduced by its demographic decline and the rise of the far western provinces' wealth in oil and other natural resources, and by the astute, bilingual Harper, who made tax cuts and economic growth good politics and brought Canada through the 2008–2009 recession with flying colours.

There had been recurrent reports of Ignatieff undercutting members of his own party. His championship of civil rights was ultimately tainted by his endorsement of oppressive collective rights in Quebec, such as the imposition of unilingual French commercial signs. Ignatieff was trying to pander to Quebec with outworn constitutional and cultural overtures. He held a portentous "thinkers' conference" that advocated more daycare and soft power (a concept that, if it works at all, only does so when the country practising it has a real power alternative).

He "lost no sleep" over the Lebanese dead at Qana one week, and denounced the events there as an Israeli war crime the next, having previously bought into the piffle about the lack of "proportionality" of Israel's response to the endless rocket attacks against Israeli civilians by Hamas in Gaza. Ignatieff's intelligence is conceded by all, but not his judgment or even his intellectual ethics.

Ignatieff's claque in the cultural establishment, such as Adam Gopnik in *The New Yorker*, who declared him prime minister presumptive in 2009, signed on to Ignatieff's right to govern. But Harper, though not especially popular as a somewhat desiccated and unspontaneous man, was yet competent and authoritative and delivered prosperity. He began to assert Canada's new position in the world as rich, benign, prepared to enter places like Afghanistan, and much better governed than the debt-ridden United States, the floundering EU, and geriatric Japan.

Canada had suffered from being a mainly resource-based economy in the long era when lack of demand meant there was a glut of almost everything Canada produced: base and precious metals, energy, forest products. But once importers China and India, with nearly 40 per cent of the world's population, began achieving economic growth rates of 6 to 10 per cent a year, Canada (and Australia) boomed.

Canada's self-conscious deference to the Americans and British, and even, at particularly grim moments, the French, ended. Harper proved an unruffled professional and a cunning political hard-baller: he ran advertising blitzes portraying Ignatieff as an elitist snob who had returned to Canada after an absence of decades to become an instant prime minister.

The opposition parties, believing they could win a campaign, passed a resolution of contempt of Parliament because one of Harper's minister's had given disingenuous answers to a parliamentary committee about the cessation of aid to a development agency that had been very censorious of Israel. The public didn't want an election, blamed it on the opposition, and considered Ignatieff not as heir to King and

Pearson and Trudeau but as an ineffectual dilettante. The harder he tried to be a populist leader, as in his implausible exhortation "Rise up, Canada!" the more absurd he became.

Quebec dumped the separatists from the federal Parliament, where they were a nonsensical anachronism, and voted for an unknown slate of New Democrat flakes and kooks, making that party, hilariously, the mainly French official opposition. The country deserted the Liberals in droves and gave Harper a strong mandate with a conveniently splintered opposition. Ignatieff was defeated in his own constituency, retired from politics the day after the election, and accepted an academic position at the University of Toronto the day after that.

His foray into public life had been a disaster. He has led the former party of government, the most successful political party in the democratic world, to the brink of extinction with less than 20 per cent of the vote, and doomed it to petition frivolous rivals for a merger. But as a result of the Liberal attempted suicide, Canada is within sight of a genuine two-party system for the first time since 1917. This is progress.

# TRUDEAU'S
# MASTER STROKE

*National Post*, March 31, 2012

As a guest of the American people, my deliveries of the *National Post* – late and sporadic as they are – comprise my principal connection, here in the tenebrous, alligator-infested thickets of Florida, with Canadian public-policy discussion. This is my excuse for commenting so tardily on the debate in Toronto on March 8 between scholars Antonia Maioni and David Bercuson over whether Canada is "bilingual, binational, and bicultural"; and also on Hugh Segal's comments about Syria, delivered in the Canadian Senate, on March 6.

The difficulty with the Maioni–Bercuson debate is that almost everything the protagonists said, as reported, was accurate. Of course, as Mr. Bercuson said, the country isn't really any of the "bi" adjectives in the title of the debate. And of course, as Ms. Maioni said, "We can't airbrush the French fact out of Canada's past and present, and shouldn't dismiss it from its future." Nor would any serious person aspire to do anything of the kind. (That, as Ms. Maioni also said, the Charter of Rights and Freedoms "has consolidated the sense of the Quebec nation as a rampart for French language and culture" is another matter, and is not invulnerable to skepticism.)

As I have had occasion to write here (and elsewhere) before, the Charter, like the enforced bilingualism in retail packaging, and access

to federal government services and television and radio outlets, which
Mr. Bercuson rather dismissively mentioned, were a response to the
threat to federalism posed by the Quebec separatists. They were an
inspired tactic of Pierre Trudeau's to muddy the waters in the federalist–
separatist debate by focusing attention on individual rights, rather than
federal and provincial government prerogatives, and to give some substance and effect to his promise formulated at the end of his vote-eve
address to the federal Liberal leadership convention in 1968, "Masters
in our own house (*Maîtres chez nous*), but our house is Canada."

It is not the case, as Mr. Bercuson claimed, that this was appeasement of the separatists. Trudeau was no appeaser of the separatists. Nor
was it, as the separatists claimed, and still claim, tokenism. Along with
the deluge of money that was collected in Ontario, Alberta, and British
Columbia and delivered upon Quebec almost as indiscriminately as if it
had been (and still is) thrown out of low-flying aircraft like ammunition
to the Warsaw Uprising of 1944, these measures were a counter-strategy
to defeat the separatists and spare Canada the agony of the attempted
secession of a province holding a quarter of its population. (The
Confederate states, by contrast, had only 19 per cent of the free population of the United States in 1861.) Under any separation scenario, a very
large number of Quebeckers would have dissented from any separatist
majority, creating an irredentist problem, and a spectacular and profound fissure would have immobilized the whole country indefinitely.

It was a masterly two-track strategy that gradually defanged the separatists. And while Canada did not become bilingual, and bilingualism was most fiercely resisted by Québécois fearful of assimilation if
the people were excessively exposed to English, the availability of both
languages on radio and television and in commercial descriptions and
instructions and government services throughout the country did reinforce the official equality of the founding cultures. This was not a high
price to pay to have comparative peace in the country. It was a fair and
reasonable, if sometimes irritating and symbolic, fine-tuning of practical constitutional matters.

But Ms. Maioni's assertion that the Charter helped the "Quebec
nation" become a "rampart for French language and culture" is a stretch.
I doubt if the Charter really accomplished much substantively beyond

unleashing Canada's underqualified judges to meddle open-endedly in social animation.

Quebec's claim to being a "nation" is a bit dodgy as well, unless the word is being used in the rather unrigorous manner that allows formerly so-called Indian tribes and castaway groups generally to describe themselves as "nations." Quebec is too heavily influenced, culturally and psychologically, by the English language and North American ambiance around and within it to be incontestably more separable than a distinct province.

The nationalists were as inexact in underestimating the problems and illogic of separation as Prime Minister Louis St. Laurent was in 1955 to call Quebec "a province like the others." Nor, for the same reason, is the distinction of the status of French in Quebec quite adequate to call it a "rampart," other than in comparison with more acculturated places, such as St. Boniface and Moncton, or less developed segments of la Francophonie, such as Djibouti or the Cameroons.

This is the genius of the Trudeau formula: it was proportionate. His bicultural program was neither binationalism nor tokenism, to deal with a restless jurisdiction that feared assimilation, was tempted by independence, but could be fairly and sensibly satisfied with a mélange of sovereignty and association – almost comedian Yvon Deschamps' old joke of "an independent Quebec in a strong Canada," except that it is not risible. It is, yet again, the confirmation of historian W.L. Morton's description of Canada as a country "strong only in moderation and governable only by compromise." It was Trudeau's great achievement, and his call on the gratitude of the country, that he steered deftly between the rednecks raving about bilingual cornflakes boxes (he suggested they turn their boxes around) and the Quebec separatists crabbing about tokenism.

It took me some decades, mainly lived in other countries, to realize that this quality is at least as much a strength as a weakness. But I have gradually seen that the ability to elaborate public policy within these constraints, though it is extremely difficult to describe in an uplifting way and is certainly unheroic, and is a spectator sport only for true aficionados, is a remarkable and benign national talent and vocation.

---

A word for my old friend Hugh Segal (and colleague in the effort to encourage the late Claude Wagner into federal Conservative politics forty years ago, still the stuff, for both of us I'm sure, of some good after-dinner stories). Senator Segal is absolutely right that Canada should assist and lead in helping the moderate opposition in Syria. The Assad regime is a sponsor of terrorism, as Gaddafi was, and like Gaddafi should be overthrown, whatever replaces it. The devil we know deserves to be ousted; we can deal with the devil we don't know later. Eventually, they will become so attached to incumbency they will cease to be devils, at least to the West.

The reason is certainly humanitarian, as the senator said, as well as punitive, as it was in Libya. But it is also part of the greater problem of Iran. Deposing its only real Arab ally and conduit to Hezbollah would help stabilize Lebanon, reduce the threat to northern Israel, reduce the Iranian potential for mischief-making generally, and possibly even assist whatever forces of reason may still subsist in the Iranian theocracy to be more cautious about nuclear weapons. Stephen Harper has an excellent record in Middle Eastern affairs; he should not miss this opportunity to add to it.

# THOMAS MULCAIR
# PROMOTES AN ODIOUS
# SPECIES OF "FEDERALISM"

*National Post*, January 26, 2013

---

New Democratic Party leader Thomas Mulcair spoke to University of Toronto political science undergraduates earlier this month, and claimed to be uttering a largely non-partisan exhortation to his listeners to participate in the political process. The leader of the opposition said he was motivated by the fact that approximately 65 per cent of Canadians between the ages of eighteen and twenty-five did not vote in the last election. This theme was unexceptionable. But not so innocuous was his version of the political evolution of Quebec.

In his January 14 speech at the University of Toronto's Convocation Hall, Mr. Mulcair started from the well-known NDP premise of the desirability of a statist, or highly *dirigiste*, society. The more enthusiastic a person is for an interventionist and authoritarian state, the more likely that person is to favour relatively high taxes to pay for these interventions – with the resultant encroachment on individual liberties being represented as merely a reflection of collectively expressed political will. As for the fact that these interventions are usually done by executive order, under only generally enabling legislation, and are implemented by unelected and largely unaccountable officials – this is something that Mulcair left to his audience to discover as they progress down the great boulevard of life.

According to Mulcair, Canada's Wheat Board – whose Western wheat and barley monopoly finally was ended after seventy-seven years in 2012 as a superfluous and meddlesome impediment to agrarian prosperity – gave farmers "an even break" and prevented the American phenomenon Mulcair claimed to perceive of "multinationals taking over more farms" (a figment of his frequently verdant imagination).

Mulcair also declared that "poor people don't have access to health care without universality," which is a complete falsehood: all advanced countries provide access to health care. Canada is the only one among them that has tried to ban large swaths of private medicine.

These are the usual liberties with the truth that assist those who desire – and particularly those who desire to direct and impose – big government. But more troubling in Mulcair's case (and something that should be elaborated as a fundamental political issue by the other political parties) is his enthusiasm for Quebec government-mandated infringement on freedom of expression in the cause of the cultural ambitions of French Quebeckers.

In his pursuit of retention of the French nationalist vote in federal elections in Quebec that his predecessor, Jack Layton, wrested from the Bloc Québécois in the 2011 federal election, Mulcair made what amounts to a pre-emptive strike against the general federalist position of the Conservatives, Liberals, and (insofar as they address the issue) the Greens, which is that French- and English-language rights should be assured throughout Canada.

In this area, Mulcair makes two false claims that are insidious and scandalously cynical. First, he credits the NDP with ending the artificial division of Quebec political allegiances along the issue of constitutional options. Second, he claims that cultural repression in Quebec is a buttress to federalism because it serves to ease French Quebec's insecurities; and that, as a result, the NDP, while it panders to separatists, in fact is the true federalist party.

In service to the first claim, Mulcair makes the argument that both the sovereigntist PQ and Quebec's federalist Liberal Party are broadtent groupings of voters reflecting a wide ideological range between socialists and conservatives. This is rubbish: both are left-of-centre parties, and the ideological difference that exists between them is fairly subtle, consisting chiefly of the PQ's enthusiasm to turn the tax and culture screws harder on the non-French in order to accelerate the process of driving them out of Quebec (thereby making it easier to get a majority of Quebec referendum voters to lead a culturally cleansed province out of Canada). The Liberals are more restrained, as almost all the non-French vote for them and now provide most of their support.

What Mulcair dismisses as an "artificial axis of sovereignty or federalism" (as between the PQ and the Liberals) is in fact the evidently principal issue of Quebec public policy. Practically all Quebeckers in both parties are addicted to the overweening state that Mulcair favours for ideological reasons, especially as the primarily English-speaking provinces of Canada are paying for much of it through transfer payments, a fact that Mulcair does not acknowledge (and cannot acknowledge without alienating the Quebec nationalists whose electoral boots he is so energetically and verbosely licking).

In regard to private schools that frustrate the Quebec government's policy (under both parties) of forcing the children of immigrants to attend schools where French is the language of instruction (and not just an important part of the curriculum), Mr. Mulcair claims that such private education alternatives are "not helpful" – by which he apparently means "not helpful to the suppression of other languages and of parental rights."

In the same vein, the NDP leader pats himself on the head and back for declaring his support for the many official restrictions on the use of English and other languages in Quebec, such as on commercial signs. Such restrictions are, in fact, completely unnecessary to the preservation of the French language in Quebec and are odious to anyone with the slightest concern for freedom of expression that is otherwise regarded as one of the cornerstones of democratic civilization. That freedom was proclaimed and assented to by all democratic countries, including Canada, in the Atlantic Charter of 1941, drafted originally and signed in Newfoundland, and was what we successfully fought for in the Second World War.

Finally, Mulcair used his University of Toronto speech to claim that French Quebeckers were "far more secure in 1980," when the independence referendum was won 60–40 by the federalists, than in 1995, when it was a hair's-breadth margin; his point here being that securing maximum protections for the French language, and restrictions on other languages, is the best way to prevent the flourishing of separatist sentiment. But language conditions did not appreciably change in Quebec during the fifteen-year interregnum he describes.

The real reason most Quebeckers are not interested in sovereignty now is because: (1) they are addicted to over $8 billion of annual transfer payments, from elsewhere in Canada, which enable them to have a low birthrate, a white-collar service economy, and have almost all the trappings of an autonomous country; (2) they recognize that English Canadians already have made a good faith effort at conciliation and will make no more substantial concessions; (3) another trick referendum question promising independence with the continued benefit of Confederation won't fly; (4) any secession would be an economic and demographic catastrophe, leaving Quebec with Greek-level debt and several hundred thousand fewer taxpayers; and (5) an appreciable number of them actually believe in Canada.

Thomas Mulcair is committing the hypocrisy of grovelling to French Quebec racists while claiming to be a successful federalist. He must not be allowed to get away with this monstrous canard. Stephen Harper [and (presumably) Justin Trudeau] must assure that he does not.[†]

---

† In the election of October 2015, they did just that.

# TURNING PUBLIC DISCOURSE INTO A NEVER-ENDING SHRIEK OF "UNCLEAN!"

*National Post*, March 8, 2013

---

This is my first foray into the subject of pornography in any form. I have never seriously looked at adult heterosexual pornography, much less aberrant or deviant forms, and I only venture here because my experiences as a prisoner for three years give me a perspective that I have not seen in the furor following Tom Flanagan's comments on the subject.

I have met the University of Calgary academic twice, and find him to be a decent and civilized man. Last week, during Q and A at the University of Lethbridge, he spoke flippantly on a terribly serious subject, child pornography, and deeply offended legitimate sensibilities. It was a bad mistake and he has apologized for it.

In the circumstances, his apology should be accepted, and he should not have been dismissed by the CBC, the *Globe and Mail*, or from any other affiliations. Sincere apologies for mistakes that are not illegalities or revelations of fundamental failings of character should not bring such heavy retribution as was inflicted on Tom Flanagan. This society's concern about pedophilia should not be taken to such an extent that insensitive – but not discreditably intended – remarks become an instant race to stone verbal offenders to death before they can utter their abject recantations. It is even a criminal offence to view explicit child pornography and then destroy it, having shown it to no one (though it is hard to prove other than by confession or security camera).

When I was in U.S. federal prisons, I met many men who had been severely sentenced for downloading child pornography. Most of what little violence there was in those low-security prisons was directed against these people, for no reason other than outrage at the nature of their alleged offences. None of the people whom I met had actually molested or even approached a child; none had created child pornography, profited from it, or distributed it. I am well familiar with the practice of convicted people to whitewash their records, especially where they are at some physical danger, as those of us who were sent to prison could be if careless, unlucky, or stigmatized by the nature of the conviction. But in the case of those I refer to, I had all of their records checked (all criminal convictions in the United States are publicly accessible), and their offences were as I have described.

Having objected to the habit of overreactive disassociation with anything or anyone to do with this kind of conduct, I will not labour my own extreme distaste and concern for the subject. Lawyers, psychiatrists, and qualified behaviourists whom I know and respect have all told me that some examples of child pornography are so disgusting that even the most worldly and experienced professionals are profoundly shaken and repulsed by them.

I am sure that that is true. But inflicting heavy prison sentences on the sort of people I met in prison, who were convicted of downloading this material in their homes – who are no threat to anyone but like watching this sort of thing and don't pay for it or share it – is wrong and part of the problem, not a step toward a solution.

Without exception, in all other aspects of their personalities that I encountered (and prisoners live at close quarters with each other), these were perfectly sociable men. They were often quite cultured; one was a chef, one a French teacher, one an art teacher. They were interesting conversationalists and their conduct as prisoners gave no hint of aggression or deviance.

I am afraid that this is a problem that surfaced in our Western societies relatively suddenly, having long been repressed, and has roused a level of hysteria that is understandable. And given the concern most of us rightly have for the welfare of children, this attitude is useful up to a point. But it is not an answer in itself, and it is not the sort of initial response conducive to finding the best possible way to address the problem.

Society does not need protection from the type of people I am writing about here. They are no more likely to inflict themselves on children or anyone else than the rest of us are. And sending them to prison for long periods, where they are ostracized and largely forced to associate with each other, and where they are apt to be beaten up at any time as unlucky props in the sociopathic frustrations and belligerency of other prisoners, dressing up their aggressivity as righteousness on behalf of the defenceless, will make things worse. It is unjust to everyone.

From what I have seen of the response to the Flanagan affair, his critics have made practically no distinction between those who derive pleasure from looking at child pornography privately and passively and those who sexually assault children. Yet few legal and moral distinctions are clearer and more honoured by time and practice than those between private contemplation of deranged or even psychotic activities and the perpetration of them.

I was not present at Tom Flanagan's session with the First Nations people in which the child pornography matter was suddenly raised at the University of Lethbridge event last week. But I have not seen that his own account of the occasion (published in these pages on Monday) has been contradicted by those who were there. And he seems certainly to have been on the better side of the question: he was just making that important distinction, albeit in negligently cavalier and provocative terms, as professors often do.

Then there is the civil rights aspect. It appears to be acceptable to society to have the police enter people's homes without notice and seize their computers and examine what they have been viewing and reading, and then to prosecute and imprison them for long periods in very hostile conditions, because of the nauseating and deranged nature of what they have been downloading for their own use – even though their imprisonment could not fail to aggravate whatever drove them to such objectively disgusting susceptibilities in the first place.

I believe that this is not acceptable, either in civil rights or correctional terms. On balance, people should be able to read and view what they want in privacy, as long as they are not profiting from or distributing such intolerable material. I agree that this sort of predilection is so abominable that society is justified in having those addicted to it discreetly identified, subjected to special scrutiny, and compelled to report for treatment and counselling. But the people I met who were convicted on these charges were not hopeless cases of psychiatric wreckage; were, I repeat, no danger to anyone, and throwing them into prison and ostracizing them in society while they are beaten up at the pleasure of other prisoners often no less legally tainted than themselves is not the response of a civilized society to a problem that requires a proper fusion of enforcement, compassion, and common sense.

It is particularly not an appropriate response given the unlimited availability of such material over the internet and the impossibility of prosecuting at the source. We are flogging the junkie, without recourse to the dealer, and then flogging insufficiently febrile commentators as well.

The scourge of child pornography is a terrible problem made more odious and unnerving by its revolting and perverted nature, and by the vulnerability of its victims. But the correct response is not to treat it like people in medieval times screaming "unclean" – not only at those suspected of being lepers but also, as in the Flanagan scenario, at those who even refer in an inappropriately relaxed way to non-contagious instances of leprosy. As a society, and for the sake of the victims especially, in reducing receptivity to child pornography and therefore the availability of it, we are going to have to do better than this.

# HARPER IN ISRAEL: A GREAT MOMENT FOR CANADA

*National Post*, January 25, 2014

Prime Minister Stephen Harper's address to the Israeli Knesset this week was one of the greatest speeches ever delivered by a Canadian leader, ranking (in content if not delivery, though that was quite adequate) with John A. Macdonald's defence of his conduct in the Pacific Scandal in 1873, Wilfrid Laurier's parliamentary response to conscription in 1917, and Pierre E. Trudeau's speech at the end of the Quebec sovereignty referendum campaign in 1980. The content of the Knesset speech was generally accurately reported in Canada, but not widely recognized as a brilliant address, as a great milestone in the rise of Canada as a power in the world, a clarification of the moral basis of this country's foreign policy, and as an episode that brings distinction on the whole country.

The prime minister emphasized the historic connection between our country and the Jews, who have been in Canada for 250 years. He said that the pride in Israel exhibited by Canada's 350,000 Jews is perfectly compatible with their Canadian patriotism. This was a worthwhile rebuttal of the hackneyed claim that Jews are compromised by "divided loyalties." In its most extreme form, this libel became the basis of Hitler's charge of treasonous betrayal in the First World War, and of Stalin's infamous persecution of Jews as "rootless cosmopolitans."

Mr. Harper declared: "After generations of persecution, the Jewish people deserve their own homeland and the right to live peacefully in that homeland." It was on this basis exactly that the United Nations *created* Israel, as opposed to merely admitting it as a member state, as the UN's five founding members did with Canada and the world's other nations. In the aftermath of the genocidal murder of half the world's Jews in the death camps of the Third Reich (along with six million non-Jews), it was agreed that the Jews should have a homeland in the land of Israel.

All the efforts to float a pluralistic Palestine or an unlimited right of return to Israel for the Arabs and their descendants who fled Palestine when Israel was founded would inundate Israel with hostile Arabs and convert the Jewish homeland into another opportunity to persecute a Jewish minority. They are, intentionally or otherwise, just attempts to reduce the Jews, one more time, to the status of a stateless and vulnerable minority. Two generations after the Holocaust, the Jewish homeland, a desert country the Jews have made fabulously successful, would be repealed and the Jews would be left once more at the mercy of their most zealous enemies.

Stephen Harper made the point that "Canada supports Israel because it is right," and he explained that in its history, Canada often has taken principled positions and made sacrifices, not because it was itself under threat, but because it was correct to do so. This was in fact what Canada did in both world wars, where, in an act unprecedented in world history, Canada, Australia, and New Zealand sent large numbers of volunteers to overseas wars to fight for the cause of freedom, although none of those countries was under any threat (except, more than two years after the outbreak of the Second World War, when Japan threatened Australia and New Zealand).

Harper acknowledged that Canada had entered the war against Nazi Germany despite our nation's failure to assist the Jews being persecuted in the Third Reich in the 1930s. In this, he accepted the moral failure of Prime Minister W.L. Mackenzie King, who, like the British leaders in the 1930s, did not lift a finger to assist the Jewish victims of the Nazis (in contrast to the United States, where Roosevelt admitted nearly 500,000 Jews, almost 20,000 Austrian Jews in one stroke after the German takeover of Austria, and without the congressional authorization that the law technically required; and withdrew his ambassador from Berlin after the unspeakable pogroms of Kristallnacht in November 1938).

Though Canada supports Israel because it is the right thing to do morally, Harper made the point that it is also the right thing to do strategically, because Israel is the only true democracy in the Middle East, and democracy, as he told the Knesset, is the only method of "assuring human rights, political stability, and economic prosperity." Moreover, "When democracy is threatened anywhere, it is threatened everywhere . . . by those who scorn modernity, loathe the liberty of others, and hold the cultures of others in contempt. [We must] stand up for a free and democratic Israel or our retreat in the world will begin." This was essentially the point that brought Canada into the world wars, and this position is consistent with our history and character.

"The Canadian commitment to what is right applies no less to the Palestinians [and to Canada's desire for] a just and secure future for the Palestinian people," Harper added. He also declared that when the borders of a Palestinian state are agreed to, Israel would be the first country to recognize it, but Canada will be the second.

The prime minister thus recorded that the principal obstacle to a Palestinian state is not Israel, but the Arab powers. Arab leaders have used the tragic fate of the Palestinians, which they have prolonged and exacerbated by keeping them teeming in wretched refugee camps, to distract the Arab masses from the despotism the Arab leaders have inflicted on their peoples while inflaming the pan-Arab world with the red herring of Israel.

Mr. Harper deplored that "the legitimacy of the existence of the State of Israel" has been compromised by world leaders' and diplomats' desire "to go along to get along" with Israel's enemies, and that this practice is regularly represented as "balanced" or diplomatically "sophisticated."

"Intellectualized arguments thinly mask underlying realities," he said. "Some openly call Israel an apartheid state. Think about the logic and outright malice behind that: a state based on freedom, democracy, and the rule of law that was founded so Jews can flourish as Jews and seek shelter from the worst racist experiment in history" is assimilated to the racist oppressions of South African apartheid. It is, he fairly stated, "sickening. . . . For too many nations, it is still easier to scapegoat Israel than to emulate your success. It is easier to foster resentment and hatred of Israel's democracy than it is to provide the same rights and freedoms to their own people."

As if to illustrate Stephen Harper's point, two Arab members of the Knesset heckled and shouted at him as the rest of the members of Israel's parliament applauded the visitor. Exercising democratic freedoms they would not have in ethnically more kindred states, the two legislators stormed out of the chamber, which rose en bloc to give the Canadian prime minister a prolonged standing ovation.

Harper did not discuss the specific issues that are now invoked to prevent progress in peace discussions, particularly the West Bank settlements. Israel demonstrated in Sinai and Gaza that it will concede settlements for real peace, but in the face of Arab claims of predestined demographic victory over Israel, gradually expanding the settlements is the best bargaining pressure Israel can apply, since, as a democracy, it cannot expel, coerce, or ghettoize the Arabs.

Nor can it engage in any more spurious land-for-peace arrangements such as Oslo, where land Israel gained in wars the Arabs started and lost is conceded for ceasefires of brief duration (if any). Yet the settlements issue is frequently invoked by those, including most of the Canadian foreign policy establishment and the opposition Liberals and New Democrats, in pursuit of the spurious "moral relativism" and "sophistication" that Harper rightly debunked.

The prime minister's speech concluded: "In the democratic family of nations, Israel represents values which our government takes as articles of faith and principles to drive our national life." Expressed in this way, Stephen Harper and John Baird's Israel policy is the first serious occasion in Canadian history when this country has taken a position sharply at variance with the United States and most of Western Europe, without truckling to powers antagonistic to the West, as Pierre Trudeau did with his sophomoric posturing as a neutral arms-control promoter. Stephen Harper has turned Canada into Israel's greatest ally; has aligned Canada with democracy against despotism, with international law and the better traditions of the United Nations against racism, bigotry, genocidal polemics, and Holocaust denial; has called the United States and the European Union back to their former and rightful views; and has erased the shame of the appeasement of the Nazis in the 1930s by the King government.

We have finally got beyond the self-righteous fairy tales about peacekeeping and "soft power." (You don't need peacekeepers in either peace or war, and soft power works only when there is a hard-power alternative.) All Canadians are ennobled by this espousal of, as the prime minister described it, what is morally imperative and strategically wise in the world's premier crisis area.

"Through fire and water, Canada will stand with you," he told the Israelis. All Canadians, including those who sympathize with the Palestinians, should support him.

# IN QUEBEC, COMMON SENSE HAS PREVAILED

*National Post*, November 8, 2014

---

The politics of Quebec are now almost Manichaean. On the one hand, the minister for Intergovernmental Affairs in the province's Liberal administration, Jean-Marc Fournier, has made reasonably constructive noises about trying to finish the task of crafting a Constitution that accommodates the entire country. On the other hand, the most visible aspirant to the leadership of the opposition Parti Québécois, Pierre Karl Péladeau, has launched a completely irresponsible attack on Quebec's most distinguished family (and a rival to his family's business).

Fournier recently spoke in Ottawa and said that the Constitution is "not taboo," a thought that arouses alarm in French and English Canada. English Canadians generally are averse to the grindingly difficult process they remember from endless federal–provincial conferences in the Trudeau and Mulroney eras, leading to the suspenseful Quebec and Charlottetown referenda; and the French Québécois do not want the financial and emotional strain that questions of independence inflicted on Quebec, bitterly dividing families and communities.

But Fournier was not asking for any of that. Although he spoke of entrenching the status of French in Quebec, as if that had not already been achieved these four hundred years, he stressed that the Constitution is "the fundamental contract of the country" and that it is unsatisfactory that Quebec has never specifically adhered to it after the patriation of 1982.

He spoke of the need for "a reciprocity of respect," a concept that has never been of much interest to the Parti Québécois. Although René Lévesque and some of his successors have been careful to avoid disparagements of the non-French in Quebec, they generally have reviled the federal government as an exploitive anachronism and a mere scaffolding, a façade behind which there is nothing except a desire to hoodwink and short-change French Quebec.

Quebec voters played along with this up to a point, as long as their governments could use the threat of independence to extract jurisdictional and fiscal concessions from Ottawa, but they have made it clear in many elections that they are not going to try to take that plunge. If a majority of Quebeckers wished to secede, there would always be millions who did not, and the Quebec nationalists could not seriously expect to drag those people out of Canada into an independent Quebec; there would have to be some sort of partitioning, which could be terribly difficult.

The public of Quebec also is reasonably numerate. And despite the perfervid efforts of separatist advocates to muddy the waters, any moron can see that Canada deluges Quebec with transfer payments, approximately $2,000 per capita annually for most Quebeckers. This is justifiable Danegeld from the federalist side to assure that the disruption of another separatist initiative doesn't get any traction.

Quebec premier Philippe Couillard made it clear in the election earlier this year that he was opposed to further oppression of the English language in Quebec and is a less ambiguous and a braver federalist than any occupant of his position since Jean Lesage or even (Colonel) Paul Sauvé. He referred last month to the possibility of trying to complete the process of securing Quebec's adherence to the Constitution, a process that was left incomplete at the federal–provincial conference of 1981 and by the failure to ratify the Meech Lake and Charlottetown agreements. The next day, however, Stephen Harper repeated his tiresomely familiar refusal to reopen the subject of the Constitution.

The problem really arises from the fact that Confederation was a pact between two peoples, French and English, originally involving four provinces, all of which, except Nova Scotia, had sizeable French or English cultural minorities. The federal Liberal Party, which governed the country for 80 of the 110 years between 1896 and 2006, imposed, under King, St. Laurent, and Trudeau, the fraud that "Quebec is a province like the others." It isn't. But in pursuing independence in gradual steps, concession after concession, the leaders of Quebec ceased to speak either for their non-French minority in Quebec or the French-Canadian minorities outside Quebec.

With the collapsed birthrate in the post-Catholic era in Quebec and the attempt to replace the unborn with immigration from Haiti and North Africa (people little interested in Quebec nationalism), the provincial leaders of Quebec have spoken for a steadily smaller proportion of Quebeckers, of French Canadians, and of Canadians as a whole. Their bargaining power has shrunk, and when English Canada voted to make no further concessions to Quebec in the national Charlottetown referendum (as Quebec voted not to accept the proposed concessions as adequate anyway), English Canada finally called Quebec's bluff and effectively told it to try to secede if it wanted to.

In 1995, Quebec came close to approving secession if greater powers could not be worked out within Canada – but only through the separatists' usual formula of a trick question offering all the benefits of federalism and independence, which has never been on offer and never will be (though I was not convinced that Robert Stanfield or Joe Clark could not have been tricked into such a thing).

With the Constitution, we can muddle along indefinitely with arrangements Quebec has not ratified, but not forever. It is important unfinished business. Jean-Marc Fournier was effectively asking for private talks; perhaps they are taking place – we need never know unless they are successful. But they should take place, and if Ottawa and Quebec can reach agreement on the terms of Quebec's unconditional reintegration into the framework of the country, then the federal government could sponsor the arrangements in all of the country and the government of Quebec could do so in the National Assembly of that province. Agreement would likely result, in this relatively serene political ambiance. While we were at it, we could modernize the time-warped relics of the Senate and the governor general and upgrade the quality of their personnel.

While the governing party in Quebec has been trying to address this concern, the likeliest successor to the headship of the almost unrecognizably battered PQ, the hyperactive Pierre Karl Péladeau, has accused the Quebec government of truckling to Alberta oil interests under the saturnine influence of Power Corporation, controlled by the family of the late and distinguished Paul G. Desmarais, which, with a Belgian partner, owns 3.6 per cent of French petroleum giant Total.

This is conspiracy theory, one that is on all fours with the claims of the far right in Quebec two generations ago of Liberal plans to assimilate the French and swamp Quebec with Jewish immigration; and of the far left a generation ago of plans to sell Quebec's resources and patrimony for a bagatelle to Americans and their Toronto quisling helpers. This from the same font of statesmanlike ideas that in the last year gave us the Quebec Charter of (bigoted and repressive) Values and its policing of headgear and sectarian ornaments.

Quebec's capacity to be distracted by charlatans has not entirely vanished. When Premier Philippe Couillard and Jean-Marc Fournier are trying to stabilize constitutional arrangements with Canada once and for all, they should not be ignored because of Harper's phobia of any controversy whose outcome cannot be conveniently preordained. There is an opportunity to act, and it should be grasped.

*Harper's spurious reference to the Supreme Court of the ability of the House of Commons almost alone to abolish the Senate, an absurd constitutional non-starter, when rejected, was invoked as an excuse to do nothing. This subject must be addressed but must not be the subject of overpublicized grandstanding contests between the provincial premiers outbidding each other in demands for federal concessions, which Trudeau and Mulroney manfully endured.*

*Harper's follow-up response to the challenge of Senate reform was simply not to name any senators. When time came for the 2015 elections, there were twenty-three vacancies; it was a childish and silly policy, which seems not to have impressed voters.*

# A JUDICIAL COUP D'ÉTAT

*National Post*, January 31, 2015, and February 7, 2015

---

January 31, 2015

Very inadequate attention has been paid to the persecution of Joseph Groia, former director of enforcement of the Ontario Securities Commission and a prominent Toronto barrister. He has been the subject of an unfeasible charge from the Law Society of Upper Canada of "incivility" in the lengthy trial of John Felderhof, chief geologist of Bre-X and sole and scapegoat defendant in one of the greatest fraud cases in Canadian history.

Tens of billions of dollars of gold reserves were alleged to have been found in Indonesia by Bre-X, and it rose from a penny stock to $286 (adjusted for stock splits) before the ore samples were discovered to be fraudulent and the mining property to be commercially worthless. The stock price evaporated. Felderhof was charged with insider trading in 1999. His trial started in 2001 but was delayed four years by the OSC's attempt to have trial judge Peter Hryn removed for bias, essentially because Hryn upheld the rules of evidence and did not allow the OSC to introduce herniating masses of uncatalogued exhibits.

Groia resisted this so successfully that, after he discovered in the commission's jungle of documents items helpful to the defence, the OSC felt obliged to require him to prove the authenticity of evidence it had originally sought to admit, before it would agree to its admission. Hryn was sustained by the Superior Court and then, on appeal by the osc, by the Court of Appeal. The Superior and Appeal courts did criticize Groia, though they also criticized the conduct of the osc prosecutors. Justice Rosenberg for the Court of Appeal added that the incidences of unprofessional conduct by the osc prosecutors were "perhaps less frequent," but Judge Hryn was affirmed. After this four-year diversion, Felderhof's trial resumed in 2005.

Groia represented Felderhof very successfully, and through most of the trial he acted pro bono, as Felderhof ran out of money. But for Groia's generous and principled nature, Felderhof would have fallen into the morass of the public defender system and been steamrollered by the osc. Felderhof was acquitted in 2007. The commission had acknowledged from the outset that it had no evidence that Felderhof had any knowledge of the fraud that was the basis of the Bre-X fiasco, and insider trading was the mousey charge born of this mountainous scam (where $6 billion were lost by trusting investors, to the more astute or lucky shareholders who sold their Bre-X stock to those left holding the bag when the fraud blew up). The osc did not appeal.

It was a classic case of someone being selected as the fall guy and symbolic defendant. It was also a classic example of the lawyer as heroic and disinterested champion of an innocent underdog. This is the stuff of much legal lore and many fine novels and films. But the greatest drama, and the most egregious persecution in this whole sequence, were yet to come. Before the trial ended, the Law Society of Upper Canada had begun to intervene, objecting to Groia's "incivility." Its internal committee that determines what activities merit close scrutiny examined the case and eventually told Groia to justify his conduct. A mystified Groia was unaware that there was any conduct he needed to justify. His apparent real offence was to have won a case and exposed the osc's effort at prosecution as unsupported by evidence and questionably motivated.

The trial judge had found nothing unprofessional in Groia's conduct. The trial had been robust on both sides and the conduct of the osc was frequently very bellicose. It was a no-holds-barred battle, but as far as is known, the OSC did not generate a complaint about Groia. This appears to have been a spontaneous brainwave of members of the enforcement apparatus of the Law Society. Their motives are not clear but should be examined in sworn testimony before this alarming saga ends.

The militants in the Law Society were heard initially by a three-person panel of the society, only one of whose members had any criminal law experience. The opening gambit of Groia's accusers was that Groia's infractions of professional and barristerial standards had emerged indisputably in the Felderhof trial and that he had no right to defend himself at all before the hearing panel of the Law Society – indeed, that even attempting to do so was an abuse of process. No such offence had been alleged or found at trial, and it was proposed to brush past the trial judge and the higher court jurists who confirmed the judge's right to try the case and the rectitude of his conduct. Groia was to be condemned on the sole authority of his almost anonymous enemies in a Law Society Star Chamber.

The purpose of the hearing was to determine the penalty to be imposed on the pre-convicted Groia. The entire notion of an accused putting up a defence of his conduct was to be rejected as not only superfluous but in itself an affront to the whole concept of due process. As I was myself rather distracted by legal travails at the time, I only followed this vaguely. But having known Groia professionally, I doubted that he would ever behave unprofessionally, and it did seem to me then, as it does now, profoundly disconcerting that officials responsible for ensuring probity and integrity in the legal system and profession should challenge the right of an accused person to any defence at all. Even the Red Queen would take evidence, albeit after the sentence (which also preceded the verdict and the charge, but given the chance the Law Society might emulate that sequence also).

Groia's counsel in these proceedings is Earl Cherniak, another eminent barrister (who has acted successfully for me a number of times). As Groia gamely wrote in a monograph about the case, which has cost him most of the last sixteen years and over $2 million in costs and fees, it is rare that a lawyer has the opportunity to fight so clearly for such conspicuous matters of principle. It shortly emerged in the initial Law

Society hearing that in addition to having the effrontery to contest his innocence of professional misconduct at all, Groia had used the word "government" as a supposedly pejorative adjective or noun in reference to the OSC, and had allegedly omitted the word "simply" in quoting a statement uncontestedly uttered by Frank Switzer, the OSC director of communications.

Groia was also held to have spoken abusively in court on a number of occasions, including when he said that the "prosecutors' statements were not worth the transcript paper they were printed on," though there was ample reason for such reflections, which, again, were not found objectionable by the presiding judge or the jurists to whom these matters were referred in the action to remove Hryn. The hearing panel was partly overruled by the Law Society's appeal panel (which had no one on it with any criminal law experience). This panel confirmed Groia's right to defend himself, but found that Groia was unreasonable in his reflections on prosecutorial misconduct, motives, and integrity, and this was held to have had a serious adverse impact on the trial, though these findings were all contrary to the opinions of the trial judge and reviewing judges. The appeal committee purported to impose a suspension of a month and costs of $200,000 on Groia, who has appealed to the Divisional Court, where the matter now sits.

Even I – after all the megalomania and intellectual corruption and professional hypocrisy I have witnessed in the last decade in the U.S. legal system, and its echoes among the Canadian quislings who abound in the entourages and committees of public institutions in this country, down to clubs and honours-dispensers, heavy with their own cowardice and inflated sufficiency – even I was astounded at the sanctimonious pettifogging of these nasty proceedings. The complainants are (in Cromwellian terms) among our traditionally most decayed servitors, the authors of what in France in successive centuries has been called "the treason of the clerisy," the abuse of petty office to betray the principles of the national society to envy, malice, faction, and self-interest. It is the shrivelled and bitter detritus of little, colonial Canada, the falsely obsequious greasers of the components of the system.

The underlying problem is that after many centuries of judicial precedent have left the conduct of trials to presiding judges, the secondary and often arbitrary or even spurious criterion of "civility" is now being invoked by anonymous tinkerers in the bar bureaucracy to ignore and repeal the powers of judges and capriciously dictate the conduct of barristers. There is no precedent for such an intrusion, no legally authoritative mandate for it, no semblance of professional or legislative consultation. It is an outright usurpation, a *coup d'état judiciaire*.

There has always been some doubt about the ability of the legal profession to regulate itself, and its attempts to do so have often amounted to a rather self-serving defence of the impermeability of the legal cartel to outside pressures whatever their merits. But this is an outrage – an unspecified faction within the bar administration emasculating the bench, ignoring most of the benchers, and randomly terrorizing the profession, the public and the public interest be damned. It must not succeed.

---

February 7, 2015

The Divisional Court, last Monday, released its decision rejecting Mr. Groia's appeal from the hearing and appeal panels of the Law Society of Upper Canada, finding him guilty of misconduct and upholding his suspension for one month from practice and awarding costs against him of $200,000. (The appeal panel had reduced the hearing panel's suspension of two months and $246,000 in costs.)

While the decision was competently written and fairly thoroughly explained by Justice Ian Nordheimer on behalf of a panel including two of his colleagues (Justices Sachs and Harvison Young), and I will not reargue my points of last week, I believe it to be an unjust and dangerous decision – which I understand will be appealed.

The Divisional Court upholds the appeal panel's reversal of the hearing panel's determination that Groia should be penalized for not showing remorse for his conduct, which the first panel held to be a danger in the future to the exercise of justice. Nordheimer pointed out that this was implausible, since it was conceded that Groia was sincere in his aspersions of the OSC prosecutors and that it was unlikely that he would be a danger, given his many years of "unblemished" practice, including over ten years since the incidents that gave rise to these proceedings. But the Divisional Court held that a good faith belief in his reasonableness did not liberate Groia from the finding of misconduct through "uncivil" behaviour that could "bring justice into disrepute."

Early in his judgment, Nordheimer laments a rise in barristerial incivility, denies that there is any incongruity in "the profession," as he rather grandiloquently describes the Law Society of Upper Canada, acting in a disciplinary role where the trial judge has not done so with no adverse reflection on the performance of the judge thereby. And Nordheimer refers a bit huffily to the O.J. Simpson trial and to film and television portrayals of courtroom proceedings generally, as if Groia was responsible for any of that.

Nordheimer writes early on that he will not go over in "excruciating" detail Groia's alleged verbal and behavioural transgressions, and the only illustrative phrase cited is Groia's reference to the vast mass of documentary evidence the OSC sought first to admit and then selectively to challenge as "wheat and chaff." While the inference is incited that both sides regularly hurled frightful abuse at each other, the evidence focuses, as I wrote last week, on rather tepid impeachments such as whether Groia meant the noun or adjective "government" in reference to the OSC prosecutors disrespectfully, and whether he misrepresented the OSC communications director's statement that the commission "simply" wanted to get a conviction (against Felderhof). Nordheimer and his colleagues brushed aside interventions on Groia's behalf from the Advocates' Society, the Canadian Civil Liberties Association, and Criminal Lawyers' Association as not relevant to the constructive point on the evils of incivility the court claimed to be upholding. The justices denied that this was any sort of "test case" or a matter that directly affected the broad "public interest," concluded that Groia had brought justice into disrepute, and while agreeing with the "profession's" appeal panel rejection of what they called the hearing panel's principal conclusion, they supported its only minimal reduction of the initial penalty.

What really brings justice into disrepute is endlessly protracted disputes (this one is far from over, sixteen years after the Felderhof case began) where relatively genteel disapprobation, engaged in by both sides in court without overly upsetting a presiding judge sustained by two higher courts in the competence of his handling of the case, is waved about like a bloody shirt by almost anonymous, self-launched inquisitors, leading to this bizarre finding. This is especially so when the decision is apparently a judicial pat on the head to the "profession" for commanding, Canute-like, the recession of the current societal wave of incivility and histrionic vulgarization of court proceedings.

At least in the United States, it is a notorious fact regularly condemned in the leading media outlets and in Congress and often by senior judges and lawyers that the civil U.S. legal system is a psychotically litigious jungle. U.S. criminal justice is a playpen for corrupt and capricious prosecutors to operate a conveyor belt to the country's hideously overpopulated and expensive prison system (the country has a 99.5 per cent conviction rate, 97 per cent without a trial, because of the manipulation of the plea-bargain system).

No one said anything about bringing justice into disrepute during the O.J. Simpson trial which so scandalized Justice Nordheimer, when every night during the trial Jay Leno's *Tonight Show* opened with "the Flying Itos," five diminutive berobed men apparently of East Asian ancestry, resembling the Simpson trial judge Lance Ito, who rushed onto the stage from the right, performed a spectacular series of cartwheels across the stage, black robes flying, and ran off the stage to the left.

In the United States, the law is generally "an ass," and a severely spavined ass at that, and almost everyone knows it. A bit of comic bathos is welcome. We haven't descended to quite such depths here, but we are on the same slipway, and this sort of proceeding accelerates the descent. Too much piety about the dignity of the process is implausible (and itself undignified).

If we had any serious leadership in the vital public-policy area of justice, we would require the "profession" to submit to a much stronger criterion of public interest and stop these enervating internecine persecutions. Radical, though well-considered, reforms would be welcome. (Joe Groia's election as a bencher of the Law Society, which he is seeking, could be a start).‡ The legal profession in Ontario has substantially failed at self-regulation and that right should be curtailed.

---

‡ He was elected.

The state's overregulation of the financial industry should also be rolled back, as in the United Kingdom, now the world's greatest international financial centre, where regulation is by the industry under the aegis of the governor of the Bank of England, and prosecutions are by the fraud section of the Crown Law Office under the authority of the non-political attorney general. An inordinate number of lawyers are traumatized by taking their incomes from clients they consider intellectually beneath them, just as, for essentially the same reason in reverse, many businessmen, to add a cubit to their intellectual stature, have squandered billions of dollars of their companies' and their own money in redundant business schools, as commerce is essentially arithmetic, a trade, and an intuition, not an academic pursuit. We should revive the high court of Parliament, but not by continuing to emasculate judges by dictating mandatory sentences in politically sensitive cases.

Pierre Trudeau emphasized individual rights in his Charter of Rights and Freedoms to distract Quebec from the quarrel over jurisdictional rights. He defeated the separatists but transformed the bench into a legion of affirmative action, idiosyncratic hobby-horse tinkerers and meddlers. It is time to clean it all up, before we all become an uncoordinated mass of Flying Itos.

# ALARM BELLS MUST
# RING IN RESPONSE
# TO THE GOVERNMENT'S
# NEW ANTI-TERROR BILL

*National Post*, February 28, 2015

---

B ill C-51, the federal government's Anti-Terrorism Act, 2015, is the principal official response to the increasing threat of terrorism, a phenomenon that infamously prorupted into the Central Block of Parliament on October 22 after the murder of a soldier ceremonially guarding the Tomb of the Unknown Soldier at the National War Memorial in Ottawa.

The purpose of the measure is given as assurance that the people of Canada "live free from threats to their lives and their security," as "there is no more fundamental role for a government than protecting its country and its people." To this end, government departments and agencies are authorized and instructed to share information that could frustrate or reveal attempts "to undermine" or "threaten the security of Canada"; the minister of public security and emergency preparedness compiles a list of people who he or she "has reasonable grounds to suspect will attempt to threaten transport security" or commit or facilitate a "terrorism offence" in Canada or elsewhere.

This sounds fairly innocuous by the standards of legislation conferring enhanced arbitrary powers on law enforcement officials, but, as is usual and to some extent unavoidable, many of the elaborations of enhanced official powers are very broadly outlined. Reading through the text of this and related bills, it is evident that the principal areas of impact are lowering the threshold for arrest, criminalizing the promotion of terrorism, conferring powers of disruption on CSIS (Canadian Security Intelligence Service), giving the power to remove designated terrorist material from the internet, permitting court proceedings to be sealed while they are in progress for protection of investigative techniques, evidence, and personnel, expanding the government's ability to stop people from leaving the country, and granting unspecified and scarcely limited powers of arbitrary, warrantless, detention.

It becomes quite troubling with the provisions that "every person who, by communicating statements, knowingly advocates or promotes the commission of terrorism offences in general . . . while knowing that any of those offences will be committed or being reckless as to whether any of those offences may be committed . . . is liable to imprisonment of not more than five years"; and that anyone responsible for "any writing, sign, visible representation or audio recording that advocates or promotes . . . or counsels the commission of a terrorist offence" may have material seized, internet excerpts deleted, and be subject to detention, indictment, and imprisonment, though the authority of the attorney general is required for such proceedings.

Even more worrisome is the provision that a person may be detained in custody without warrant if a peace officer "believes on reasonable grounds that a terrorist activity may be carried out," or that such arrest and detention "is likely to prevent the carrying out of the terrorist activity," pending ratification of the action by a provincial court. Most Canadians would not be too much disturbed by the requirement that such a suspect be "prohibited from possessing any firearm [or] crossbow," or be confined to a geographic area temporarily.

But alarm bells really must ring at "If there are reasonable grounds to believe that a particular activity constitutes a threat to the security of Canada, the service [CSIS] may take measures in or outside Canada, to reduce the threat." These are unspecified, and must be "reasonable and proportional," but they are unlimited except by the admonition not to violate the Charter of Rights and Freedoms or any other law, unless "authorized to take them under a warrant," but there are no further guidelines on the issuance of warrants. It is not altogether comforting to read that the authorities are forbidden to "cause intentionally or by criminal negligence, death or bodily harm," or "wilfully [to] attempt in any manner to obstruct, pervert, or defeat the course of justice; or violate the sexual integrity of an individual."

Those representing the public security and emergency prepared-ness minister may decide whether a warrant is necessary for any of these initiatives, in Canada or in any other country: "Without regard to any other law, including that of any foreign state, a judge may, in a warrant . . . authorize the measures specified in it to be taken out-side Canada." Obviously, no foreign jurisdiction would accept that a Canadian authority has any standing to approve such an intrusion, and it is fervently to be hoped that no one in the federal government imag-ines that it would be a good thing to exchange empowerments for the execution of such warrants with other countries, provoking a regime of reciprocal extra-legal, official outrages across international frontiers.

All of these steps create problems on the civil liberties front. As presented, Bill C-51 makes a Swiss cheese out of due process, and the three national political parties have approached the problem from dis-tinctly different angles. The government have swaddled themselves in Stephen Harper's default-toga of protecting the public, aspersing civil liberties concerns, and uttering tired pieties that "the law enforce-ment agencies are on our side," presumably referring to their objectives rather than their political preferences. It is easy to be cynical about this and resignedly conclude that Vic Toews and Julian Fantino ride again (itself a terrorizing thought, and thought-terror is assumedly covered in the vast sweep of this bill). The government is responsible for pre-venting terrorist outrages from happening and it has to be given some licence to protect the country and everyone in it. But it is hard to be overly sanguine about the medieval antics of the government that took the giant leap backwards that was the omnibus crime bill. Nor is it reas-suring that Mr. Harper, as is his frequent custom, is imposing a short-ened debate on Parliament.

The Liberals have accepted the bill but claim to seek a clearer and heavier oversight than is now provided. This has been much mocked as toadying to reactionary opinion, but again, it is an attempt to reconcile the conflicting goals – though the unofficial opposition is no more specific about increased oversight than the government is about the many open-ended powers it wants to give the whole range of law enforcement agencies. The New Democrats and their leader, Thomas Mulcair, deserve credit for tackling this sloppily worded measure head on. He and his colleagues have said that the failure to give more precision to "disrupt" and many other new official rights is careless, that anyone protesting even the construction of a pipeline could be a target for some of these actions, and that there is insufficient focus on "deradicalization," but that the NDP could support a bill adequately clarified.

We have ample proof, from the McDonald Commission's 1981 report and elsewhere, that the law enforcement agencies in this country, as in others, are capable of outrageous and unfathomably stupid abuses, and anyone who has had anything to do with any arm of the law knows it (although most people in these occupations are reasonably dedicated and honest). Definitions have to be tightened; oversight has to be stringent and prompt and answerable to parliament, and we should be careful of too much reciprocity with foreign governments. Only ten or twelve other countries have as much respect for human liberties as Canada does and must retain; the United States, with its 99.5 per cent conviction rate and stacked rules and bloated prison industry, is not one of them. If we go to sleep in Canada, we will wake up in an unrecognizable despotism, like Argentina, Turkey, or Louisiana.

# CANADA AND
# THE UNITED STATES

Unpublished

In early 2010, I was invited by a professor at the University of Toronto to contribute a piece to a book that would be published by the university – a collection of reflections about public intellectuals. This was what I wrote, but on submitting it, I was invited to write instead about my then current legal difficulties. This was the first suggestion of this and I declined and withdrew from the project.

---

It is with natural Canadian reticence that I hesitate to claim the status of a public intellectual, though it is certainly flattering to be so described. In this essay, there is great emphasis on salient aspects of the history of the United States, but particularly on their impact on Canada, and this is more a discussion of Canada's response to those events and personalities than a recitation of reasonably familiar chapters of American history. The point of the essay is that the relationship and underlying correlation between the two countries have shifted substantially, and if those holders of public offices that occupy themselves with continental relations are slow to grasp this, and the media are unlikely to find it close enough to the surface of daily events to notice, this is a fine example of where public intellectuals can usefully attract the attention of a wider echelon of opinion.

The emergence of Canada as a major power in the world has been predicted as regularly, for almost as long and just as imminently, as the deafeningly trumpeted rise of Brazil. Unlike Brazil, the problem has not been that Canada has been a late bloomer among the world's important countries; it is that Canada has so long measured itself against what General de Gaulle identified in 1944 as "the overwhelming contiguity" of the United States. It has an almost neurotic aversion or inability to recognize or believe that it has added a large cubit to its absolute and comparative stature as an important country. It has always thought itself a rather virtuous country, sometimes to a fault, as well as a pleasant place to live, but not as one that had much capacity to act as an influential autonomous force in the world.

When Canada, in the mid-eighteenth century, was hostile zones of English and French colonial soldiers, the American colonists (slave-holding and otherwise) were uniformly British, more than fifteen times as numerous, and in a more temperate clime. By 1775, the Americans had nearly 40 per cent of the population of Great Britain (excluding an increasingly fractious Ireland), a higher standard of living than the Mother Country, and were advantageously represented in London by Benjamin Franklin (1757–1762 and 1764–1775) and others. It served the convenience of the British in their postpartum hauteur, and of the Americans in their national creationist myth-making, to represent the thirteen colonies as puny and sparse, and they were rough and ready places, but they were already a geopolitical factor in the world by 1775, as impending events were about to demonstrate.

From 1775 to 1860, America waged and won its Revolution and developed its genius for the spectacle, the generation of legends, and the star system, which has never deserted it. The founders, Washington, Franklin, Hamilton, Jefferson, Madison, and Adams, became an almost instant pantheon of epochal personalities. They were an unusually talented group, and a couple of them possessed genius, but not necessarily more so than some of their contemporaries in more venerable countries, such as Burke, both Pitts, Fox, Wellington, Talleyrand, Metternich, and of course, the master legend-maker and supreme adventurer of all time, Napoleon.

It was an astounding feat of public-relations legerdemain that Jefferson, Thomas Paine, and a few others managed to sell the American

Revolution as a triumph of democratic government, of "self-evident truths," and "inalienable rights" to the establishment, and retention of which was pledged the "sacred honour" of the insurgents. Benjamin Franklin, as agent of Pennsylvania in London during the Seven Years War, was instrumental in persuading the British to expel France from Quebec, and not, as was of more interest to many in British public life, from the Caribbean, although the French king, Louis XV, and his chief minister, Choiseul, couldn't wait to be done with Canada, which had never returned the heavy costs of establishing and defending the colonies there. All they sought to retain was the right to fish off Newfoundland and service their fishing fleet at St. Pierre and Miquelon. Voltaire's infamous disparagement of Canada as *"quelques arpents de neige"* rankles yet in Quebec. Without the removal of France from Canada, the American colonists could not have dared to rebel against Britain, and no substantial English settlement around what is now Toronto would have arisen, built up as it was by Empire Loyalists fleeing America, who moved the centre of English-speaking Canada to the west of the French and replaced Quebec as the principal gateway to the west.

Britain's national debt almost doubled in the Seven Years War, and when the British set out to collect from Americans, by taxation, some of the heavy cost of removing France from the colonies' borders, the Americans balked. The "King's friends" were able to prevail in Parliament and impose an insane policy of tax collection that had no possibility of being implemented peacefully. It enflamed the colonists but was not especially unjust, though it was high-handed. Approximately a third of the British dissented from the George III's American policy, and about a third of Americans, according to John Adams, opposed the Revolution. No subsequent monarch would have been able to execute so unpopular and unsuccessful a policy.

If George III had listened to the best of his legislators and colonial officials, the great schism of the English-speaking world would not have occurred, power would gradually have migrated from the old to the new part of the British Atlantic community, and America, including Canada, would have predominated within it sometime in the nineteenth century. After 1840, the United States surpassed Britain's population. Britain might have been able to assist in a less tense and sanguinary end to American slavery. There could even have been cross-representation in parliaments, a partial American residence for the royal family, or a federation of a monarchy and a republic. Any coherent joining, or even an intimate alliance between fully independent entities, at the level of highest foreign policy coordination of the British Empire and American republic would have been powerful enough to prevent the world wars that so horribly scarred the first half of the twentieth century. Ultimately, the Americans could have taken over the whole British Empire if they had wanted it.

Benjamin Franklin came to the rescue of the nascent American project again (following his influence on the removal of France from Canada) in 1778, when, in one of the great diplomatic triumphs of all history, he persuaded France to go to war in favour of American republicanism and secessionism, without which America would not have won, or at least not as soon and completely as it did. In France, there had been nothing resembling a parliament since the young Richelieu had dismissed the Estates General in 1614 with such finality that it did not presume to reconvene for 175 years. Without this mad assault on Britain, in pique after the fiasco of the Seven Years War – with the loss by France of Canada, India, and some of the Caribbean – France might quite possibly have avoided its own terror-stained revolution and spared Europe almost twenty years of continuous war across the entire continent, from Cadiz even unto Moscow, killing over a million people.

The American Revolutionary War was largely a guerrilla war and Washington kept luring the British inland, where their armies melted away among the indistinguishable locals. They had to be supplied by sea and it was hazardous for the Royal Navy to be so concentrated in American waters when there was a large French army on the English Channel. Unless the Americans gave up, they would win eventually.

That Benjamin Franklin was able to manipulate the world's greatest powers to assist the fledgling Americans in being rid of both of them as retardants or threats to an independent America was a stunning achievement, but in the midst of it came the greatest setback of Franklin's career, in Canada of all places. As American discontent rose, one of North America's greatest statesmen, Guy Carleton, later Lord Dorchester, negotiated the Quebec Act of 1774 with the woebegone French-Canadian authorities, such as they were after the withdrawal of the French, who took all but the slate roofs from Quebec when they sailed away (only the clergy remained). French Canada would be loyally subject to the British Crown, and the civil law, Roman Catholic religion, and French language would be protected. Franklin and the then loyal revolutionary Benedict Arnold were sent packing from Montreal when they tried to incite the French Canadians to join the American revolutionaries in 1776.

This coup of Carleton's, too, was a brilliant act of statesmanship, and unlike Franklin's triumph in Paris, it worked for both sides in Canada. Without it, neither British nor French Canada would have avoided absorption into the United States. The French intervention in the Revolutionary War saved the revolt of the colonists but was a disaster for the French, who were deserted by Washington and Franklin, who made a separate peace as soon as Britain offered the Americans acceptable terms. The debt incurred in this struggle helped precipitate the descent to the French Revolution. In its way, North America was already playing an important role in the world.

Franklin's diplomacy and Washington's ability to keep a largely unpaid army of irregulars going for seven years, won the Revolution. Their joint leadership of the Constitutional Convention of 1787–1788 in Philadelphia enabled the arguments of Madison, Hamilton, and John Jay to furnish the nation its Constitution. The Declaration of Independence, chiefly authored by Jefferson, between its splendid top and tale polemical flourishes, was a Nuremberg Trials–level indictment of poor old "Farmer George," a benign, if limited, monarch, intermittently incapacitated by porphyria, and a blood libel on the American Indian. In its initial version, Jefferson, a slaveholder, raged against the British for importing slavery into America. It was suggested that this was imprudent, given Jefferson's intimate and notorious relations with his comeliest female slaves, and his insufficient moral concern about slavery (which he famously called "a firebell in the night") to emancipate his own slaves (even at his death at the age of eighty-three in 1826).

In the sixty years from the retirement of Washington to the rise of Lincoln, the history of the United States was not overly distinguished or even successful. The British provoked America into the War of 1812, especially by the impressment of American sailors into the Royal Navy, an outrageous effrontery to a sovereign country. The British had offered the end of the *casus belli* before the war began, but word of it did not reach America on time.

The Americans scored what would have been a decisive victory two months after the war ended, with Andrew Jackson's victory at New Orleans. But if the war had not already ended, the British would have probably sent the Duke of Wellington and his battle-hardened Peninsular Army to Canada and he could have taken back the territory down to the Ohio River. A British shore party had burned out the White House and the Capitol and all other public buildings in Washington in 1814 in revenge for the destruction of York (Toronto), and Mrs. Dolly Madison fled the White House with a painting of George Washington under her arm. The British had been distracted by the Napoleonic Wars and the Americans did well enough to draw this war.

Jackson sacked a large swath of the civil service on entering office (the "spoils system"), entrenched slavery, warred against and betrayed treaties with, and transported to the west, many hundreds of thousands of American Indians, and ruined the U.S. economy for almost a decade by abolishing the central bank. Yet he saved the Union for thirty years by promising to crush secessionism, including the threat to hang his own vice-president, John C. Calhoun, of South Carolina, otherwise known, with the usual effusive hyperbole of the American star system, as "the American Demosthenes." America's greatest orator of the time, the formidable but somewhat erratic Daniel Webster, was "the God-like Daniel," and the greatest congressional figure and three-time presidential candidate, Henry Clay, was "the Great Pacificator." The last great leader of the Democrats before the Civil War was Stephen A. Douglas, "the Little Giant," who helped bring on the war with his concept of "squatter sovereignty," which effectively meant preliminary civil wars in each territory seeking statehood to determine whether the new state would be slave or free.

As America manufactured heroes from skirmishes with Indians or Mexicans, and famous military figures ran for president or vice-president in nineteen of the twenty-four elections from 1788 to 1880, Canada became grumpy about the absence of responsible (i.e., elected and largely autonomous) government, resulting in a couple of almost bloodless uprisings (led by Mackenzie and Papineau), and spent twenty-five years in the official pursuit, by acculturation, not force, of the assimilation of the French.

As the United States wavered eerily toward the terrible War Between the States, fobbing off each new mediocre pair of quadrennial presidential nominees as epochal leaders of the New World, Canada quietly and soporifically wrestled, as it would, with numbing repetition and earnest for another 150 years, with the French–English conundrum. Thus, Lord Durham, dispatched to examine the issue after the Mackenzie–Papineau fracases, described Canada as "two nations warring in the bosom of a single state." This was accurate, but his proposed solution of relieving the French of the insufferable burden of being French was as far from a sensible policy prescription as it was possible to get. It was such a mad enterprise, that failed so completely, that a barely adequate majority of French and English Canadians resolved to have a try at being a sovereign country together, albeit under British sponsorship and protection. Both the British and French Canadians were motivated almost exclusively by fear of absorption by the United States, the British from loyalty to the Mother Country, and the French from fear of cultural assimilation. There were both annexationists (Goldwin Smith) and French independentists (A.A. Dorion), and the achievement of Macdonald and George-Étienne Cartier and others in agreeing the terms of Confederation was very considerable. Canadian Confederation could scarcely have followed an apparently more different and less heroic route to fruition than American independence, but that appearance is largely deceptive. And the contrast between Canada and the United States in the period between the American Revolution and the end of the U.S. Civil War and Canadian Confederation could hardly, again at first glance, have been greater. The one was a string of unsure settlements, historic castaways, a demographic ribbon along the U.S. border; the other a mighty republic born as a "new order of the ages" from "a shot heard round the world." But as so often in the history of the two countries, appearances were deceiving, precisely because the United States had mastered the genius of presentation and Canada had not attempted it, and then awkwardly represented this oversight as virtue. Therein, largely, is the tale of the two countries.

Apart from scale and showmanship, the main factor in Canada's constant wariness about invidious trans-border comparisons has been that at every stage the Americans were one full phase of national development ahead. Canada just managed to get the French on side and in the British Empire as the American Revolution for outright independence from the Empire was getting under way. Mackenzie and Papineau were agitating somewhat farcically for an elected legislature with autonomous authority as the United States passed Great Britain in population and prepared to seize Texas, California, Arizona, and New Mexico for the expansion of the slaveholding section of the country (and Utah and Colorado, as free states, covering this rather shabby exercise to keep the slaveholding states from revolting with a lot of Yankee-Doodle bunkum about "manifest destiny"). And Canada was just cohering as an autonomous confederation strung out along the U.S. border as the United States crushed secessionism after a horrible but courageous war that took the lives of over 700,000 Americans in a population of thirty-one million but enabled Abraham Lincoln to lead it into the same paddock of the world's greatest powers as Palmerston and Disraeli's British Empire and the about to be born German Empire of Bismarck. These were statesmen of gigantic stature, but Sir John Macdonald, considering he was only representing three million emerging colonists, was of great stature and cunning also. His astuteness, balancing the British and Americans, the English and French Canadians, not only founded the country but preserved it for twenty-five years, in considerable measure because he was a good deal more astute than the seven U.S. presidents he dealt with: Johnson, Grant, Hayes, Garfield, Arthur, Cleveland, and Harrison. (Grant, of course, was a great general and world historic figure but, though better than is generally believed, not an overly effective president.)

Again, appearances are deceptive. Canada's climate never was amenable to growing cotton, so there was no economic need or justification for the importation of slaves, and at the time of the outbreak of the U.S. Civil War, the only blacks in the country were 40,000 fugitive slaves who fled their bondage to a regime without significant official prejudice in Canada. There is a considerable and moving literature of letters from self-emancipated fugitive slaves to their former owners in the Southern states, rejoicing in their freedom and dignity.

A significant number of Canada's native people were similarly fugitives from the relentless expansion of white America. The fact that Canada was settled later and had much less arable and easily habitable territory mitigates the comparative moral decency of the Canadian native people's regime, and no informed Canadian can be unaware of the limitations of the country's native people's policy to this day. But the fact remains that treaties signed with the Indians by Canadian authorities, private and public sector, were rarely as grossly violated as they were in the United States, and Indian agents in Canada were generally honourable, Lord Strathcona being the most famous and one of the most durable. A great many analogous American officials were sadistic and corrupt scoundrels. Once more, it would have been a challenge even for the most ingenious and bold American propagandists, Paine and Jefferson themselves, to build a national legend on comparative civility to indigenous and indentured minorities, but Canada could have been less easily gulled by the riptide of revisionist flim-flam with which the United States, as a matter of policy, has until very recently obscured some of its less salutary traditions.

When Andrew Jackson uprooted 250,000 American Indians living in the Southeast and South, under treaty, and forcibly removed them to west of the Mississippi, the Supreme Court of the United States ruled his conduct unconstitutional. The president replied, of the illustrious Chief Justice John Marshall, "The chief justice has made his decision; now let him enforce it." This was a distinguishably un-Canadian approach, especially as Jackson undertook this enterprise for the purpose of replacing the natives with 250,000 more slaves to deliver on his promise to protect slavery in part of the Union while protecting the integrality of the Union as a whole. This policy bought the time for the North to grow to such demographic and industrial maturity that Lincoln was able, by the narrowest of margins, to subdue the insurgency when it came, though there is no evidence that Jackson foresaw the suppression of the South or the emancipation of the slaves.

Though there were a few rabble-rousing comparisons from nationalist Quebec demagogues in bygone years of French Canadians to African Americans ("white niggers" of North America), there is little comparison, starting with matters of pigmentation, nature of arrival in the New World, and civil status. Yet Canada did very cleverly employ a variant of the Jackson policy to slavery in conserving Canadian Confederation against English–French stresses. As the Jefferson–Jackson–Polk Democrats stood as the party that knew and would protect the South but preserve the Union, so the Canadian Liberals would plausibly present themselves as the party that knew Quebec and would make Canada work for the French Canadians, while keeping the French in Canada by an artistic combination, depending on the targeted audience, of *bonne entente* and *force majeure*. There is no evidence that the Liberals consciously emulated the Democrats, but the formula was essentially the same: we will appease this prickly region up to a point, and collect almost all its votes, but we will preserve the nation. Thus did the Democrats win thirteen of the fifteen presidential elections between 1800 and 1856 (and govern for fifty-two of sixty years up to 1861), and the Liberals win seventeen of the twenty-three general elections from 1896 to 1980 (not counting one drawn election and one that was won by a wartime coalition) and govern for sixty-seven of the eighty-eight years ending in 1984. The astuteness and agility of the Canadian emulators was not markedly less than their American trailblazers, and though Laurier, King, St. Laurent, and Trudeau do not bulk as heavily in history as Jefferson, Madison, Monroe, Jackson, and Polk, they were, on balance, as capable government leaders as those illustrious presidents, and they were well-regarded by their contemporaries in the White House (it being understood that much of the greatest service of those American eminences was not rendered as president).

It is not the object of this essay to debunk the great men and events of American history. The rise of the United States from scattered colonies with a population smaller than that of today's metropolitan Montreal to be, in one long lifetime, one of the greatest powers on earth, and in one long lifetime after that to half the world's economic product, overwhelming military power including a nuclear monopoly, and immense popular cultural and moral influence, is a rise unexampled in the history of the nation state. As Winston Churchill said in his parliamentary eulogy of Franklin D. Roosevelt, he had raised "the strength, might, and glory of the Great Republic to a height never attained by any nation in history." And the principal authors of that progress were among the great figures of world history. The implications of this almost vertical ascent of America, sustained virtually without interruption for approximately 225 years, are not blunted or bent by the fact that it could not have begun without Franklin's masterly diplomacy at the creation, and the sublime statesmanship of Lincoln and Franklin D. Roosevelt at the direst moments of the country's history.

No more is Canada's rise compromised by the essential role of Carleton's brilliant placation of the French Canadians just before Franklin's recruitment of the continental French to the colonists' cause; or, just as the United States was emerging from the horrors of civil strife, by the narrow margin with which Macdonald assembled a consensus for a new nation, bound by rail and built behind tariffs, and based on a novel official bicultural respect. However difficult and tumultuous French–English relations have been in Canada, it is a creditable and adaptable and unique framework for a country, the only bicultural, transcontinental parliamentary confederation in history.

Again, this is not the sort of thing that patriotic lore is made of, but the allowances for irredentist minorities within the Canadian provinces have been less cynical than the U.S. Constitution's attribution to slave states in the Electoral College and House of Representatives of delegations representation reflecting three-fifths of the slave population; that is, for purposes of representation in the House of Representatives and in the Electoral College that chooses the president, though no slaves could vote, three-fifths of them were counted. Other than by reference to the fact that the South would not have joined the Union on terms less favourable to it, this was an outrageous arrangement. It was made even more egregious after the slaves were emancipated, the Union army was withdrawn from the South, and, from 1880 to 1964, the African Americans in southern states were almost entirely prevented from voting, but those states enjoyed congressional and Electoral College representation reflecting the entire African-American population. For the first 175 years of U.S. history, the entire South, between 40 and 25 per cent of the whole population, was a rotten borough, as well as a fetid cauldron of racial oppression, with an inordinate influence in Congress.

The point is that Canada has traditionally underestimated itself and adopted a defensive comparative posture, frequently tinged with deprecatory envy, but it has itself followed a sharply rising trajectory. It did not master the genius of national self-promotion or adopt what amounts to a widely accessible, self-amplifying system of manufacturing greatness or at least distinctiveness, as America did, the absence of which contributes to the spirit of envy that often afflicts Canadian public attitudes. So Canada tends not to realize the extent of its own national accomplishments, and tends not to notice, precisely because U.S. history is not the normal business of Canadians, the extent to which the American story is a patch-up of convenient myths and coincidences.

And finally, and most timely, it is my purpose here to make the point that the rise of Canada is quickening and that of the United States has slowed or stopped, at least temporarily, and that the correlation of forces between the two countries has finally started to shift. It is like a chase, where one participant starts early, runs strongly, and the initial gap is maintained but not increased, because the newcomer to what has become a distant chase is moving just as quickly, and where the lead protagonist starts to slow after a tremendous sprint and the latecomer then starts, finally, to gain ground. If Carleton's Quebec Act was roughly parallel to Franklin's recruitment of France into the Revolutionary War, ninety years were necessary for Macdonald to translate the French–English relationship into an autonomous and largely sovereign state. Canadian Confederation emerged as the United States suppressed insurrectionism and abolished slavery, and Canada effectively resolved its severe internal stresses about 140 years after the United States ended slavery, but only about forty years after it finally got to grips with segregation and voting rights that made the emancipation of the slaves ineffective beyond elimination of its most infamous barbarities. In the long march to the front rank of nations, the gap in political maturity between the North American neighbours had narrowed appreciably, from ninety years between dates of independence to about forty years between the years of resolution of the most severe regional disharmony.

For the first phases of their histories as sovereign countries, the principal service of the United States and Canada to the world was the reception of disadvantaged immigrants, generally fleeing the poverty, oppression, or conflict of Europe and Asia. For geopolitical reasons, to celebrate America's role in the world and the centenary of its victory in the Revolutionary War, and France's mythologized status as fighting midwife to America's Revolution and as the world's other great republic, France presented the Statue of Liberty to the United States in 1886. France had been surpassed by both Britain and Germany earlier in the nineteenth century. It was soundly militarily defeated by each of them (Britain as the head of the coalition) and had endured the occupation of Paris by each. In the intervening century, France had been through three monarchies, two brief restorations, two republics, two empires, a directory, and a consulate, and nearly half its people were monarchists at heart. (France ignored the French Canadians.)

Both Canada and the United States were accepting foreigners to their shores in approximately equal proportions. The United States was the indispensable country in democracy's supreme trials in the twentieth century, providing the margin of an incomplete victory in the First World War, leading the Allies to absolute victory in the Second, and providing the overwhelming share of the strength and ingenuity necessary to the success of containment of Soviet communism in the Cold War, until the U.S.S.R. majestically imploded, and the inducement of China into a largely market economy.

Canada's achievement in joining both world wars at their outsets, and providing relatively very large contingents of first class warriors almost entirely as volunteers, even though Canada was itself under no threat, was, along with a comparable effort by Australia and New Zealand, one of the prodigies of world military history. Nothing like it had ever happened. Of course, this is not universally recognized, and is not, in itself, a substitute for the 250 divisions, staggering war production, and immense sea and air fleets of America, and it was largely prompted by loyalty to an overseas crown and country. But the fact remains that Canada opted, totally voluntarily, to fight an aggressive and racist dictatorship and gave to the struggle all it had, including the service of a million men, even though a painless avoidance or exit were available throughout.

American folklore, from the nation's beginning, held that it was "a light unto the nations" and "a new order of the ages," essentially in

its espousal of democracy. There is no doubt that the American project attracted conspicuous attention when undertaken, and the United
States has never been absent from the world's concentrated attention
since. But its contribution to democracy was entirely by example, by
flag-waving, and by its own expansion across the continent. Americans
were not possessed of appreciably greater rights after their Revolution
than before, other than in the collective sense of having their own
government in situ, nor of more rights than the British, against whose
monarch they revolted (most of them). The democracies in the world
at the end of the American Revolution were America, Great Britain,
Switzerland, and parts of the Netherlands and Scandinavia. At the
end of the Second World War, the world's democracies were essentially almost the same countries, the British Isles and three dominions, Switzerland, the just liberated Low Countries, France, and
Scandinavia, a very small advance to show for the passage of 162 years.

It was only when the Cold War began in earnest that the great
American strategic team that had been assembled by Roosevelt –
Truman, Marshall, Eisenhower, MacArthur, Acheson, Stevenson,
Bohlen, Kennan, and others – determined that what was afoot was a
mortal contest between the godless, totalitarian communist and the
Free World, including in its polyglot ranks Franco, Syngman Rhee, the
Shah, Salazar, Chiang Kai-shek, and the juntas of South America, so
collectively bemedalled they could scarcely get into their tunics and
could have kept the pawn shops of the world going for decades with
their self-awarded decorations (celebrating an extreme paucity of events
involving live fire). This was the Free World, yet the United States conducted the Cold War so successfully, with only occasional mistakes
such as Vietnam, that communism collapsed.

All of Latin America except Cuba and perhaps Venezuela became
democratic. So did all of Europe except a couple of units of the old,
defunct U.S.S.R. Most of South and East Asia except China, Vietnam,
and North Korea, and large and important countries that had been shabby
despotisms, such as Indonesia, Brazil, Spain, Poland, and Colombia,
became democratic pillars. American protégés, including Israel, Taiwan,
and South Korea, flourished as democracies, the last two having begun
their national lives as dictatorships. The roles of Canada and other

consistent allies were valuable and impeccable, but let no one doubt that the triumph of democracy in the Cold War, once it ceased to be a mere posture and became the chief criterion for victory in America's struggle with its last remaining rival, was pre-eminently gained by the power of America's ideology and popular culture, the mighty American economy, the ingenuity of its statesmen, including nine presidents of both parties, and the courage of its armed forces, including nearly 100,000 who died in Korea, Vietnam, and the Middle East.

When the academic seekers of freedom in China sought to slough the shackles of Communist dictatorship, they gathered around a model of the Statue of Liberty they set up in Tiananmen Square. And when the analogous groups in Prague, Budapest, and Warsaw demonstrated for the same goals, they read to their supporters from the works of Jefferson and Lincoln. The uneven implementation of those ideals in the country of their origin did not reduce their power in exhorting those who had suffered under the hobnailed jackboots of the red armies. And here lies the irony of the latest lap in the subtle competition between the United States and Canada.

The United States secured the triumph of democracy and of capitalism, the victory of the American economic system extending even to the bowels of China and the vastness of India, the two ancient behemoths holding nearly 40 per cent of the population of the world. The United States had sponsored Canada as one of the G7, albeit chiefly because it and Japan did not want the membership swamped by Europeans, who were all on the rocky road to integration anyway. But 85 per cent of Canada's exports were to the United States, about 43 per cent of the country's GDP, and Canada was more closely integrated into the U.S. economy than was California. Canada was prosperous, secure, and well-regarded, but not deemed to be, nor in fact, very distinct from the United States and, apart from Quebec, barely distinguishable from the northern states of the United States.

But in the depth of the serenity of the American age, deep within America's cult and practice and incandescent fact of success, and ingrained in the caution and diffidence and methodical foibles of Canada, was an astounding shift of national efficacy and coherence. After a strategic golden age – from Roosevelt's "all aid short of war" for the democracies, from 1939 to 1941, and the brilliant conduct of the war by the president and his chiefs, Marshall, Eisenhower, Nimitz, and MacArthur, and the containment strategy devised and promulgated by the Roosevelt entourage but extending through the gifted policy innovations and execution of Nixon and Reagan and George Bush Sr. – the United States adopted a catastrophically misconceived and negligently pursued strategy that has made the skyrocket rise of America seem less legitimate, as well as much less unchallengeable. It allowed the price of oil to rise from less than $5 a barrel in 1970 to between $80 and $130 forty years later, while more than doubling its consumption of oil and increasing its dependence on foreign-originated oil from under 20 per cent to 60 per cent of its needs.

And among the chief beneficiaries of its petro-thirst has been Saudi Arabia, an accidental state that is a joint venture between the royal House of Saud and the jihadist Wahhabi establishment. Saudi Arabia finances more than 90 per cent of the Islamic institutions in the world, and is the chief paymaster of militant Islam, effectively putting the United States on both sides of the War on Terror when that war struck America in the late nineties and especially at the World Trade Center and the Pentagon on September 11, 2001. The United States outsourced millions of low-paying jobs while it allowed the illegal entry of up to fourteen million unskilled immigrant workers. Employment was exported while unemployment was imported. The country became addicted to luxury goods, which benefited Western Europe and Japan while aggravating an unsustainable current-account deficit, ultimately totalling over $800 billion annually, for years, while the Europeans and Japanese sanctimoniously lectured the United States about its international deficit.

And, the crowning diadem to this blinding galaxy of blunders, the Executive, Congress, and Federal Reserve promoted family home ownership (as well as vertiginous speculation) with mandated and legislated non-commercial residential mortgages and low interest rates that could not fail to weaken severely the quality of the loans of the nation's banking system. Securities regulators facilitated the issuance of trillions of dollars of real-estate-backed instruments that were enthusiastically peddled by the most sophisticated lenders and transactional houses of Wall Street and were certified as investment grade by the leading rating agencies. The United States borrowed trillions of dollars from China and Japan to buy goods – which it could and formerly did manufacture itself – from China and Japan. At the bottom of the Vietnam quagmire, President Nixon warned America (in 1971) that it must not become "a pitiful helpless giant." That, incredibly, is the condition, nearly forty years later, that it approaches. Debt-ridden, with a special-interest, money-raddled political system that is intolerably corrupt and riven by fierce policy divisions, afflicted by obsessions and fads in its administrations that have squandered its energies in misconceived Middle Eastern nation-building and overreaction to alarmist environmental fears, a sequence of presidents who should have been weeded out by the voters well before they got near the White House for their sleaze, unworldliness, or chippy and amateurish and slightly subversive combativity, the United States is again, for the first time since 1932 and the second time since 1860, in desperate need of a great epochal leader. Can America do it three times in a row? the world wonders. Perhaps the most serious concern is that, unlike the Great Depression and the Civil War, practically no one except a couple of eccentric academics saw this disaster approach. As the nation borrowed and borrowed for the acquisition of depreciating or at least fungible and overvalued assets, it was taken over the (oil) barrel by those who do not wish it well, and became a Ponzi scheme of Brobdingnagian proportions.§

Canada ran steady budget and current-account surpluses. As China leapt on the capitalist bandwagon, with the socialist shambles of Nehruist India, in all its delusional poverty and pretension, finally trotting and then running behind, Canada, one of the world's pre-eminent hewers of wood and drawers of water, the first victim of commodity price valuations, vulnerable to the efforts of natural resource importers such as Japan endlessly to produce new sources of supply, was suddenly in the economic driver's seat. There was full demand for all Canada's base and precious metals, energy, forest products, and agriculture. The share of Canada's exports that went to the United States has declined significantly and the branch-plant history of the country is fading. By a combination

---

§ Five years after this essay was written, the United States was sharply reducing energy imports and the current-account deficit.

of economic and demographic forces, the undoubted goodwill of English Canada and the hard-nosed pecuniary nous of their Norman and Breton ancestors, French Canadians have effectively given up the dream and the threat of secession. Though, again, any comparison between French Canadians and African Americans is extremely tenuous, this problem has been solved, not dealt with in increments after immense crises, as the civil rights question still unfolds in the United States.

Canada is a treasure house, sparsely populated by thirty-three million relatively well-educated and law-abiding people in a stable and institutionally sophisticated country. If it had half the population of the United States, it would be as great a force in the world. America faces a mighty task of self-help, Canada a stirring challenge of filling its potential, now that it is no longer a notion that is decades or a century away. While American foreign policy strategists were preparing to lead the world, O.D. Skelton, Lester Pearson, and the other founders of the Canadian External Affairs service were learning how to put Canada's marginal differences with senior allies essentially as effective and not servile courtiers. Canadians, who are habituated to tugging at the trouser legs of the United States and even Britain, face the challenge of striking out into the world and could learn from such Americans as Franklin, John Jay, John Quincy Adams, Lincoln, Woodrow Wilson, and the Roosevelts. Americans, faced for the first time with the realities of retrenchment and national reappraisal, can find lessons in their own past but could do worse than look at some of the tactics, miniaturized though they were, of Macdonald, Laurier, and King.

There is no room in any of this for envy, spitefulness, or a lack of appreciation for the greatness of America and, on balance, its immensely positive contribution to the world. Nor is there room, any more, for the righteous piffle about the peacekeepers of the pure North with which Canadian self-consciousness has tried, these many decades, to swaddle itself in feeble dissent from the mighty swath of America, while being hypnotized by American entertainment, living off the American economy, and vacationing in most states of the United States. America is fallible, and Canada is not punching above its weight.

But for these purposes, the greatest failing has been in the perceptions of the Canadian nationalists, not that Canada is not worthy of national pride but precisely because it is a stronger and more accomplished subject of national pride than most of its espousers recognize. In the absence of the political leadership that could spontaneously adapt to these new and promising circumstances, it devolves to public intellectuals to fill that long awaited, very necessary role.

# THE PACIFISM
# OF FOOLS

*National Post*, April 25, 2015

t is hard to avoid the sinking feeling that former NDP federal secretary
and national campaign chairman Gerald Caplan was speaking for his
party and its current leader, Thomas Mulcair, in the *Globe and Mail*
on April 17. Caplan wrote that our only problem with Muslim terrorists is their objection to America's dispute with Saddam Hussein, after
he seized Kuwait in 1990, was expelled from it, and defied seventeen
United Nations Security Council resolutions in support of the ceasefire
at the end of the Gulf War. Caplan cited Osama bin Laden, entirely
neutrally, when he denounced the "hundreds of thousands of Iraqi
children who died from lack of food and medicine due to American
sanctions"; the founder of al Qaeda, he explained, "resented the deployment of American forces throughout the Gulf states, particularly in his
homeland, Saudi Arabia."

Caplan further claimed that "Canadians were given the same
reasons by Michael Zihaf-Bibeau, who murdered Corporal Nathan
Cirillo at the War Memorial in Ottawa [that] his actions were spurred
by Canada's military involvement in Afghanistan and Iraq." Of course,
that isn't the same thing at all. Bin Laden was speaking in 2001, in
the wake of the attacks he directed against the World Trade Center in
New York and the Pentagon, at which time there was no Canadian (or

American) military involvement in Afghanistan; Canada's only involvement in Iraq had been ten years before, in an operation approved by the United Nations, NATO, Egypt, Syria, Turkey, Saudi Arabia, the Gulf states, and the Palestinian Authority (led by Yasser Arafat, who purported to donate blood to assist victims of bin Laden's terrorist assault on the United States).

This is a fantastic exaggeration of the effect of international sanctions on Saddam Hussein, imposed by an almost unanimous United Nations, for his violations of international law (hundreds of thousands of Iraqi children did not die, and food and medicine were largely exempted from the sanctions, which were porous anyway). And Caplan's explication of the motives for these massacres of innocent people (as bin Laden acknowledged them to be) is a Swiss cheese of inconsistencies. Are we to understand the former NDP campaign chairman attaches some credence and approval to these motives? Practically the only country that dissented from the eviction of Iraq from Kuwait was Jordan, whose opposition was based on King Hussein's desire not to antagonize his Iraqi neighbour, not any approval of Saddam's seizure of Kuwait.

Caplan is on safer ground alleging the hostility of Islamist militants to various long-standing U.S. policies, including recognition (along with the rest of the United Nations Security Council and most of its members) of Israel's right to exist as a Jewish state, as well as a modest American military presence in the Middle East, invariably at the request of the governments of the host countries, including several of the Gulf states, most conspicuously Saudi Arabia. The countries that requested American military collaboration did so because they felt threatened by the ideological and sectarian soulmates of bin Laden, which was understandable given the attempted assassination of the Saudi royal family at the principal mosque in Mecca in 1979, and many other infiltrations. If Caplan believes that the United States has no right to defend what it considers to be its strategic interests when asked to do so by sovereign governments in the Arab world, and has no right to avenge itself against groups that have murdered thousands of its civilians in vile acts of terrorism, he is enunciating a version of pacifism that is entirely original.

Even Gandhi accepted the legitimacy of military action in certain circumstances (he had little objection to the great Japanese offensive in the Pacific starting in 1941), as did Nelson Mandela, former commander of "The Spear of the Nation." Caplan has a point to the extent that he regards as simplistic the George W. Bush–Stephen Harper imputation of objections to democracy as the Muslim terrorists' sole motive in their attacks on the West. But I believe it is widely understood that bin Laden and other terrorists have vehemently objected to any Western cultural influence in the Muslim world and have disputed the right of the Arab powers to develop military relations with the West, the United States in particular.

The readership of the *Globe and Mail*, and the democratic world generally, are not truth-starved and were not gasping in ignorance of this point, awaiting enlightenment from the former NDP campaign chairman. Neither Bush nor Harper have denied this, and while I am not an apologist for them, they are entitled to mention other factors, and their record in countering terrorism has been very defensible. Caplan might wish to recall the bloodthirsty and blood-curdling videos that bin Laden released in the year following the 9/11 assault, promising much more of the same. Instead, despite bin Laden's professed desire to die righteously and go to his reward in paradise, terrorist attacks in the West have been comparatively few, and bin Laden hid like an animal until he was found and executed by American forces in Pakistan. Doubtless, bin Laden objected to that American action too.

Caplan goes on to quote, again with matter-of-fact neutrality, Richard Reid, the shoe bomber who tried to blow up a commercial airliner bound from Paris to Miami in 2001 "to help [expel] the oppressive American forces from the Muslim lands," and one of the terrorists who blew up 202 tourists in Bali in October 12, 2002, in "revenge" for "what Americans have done to Muslims." (The Bali bombs killed eighty-eight Australians, thirty-eight Indonesians, twenty-seven British citizens, and seven Americans, so it was a rather poorly targeted act of vengeance on Americans.)

Caplan even dredges up Mir Aimal Kasi, who attacked several people in front of the CIA headquarters in 1993 as "retaliation" for "American support of Israel." He quotes *The Guardian*, a more anti-American news outlet even than Al Jazeera, to ascribe the evolution of the Houthi movement – bankrolled and supplied by Iran in the Yemeni civil war – from peaceful coexistence to its present militancy, because of the "2002 U.S.-led invasion of Iraq." Finally, the punchline: ISIS (a "brutal movement") is responding to "the humiliation that Muslims have suffered at the hands of foreign powers and local dictators ever since the First World War." And: "Are there hard lessons here for Canada and its allies?"

I don't think so. I think we knew all that, but the humiliations did not begin in 1918; they started with the expulsion of the Moors from France after the Battle of Tours in 732, continued through the expulsion from Spain, the repulse of the Turks from the gates of Vienna in 1529 and 1683 (all defeats of naked Muslim aggression), the French and British seizure of Egypt in the Napoleonic Wars, the colonization of North Africa in the nineteenth century, and the defeat of the Ottoman Empire and Anglo-French carve-up of Arabia after 1918. The same sense of humiliation assimilated the British, American, and French discovery of oil in the Middle East cheerfully enough, but has never really accepted the Maronite Christians of Lebanon, nor other Christians in the Muslim world, much less a Jewish state.

We know all that too, and Stephen Harper and even George W. Bush know that. The solution for these antagonisms and the violence that results from them is better government in most of the Muslim world. But does Caplan, a learned authority on the Rwanda genocide, recommend Western appeasement of terrorists, the abandonment of the Muslim world to its most extreme inhabitants, and the renunciation of any legitimate Western interest in it, including its Christian and Jewish minorities? Has he similarly no concern for the fate of nuclear non-proliferation, the region's pro-Western governments, Europe and Japan's oil supply, or the existence of a Jewish state in any borders? Where, if at all, do humanitarian considerations fit into this world view?

What is Caplan's plan of action for all these problems, and will the real Thomas Mulcair please stand up with him and stop waffling about helping refugees and avoiding mission creep? These criminally diseased Islamist lunatics are attacking all civilization, including Muslim and Western civilization. We can't just dump it on the Americans and respond with blankets, Spam, pamphlets, rosewater, and sanctimonious obfuscation.

# WHY WE HONOUR
# QUEEN VICTORIA

*National Post*, May 23, 2015

Tomorrow is the 195th birthday of Her Imperial Britannic Majesty Victoria, Queen and Empress, which we celebrated with the holiday last Monday. All my youth, with the fireworks displays, it was one of my favourite holidays.

I recall with particular pleasure when the metal rod from which my father was launching May 24 rockets slipped and the already lighted rocket took off almost horizontally and went through a neighbour's window, buzzed about the walls emitting small flames and erupted spectacularly over about ten blazing seconds. After another ten seconds, as my father expressed the hope there had been no one in the room, an ancient grey head festooned with curlers and still sizzling sparks appeared, shaky but purposeful, and emitting an unholy rage. She shook her fists, screamed a few epithets, and receded, like a geriatric cuckoo-clock bird, slamming the window and pulling closed the curtains, as we were all splitting our sides with unhoped-for holiday mirth.

My father, a literate man with a formidable deadpan sense of humour, replied, for our benefit, with the famous line from John Greenleaf Whittier's poem about Barbara Frietchie, who defied General Stonewall Jackson by waving the Union flag and shouting, "Shoot if you must this old gray head, but not" – and here my father improvised – "your neighbour's children," continuing, from Whittier, a bit late, "Who touches a hair on yon gray head dies like a dog." All in all, it was the most riveting fireworks display I have witnessed.

In so far as there is a point to any of this, it is that we all happily observed Queen Victoria's birthday without a thought of why we were doing it. Of course, she was a long-serving Queen of England and affiliated jurisdictions, including Canada, but not one person in a hundred then, nor, I suspect, one Canadian in ten thousand now, could say why anyone in this country should observe that Queen's birthday. In fact, it is the least we can do. When still in her twenties, Victoria, in her first of over six decades as Queen, dissented from what Stephen Leacock described (in the case of colonial secretary Lord Stanley) as the "magnificent stupidity" of trying to retain the government of Canada in the hands of colonial governors with no system of popular approval. She took matters into her own hands and insisted on the appointment as governor of Canada of the enlightened former governor of Jamaica, Lord Elgin, in 1847, with a clear mandate to bring in "responsible government": autonomy in domestic matters for ministers responsible to an elected legislature of what was then called the united Province of Canada, effectively Quebec and Ontario together.

There followed a gradual recognition that unless they were united, the provinces north of the United States would have no ability to resist the magnetic power of that country even in peaceful conditions, much less if the United States resorted to force after its sanguinary Civil War. The Americans emerged in 1865 from that war forcibly united at a cost of 750,000 dead (in a population smaller than Canada's is now), with the greatest army and most talented generals in the world and unencumbered by any affection for Britain or Canada, as Britain had almost overtly favoured the Confederacy in the late war.

The leaders of the drive for responsible government in Canada, Robert Baldwin and Louis-Hippolyte LaFontaine, had recognized that to become a successful and independent country, Canada would have to be governed by the English- and French-speaking populations jointly and that a majority would be required from both communities on very important questions; the country would not function if the English simply imposed their majority on the French. This message was carried forward by their successors, John A. Macdonald and George-Étienne Cartier; these men, with George Brown and others and with the encouragement of Queen Victoria, directly (when they visited her in the mid-1860s) and through her governor general Viscount Monck, negotiated Confederation.

Canada became and remains the only transcontinental, officially bicultural, parliamentary confederation in the history of the world. Despite considerable skepticism in the British Parliament and in the United States, that Confederation has endured and generally prospered these 148 years. Of the world's countries with a population as large as Canada's, only the United Kingdom and the United States have been governed by the same political institutions for a longer time. At the time of Confederation in 1867, France and Russia and the Central European congeries of nationalities grouped around Austria and Hungary were all empires, Germany and Italy were fragmented in various kingdoms and principalities, and Japan was an underdeveloped hermit kingdom.

Victoria saw clearly that Canada had the potential to be an important country, and that the French Canadians could not be treated as a conquered people (which they never were – the British army defeated the French army at Quebec and Montreal, but no one has ever conquered any significant part of Canada). She and her enlightened consort, Prince Albert, were in a minority in the British establishment that did not favour a Confederate victory in the U.S. Civil War and realized that Britain could not, even tacitly, favour slavery and secessionism.

Queen Victoria took a great and helpful interest in Canada throughout her reign, which began at the time of the Gilbert and Sullivan rebellions of Mackenzie and Papineau in 1837. She sent the Prince of Wales (later King Edward VII) to Canada on a visit in 1860, during which he opened the Victoria Bridge in Montreal, then the longest bridge in the world, and laid the cornerstone for the Parliament Buildings in Ottawa. She sent her son-in-law the Marquess of Lorne to serve as governor general of Canada from 1878 to 1883, and always treated Macdonald and Sir Wilfrid Laurier with great respect when they came to England. They served her as prime minister of the dominion or co-premier of the united province for a total of forty-three years.

When Macdonald won the 1891 election on an anti-annexationist platform, Victoria sent him congratulations via Governor General Lord Stanley (son of the sluggish colonial secretary from forty-five years before); when Macdonald died later that year, she had Sir Casimir Gzowski (ancestor of the popular broadcaster) lay a wreath of roses from her on his coffin. Macdonald's preferred successor, Sir John Thompson, died while on a three-day visit to Windsor Castle in 1894. She arranged, unprecedentedly, a Roman Catholic state funeral for him in London and had a Royal Navy cruiser painted black for the return of Thompson's casket to Halifax.

She was respected by all the ten British prime ministers who served her in seventeen different governments, including some of the most distinguished in British history: Peel, Russell, Palmerston, Disraeli, Gladstone, and Salisbury (though she exclaimed, "Not that bore again!" when informed she had to invest Gladstone for a fourth time). She and her grandsons, the last emperors of Germany and Russia (Czar Nicholas II was her grandson-in-law but purported to regard her as a grandmother), reigned over a majority of the land surface of the world, while Britain famously ruled the waves. She reigned for sixty-three years and seven months, through the supreme decades of British ascendancy. (Queen Elizabeth II will pass her record for longevity this coming September 10.)

Next to Britain itself, there was no country Victoria liked more than Canada, and no outsider has done as much for Canada as she did. We are right to celebrate her birthday, with fireworks.

# CANADA'S TREATMENT OF ABORIGINALS WAS SHAMEFUL, BUT IT WAS NOT GENOCIDE

*National Post*, June 6, 2015

---

I yield to no one in my fervour to make amends to the native people for violations of treaty rights and other mistreatment, but the phrase "cultural genocide," as I wrote here last week in reference to the chief justice of Canada's use of it in a speech given in honour of the Aga Khan, is deliberately provocative and sensational. We might as well accuse Canada and the United States and all countries built on immigration (ultimately almost all countries) of cultural genocide, of the natives or the arrivals, though of course immigration is voluntary. All words bearing the suffix *-cide* refer to physical extermination: suicide, homicide, genocide, regicide, etc.

The native people, or First Nations, were here first, but there were not more than a few hundred thousand of them in what is now Canada in the seventeenth century. They had a Stone Age culture that had not invented the wheel, and which graduated, however brusquely, to more sophisticated levels of civilization, but the culture was not exterminated. Apart from a few mid-western farming tribes and Pacific and Great Lakes inhabitants of log dwellings, the First Nations did not have permanent buildings or agriculture, metal tools, or knitted fabrics. They were nomads, clothed in hides and skins, living in tents, surviving on fish and game, and usually at war, which included the torture to gruesome death of prisoners from other tribes and nations, including women and children.

They were genius woodsmen and hunters and craftsmen, and had artistic abilities, and I am not suggesting and do not accept that they were anything but the complete natural equal of the arriving Europeans. Some European notables, such as Champlain, were interested in and generally respectful of the native people; some made expedient alliances with them; but generally, traders bought their animal furs for consideration the natives sought, including alcoholic beverages and firearms, and settlers encroached on their land, moving inland from the ocean shores and river banks. There were certainly unjust provocations by the Europeans. The British promised the natives occupancy of the land between the Ohio River and the Great Lakes, even as they signed the same territory over to the successful American Revolutionists. (Somewhat as, 135 years later, the British promised Palestine, then occupied by the Turks, simultaneously to the Jews and the Arabs. Selling the same real estate to two different buyers at the same time is complicated on every continent.)

Even that eminent humanitarian Thomas Jefferson, one of history's prototype limousine liberals, described the native people in the Declaration of Independence as "merciless Indian savages whose known rule of warfare, is an undistinguished destruction of all ages, sexes, and conditions." The Shawnee chief Tecumseh greatly helped General Isaac Brock and the Canadians and the British in the War of 1812; Colonel Richard Johnson took credit for killing him, being elected vice-president of the United States in 1836 on the slogan "Rumpsey, Dumpsey, Who Killed Tecumseh?"

When President Andrew Jackson transported 250,000 native people westwards to open up more land for the importation of slaves, and was found liable by the Supreme Court, led by Chief Justice John Marshall, of treaty violations against the native people, Jackson, in control of Congress as well as the administration, replied, "The chief justice has made his decision; now let him enforce it."

As the settlement of the United States by Europeans proceeded much more quickly and on a much larger scale over a more temperate country than the corresponding development of Canada, and the British and Canadian officials dealing with the natives were generally less corrupt than their American analogues, our relations with the native people stayed largely clear of the violence so fabled in American history, including the death of General George Armstrong Custer and his Seventh Cavalry at the Little Bighorn in 1876.

Once the white men were indisputably pre-eminent in this continent, administration of native affairs was largely unsatisfactory, frequently corrupt, and sometimes brutal. The Canadians and Americans did not simply massacre them all, as the Argentinians did (that was genocide), and there were many sincere and entirely benevolent contacts among the natives, including from most of the Christian churches. It was widely assumed that assimilating the native people was the ultimate compliment and service. Lord Durham assumed the same about the French Canadians, and the united Province of Canada, Ontario and Quebec today, was set up for that purpose. Of course, it was all nonsense and an outrage, and the French Canadians easily resisted this clumsy and arrogant effort to relieve them of their culture. Their numbers and importance within Canada as a whole were such that they had the political muscle to be a coequal race when Canada was swiftly launched in 1867 in the tenuous hope that it could retain its independence from the post–Civil War United States and its Grand Army of the Republic.

The native people were less fortunate, fewer, and less politically powerful than the French Canadians, and there is no doubt that they were shortchanged, condescended to, and, in a heartbreaking number of individual instances, mistreated: the Truth and Reconciliation Commission's belief that 5 to 7 per cent of native students in residential schools died in those schools is a horrifying accusation. But none of it justifies the invocation of the word *genocide*, which is a contemptible device to tar esteemed people like John A. Macdonald with the brush of Hitler, Stalin, Pol Pot, and others who set out to murder millions of totally innocent people.

The policy, which was one of assimilation, acculturation, or even deracination, was misconceived, frequently unjustly administered, and the horror stories of what happened in the residential schools are the very worst of it. But the fact that the Truth and Reconciliation Commission employs the term "cultural genocide" is neither true nor conciliatory, though I wholeheartedly support the official purposes of the commission, and am mortified by the summary of its findings I have seen. We must know the proportions of wrongs committed, and do whatever we can to make amends.

But we are dealing with a policy of using high office for unctuous national moral self-flagellation; the country didn't murder native schoolchildren and at every stage would have been just as shocked as we are now to learn of it. In the same address, the chief justice lamented that West Coast Japanese Canadians were rounded up without trial, their property seized, and bustled into "concentration camps." It was a shameful policy, made more odious by it being a heel-clicking imitation of the United States' policy devised by some of its greatest modern liberals, including Franklin D. Roosevelt, John McCloy, Felix Frankfurter, and William O. Douglas (and was chiefly opposed in that country by J. Edgar Hoover, a fact the left has almost airbrushed from history).

But the victims were not in "concentration camps," as the chief justice perfectly well knows; they were in boredom camps, with their families, where they had nothing to concentrate on. It was shameful and was recognized as such in the Mulroney government's commendable restitution and apology of 1993, but the efforts in high and authoritative places to invoke the Nazi and communist vocabulary of oppression in respect of the morally insalubrious official episodes in this country's history, compound, and do not ameliorate, the shame.

There appear to be terrible strains in the native community between the emotional attachment to traditional life and the notorious temptations and diversions of modern Western life. It is not the case that the Europeans have no right to be here, and we have made vastly more of this continent than its original inhabitants could have done; it was only the mighty continent of North America that prevented the triumph of real genocidal regimes in Europe and the Far East in the great wars of the last century. It ill behooves the chief justice to rail against the proximity to the Supreme Court of a monument to the victims of communism, while imputing to the society whose senior jurist she is the practice of any form of genocide. Nor should the federal government be building superfluous prisons and deliberately worsening the conditions of the incarcerated, especially when it can be certain that an inordinate number of the occupants of these prisons will be native people, a policy that is a triple declaration of bankruptcy: in criminal justice, rehabilitation, and native people's policy.

In fairness to the Harper government, it did its best in agreeing to a $2 billion education catch-up program for native people; their leaders rejected it and forced out the First Nations' national chief, Shawn Atleo, who negotiated it. The relationship between official Canada and the First Nations is full of sadness, mistakes, and dishonour, but both sides share it, and respect for native government often results in grievous corruption and despotism by the native leaders.

Despite everything, even the First Nations should be grateful that the Europeans came here. There has been quite enough shameful conduct to go round, including by some of the natives. Let us all repent past wrongdoing without demeaning histrionics and hyperbole and be proud of whatever we are ethnically: all cultures and nationalities have their distinctions. The whole country must do what it can to atone for the past, but a continuing orgy of recriminations will be unjust in itself, produce a nasty backlash, and will aggravate grievances.

# CANADA IS AFFLICTED BY A PANDEMIC OF DEFECTIVE MORALIZING ON NATIVE ISSUES

*National Post*, June 13, 2015

---

S tephen Maher wrote here yesterday that (apart from those that were already extinct) "aboriginal people across Canada have attacked (me) for writing that 'even the First Nations should be grateful that the Europeans came here'" and "for rejecting the idea that they were the victims of attempted cultural genocide." Maher disputed my point that the "Europeans have made vastly more of this continent than the original inhabitants could have done." He accused me of exaggerating the "gulf" he admits existed between the European and aboriginal civilizations and dilated on the accomplishments of the Aztecs, Incas, and Mayans (which are not at issue and are not relevant here).

Nothing remotely close to the fifty million native people, he claims, could have perished in North America from European-carried diseases, as that is about ten times the native population at the time the Europeans arrived. There was a tragic and unknown vulnerability to these diseases, but there was never a policy to infect natives with diseases, other than possibly in the one incident in 1763 that Maher mentions, that which was the act of British authorities in what soon became American territory (and was unsuccessful if it was really attempted – all that is known is that it was discussed).

Maher implies that the natives of North America lived largely in permanent, constructed dwellings, cultivated crops, had serious political institutions that were more democratic than those of France and inspired Karl Marx and James Madison, and that they were no more violent warriors and captors than the French and British.

They were wonderfully adept and admirable in many ways, but they had not discovered the wheel, metal tools, or the knitting or sewing of fabrics, were mainly nomads and often compulsively belligerent and routinely tortured female and child prisoners to death. France had no democratic institutions until the Revolution (one of its principal causes), but the British and Dutch did. The Iroquois claim to democracy Maher makes is an acrobatic stretch.

The natives may have been hardier than the more urban Europeans, but both populations had approximately equal life expectancies, leaving out the native propensity to kill each other in large numbers at premature ages. Both sides share responsibility for the sad history of aboriginal–white relations, but it is not the tear-jerking myth that has been endlessly portrayed of a barbarous European onslaught against the pure idyll of a bucolic native paradise. None of the first three hundred years of the relationship is Canada's responsibility.

Yet Canada is afflicted by a pandemic of defective moralizing. There was a prolonged official attempt to assimilate native people to the Euro-majority in Canada, but it was not motivated by hate or malice but by the common misconception in Victorian times and for some while afterwards that the world would be better if minorities in English-speaking countries were relieved of the burden of not being Anglo-Christians. As I wrote here last week, assimilation was insanely proposed by Lord Durham, the British governor general, as the cure to French-Canadian grievances and was the reason for the unification of Quebec and Ontario in 1840. Instead of eliminating them, it led to the recognition, finally, of French Canada's coequal status in the new Confederation that was founded and has served us well these 148 years.

Assimilation was an extension of the Canadian and American practice of integrating newly arrived people in the majority cultures. However mistakenly and patronizingly conceived and at times barbarously executed, the authors of the residential schools program, starting with John A. Macdonald, imagined they would be benignly solving the problems of the native people.

We are now in danger of being overwhelmed by an unholy coalition of the charlatans of the victimhood industry, the corrupt elements of the native leadership, and those officials who seek an expanded jurisdiction or political advantage in national moral self-flagellation. Let there be no dispute that the residential schools program was in large measure a tragic and cruel failure, as it wrenched children from their families and subjected them often to physical and sexual abuse as well as severe emotional neglect. But in most cases the conditions from which these children were plucked were unsanitary, penurious, sociopathic, and hopeless.

Between the 1880s and 1996, there were about 150,000 students in the native residential schools, which was too narrow an echelon of the aboriginals to qualify as the attempted assimilation of the whole population. Allegedly 5 to 7 per cent of the students in these schools died in the schools, but we have no way of measuring those appalling figures against what would have happened had they been left where they were, or would have happened to students of other sociological origins sent to schools in isolated locations where there were not adequate medical facilities. It was a time of frequent epidemics, and aboriginals were still vulnerable to a number of diseases inadvertently transmitted by Europeans.

There was a great deal of severe physical punishment in most of these schools, and doubtless much of it was outright savagery. But it was a culture that didn't spare the rod anywhere. While few schools would bear comparison with the failings of these residential schools, a glance at Dickens and other authors, even my classmate John Fraser's *Telling Tales*, confirms that a huge number of students in the nineteenth and first half of the twentieth century, in the British world at least, were subjected to a good deal of sadistic and deviant authority. This is context, not mitigation. Almost half of the approximately 80,000 residential school alumni alive now have filed complaints of sexual abuse, which include many acts of excessive force that may not have been explicitly sexual. It is unlikely that all these claims are well-founded, but many of them must be.

What is enormously divisive is the attempt to aggregate the failings of aboriginal policy into "cultural genocide." I don't really fault advocates like Maher or my generally cordial acquaintance of many years John Saul for pushing on an open door for a good cause. But the main promoter of the complex of unearned collective guilt is the chief justice of Canada, Beverley McLachlin, within her long-running constitutional putsch based on the claim that the Charter of Rights and Freedoms has made the courts the "arbiter between the legislatures and the people."

In her "Pluralism Lecture" on May 28 in Toronto, she referred to "the buzzword of the [nineteenth century], 'assimilation'; in the language of the twenty-first century, 'cultural genocide.'" That was the leap from fair allegations against bad Victorian policy to a charge of Satanic modern crimes, and she must not be allowed to take the rest of us with her. Assimilation was never a buzzword; like acculturation and deracination, it was an objective for some and a fear for others throughout Europe's irredentist communities and in native communities in much of the New World and colonial world. It is still a concern with some Quebec nationalists, though it can only be kept alive at all because of the collapsed French-Canadian birthrate. Peoples that don't have the energy to procreate will be assimilated eventually.

"Genocide" means physical extermination, and the argument that it has been broadened is based on the United Nations Convention on the Prevention and Punishment of the Crime of Genocide of 1948. That convention refers to various assaults on a "national, ethnical, racial, or religious group." It says precisely nothing about culture. There is no evidence that John A. Macdonald and his collaborators could be accused even of seeking culturicide, as they only wanted native children to be assimilable in one of Canada's official cultures, whatever interest they retained in their own traditions.

The chief justice's address had the air of a banal and unrigorous stitch-up. Various portentously invoked sources were cited in favour of pluralist tolerance, such as John Milton, a sublime poet, but, as Dr. Johnson said, "a surly and acrimonious" regicide who was tolerant of all Protestants but intolerant of everyone else, especially Jews, Roman Catholics, atheists, and Muslims (i.e., most of Europe and the world and a large percentage of his countrymen). It was here that the chief justice invented the "concentration camps" in which Japanese Canadians were supposedly confined in Second World War. (Their detention was an outrage but it did not occur in concentration camps.)

In the same speech, last month, she said "slavery was not absent from" Canada. It almost was, and the choice of words was misleading. The largest concentration of slaves was by and of the native people, as many as a third of the northwest Pacific tribes were slaves. New France had about 4,000 slaves at its end, and Upper Canada, when set up, a few hundred. Their numbers dwindled and all were emancipated in 1833, when slavery was abolished throughout the British Empire. In the meantime, Quebec governor Guy Carleton had refused to give back 3,000 slaves to George Washington at the end of the Revolutionary War, and the Underground Railway admitted approximately 40,000 fugitive American slaves to their freedom in Canada, and many U.S. antislavery leaders lived at times in Canada, including John Brown, Josiah Henson (Harriet Beecher Stowe's original Uncle Tom), and Harriet Tubman (who regarded herself as a Canadian). On balance, Canada's record in these matters, though not perfect, was very creditable.

Truth and Reconciliation trumpeted the same war cry of "cultural genocide." Liberal leader Justin Trudeau embraced all of the ninety-four recommendations instantly and before he could have seriously read them: the final report won't be out for months. Thomas Mulcair rushed to the head of the teeming, piping, counter-genocidists by demanding that Stephen Harper ask Pope Francis for an apology over the residential schools when they met this week. (The prime minister made no such request.) Only about two-thirds of the schools were Roman Catholic and they were carrying out federal education policies, not operating in the separate school system. The party of Tommy Douglas, David Lewis, Ed Broadbent, and Jack Layton, in its febrile ambition not to seem lacking in self-hate, wants to assist the first Canadians by pillorying Canada's largest religious denomination.

All people of goodwill will support an approach that is respectful of native tradition, makes good on treaty violations, and makes the
country fully accessible to the native people. But the great majority
of Canadians will not tolerate any theory that this country or its chief
founder practised or countenanced any plausible definition of genocide
ever or anywhere. The natives and their champions are making a terrible mistake if they think that Canadians, indulgent as they are, will roll
over for any charge of genocide. The premeditated enthusiasm of the
chief justice to inflict this blood libel on English and French Canada,
and the reflexive falling in with it of the federal opposition leaders, is
a disgrace. Stephen Harper, by contrast, has handled this issue with
comparative distinction.

# STEPHEN HARPER HAS BEEN A DISTINGUISHED PRIME MINISTER BUT IT IS TIME FOR HIM TO GO

*National Post*, October 17, 2015

---

The arguments for voting for Conservative Leader Stephen Harper are numerous and persuasive. He has been a competent and diligent prime minister who has avoided fiscal imprudence, brought us well through the 2008 financial crisis, and has gone to great and imaginative lengths to keep taxes down and shrink public-sector spending as a share of GDP.

His government has cleaned up a mess in immigration, has been creative with native people's questions without signing on to the nationally self-administered blood libel of "cultural genocide," and shown good judgment and restraint in not going into the deep end over unproved ecological alarm. (It was a credit to him that our peppy itinerant Marxist, Naomi Klein, denounced Harper last week in the world-renowned Sydney Opera House as a "climate criminal.")

His foreign policy has been robust in joining the coalition against ISIL, in not appeasing Russian aggression, and in unambiguously recognizing Israel's right to exist as a Jewish state. (The Palestinians could have their state next week if they abandoned their claimed right to inundate Israel with millions of returning Palestinians. The right of Palestinians to return must be to Palestine, not Israel.) He has neither antagonized the United States as former prime ministers John Diefenbaker and Pierre Trudeau did, nor been subservient to it.

He has shed the cozy myth that we are a nation of beloved peacemakers enlightening the rabidly anti-Israel and anti-West blocs in the United Nations: it is a badge of honour that Canada has not been patronized by those corrupt despotisms that have hijacked much of the UN apparatus. Harper has earned our gratitude by banishing from our foreign policy what the distinguished American (and half Canadian) secretary of state Dean Acheson accused us of sixty-five years ago: "arm-flapping moralism."

As I wrote in my history of Canada (*Rise to Greatness*) last year, Harper ranks now with Louis St. Laurent, Lester Pearson, and Brian Mulroney as an important prime minister, just one level below John A. Macdonald, Wilfrid Laurier, William Lyon Mackenzie King, and Pierre Trudeau. He had to put two quarrelling parties together to become a challenger for that office, and he led his reunified party to steadily better results in four straight elections up to 2011. (No other democratic leader has done this – not even Franklin D. Roosevelt, who was elected U.S. president four times, but not with increasing pluralities.)

These are remarkable achievements, and it was an honour to have been of some assistance to him in the earlier stages of his progress. It was partly to help reunite the Conservatives and promote an alternative to what had almost been one-party Liberal rule for a century (73 of the 103 previous years) that Ken Whyte and I founded the *National Post* in 1998, and I tangibly supported Harper as head of the National Citizens Coalition, the Canadian Alliance, and the reunified Conservatives for many years.

On the other side of the ledger as we approach this election, his government has, with a parliamentary majority, become sclerotically rigid, media-inaccessible, authoritarian, and peevish. Strong ministers such as John Baird and the late Jim Flaherty have not been properly replaced, and there is no discernible policy goal or imagination: only the relentless pursuit of extended incumbency. It is a humourless and often paranoid regime where all spontaneity in cabinet or in the governing caucus in Parliament is stifled and punished.

Harper regularly forbids colleagues from being in contact with people of whom he capriciously disapproves. He will not allow Canada, unlike most serious countries, to have a completely non-partisan, individually conscientious, legislative debate about abortion – essentially the issue of when the rights of the unborn start to rival those of the mother – because it is divisive. He will not respond to Quebec's desire to try to complete the constitutional reforms of Pierre Trudeau and Brian Mulroney, because that, too, is not an easily manageable issue. Leaders are not elected to deal only with what is easy.

Harper claimed the Supreme Court made constitutional change impossible when it determined, as any imbecile knew it would, that the House of Commons could not simply abolish the Senate¶. His response to the questions surrounding the Senate is not to name any new senators – almost a quarter of its seats are now vacant. The real answer is to name distinguished senators, even if they only undertake to serve for a few years.

While the prime minister's foreign policy is principled and rigorous, he has allowed our military capabilities to atrophy to the point that we are the mouse that roars. No one, except Israel, which can take care of itself and is grateful for verbal support, pays any attention to us, especially not Russian president Vladimir Putin. If Putin were to test our Arctic sovereignty, we would only have native people in kayaks to defend it.

Harper has gagged Parliament (and probably misled it in the Mike Duffy affair) and garrotted his own cabinet and caucus, but has sat as silent and inert as a wax dummy while the courts of the country, incited

---

¶ With trivial additional concurrences.

by the jurisdictionally putschist chief justice, Beverley McLachlin, have steadily assumed the rights of the federal and provincial legislatures under the authority of the Charter of Rights and Freedoms. Pierre Trudeau promoted the Charter as an antidote to endless dispute over the federal–provincial division of powers, not as a matrix for the emasculation of legislators.

Instead of counter-legislating, or invalidating ultra vires decisions (of which there have been many) by invoking the notwithstanding clause, Harper assailed the chief justice's personal integrity, almost the only relevant area where she is invulnerable. He has appointed most of the incumbent Supreme Court justices, and a great many judges on junior federal courts, and has only himself to blame for this jurisdictional chaos. The supreme democratic authority of Parliament is being squandered by a control-addicted prime minister and by the falsely righteous depredations and tinkerings of an unchallenged and usurpatory bench.

The entire reactionary agenda is obnoxious to traditional Canadian respect for rights and due process. The omnibus crime bill imposed arbitrary and draconian sentences (Parliament's one counterattack on the rapacious judiciary). It built more prisons in response to a declining crime rate, reduced rehabilitative activity and inmate access to families, and is in sum an unrelievedly retrograde, total-immersion plunge into primitivism. Native people will be the chief occupants of the new prisons, which should be repurposed at once as assisted housing. The bill is a disgrace and should be repealed, even by this government if it is re-elected.

Bill C-51 in defence of national security from terrorism has unexceptionable objectives, but dispenses with due process and cannot fail to be abused in a way profoundly offensive to Canadian traditions of respect for individual rights and the rule of law. The leaders of the NDP and the Green Party, Thomas Mulcair and Elizabeth May, were magnificent in their opposition, and even Liberal leader Justin Trudeau's call for greater oversight was reassuring.

The gratuitously self-awarded right to expel dual citizens convicted of terrorist acts from Canadian citizenship is another worrisome step toward un-Canadian, if not totalitarian, measures. We can punish our own citizens without expelling them. Trudeau's objections to this mob-pleaser were also impressive.

Finally, to make a major election issue out of a woman wearing a face-covering niqab at a citizenship swearing-in ceremony after privately identifying herself is a shabby act of desperation. (Public security requires that everyone be identifiable when in public, but in particular ceremonies exceptions can be made for religious reasons as long as the individuals privately prove their identity to officials.) There is no reason for the government to do any of this except pandering to knuckle-dragging authoritarians in no danger of straying toward the Liberals or NDP. It all incites worried curiosity about what cloven-footed, horned, and furry-headed motivational beasts may lurk within Harper's mind.

It was, until fairly recently, a good government, but it has not renewed its personnel or its program and has become frightening in its disregard for democratic institutions and the rights of the citizens to whom it must answer and is sworn to serve.

Mulcair has fought an admirable campaign as leader of the opposition. He is not an extremist. But the NDP favours abstention from military action against ISIL, recourse to the eco-lunacy of Kyoto and cap-and-trade, unsustainable increases in public spending and taxes, the effective abolition of the English language in the federal workplace in Quebec, repeal of the Clarity Act, and a direct pitch to Quebec's defeated separatists (though Mulcair's stance on the niqab has been admirable). The NDP can only do limited damage in a provincial government; if elected federally, well-intentioned to the end, it would take this country over Niagara Falls.

Justin Trudeau took the headship of a shattered Liberal Party that was widely assumed to be beyond recovery. He has been flexible on public finance, principled on the issue of expulsion from citizenship, wants to fund the armed forces, and has stepped with self-possession into a daunting role opposite more experienced adversaries at the head of bigger parliamentary parties. He remains a largely unknown quantity, but he has a very alluring personality, a quick intelligence, and an apparently reasonable combination of principle and openness. (He also has his lapses, as in his tasteless and nasty attack on popular former Toronto mayor and recovering cancer patient Rob Ford.)

I wrote here earlier this year that the Conservatives' best chance of re-election was for Harper to follow the example of King, Pearson, and Pierre Trudeau, and hand over the leadership of his government to his partisans' choice as a successor; and I wrote that the Conservatives would make a serious mistake if they assumed that Justin Trudeau would make an air-headed ass of himself in an election campaign. Trudeau and Mulcair are right, given Harper's now almost sociopathic personality, to say that they will support each other rather than a Harper minority.

Needlessly, Harper is now likely to follow the route of greater statesmen who didn't know when to leave: Winston Churchill, Konrad Adenauer, Charles de Gaulle, Margaret Thatcher, Helmut Kohl. He was a good prime minister, but it is time to see him off. Trudeau, with a minority, will grow or go. I believe the former, but he has earned his chance. We really cannot have another four years of government by a sadistic Victorian schoolmaster.

# UNITED·STATES

## A YEAR AFTER CHICAGO: HOMAGE TO LBJ

Sherbrooke *Record*, August 26, 1969

Former president Johnson celebrated his sixty-first birthday
on Wednesday. Conrad Black, publisher of the *Record*, has written
this article to honour the man and his achievements.

Lyndon Baines Johnson left Washington seven months ago, after more than three decades there, and home again under "the tattered skies of Texas" he reflects on a uniquely long and productive career.

As secretary to a congressman he arrived in Washington in the vanguard of the New Deal in 1932, and after two years in the National Youth Administration was elected to Congress in 1937, aged twenty-nine.

Throughout his public career, Johnson advocated liberal domestic policies, military preparedness, and full international participation. He led the fight which resulted in irrigation, flood and drought control, and rural electrification for almost one-sixth of all Texas; supported aid to embattled Britain and peacetime conscription in 1940 and 1941, and large postwar foreign aid programs, starting with the Marshall Plan.

Despite his reputation as a liberal and international maverick, Johnson was elected senator in 1948, following a hotly contested primary which he won by 87 votes out of 988,000 cast. This precarious result was upheld in subsequent investigations, and Johnson took his place in the Senate as one of the few southerners who had remained loyal to the administration after the succession of Harry Truman, who advocated extension of civil rights for African Americans, alienating much of the old South.

It is generally agreed that Lyndon Johnson was one of the most effective, ingenious, and picturesque figures in the history of the United States Senate. He became the youngest majority leader in history in 1955, and except during elections was the most powerful member of the Democratic Party throughout the Eisenhower years. These were lean times for American liberals and Johnson was the nation's principal source of progressive legislation. He exposed huge wastes in defence procurement during the Korean War; engineered, with vice-president Richard Nixon, the downfall of the immensely distasteful Senator Joseph R. McCarthy and the dissolution of his witch-hunting committee in 1954; and secured passage of civil rights bills in 1957 and 1960, the first initiatives taken by Congress in this field in eighty years. In passing this act, he had to put down a full-scale filibuster by southern Democrats. One of the leading opponents, then as subsequently, was William Fulbright of Arkansas, who recently has demanded for the people of South Vietnam liberties whose extension to the African American he has stertorously denounced as unconstitutional.

Johnson's judgment of the mood of the Senate was unfailing and he became a ubiquitous, mysterious potentate, always in motion, surrounded by scurrying aides and bourbon-sipping cronies in a gothic tableau already very much of another era.

Johnson was an early advocate of missile development and space exploration, was the first chairman of the Aeronautical and Space Sciences Committee set up after the original fiascos of the American space program, and continued to have responsibility for this program under President Kennedy. He has always defended it against budgetary critics, and has overseen its growth from a retarded and embarrassing infancy to the recent outstanding successes of the Apollo series.

## THE NEW FRONTIER

In 1958, Johnson brought forth a comprehensive program of reform that was the manifesto for his party's sweeping congressional victory that year. It was a plan "to extend the American frontier," the inspiration for the slogan "New Frontier" that Kennedy made famous in 1960. Johnson came second to Kennedy in the quest for the Democratic presidential nomination in 1960, and surprised many by accepting second spot on the ticket. Kennedy's assistant, Theodore Sorensen, has written that Kennedy regarded Johnson as "a senator's senator" who had accomplished more in Congress in the previous eight years than Eisenhower. Kennedy admired from first-hand observation Johnson's tireless ability to campaign, cajole, and persuade, his leadership of the party in its dark days, and his sure-footed finesse in the Senate. Refusing to back down on civil rights, Johnson brought persuasive pressure to bear on southern senators, governors, and local leaders who had theretofore refused to work for a politically unpopular ticket. In one of the closest elections in U.S. history, Johnson provided the margin of victory to the south, and was the only person who could have done so. Probably neither Kennedy nor Johnson would have become president without the other (and it is not clear that either would have been president if Richard Nixon had exercised his right to a full recount).

As vice-president, Johnson concentrated on the space program, foreign visits, especially in Berlin and the Far East, and the Commission on Equal Employment Opportunity, where he continued to work for racial understanding.

## NOVEMBER 22, 1963

Never has a president been sworn in who was better qualified by experience, and never in more tragic circumstances, than Lyndon Johnson, hastily inaugurated at Dallas Airport on November 22, 1963, following the assassination of his popular and talented predecessor.

The contrast between the styles of the old and new presidents was sharp and continued to grate on many who fondly remembered the facile elegance of Kennedy and his principal collaborators. Though the transition was carried out with dignity, the initial spirit of national unity created around the new leader gave way to a feeling among many that Johnson was an illegitimate president, and even a usurper.

Kennedy had achieved passage of only 39 per cent of the bills he had sent to Congress. This shockingly low figure attests to the amateurishness of his approach to Congress and to the lethargic performance

of Mike Mansfield, Johnson's bland and ineffectual successor as majority leader. Johnson's view had been that Congress should be as productive as possible, regardless of the party standings, and he helped
secure passage of 46 per cent of the Eisenhower program. As president,
Johnson gained adoption of a phenomenal 66 per cent of his proposals,
and when he entered the White House, committee chairmen accustomed to whimsically delaying presidential priorities indefinitely soon
learned that there was a new hand on the regime.

Johnson resurrected from committees where they had languished for
many months Kennedy's civil rights and tax-cut bills, and cleared them
through Congress. Similarly, Kennedy's agriculture bill which had been
continually rejected by Congress, and finally by farmers themselves in a
referendum, was passed with minor alterations for Johnson's signature.

## THE GREAT SOCIETY

President Johnson unveiled his Great Society program before
90,000 people at Ann Arbor, Michigan, in May 1964. A plan for
massive social and political change, it was the platform from which
LBJ led his party to the greatest electoral victory in American history that autumn. The opposition was Senator Barry Goldwater and
his following of more conservative Republicans than had prevailed in
the party since the days of Herbert Hoover. Goldwater had alienated
millions of American moderates with his call for the dismantling of
most of the gains made by American liberals since Roosevelt's day. It
is hard to believe now, but in that year many felt liberalism was endangered by the long-stifled forces of reaction. Perhaps the most damaging
issue for Goldwater in that campaign was that, since he had suggested
nuclear defoliation of the jungles of Vietnam, he might be tempted, in
General LeMay's inimitable phrase, "to lob one into the men's room in
the Kremlin."

As the American involvement in Vietnam grew, so did the illusion
that Johnson had pledged himself in that campaign to avoid escalation
of the Vietnam War. He pledged to respond with appropriate measures
to the actions of the enemy; he pledged to seek cooperation with the

communist powers, especially the Soviet Union; and he commended himself to the U.S. voters as indeed more moderate in word and therefore also, action than his opponent. History will record that he kept his pledge, though it is unclear that it has been a successful policy.

Johnson used the immense harvest of votes in 1964 to press his domestic program. The Great Society legislation was one of the finest, if least fully appreciated, hours in the fretful history of American liberalism. The last five years are rivalled as a period of legislative productivity only by the first four years of the New Deal, and when current emotionalism subsides LBJ will take his place beside FDR in the pantheon of American reformers, though it will be difficult to assess the success of his social programs for some time.

## CIVIL RIGHTS

Those who had despaired of the cause of justice to the African American when a southerner became president, who flourished alleged quotations from a Johnson twenty years younger campaigning for election in rural Texas, were silenced by the president's words to Congress and the nation March 15, 1965. Speaking of blacks then demonstrating in and around Selma, Alabama, he said, "Their cause must be our cause too. Because it is not just negroes, but really it is all of us, who must overcome." Martin Luther King commented that the speech was "one of the most eloquent, unequivocal, and passionate pleas for human rights ever made by a president of the United States. He revealed great and amazing understanding of the depth and dimension of the problem of racial injustice."

The voting rights bill that the president then sent to Congress, which approved it, was the most significant forward step for American blacks since the Proclamation of Emancipation. Johnson was the first president since Abraham Lincoln to do something to improve the lives of all blacks, and through two civil rights acts and numerous economic and social laws, he did a great deal.

The initial steps toward the Great Society were leftovers from the Kennedy program: the War on Poverty and the Appalachia relief and road construction bill, but the program broadened into a concentrated attack on all the roots of dispossession and underprivilege in America. Poverty was combatted through stimulation of small businesses, advanced and improved education for the children of poor families, creation of a National Teacher Corps, job retraining for the unemployed for all ages, aid through incentives to depressed areas, and community development programs, some of them managed by the most novel forms of local administration.

## SOCIAL PROGRESS

The War on Poverty was much criticized for overlapping, bureaucratic inefficiencies, and the Orwellian implications of expanding big government. The president himself admitted there was waste and agreed that streamlining was in order. Despite difficulties, most of the program will be retained by the new administration, and the number of Americans hobbled by conditions of poverty according to an inflation-adjusted scale declined from 1963 to 1968 by more than six million.

When Johnson first attained elected office, President Roosevelt spoke of "one-third of a nation" mired in poverty; as he left public office after thirty years, the fraction was one-seventh.

Johnson did more for the expansion and availability of medical facilities than any previous president, passing several far-reaching but not coercive measures. Most important was the Medicare bill, a leftover from the Truman days and supposedly the principal policy difference between Kennedy and Nixon in 1960 (apart from the nonsense about the "missile gap"). It was passed under Johnson's artful prodding after twice being rejected during the Kennedy administration.

Unquestionably, Lyndon Johnson has done more for the development of American education than any other individual in the country's history. The much admired former secretary of health, education, and welfare, John Gardner, described a conversation about education with the ex-president as "one of the most exciting moments of my life." According to the *New York Times*, "Education has been the interest closest to the President's heart, and a national leader could have no more important concern. He has signed into law more than forty separate pieces of legislation to support education, from pre-school projects to graduate education. The federal government has nearly tripled its investment in education, and has for the first time, brought federal money directly to the slum schools which need it most."

Lyndon Johnson was the first president seriously to tackle the whole complex of urban problems that had been allowed to fester virtually unattended for the entire history of industrial America up to his intervention.

Housing: from a plodding and grossly underfunded throwaway, building about 30,000 units a year for low-income families in the Kennedy era, he expanded the federal program to the projected construction of 300,000 units this year, and over six million in the next ten years. Besides new construction, the president's program, one of the most imaginative and extensive ever devised, emphasizes home improvement in shabby but not irreparable areas, rent supplements for hundreds of thousands of families, and the enlistment for the first time of private industry, through tax incentives, in the construction of housing.

Government departments of Housing and Urban Development, and of Transportation, were set up to concentrate the federal approach to these problems, and a Model Cities Act was passed whereby Washington has already subsidized more than 150 locally devised schemes for the improvement of the local urban environment. Mindful of the problems created by entrusting too much of the War on Poverty to the federal bureaucracy, Johnson here, as with housing, involved private industry and local authorities as builders and planners, while the federal government served as a catalyst and financial guarantor.

Lyndon Johnson, the Texan rancher, in the mastering of the corrosive problem of environmental pollution and in the conservation of wildlife and natural resources, has made a contribution unique in his country's history. He has added millions of acres to the domain of the national parks, secured passage of multi-billion-dollar schemes for the cleaning up of the Great Lakes, for the disposal of solid wastes, the beautification of rivers and highways and federal property, the depollution of the air and shores of America, and the creation of greater recreational facilities for its people.

The Johnson program could also be cited for many other advances: the dissemination of birth control information (the first administration to legislate this controversial subject), and consumer protection through an assortment of bills including landmark measures for truth in packaging, and money lending, auto-safety standards, and cigarette-smoking health warnings. The Safe Streets and Crime Control Act has made law enforcement more efficient without reducing individual or collective liberties. There were also bills for the financing of presidential campaigns and control and licensing of firearms, which although more modest than the administration requested, were at least a beginning.

*Congressional Quarterly* reports that in the five years of the Johnson presidency, five times as much important legislation was passed than in the previous ten years under Eisenhower and Kennedy. Lyndon Johnson also sought, without great success, to be one of the few presidents to change the structure of American political life through the almost impossible procedure of constitutional amendment. Under his administration there was an amendment providing that the vice-presidency should never be left vacant, as it was for fourteen months after the death of President Kennedy. Some of his other principal proposals, though not yet acted upon, may be considered of a prophetic nature: lowering the voting age to eighteen; lengthening the term of the House of Representatives to four years; and abolition of the Electoral College to eliminate the possibility of a hung election such as almost occurred in the 1968 Nixon–Humphrey–Wallace race (although if the votes cast in Alabama for a renegade Democrat had not been allocated to Kennedy, Nixon would have won the election by popular vote).

It is the primordial cliché on the subject of Johnson to say that the ghetto riots and the Vietnam War did him in. Most African-American leaders, excepting Eldridge Cleaver, Bobby Seale, and other members of the criminal lunatic fringe, are in accord that the era of the big riots is over, and there have been no significant riots since shortly after the death of Martin Luther King in April 1968. The exodus from the southern cotton fields to the northern ghettoes is now almost at an end, and the population of some ghettoes is already declining. The United States is now enjoying high employment and has committed itself to equalizing standards of education, hireability, housing, and sanitation between the black and white communities among lower economic groups, and for the first time most African Americans are now in the middle class. There is some reason to believe, therefore, as newscaster Chet Huntley remarked, that the riots of recent years "were not signal-fires of the future, but funeral pyres of the past." It is difficult to see, in any event, how this painful period of adjustment could have been avoided, and what more Johnson could have done for racial justice.

## VIETNAM

V ietnam is a story too well-known to require a long telling, yet too agonized and uncertain to be dealt with briefly. However, several points are worth recording already. President Johnson inherited a deteriorating situation from his predecessor and was advised by all those whose advice he also inherited (Bundy, Rusk, Taylor, McNamara, et al.) to intervene forcefully. Indeed, as even dovish columnist Stewart Alsop remarked, it was surprising that Kennedy's attempt to win the war "by proxy" took as long as it did to fail. Throughout the time of active American involvement in Vietnam, Johnson has stated that his country's motives were not total victory but honourable compromise: his speech at Johns Hopkins University in Baltimore, in June 1965, was one of the more important of such restatements, and to this end he called three bombing halts prior to 1968. The principal motives of the American involvement in Vietnam were: to prove that the murderous euphemism of "the people's war of liberation" is not an invincible means of territorial expansion; to aid in the construction of a balance of power in East Asia by developing a coalition of states as a counterweight to China; to contain and deter the eruptive and aggressive force of revolutionary China-Vietnam; to prevent one of Asia's most strategic areas (before the war, South Vietnam was the greatest rice exporter in Asia) from falling by default into the hands of America's self-proclaimed enemies; and to honour the original SEATO commitments signed by President Eisenhower and Prime Minister Churchill in 1954.

In these objectives, the United States has been supported by all the con-communist states of the area, except Cambodia. The recent stirrings of the Philippines and Japan from slumber under the American umbrella, and the downfall of the pyrotechnic President Sukarno in Indonesia, augur well for the American goal of an independent and self-reliant coalition of non-communist states in the Far East. The other objectives will be achieved if the peace that seems slowly to be emerging from the tortuous roundel at Paris is the honourable compromise President Johnson long ago pledged himself to pursue.

Except for the hysterical and apocalyptic, to whom the tedious refrain of genocide, war criminals, etc., comes automatically, the principal objection to the Vietnamese policy has been on the grounds that the energies expended in the war could never be justified or repaid, even by the war's victorious conclusion. This is a serious argument that may never be resolved, and certainly not before the war is ended and its cost can be estimated. At no time did the war absorb more than 15 per cent of federal government expenditures. The loss of 34,000 men over seven years is of course an immeasurable tragedy, even in a country which loses over 50,000 dead a year on its highways. However, the cost of abandoning Vietnam and with it the objectives enumerated above would also have been heavy. Perhaps President Johnson was being somewhat theatrical when he said, "Not even blood is a high price to pay for civilization," but before dismissing the war a sanguinary fiasco, critics should assess the implications of the alternatives, an exercise that few critics have troubled to attempt. What has seemed to hamper the progress of the U.S. war effort has been Johnson's tendency to de-escalate in hopes that this will be reciprocated. To date, it has not been, and unfortunately there is no sign that it will be.

The war was never a holy crusade against communism, and those who accuse the ex-president of having an irrational fear of the "international communist conspiracy" (words which neither he nor any other administration spokesman has uttered since the Dulles era) ignore the fact that he negotiated the Nuclear Non-proliferation Treaty, a trade expansion and encouragement plan, a consular agreement, and the beginnings of general armaments-control talks, all with the Soviet Union. All of these were stalled or rejected by the Senate, or had to be postponed because of the Soviet invasion of Czechoslovakia. Johnson also assembled a staff of China experts who were designated to occupy the U.S. embassy in Peking when conditions eventually permit mutual recognition between the two countries.

## ABDICATION

When Lyndon Johnson announced on March 31, 1968, that he would not seek re-election, it was the greatest bombshell in an American political generation. Senator Eugene McCarthy had come close to defeating the president in the New Hampshire primary, but he was certainly not a serious threat to his authority. McCarthy's urbane but supercilious waspishness finally irritated as many people as it impressed and his recent erratic conduct has caused many to wonder if he is even fit to continue as a mediocre, lazy, and temperamental senator, let alone preside over the nation. His campaign was based on three factors: peace at almost any price in Vietnam; a scatter-gun demand for reduction of the powers of the presidency; a vague and rather maudlin recollection of the tranquil, Midwest, mid-twenties America of Sinclair Lewis (the bandshell-in-the-park, Norman Rockwell and Walt Disney); a flimsy platform indeed. Furthermore, McCarthy seems to be a political masochist: his hero is Sir Thomas More, and it is difficult to shed the impression that he, too, wanted to be beheaded by Henry VIII / LBJ.

But McCarthy's performance did smoke out the real opposition: Bobby Kennedy was moved to make yet another "reassessment" of his "non-candidacy." He would enter the lists to have the very liberalism Johnson had fought ten years to advance and to deliver the nation from Richard Nixon. Johnson never doubted who Judas would be. In the last two years of his regime, Johnson was obliged to deal with a steadily increasing barrage of hysterical and sometimes infantilistic abuse from reflex liberals in Congress, the Democratic Party, and the press. Bobby Kennedy bubbled naturally to the top of this cauldron – the wartime president's traditional cup of hemlock.

Even Stewart Alsop, the apogee of the Georgetown liberal, recently wrote that "a lot of people, especially journalistic admirers of President Kennedy, including this one, have been brutally unfair to Lyndon Johnson." Many of the same writers who decried Congress in Kennedy's day as cumbrous and obsolescent insinuated that Johnson was an immoderate and power-hungry autocrat when he made the system work. Many of the dispossessed Kennedyites who criticized Johnson for pirating the unhatched brain-children of his "martyred" predecessor blasted him in equal voice for unimaginative and antiquated solutions to the problems of the 1960s; doubly irritating criticism considering the source. The same elements which denounced Johnson for appointing a commission to investigate the cause of riots because it would bring forth humdrum recommendations paused only to draw breath before attaching him for not requesting immediate congressional action on the commission's very penetrating and even radical report.

The president suffered the defeat of an open housing and civil rights bill, and of a bill giving home rule to Washington, D.C., a predominantly black city, though his manner of getting around this and appointing a negro mayor in spite of Congress prompted liberal writer Richard Rovere to reaffirm that Johnson was a great president in all respects except Vietnam. The Riots Commission reported that "white racism" was the principal cause of African-American violence, and true though this perhaps was, the president was understandably reluctant to send to Congress a controversial measure that would have no chance of success. Many of the critics who accused Johnson of being too intractable with the communist powers cried like stuck pigs when it occurred to them that he might meet with the Soviet leadership even after the Soviet invasion of Czechoslovakia.

Arthur Schlesinger, almost part of the Kennedy family, lightly criticized Kennedy for Vietnam ("He never gave it his full attention, it was the greatest failing of his administration.") but condemned Johnson for being "obsessed" with the subject.

*Time* magazine, which three years before, when it was beating the drums for Vietnam, had declared that General William Westmoreland was the "Man of the Year," had the effrontery to accuse Johnson of praising the general too highly when he promoted him from the Vietnam command to be army chief of staff. (In fact, Westmoreland's failure to cut the Ho Chi Minh Trail was a disastrous one.)

Last and certainly not least, Norman Mailer, the bedraggled warhorse of American blowhardism, whose effort to become the moral arbiter of modern America was hindered somewhat by his stabbing of his first wife, and who by his own admission is "full of crap," was taken seriously for the first time in twenty years when he uttered the most specious and irrelevant opinions about Johnson.**

Some merely misunderstood Johnson; many others subjected him to the most disgusting abuse. Stokely Carmichael called him a "hunky, a buffoon, and a liar." And H. Rap Brown suggested that Johnson and his wife "should be shot." Robert Sherrill described Johnson as "treacherous, dishonest, manic-aggressive, spoiled," and he was referred to in the play *MacBird!* as a "canker, tyrant, villain, traitor, cur." The campaign of youthful vilification against the president reached a sickening climax in Chicago last August. Thousands of youths marched around Grant Park shouting the ultimate obscenity at Johnson, and finally fed a birthday cake to a pig in commemoration of his birthday. Johnson said only that if he were a young person he would probably feel like protesting too; a less patient and dedicated man, when taunted incessantly with the chant "Hey, hey, LBJ, how many kids have you killed today?" might have been tempted to reply, "None, unfortunately."

## BOBBY

The aspiring head of all the opposition, responsible and not, was Bobby Kennedy, who regarded Johnson as a crude interloper, tainted by long years of public service in previous eras less enlightened and edifying than the Kennedy Camelot. As the senior surviving Kennedy brother, he felt that he had not only the right but the obligation to keep faith with the honoured dead by ending this usurpation. His statement the previous July that Johnson was "a great president," like his long-standing enthusiasm for the Vietnam War before public support for it fell off, he dismissed with a glazed pall of prevarication and the comment that the "only sin is to be too proud to admit mistakes."

---

** Norman and I became friends thirty years later and he acknowledged that he had been unfairly critical of LBJ.

Johnson looked on Bobby as the man who had worked for Joseph McCarthy, American liberalism's greatest enemy, whom Johnson (and Nixon) overthrew; as the man who had objected to Johnson's nomination as vice-president in 1960 but was overruled by his brother, who fortunately for the Democrats had a better knowledge of political arithmetic; as the man who as attorney general had been the foremost wire-tapper in U.S. history; who had been caught publicly lying by the FBI, who had suddenly discovered a hatful of votes in civil rights after Johnson had worked for racial understanding for years in the unfertile south; as the man who in running for his first elective office, as senator from New York, had got into trouble on the carpet-bagger issue, requested the aid of the president's coattails, and trailed Johnson into office by two million votes in New York; and as the man who spoke as if he had discovered the word *meritocracy*, yet had inherited access to more money and popularity than any politician in U.S. history.

There wasn't room for both of them in Washington, and shortly both were gone. Even if they had contested at the convention in Chicago, Johnson would have surely won. At the time he withdrew, all surveys showed him with an easy and assured majority of the delegates, most of them unshakeable Johnson loyalists, friends accumulated over a long career of influential back-scratching. In view of the close race run by his stand-in, Hubert Humphrey, he might even have won re-election. His withdrawal was motivated in part by health reasons, and in part by a fear of electoral defeat, which would have been a humiliating last hurrah. But even the jaded Washington press corps managed to find more important reasons. The serried ranks of American punditry wavered badly in the Johnson years: the cavernously pontifical Walter Lipmann changed course so often, but always with such oracular pomposity, that one was tempted to ask if the real Walter Lipmann would please shut up; and the remarks of the eternally smug and smarmy Tom Wicker were rarely deserving of attention. But Stewart Alsop raised himself above his peers long enough to give this assessment of Johnson's withdrawal: "Lyndon Johnson could almost certainly have bulled his way through to renomination, and quite possibly re-election. To abandon power goes against the man's every instinct; yet he chose to do so. He so chose for several reasons, some not unconnected with his colossal pride. But the main reason, surely, was simple love of country. He knew the country would have to pay a terrible price in what he called, in his March 31 speech, 'divisiveness,' if he ran again. He chose not to make the country pay that price. For that, as well as for much else for which he has received little credit, Lyndon Johnson deserves the heartfelt thanks of his countrymen."

## HISTORY'S JUDGMENT

The *Chicago Sun-Times* said that the nation had failed him more often than he had failed the nation; more likely, neither had failed. As Johnson left office, racial tensions were declining somewhat; Vietnam was going better militarily, and peace might be in sight; there were two consecutive balanced budgets; the official balance of payments was favourable again after ten years of chronic deficits; and employment was almost full. Inflation was admittedly a serious problem but the tools to combat it were at hand. The *New York Times* said, "Mr. Johnson has presided over a new age of progressivism. He laboured mightily on behalf of this nation and always tried to serve the best interest of all the people. He has no reason to fear history's judgment."

Indeed many serious historians such as Allan Nevins, Clinton Rossiter, and James MacGregor Burns already regard him as an outstanding president.

The reforms achieved by Johnson differed from Roosevelt's in that they were aimed more at economic rehabilitation than emergency relief, and in contrast to the Depression president, he attacked poverty and underprivilege without baiting the rich. His objective was not a redistribution of the wealth of the country, a Robin Hood–like taking from the rich to give to the poor. The rationale for the Great Society was that the natural premium on the growth of the American economy could be used to raise up the disadvantaged to the level of economic participation. The poor could be helped without hurting the rich, said LBJ, and the same president who cut the maximum personal income-tax rate by 26 per cent also raised welfare and services expenditures from $30 billion to $68 billion. The same President Johnson who was derided by liberals as an heirloom from the New Deal first sponsored the involvement of business in the reconstruction of society through a program of grants and incentives. The first southern president in over a century, to a certain extent he reintegrated the south in the political processes of the country. The president who routed the extreme right in 1964, he also helped to save the country from the extreme left in 1968.

His one really serious mistake was to send 540,000 mainly conscripted soldiers to a foreign war without express congressional authorization and with an objective short of victory and not indisputably in the national interest. He could have obtained such approval, in February 1965, almost unanimously, and a man of Johnson's experiences should have known better than to embark on that enterprise on such vague authority as the Gulf of Tonkin Resolution, which only urged him to take the steps necessary for the defence of American interests. These were practical and possibly strategic, but not moral, errors.

If there was a second mistake, it was his handling of the Detroit riot in 1967, when he insisted that Michigan governor Romney admit that he had lost control of the situation before the dispatch of federal troops. This gave the impression of playing politics with lives in one of the nation's largest cities.

Some critics claim the Dominican Republic intervention in 1965 was a mistake, but the operation was quite successful: a communist takeover through front organizations was avoided, and in impartially supervised free elections, the anti-communist candidate won a landslide victory.

More damaging than any blunder: Johnson was not, as his old mentor Franklin D. Roosevelt had said the president must be, "pre-eminently the head of the American people for the presidency is a place of moral leadership."

In person, Johnson could be very impressive. His technique of personal persuasion, an overpowering hard sell of cajolery and bullying, was almost irresistible, and many strong-minded men, including George Wallace, buckled under it. Even Bobby Kennedy called him "a very formidable man" after a meeting. He was also both clever and intelligent. Richard Nixon called him "one of the greatest political craftsmen of our time," and J.K. Galbraith said of him, "He's genuinely intelligent, imaginative, flexible, and he wants to do things." James Reston described him as "one of the most eloquent and persuasive advocates of this generation." He could be a prodigious and effective campaigner.

But in addressing himself to the whole nation, Johnson did not always achieve the full status of his office. Whether because of his regional mannerisms, accent, or old Senate habits of secretiveness and even double-talk, he sometimes had problems of communication, but he was also the victim of what the *New York Times* called "vulgar snobbery," and the credibility gap was an almost entirely phony issue. Johnson was as forthright as most presidents and more so than many (including Roosevelt, who was saved, however, by managing to sound like an apostle when he was lying). But Johnson's critics, in one of American history's most effective and insidious hatchet jobs, managed to sew mistrust between the people and their president.

Johnson's abdication, like that of Cincinnatus, was a classic example of the voluntary surrender of great power, a very dramatic act. All knew that a titan had passed whose like would not be seen again. His talents, his ego, his compassion, determination, and capacity for work were, like his services to the nation and his much-caricatured ears, very prominent.

And so an epoch in American and world affairs, which only began with the intercession of tragedy, ended prematurely, and the plane in which Lyndon Baines Johnson was inaugurated president at Dallas, and which carried him and the corpse and the widow of his predecessor back to Washington in 1963, carried him also back to Texas at the end of his public days in 1969. Thousands bade the president a friendly farewell at the Washington airport, and the largest and most appropriate sign they held aloft read "Vaja con Dios, LBJ."

*The information officer in the U.S. consulate in Montreal read this comment in the Sherbrooke* Record *and sent it to President Johnson's office. That office gave it to the congressman in Austin, Jake J. Pickle, an old LBJ protégé, who inserted it in the congressional record, and President Johnson sent me a very gracious note of appreciation on September 9, 1969, and I visited him at his ranch in the spring of 1970. He facilitated my extensive trip to East Asia later that year, and especially my stay in South Vietnam, where he enabled me to interview the president and vice-president of that country, the U.S. ambassador, and theatre military commander (General Creighton Abrams). My interview with President Thieu was very widely carried, including by the* New York Times, London Times, Daily Telegraph, *and* Le Monde. *I have never lost my admiration for LBJ, even as he became a tragic figure. If he had cut the Ho Chi Minh Trail and intensified the bombing of the North, or even, after the great but disguised Allied victory of the Tet Offensive, given the Silent Majority speech Richard Nixon gave nearly two years later and relaxed draft calls and begun troop withdrawals, he would have been re-elected and might have had a successful last term and served longer than any president of the United States except Franklin D. Roosevelt. History is full of such might-have-beens.*

# AMERICA CAN
# DO BETTER THAN THIS

*National Post, Chicago Sun-Times,* and *Daily Telegraph,*
December 21, 1998

---

The shambles in Washington is one of the most profound political impasses there since before the Civil War. Even in Watergate, Richard Nixon was so swiftly deserted by his own party, there was not such a stand-off. President Clinton has convinced the public that his offences are insufficient to justify removal from office (which is, of course, true, but so were Nixon's, and Andrew Johnson's in 1868), but he has so antagonized Republican leaders in Congress that they seem prepared to go to almost any lengths to force him out. They cling with a tenacity the voters consider pedantic and sadistic to the notion that even a relatively trivial act of perjury in a spurious proceeding is a crime disqualifying its author from continuing as president.

A little like Paul Newman in the early 1960s film *Hud,* President Clinton is a naughty southern boy who tempts and taunts those who would catch him doing bad things while winking mischievously and even beguilingly at onlookers, in this case his countrymen and the whole world.

The more President Clinton professes smilingly to be a reborn man of virtue, the more paroxysmally the Republican leaders run out and sermonize about his debauching the great office of Washington,

Jefferson, Jackson, Lincoln, Wilson, and the Roosevelts. Both the presidency and Congress are falling into a state of disrepute that may not be just dangerous but farcical. It makes the world's most important country look like a banana republic, lacking only in chubby and bemedalled junta-aspirants.

All that can now be foreseen is more of the same indignity. Barring the sudden emergence of incriminating evidence in more substantive areas than the president's sex life, there is little chance of attracting sixty-seven Senate votes to remove him from office. A reproach, passed as a bill and signed by the president with a plausible apology – not another exercise in finger-crossing casuistry – might mercifully end the nonsense.

But the present cast – the president's fixers and managers, a noisy riff-raff clamouring about popular sovereignty and repossession of the Constitution, and the Republican congressional leaders unctuously posturing like pompous, otherworldly, Victorian clergy – is unlikely to produce such a result.

Perhaps the looming presence of the chief justice and the talk of bringing back Howard Baker, George Mitchell, and Bob Dole in a mediating role might produce something useful. Failing that, we will have a trial that will be as dignified as possible, given the tawdriness of the facts to be adjudicated.

The president will not be dislodged; there will be no further apology from him; and he will limp to the end of his term, well-liked but tainted, profoundly disappointing, and ineffectual. The Boniors, Daschles, Lotts, Gephardts, Armeys, and whoever may occupy the ejector seat of the House speakership will then go on flailing pathetically at each other like rubber-legged prize-fighters.

Such a scenario – at present the most probable one – will bore and embarrass America and its foreign friends, and confirm others in their suspicions that the United States is fundamentally a vacuous country, leavened only slightly by unbecoming prurience and imperishable naivety.

Surely America can do better than this. What should happen is that the Senate should pass a bill more or less incorporating what the House Democrats offered. Congress should adopt a sensible definition of high crimes and misdemeanours for these purposes. It should reform the independent counsel law to discourage not so much the overmaligned Ken Starr as prosecutorial lunatics like Archibald Cox (transmogrified by his brief experience into the self-appointed "conscience of the nation," the subtitle of his admiring biography referred to in the piece from *National Review Online*, September 25, 2014, which appears later in Part 2) and Lawrence Walsh, whose indictment of Caspar Weinberger in the Iran-Contra affair was the single most outrageous abuse of the statute. Recourse to independent counsel should be made less easy and subject to more precise guidelines. There must be legal discouragements both to power-mad Torquemadas like Cox and Walsh and to Janet Reno's unreasonable refusal to investigate seriously the morass of campaign financing abuses (which is much more worrisome than the president's peccadilloes and his shortcomings as a grand jury witness).

Finally, Congress should acknowledge that it is not at all clear that Richard Nixon, given a fair trial, would have been found guilty of high crimes and misdemeanours worthy of removal from office. The combination of fanatical hostility from the liberal media, which had never forgiven him for being right about Alger Hiss (or calling Helen Gahagan Douglas "the Pink Lady" when he defeated her for the U.S. Senate in 1950, and she often called him "Tricky Dick"), and his own psychological complexities in Watergate have caused Richard Nixon to be uniquely and undeservedly dishonoured.

It is hard to be optimistic that the present congressional leadership of either party could be capable of making anything useful out of this debacle. This Congress has performed more poorly with the voters than any opposition Congress facing an administration's second midterm election since President Monroe in 1822. In two years, the country will elect a new president who will, presumably, be aware of the need to execute the office with more probity than has the incumbent. It is within the bounds of reason to hope that that president will bomb a Saddam Hussein when the national interest requires it. But will Congress respond with support for the commander-in-chief or, as this one has, with churlish imputations of unworthy motives for carrying out the policy it had long recommended?

America and the world need a U.S. president who will, if necessary, be believed in addressing Congress in Cromwellian terms: "You have been sent here to redress the nation's grievances and you are now the nation's greatest grievance," and a Congress which will make such assertions unjust and unnecessary. Almost everything one would hope for is lacking now – except a great people, a mighty nation, and a system of government that usually works, and will work again, eventually.[††]

---

[††] It was too hopeful; it all got steadily worse for four consecutive presidential terms.

# ROOSEVELT
# AND THE REVISIONISTS

*National Review Online*, March 5, 2009

---

As the current financial crisis has unfolded, Franklin D. Roosevelt has been frequently traduced for the economic policies he used to lead the country out of the Great Depression.

On Inauguration Day 1933 (then March 4), there were machine-gun nests at the corners of the great government buildings in Washington for the only time since the Civil War. Almost all banks in thirty-eight states had been closed sine die. In most of the other states and Washington, D.C., withdrawals were limited to 5 per cent of deposits, and in Texas to $10 per day. The New York Stock Exchange and the Chicago commodity exchange had been closed, indefinitely. The financial system had effectively collapsed. In a fever of activity, Roosevelt guaranteed bank deposits, made the federal government a temporary non-voting preferred shareholder in thousands of suddenly undercapitalized banks (more than half the banks in the country), refinanced millions of residential and farm mortgages, put millions of people to work in relief and conservation programs, tolerated cartels and collective bargaining in order to raise prices and wages, increased the money supply, effectively departed the gold standard, repealed Prohibition of alcoholic beverages (wrenching one of the nation's largest industries out of the hands of the underworld), and legislated reduced working hours and improved working conditions for the whole workforce. In the next two years, he set up the Securities and Exchange Commission, created the Social Security system, broadened the powers of the Federal Reserve to equal those of other nations' central banks, and imposed some entirely political tax changes to stave off Huey Long and other extremists in what became known as the Second New Deal.

The Hoover agricultural policy had been to dump surpluses abroad, lend foreign governments the money to buy them, and then pursue the debtor countries aggressively when they defaulted. Roosevelt had farmers vote, by category of what they produced, on agreed production cutbacks, assuring sustainable agricultural prices, and compensated farmers for the production they had curtailed. The more extreme revisionists now claim that Roosevelt should not have stabilized food prices and financed, through public-works projects, flood and drought control and rural electrification, because it would have been better to starve these people off the land and to the cities, where, a generation or more later, they would have had higher standards of living. Apart from the fact that the resulting human misery would have been morally and politically unacceptable in the United States, the already militant farm unions would have disrupted the nation's food supply. Such a policy would have put Roosevelt in the same general category of agrarian reformers as Stalin and Mao.

The key to evaluating Roosevelt's performance at combating the Depression is the statistical treatment of many millions of unemployed engaged in his massive workfare programs, which were called "internal improvements" in Jackson's time, and are called "infrastructure" now. The government hired about 60 per cent of the unemployed in public works and conservation projects that planted a billion trees, saved the whooping crane, modernized rural America, and built such diverse projects as the Cathedral of Learning in Pittsburgh, the Montana State Capitol, much of the Chicago lakefront, New York City's Lincoln Tunnel and Triborough Bridge, the Tennessee Valley Authority, and the heroic aircraft carriers Enterprise and Yorktown. They also built or renovated 2,500 hospitals, 45,000 schools, 13,000 parks and playgrounds, 7,800 bridges, 700,000 miles of roads, and a thousand airfields. They employed 50,000 schoolteachers, rebuilt the entire rural school system of the country, and employed 3,000 writers, musicians, sculptors, and painters, including the young Willem de Kooning and Jackson Pollock.

Even pro-Roosevelt historians such as William Leuchtenburg and Doris Kearns Goodwin have meekly accepted the characterization of millions of people in the New Deal workfare programs as "unemployed," while comparable millions of Germans, Japanese, and eventually French and British also, who were dragooned into the armed forces and defence-production industries in the mid and late 1930s were considered to be employed. This made the Roosevelt administration's economic perfor-mance appear uncompetitive, but the people employed in government public-works and conservation programs were just as authentically (and much more usefully) employed as were draftees in what became the European and Japanese garrison states, while Roosevelt was rebuilding America at an historic bargain cost. If these workfare Americans are con-sidered to be unemployed, the Roosevelt administration still reduced unemployment between 1933 and 1936 from 33 per cent to 12.5 per cent, to less than 10 per cent by the end of 1940, and to less than 1 per cent a year later, when the United States was plunged into war. If the federal workfare employees are accepted as employed, the corresponding num-bers are 33 per cent, 7 per cent, 3 per cent, and 0.5 per cent. Virtually all the genuinely unemployed received basic social-benefit payments from 1935 on.

After the Second New Deal, in 1934–1935, came a period of rela-tive inertia and reduction of welfare spending, to test traditional capi-talist theory, which provoked what Republicans tried to promote as a "Roosevelt Recession" (having noisily demanded the measures that led to it). The Third New Deal, in 1938, involved a massive return to work-fare programs, whereupon economic progress resumed. The Fourth New Deal was the greatest defence build-up in history, starting in 1939, including the first peacetime draft in U.S. history in the midst of the 1940 election campaign. Finally, there was the GI Bill of Rights in 1944, which, posthumously as to Roosevelt, transformed the American working class into a middle class. In the late 1940s, half the students in U.S. universities were on GI Bill of Rights student grants.

In the vacuum created by Roosevelt's unexpected death in office, without memoirs or a literary executor, a spontaneous coalition of

McCarthyite Republicans, disgruntled British imperialists, and Euro-Gaullists propagated the Yalta myth – i.e., that Roosevelt had been swindled by Stalin at Yalta into handing over Eastern Europe to the U.S.S.R. In fact, the Yalta agreement promised freedom and independence for Eastern Europe, as Eisenhower pointed out to Khrushchev at the Geneva Conference in 1955. If Roosevelt and Churchill had given Stalin everything he wanted, he would not have felt the need to violate every clause of that agreement, as he did. FDR had no sooner been acquitted on that score than some supply-side economic purists started alleging that he actually prolonged the Great Depression in the United States.

Roosevelt expressed frustration to Felix Frankfurter and others that his opponents didn't recognize that he was "the greatest friend American capitalism ever had." He wanted to, and did, make America safe for people who lived in forty-room houses on thousand-acre estates. He directed all the anger and frustration of the Depression into a cul-de-sac of mythological characters – economic royalists, war profiteers, monopolists, malefactors of great wealth, money changers, and speculators – and preserved the moral integrality of the nation to focus hostility on its real enemies: Nazism and Japanese imperialism. He was no bleeding heart, and he reduced welfare outlays in the summer, explaining, "No one ever dies of starvation in this country in the summer."

It is, to say the least, unrigorous for current spokespeople of the intelligent right to claim that Roosevelt's peacetime elimination of unemployment was a failure, that war-mongering was his real antidote to economic depression, and that the grateful electors of the most successful politician in the country's history were hoodwinked, as FDR would have said, "again and again and again." Instead of trying to debunk FDR, Amity Shlaes, Holman Jenkins, and even Jim Powell should complete his liberation from leftist kidnappers and claim him for themselves. He was a reformer, and also one of the very greatest conservatives in American history.

# LIES THAT ARE DISPUTED

*National Review Online*, October 26, 2009

M ost thoughtful commentators bemoan the decline of bipartisanship and the coarsening of political discourse in the United States. The president promised to reach out to the opposition and hoped for eighty Senate votes for his stimulus bill. But he disregarded all Republican suggestions for the bill and acquiesced in its Pelosification into a groaning, creaking, Democratic gravy train.

I remember, as a very young person, the august comparative tranquillity of the Eisenhower era, when the president requested national air time only for matters of indisputable national interest. He never abused this privilege, and there was no call for equal time. The morning after his addresses, two giant-finned Cadillac limousines would convey the Democratic leaders of Congress, Speaker Sam Rayburn, and Senate majority leader Lyndon B. Johnson, up Pennsylvania Avenue to the White House to assure the president and the media of the rock-solid support of Congress.

At the heart of the degeneration from that level of trust is an embittering partisan difference over the national interest, built on competing versions of recent U.S. history. Those Democrats who think about these things believe that the Kennedy administration's response to the Cuban Missile Crisis of 1962 was a masterpiece of crisis management, an almost scientific path to a bloodless triumph. They believe the Kennedys would never have plunged into Vietnam, that Lyndon Johnson, despite his inestimable services to civil rights and the growth of the compassionate welfare state, blundered into a hopeless war (urged by the same people who had advised Kennedy during the Missile Crisis), and that he misled the public and provided a cautionary tale showing why the United States should commit forces to foreign combat only in precisely limited multinational operations of unquestionable virtue.

They believe that President Nixon took over the Vietnam War as his own, also misled the nation, and squandered 30,000 American lives in a shameful pursuit of a "decent interval" between the U.S. withdrawal and the collapse of the Saigon regime. According to this account, the Democrats forced a brave termination of the war with a shutdown of all aid to South Vietnam, and then redeemed the integrity of the U.S. government by forcing the departure of Nixon, a uniquely sleazy and villainous president. This version was frozen and fed to the public by the national media, who touted themselves as the heroic exposers of "imperial" government misfeasance, in Vietnam and Watergate.

Kay Graham's version of what her late husband called the "rough first draft of history" became liberal holy writ. It was genuflected to like the Infant of Prague, and defended with the tenacity of the garrison of the Alamo. The conservative talk-show personalities who have grown like dandelions in opposition to this orchestrated groupthink, and the media controlled by Rupert Murdoch (Fox and the *Wall Street Journal*), are reviled as rabble-rousing muckrakers. (Murdoch is a more astute political manoeuvrer than has been seen in Washington for decades.)

The same liberals tend to believe that Ronald Reagan was "an amiable dunce," though a "great communicator" and "Teflon man" (as opposed to a great orator and clever statesman). They claim Gorbachev ended the Cold War and Reagan seduced the country with a fools' paradise of vulgar and easy self-gratification. It need hardly be added that George W. Bush has passed into these canons as a belligerent, pigheaded, semi-literate oaf.

Taken as a whole, this is a vulnerable catechism. We now know that there were 40,000 Soviet soldiers in Cuba in October 1962, and that the nuclear warheads were already in the country and could have been installed and fired in twenty-four hours. A disaster was avoided not by the portentous calibrations of Kennedy's entourage, but by the president's own, inspired, intuition. And it was no great strategic victory; in exchange for Soviet non-deployment in Cuba, the United States began the destabilization of the Turkish alliance by removing its long-deployed missiles in Italy and Turkey.

Lyndon Johnson had basically thrown in the towel in Vietnam in October 1966, when he offered Hanoi reciprocal withdrawal of forces from the South. If Ho Chi Minh had not thought that he could militarily defeat the United States, he would have accepted that offer and crushed the South six months after the U.S. withdrawal. Johnson would not have tried to reintroduce ground forces, but Ho wouldn't give the United States any cover for its disengagement; he was determined to humiliate it completely.

In April 1972, between Nixon's historic visits to China and the U.S.S.R., the South Vietnamese defeated the North Vietnamese and Viet Cong invasion and offensive, with no U.S. ground support but with heavy air support. This formula might have kept South Vietnam afloat for fifteen years, until international communism collapsed. In his Silent Majority speech of November 1969, Nixon said that North Vietnam could not "defeat or humiliate the United States. Only Americans can do that." This is what happened, and the Democrats and the national media have been in steadily more implausible denial for over thirty years.

Watergate was nonsense. The House Judiciary Committee was a shameful riff-raff of grandstanding poseurs. Counsel John Doar's charges against Nixon were a Stalin-worthy fantasy of what Kafka called "nameless crimes." The "smoking gun" was tawdry but innocuous, and the only legal vulnerability was the payment of Watergate defendants' expenses in possible consideration for altered testimony. This may have happened, but in a serious proceeding it would have been very difficult to prove Nixon knew anything about it. He had a direct connection only to the supplementary payment to Howard Hunt, and it isn't exactly clear what the consideration was. These were, and were not necessarily more than, what Nixon called "horrendous" mistakes "not worthy of a president."

Nixon's only full term was, except for Lincoln's one and FDR's first and third, the most successful in history (founding the Environmental

Protection Agency, ending the riots and assassinations and hijackings, ending the draft, reducing the crime rate, stopping inflation, the opening to China, SALT I, the Middle East peace process, and the undefeated withdrawal from Vietnam). His ethics were no more unprecedentedly deficient than his presidency aspired in any way to being imperial. Nixon was impeccably honest financially and an unwavering patriot. He had some infelicitous foibles that were worrisome, but they were grotesquely exaggerated by the media.

Thus did the Democrats discover the joys of criminalizing policy differences, which corresponded with the relentless rise of the powers of prosecutors in the country generally. They tried it again in the Iran-Contra foolishness, and the exemplary Caspar Weinberger briefly faced criminal prosecution. The Republicans returned the favour by deposing Speaker Jim Wright, sending Ways and Means chairman Dan Rostenkowski to prison, and taking President Clinton's demeaning but hardly unprecedented peccadilloes to the only Senate impeachment trial of a president since Andrew Johnson.

Along with Truman, Nixon and Reagan did more than anyone else to win the Cold War, the greatest and most bloodless strategic victory in the history of the nation state. Nixon was a master chess player, from propagator of the Red Scare in the 1940s to architect of détente in the 1970s, to friend of Yeltsin in the 1990s. And Reagan was a great poker player; he raised the ante with his Strategic Defense Initiative, which the Democrats mocked, until the U.S.S.R. was bankrupt. The United States now faces the consequences of the Democrats' crucifixion of the one and overmockery of the other.

The truth in all these controversies is between the poles, but the indigestible fact is that Rush Limbaugh and Ann Coulter are closer to it than the *New York Times* and the traditional networks. In this vortex, the gerrymandering of congressional districts and entrenchment of special interests in campaign financing has gridlocked legislation as an earmark contest and an endless war of attrition waged through sound bites, sniping, posturing, and poll-taking. The political class has taken an almost vertical dive in respectability since Stevenson and Eisenhower, or Kennedy and Nixon, contested the presidency.

This is not a culture war. The prevailing ethos rests on the vibrating pillars of the demonization of Nixon and the myths of Vietnam. Napoleon famously described history as "lies agreed upon." What we have now are lies that are disputed. The liberals must relinquish their claimed monopoly on virtue. The conservatives must cease implying that the liberals are traitors. And the national media must re-earn public confidence or be swept into a cul-de-sac by Murdoch, Limbaugh, and the rest.

# LESS EXCEPTIONAL
# THAN YOU THINK

*National Review Online*, March 11, 2010

---

t is with regret and trepidation that I take some issue with Richard
Lowry and Ramesh Ponnuru's stimulating essay on American exceptionalism in the March 8 issue of *National Review*. I am afraid they
exaggerate the pristine idealism of the founders of the United States,
and the current state of the effervescence of its democracy. They state
that America has always had "a unique role and mission in the world:
as a model of ordered liberty and self-government and as an exemplar
of freedom and a vindicator of it."

There is no doubt that this is the country's long-standing self-image,
and the American genius for the spectacle, for public relations and
advertising, which is as old as the republic, gathered much credence for
this version of events, through the polemical talents of Jefferson, Paine,
Patrick Henry, and others. In fact, though King George III and his
prime minister, Lord North, handled it incompetently, they were really
only trying to get the Americans to pay their fair share of the costs of
throwing the French out of Canada and India in the Seven Years War.

Lowry and Ponnuru are correct that America was already the
wealthiest place in the world per capita, and it had 40 per cent of the
population of Britain and was the chief beneficiary of the eviction
of France from Canada. The colonists should certainly have paid

something for the British efforts on their behalf, and "no taxation without representation" and the Boston Tea Party and so forth were essentially a masterly spin job on a rather grubby contest about taxes.

In its early years, the United States had no more civil liberties than Britain, Switzerland, the Netherlands, and parts of Scandinavia. About 15 per cent of its population were slaves and, in the Electoral College, the slaveholding states were accorded bonus electoral votes representing 60 per cent of the slaves, so the voters in free states were comparatively disadvantaged. (If America had stayed in the British Empire for five years beyond the death of Jefferson and John Adams, the British would have abolished slavery for them and the country would have been spared the 750,000 dead of the Civil War.)

The authors write: "We are a nation of Franklins." I don't think so. Franklin was the principal architect of one of the greatest triumphs of statesmanship in modern history: America's enlistment of Britain to evict France from Canada and of France to eject Britain from America, without which the colonists would not have won the Revolutionary War. America's precocious manipulation of the world's two greatest powers was brilliant, but not exactly heroic.

Nor was the United States much interested in exporting democracy. One of its greatest secretaries of state, John Quincy Adams, spoke of being a brilliant light and example but of avoiding attempts to influence other countries except by example. After the country was established, there was almost no focus on foreign affairs generally until John Hay, Theodore Roosevelt, and Elihu Root, and then Woodrow Wilson (whom I do not accept to have been a non-believer in the goals of the Revolution, as the authors suggest). Then there was another lapse until the late 1930s, when the objective emerged of getting rid of the Nazis and Japanese imperialists, and Stalin was eventually sustained in doing most of the heavy work with the Germans. As late as 1944, the only democracies in the world were the United States, the British Isles and dominions, Switzerland, and the unoccupied parts of Scandinavia, though the French, Danes, Norwegians, and Benelux countries had legitimate hopes of democratic restorations.

The brilliant achievement of Roosevelt and Churchill in salvaging – from the disasters of 1939–1941 – France, Germany, Italy, and Japan for the West, and of Roosevelt's lieutenants (especially Truman, Marshall, MacArthur, and Eisenhower, with outstanding indigenous statesmen such as de Gaulle, Adenauer, and De Gasperi) in reconstituting those countries and their neighbours as democratic allies, took democracy decisively forward. So did the success of a number of American pro-tégé countries that were or became democracies, such as Israel, South Korea, Taiwan, Chile, and Spain.

The propagation of democracy emerged as a goal only in the Cold War, and exceptions were made for all manner of dictators, from Franco to the Shah, Sadat, and Chiang Kai-shek. And the American-led victory in the Cold War brought the long-suffering Poles and Czechs, the Slovenians, Baltic countries, and others into the demo-cratic column and crowned democracy with the laurel of a mighty and relatively bloodless geopolitical victory.

The wages of this victory have included the stale-dating of the authors' claim that America "is freer, more individualistic, more demo-cratic, and more open and dynamic than any other nation on earth." It is more dynamic because of its size, the torpor of Europe and Japan, and the shambles of Russia. But Americans do not do themselves a favour by not recognizing the terrible erosion of their country's education, justice, and political systems, the shortcomings of U.S. health care, the collapse of its financial industry, the flight of most of its manufacturing, and the steep and generally unlamented decline of its prestige. Unionized teachers have destroyed much of the state school system. (The antics of rampaging and often lawless prosecutors were described but are omit-ted here as they are the subject of other pieces in this book.)

Most of Congress is an infestation of paid-for legislators from rot-ten boroughs, representing the interests that finance their elections and exchanging earmarks with their colleagues like casbah hucksters. Many other countries are better functioning democracies with better legal and education systems. American doctors are very good, but annual medical care costs $3,000 per capita more than in other countries where stan-dards of care are comparable and care is more widely accessible.

The fact that Western Europe is dyspeptic and is paying Danegeld in back-breaking amounts to industrial workers and small farmers does not mean that the United States has not already sloughed much of its exceptionalism. Of course the authors are right that the Howard Zinn–Noam Chomsky view of U.S. history is an almost complete fraud, but it was made plausible only by the Washington's-cherry-tree school of myth-making.

The United States is still much the world's greatest power, and its military is very efficient. The people are hard-working and productive; not demotivated and pretentiously world-weary like Europeans, nor encumbered by hundreds of millions of primitive peasants like the Chinese. But half the horses of American exceptionalism have already fled. Where I agree emphatically with Richard Lowry and Ramesh Ponnuru is that President Obama is aggravating the problem. It is not nearly too late and can certainly wait for another president. But the problem will not be improved by endless repetition of the time-worn mantra about American virtue and superiority.

*I wrote this column in the first week after I self-surrendered to a U.S. federal prison. I had my own views of American exceptionalism.*

# THE DRUG WAR FAILURE

*National Review Online*, October 28, 2010

It is indicative of the failure of the current election to deal with real issues, apart from unease about deficits and curiosity about the endless military effort in the Near East, that, once again, almost nothing is asked or uttered about the proverbial War on Drugs, even as the near civil war it has caused in Mexico is amply publicized. Almost everyone agrees that hard drugs are a criminal problem, even if there is disagreement about how to fight them and dissatisfaction with the progress to date in doing so. But marijuana, cannabis, is an astonishing story of the hideously expensive and protracted failure of official policy.

There was an increase of 600 per cent in the federal drug-control budget, from $1.5 billion to $18 billion, between 1981 and 2002, and it is almost certainly now over $25 billion, and yet cannabis as an industry is an almost perfect illustration of the unstoppable force of supply-side economics. Between 1990 and 2007, there was a 420 per cent increase in cannabis seizures by drug-control authorities, to about 140,000 tons; a 150 per cent increase in annual cannabis-related arrests, to about 900,000 people; a 145 per cent increase in average potency of seized cannabis (delta-9-tetrahydrocannabinol content); and a 58 per cent decline, inflation-adjusted, in the retail price of cannabis throughout the United States.

The laws governing cannabis growth, sale, and use, though under review in California, where it is the state's largest cash crop, have not been proposed for serious amendment, although 42 per cent of Americans acknowledge that they have used cannabis at one time or another. Despite the Drug War's official costs of over $2.5 trillion over about forty years, comprehensive research by the authoritative International Centre for Science in Drug Policy (ICSDP), a Canadian organization but with wide international expertise and collaboration, reveals that cannabis is almost universally accessible to twelfth-graders in all parts of the United States, and that cannabis use by American twelfth-graders has increased from 27 per cent to 32 per cent between 1990 and 2008; and, furthermore, that among all Americans between the ages of nineteen and twenty-eight, use increased in the same period from 26 per cent to 29 per cent. The argument has been made that growth of cannabis use would have been greater without the Drug War assault on it. But it is hard to credit that official discouragement is very closely related to drug use at all, since 900,000 annual arrests, about half leading to custodial sentences, and with very heavy sentences of up to forty years for large-scale production and sale, have failed to discourage cannabis use and traffic.

Extensive U.S. federal government research indicates that the $1.4 billion National Youth Anti-Drug Media Campaign has been completely ineffective and may even have incited increased drug use by needlessly publicizing it. Given the abundant evidence of the ineffectuality of efforts to restrict and reduce cannabis use, it is astonishing that there has been so little public discussion in the United States of alternative policy courses. The Netherlands, which has effectively legalized cannabis use, has roughly half the incidence of per capita use as the United States. And the United States has approximately four times the per capita level of cocaine use of a broad selection of countries, including France, Germany, Italy, Ukraine, Spain, Israel, Lebanon, South Africa, China, Japan, Mexico, and Colombia. Differing regimes of cannabis decriminalization have been instituted by Mexico, Peru, Brazil, Paraguay, Argentina, and Portugal, of which the latter country, even nine years after decriminalization, has among the lowest cannabis-use levels in the European Union. There is a great range of policy options available, and observable in other countries, including restricting places of use, registering and rationing, increasing emphasis on treatment methods, and separating medical (use) from criminal (distribution outside official channels) aspects.

The argument that marijuana is "the gateway drug" that leads to more dangerous drugs and must therefore be evaluated for its consequences as well as its direct effects may have some validity. But the ICSDP judges that from 76 to 83 per cent of the world's 155 million to 250 million annual drug users use cannabis, which may make it a gateway but also makes it by far the greatest enforcement problem, even though two-thirds to four-fifths of cannabis users do not use it as a gateway into hard drugs. A U.K. medical and scientific panel, using a nine-category measurement of social and physical harm, rates cannabis less damaging and dangerous to society than alcohol or tobacco. Those who start on cannabis early and continue intensive use over long periods can suffer a range of psychological problems and motor impairment, become vulnerable to respiratory ailments, and become accident-prone, especially if driving motor vehicles or other sophisticated machinery. But this does not make up as great a risk of societal damage, or as high a challenge to individual health, as legal but controlled substances.

There are also profound social and foreign policy questions involved. It is fundamentally inconceivable that if the United States were absolutely determined to reduce drug use substantially, it could not do a much more thorough job of suppressing use within, and of preventing the entry of foreign-originated drugs into, the United States. The greatest military power in the world, with, by most measurements, greater military strength than all other countries in the world combined, could seal its own borders to drugs (as to illegal immigration) without disturbing legitimate commerce and tourism. And the public-policy decision has been informally concerted to leave middle-class, prosperous American secondary-school and university youth alone with at least their soft drugs, while trolling relentlessly through poor African-American areas, rounding up dealers and users, and imprisoning them en masse.

For blacks, the chances of being arrested and charged and convicted for cannabis offences are 300 per cent greater than for whites. Sending nearly half a million cannabis offenders to prison each year inflicts a $40,000 annual charge per prisoner, not counting the processing costs of the mass-convict-production U.S. law enforcement system. Domestic consumption of cannabis is an approximately $140-billion industry in the United States, which, despite large domestic production, requires large imports, especially from Mexico, Canada, and Colombia. In Mexico, 20,000 metric tons of cannabis are shipped annually to the United States, and the United States is in the position of telling foreign nations to cease production, while it will not impose the same solution on itself nor even make an all-out effort to discourage imports. The result is almost a civil war in Mexico, where 28,000 people have died in drug-related violence in the last four years, five times the number of Americans who have died in Iraq and Afghanistan in the last nine years. The beneficiaries of official American policy are the drug cartels, who make billions on it annually and maintain private paramilitary forces, including armoured vehicles, submersible drug-transport ships, and a range of aircraft.

There is room for legitimate argument about what course the United States should follow in drug-control policy, but there is no possible dispute that the present course has been such an unmitigated failure that it has aggravated the societal problem, strained relations with friendly foreign countries and destabilized some, and, as Milton Friedman said in 1991, constituted a protectionist bonanza for the most virulent and sociopathic elements of organized crime. In comparison, Prohibition, which handed the liquor business to Al Capone and his analogues, was a howling success, and it was repealed after fourteen years. Surely we can do better than this. But as with most other urgent issues, we are completing a pyrotechnic midterm election campaign with scarcely a peep being raised on a subject that affects almost half the population of the United States.

# THE DECLINE OF LIBERALISM

*The American Spectator,* February 21, 2011

American liberalism, synonymous today with big government, the exact opposite of the liberalism of Edmund Burke and other British champions of individual liberty, arose essentially from the use of the state to alleviate the most severe economic inequalities in society. In Great Britain this began in the competition between the Liberal and Conservative leaders, William Ewart Gladstone and Benjamin Disraeli, between 1865 and 1880, and among major European powers with the quest for an unthreatening working class with the founder and first chancellor of the German Empire, Otto von Bismarck. Britain had a great battle over pensions under the chancellor of the exchequer just before the First World War, David Lloyd George.

The assassination in 1914 of the distinguished French socialist leader Jean Jaurès, for advising against a headlong plunge into general war, was a grim harbinger of what was to come: ineffectual socialist pacifism that facilitated the advance of totalitarian regimes of hitherto undreamed of evil. Between the wars, in the aftermath of the hecatomb of the First World War and through the Great Depression, there was a general drift to higher taxes, a more extensive social safety net, and the rise in Britain and France of democratic socialist parties to principal opposition status and a few turns at government (Ramsay MacDonald and Léon Blum). In Germany, where the picture was much complicated by the bitterness of defeat in war and rampant inflation in its aftermath, the democratic socialists were outflanked and outmatched by the Communists, the National Socialists, and the principal upholders of Germany's fragile democratic heritage, the mainly Catholic Christian democratic parties that were revolted by the authoritarian paganism of the Nazis and the totalitarian and atheist materialism of the communists. The triumph of the Nazis and the dithering and waffling of France and Britain between conservative appeasers and pacifistic socialists, when crowned by the most cynical alliance in world history between Hitler and Stalin, infamously catapulted Europe into the Second World War.

From 1865, while the more advanced European countries were slowly conceding a larger share of public-policy concern and fiscal largesse to improving working conditions, tighter restrictions on commercial fraud and exploitation of consumers, wider franchises and education, and some concessions to organized labour, and financing these reforms with increased taxation on higher incomes, the United States was in the full flower of economic growth, fuelled by a colossal sixty-year wave of immigration and economic growth rates that generally exceeded 5 per cent annually for most of that time. In such a climate, nearly twenty-eight million immigrants arrived in America between the Civil and First World Wars, helping almost to triple the country's population from thirty-three million to ninety-eight million. In this heady atmosphere, while there was labour unrest, individualism and pure capitalism reigned, and American exceptionalism had little time for what was generally considered proletarian, foreign-originated snivelling on behalf of the self-pitying indolent. Theodore Roosevelt and Woodrow Wilson made a few gestures to restrain monopoly, assure a stable money supply, and discourage fraud in vital industries such as food processing and packaging. Several of these attitudes showed twitches of meliorism in respect of the working class, but it didn't go much further. Immigration was rolled back in the 1920s. Federal taxation of incomes was only made constitutional in 1913.

What is called liberalism in America today had scarcely seen the light of day in the United States until Franklin D. Roosevelt was inaugurated president on March 4, 1933, to face an unemployment rate generally reckoned at somewhere between 25 and 33 per cent, with the banking and stock and commodity exchange systems collapsed and shut down, no direct federal relief for the unemployed, farm prices beneath subsistence levels for 75 per cent of farmers, nearly half of residential accommodation in the country threatened by mortgage foreclosure, and no guaranty of any savings deposits. FDR led the country out of the Depression, saved 95 per cent of the existing institutions and social framework with emergency relief and by bolting a safety net onto them, and channelled economic envy and anger against non-existent groups (economic royalists, war profiteers, monopolists, munitions makers, malefactors of great wealth, etc.) and ultimately against the nation's real enemies: the Nazis and Japanese imperialists. If he had once named any plutocratic wrongdoers, mobs would have burned down their houses, but he preserved the moral integrality of the country.

His New Deal unfolded in five phases [as described in greater detail in "Roosevelt and the Revisionists" from March 5, 2010]. The first New Deal (1933–1934) consisted of gigantic workfare projects to absorb the unemployed in conservation projects and what would today be called infrastructure construction; a comprehensive banking reorganization with guaranties of deposits; agreed rollbacks of agricultural production, voted by sector, to assure viable pricing; encouragement of cartels and collective bargaining to raise wages and prices; devaluation of the dollar and a departure from the gold standard apart from international transactions; and legislated improvements in working conditions. The Second New Deal (1934–1938) included social security, the Securities and Exchange Commission, some remodelling of the pyramidal corporate structure of the hydroelectric industry, and higher taxes as a sop to the demagogic political movements chipping at the two-party system. In the latter half of this phase, the workfare and conservation programs were rolled back, and the federal deficit was reduced. Depressive conditions began to reappear and Roosevelt reapplied workfare pump-priming on a massive scale in 1938–1939 (Third New Deal) and shifted to the greatest peacetime arms build-up in history, including America's first peacetime conscription, the Fourth New Deal phase, which carried into the war, 1939–1945. Counting the workfare program participants as employed, (which is as logical as including European military draftees and defence workers as employed), unemployment was severely reduced by 1935; counting them as unemployed, the unemployment numbers came down to the low teens by 1936, descended below 10 per cent in 1940, and unemployment was completely eliminated before the Japanese attack plunged America into war in December 1941. The final phase of the New Deal came posthumously to Roosevelt, 1945–1949, but was his GI Bill of Rights, which gave university tuition and a stake to start a business or buy a farm to thirteen million returning American servicemen (almost 10 per cent of the entire population), and effectively turned the working class into a middle class, having saved them from joblessness, trained and led them to victory in war, and staked them to new careers. The Roosevelt program kept extremists from making any headway in American elections. The Socialist Party vote declined by 85 per cent from 1932 to 1936, and when asked if Roosevelt wasn't carrying out the Socialist program, perennial Socialist Party presidential candidate Norman Thomas replied, "Yes, carrying it out in a coffin."

There has been a good deal of revisionist comment recently that Roosevelt's policies did not end the Depression, but as U.S. GDP doubled in his twelve years in office and unemployment declined from roughly 30 per cent to 0.5 per cent, that case is difficult to sustain (and is in fact nonsense). From this point on, the tussle between American liberals and conservatives has been over what emphasis to give unrestricted economic activity, which promises relatively high growth but with sharp cyclicality of booms and busts; and alleviation of substandard social conditions through anti-poverty and health-care programs. Most of Western Europe, as it rebuilt from the devastation of war, fearful for notorious historic reasons of the anger of the urban working class and of small farmers, has been lumbered by a system of social-benefit and subsidized living that paid Danegeld to traditional disturbers of social peace at the price of minimal economic growth, though they are relatively high income societies.

In the United States, conservative and liberal issues became tangled in foreign policy as well, as liberals tended to believe that stability in the world could be had with minimal recourse to force and reliance on international organizations, while retaining a military adequate to deter direct national attack on the United States and defend its principal allies, and conservatives have been generally more proactive in seeking an improved strategic balance, by a combination of diplomatic innovation and assured peace through enhanced military strength.

In foreign affairs, President Truman devised the great instruments of anti-communist containment, NATO, the Marshall Plan, etc., and defied Stalin with the Berlin Airlift and resisted the communist take-over of South Korea. President Eisenhower, the first Republican in twenty years, maintained virtually everything FDR and Truman had done, but did not expand the state socially (though he did build the Interstate Highway System and the St. Lawrence Seaway), and in foreign affairs he ended the Korean War along the compromise lines sought by Truman, contrary to the wishes of more conservative Republican hawks, including Douglas MacArthur, Richard Nixon, and John Foster Dulles. Eisenhower refused to touch Vietnam as the French were pushed out of it, and cut the defence budget while relying on "more bang for the buck": massive retaliation to deter aggression. He threatened a nuclear response to everything, even over the trivial Formosa Strait islands of Quemoy and Matsu. It was brinkmanship, but it worked. Eisenhower also began the de-escalation of the Cold War, with the first summit meeting in ten years, at Geneva in 1955, where he proposed his Open Skies program for reciprocal aerial military reconnaissance.

Roosevelt's social programs were left essentially unaltered for twenty years after he died, until President Lyndon Johnson cut taxes while expanding the social ambitions of the federal government with his Great Society's War on Poverty and massive job retraining efforts, coupled to great and long-delayed advances in civil rights. Kennedy and Johnson favoured civil rights more actively than had their predecessors, and backed conservatives into pious humbug about the Constitution not allowing for federal imposition of voting rights and official social equality for African Americans. Johnson overcame that opposition and it was one of liberalism's finest hours. But the long Roosevelt–Truman–Eisenhower consensus frayed badly when Johnson, who had been a congressman during the New Deal years, determined to take it a long step further and proposed a policy extravaganza that promised to buy the end of poverty through social investment. As all the world knows, it was a disaster, which destroyed the African-American family and severely aggravated the welfare and entitlements crises.

And in foreign and security policy, Kennedy abandoned massive retaliation, promised limited war by limited means for limited objectives, in unlimited locations, and the communists took him up on it. Having claimed a non-existent missile gap, he then squandered the U.S. missile advantage in favour of Mutual Assured Destruction; i.e., no advantage. Worse, he drank his own bathwater over Cuba. Before that crisis (1962), there were NATO missiles in Italy and Turkey, no Russian missiles in Cuba, and no assurance against U.S. invasion of Cuba. After the crisis, there were no NATO missiles in Italy or Turkey, nor Russian missiles in Cuba, and a guaranty of no U.S. invasion of Cuba. U.S. intelligence had not realized that there were already 40,000 Soviet troops in Cuba in the autumn of 1962, and that the nuclear warheads were already there and could be attached in twenty-four hours. The famous and photogenic sea blockade was closing the gate after the Trojan horse had entered. It was a triumph for Kennedy, in that he didn't commit to an invasion that would have been a very rough business in a nuclear-capable theatre and that would presumably have precipitated countermeasures in Berlin. (Khrushchev could not have sat inert while the United States overpowered two Soviet divisions in Cuba.) But it was no strategic victory, and discerning judges, especially de Gaulle and Mao Tse-tung and Richard Nixon (who lost the race for governor of California as a result of the perceived Kennedy tour de force in Cuba), saw that. However, the liberal leadership thought they had a new and foolproof technique of crisis management, the critical path of graduated escalation, and that led us straight into Vietnam, with no notion of how to fight such a war; while LBJ's application of overreach to domestic affairs drove America into the mire of the Great Society.

Richard Nixon ended Mutual Assured Destruction by starting anti-missile deployment, pursuing what he called "nuclear sufficiency," which in practice was a restoration of U.S. nuclear superiority, based on technological advantages, especially multiple independently targeted warheads on the same missiles (MIRVs), and using this strength to "build down" through the SALT process, thus impressing hawks with his enhancement of American military strength and doves with the greatest arms limitations agreement in history, in 1972.

Vietnam by 1966 was killing two hundred to four hundred American draftees every week with no prospect of victory. The greatest military blunder in U.S. history was the failure to cut the Ho Chi Minh Trail, when public opinion would have supported it. President Johnson effectively gave up in Vietnam in October 1966, when he offered a joint withdrawal of all non-South Vietnamese forces from the South. Ho Chi Minh declined this, because he wished to defeat the United States directly, signalling a decisive victory in the Cold War of the communists over the West. He could have won his declared objectives by accepting the joint withdrawal and then returning six months later. He knew the United States would not commit ground forces again to the war. That he did not accept Johnson's offer demonstrates the fervour of his ambition to defeat the United States itself. Richard Nixon handed the Vietnam War over to the South Vietnamese, bought them time to ramp up their war effort by wiping out the North Vietnamese sanctuaries in Cambodia as he drew down U.S forces, and he resumed heavy bombing of North Vietnam when that country overtly invaded the South in 1972. Nixon opened relations with China, which helped propel a reduction in tensions with the U.S.S.R., and he detached both the Chinese and the Russians from support of Hanoi's effort to defeat the United States, as opposed to just unifying Vietnam. Nixon enabled the South to hold its own on the ground with heavy U.S. air support. He ended the Vietnam War with a non-communist government in place in Saigon and believed it could have been preserved if the United States had retained its readiness to respond with heavy air reprisals to a renewed North Vietnamese invasion of the South. For that reason, he sent the peace accord to the Senate for ratification, although he was not obliged to do so, to gain Senate support for the enforcement of the treaty if necessary.

The great watershed of modern American politics was the tawdry Watergate affair. Historians will long debate whether Nixon actually committed crimes or whether, as he claimed, he committed "mistakes unworthy of a president" but not crimes. Certainly, the impeachment counts presented to the House Judiciary Committee were outrages of partisan hysteria, and liberals in Congress and the national media grossly exaggerated the significance of what was uncovered. Assisted by Nixon's inexplicable mismanagement of the affair, they hounded

Nixon from office, diminished the presidency as an institution, and then, for good measure, cut off all aid to South Vietnam, ensuring that that country would fall to the communists, that the United States would be completely humiliated, and, although they would not precisely have foreseen this, that millions would die in the Killing Fields of Cambodia and drown when forced to flee Vietnam as boat people. And for Watergate and the debacle in Vietnam, the liberal political and media establishment took a decades-long bow and claimed the status of redeemers of American democracy and integrity in government.

Nixon had saved America from the liberal debacle in Vietnam and the self-imposed cul-de-sac in the arms race, and Nixon ended school segregation without falling into the catastrophe of compulsory school busing between districts as was being ordered by the courts. He proposed, but did not get to enact, welfare reform, founded the Environmental Protection Agency, which he foresaw would become another faddish leftist hobby horse if conservatives were not sensible, abolished the draft, and reduced the crime rate. He had taken a great deal of the liberals' clothes, while holding the conservative majority in place, and his re-election by the greatest plurality in American history in 1972 (eighteen million votes and forty-nine states) showed the extent to which liberalism's failures under Kennedy and Johnson had been recognized and corrected.

Though many liberals were doubtless sincere in believing that Nixon was a menace to constitutional government, and he did have some completely unacceptable notions of executive privilege in national security matters (such as the claimed right to ransack the Brookings Institution and break into the office of a dissident Vietnam consultant's psychotherapist), Nixon was a patriotic American, a very capable president, and he did much more to stabilize constitutional government than to undermine it. The effect of the Watergate and Vietnam disasters was to criminalize policy differences and help turn the United States into a prosecutocracy terrorized by overzealous U.S. attorneys; propel the media to depths of investigative cynicism that made the lives of anyone trying to accomplish anything newsworthy unprecedentedly difficult; temporarily reduce the executive branch to less than its constitutionally allotted position of equality with the legislature and judiciary; cause scores of millions of Americans to be disillusioned with government and to abandon the national media for competing and new technology rivals as they became available; and lead to a period of aggressive Soviet expansion in southern Africa, Central America, and Afghanistan.

But Watergate and Vietnam hastened the decline of American liberalism. Jimmy Carter squeaked into office in the aftermath of Vietnam and Watergate, and failed in his quest for a more liberal state and a safer world through accommodation of the U.S.S.R. Ronald Reagan led the definitive takeover of the Republican Party by conservatives; he was as much to the right of Nixon as Nixon had been to the right of Eisenhower. He cut taxes and promised a defensive anti-missile system that effectively cracked the Soviet Union completely. Unable to envision a further increase in the percentage of GDP devoted to defence, scarcely able to maintain its hold over Eastern Europe and its own restive ethnic minorities, the Soviet Union quietly imploded and international communism collapsed, as China, partly under the influence unleashed by Nixon's opening to it, became a hotbed of state capitalism. Reagan led the country to huge productivity increases, the creation of eighteen million net new jobs, and the adaptation of the American economy to new techniques and technologies. Conservatism was triumphant.

Americans calling themselves conservative as opposed to liberal were now at a ratio of about three to two. After the chaotic and violent convention of 1968, the Democratic Party took the nomination process away from the party bosses who had chosen and supported Roosevelt, Truman, Kennedy, and Johnson, as well as the less successful but respected Adlai Stevenson and Hubert Humphrey, and the elevation of a very improbable sequence of candidates resulted, from George McGovern in 1972 to Michael Dukakis. After Reagan's vice-president, George H.W. Bush, succeeded him and mismanaged the economy, broke his pledge of "no new taxes," and ran a very inept re-election campaign after allowing an eccentric Texan billionaire to seize a chunk of Republican support, the Democrats won with a young Ivy League educated southern governor, who ran as a "new Democrat," which in policy terms meant essentially a Republican. Bill Clinton tried a turn to the left, especially on health care, was beaten badly in the midterm elections in 1994, and then produced budget surpluses, engaged more policemen, and proved too agile for the Republicans to catch. The country was, however, and in the new Watergate tradition, reduced to a demeaning impeachment hearing based largely on the president's rather undiscriminating extramarital sex life. In the midst of it, the Republican leaders in Congress finally rolled back much of the shambles of the Great Society and rammed through comprehensive welfare reform.

The 2000 election was an uncertain draw between Clinton's vice-president and Bush's son. The eight Bush years that followed were clouded by the preoccupation with terrorism after the suicide attacks on New York and Washington on September 11, 2001. Bush mismanaged the budgetary deficit, and the Clinton-originated practices of immense current-account deficits and the encouragement of the issuance of trillions of dollars of worthless real-estate-backed debt, supposedly to facilitate home ownership, came home to roost in severe recession while the country's entire conventional armed forces capability was mired for five years in Iraq and Afghanistan. President Barack Obama is the result, after he deftly took the Clintons' party out from underneath them and liberated white America from its guilt complex after 350 years of mistreatment of the blacks (and as a bonus liberated them also from having to listen to charlatans like Jesse Jackson and Al Sharpton and Charlie Rangel as African-American leaders). Mr. Obama broke the glass ceiling barring non-whites from the highest office but tried to use the economic crisis to justify a sharp turn to the left, expansion of the state in health care and the environment, tax increases, and outright bribes ("refundable tax credits") to the indigent. The resulting political and economic debacle gave a no-name, leaderless Republican Party a huge sweep as a reward for unimaginative denigration of the administration in November's elections, and if Obama is to have a chance of re-election, it will be by turning the balance of this term into, as has already begun, a tutorial from Bill Clinton on how to masquerade as a Republican. All polls now indicate that there are twice as many self-designated conservatives as liberals, but also almost twice as many independents as liberals.

Americans are worried about debt, tax increases, distrustful of government regulation, concerned at extreme income disparity and the loss of huge chunks of business, including energy supplies, to foreigners, and they associate liberalism with extravagance, the use of the welfare system to buy the votes of the underperforming (whether with a legitimate excuse or not), the belittling of America in the world, and a general erosion of cherished values. And the last liberal leader the people really liked was John F. Kennedy, and in that they are largely buying a public-relations confidence trick, amplified by the horrible tragedy of his premature death. If the Republicans have a plausible leader, and the Bushes were no world-beaters, their program will win for them. Leaders of unusual stature or agility, such as Eisenhower, Nixon at his best, and Reagan, win heavy majorities.

Liberalism saved America and led it to its greatest days under Roosevelt and Truman. And it essentially continued under Eisenhower, a non-partisan war hero who pretended to be above politics. Under Kennedy and Johnson and their inept Democratic successors, liberalism ceased to be perceived as helping the deserving and instead became taking money from those who had earned it and giving it to those who hadn't in exchange for their votes. Nixon saved the country from the Kennedy–Johnson failure to redefine liberalism successfully, but freakishly squandered the political credit for doing so. Reagan won the battle for the conservatives against the liberals, and the Democrats have only won since when they ran an ostensibly moderate candidate against a very weak Republican. (Bob Dole and John McCain, whatever their merits as senators, were hopeless blunderbusses as presidential nominees.)

Liberalism will revive, as conservatism did, when it redefines itself as something that is new, looks likely to succeed, favours economic growth, and is no longer tainted by envy, hypocrisy, and the mere bribery of voting blocs. This will take a leader of the stature of a Roosevelt or Reagan. No such person is now visible, in either party, but neither were those two seen in that light before they were elected and became candidates for Mount Rushmore.

# ALEXANDER HAMILTON
# AND 9/11

*National Review Online*, September 22, 2011

---

aving just spent four pleasant months in New York City, it was my
misfortune to have to leave to return to prison after fourteen months
on parole following vacation of my convictions just before the opening
of two historic sites that demonstrate the long-standing, dramatic importance of that city.

The relocation and renovation of Alexander Hamilton's house, the
Grange, reminds us that New York has been an influential city in the
world since before Napoleon was emperor of the French. The house
was built in 1802, two years before Hamilton died in the still hotly
debated duel with Vice-President Aaron Burr. It is, as one reviewer said,
not Mount Vernon or Monticello – but then, Hamilton was the illegitimate son of a wandering Scot from the Caribbean island of Nevis, not
a member of one of the First Families of Virginia, rich in land, slaves,
and connections. But, from pictures, one can tell that it is a somehow
surprisingly well-proportioned, airy, cheerfully coloured and situated,
and gracious home, now very close to its original location on Hamilton
Heights in northern Manhattan, on the greensward that is left of its
original thirty-two acres overlooking the Hudson and Harlem Rivers.

Hamilton was rivalled in his time as the most important New York
political figure by Burr and nine-term governor George Clinton. Burr

tried to pretend that the electoral votes cast for him in the 1800 election were for president and not vice-president, as they were not differentiated at that time, and he drew with the real presidential candidate, Thomas Jefferson, and both came ahead of the incumbent president, John Adams. Hamilton and Adams, despite their dislike of Jefferson, judged him morally more suited to the office, and eventually put him across in the House of Representatives. Jefferson ditched Burr and amended the Constitution to avoid this anomaly, and selected Clinton for vice-president in 1804. In 1808, Clinton had the distinction of running simultaneously for president and vice-president, and therefore against himself (as the same person cannot hold both offices), and was defeated by Madison, whom he then served as vice-president. The other great New York public figure of the time was John Jay, a prominent federalist in constitutional discussions, the first chief justice, Washington's emissary to complete peace terms with Britain, and governor of New York, but never a man with a great deal of political traction.

Though Burr and Clinton were as politically prominent as Hamilton, they were not as esteemed and were far from being founding fathers of the country. As Washington's chief of staff in the Continental Army, principal spokesman for New York at the Constitutional Convention, principal author (next to Madison) of the Constitution, and first secretary of the treasury – the man who gave the United States sound money, a high national credit rating, and sophisticated fiscal institutions, and foresaw and facilitated the mighty industrial development of the nation – Hamilton ranks with Washington, Franklin, and Jefferson as one of the principal founders of the United States. It is certainly right that his home should be restored, and a bonus that it is so easily accessible to so many in the middle of the nation's largest city. The renovation and relocation (by 250 feet) of Hamilton's house required five years and $14.5 million.

Hamilton was a turbulent man and an unfaithful husband, with undemocratic and even slightly Bonapartist tendencies (who wished to lead armies of liberation, i.e., conquest, across Latin America), and it is enlightening to see that at home he was in a tasteful, semi-rural place of calm and refinement, where he played a fine piano (still there) with his daughter. He worked better as a chief collaborator of Washington's than autonomously, and was prone to tactical lurches and improbable schemes, and his impetuosity undercut Adams and helped to destroy their Federalist party. He inadvertently was instrumental in delivering the country to Jefferson, whom he regarded, with some reason, as a prototype limousine liberal selling a rustic and patrician vision of America that was self-serving primitivist moonshine. Like Adams and Franklin, he was effectively an abolitionist.

Hamilton was a historic giant, who, though only forty-nine when he died, changed the world. He was regarded by France's chief foreign policy architect for nearly forty years through a kaleidoscope of constitutional regimes, the timeless and cunning Talleyrand, as (with Napoleon and Charles James Fox) one of three men of genius he had known. (Talleyrand never met Franklin and was not much impressed by Jefferson; when he was in America fleeing the Terror of the Committee of Public Safety, Washington refused to receive him because he was openly cohabiting with a black woman.)

At the other end of Manhattan, at the site of the World Trade Center Towers, the memorial to the victims of the September 11, 2001, terrorist attacks opened to the public the same week as the Grange. This is admittedly harder to assess while relying entirely on photographs, television, and others' descriptions. But I must dissent from the somewhat negative comments of several knowledgeable critics. Designer Michael Arad was given a difficult brief to work with, as it had been resolved that nothing could be built over the fallen towers, and his initial plan for a ramp down from the planned eight-acre plaza was judged impractical and too expensive.

Altering his initial design, Arad has produced two stark, square granite depressions at the bases of the old towers (and encompassing the site of the initial bombing in 1993), two hundred feet on each side and thirty feet deep, with the names of the three thousand victims etched on a bronze plate around the edges, and a steady waterfall all around the two depressions. The water flows into deep squares in the centres of them, their depth too profound to be discernible from the sides. The eight-acre park has light-shaded stone pavements and apparently haphazardly placed oak trees throughout, that do, in fact, form orderly avenues after followed for a few yards, and will grow to produce a canopy, as is popular in more southern climes, such as Provence.

I find the concept and execution inspiring. The contrast between the accessible and commodious and tranquil green and stone park, at one of the densest points in the city, and the huge and gaunt openings, under the soaring and reflecting façades of successor buildings to the destroyed towers, promises to be a memorable unity of the peaceful and contemplative with a forceful allegorization of the enormity of what assaulted the site on that awful day.

At least one critic has bemoaned that the use of water is not the purifying and soothing burble more often found in monuments, but is noisy and distracting. But this isn't a monument to a great statesman long dead, or to the sacrifices and victories of a war fought over a long period and far-flung areas. It commemorates the victims of a swift and horrible act of suicidal terror, premeditated and planned as an infamous gesture of nihilism, an unforgettably spectacular and repulsive massacre of innocents. For such an act, a division between the peace of the living and the dead, and the dramatic portrayal of irreplaceable loss to treachery and barbarism, is entirely appropriate. And the relatively constant and not-at-all-bucolic sound of always-appearing-and-disappearing water in vast, dark, square accesses to the bowels of the earth is a brilliant metaphor for what it commemorates.

The attack on the World Trade Towers was unlike anything else in American or modern world history, and what was required was appropriate measures of mourning, outrage, reflection, homage, and resilience, and from this distance it seems that Michael Arad and the overall project planner, Daniel Libeskind, have done brilliantly.

These two historic sites also express the metropolitan historic force of New York City. The soft-coloured, verandah-girt receptive retreat of a brilliant but tempestuous man who never recoiled, built much, and departed this gentle place for his violent and very unnecessary death is the civility and sacrifice of the great man. The 9/11 memorial is to the patience, strength, and dignity of the people, savagely and mindlessly assaulted in the noiseless performance of their daily work, and to those who provide them basic services: firemen, policemen, and emergency medical personnel. These are the power and grandeur of the historic statesman seen in private, and the immutable strength of the ordinary people: the historic building blocks of America, at the geographic poles of Manhattan.

And as is so often the case with historic American men and events, from Hamilton to Lincoln, to the Kennedys and Martin Luther King and even Harvey Milk, to 9/11/01, both are defined by unprovoked violence nobly borne. This overbearing recourse to violence and tragedy is what mainly turns the importantly effectual and consequential, the historic staple of Boston and Philadelphia, of Faneuil Hall and Independence Hall, to the dramatic. New York, too, has been generating history for over two hundred years, but producing great drama also, on a grand scale, and still does, and knows how to preserve the memory of it.

# JUSTICE DISTRACTED

*National Review Online*, October 14, 2011

The vast recognition of the astounding accomplishments of Apple's Steve Jobs seems not much to have focused on the fact that – according to the moral views that have prevailed in the United States for most of his adult life – he, as the unintended issue of a young, unmarried couple of limited means, was a prime candidate for abortion, which the Supreme Court has determined to be a matter of a woman's privacy and sole authority over her own body.

My purpose is not to reopen the vexed abortion debate, only the questionable reasoning behind the current state of the law, and the unrigorous philosophical selectivity of some leading jurists. The abortion issue depends on the point at which the unborn are deemed to have obtained the rights of a person, when their right to life supersedes their mothers' right to control all that occurs within their own bodies. Perfectly good arguments can be, and have endlessly been, made for every option, from conception to birth at the end of term. Majority opinion in most Western countries is that it's the point at which a baby is reasonably likely, with sophisticated medical attention, to survive: about five months.

The intensive activities of the pro-life faction, especially the Roman Catholic Church, have debunked the theory with which the pro-abortionists began, that it was exclusively a female-privacy issue of no more moral significance than disposing of a dishcloth. If Steve Jobs, who has been rightly claimed to have been one of the great commercial and marketing geniuses of world history, had been conceived ten years later, in 1965, or after, his parents would have been aggressively counselled to abort him. And that advice – and, if it were followed, the procedure itself – would probably have been government-assisted, even if only indirectly, by tax-favoured treatment of the counselling agency.

The issue of disposing of large numbers of conceived but unborn people involves practical as well as moral considerations. At the time Steve Jobs was born, in 1955, concern was already rising about the world population explosion, and the need to seek zero population growth. In this area, almost all advanced countries have been overachievers and have fallen into chronically low levels of demographic regeneration.

Instead of addressing abortion, as they should have done, on the basis of when the rights of the unborn rival the rights of the unenthused mother, Congress and state legislators waffled, abstained, and failed to do what legislators are needed, elected, and paid to do, and left it to the courts, a shameful abdication. It was a dereliction on all fours with Congress's refusal to deal with immigration as millions of unauthorized and unskilled people poured into the country, and scores of millions of low-paying jobs were outsourced out of it.

There has been no serious public discussion of trying to promote – by incentivization, not coercion (as first India and now China have unsuccessfully tried) – an optimal demographic policy, even as the population ages and the richest nation in history stares myopically at the impending bankruptcy of its public sector. America is being led into the slaughterhouse of insolvency by the Judas goat of unbalance-able social programs, as a shrinking proportion of earners creaks under the burden of an ever-larger number and proportion of medically expensive elderly and young recipients of benefits.

This leads to the even more delicate issue of the moral precepts that guide the judges and justices into whose inept laps these issues have been dumped by the moral and political cowardice of legislators of all ideological shadings, in both parties, at all levels, for decades.

President Eisenhower's patronage recognition of the nearly 25 per cent of his countrymen who were Roman Catholics was the nomination to the Supreme Court of Justice William Brennan (where

Roman Catholics, starting with the infamous Chief Justice Roger Taney, 1834–1863, had preceded him). Now we have three Jewish and six Roman Catholic members of the Supreme Court, though probably only about four of the Roman Catholics appear to be particularly attuned to the official positions of their church on the types of issues apt to come before the high court.

But some are, including Justice Antonin Scalia, who, as Maureen Dowd wrote in the *New York Times* on October 2, has attacked the complainant in a civil suit to stop the banning of co-ed dormitories at the Catholic University of America in Washington, D.C. As Ms. Dowd pointed out, Justice Scalia has not hesitated prior to this to volunteer publicly either his solidarity with his Church militant, or his dissent from it. But in the case of the Roman Catholic Church's long-held and oft-expressed (by four recent popes) hostility to the death penalty, Justice Scalia recently told Duquesne University in Pittsburgh that if he thought "that Catholic doctrine held the death penalty to be immoral, I would resign." Since he could not possibly be unaware of the views of the Holy See over the past fifty years (John Paul I was the only pope in that time who did not reign long enough to opine on the subject), nor of the authority of the pope to speak on such matters for the whole Church, it is not clear why he is not delivering his letter of resignation to the president instead of sticking his nose into the dormitory rules in one of the national capital's universities.

To move the inquiry that Ms. Dowd usefully started to entirely secular matters, there could be searching questions about why the Supreme Court has sat like a great inert toad for decades while the Bill of Rights has been raped by the prosecution service with the connivance of the legislators, a tri-branch travesty against the civil rights of the whole population, but I will spare readers another dilation on that subject. However, Justice Scalia's preoccupation with the dormitories of the Catholic University of America (a matter that is now, to the justice's chagrin, sub judice), is, in the circumstances and to say the least, bizarre.

Leaving that aside, the report card on the coequal branches is not uplifting: the legislators and the executive wimped out on abortion and immigration. The beehive of conscientious jurists on the Supreme Court applied a completely amoral test to get to a defensible conclusion on abortion when it was dumped by default on them to determine. And its most vocal current Roman Catholic member, swaddling himself in his faith, upholds the death penalty in contradiction to the popes, holds in pectore his views on abortion (which is not now before the high court, though not for absence of petitions), and thunders fire and brimstone about coeducational university dormitories, which is not, I think, a subject that the See of Peter has addressed.

The executive and legislative branches do nothing to encourage a higher birthrate, having ducked abortion, nor to promote the most assimilable immigration, having flunked in dealing with the more prevalent, illegal categories of immigration. Justice Scalia's responses to the moral positions of his church are between him and his arch-bishop, even when he trots them out publicly, but the failure of the whole inter-branch U.S. government to address any of these immense issues that ramify profoundly, morally, or practically, has created a potentially lethal threat to the country's fiscal and social stability.

Justice Scalia's conduct may or may not be, by the canons of his church, as Maureen Dowd suggested on October 2 in the *Times*, "cooperating with evil," but it is, in some respects, in a phrase of the Blessed Cardinal Newman's, "shovel-hatted humbug." America needs more people like Steve Jobs, from conception even unto elegiacs.

# DON'T LOOK
# TO CANADA AS A MODEL
# OF HUMAN RIGHTS

*Huffington Post Canada*, February 9, 2012

---

S upreme Court Justice Ruth Bader Ginsburg has come in for some
criticism for telling an Egyptian television network that as Egypt
devises a new constitution, it should not look to the Constitution of the
United States to provide whatever protection for human rights it is seeking. (The existing Egyptian constitution probably reads quite purposefully on the point; the problem would be in the execution. The same
will almost certainly be said of the incoming regime dominated by the
Muslim Brotherhood, and the same can be said of the United States
also, as the justice implicitly acknowledges.)

Justice Ginsburg counselled her Egyptian viewers to look at the South
African constitution's guarantee of basic human rights and an independent judiciary, and further commended the Canadian Charter of Rights
and Freedoms and the European Convention on Human Rights.

The justice's concern for the adequacy of protection of due process in the United States is well-founded, but her choice of jurisdictions that are more exemplary is open to some question. South Africa
is a country where even the sainted President Mandela described the

high frequency of break-ins and robberies in wealthy white districts as a form of wealth redistribution.

When management of the South African hydroelectric power authority was outsourced to a Japanese company because of the occurrence of unacceptable and unprecedented power shortages, the deal was sealed with a publicly disclosed, outright *ex gratia* gift by the hired manager of $1 billion to South Africa's governing African National Congress. These aren't strictly civil rights matters, but they are symptomatic of a chronically lawless condition, whatever rights the country's constitution may purport to enact and protect.

Canada's Charter of Rights and Freedoms was devised by the former prime minister Pierre Trudeau for fifteen years up to 1984, and his principal mandate was to prevent the secession of the mainly French province of Quebec, to distract voters from the issue of the division of powers between the federal and provincial governments, and to focus instead on the rights of man in flamboyant, Rousseauesque fashion.

As a recitation of civil liberties, it is quite comprehensive, but the federal Parliament and the legislatures of all the ten provinces can vacate the property and civil rights clauses of the Charter on a case-by-case basis as it applies to each jurisdiction. This is not a very iron-clad guarantee of the people's rights, and the escape clause has been invoked occasionally for dubious purposes. But the Canadian provinces have their own civil rights legislation, the common law is strong in these areas, and Canada does have one of the best civil rights records of any country in the world, but not particularly because of Trudeau's Charter (which did largely succeed in its tactical political objective of out-manoeuvring the Quebec separatists).

The European Convention is, again, a ringing affirmation of the rights in question, but it has practically no enforcement powers. Where it is applied within the European Union, most countries will act on rulings based on it, but the delinquent jurisdiction can re-legislate for another ten years or so as the process repeats itself.

The perversity of legislatures is a tenacious condition. With that said, such an assertion of rights over twenty-seven contiguous countries, where within living memory twenty-one of them were governed by communist, fascist, or Nazi dictatorships, whether indigenously generated or imposed by military occupation, is a great achievement. But its relevancy as guidance from a U.S. Supreme Court justice to the eighty million rights-starved people of Egypt is not entirely clear.

Where Justice Ginsburg deserves great commendation is in recognizing the erosion of the United States as the haven of human rights it has always proclaimed itself to be. It is one of the great ironies of modern times that the United States, in the Second World War and the Cold War, led the world to the triumph of democracy but is not now itself one of the world's better functioning democracies.

From the end of the Revolutionary War and the independence of the United States in 1783 to the landing of the Allied armies in Normandy in 1944 to liberate Western Europe, there had been a net diminution of democratic rule in the world, other than in the demographic growth of its original beneficiaries: the British Isles and advanced colonies, later the dominions (Canada, Australia, etc.), and the United States, Switzerland, and parts of Scandinavia. The Netherlands had enjoyed some democratic rights in 1783, as had the Danes, Norwegians (though part of Sweden), and as had, subsequently, France, Belgium, Greece, and the Czechs, but in 1944 these countries were awaiting deliverance from Nazi occupation.

Once the Cold War got underway, the U.S. grand strategists brilliantly defined it as mortal combat between godless, totalitarian communism and the "Free World," never mind that among the free were many dictators.

The Free World won and democracy prevailed in all of Europe west of the Ukraine, almost all of Latin America, much of the Far East, South Asia, Australasia; almost everywhere except China, Russia (and there are flickerings there), North Korea, Vietnam, Cuba, and much, but not most, of the Near East and Africa.

But in the United States, politics is more financially corrupt than ever; the political class has dodged dealing with immigration, abortion, wealth disparity, and now the deficit – almost anything seriously contentious. The media has dumbed down discussion to the subterranean level of CNN and MSNBC on the left and Fox News on the right. The national conversation is between Paul Begala, Sean Hannity, and their sound-alikes. Public education has been effectively hijacked and destroyed by the teachers' unions, academia has been seized by the American self-hating left, and the criminal justice system is a neo-fascist parody.

The United States has gone in thirty-five years from having a per capita number of incarcerated people at the average for advanced countries to six to twelve times the number in Australia, Canada, France, Germany, Japan, and the United Kingdom. A $2 trillion phony War on Drugs has been waged and lost, and over 97 per cent of prosecutions are won, over 95 per cent of those without trial, as the prosecutocracy enjoys a huge evidentiary and procedural advantage and extorts and suborns perjury under the plea-bargain system (under which everyone around a target is threatened with prosecution, unless their memories miraculously disgorge carefully rehearsed and long forgotten recollections of the wrongdoing of the benighted target).

Defendants are routinely deprived of the means to defend themselves by *ex parte* seizures or freezes of their assets often on the basis of false FBI affidavits alleging that their assets were ill-gotten gains. Criminal charges come down immediately, staying these spurious proceedings and often forcing the defendants into the hands of the public defenders, most of whom are just Judas goats for the prosecutors.

Grand juries are rubber stamps for the prosecutors; most judges are ex-prosecutors, and the whole country has been whipped into a cretinous frenzy by screams of "law and order" from all the media and the gimcrack majority of the political class from left to right. Almost everyone is convicted; almost all of those convicted are oversentenced by civilized international standards, and the living conditions of probably a million (out of 2.5 million in total) American prisoners are barbarous.

Justice Ginsburg is right to be disappointed by the deterioration of human liberties in America, and she dissented admirably on the Thompson case last year where an absolute immunity was granted prosecutors who had left the complainant on death row for fourteen years while deliberately suppressing DNA evidence that ultimately exonerated him.

The justice is correct, but she gives no hint of where the Supreme Court has been for the nearly twenty years that she has been a member of it, as the Fifth, Sixth, and Eighth Amendment guarantees of the grand jury as insurance against capricious prosecution, of due process, against seizure of property without due compensation, of an impartial jury, access to counsel, prompt justice, and reasonable bail have been put to the shredder.

The Supreme Court is complicit in the destruction of the people's rights, and Justice Ginsburg and the rest of them should be doing more about it than advising the Egyptians to look elsewhere for guidance on civil liberties, unexceptionable though that advice unfortunately is.

# THE WAR ON NIXON

*National Review Online*, June 14, 2012

---

B ob Woodward and Carl Bernstein (Woodstein for our purposes) now claim, in a *Washington Post* piece, that Nixon was "far worse than we thought," and accuse him of conducting five "wars": against the anti-war movement, on the media, against the Democrats, on justice, and on history. In evaluating such a volcanic farrago of pent-up charges, the facts must be arrayed in three tiers: the facts of Woodstein's activities and revelations; the facts of the Watergate case and related controversies; and the importance of Watergate in an appreciation of the Nixon record.

Woodstein were showered with the prizes and awards the media narcissistically pour on one another to deafening collective self-laudations, and became the pinup idols of two whole generations of aggressively investigative journalists. Other media outlets were hotly pursuing and uncovering disturbing stories of campaign skulduggery, but the *Washington Post*, led by Woodstein, under the inspiration of editor Ben Bradlee, confected the Brobdingnagian fraud that Nixon was trying to perpetrate a virtual *coup d'état* by imposing an "imperial presidency" on the prostrate democracy of America.

Woodstein showed no great enterprise; they stumbled upon a senior official of the FBI angry that he had been passed over as successor to the deceased J. Edgar Hoover. Mark Felt – Deep Throat, as he became known to history – provided almost all of the *Post's* investigative initiative in a squalid and envious attack on the nominated heir to Hoover,

L. Patrick Gray. The reporters, who were effectively note-takers, and their editor parlayed it into an impeachment controversy, assisted by the uncharacteristic ineptitude of Nixon in dealing with what he would normally have recognized as a potentially serious problem. (Here's an indication of the bigotry of the Woodstein school: When Felt was charged by the Carter administration with criminal violation of the privacy of the Weather Underground, Nixon insisted on speaking in his defence at the trial even though he suspected Felt was Deep Throat, and persuaded incoming President Reagan to pardon Felt after he had been convicted – and yet neither Felt in his memoirs, nor Woodstein ever, nor the left generally, even recognized Nixon's generous actions. That would have been inconvenient to the demonizing narrative.)

The facts of Watergate have been wildly exaggerated. Neither in financing techniques nor in the gamesmanship with the other side was the Republican campaign of 1972 particularly unusual. And it was puritanical compared with what appears to have been the outright theft of the 1960 election for Kennedy over Nixon by Chicago's Mayor Daley and Lyndon Johnson. And perhaps the all-time nadir in American presidential election ethics was achieved in 1968, when Lyndon Johnson tried to salvage the election for his vice-president, Hubert Humphrey, with a completely imaginary claim of a peace breakthrough in the Vietnam talks a few days before the election. LBJ announced an enhanced bombing halt and more intensive talks in which the Viet Cong and the Saigon government would be "free to participate" (i.e., Saigon declined to attend since there had been no breakthrough).

In Watergate, Nixon knew nothing of the break-in, nor had he known anything of the earlier break-in at the office of Dr. Fielding, the psychotherapist of both the thief and the publisher of the Pentagon Papers, Daniel Ellsberg. These papers reflected badly on Kennedy and Johnson, but had nothing to do with Nixon, and his opposition to their publication was based on the notion that secret government documents should not be stolen and published when national security is involved.

The congressional treatment of Nixon was an unmitigated outrage. The president's counsel, John Dean, a slippery weasel who was up to his eyebrows in unauthorized illegal practices, made a plea-bargain deal and then gave perjured evidence against his own client, which would have been completely inadmissible in a law court. The House Judiciary Committee was a mockery. Its counsel, John Doar, a foaming-at-the-mouth partisan on a par with Bradlee-Woodstein, produced five counts of impeachment, of which four were farcical on a Kafkaesque scale: articles 2 to 5 of the impeachment alleged that Nixon "endeavoured" to misuse the IRS (not that he had actually done so) and had violated his oath of office and the rights of other citizens. (By this last criterion, historically guilty parties would have been numerous and distinguished, including FDR, the Kennedys, and LBJ.) Article 3 impeached him for resisting Congress's right to 147 tapes; presto, Nixon had no right to try in court to retain tapes of private conversations, which he handed over when ordered by the Supreme Court to do so.

Even the rabid House-committee kangaroos voted down the last two counts: that Nixon had usurped Congress's power to declare war by bombing Cambodia and that he had cheated on his tax returns and improperly charged the government for improvements to his home. (Regarding the latter count: The IRS had revoked Nixon's tax credit for his vice-presidential papers – an arrangement similar to others that had been made by national office-holders – but refused to return the papers. This was an outright theft, and it required many years to have it undone by the courts. And Nixon eventually secured a court order requiring the government to remove from his property in California the vast eyesore of security apparatus and staff quarters that middle-level officials had installed there.)

The impeachment count worthy of consideration was the charge that Nixon had "made it his policy" and acted "directly and personally through his close subordinates . . . to delay, impede, obstruct . . . cover up, protect, and conceal," etc. Most of this was sanctimonious claptrap, and the so-called smoking gun consisted of his allowing subordinates to ask the director and deputy director of the CIA to ask the FBI not to investigate Watergate because it might back into national security matters. The two officials (Richard Helms and Vernon Walters) said they would follow a presidential order but would otherwise not interfere, and Nixon declined to take it further. This was not an offence, though the idea should never have been considered.

Nixon always claimed he approved payment for normal expenses, the defendants' families, and legal fees, not for altered testimony, and the tapes are ambiguous. He would probably have won in a fair trial, but not after prosecutors had done an elephant walk through the book of practice and rolled over most of his staff on false plea bargains with Bradlee–Woodstein shrieking from the rooftops of the nation that Nixon had cloven feet and wore horns. There is also the whole question of the Fifth Amendment right against self-incrimination raised by the tapes; and Nixon had had a conservative view of the national security privilege of the president throughout his public career (as did Roosevelt, Truman, and Eisenhower), and that issue remains a constitutional grey area. But a lynching was in progress and Nixon had no exercisable rights.

This raises the third assessment of Watergate: its place in the Nixon presidential record. When Nixon entered office in 1969, the country was torn by assassinations and race and anti-war riots, and President Johnson could scarcely visit any part of the country without being beset by demonstrations. Johnson had 550,000 draftees in Vietnam on a flimsy legal pretext, and 200 to 400 were returning in body bags every week. Hanoi would give no incentive at all for an American withdrawal from Vietnam. Johnson offered joint withdrawal of all foreign forces from the South in 1966. Hanoi could have taken this and returned six months after the American departure, and Ho Chi Minh would have lived to return to Saigon, but he insisted on defeating the United States directly. Nixon won that war. Nixon had extracted American forces, and the South Vietnamese defeated the North and Viet Cong in the great battle of April and May 1972 with no American ground support, but with heavy air assistance. Nixon sent the peace agreement to the Senate for ratification, though he did not have to constitutionally, to ensure Democratic support for a return to bombing the North Vietnamese when they violated the peace agreement.

Watergate enabled the Democrats to cut off all aid to South Vietnam and ensure American defeat in a war their party entered and had effectively lost, before Nixon salvaged a non-communist South Vietnam while effecting a complete American withdrawal. They are complicit in the murder of millions of Indochinese, from the Killing Fields of Cambodia to the boat people of the South China Sea.

Nixon's term was one of the most successful in the country's history: Vietnam, China, SALT I, desegregation, the EPA, ending the draft. He proposed non-coercive universal health care and welfare, and tax and campaign-finance reform. And he was re-elected by the largest plurality in the country's history (eighteen million).

The Watergate affair was sleazy and discreditable, but Nixon was an unusually talented and successful president. The war on history has been conducted by his enemies. There have been indications before of Woodward's desperation to conserve his status as a dragon-slayer, in particular his outright invention of a conversation with a comatose and heavily guarded William Casey on his hospital deathbed, confessing guilt in the spurious Iran-Contra affair. In sum, Bradlee–Woodstein bloodlessly assassinated the president, routinized the criminalization of policy and partisan differences, grievously wounded the institution of the presidency, and enjoyed and profited from doing so.

# GOD, THE FOUNDERS, AND GEORGE WILL

*National Review Online*, January 9, 2013

George Will's address at Washington University in St. Louis on December 4 has been rightly hailed as a seminal statement on the role of religion in Western and especially American society, and on the conflicting constitutional ambitions and their consequences of two of George Will's most eminent fellow Princetonians, James Madison and Woodrow Wilson. It is clear that George Will put a great deal of thought into the address, which required about forty minutes to deliver, and as would always be the case with anything he thought seriously about, it is a learned, insightful, and stimulating argument. He makes three principal points: that, in most cases, religion is a desirable belief for a society in general to hold, one that benefits equally all members of that society, including those who, like himself, have no religious beliefs; that Madison, as chief author of the Constitution, instituted the system of checks and balances among three coequal branches of the government to restrain the federal government from too *dirigiste* an intrusion in the rights and freedoms and natural course of the lives of the citizens; and that Woodrow Wilson compromised this with the assertion of the federal government's right and duty to be more directly interventionist than the authors of the Constitution wished.

George Will holds Wilson's emulators responsible for unconstitutional deviations that have resulted in the wholesale acquisition, with the taxpayers' money, of the political support of special-interest groups, and the redefinition of the role of government to one of almost unlimited tinkering and meddling in areas that the authors and initial adopting legislators of the Constitution did not intend and would not approve, a meddling that is objectively regrettable and, on balance, unsuccessful and dangerous.

In what must rank as one of the greatest intellectual tours de force ever written by an American journalist (and one that has very few rivals from journalists of other countries since Swift), Will establishes a sequence, starting from the recognition by the principal founders of the country (Washington, Franklin, Jefferson, Adams, and especially Madison, but not Hamilton, are mentioned), that religion is central to a concept of natural rights, as in the assertion in the Declaration of Independence that the "Creator" endows all men with "inalienable rights," and that all are "created equal." Will said in St. Louis that "natural rights are especially firmly grounded when they are grounded in religious doctrine." Though Will effectively asserts that none of the founders was religious at all, they invoked religion, rather as he does, as useful because it "fostered attitudes and aptitudes associated with, and useful to, popular government." (He exaggerates: Washington, Adams, and even Hamilton had their moments of conventional religious practice, and the others did more at times than, as is claimed, just doff their caps to religion.)

Will reminds us that Madison was most concerned about the tyranny of a majority and had created the system of checks and balances between three coequal branches of government to prevent the installation in authority of a durable, tyrannizing majority. "A government thus limited is not in the business of imposing its opinions about what happiness or excellence the citizens should choose to pursue," he said in St. Louis. The core of his thesis – which he developed, as time allowed, with recondite extracts from Machiavelli, Luther, Hobbes, Tocqueville, and Irving Kristol, and references to Locke and Kant – is that Madison's Constitution and his mentor Jefferson's Declaration held the truths of natural rights to be "self-evident," that the purpose of government is to "secure" these rights, and that the founders considered religion reasonable because it secured those rights.

He credits Madison as "the wisest and most subtle" of the founders, and Wilson he decries as opposed to Madisonian limits on government as a "cramped, unscientific understanding of the new possibilities of politics." He quotes Wilson's social scientist's view of the opportunity for politics to quicken "in every suitable way . . . both collective and individual development," and takes issue with Wilson's sanguine view that though "great passions" may be stirred, these passions will, if they seize the public, "find a great spokesman." Will disagrees strongly with this; he says that the United States, "steeped in and shaped by Biblical religion, cannot comfortably accommodate a politics that takes its bearings from the proposition that human nature is a malleable product of social forces, and that improving human nature, perhaps unto perfection, is a proper purpose of politics." As "Biblical religion is concerned with asserting the dignity of the individual," the Wilsonian conception of government is, in effect, un-Christian. Will agrees with Irving Kristol that "it is crucial to the lives of all our citizens, as it is to all human beings at all times, that they encounter a world that possesses a transcendental meaning, a world in which the human experience makes sense. Nothing is more dehumanizing, more certain to generate a crisis, than to experience one's life as a meaningless event in a meaningless world."

Will concludes that "we may be approaching what is, for our nation, unexplored and perilous social territory. . . . When many people decide that the universe is merely a cosmic sneeze, with no transcendent meaning; when they conclude that therefore life should be filled to overflowing with distractions – comforts and entertainments – to assuage the boredom; then they may become susceptible to the excitements of politics promising ersatz meaning and spurious salvations from a human condition bereft of transcendence."

It was, as it has been acclaimed to have been, a brilliant speech, from a brilliant man (who is also a good and loyal friend whom I have known, liked, and admired for more than thirty years), and I agree fervently with his conclusion, and most of the reasoning that generated the conclusion. But unfortunately, there are a few problems with it.

First, it is slightly disconcerting to have a professed atheist pat those of us who practise a religion (I am an observant, though not uncritical or intolerant, Roman Catholic) on our heads and urge us to carry on with something that he implicitly considers to be rubbish but is one of the pillars of American civil society. It is like Charles Maurras's Action Française, which endorsed the stabilizing influence of Roman Catholicism in France a century ago even though Maurras himself regarded Catholicism as superstitious obscurantism and unfounded conjurations. And for George Will to imply that this position is close to that of the Founding Fathers of the country won't fly. Washington was a vestryman in his church; Hamilton and Adams were frequent church-goers; and even Franklin, Jefferson, and Madison, evolving Unitarians or deists as they were, would not have described themselves as "nones," where Will places himself in the Pew Foundation survey.

More worrisome, Will effectively states that American democracy reposes in large part on beliefs and activities that he does not consider intellectually persuasive on their objective merits. I find this undermines the credibility of his faith in the ability of the United States to defend a system of natural rights as he knowledgeably defines it.

Second, I don't agree that Madison's constitutional stipulations of divided and restrained powers, no matter how faithfully adhered to, would have prevented the crisis that George Will rightly fears is upon us – a society that looks to government to cure all ills as a matter of right. That process is the result of a universal franchise, which, though Madison and Jefferson favoured a broader electorate than did Washington, Adams, or Hamilton, is not what any of them, including Franklin, sought. Democracy was going to open the whole process to a supreme test of the maturity and political sobriety of the people, and the people's will was never going to be frustrated indefinitely by recourse to the limited jurisdiction of the federal government. The idea that in what is essentially a free country the majority could be denied what it wants, even if its desires are incited by demagogues and charlatans, is moonshine.

Third, I do not agree with Will's Manichaean portrayal of the two Princetonian presidents. Madison wasn't the wisest and subtlest of the founders, as Will claims; he was a subtle legal theorist and draftsman, but he was not as wise nor as subtle a mind or personality as

Washington or Franklin. As president, Madison blundered into a war with Britain and Canada, which he managed not to win, and which raised the northeastern states to a condition bordering on revolt. He could have doubled the size of the United States by taking Canada, as Jefferson had done with the Louisiana Purchase, but instead he was chased out of Washington on foot as the British burned down the government buildings there. Madison was reduced to naming Monroe simultaneously secretary of state and of war to try to end the War of 1812 both militarily and diplomatically. He ranks as the greatest lawgiver since Moses (who was, after all, a messenger), surpassing, among others, Hammurabi, Justinian, and Napoleon. But his Constitution is not working well now, with a severely corrupted and deadlocked political process. This is not the consequence of anything Wilson did.

Wilson is rivalled not by Madison but perhaps by Jefferson and John Quincy Adams as the greatest intellect who ever lived in the White House. He believed that the security to which the Declaration of Independence referred depended on an educated electorate, exercising its democratic rights. He was a contemporary democrat and a serious Christian (son and grandson of Presbyterian ministers), unlike Madison and Will, and introduced a serious moral yardstick to American foreign policy and was the first person to inspire the masses of the world with the visions of enduring peace and of the government of a coherent international law. At the conclusion of his war message of 1917, he meant it when he said, "God helping her [America], she could do no other." He never uttered a word about the perfectibility of man, and the imputation to him of that Marxist heresy is little short of an outrage.

His expansion of government consisted of the Federal Reserve, the Federal Trade Commission, and the Clayton Antitrust Act. These did not sap the marrow of American liberty, and Wilson cannot be blamed for the errors of those who have governed in the last fifty years. Wilson's concern about the Constitution was that in such a separation of the executive from the legislative, it could become completely ineffectual. It has, and a penitent retrenchment to Madison won't renovate it. Only a resurgent national will to American greatness and the ideals espoused by all distinguished American leaders and political thinkers, including James Madison, Woodrow Wilson, and George F. Will, will achieve that.

# BROKEN JUSTICE

*National Review Online*, February 28, 2013

I observed Washington's birthday by participating in a Federalist Society telephone forum on the American justice system with two other panellists. The chairman, Dean Reuter, and the other panellists, Professor Ellen Podgor, of Stetson University Law School in Florida, and Professor William Otis, of Georgetown University Law School, could not have been more polite, and all the callers at the end of our introductory remarks were intelligent and courteous, and posed stimulating questions. It was my first direct contact with the Federalist Society, though I had often read material associated with its members and had always found it high-quality work. (The Federalist Society will be making available a podcast of the forum in the next couple of weeks.) I did not realize until just before we began that we were to make introductory remarks of five to eight minutes, but since I have uttered my views on the subject of U.S. justice, especially criminal justice, so often, including in this space, it was not a great challenge to muster a tolerably fluent recitation of the highlights.

These are, in the briefest synopsis, that American prosecutors win 99.5 per cent of their cases, a much higher percentage than those in other civilized countries; that 97 per cent of them are won without trial because of the plea-bargain system, in which inculpatory evidence is extorted from witnesses in exchange for immunity from prosecution, including for perjury; that the United States has six to twelve times as many incarcerated people per capita as do Australia, Canada, France, Germany, Japan, or the United Kingdom, comparably prosperous democracies; that the United States has 5 per cent of the world's population, 25 per cent of its incarcerated people, and half of its academically qualified lawyers, who take about 10 per cent of U.S. GDP; that prosecutors enjoy very uneven advantages in procedure and an absolute immunity for misconduct; that they routinely seize targets' money on false affidavits alleging ill-gotten gains so they cannot defend themselves by paying rapacious American lawyers, most of whom in criminal defence matters are just a fig leaf to provide a pretense of a genuine day in court before blind justice; that the Fifth, Sixth, and Eighth Amendment rights that are the basis of the American claim to being a society of laws don't really exist in practice; and that far too many judges are ex-prosecutors who have not entirely shed the almost universal prosecutorial will to crucify.

Professor Podgor followed me and agreed in general with my comments and added some very learned points, such as that there are now 4,500 criminal statutes, and that prosecutors have become specialists in applying catchall laws such as RICO (Racketeer Influenced and Corrupt Organizations Act) and obstruction of justice, or against untruthfulness in the case of the slightest variance in what has been said about even slightly related matters, so they often never have to prove the charge that gave rise to the proceedings. Mr. Otis followed with a mellifluous and integral whitewash of the justice system as seamless, leak-proof, and almost perfect. American prosecutors are so successful because they are better than those in other countries and never charge mistakenly (despite the endless popping up every week or so of the most shocking cases of deliberate prosecution suppression of evidence). The United States, in its prosecutors, has an almost flawless functioning of the rule of law that is responsible for a heavy decline in the crime rate. It is efficient, unlike the welfare system – as if Ms. Podgor or I had been defending the welfare system or had even mentioned it.

Otis retreated only in microscopic increments and sideways, when we responded. Yes, he allowed, the aging of the population, improved police techniques, and the profusion of security cameras might have had a marginal effect on the reduction of crime. Despite the undisputed comparative percentages of incarcerated people, he claimed that there were only three-quarters of 1 per cent of the population in prison at one time; but he had no reply to my question of whether, in light of the fact that there are forty-eight million Americans with a criminal record, albeit many of them for DUI or university-age disorderly behaviour many years ago, he thought that one-sixth of Americans, and one-quarter of American adults, really deserve to be considered criminals. To my comment that 15 per cent of convicted people were innocent, he replied with a red herring about an Innocence Project estimate that 3 per cent are innocent, although it was clear that I was speaking of all people convicted of crimes and the source he cited was referring only to those successfully accused of violent crimes.

Ms. Podgor and I challenged Otis's serene platitude that "juries convict and judges sentence" by pointing out that the juries are snowed by the procedural inequalities, and that the judges' hands are tied by usurpatory legislative grandstanding such as mandatory minimums and "three strikes and you're out." He met us with a glazed pall of impenetrable prevarication. And the comments of both of us on the human wreckage needlessly created in the justice system by the conduct of prosecutors who would be disbarred in any other serious country caused me to be gently disparaged as – a real and rather agreeable novelty – an almost hemophiliac bleeding heart. When Mr. Otis said that if the conviction rate were as low as those in Britain and Canada (50 and 60 per cent) the prosecutors would be reviled for dragging the innocent through ineffectual proceedings, I resisted with difficulty the temptation to reply that if that was his view of how the system should work, we might as well talk about goldfish. Ms. Podgor came in admirably with well-formulated concerns about the commoditization of convicted people.

Former senator Jim Webb (Democrat, Va.) spoke out a few years ago about the imbalance of American criminalization and the record of other advanced countries and concluded that either the other countries (named above) were not interested in crime, which is nonsense, or Americans were uniquely prone to commit crimes, which is nonsense, or the system isn't working well. Bingo, but Mr. Otis gave us a new explanation, which I called the providential and almost uniform moral and professional superiority of American prosecutors. Senator Webb's proposed commission on these issues was never set up and would not have achieved anything anyway: there have been countless such commissions and they never achieve anything. But self-coronations for global superiority are disturbing, and unbecoming to Americans. Mr. Otis's presentation was like that of an unscrupulous televangelist: all was fine, there was a ready explanation for everything, and when a question could not be answered, just answer a different one and pretend it is an answer.

The War on Drugs has cost over $1 trillion and resulted in the imprisonment of two million people, and yet drugs are more plentifully available, in better quality, at cheaper prices, than they were when the war began. Prohibition was a master stroke of public policy in comparison. In Canada, only 60 per cent of prosecutions are successful, plea bargains are rare, and a third of those convicted do not receive custodial sentences.

Winston Churchill regarded the use of imprisonment as "the test of civilization"; the United States has flunked the test. There are at least 750,000 more convicted people to add to the forty-eight million there already each year. Many, certainly, are for unstigmatizing events, but because of the U.S. government's passion for extraterritoriality, even those so charged are, at American official request, barred entry to friendly countries such as Canada (which admitted scores of thousands of fugitive slaves and draft evaders and deserters). It is all part of the larger problem of too many lawyers and too many laws and regulations, as the legislating lawyers at all the sources of lawmaking and regulation in the country spew out more restrictions and penalties as furiously as the national debt rises. On the civil side, the Bank of America has set aside $42 billion in two years to deal with lawsuits arising from bad acquisitions.

Every resident of or frequent visitor to the United States should rejoice at the Supreme Court's decision last week expanding the rights of defendants to effective counsel in plea-bargain negotiations. As Justice Anthony Kennedy wrote in the majority opinion, the country no longer has a "trial system" but rather a system in which "the negotiation of a plea bargain, [instead of] the unfolding of a trial, is almost always the critical point for a defendant." In federal cases, 97 per cent of convictions – and in state cases, 94 per cent of convictions – are the result of plea bargains.

Justice Kennedy, perhaps without realizing it, turned over the rock that hides the ghastly infirmity of the whole American criminal justice system when he emphasized that the plea bargain is "the critical point for a defendant." He didn't say "for a convicted defendant" or "for a guilty defendant" – and thus implicitly recognized that over 90 per cent of those charged are convicted. The sluggishness of the Supreme Court to grasp the implications of this makes the gently downward movement of molasses and even that of fresh cement seem like the rush of the Niagara River toward the Falls, but at some point the high court is going to have to come to grips with this degeneration of American justice into virtual Star Chambers.

It was accepted by the Supreme Court in the cases decided last week that defendants frequently receive inept advice. It is also frequently the case that the government spuriously seizes the assets of defendants as ill-gotten gains – on the basis of fraudulent affidavits in *ex parte* actions – so that the defendants can't engage the counsel of their choice, and then stays those proceedings while the criminal case is decided without the presence of a serious defence counsel.

It is also usually the case that the public defender, provided in response to the much-mythologized *Gideon v. Wainwright* case of 1963, is an underfunded and docile dupe of the prosecutors who is paid according to the number of clients he represents and not his performance, thus incentivizing minimal service and maximum turnover.

It put me in mind of a friend who had happened to see that ineffably tedious television personality Dr. Phil recently assuring a caller on his program that the United States "has the best justice system in the world," as if this subject had much to do with his field of specialty. The United States has done well with a systematic and saturating policy of self-praise, from workers' putting flag decals on their hard hats to Senator Marco Rubio's responding to every encouragement to say anything with an encomium to "the greatest country in human history" to intellectuals' celebrating American exceptionalism in recondite ways. All countries need some boosterism and all people should be proud of their collective identities, national, ethnic, and sectarian, and usually even vocational. There are dangers in cynicism, as the Italians and the French – who generally regard politics as an absurd and inherently corrupt and contemptible activity and their countries as likeable but raddled old harlots – demonstrate. But there is something potentially delusional in this endless American incantation of self-laudations. Even President Obama, a dissenter before his elevation, is grating with his completely false claims to have re-established America's prestige in the world, as he runs, not walks, from every problem. This can only be intuition, but I suspect the increasing anti-Americanism on U.S. campuses may in part be a response to this relentless impulse to mindless national vanity.

Part of the difficulty is that almost all America's traditional peers, the old Great Powers, are crumbling too, except Germany and Canada, the only major countries that still impress the unconscionable scoundrels in the thoroughly disgraced rating agencies. When Britain, France, and Japan, not to mention Italy and Spain, are floundering, Russia is a gangster state, and no one can believe a word or number emanating from Beijing, it is easier to continue like Victorian elocution-school students to repeat a mantra – in this case, that America is the greatest. This practice has its rewards and its hazards, but indulging the conveyor belt to the steroid-fed U.S. prison industry that is its criminal justice system in such a full-body immersion of misplaced praise is not just unrigorous and unwise. There is something totalitarian, pagan, psychotic, and thus profoundly un-American, about it.

# WHY JFK?

*The National Interest*, November 2013

F ifty years after the murder of President John F. Kennedy, the event is scarcely less shocking and saddening than it was in its immediate aftermath. It must rank with the terrorist attacks of September 11, 2001, as the most graphically shocking and horrifying memory in the minds of the hundreds of millions of people who remember that day. The reason it is such a vivid memory is not just that it was the murder of a president; the United States had endured that three times before, though not in the electronic age, and the assassination of President Abraham Lincoln was a greater tragedy for the country, in terms both of the greatness of the deceased president and in what could legitimately be expected of him had he finished his term. In the case of Lincoln, and James A. Garfield, in 1881, and William McKinley, in 1901, the assassinations were vividly sketched and described, and the country was profoundly shocked in every case, but the endless televised reruns of the motorcade in Dallas, and the solicitude of Mrs. Kennedy and then the horror within the presidential car and on the roadside when it was clear that a terrible wound had been sustained, is a ghastly and indelible recollection to everyone, in a way that a drawing, however skilfully executed, cannot be. (Contemporary sketches of Lincoln being shot in the head at point-blank range in his box at the theatre, beside his wife, were, and remain, very chilling.) And though President Kennedy was not a gigantic statesman who had saved the Union and emancipated the slaves and seen the country through a horrible war in which more Americans died than in all other American wars combined, he was only forty-six and was not three years into his presidency. Lincoln announced that he was "an old man" in his famous leave-taking at Springfield, Illinois, in 1861 as he went to his inauguration "not knowing when, or whether ever, I shall return," though he was only fifty-two. It was a century earlier, and Lincoln had led a hard life. And he was departing his home to assume the headship of a country that was already in the deepest crisis in its history, with states seceding pre-emptively every week.

The greatest contrast with previous analogous tragedies in American history was that JFK was glamorous; he was a star. Abraham Lincoln, for all his greatness, and partly because of it, was not glamorous, and certainly his harridanly and somewhat maladjusted wife was not glamorous. John F. Kennedy was a fair and tousle-headed, intelligently ingenuous, stylish scion of a wealthy family. It was an altogether different appeal from that of the craggy product of the log cabin and the rail-splitting youth and itinerant frontier lawyer, Abraham Lincoln. Jacqueline Kennedy was only thirty-four when her husband was murdered, and was an elegant, trilingual, stylishly dressed, and refined woman. Garfield had been a university head in his twenties (Western Reserve), and a distinguished combat citizen general in the Civil War, and was the only person ever to make the jump directly from congressman to president (though he had already been elected senator but not installed), but he was not glamorous, and glamour was not in 1880 what it was in the 1960s. William McKinley had had a good war as a middle officer, and the war with Spain was a walkover. He was a journeyman senator, a solid plough horse, but he was in no sense glamorous.

Of presidents who died in office, the closest in some respects to President Kennedy was Franklin D. Roosevelt, who was a great star, who at least lived in the era of films, newsreels, and glossy magazines, and who captured and held the imagination of the nation and the world in a way that Kennedy consciously tried to replicate, down to the smiling countenance and the identification by his three initials. But FDR, though only sixty-three when he died, passed on from exhaustion in his great office in his fourth term, was seventeen years older than JFK, and cannot be claimed to have died entirely prematurely. The deaths of FDR and JFK provoked the two greatest outbreaks of public grief in the nation's history, apart from the death of Lincoln. Two million people stood silently beside the track at all hours of the day and night as the funeral train bore the casket of President Roosevelt back from Warm Springs, Georgia, to Washington, and on to his ancestral home at Hyde Park, New York.

The shocking televised record of President Kennedy's murder, the premature demise of this popular and attractive young leader, have made it such a timeless tragedy, a piercing wound to the world's conscience and sensibilities that does not much heal or abate, not his actual performance in office. As president, he followed and concluded what must with perspective be considered a golden age of the U.S. presidency, through the distinguished incumbencies of Franklin D. Roosevelt, Harry S. Truman, and Dwight D. Eisenhower. The accomplishments of those leaders, taking the country out of the Great Depression and to victory in the Second World War, and through the worst phase of the Cold War, founding NATO and creating the Marshall Plan, defending Korea, and proposing Atoms for Peace and Open Skies, and delivering a peaceful and prosperous America beginning to desegregate to the young President Kennedy, were probably the greatest sustained period of presidential accomplishment in the history of that office.

John F. Kennedy moved it forward a whole generation (his three predecessors were born between 1882 and 1890), but apart from the appearance of vigour (which disguised severe medical problems and excessive medication, not to dwell upon apparent satyriasis), his record in office was thin and composed more of promise than fact. JFK came late to the correct conclusion on civil rights and taxes, but couldn't move them legislatively, and it was his successor, Lyndon B. Johnson, who got those measures adopted. He probably deserves the benefit of the doubt that he would not have made such a terrible mess of Vietnam as his successor did; would have avoided it, or, if he had intervened directly, would have followed the advice of Eisenhower, Douglas MacArthur, and other serious military experts and cut the Ho Chi Minh Trail. As it is, the chief responsibility for turning Laos into a superhighway of North Vietnamese infiltration of the South resides with Kennedy for the Laos Neutrality Agreement, which Richard Nixon (who may well have been the real winner of the 1960 election and has received minimal credit for not contesting it and immobilizing the country) called "Communism on the installment plan." Kennedy did sign the Nuclear Test Ban Treaty, but most of the preparatory work was done by Eisenhower. His great triumph is commonly held to be the Cuban Missile Crisis of 1962, and he does deserve much credit for distrusting blasé military and intelligence assurances of an easy possible invasion option, when there were in fact short-range missiles with nuclear war heads and two Soviet divisions already in-country. But at the start of the crisis, there were NATO missiles in Italy and Turkey and no Soviet missiles in Cuba and no guaranty by the United States of non-invasion of Cuba. At the end of the crisis, there were no missiles in Italy, Turkey (contrary to the wishes of those countries), or Cuba, and the United States had undertaken not to invade Cuba. It was prudent management, but as Charles de Gaulle and Richard Nixon pointed out, it was no American strategic victory.

John F. Kennedy was probably an above-average president, and might have been a very talented two-term president, but that is rank conjecture. All the bunk about *Camelot* (a musical he didn't even enjoy) has burnished a rather humdrum record, but he will always remain an admired and lamented man, whose life and death were an evanescent source of encouragement, and a permanent tragedy.

# A NEW GREATEST
# GENERATION?

*National Review Online*, January 29, 2014

---

ast week I received a message from a distinguished retired general
and head of a strategic institute in Canada, wringing his hands at
the pusillanimity and ambivalence of most current world leaders and
the apparent lack of any public appetite for the assertion of any recognizable principles in international affairs. He asked whether I thought
the contemporary West could chin itself, if necessary, on facing the
sort of challenges that were served up to and mastered by, as they have
become known, "the greatest generation." (This was Tom Brokaw's
coinage, referring to the generation of Americans and, broadly, British
and Canadians also, of the period from 1930 to 1960.) I replied that
I did not think it was such a great generation spontaneously; it rose
to great challenges, and lived in what was ultimately an immensely
successful time, because of the leadership it enjoyed. That leadership
devised and executed the strategy that brought the West through the
Great Depression and Second World War, and to the creation of the
alliances and institutions that won the Cold War and secured the triumph of democracy and the free-market economy in the world.

When Franklin D. Roosevelt was inaugurated in 1933, estimates
of the level of unemployment varied from 25 to 33 per cent (the figures were compiled by the states, and rather unreliably in some cases).

The economic system had collapsed. The Hoover administration's policy prescription, as we now know, was the worst that could have been devised: higher taxes, higher tariffs, and a shrunken money supply, all of which inadvertently poured gasoline on the fire of the Depression. President Hoover, as future *Washington Post* publisher Katharine Graham's mother put it, left office "to the sound of crashing banks." Thousands of them had failed, and there was no deposit insurance. The whole nation, and the whole Western world, was terrified by the mighty and voracious Depression.

Immense controversy continues still about the relief and reform program put through by the new president. Though an economic conservative, I have waged the battle, here and in many other places, including my biography of Franklin D. Roosevelt, that he deserves, as Alan Greenspan once put it to me, "a solid 67 per cent pass for economics, but an almost perfect 99 per cent score for catastrophe avoidance." He began his presidency with the famous encouragement that "the only thing we have to fear is fear itself," provided emergency funds for the banking system (which became preferred shares which the government sold profitably as conditions allowed), reopened and merged banks as appropriate, guaranteed bank deposits, and – of the seventeen million unemployed – put seven million to work in the first year of his administration on workfare programs in conservation and in what would today be called infrastructure but were then known as public works. The workers also planted tens of millions of trees; Eugene O'Neill taught people how to write and perform plays; the whooping crane was saved; and, "as the storm clouds gathered across the sea," the aircraft carriers *Yorktown* and *Enterprise* (destined to be decisive at Coral Sea and Midway) were constructed by the unemployed, all supervised by army engineers and navy shipbuilders. Natural recovery and statutorily reduced hours absorbed another five million of the unemployed, and the Social Security system enacted in 1935 provided the safety net for the rest. Farm incomes were reinforced by a referendary agreement among categories of farmers to reduce production, store surpluses, and raise commodity prices to levels at which the agricultural community could survive. This was the successor policy to Hoover's dumping of surpluses on the global market and enduring the default in payment of the buyers, while the American farmer was forced off his land by the combined fury of economic hardship, drought, and cyclonic soil erosion.

There were many other measures in the New Deal, ranging from genius to poor, but Roosevelt gave the nation hope, got the country through, and eliminated unemployment – by recourse to workfare (which is traditionally, and unfairly, not counted in the statistics of employed people), and then by rearming America in response to the world crisis (which is how the European powers and Japan reduced unemployment – by drafting everyone into the armed forces and defence-production industries). Having been terrified by economic impoverishment, the young and early-middle-aged people of the country learned the virtues of work, collegiality, and a practical application of national spirit. The president led the distressed and afflicted people in coordinated self-help.

Roosevelt recognized that without America, the forces of democracy in the world would be insufficiently strong to prevent the totalitarians from dominating the entire Eurasian land mass, and, as FDR put it in a conflation of two of his speeches, in the tense year of 1940: "We in this hemisphere would be living at the point of a gun . . . fed through the bars of our cage by the pitiless and contemptuous masters of other continents." He broke a tradition as old as the republic by seeking and winning a third term and mobilized opinion behind supporting the democracies (Britain, Canada, and Australia) against Germany and shutting off the supply of oil and the ingredients of steel to Japan unless it ceased its aggression against China and Indochina. When Japan attacked the United States and Great Britain at Pearl Harbor and across the Pacific, he led a united country into war for the only time in American history (there was practically no dissent); thirteen million men volunteered or were conscripted, and Roosevelt's appointee-generals George C. Marshall, Dwight D. Eisenhower, and Douglas MacArthur, and Admiral Chester W. Nimitz, led the United States and its allies to the unconditional surrender of Germany in the West and Italy and Japan altogether. Three hundred thousand Americans died, every one a tragedy, but a 2.5 per cent fatal casualty level against such fierce, powerful, and courageous enemies as Nazi Germany and

222 | BACKWARD GLANCES

imperialist Japan was a miraculously light price to pay, strategically, to bring Germany, Japan, France, and Italy into the West as flourishing democratic allies and to ensure the victory of democracy and the free market in most of the world.

And, posthumously, FDR had two other bequests to what is now regarded as the Greatest Generation: his GI Bill of Rights gave a free year at university for every year in the armed forces and interest-free loans for the start of a small business or acquisition of a farm. He enabled the unemployed of the 1930s to become the middle class of the 1950s. And when Stalin made the stupefying mistake of unleashing the Cold War, it was FDR's strategic team – Truman, Marshall, Eisenhower, Dean Acheson, George Kennan, Charles Bohlen, and others – who devised the containment strategy. This led, with refinements by Richard Nixon, Henry Kissinger, and Ronald Reagan, to the implosion of the Soviet Union and of international Communism.

Thus, an American born in 1920 who remained active to his or her early seventies saw the country plunged to the depths of economic and psychological depression, pulled up from those depths, attacked by the forces of militant evil, and emerge victorious in the ultimate just war when led by outstanding commanders. That American saw the country challenged by its erstwhile ally (the U.S.S.R. took over 90 per cent of the casualties in subduing Nazi Germany, but the West took 90 per cent of the geostrategic assets at stake) and saw the victorious conclusion of the struggle between the superpowers without a general war. It was a great generation that did all this, but it was inspired leadership that gave that generation the opportunity to be great. Of the ten presidents, five of each party, who contributed to this magnificent sequence, the only one who was not altogether adequate was Jimmy Carter, and he had his moments. The rest ranged from the brave decency of Gerald Ford to the uneven qualities of JFK, LBJ, and Richard Nixon, to the solid distinction of Truman and Ike, to the uplifting success of Reagan, to the genius of FDR – but the really great thing about the Greatest Generation was that it elevated fine leaders. If this generation of Americans would do the same, it would be great also. They are capable of it, of attracting and electing great leaders and of responding to them. In a democracy, it starts and ends with the people; if the people want greatness, they have to find leaders who will bring it out of them. It can be done, and looking at the deterioration of the United States in absolute and relative terms in the past twenty years, it must be done, and so, it will happen. "The fault, dear Brutus," (who was an assassin) "is in ourselves." So is the greatness.

# A FARCE AT FORTY

*National Review Online*, September 25, 2014

Over the summer, the fortieth anniversary of the resignation of President Richard Nixon and President Gerald Ford's pardon of him passed not, unfortunately, without the usual clangorous outburst of self-righteous claptrap and exercises in pseudo-historical mind reading and amateur psychoanalysis. Many years ago, I happened to have dinner with the former president a few days after the *New York Times* had run another speculation about his psychological makeup, and when I volunteered that he probably didn't enjoy these pieces, though he must by then have been used to them, he replied that the first such published insight into his psyche was in a California newspaper when he was only a second-term congressman. Nixon said, "The author committed suicide a few years ago, which, though unfortunate, confirmed me in my original view that her mental equilibrium was a good deal less stable than mine was."

Even my distinguished friend George Will got into the act this year, by suggesting that Nixon may have resigned to avoid having to deal with his recorded instruction to his chief aide, Bob Haldeman, to break into the liberal Brookings Institution and "clean out the safe." This was, to say the least, a bad idea, and even Haldeman, who had no shortage of improvident brainwaves himself, ignored this particular instruction. But that is the point: it was never attempted. The release of the tape containing that order to Haldeman was certainly an embarrassment, and is a disturbing impulse from the holder of so great an office, but people are not impeached and removed from an office to which they have been elected (in this case by the greatest plurality in American history) for voicing an insane thought, even when that thought, if enacted, would have been a very serious crime.

The same could be said of the so-called smoking gun, which precipitated Nixon's resignation and was effectively the last straw to a public that had been whipped into a righteous frenzy by a media campaign that seized upon and magnified every instance of Nixon's uncharacteristically inept handling of the whole series of revelations and allegations that started with the forced entry of the Democratic National Committee headquarters in the Watergate complex in Washington. Aides suggested that they ask the director and deputy director of the CIA (Richard Helms and Vernon Walters) to intervene with the FBI to stop the Watergate investigation for the stated reason that it could back into CIA covert operations against Cuba in which some of the Watergate intruders had once been involved. It was a tawdry as well as an insane proposal, and even if successful would not have accomplished anything, because the investigation was being carried out by District of Columbia police. But Helms and Walters said they would do so if ordered by the president himself to make that request, and when informed of this, Nixon declined to give any such order and told his aides not to proceed. This was a contemptible and foolish idea, but it was not pressed or acted upon and did not constitute obstruction of justice, or anything that justified disembowelling a presidency.

One of the more irritating anniversary comments was a piece in the *Wall Street Journal* commending President Ford for pardoning Nixon. It was annoying not because its conclusion was mistaken but because of the sanctimonious presumptions that were invoked in support of the intelligent conclusion that Ford was in all respects correct to issue the pardon. The op-ed piece, which was published on September 6, was written by Ken Gormley, dean of law at Duquesne University and author of a biography of Archibald Cox, Watergate special prosecutor and former solicitor general of the United States, and David Shribman, executive editor of the *Pittsburgh Post-Gazette*. The authors claim that, in accepting the pardon, Nixon "acknowledged his guilt." He did not;

he maintained all his subsequent life of twenty years that he had made serious errors but had not committed illegalities. Their authority is a 1915 case that found that a presidential pardon carried "an imputation of guilt." It may, but it does not necessarily do so, or at least not an irreversible imputation of guilt.

These authors also assert that President Ford had not made a deal with the president who appointed him vice-president and then stood aside to elevate him to the presidency, trading a pardon for the country's two national offices over ten months. Many pundits as well as the dense ranks of Nixon's opponents (they almost completely overlapped for a long time) screamed this at the time, including relatively sober commentators such as Joseph Alsop, but there was never a shred of evidence of it and such a thought arose only in the perfervidly malignant atmosphere confected by the anti-Nixon media, with, it must be admitted, what amounted to the cooperation of Nixon himself in his incompetent handling of the issues from the Watergate intrusion of June 1972 right up to his resignation in August 1974. Of course there was no such arrangement, the suggestion of it was always scurrilous and defamatory of both presidents, and to proclaim triumphantly forty years later that they are now free of that suspicion is fatuous.

These authors also claim that Ford acted to "preserve American history." But there was never any suggestion that Nixon, having complied with the Supreme Court order to hand over the tapes of his private conversations, would destroy any documents. As was ultimately determined by the courts, when cant and emotionalism had finally subsided to manageable levels, Richard Nixon had the same right as other presidents to presidential materials, and the intervention of Congress to deny him that access was illegal, just as the IRS's revocation of its previous agreement on the tax treatment of his contribution of his vice-presidential papers, which mirrored what other vice-presidents had done, was illegal, and was, in effect, an act of theft, as the government retained the papers. (Could anyone today imagine that the IRS had any lessons in ethics to give Richard Nixon or any other taxpayer?) Richard Nixon had to build his own presidential library, with the financial support of many thousands of admirers throughout the country and in every walk of life, and litigate to gain possession of papers that were his by right. The scandal in this aspect of the Watergate controversy is that it has taken forty years for even a dean of law to realize that Gerald Ford was an honest man. But to judge from this piece, it may take some while longer for him to realize that Richard Nixon did not cease to possess any rights over what is traditionally a president's property, with an obligation to preserve it, with or without a pardon for offences of which he was never officially accused.

The authors are of course correct to endorse President Ford's action, and it was to the Kennedys' credit that Edward Kennedy and others awarded him the Profile in Courage Award in 2001 for granting Nixon the pardon (which Senator Kennedy, a renowned pillar of official probity, had opposed at the time). If even Teddy Kennedy figured that out ten years ago, one wonders why it is still judged a ponderously weighty conclusion today. Mr. Gormley's book about Archibald Cox was subtitled "Conscience of a Nation." I think not. (That was the title of egregious former Irish prime minister Charles Haughey's autobiography, with no more justification.) Cox was a well-qualified lawyer, but he was a raving partisan Kennedy Democrat whose interest from beginning to end was the lynching of the man from whom the Kennedys probably stole the 1960 presidential election to put themselves in the White House (and install Cox as solicitor general). He was so far from America's conscience that, when President George H.W. Bush obtained congressional approval for the great alliance that forced Saddam Hussein to disgorge the state of Kuwait that he had seized, Cox wrote to the governments of the member states of the United Nations urging them not to cooperate with the United States. Most UN countries approved the alliance action and it has never been clear to me why Cox was not accused, even if only informally, of violating the Logan Act and trying to conduct American foreign policy as a private citizen without authority or standing to do so. (This first intervention in Iraq is almost universally considered to have been justified and successful; it lasted only a few days on the ground and the allies incurred very few casualties.)

At some point, even if it is the centenary or bicentenary of Watergate, America is going to have to realize that there was never an adequate reason to drive from office one of the country's most successful presidents.

Richard Nixon extracted the country from the Vietnam War while pre-
serving a non-communist government in Saigon, reopened relations
with China, signed the greatest arms-control agreement in history with
the U.S.S.R., founded the Environmental Protection Agency, ended
school segregation without recourse to the mad, court-ordered busing
of schoolchildren all around metropolitan areas for racial "balance,"
ended the draft, stopped the endless riots and skyjackings, started the
Mideast peace process, and calmed the nation, which rewarded him
with a mighty landslide re-election. There is some legitimate question
about his motives in advancing funds to Watergate defendants, but
there has never been what a proper court of justice could call a clear
case that Nixon committed crimes.

Watergate delivered Indochina to the North Vietnamese and
Khmer Rouge; unleashed the U.S.S.R. in Angola, Central America,
and Afghanistan; poisoned the wells of American public life to this day;
fragmented the national media; and undoubtedly helped reduce the
quality of candidates for high offices, including the presidency (vide
the last four elections). Forty years after this shameful travesty, and
long after Woodward and his claque have been exposed as all-season
myth-makers, much of American opinion is still sleepwalking through
a stilted morality play and congratulating itself on the inexorable work-
ings of its democracy. The distinguished British writer Muriel Spark
was much closer to the truth when she allegorized it as the theft of
a thimble in a convent in her book *The Abbess of Crewe*. As George
Stade, head of the English department of Columbia College, wrote
in the *New York Times* forty years ago next month (October 20, 1974),
Ms. Spark was the first writer to demonstrate that the Watergate affair
was, in fact, "a farce." Though it was on all sides a tawdry farce, the
farce lingers yet.

# INJUSTICE SYSTEM

*National Review Online*, October 9, 2014

---

Every week there are new revelations of the decrepit and often bar-barous state of the U.S. criminal justice and prison systems. The most egregious aspects of its dysfunction are not the absurdly severe sentences and world-record incarceration levels, or the North Korean conviction rates, or the frequent murders of prisoners by correctional officers in some of the state prisons, but the politically motivated antics of the prosecutors. I was one of those who warned of the criminaliza-tion of policy differences in the Watergate affair, but unfortunately the inexplicable and uncharacteristic mismanagement of the whole taw-dry sequence of events by President Nixon made it relatively easy for his enemies to drive him from office. It was bound to be an intoxi-cating experience, and beneath the confected sanctimony of many of the Watergate principals in the media and law enforcement, the joys of the assassin were evident. Ben Bradlee, editor of the *Washington Post*, whose notes reveal that he distrusted Woodward and Bernstein's Watergate reporting, was audibly rubbing his hands with glee at the prospect of going over the same ground again in the piffling Iran-Contra affair of 1986.

It was hard to resist the temptation to believe that the overreaction to President Bill Clinton's peccadilloes was just tit for tat over Watergate. There were never grounds to impeach him, any more than there had been in the one previous impeachment of a president, Andrew

Johnson's, in 1868, but, to adapt the metaphor of Mark Steyn, Air Force One got back to its hangar only with difficulty. The pursuit of Governor Don Siegelman of Alabama was always dubious, and the long persecution of the former House majority leader Tom DeLay, of Texas, has finally collapsed as the scandalous abuse of a partisan prosecution service that it always was. The infamous Ted Stevens affair has already been exposed as fraudulent withholding of evidence by the prosecutors, but only after the seven-term senator narrowly lost his bid for re-election and one of the prosecutors committed suicide. The protracted persecution of long-serving New York Senate leader Joseph Bruno has been another glaring example of the political corruption of the bench and the prosecutors. Most recently, the harassment of Republican governor Scott Walker of Wisconsin by the Democratic district attorney of Milwaukee, the pursuit of conservative commentator Dinesh D'Souza, the partisan indictment of Governor Perry of Texas for exercising his veto right, and the antics of the IRS (including the comically evasive and self-righteous appearances of IRS director John Koskinen at congressional hearings) demonstrate how resistless these prosecutors are against the temptation to use their unchecked powers for brazenly partisan ends.

In the assault on Governor Scott Walker, Democratic district attorney John Chisholm's long-running criminal investigation of the governor and his entourage ended in 2013 and has been followed by a criminal investigation into the most prominent individuals and organizations that support the governor, expressing concern about improper collusion in support of the governor's political, if not statutory, offence, which was to curb rapacious and irresponsible public-sector unions. This is a John Doe investigation (so called because it is a blind search into whether a crime was committed at all, and if so by whom – a procedure certain to lead to abuse). Nothing is said in public, except that evidence of the existence of the investigation is conveniently leaked, and the subjects cannot speak about it. Unfortunately for Chisholm, a long-time friend of his and his wife's (she is a militant shop steward for the teachers' union) brought forward extensive allegations of the political and spousally generated motives behind the investigations. One of the governor's supporters, Eric O'Keefe, of the Club for Growth, won a lift on the gag orders and a suspension of the whole investigation by a federal court, claiming a violation of freedom of speech and a partisan political vendetta. This judgment was overruled the next day by the Seventh Circuit Court of Appeals in Chicago, on grounds that a federal court did not have jurisdiction in such matters. The redoubtable trial judge, Rudolph Randa, came back just as quickly and upheld the investigation again on grounds where he had a clear jurisdiction. The whole endeavour by Chisholm and his Democratic claque is a disgrace.

The Dinesh D'Souza affair is another straight political prosecution traceable to the accused's acerbic criticisms of the present administration: he was dragged through a criminal trial on the trivial pretext of a minor violation of campaign-finance laws, a tenebrous jungle of layers of legislated self-interest through which even the most incorrigible specialist in the legal cartel has difficulty beating a path. At least the judge in this case had the decency not to imprison the defendant after, like 99.5 per cent of American criminal defendants, he was found guilty, but he was sentenced to probationary community service and therapeutic counselling. There was nothing in the proceedings or allegations to suggest that D'Souza was in any need of such therapy, which is almost entirely useless charlatanism anyway. In a number of areas, the United States is drawing closer to the justice of totalitarian countries. The Soviet Union took to describing all designated wrongdoers as mentally ill, and the D'Souza sentence confirms this tendency in the United States, where conviction rates are already equal to those of the Soviet Union and the numbers of incarcerated people at least equal to those of the Brezhnev-to-Gorbachev last phase of the U.S.S.R.

Another imitative feature has been the "allocution." As 97 per cent of the 99.5 per cent found guilty are intimidated by the manipulation of the plea-bargain system into pleading guilty to spare the state the irritation of a trial, the defendants accept the abandonment of 147 of the 153 counts against them, plead guilty, and are rehearsed in a catechetical process by the prosecutors to accuse themselves of cowardice, hypocrisy, sociopathic turpitude, and often outright evil, and profess their gratitude for the sentence they are about to receive. It smacks of nothing so much as the Stalin system of torturing the innocent until, to spare their families, they proclaimed their guilt, fulminated an allocution of coruscating self-loathing and self-righteously bellowed their demand to be executed immediately, and were led away by Stalin's obliging jurists, and often dispatched, mercifully in the circumstances, in the basement of the courthouse. (Successive secret-police chiefs were themselves executed by Stalin, or, in the case of the infamous Beria, by Stalin's successors, in the only step they could agree upon before a rending struggle for power between themselves.) The United States certainly has not plumbed these depths, but the allocutions are just as nauseatingly excessive and obviously extorted by terror in sentencing – psychological, as opposed to physical, torture.

This brings us to the excruciating and horrifying saga of the Internal Revenue Service. It is clear, despite an administration effort to muddy the waters and strangle the congressional investigation, that the president and his party's leaders in Congress launched a Herculean effort to bully the IRS to silence conservative organizations critical of the administration, and that the IRS, led by the head of the tax-exempt-organizations section, Lois Lerner, did its best to comply with this request. The extent of the collusion has been made difficult to fix with precision, because Ms. Lerner's hard drive disappeared and she has declined to answer congressional questions, exercising her right to avoid self-incrimination. No one believes that her emails vanished accidentally, but let us note the contrast between the complacency with which the Democratic national media have assimilated this news with the hysteria that followed the revelation that Rose Mary Woods, Richard Nixon's assistant, had lost only eighteen minutes of a Watergate tape. Because of synchronized IRS non-cooperation and the likely destruction of evidence, it is hard to be sure of the extent of the contact between Democratic eminences and the national tax collector, but the existence of many meetings and email exchanges has been established. (New York senator Chuck Schumer had publicly urged the IRS to crack down on the "extraordinary influence" of the Tea Party and other Republican groups.) Ms. Lerner eventually took leave from her position and was accused of contempt of Congress. It is hard not to be contemptuous of Congress, but that does not excuse refusal to answer amid the heavy suspicion of destruction of evidence.

President Obama installed John Koskinen, a "turnaround" expert from Fannie Mae, to clean up the IRS. But he has construed his role to be the obstruction of the congressional investigation, in appearances that were sanctimonious filibusters to explain the IRS's conduct by standing on what he fancies to be his dignity and fuming with righteousness when the committee members suggested that he is not cooperating (which, of course, he isn't). The administration's own investigation has been a slapstick farce, largely led by Ms. Lerner's chief associate in persecuting Republican political organizations, Jack Smith, now head of the public integrity unit of the Justice Department. The administration is determined to kill the whole investigation, and there is little doubt that a thorough airing of the matter would show the conduct of much of the senior levels of the administration to be, to say the least, discreditable.

This is a justice system in which the conservative majority on the Supreme Court overruled lower courts and denied a man (John Thompson) the $14 million that lower courts had awarded him for spending fourteen years on death row for a crime prosecutors knew he had not committed because of their possession of DNA evidence that they withheld (*Connick v. Thompson*, 2011). The elephantine prison system, the unstoppable prosecutors, the entire legal cartel, and the slumbering higher bench, quiescent in the shredding of the Bill of Rights, have created a terrible problem that, even now, the country is largely ignoring. It is hard to imagine what new outrages have to occur before the public demands a restoration of America's status as a society of reasonable laws, where a day in court is a reassuring thought for the innocent.

# A PLEA AGAINST PLEADING

*National Review Online,* November 12, 2014

Judge Jed S. Rakoff of the federal district court in New York has written a much-circulated piece in the November 20 issue of *The New York Review of Books,* in which he laments the breakdown in American criminal justice caused by abuse of the plea-bargain system. He writes, correctly, that "the criminal justice system in the United States today bears little relationship to what the Founding Fathers contemplated, what the movies and television portray, or what the average American believes." He quotes Jefferson's expression of faith in the jury trial as "the only anchor yet imagined by man by which a government can be held to the principles of its constitution." The Fifth, Sixth, and Eighth Amendments famously guarantee the grand jury as an assurance against capricious prosecutions, and also due process, no seizure of property without just compensation, prompt justice, an impartial jury, access to counsel (of choice according to judicial interpretation), and reasonable bail. Almost none of this really exists in most cases today, and Judge Rakoff writes: "The drama inherent in these guarantees is regularly portrayed in movies and television programs as an open battle played out in public before a judge and jury. But this is all a mirage. In actuality, our criminal justice system is almost exclusively a system of plea bargaining, negotiated behind closed doors and with no judicial oversight. The outcome is very largely determined by the prosecutor alone."

Eight to 10 per cent of federal and state cases are dismissed because of a technical error or because a defendant chooses to cooperate, but of the rest, 97 per cent of federal cases and about 95 per cent of state cases are resolved by plea bargains, and, in practice, these are almost invariably dictated by the prosecutor. Up to the Civil War, Judge Rakoff writes, almost all prosecutions were tried, but the strains of that war and the very heavy immigration that followed for decades afterward raised crime rates and – uniquely among judicially advanced countries – the United States adopted the plea bargain, by which more-severe charges were withdrawn in exchange for guilty pleas on others, to relieve the strain on the courts. This was an inexcusable failing in the first place: Canada, Australia, and some other advanced countries had proportionately as heavy immigration, but their justice systems were not allowed to mutate by allowing the prosecutor to decree a sentence while binding the hands of judges with legislative usurpations of the power to sentence. By the end of the Second World War, about 80 per cent of American criminal cases were resolved by plea bargains.

But in the 1960s and 1970s, crime rates rose steeply, largely in drug-related and race-related activities, and legislators vastly increased sentences, many of which were made mandatory (as in liberal New York governor Nelson Rockefeller's mandatory sentence of fifteen years in prison for selling two ounces or possessing four ounces even of marijuana). The severity of sentencing was enhanced by making sentences on individual counts consecutive, so even relatively minor offences could be aggregated into appallingly long prison sentences. The whole political community from right to left got on the law-and-order bandwagon, and dissenters were dismissed as permissive kooks and mollycoddlers of crime. The percentage of federal prosecutions tried by juries declined from 19 per cent in 1980 to 3 per cent today, as prosecutors have huge advantages over defence counsel and throw a great raft of counts against a defendant who declines to roll over. The prosecutor wins most of the cases that are tried and, as he can decide on the number and level of gravity of counts charged, defendants can face as much as ten times as heavy a sentence if they plead guilty as they would if they try the case and, as usually happens, lose. Rakoff does not mention that the high probability of successful prosecution is enhanced by plea bargains with witnesses who are threatened with prosecution for conspiracy to obstruct justice if they do not jog their memories to recall damaging evidence against an accused in exchange for immunity from prosecution, including for perjury. Rakoff does make the point that defence counsel are subject to allegations of "ineffective assistance of counsel" if a plea-bargain offer is rejected peremptorily, even as a negotiating ploy to extract a less onerous proposal from the prosecutor.

Thus do prosecutors acquire control of all relevant aspects of most cases. They target someone, throw a mass of charges against him, hustle the defendant and defence counsel (and – though Rakoff does not say this either – that counsel is often a hopelessly overworked public defender who is bulldozed by the prosecutor), and whatever he or she agrees to is apt to be repudiated by the prosecutor in court to reach for a stiffer sentence under mandatory minimums and legislated guidelines. The judge writes, "The Supreme Court's suggestion that a plea bargain is a fair and voluntary contractual arrangement between two relatively equal parties is a total myth: it is much more like 'a contract of adhesion' in which one party can effectively force its will on another party." He also makes short work of the academic argument that the plea bargain is equivalent to a regulatory process, as there are no regulations and the prosecutor just forces the result he wants. As Rakoff summarizes, the system is terribly one-sided, contrary to the image of impartial justice weighing these matters in finely balanced scales. The plea-bargain discussions are conducted in secret and are not subject to serious review, no matter what level of intimidation is employed; and many people become so terrified by the Stalinesque arithmetic of successful prosecutions (the conviction rate in Canada is about 60 per cent and in the United Kingdom just over 50 per cent) that, even when completely innocent, they plead guilty for a sentence much reduced from what a guilty finding at a trial would produce, given the ability of prosecutors to secure convictions even of the innocent.

Judge Rakoff reckons that from 2 to 8 per cent of defendants are innocent. On the basis of my observations, as someone who was wrongly convicted and imprisoned, though the Supreme Court ultimately vacated my four convictions (four having been abandoned and nine rejected by jurors), the number is probably 10 to 15 per cent, but if we take 6 per cent, that means that there are 150,000 innocent people today in American prisons and jails, and that nearly three million of the United States' forty-eight million ostensible felons are innocent; three million convicted felons who are innocent, the population of Montreal. At the end of his piece, the judge proposes the involvement of judges in the plea-bargain process, which he admits is "not a panacea," but which he puts forth as a palliative to the "shame of sending innocent people to prison." The mountain of corruption and hypocrisy gives birth to a mouse of reform.

The judge does not refer to any other infamous aspects of this terribly corrupt and abusive system (which were described in this piece originally, but are omitted as they have been described elsewhere in this book already). This happened to me, but my assets are largely in Canada and the United Kingdom, I am not an American citizen or resident, and those countries refused to hear of any such Star Chamber asset-freeze proceeding, though attempts were made to achieve them, through misinterpretations of the mutual legal assistance treaties with those countries.

A friend of mine who is a nationally recognized authority on the vagaries of the American criminal justice system wrote of the Rakoff piece: "Would that Rakoff would go one step farther and conclude his piece with a paragraph like this: 'And so, with the interests of true justice in mind, I announce that henceforth I will not play this game that is characterized by coerced testimony (*cooperation*) that is of dubious credibility. I will not take prosecutors' sentencing recommendations. I will dismiss indictments that are brought in order to bring pressure on an individual to cooperate by giving testimony pleasing to the government, or to punish said individual for refusing to cooperate, and I will state, in written opinions, my reasons for dismissing those indictments. Since I consider the entire system described in my *NYRoB* article to be unconstitutional as well as immoral and unethical, I will simply bow out of the game and allow the appellate courts, whose members know full well what I have written is true, to reverse me if they want to see a corrupt game continue.'"

It is astounding and depressing that there is little public outrage and media exposure of this awful blight on America. Last week, as on

every election night, we got winning and losing candidates of both parties and every state repeating the same tired pieties about "the greatest country in human history" (which in some respects may be true
but is not beyond debate). Above all, I lament the negligent absence
of the collectively narcissistic Supreme Court with its large staffs and
extended vacations, the ultimate guardians of the Constitution. I regret
to advise my American friends that, to well-disposed outsiders, this
atrophied mockery of a justice system is, next to the scale and vigour
of the country as a whole, the principal evidence of the much-touted
American exceptionalism. This is the original "land of the free"; but
when Americans finally awaken, it will be in a country whose legal system is more like North Korea's than that of the America they thought
they knew.

# EUROPE

## CENTURIES IN THE MAKING

*National Post*, November 7, 2009

Twenty years ago, like scores of millions of others, I watched in delight as the Berlin Wall, the "anti-fascist defence barrier" as it was officially called, came down. A huge crowd stood in front of the Brandenburg Gate, waving the flag of the Federal Republic and singing the current words of the country's stirring national anthem, composed by Haydn. This piece is still better known outside Germany as "Deutschland über Alles," but now extols peace, unity, and freedom.

It was a rare, seismic event, and it produced a kaleidoscopic variety of perspectives on Germany, Europe, and the whole world. For Germany, it was clear that the imposture of the Democratic Republic (East Germany), an artificial creation of Stalin's Red Army in 1945, was over. It was like watching a fly after a blast of insecticide, buzzing furiously about, in denial that it was about to drop down dead.

I remembered the aftermath of the popular unrest in 1948 and 1953, of East German dictator Walter Ulbricht's assertion that the "state had lost confidence in the people," prompting disillusioned communist writer Bertolt Brecht to ask if the regime intended to choose another population to misrule.

Like all who lived through the Cold War, I saw the steady departure of huge numbers of East Germans to the West, through Berlin, and Khrushchev's construction of the wall in 1962, the first "national" physical enclosure to keep a population in rather than invaders out. And I watched the agony of fugitives being murdered by the East German police as they tried to cross over the wall, and the immense demonstrations on the western side, with swaying masses locking arms and singing the mournful and moving German dirge "Once I Had a Comrade."

What the Americans had mockingly called "the Pankow regime" had been backed into announcing the opening of the wall. Ulbricht's successor, the equally leaden Erich Honecker, when sacked by his central committee as the state crumbled, dutifully voted for his own dismissal and censure to preserve unity. His successor, Egon Krenz, bustled purposefully around, explaining how much East Germany had to teach West Germany: "In [East Germany], we don't have to take our car keys out of the ignition when we park our cars."

All Germans were aware of the ability of totalitarian police to discourage street crime, and also of the limitations of East Germany's absurd little plywood, 40-mph national car, the Trabant. (When they strayed unsuspectingly out onto the Federal Republic's unlimited-speed autobahns, the Trabants were regularly run down, and over, by the mighty Porsches and Mercedes and BMWs of the west.)

The only becoming face of East Germany was that of the graceful and beautiful figure-skating champion Katarina Witt, the poster girl of the Communist government, who often concluded her performances by reclining on the ice, on her side, an allegory of female allure. She was much indulged by the regime, but carefully monitored, with officials listening pruriently to bugged recordings of the highlights of her allegedly energetic but quite conventional sex life.

In the only place where heavily armed Soviet and American soldiers had faced each other in the Cold War, at the world famous Berlin checkpoints, there was now an immense flow of traffic, and thousands of people tearing down the wall, as U.S. leaders from John F. Kennedy to Ronald Reagan long had demanded. Now its relics could join the other nearby alluvia of previous German states, like the rings of a tree: Frederick the Great's Brandenburg Gate; Bismarck's Reichstag; the pretentious Hohenzollern Lutheran cathedral, with implausibly heroic tombs of deceased infant princes; a few stark, Teutonic, Albert Speer exemplars of Hitler's pre-nascent Germania (the Führerbunker remains, sealed, the subject of intense controversy); and Stalin's grotesquely large socialist-realist Soviet embassy.

All these heirlooms of Germany's unsuccessful search for responsible government are jumbled together in half a square mile, and they would be joined by the magnificent monuments of a reunited Germany: the brilliantly restored (by British architect Norman Foster) Reichstag; the immense but benign, white Chancellery; and, soon, the restored schloss of the Wilhelmine emperors.

These chronological layers of Germany's terribly disturbed history express the truisms that Germany was too late unified (centuries after France, Britain, and Russia), had always been ambiguous about whether it was an eastern- or western-facing country, and could not assure its own security without destabilizing its neighbours.

Twenty years ago, communism itself was crumbling along with these deep-seated German political neuroses. Part of the Hungarian border was opened. Romania's Ceaușescu was publicly booed, fled his palace in a helicopter, and was hunted down by his former collaborators; he and his wife were finally executed by one of history's largest firing squads, so eager and numerous were the volunteers for it.

In Prague, students conducted large sit-ins and occupations of the universities and public places, and read out some of the most lapidary works of Jefferson and Lincoln. Poland was already under martial law and committed to elections that were sure to send the communists packing (these being the elections Stalin had promised at Yalta forty-four years before). Soon, Poland would join NATO and the European Economic Community, finally fulfilling the decision of Britain, France, and Canada to go to war to defend Poland when it was attacked by Hitler and Stalin in 1939.

The eastern border of the Western World would not be a German border. Germany would be encased in the West. The Cold War, and in a sense the Second World War, would end in a mighty and bloodless triumph of democracy, and, more or less, market economics.

I lived in Britain then, and though not a Euro-federalist, I did not doubt the sincerity of German chancellor Helmut Kohl's formulation "A European Germany and not a German Europe." After forty years of professing to seek the reunification of Germany, the British and French governments (led by Margaret Thatcher and François Mitterrand) fell to lobbying Soviet president Mikhail Gorbachev not to allow it to happen. But it was soon clear that Gorbachev was powerless to stop it, and the United States, unlike the United Kingdom and France, had no fear of a united Germany. President Bush (senior) and his agile secretary of state, James Baker, worked skillfully with Chancellor Kohl, and turned the Open Skies meeting at Ottawa into a German reunification meeting.

All this was easily foreseeable, even inevitable, twenty years ago. What was not so clear was that the Soviet Union would itself disintegrate, and that the emergent era of one overwhelmingly powerful country in the world would be such a fragile vacuum.

The spirit of reconciliation and relief that rippled out from the Brandenburg Gate uplifted the world. I assumed that the United States, at the supreme coruscation of its history, would have a long, successful, and benign eminence in the world. In these twenty years, it has come close to fumbling, but has not forfeited, its status, unique in the world since the Roman Empire. It will presumably recover its balance, if not its dominance. America was there when civilization needed it, and when only America could lead. Twenty years ago, almost the whole world was grateful to America.

The world turns, but it should not forget.

# ROYAL WEDDING A REMINDER OF WHY THE MONARCHY REMAINS USEFUL

*National Post*, April 23, 2011

---

Since the wedding of Prince William and Kate Middleton is the first first-time wedding in nearly thirty years of a British royal who has a serious prospect of being the monarch, and only the fourth in the last century, it is natural that it would generate some interest. There seems to have been some sniggering that the couple are unexciting, and even a few assumptions of loftiness that the bride is not in *Debrett's* (the almanac of British peerage, baronetage, and knightage). I cannot claim to have yet seen the antiquarian word *morganatic* fetched out and plunked down like a Victorian antimacassar, but I think the betting is only even that we will get through to the nuptials without it, and am prepared to fear the worst.

There has naturally been a slight deflation of expectations because of the marital difficulties that have afflicted three of Queen Elizabeth's children. But those problems should be seen not as an erosion of the seriousness of marriage vows in that family but rather of the relatively recent impossibility of relying on their royal status to assure that even the most frightful infidelities would not lead to the breakup of the marriage. If the same criteria had applied in bygone days, many marriages in that family would have come completely unstuck, including, most notoriously, Charles II, George IV (whose marriage did effectively collapse very publicly), and Edward VII, as well as some others whom it would be indiscreet to mention.

Viewed from this perspective, the British royal family could be said to be becoming more firmly principled, rather than more cavalier, about the institution of marriage. If Princess Diana had been prepared to be treated like Princess and Queen Alexandra and remain uncomplainingly with her children while her husband careened about London society like a rutting panther as Edward VII did, her marriage would have survived. (Edward VII even made a joke of it by filling the royal box at his coronation with his principal dalliances, including Winston Churchill's mother. The royal box was renamed "the loose box" for the occasion.) In fact, horrible though it was, the death of Diana was the watershed that marked the beginning of the *revival* of the monarchy from one of its periodic dips.

Diana had been running a parallel monarchy: she declined, unlike Queen Alexandra, to be a silent and indulgent pretty face and girlish figure while her husband ran an open-plan marriage. The media were thoroughly manipulated by Diana as she leaked damaging information to selected reporters, while the more irresponsible sections of the press hacked the Prince of Wales's cell phone and even recorded his ill-considered descent into scatology in conversation with his later wife, the Duchess of Cornwall. ("Tampax Britannica" was the headline in the *Spectator* magazine – which my associates and I owned at the time – after he compared himself to a tampon.) The marriage disintegrated before the titillated and prurient eyes of the nation and the world.

No one knows what goes on in someone else's marriage, but Diana had no difficulty establishing herself as the wronged party and the popular favourite; and the Palace, unaccustomed to being on its back foot, looked like a superannuated heavyweight blinking in disbelief at the blows being rained on it by an agile underdog opponent.

When Diana died, the Royal Family remained in Scotland, and, as was then the custom when the Queen was not resident in London, there was no flag over Buckingham Palace to lower. The prime minister, Tony Blair, advised the Queen emotions were unprecedentedly profound and visible in London and she had to become more involved. The *Daily Mirror* bannered on its front page: "Show Us You Care, Ma'am."

The Queen returned to London, the royal standard was raised to half-staff, and she decreed a ceremonial funeral at Westminster Abbey. She spoke to the nation briefly but eloquently on television and radio on the eve of the funeral, and expressed her sorrow "as a grandmother and as your queen."

The seventy-six-year-old Prince Philip walked with the Prince of Wales and the princess's sons and brother behind the caisson bearing her casket; the ninety-seven-year-old Queen Mother stumped majestically up the aisle, and the House of Windsor paid its respects with immense dignity and moved into a new era.

The following is a retroactive note from 2016: The media got off Prince Charles's back, the Queen Mother passed on, and the Queen soldiered through her fiftieth and sixtieth anniversaries as monarch, and closes in on Queen Victoria's record of almost sixty-four years, the mother of the nation at last.

She is not always the most imaginative or evidently vivacious sovereign, but she is intelligent and dutiful, and has never offended or embarrassed her subjects these sixty-one years, not once, a performance of astounding virtuosity.

There is not a twitch, whisper, or wisp of republican sentiment in Britain today. Everyone knows that Britain can't unite the roles of chief of state and head of government in the same person, as France and the United States do.

Surely it is a good thing that Prince William's fiancée, Kate Middleton, is a solid member of the prosperous, hard-working, reasonably educated middle class, the backbone of Britain and of all advanced societies. As the Queen has cut the budgets and perquisites of some of the lesser royals in response to political complaints these past decades, it has been sad to see them, untrained for anything but a ceremonious role, scrambling for income, with mixed results. Princess Michael of Kent, though much criticized, has been imaginative and rather successful as an author and art dealer, where the Duchess of York did well with Weight Watchers but was so starved for money she made some other, more unfortunate, commercial decisions.

Nor should there be lamentations that this attractive young couple is not flamboyant enough. One of the secrets of the comparative success of the British monarchy is that since William IV (1830–1837) it has been a bourgeois monarchy, that though it lives in palaces and travels in elongated Rolls-Royces, it also clearly has middle-class tastes in decor, behaviour, and interests – such as dogs, and even bawdry jokes. They work hard and always identify very emphatically and doubtless sincerely with average people.

George IV had style, as he showed at the Brighton Pavilion, and as did his friend Beau Brummell, but he almost bankrupted the royal family and aggravated his father's porphyria. Edward VII had great style (he invented the dinner jacket on his tour of India) and made Biarritz so popular a summer resort that even the Czar and Bismarck came there; and he was a popular and successful king. But that was because he was unusually talented. Edward VIII had style but was erratic and headstrong and only lasted a few months before being forced out. George V and George VI were very plain men, but popular and diligent kings. When accused of being a "boring alien" (meaning German), George V replied, "I may be boring but I'll be damned if I am an alien."

Prince William and Kate Middleton look like competent, pleasant young people, with whom most people can relate; they have no affectations or delusions and show no sign of being prone to the sort of ponderous comments of the Prince of Wales that have so delighted satirists and anti-monarchists. These arise almost inevitably from some of his architectural and environmental crusades and his championship of exotic religions, and obscure the Prince's undoubted achievements in helping young offenders relaunch their lives, and other good works. The British always carry off royal spectacles well and there is no reason not to watch and enjoy this one.

For Canada, the royal connection is becoming gradually more tenuous. The concept of a non-residential monarchy for a serious country was always going to become a difficult one. Canada is a G7 country, and having a chief of state who is only here for a couple of weeks every two or three years creates problems. And the stand-in, a governor general, is bearer of a traditionally colonial title. I have long advocated an update to such arrangements.

Great Britain is a strong historic association and a close ally, and I think the most promising multinational arrangements we could make are with an upper tier of the Commonwealth: the United Kingdom, Australia, New Zealand, India, and Singapore. The wheels have come off the European Union and the American economy, as the world's leading bond house (PIMCO) shorts U.S. treasuries. Canada should not become cozier with the United States until that country recovers its talents at self-government, and should associate with more reliable, yet kindred countries.

In such an international context as this, the monarchy could play a role, such as providing a co-chief of state in the senior Commonwealth countries apart from Britain, to serve alongside a domestically chosen associate head of state. Canada could thus have the British monarch and head of the Commonwealth as co-chief of state, operating with a president/governor general, who could tacitly represent the republicans in the country. The monarch, apart from representing the admirable tradition of the British (and Canadian) Crown, would also be a valuable link in an international organization that would be largely united by the English language, the common law, democratic traditions, and much history.

It is premature to discard the monarchy for the sake of becoming just another republic with a ceremonious head of state like Germany or Italy, where the presidents are just stand-ins for deposed dynasties. And adapting to the American or French model of a president who is chief of state and also head of government would be a drastic change to Canada's system, for which there does not seem to be any need or mandate. While we await some imaginative thinking about our institutions, William and Kate, like any newlyweds, deserve the goodwill of all.

# ITALY SENDS IN THE CLOWNS

*National Post*, March 2, 2013

I n the incomprehensible stock market flutter that followed the result of the Italian elections, the singular service that France and Italy have paid the world by their political initiatives in the last year seem to have gone unrecognized.

Canadians tend to take politics seriously, and up to a point so do British and Americans. In all but the most gripping circumstances, such as the First World War, the French know better, and the Italians threw in that towel after the reign of Constantine I (AD 306–337), if not before. And so it is to France and Italy that we must turn our weary eyes, thirsty for entertainment from our public men and women.

Italy's election last weekend produced a refreshingly preposterous result. The slightly left-of-centre Democrats and their allies came first with just under 30 per cent of the vote, and thus get a majority in the lower house under Italian electoral rules, followed within half a point by the coalition led by the utterly ineffable Silvio Berlusconi, the wealthiest and most outrageous figure ever elected to lead a large democratic country, less than two years after being turfed out more or less in disgrace. He managed this by using his dominance over private-sector television to tout himself ad nauseam, and capped it with the delivery to every household in the country of a rebate of its property tax, a grandiose electoral gambit that in most advanced countries would have infringed campaign financing rules.

But the star of the piece is the third candidate, comedian Beppe Grillo, a hirsute gadfly who polled 25.5 per cent of the vote at the head of his Five Star Movement, the country's largest single party. He has a genuinely heroic CV as a crusader against corruption in Italian affairs. It is twenty-five years since he helped drive out socialist prime minister Bettino Craxi for corruption, causing him to flee to Tunisia, where he could not be extradited. In 2007, he famously said on his television program that the most crime-ridden district of Naples, Scampia, which has the highest crime rate of any urban district in the European Union, had a lower crime rate than the Parliament of Italy. He has used the internet and his widely read blog to mobilize his followers.

With his commendable crusade for cleaner government there goes a taste for bombast and salacity that strains toleration, even in Italy. He had to pay a substantial libel award in 2003 to Rita Levi-Montalcini, a ninety-four-year-old senator and winner of the Nobel Prize for physiology and medicine, whom he had described on his television program as an "old whore." In 1980, he was found guilty of manslaughter for being criminally negligent in causing a car accident that killed three people. In the 1990s, he was regularly banned from television, and finally banned completely for some years, but when he finally returned to the airwaves after one lapse, in 1993, he attracted about 40 per cent of the entire population above the age of twelve.

In September 2007, he organized, by blog, a "V-Day celebration." The V stands for *vaffanculo*, Italian for f\*\*\* off. More than two million Italians participated in this rally, though Italy is no more given to this level of coarse language than the main English-speaking countries are.

While Grillo is an endearing character and is apparently sincere, Five Stars does not seem to go much further than rail against corruption and espouse environmental causes. But between the Democratic leader, Pier Luigi Bersani, Berlusconi, and Grillo, as the Senate is severely splintered between those and other parties, they have created an apparently intractable parliamentary farce: vanished, with the illusion that Italy was ready to sign on to the professorial tutelage of the desiccated and apolitical Mario Monti, is the delusion of public support for an austerity program.

France, unlike Italy, is an intermittently politically serious country. And unlike Italians, the French do take themselves quite seriously.
Last year, in response to the antics of the hyperactive Nicolas Sarkozy,
the French did something almost Italian in its perversity, and elected
François Hollande as president. He is a man from a small town, short,
dumpy, with no uplifting qualities, whose career has essentially been a
creeping advance within the cadres of the French Socialist Party.

Six years ago, he was abruptly side-swiped as party nominee by
his long-time unmarried companion and mother of his four children,
Ségolène Royal, who put up a peppy campaign in mini-dresses and
exiguous trousers and tops, but had no grasp of the issues. However, she
benefited from French gallantry in avoiding a severe defeat by Sarkozy.
(Mr. Hollande and Ms. Royal have parted company.)

As the last election approached, Hollande was assisted by the lawless prosecutors of America, who spuriously threw the leading Socialist
contender and head of the International Monetary Fund, Dominique
Strauss-Kahn, into the teeming cesspool of the Rikers Island criminal
detention centre on the complaint of a chamber maid in his New York
hotel (who is eight inches taller than he is). The charges were dropped
after the normally terminally rabid prosecutors realized that the complainant might be an "unreliable witness," but Strauss-Kahn paid her
$6 million to be rid of her civil suit, a pretty good turn for that kind
of work. (Strauss-Kahn may be back; consider that socialist icon and
former president François Mitterrand came back from simultaneously
aiding the communists and the Nazis during the Occupation and from
a faked assassination attempt.)

In office, Hollande has been dogged by relentlessly rising unemployment (10.5 per cent). His tax increases and rhetorical attacks on the
wealthy and effusions on behalf of France's Marxist labour movement
have produced €25 billion monthly capital departures. Actor Gérard
Depardieu, saying that he had paid €189 million of income tax to the
French government in his career, though officially reviled as "a drunken,
incontinent windbag," was widely approved for seeking Belgian and
Russian citizenship, and on acceptance by Moscow he praised Vladimir
Putin's "great democracy."

Hollande is so clumsy, he even managed to unite all sides against him on the gay marriage issue. He backpedalled on complete marital liberty under pressure from France's beleaguered Catholic community after Paris's cardinal archbishop pitched his opposition to gay marriage on the rights of children. The cardinal whistled up a demonstration of a third of a million people in protest, a respectable-sized mob even in Paris, and Hollande then climbed down and left it as a matter of conscience to the municipal mayors who perform civil marriages. But then he resurrected his initial bill when the gay, lesbian, bisexual, and transsexual alliance came snorting out to assert itself. The president enjoyed a slight rise when he sent a brigade of three thousand men to liberate Timbuktu from terrorists, but *beau geste* military derring-do are rarely durable poll-lifters.

France elected a bonze to the great monarchical office created by Charles de Gaulle (for himself), as a gesture of perversity, and Italy has given the balance of power to a "clown prince" as a protest. Neither step will accomplish much that is useful, but they should remind us that, in all our sobriety and earnest, Canadians have much to be thankful for, and could lighten up a little.

# A HISTORIC SETTLEMENT FOR A LONG-BLOODIED UKRAINE

*National Review Online*, February 21, 2014

---

Ukraine has never been a homogeneous country; it was born of an uneasy congeries of Mongols, Lithuanians, and Poles in the fourteenth century, which eventually led to the pre-eminence of the Poles. In the seventeenth century, most Ukrainians turned to Moscow for assistance, and after the partitions of Poland between the Prussians, Austrian Empire, and Russia, what is now Ukraine was divided in 1795 between Austria and, mainly, Russia. After the First World War and the Bolshevik Revolution, there were civil wars in Ukraine, in Russia, and a war between an independent Ukraine, generally recognized in the West, and the emergent Soviet Union. Ukraine was crushed by the Red Army, and for good measure Stalin engaged in mass repressions of Ukrainian culture and intellectuals, and millions of Ukrainian small farmers were starved to death in the infamous Holodomor, the slaughter of the kulaks, in the 1930s. It was not surprising that many Ukrainians warmly welcomed the German invasion of 1941, until they got a clear view of the Gestapo in action.

No European country has had a more tragic history. Following the murder of 10 per cent of the population in the 1930s, approximately a fifth of the survivors, about seven million people, perished in the Second World War, including the massacre under Nazi occupiers of perhaps 90 per cent of the Jews (who in the late 1920s had comprised 37 per cent of the population of Odessa and 27 per cent of the population of Kyiv, and are not 2 per cent of the population of those cities today).

At the Tehran Conference of 1943, Churchill, Roosevelt, and Stalin agreed that Soviet – i.e., Ukrainian – borders would be moved two hundred miles to the west as a reward for the U.S.S.R.'s twenty million deaths at the hands of the Nazi invaders. (As between the Big Three, the Soviet Union took over 90 per cent of the casualties in subduing the Nazis.) As the Red Army was going to occupy the territory anyway, the Western Allied leaders overlooked the fact that the war only began with the Nazi–Soviet Pact of 1939, which partitioned Poland. Western leaders deftly plucked France, Italy, over 80 per cent of Germany, as well as Japan, as occupied territory to be transformed by enlightened administration into flourishing democratic allies of the West in every case, while Stalin squatted improvidently and temporarily in Eastern Europe. Poland was compensated for the loss of two hundred miles off its eastern border with a two-hundred-mile western move of its western frontier at the expense of the Germans, eight to twelve million of whom moved westward into the comparative civility of occupation by General Eisenhower's Western Allied armies to escape the joys of Stalinist custody.

Crimea, the former Khanate of the Mongols, was transferred to Ukraine only in 1954. It naturally rankles with the Russians today that Moscow has to rent naval bases from Ukraine in the Crimea to dock its Black Sea fleet. And Ukraine, though it has a population of forty-six million (down from fifty-two million in 1994, due to emigration and a falling life expectancy because of intense pollution, poor diet, heavy smoking, pandemic alcoholism, and inadequate medical care), is in all respects a fragile state.

All of European history since Augustan times two millennia ago has been a demarcation of Western and non-Western influences, a line that fell along the Rhine and the Danube then and generally remained there for fifteen centuries. When pre-Reformation Christianity prevailed, the

Turks were unable to seize Vienna or gain control of the Mediterranean, while the always-divided Germans were until relatively recently unsure whether they were an eastern- or western-facing people.

Germany joined the West under the sponsorship of the post–Second World War American occupiers, who, unlike the British, French, and Russians, were not afraid of a united Germany. They brought Germany into NATO as a respected ally, and enabled reunification as part of the American-led victory in the Cold War. The envelopment of Germany in the West was reinforced by the admission of Poland to NATO and the European Union, where it has been successful and has enjoyed the happiest years in its long and very disturbed history.

Thus did the eastern border of the Western world arrive at the western edge of Ukraine, independent since the disintegration of the Soviet Union in 1991, a status Moscow has never really accepted. About one-third of the people in western Ukraine work or have relatives in the West. About 78 per cent of Ukrainians are ethnic Ukrainians, to 17 per cent Russians. About two-thirds of the people speak principally Ukrainian, to about 30 per cent who speak Russian; 75 per cent of Ukrainians claim to believe in God, 22 per cent are declared atheists, and of the believers just under 40 per cent are practising Christians, 71 per cent in various branches of Eastern Orthodoxy and 17 per cent as Roman Catholics. Ukraine has never really had a day of what anyone in the West would call good government. (But the same is not true of Ukrainian immigrants to Canada. With 1.2 million people of Ukrainian ancestry, we have the third largest Ukrainian-originated population in the world after Ukraine itself and Russia.)

Almost every country that is not culturally and politically in the West has a continuous tension in its own population between nativists and Western emulators, most markedly in Russia but also in such important countries as Turkey and India. Vladimir Putin is playing the Tolstoyan, Solzhenitsyn, nativist anti-Western card in Russia, railing against the West and pretending that Mother Russia was not shorn of its arms and legs and more than half its population at the demise of the communist dictatorship he served.

Viktor Yanukovych, the pro-Russian president of the Ukraine, won election four years ago only because the leader thrown up by the democratic Orange Revolution, Viktor Yushchenko, split the vote and narrowly denied victory to the glamorous former prime minister Yulia Tymoshenko, whom Yanukovych put in prison (where she has remained despite widespread protest and a serious illness) as he has raped the democratic constitution. (Yanukovych was no Eagle Scout in his youth, having been convicted of theft and vandalism, though in a profoundly suspect justice system.)

Having negotiated a treaty of close cooperation with the European Union, whose prosperity and freedom are much more attractive to most Ukrainians than the Russian alternative, Yanukovych, under pressure from Putin, executed a 180-degree turn. Putin (whose popularity at the Sochi Olympics was clearly not very heartfelt, despite his undoubted success in bringing the games off with great showmanship and in perfect security, albeit with profligate extravagance) has backed Yanukovych. Most Ukrainians clearly oppose their government, now reduced to firing grenades and machine-gunning demonstrators, killing more than fifty of them in Kyiv on Thursday alone.

Stephen Harper and President Obama were right to condemn Yanukovych and threaten sanctions, ahead of Europe. Germany, now Europe's pre-eminent power again, is the key. Chancellor Angela Merkel has led Europe into a sanctions policy and has warned Putin – who finally retreated on Friday after the Ukrainian parliament censured Yanukovych, and the military command, as generally happens, refused to fire live ammunition at civilians representing a popular majority. At time of writing, Yanukovych has pledged early elections, a new constitution not redacted by himself, release of Ms. Tymoshenko, and a transitional coalition government.

This will be a great victory for the West if it supports an independent Ukraine against almost certain agitation from Putin. And altruistic Germany can prevail peacefully over Putin's gangster regime in truncated Russia. It will be a victory of Western principles over the fatuous urge to appeasement of the professional Europeans, exemplified by former Italian premier Romano Prodi, who last week in the *New York Times*, blamed much of the violence on extremists among the protesters, credited Yanukovych with having, for a time, been an exemplar of "democracy at its best," and urged discussions with Putin to "restart . . . integrating the Ukraine into the rest of Europe," as if that were not precisely what Putin was determined to prevent.

There are four possible outcomes. In the first, Ukraine is defended in its post-Crimean borders by the West and takes the Merkel deal. In reality, this won't happen, because no one in the West except the Poles (with distant cheerleading from Canada) has the stomach for such a thing, and heavier influences will be necessary to face down Putin, palsied though Russia is, despite its president's Mussolini-like strutting and posturing. The second possibility is what was called during the Cold War "Finlandization," in which Ukraine is neutral but does nothing to offend Russia and contains ethnic Russian "autonomous zones" used by the Kremlin to represent its interests within Ukraine. This appears to be Putin's current objective, and the weaklings who mainly lead the West now could set it up for him, while pretending to do better for the Ukrainian nationalists.

Third is a de facto partition of the country, in which the Russian areas secede and join Russia and the continuing Ukraine is made less ambiguous politically. It could then join the West, having adopted a consensus to behave fiscally and politically like a serious country, something it has never managed before, in distant or recent history. The West should be pulling itself together for the achievement of this objective, which is distinctly attainable.

Last is the nightmare scenario that Putin would execute if he could: the reconquest and reabsorption of all of Ukraine into Russia. There can be little doubt that this is Putin's long-term objective, but he is pursuing it in two or more bites, because an outright Russian invasion of the whole of Ukraine would lead to a terrible guerrilla war and provoke even helpless flounderers like Obama, Hollande, Cameron, and the Italian leaders (whoever they may be) into doing something that would be a serious inconvenience to Putin. It could even elicit a response from China, which is not so comatose as the West has become.

It is a choice between options two and three; experience would indicate two but inextinguishable desire screams for three. In the circumstances, no sensible person can fail to fear the worst, and to wonder again how the West got to this pitiful point less than twenty-five years after we won the Cold War.

The Ukrainian drama is an important part of a much greater contest. The West must always resist oppression and must now embrace and assist its friends in Ukraine, not only from compassion for them but to bring closer the adherence of Holy Mother Russia to the West and to stretch the West from the Americas across the Eurasian land mass to the Far East and Australasia.

Nothing less is at stake. And led by Germany for the first time as Europe's greatest power on the progressive side of international affairs, the West, however unstable the present compromise in Ukraine, will have won a great humanitarian victory in the carnage of the streets of Kyiv, if it doesn't fumble it all away through irresolution.

# VIVE LA FRANCE!

*National Review Online*, January 13, 2015

long ago predicted in this space that France will show the way to the appropriate response to Arab extremism. It is not the least irony that this should happen under the most improbable person to lead the French state in its history, not excluding the ill-favoured trio of Charles (II) the Bald, Charles the Fat, and Charles the Simple (the latter two both known as Charles III). President François Hollande has never held a serious job, only an executive position in the French Socialist Party and an aldermanic post in a town of about three thousand. When his unmarried companion and mother of their four children, Ségolène Royal, ran ahead of him in a presidential nomination race in 2007, their relationship ended, and he succeeded her as Socialist presidential candidate and was elected in 2012.

M. le Président's succeeding companion departed the Élysée Palace in high dudgeon when it came to light that His Excellency had his official driver convey him, helmeted, on a motor scooter to the abode of his current companion-in-chief. Mlle. Royal currently serves in the cabinet of the prime minister. These matters may not be strictly relevant to the incumbent president's aptitudes as a statesman, but they indicate the farcical nature of this regime, which has conducted *la douce France*, a naturally very rich country, to negative economic growth, with absurd socialistic measures incentivizing idleness and punishing initiative and success. The French are among the world's most intellectually accomplished peoples, and among its most avaricious, and this phenomenon of a petit bourgeois redistributionist at the head of such a country must be seen as further evidence of the perversity of the French and of their tendency for *le choc*, the absurd, or whatever will startle convention. (Hollande would not have been nominated to the presidency if the New York prosecutor Cyrus Vance Jr. had not bought into a confected charge of sexual assault by an African hotel maid in Manhattan against World Bank president Dominique Strauss-Kahn and had him removed to very rough prison for the fortnight required for the false charge to collapse, wiping out his presidential candidacy also. The consequences of the rogue American prosecutocracy ramify far beyond the United States.)

Few politicians could have been less likely than François Hollande to demonstrate the exactness of de Gaulle's closing comment in his astonishingly eloquent war memoirs: "Aged France, wracked by wars and revolutions and weighed down by history but revived, century after century, by the genius of renewal." And yet it is this very M. Hollande, cloaked in implausibility, unencumbered with any obvious qualification for any position more exalted than that of a rural railway stationmaster, who has, these past months and culminating in the March of Unity in Paris on Sunday, written a new chapter in the greatness of his people.

Where other countries had quailed and waffled, France intervened in Mali and the Ivory Coast, former French colonies, to end terrible bloodletting and deny victory to Muslim extremists. After France had built two aircraft carriers for Russia, Hollande – as a punishment for Russian aggression in Ukraine – withdrew them from sale and is offering them elsewhere. (Canada is the country that should buy at least one of them, given Canadian prime minister Stephen Harper's tough talk about the Middle East and Russian behaviour – the carriers have ice-breaking capability – but Harper seems to be, as the British say, all talk and no trousers.) And when twelve people were murdered in the *Charlie Hebdo* magazine attack, and four more in the hostage-taking at the Paris kosher market, Hollande called the incidents what they were: an assault on freedom of expression and an outright and disgusting act of anti-Semitism. *Charlie Hebdo* is a crass, vulgar, offensive magazine, which sets out to offend everyone and has little wit or style, but has been threatened only, though repeatedly so, by displeased Muslims. Hollande and virtually all of his countrymen avoided the usual Anglo-Saxon pusillanimities about hot buttons and need for concern about the ruffled sensibilities of Muslims. He declared that, above all other characteristics, France was a democracy, that there was no democracy without freedom, that there was no freedom without freedom of speech and expression and a free press, and that anti-Semitism was racial and sectarian hatred that, when violently enacted, was the most vile and intolerable of crimes, whomever the victims. He called for a march of unity on Sunday and invited widespread public participation. There were none of the overworked patriotic pieties of other countries (often including the United States, where few politicians can avoid the well-trodden platitudes of superlative national self-praise). France does not claim to be perfect or superior to other countries (though it believes that in some respects it is), just to have principles embraced by almost everyone in the country, whose violation the republic will not tolerate. It was to be a silent march of unity, refusal to be intimidated, and determination to protect the nation and its highest ideals.

The people came: nearly two million in Paris, and almost as many in other French cities. From the Place de la République to the Place de la Nation, a somewhat ethnically varied route between squares redolent of mass political activity in French history, they walked, led by Hollande and the presidents or prime ministers of the European Union, Gabon, Germany, Great Britain, Hungary, Israel, Italy, Jordan (king and queen), the Palestinian Authority, Spain, Tunisia, Turkey, and Ukraine, and the foreign ministers of Algeria, Egypt, Russia, and the United Arab Emirates. Not all of these countries are overly observant of human liberty, but that is not the issue. The point is opposition to terror, and this was a beginning in forcing many Arab governments to stop trying to suck and blow at the same time: to give lip service to disapproval of terrorism while doing nothing to combat it. The presence of Mahmoud Abbas, Arafat's successor as head of the Palestinian Authority, only five people away from Israeli prime minister Benjamin Netanyahu in the front row of the immense throng, while it is unlikely to indicate a change of heart in the PLO, may presage greater care before trying to incite the murder of Israelis. The chief imam of Paris prominently participated in the march, as did Jewish leaders and many thousands of members of both communities. The board of French imams signed a joint condemnation of violence with the Holy See. France will not tolerate a challenge to the right of the French to enjoyment of their country. It is likely that the government, with broad multipartisan support, will sharply increase security within all cities and infiltration of questionable organizations, while accelerating efforts to integrate Muslims into French life and reduce unemployment and poverty throughout the Muslim community of about 4.7 million people (out of 64 million people in France).

The violent deaths of seventeen people in three days in a great city like Paris, at the hands of Islamist extremists, would not in itself generate such an immense reaction. But the fact that most of them were on the staff of a scurrilous magazine shows that the whole country will rise on the issue of freedom of expression and the unacceptability of suppression of press freedom. The fact that even many questionable elements of the Muslim world have lined up behind the West shows the power of the West to compel more respectful treatment from many of these bedraggled countries that have routinely imagined that the principal Western powers can be cuffed about with impunity and that the niceties of civilized conduct can be observed while giving aid to the most odious terrorists, as Pakistan's hosting of Osama bin Laden while that country received heavy assistance from the United States indicated. The terrorist movements are a terrible nuisance but they do not threaten our entire civilization as Nazi Germany and Soviet communism – fanatical ideologies installed in Great Powers and directed by formidable totalitarian dictators – did.

What the Paris march and the spirit that prompted it may have achieved is to put pressure on the Islamic world to divide between pro- and anti-terrorist states, and on the rest of the world to organize a consensus, which would require the adherence of the Chinese and Russians, to deal with failed states. Afghanistan, Somalia, Sudan, Yemen, Syria, Iraq, Libya, and other countries that could disintegrate must be prevented from becoming breeding grounds and sanctuaries for terrorist organizations. Where it will be very complicated is the case of Saudi Arabia, which, in exchange for untroubled incumbency by the House of Saud, has parcelled out a sizeable proportion of its oil revenues for decades to the Wahhabi sect, which is the chief propagator of the ecclesiastical rationale for Islamist violence. We owe the Saudis, as has been discussed in this space in recent weeks, the reduced oil price which has exposed Vladimir Putin as a penniless mountebank, and they have pushed him out of Ukraine. And the bonanza of the reduced oil price has been a rod on the back of Iran, which is the last stop before the arrival of the Israeli air force in preventing a nuclear-armed theocracy in that country. It is only the self-enfeeblement of Western political leadership that has thrust such power into the improbable but willing hands of the Saudis. Perhaps the Paris march may even start the West's political recovery from the narcoleptic torpor that has made the whole palsied alliance that won the Cold War, in Richard Nixon's chilling but prophetic phrase, "a pitiful helpless giant."

Given what was at stake and how clear the issues and strong the historic relationship with France, the land of Lafayette and the Statue of Liberty, are, the Obama administration will have to explain more credibly than it has why the United States was represented in the march only by its ambassador. The attorney general, Eric Holder, was in Paris; he would have been wholly inadequate, because his office is insufficiently exalted and his exercise of it has been incompetent, but he outranks the ambassador, and he did not attend, though all eleven of the other delegates at the security ministers' conference he was attending managed to join the march. In addition to the long catalogue of its other failings, this administration has a cloth diplomatic ear. The same mentality that packed up the bust of Winston Churchill and gave Queen Elizabeth II an iPod as a state-visit present was represented by the lowest rank of official of any of the fifty countries present at the Paris march. This was much commented on by the French media, on the day of the greatest public statement of solidarity since General de Gaulle walked down the Champs-Élysées in the liberation of Paris on August 26, 1944. The least the French had a right to expect was elemental courtesy from the United States, which has as much to benefit from the goals of the Paris march as any country in the world.

# THE FRENCH FIGHT

*National Review Online*, January 20, 2015

The aftermath of the French terrorist attacks has, so far, confirmed the helpful resolve that was the general French response to the *Charlie Hebdo* and kosher market murders in Paris. The realistic objective after these outrages and the great march was that the national and religious Muslim leaders would be forced to abandon their infuriating collective ambivalence and denounce Islamist violence or, by declining to do so, to effectively condone it. This was the point President George W. Bush tried to make on the evening of September 11, 2001, when he said that the United States would make no distinction between terrorists and regimes that supported terrorism, and that all countries would have to decide whether they supported or opposed the impending American counterattack on terrorism. President Bush did not succeed in producing this Manichaean divide, and most of the Muslim world sank contentedly into pious demurrals from the antics of their belligerent co-religionists, while, within the community of Muslim states, avoiding a breach with Islamist militants and often tacitly commending them on their feisty assault on Islam's ancient sectarian foes.

Most of the senior Muslim officials who attended the Paris march – the king and queen of Jordan, the presidents of Tunisia and the Palestinian Authority, the prime minister of Turkey, and the foreign ministers of Algeria, Egypt, and the United Arab Emirates – have been criticized at home for truckling to the West. This is the root of the problem: the incompetence of the Muslim world west of Malaysia at self-government and the tendency to blame the West for its own failures as mature political societies. This has created a division in technique between the Muslim states that have openly sympathized with the cutting edge of militant Islam and those who have done the necessary to remain officially cordial with the West, although most of the latter were effectively emulating the sleazy ambivalence of the Chinese toward the demented regime in the hermit-despotism of North Korea: Beijing purported to join with Japan and the Western powers in disapproval of the un-house-trained Kimist regime, which could not, in fact, discharge a sidearm without the complicity of the Chinese; and many Muslim regimes mouthed civilities at the West but furtively played footsie with the jihadists.

Any process of inciting better, or at least more consistent, behaviour from the Arab powers would have to allow for the special status of Saudi Arabia, the feudal, misogynistic paymaster of the Wahhabi Islamist extremists, which is also the temporary light of the West for using the reduction in the world oil price it has generated by increasing production to discourage Iran from its nuclear ambitions, to deter Iranian and Russian meddling in Syria, and, by a fortunate accident, to evict Putin from Ukraine. The West had no right to expect its own irresolution to be redeemed by deliverance from so improbable a benefactor, but in our present state of threadbare Western leadership, we must take success where and how we get it. The cross-currents of Middle Eastern ambitions and loyalties are so treacherous and complicated they are almost impossible to plan for durably. But presumably the Saudis will eventually, if they haven't already, circumscribe Wahhabi subversion.

The second post-Paris objective, after forcing the Muslim governments to stop being ambivalent about Islamist terror, is to evoke this problem from the mists of the evasive pretension in the West that all is well with the Muslim world apart from a few unrepresentative psychotics, the inevitable rogues and strays that pop up in such a robust religious culture as Islam. (It was pitiful and distressing to listen to a five-minute official explanation last week of the U.S. administration's reluctance to use the phrase "Islamic extremism." Who do they think

knocked down the World Trade Center – a group of angry shareholder activists? The flipside of this see-no-evil approach was the bunk about hot buttons and sensitive people, implying that insulting Islam or the Prophet invited and made explicable, if it did not justify, the murder of the authors of the disrespectful comments.)

In company with this version of events, Pope Francis's offhand comment, after unequivocally condemning the Paris outrages and sectarian violence generally, that insulting any religion was uncivilized and hazardous was seized upon by Rome's habitual critics as an attempted papal whitewash of the Paris murders. The Vatican reiterated Francis's condemnation of those acts and his support for the anti-ISIS military alliance. No Muslim organization claimed the pope had endorsed violence; it was entirely the figment of the imagination of jumpy or anti-Catholic Westerners.

The French, who were pushed to the forefront of the Western response to Islamist terror by the Paris incidents, have manfully raised the bar for the rest of us. The associate publisher of Le Figaro, with Le Monde one of France's two most influential newspapers, reissued a forceful "Declaration" last week in the splendid tradition of Emile Zola's "J'accuse!" in the Dreyfus case, leaving no doubt of the scope of the contest now well underway. (It had originally been published some years ago.) He wrote, "It is high time that we realized finally that a new religious war has been declared and this time on a planetary scale. Islamists massacre Christians in Egypt, Iraq, Philippines, Indonesia, Pakistan, Nigeria; all over in fact. We have the strong impression that this century is going to see the pitiless unleashing of a renascent Islam, seeking to dominate the world and make Christian civilization pay for the centuries in which it ruled the world. This hatred of Christianity vastly exceeds all problems of faith. Attacking churches, priests, other religious personnel, and the faithful, Islamists wish to destroy Western civilization, democracy, capitalism, what they call 'neo-colonialism,' equality of the sexes, the Rights of Man, all progress as we conceive it. Marx, Lenin, and Stalin have been replaced [as threats to the West], by Allah and the Prophet. Bellicose imams have taken the places of the political commissars. The 21st century will be a war without mercy and the immense Islamized masses of the Third World and our great metropolises could

be more dangerous than the tanks of the Warsaw Pact were. We weep with our usual crocodile tears for the Copts massacred at Alexandria and the Christians assassinated in Baghdad, but we passively sit with folded arms."

The author wrote of the "Belle Époque" of Saddam Hussein, surely the ultimate debunking of the ill-considered war against him (though, like the Warsaw Pact comparison, this is an exaggeration), and he was particularly exercised by a spectacle familiar to all of us: "a useful imbecile who lengthily explained on television that Egyptian Islamists massacred Copts because these Nile Valley Christians were representatives of the West, ambassadors of European culture, living symbols of capitalism, neo-colonialism, the dollar, and Coca-Cola, and thus they had a perfect right to wish to eliminate these surviving relics of a detested past," though the Copts antedated their Muslim oppressors in Egypt. The *Figaro* associate publisher demanded an end to nauseating platitudes about "Islamo–Christian amity . . . and the harmonious cohabitation of our three monotheisms," avoidance of "absurd and sometimes odious references to the most sober hours of our history," and the cessation of "our repentances and cowardices."

It was a magnificent polemical screed in the French manner, and showed again that France alone, of the great European powers, apart from the intermittent attendance of the British, has the instinct of a unitary national state united by principles of liberty and prepared to act like a warrior-people in defence of them. The rest of Western Europe is retarded by Germany's unending guilt and shame and anesthetized by the gelatinous Orwellian monster of the European Commission, where all is homogenized relativism. The current Islamists are not a more serious threat than Soviet and international communism was, not to mention the preceding mortal peril of Nazi Germany, whose hobnailed jackboot was on the throat of Paris itself from 1940 to 1944. Islam is not a totalitarian force (though it aspires to it) and does not govern a Great Power. While the Muslim world is better disposed to and more complicit in these attacks on Christian minorities and the West generally than their spokesmen and most Western governments and commentators admit, it remains a legitimate objective to separate the sane from the murderous Muslims. But the determination to get to the

bottom of this problem, in France and the world, and to use whatever degree of force is necessary for the defence of our civilization and interests, is correct and vastly exceeds anything heard or seen in comparably influential media outlets in the English-speaking countries (except, for special reasons, India).

The United States and Canada are made of sterner stuff, despite the moral paralysis of the Obama administration, reduced last week to recruiting the almost equally diffident British prime minister, David Cameron, to help President Obama plead to Congress not to threaten Iran with re-escalated sanctions; and France, if it remains firm, is strong enough politically to propel the whole European Union forward. In addition to a protocol to prevent failed states from becoming terrorist sanctuaries and training grounds, and the will to enforce the protocol, obviously new counterterrorist techniques will have to be developed. Just killing the leaders with drones, while useful, will not slay this Hydra-headed monster. Massive infiltration will have to be implemented. The collaboration of Algeria, which has a battle-hardened army and has successfully fought a long civil war with Islamist extremists, could be helpful in this.

One dividend of this expanding problem is that the ability of the Israelophobes to keep the Arab powers focused on the Palestinian question is faltering. In the same measure, as the entire West slowly rises to the challenge, the isolation of Israel – as the premier target and doughtiest enemy of the jihadists – declines. While the venom of the Islamist fanatics is heightened against the Jewish state because of the fraudulent claim of geographic usurpation, we of the Judeo-Christian tradition, including the irreligious and the atheists, are increasingly all in this together. It will become less of a free shot for the petty despotisms of Africa voting at the United Nations in lock-step with the Arabs. The spirit of France, added to that of Israel, if contagious, as it should be, can conquer all.

# IT'S TIME TO DESTROY ISIS

*National Review Online*, November 16, 2015

There are a few comparatively bright spots in the otherwise unspeakable horror of the terrorist outrages in Paris. As I wrote here after the *Charlie Hebdo* and Jewish market murders in Paris in January of this year, the French know better than any other democracy how to deal with monstrous assaults on civilization of this kind. Their security prevented the entry of suicide bombers at the premier stadium of France, where the terrorists had clearly hoped to kill and wound thousands of spectators, preferably including the president of France, while on television as all Europe watched a France–Germany football game. President François Hollande, the least impressive and least successful of the six successors to General Charles de Gaulle as president of the Fifth Republic, effortlessly assumed the dignity, eloquence, and inflection of the holder of his great office in these moments of the utmost extremity. Calm, unflinching, in spare, improvised, and perfect fluency, as if his words had been composed by Camus, or by a French Orwell, he described the terrorist incidents, still unfolding, as "an act of war," and declared a state of emergency, closed France's borders, effectively declared martial law in Paris – a metropolitan area of approximately thirteen million and a city that has been for four centuries one of the greatest, most beautiful, civilized, admired, and beloved urban sites in the world.

There was not the slightest hesitation – as there has been in some English-language media, in the United States, the United Kingdom, and Canada – to describe the incident as Islamist terrorism, nor did the French authorities dither with pious insipidity before detaining and interrogating all the families and relatives of the prime suspects, while deploying their air force to plaster the guilty ISIS in its lair in Syria.

Paris and the Paris police know all about violence. There was never in France going to be any ghastly waffling and snivelling about the causes of the discontent of the terrorists. Of the ten cardinal archbishops of Paris between 1781 and 1871, two fled for their lives, four were executed or murdered, and four died naturally in their cardinalitial palace and were mourned with suitable formality in Notre Dame. The Paris mobs overthrew regimes in Paris seven times between 1791 and 1871 and were suppressed many times during the first four republics, two empires, and the last three monarchical dynasties, including a restoration, and without counting the general disorder around the Liberation of 1944, during which the Gaullist victors executed rough justice among their communist and Nazi-collaborationist enemies. The Paris mobs even erected barricades and hurled paving stones at the police in 1962 and 1968. Paris has seen it all before. As General de Gaulle famously said to the International Red Cross when it remonstrated with him about the severity of French techniques in the Algerian War, "Blood dries quickly."

It does in France, but the French, as a people, know, as the major Western democracy with the largest Muslim population and the greatest experience with Islamic countries and with trying to govern them directly and not through suborned satraps as the British generally did, that blood spilled by this form of atrocity can dry only when it is avenged, as the gentle socialist François Hollande, transformed by the affront and by his office, said, "pitilessly." France knows when liberty, equality, and fraternity, like life, liberty, and the pursuit of happiness – which President Obama invoked in his predictably platitudinous, though sympathetic, comments – must give way to savage and counter-terrifying violence. The emergency Hollande has declared in France has already produced a good deal of information about the perpetrators, which presumably induced ISIS to claim the authorship of the crimes, as it was about to be outed anyway.

France will lead the world in the following wholesome understanding: a substantial part of the fundamental texts of Islam is violently hostile to non-Muslims, and to many categories of pallid Muslims also. ISIS is Islamic terrorism, and has no mitigating qualities. It is both evil and incapable and undesiring of coexistence with the West and its values, Judaeo-Christian in origin but of equal application to religious skeptics. It is also irreconcilable with regimes of other kinds, such as India, China, North Korea, and many of the quasi-tribal African countries, but they will eventually figure that out for themselves. Fortunately, France is a powerful enough country to force the world forward in what must be a war of extermination against ISIS; it would galvanize the world, including most of the Muslim world, cowering in equivocations, and could achieve the end of this phase of the struggle with terrorism.

The ghastly, unutterably contemptible quavering about ISIS must end: it is an unmitigated evil with almost no support – perhaps 50,000 active warriors in all Islam, and the usual riff-raff of useful idiots scattered about different countries prepared to become human torpedoes against all forms of civilization, starting with Muslim civilization, such as it now is. ISIS must be physically exterminated, let us be clear, in a just and virtuous act of war: anyone who favours, and becomes an armed agent to carry out, acts of indiscriminate terror, the slaughter of innocents (such as the attractive young couples and decent older people at the restaurants and concert hall in Paris on Friday), unless they believably repent, must be exterminated, and this monstrous moral, theological, and political heresy of an ISIS Caliphate must be crushed into non-existence by the application of whatever level of military force and punitive retribution is required.

The next CNN or MSNBC commentators who inflict upon viewers excessive conditionality about the unambiguous wickedness of this enemy should be relieved of their misspeaking tongues with red-hot tongs, but not on a cell-phone camera for the delectation of the devotees of the antics of ISIS. For my part, I have given up hope that Obama or Kerry is capable of doing anything except dissembling and bloviating and swinging in the wind as issues absolutely vital to the values of our civilization are determined by, in Bismarck's phrase, "blood and iron," in fierce exchanges of fire. Obama and Kerry will be oblivious and fatuously placatory as deadly projectiles ricochet around them. It has become a Buster Keaton film. If Hollande asked Obama for assistance, the U.S. president – who, on television the morning of the Paris massacres, announced the "containment" of ISIS, as if it were a state with borders – would send twenty veterans of the Peace Corps to advise the Paris police on how to deal with grumpy people of another pigmentation.

Just as France must be seen in a historic context to show what a terrible mistake ISIS has made in targeting it, U.S. national security policy must be seen as it has evolved. Franklin D. Roosevelt was a well-travelled and multilingual man and knew that the United States had to be engaged in Western Europe and the Far East to prevent mortal threats from reaching American shores. In January 1941, he warned the nation against those who would, "with sounding brass and tinkling cymbal, preach the 'ism' of appeasement." In his war message of December of that year, following the attack on Pearl Harbor, he promised that, after winning the war just unleashed, "we will make very certain that this form of treachery never again endangers us." The United States eschewed appeasement and deterred direct aggression for fifty years. America's enemies struck upon a method of evading Roosevelt's defences, by launching terrorist attacks from organizations not obviously linked to any government and nurtured in failed states where the ostensible government was not apparently involved. Unfortunately, after the terrorist attacks of September 11, 2001, George W. Bush took it as his mission to establish responsible government in places where it had not existed before, rather than merely punishing the authors of crimes against America and humanity.

Roosevelt's advice was followed until Barack Obama determined that appeasement was a useful antidote to past American wrongdoing, against Iran, Cuba, and the Palestinians, and, very tentatively, at least certain varieties of Muslim terrorists. Administrations between Roosevelt and the senior Bush saw that the whole non-communist world had to be enlisted to prevent the triumph of totalitarian communism directed, initially, from Moscow. Soviet–Chinese divisions were very intelligently and prudently exploited by Richard Nixon and Henry Kissinger, and Ronald Reagan ultimately exposed, in very pacific terms, the inadequacies of the Soviet system, which fell like a soufflé before him.

The pursuit of U.S. foreign policy since – from George H.W. Bush's intelligent but largely unformed New World Order, to Bill Clinton's ad hocery (fairly agile, except for his feeble underresponse to the first terrorist attacks), to George W. Bush's trigger-happy and unwise desire to turn Iraq into the State of Connecticut, to the incumbent's mad effort to apologize for the American national interest and befriend America's mortal enemies – has descended ever more swiftly to the present depths, in which Obama naturally expresses regret that innocent Parisians have been murdered in large numbers, but, apart from invoking Lafayette and normal human sympathy, evinces not the slightest notion of what to do about what his own paralytic moral enfeeblement and overhasty departure from Iraq have encouraged.

One thing that should *not* happen is that the door be slammed even more severely on the masses of poor refugees who are fleeing precisely the terror that has just afflicted the magnificent boulevards of Paris. The Syrian refugees, especially the very large proportion of them who are Christians, are unlikely to be jihadists, and it ill behooves this country, which, with the best of intentions, smashed up much of the Middle East, to accept only a numerically contemptible token of the refugees from its ill-considered policy there. It is unlikely that Hollande has quite the panache to do it, but if he announced the insertion of the core of trained French soldiers in a proposed boots-on-the-ground allied force of 50,000 (i.e., 1,000 times more than the sub-tokenistic addition Obama triumphantly announced a couple of weeks ago) to exterminate ISIS – to kill every member, or every reasonably suspected active and able-bodied member – all serious countries would join. This expedition should be followed by a Turkey–Egypt–Iran–Saudi Arabia Conference, under the co-sponsorship of the traditional Great Powers, to divide Syria and Iraq between them and ensure an autonomous Kurdish state; to put an end to Iranian meddling in Lebanon and Gaza; to recognize a Palestinian state with realistic borders and a right of return to Palestine and not Israel; and to declare a protocol for identification of the criteria of a failed state and for the obligation of international intervention in such states. Since the G20 is meeting now in Turkey, the members should advise their hosts that Turkey will be expelled from the G20 and from NATO if it furnishes so much as one more handgun in assistance to ISIS.

Great things could come from this horrible tragedy in Paris, but only with leadership. No sane person could expect such a response from the incumbents in Washington, but it may not be too late for Paris (especially given that this is the only possible road to re-election for François Hollande).

# INTERNATIONAL AFFAIRS

## MAKE NEW FRIENDS, AND DUMP THE OLD

*Report on Business, Globe and Mail*, February 1987

J oe Clark and Brian Mulroney have received inadequate credit for the coherent and effective management they have given Canada's foreign policy. The syncopated lurchings of the previous fifteen years – with all the ill-considered quixotries of the Third Option, North-South, the Third Track; the embarrassing trucklings to Castro and Manley; the infatuation with Nyerere – have been replaced by a comparatively sensible and consistent policy.

Seldom in contemporary affairs has a statesman had such an uneven record as Pierre Trudeau. The clarity, dexterity, and courage he showed in reconciling French and English Canada were precisely the qualities often missing from his management of our external relations.

Thus, he was gulled almost effortlessly by Soviet bloc propaganda into stating that NATO's neutron warhead, which West Germany and others had requested, was an escalation in military inhumanity; that the shooting down of a Korean airliner, killing 269 people, including nine Canadians, was "an accident," as if the crash were provoked by spontaneous engine failure; and that General Jaruzelski's imposition of martial law in Poland in December 1981 was not "inherently . . . bad" and that "there are circumstances where order has to be imposed."

In fact, Solidarity was only asking for adherence to the Gdansk accord of August 31, 1980, which the Polish government signed and almost ignored. In all of 1981, Solidarity's strikes caused only five hours of lost production, yet Trudeau responded to the Soviet-backed suppression of Solidarity (and of all Poland) with the astonishing hope that "the Polish people would exercise the proper amount of restraint and good judgment."

This was not the tenor of the harangues he delivered from his Mercedes-Benz at the romanticized Duplessis-era strikes of Asbestos and Murdochville.

He added, in what unfortunately became one of the most hackneyed themes of his last years in office, "A lot of us would like to prevent a Third World War." The later Trudeau often pandered almost unreservedly (and to no discernible advantage to himself) to the Soviets' interest, as virtually any criticism of the Soviet Union was deemed to advance the date and certainty of a Third World War.

Three weeks after this press conference (December 18, 1981), the External Affairs Department was dragooned into giving a briefing in support of the prime minister's appeasement interpretation. An unnamed spokesman asserted that the Soviet Union had shown tolerance by not intervening in Poland earlier; that martial law was exclusively a Polish decision and that Moscow exercised only moral suasion on the Polish government (Gerald Ford lost the 1976 presidential election over a less naive comment about Poland); that only ten to fifty people had been killed and five thousand arrested under Polish martial law; and that, occasionally, martial law has to be used.

Trudeau's comments were approvingly cited by the Polish authorities for their own propaganda purposes, a shameful fact that to my knowledge was only reported in this country by the *Globe and Mail* on January 2, 1982.

Trudeau professed to find the American intervention in Grenada, overturning a Cuban-dominated clique of Maurice Bishop's assassins who had placed the entire population of their country under house arrest, "an unjustified use of force." The arrival of the Americans was greeted with universal jubilation by Grenadians and legitimized by subsequent free elections.

Trudeau's principal foreign policy initiative was the Third Option, designed to increase our trade with Western Europe, as opposed to the United States, but unrelenting efforts over eleven years failed to arrest a 50 per cent decline in Canada's trade with Europe. In his final term, Trudeau produced North-South and the Third Track. North-South, in which all the world's less developed countries were grouped together under the rubric "South," was an attempt to institutionalize transfers of money and expertise from the wealthier countries and to overhaul world trade arrangements. Trudeau is generally credited with a superb performance as co-chairman of the Cancun conference, and Bernard Wood's North-South Institute has been a creditable endeavour, but the whole effort was rather far-fetched.

The Third Track was Trudeau's humdrum arms-control plan, based on his United Nations "suffocation" speech, a proposal for the winddown of the nuclear arms race by unverifiable reciprocal agreements on reduced defence research expenditures. The other elements were old wine in new bottles, and the amateurish (though well-intentioned) approach to one of history's most complicated questions, by the leader of a country that could have no possible significant influence on the powers that possessed the weapons under discussion. The timely death of Soviet leader Yuri Andropov enabled Trudeau to visit his concerns upon the geriatric successor, Konstantin Chernenko, at the Kremlin funeral reception (he had attempted to turn Dwight Eisenhower's funeral in 1969 into an opportunity to buttonhole General de Gaulle and discuss Quebec and Canadian federalism). Thus unburdened, Trudeau returned from Moscow and announced his retirement from public life.

Trudeau's knee-jerk reaction to President Reagan's Strategic Defense Initiative (SDI, which was unveiled in March 1983, on the exact evening that Trudeau was entertaining Vice-President Bush) was that it was "destabilizing."

It was never possible, even for the most brilliant and authoritative administration spokesmen, such as assistant defence secretary Richard

Perle, to make the point with Trudeau that what was really destabiliz-ing was Mutual Assured Destruction (MAD), the condition SDI (a non-nuclear and entirely defensive system) was designed to combat, and the condition by which the superpowers reciprocally hold their civilians (and the whole world) hostage to their nuclear arsenals. If technically deployable, SDI would deliver us from the spectres of world nuclear incineration, or a third conventional world war. Even today, perhaps because of its diminutive caucus, the Liberal Party is not long on stra-tegic thinkers.

Thus, in November, in response to Clark's rather magisterial treat-ment of the subject, we heard not only the lobotomous neutralist drivel of the NDP, forever marinating in its own sanctimony: unfortunately we also heard Don Johnston, who would have known better if he had had half an hour to think about it, demanding the abandonment of SDI in exchange for the Soviet concessions at Reykjavik (which SDI had elic-ited), just as his former leader had insisted that SDI never be researched in the first place, when there were no Soviet concessions, or any pros-pect of them.

Joe Clark, in a speech to Parliament on the Reykjavik summit, showed an appreciation of the progress that SDI had made possible toward reposing world security on a firmer and less nerve-racking basis than the Stalin-Dulles era concept of massive retaliation.

Mulroney and Clark have rebuilt relations with the United States (Trudeau never understood why Americans considered Reagan a better president than Jimmy Carter) without making unilateral concessions. They have retained good relations with the Third World without being mesmerized by the sort of charlatans and communist despots whom Trudeau found so beguiling.

Mulroney, with the help of his inspired choice as ambassador to France, Lucien Bouchard, has strengthened relations with the world's French-speaking countries to their highest point in our history. Stephen Lewis's attacks at the United Nations on the Soviet invasion of Afghanistan are an uplifting effort of their type, and probably make up for his clan-gorous tambourine-rattling on behalf of the United Nations. (If only he could now persuade his columnist wife, Michele Landsberg, to moderate her pathologically anti-American ravings in the *Globe and Mail*.)

Apart from some overzealous grandstanding in support of an opportunistic policy in South Africa, and mealy-mouthed posturing over Central America (including a lamentable United Nations vote in November against American policy), the Mulroney government's conduct of foreign policy has been very sensible.

Foreign policy is rarely a determining issue in domestic Canadian politics. If it were, Trudeau would not have remained in office fifteen years, and this government would have been in better standing with the voters through 1986 than the polls indicate it was. Those, especially those on the right, who spend much of their time bemoaning the present government, might do themselves a favour by remembering what the previous regime was like.

# BRITAIN'S
# ATLANTIC OPTION – AND
# AMERICA'S STAKE

*The National Interest*, Spring 1999

Ninety years ago, Lord Curzon – an intellectual grandee and holder of high offices, including viceroy of India and foreign secretary – opined that, without its empire,

> *England from having been the arbiter will sink at best into the inglorious playground of the world. Our antiquities, our natural beauties, our mansion houses and parks will attract a crowd of wandering pilgrims. People will come to see us just as they climbed the Acropolis at Athens or ascend the waters of the Nile. England will become a sort of glorified Belgium.*

This, it has turned out, was unduly pessimistic. While the Empire is all but gone, Britain remains one of the eight or so countries, grouped in the second rank behind the United States, that retain some world role. The United Kingdom's status in the world owes less to its nuclear weapons and permanent seat at the United Nations Security Council than to its prosperity on the edge of Europe, and its central historical and cultural position in the English-speaking world which it founded. In an international political universe of over 190 countries, Britain's status is not an unenviable one, and from this platform of deserved respect it is possible to envision several alternative courses for Britain's future.

At any rate, it should be possible. But the discussion of the British future today evidences almost no hint of open horizons. Instead, the British national imagination is staggering in a sludge of inevitability about a progressively tighter European Union. While there is virtually no enthusiasm in Britain for plunging deeper into such a Union – all the polls show a profound disenchantment with the Brussels bureaucracy, a deep reticence about monetary union, and growing skepticism about the economic implications of a British future in Europe – the general sense is that it will happen anyway.

The Blair government is both a microcosm of this state of affairs and a contributor to it. It has kept Britain away from the euro for the time being, yet its body language suggests grudging accession in a few years – unless, of course, catastrophe overtakes the experiment in the meantime. It is not entirely clear whether the Blair government's reluctance to embrace the Union reflects real doubts about its viability and logic, or about whether entry would best serve Britain's interests, or, again, whether it is merely that political expediency has suggested a slow approach to an accepted end. Whatever the motives, the resulting uncertainty is demoralizing.

Advocates of immediate entry into the European Monetary Union certainly exist in Britain. But while a grandiose vision of a united Europe is the chief argument for Euro-federalism bandied about in continental Europe, in Britain the federalists, apart from a few people in transactional financial businesses, are reduced to a fatalistic advocacy that Britain should be part of a tight European union – one culminating in federation – if only because staying out may be more harmful than going in. The truth is that many in Britain fear isolation and, with it, marginalization. Without an empire, there is a widespread view that the country must associate with some larger group, and Europe appears to most to be the only such group at hand.

What seems to have been forgotten at least until recently is that, unlike any other European country, the United Kingdom has both an

Atlantic and European vocation. Europe and North America are both plausible associations for the British, the latter much superior to the former in many ways. Unfortunately, Britain's North American alternative is underdeveloped in public discourse. It is the main purpose of this essay to unfurl its logic, which, it turns out, is a wholesome one not only for Great Britain, but also for the United States and Canada.

## THE AMBIVALENCE OF BRITAIN

Britain coped with the loss of empire with more dignity than other great imperial powers. But the country is still afflicted by an existential loneliness, dating at least from the Suez fiasco of 1956, and the history of Britain's ambivalent association with the European project reflects that loneliness.

Less than a year after the Suez Crisis, the Treaty of Rome was signed. The final loss of what had become the imperial illusion thus dovetailed almost perfectly with the rise of the European integration project. The four decades that followed were marked by British uncertainty and inconsistency toward Europe. Harold Macmillan, prime minister from 1957 to 1963, tried to combine a special closeness to the United States (affecting to play the sage Greek to Kennedy's Roman) with membership in the Common Market – only to be harshly rejected by de Gaulle, who found such a combination unacceptable and vetoed Britain's Common Market application in 1962. Harold Wilson (1964–1970) was initially Euroskeptical, then cautiously pro-European in his second term (1974–1976), but always ambiguous and evasive. There was nothing ambiguous about the nearly pathologically anti-American Edward Heath (1970–1974), who did his best to deconstruct almost any relationship with the United States. One of nature's corporatists, while advocating a modest common market he strove to promote practically unlimited European supranationalism – but he could bring neither his party nor his countrymen along with him to any appreciable degree.

Margaret Thatcher (1979–1990) rebuilt the American relationship, demonstrated that Britain could influence U.S. policy-making, and showed that Britain retained autonomous moral authority in the world.

Toward Europe she was less consistent. She was one of the instigators of the Single European Act, which required some surrender of sovereignty on the part of the members, and under cabinet pressure took Britain into the Exchange Rate Mechanism, fixing the relationship between members' currencies. Then she declared her implacable opposition to a more supranational Europe. John Major (1990–1997) started out believing Europe could be placated with gestures stopping well short of integration, but discovered otherwise. (The revival of British prosperity began when Britain fell out of the Exchange Rate Mechanism in 1992.)

Tony Blair's ambivalence, already noted, is almost impenetrable and rather illogical, especially for a new leader with an impregnable position in Parliament and the polls. Mr. Blair has said he will pool sovereignty without surrendering it and will be governed by the British national interest in monetary union and other euro questions. This would suggest that choices are available. But to say so outright would not be compatible with the basic argument propounded by British Euro-federalists – with whom Blair and his party are closely associated – that Euro-integration is inexorable and Britain should get in step with the ineluctable forces of history if it wants to exercise any influence in Europe. Blair is right: he not only has a choice, but he will have to make it sooner or later. Unfortunately, like most of his countrymen, he seems to have an impoverished notion of the alternatives.

## TWO POLITICAL CULTURES

During most of the period just outlined, British public interest in the European question was tepid. Certainly, the 1975 referendum on whether to leave or remain in the Common Market produced a burst of furious debate, but for ten to fifteen years after that there was a kind of intellectual demobilization. It was only as the Common Market became the Community, and the Community finally became the Union, that unease grew rapidly at the spectacle of a Britain increasingly isolated and often outvoted eleven to one. That uneasiness grew further when evidence accumulated that Jacques Delors's soothing notions of subsidiarity within the Union – essentially the promise that local matters would still be decided close to their point of origin, by local and not central EU authorities – was simply a scam. Increasingly, polls indicated that the British public was becoming disillusioned with the endless cascade of authoritarian directives from Brussels, which, in the interests of "harmonization," sought to regulate even the most obscure aspects of British life, from the stacking of fruit in supermarkets to seasons for bird-shooting in the northern counties. By now, almost all polls show that 70 per cent of the people oppose any further move into Europe and that a significant minority would be happy to depart Europe politically altogether, while keeping the free-trade arrangements.

The British consistently support the Common Market's free movement of goods and people, and few want to give up such a common-sense advantage. But increasingly there is resentment that it has been encumbered with all sorts of unwanted economic policy costs and dangers. Recently, these dangers have been highlighted by remarks from the new German finance minister and governing party chairman, Oskar Lafontaine, calling for Britain to accept higher tax rates, greater social spending, and an increased EU annual membership fee; and from the German foreign minister, Joschka Fischer, calling for an end to individual country vetoes and a majority voting system in which Britain would be swamped. Even more recently, the revelation by the normally docile EU Court of Auditors that $5 billion annually is squandered by the European Commission in fraudulent or grossly wasteful spending has further shaken the federalists.

The problems transcend economics. The prevailing British view is that British political institutions, which have served the country well for centuries, should not be stripped jurisdictionally to clothe Brussels and Strasbourg, which are unaccountable and authoritarian by Anglo-Saxon standards; that Britain should not go back to the pre-Thatcher European levels of taxation and industrial strife; and that Britain should not slam the door on its relationships with the United States and Canada. These relationships (along with the geographical fact of the English Channel) have been Britain's greatest strategic asset in this century, and the British are understandably reluctant to dismantle them. So for that matter are the Canadians – and so too should be the Americans.

But the logic of the Atlantic connection does not come solely from strategic considerations. It is also grounded in political culture. The French and Germans, for well-known historic reasons, have social safety nets that have effectively become hammocks. Out of fear of the role of discontented mobs in their history, a role that has no real parallel in the history of the English-speaking countries, France and Germany have tax and benefit systems which, at least by Anglo-American standards, subsidize unemployment and destroy the incentive to work. By British and North American standards they have semi-dysfunctional *dirigiste* economies, with excessive levels of taxation and unemployment, largely because they are paying huge quantities of Danegeld to the urban masses and uneconomic small farmers. Their political traditions are corporatist not liberal, arising in the case of France from such illustrious but thoroughly authoritarian figures as Richelieu, Colbert, Napoleon, and de Gaulle.

As for Germany, it is a cliché to say that it was unified too late, had great difficulty determining whether it was an eastern- or western-facing nation, and that whenever it set out to assure its own security it ended up making its neighbours insecure. Clichés aside, while Germany is now well unified in accepted borders, and while the extension of NATO to Poland will have the highly desirable effect that the eastern border of the Western world is not also a German border, that country still projects its own sense of historical loneliness. It is possible, and feared by some, that the German desire for security could cause it to exert pressure on other countries to immerse themselves more completely in Europe than many of their citizens, including a strong current majority of the British, find comfortable.

In sharp contrast to Britain and the United States, none of the largest continental European countries has durably effective political institutions. Those of Germany date from 1949; France's from 1958; Spain's from 1975. The Italians are still trying to reform their constitution. It is understandable that countries so placed might feel that they are not giving up much in institutional terms by moving toward federation. Indeed, some favour federation as a way of bypassing national institutions that have become sclerotic and ineffectual. Most British, for good reason, do not.

The British electorate's instincts against political immersion in Europe are sensible, but to turn away from Europe altogether to embrace Britain's post-imperial solitude is to court Curzon's curse. So both the Major and Blair governments have temporized at a fundamental level, suggesting that Britain can be a political contortionist: "at the heart of Europe," at the side of the United States, and at the head of the Commonwealth, all at the same time. Both Euro-integrationists and ambivalent dissemblers of both major parties imply that Britain can cede sovereignty without surrendering it, build up Brussels and Strasbourg without reducing Westminster – in short, have its cake and eat it too.

This is the illogic of the present position of the British government, and the only way to resolve it is to imagine that there could be a multi-speed or variable geometry Europe – in other words, a European Union flexible enough to negotiate singular relationships with a variety of its members. That, however, is not the emerging pattern either in Brussels or Strasbourg; that pattern is one of imposed uniformity, not of variety and flexibility to accommodate individual needs. To date, so-called opt-outs have been shown to be of limited value, and in all probability any further ones would only once again delay Britain's reckoning with Europe.

## THE ATLANTIC OPTION

It should be clear by now that Britain's options are not limited to embracing the European Union or settling for loneliness. Others are available. One is for Britain to join the European Economic Area (EEA) with Norway, Iceland, and Liechtenstein. EEA membership would maintain Britain's full access to the single market, avoid further political integration, and save most of the present financial cost of the EU. Then there is the Swiss option – embracing the European Free Trade Association (EFTA) but not the EEA. This would give almost as good an access to the EU market but would allow only free movement of goods, not of people. It would also impose delays on British citizens travelling to EU countries. Even the most ardent Euro-skeptic would not regard that as progress. Britain could in any case use the existence of

its veto right and its large current-account deficit with the EU to negotiate complete reciprocal access of goods and people and withdrawal
from the political and judicial institutions, thus emancipating itself
from the herniating mass of authoritarian Euro-directives with which it
has been deluged – now totalling over 230,000 pages of mind-numbing
regulations.

I have listed these options for the sake of completeness, but none
of them is commensurate with the scale of Britain's problem – which is
to find for itself a place in the world that is appropriate to its history, its
political culture, its economic interest, and its strategic needs. The alternatives listed either embrace isolation or simply associate Britain with
other relatively isolated countries. There is another option, however, that
does meet the test of proportionality, and that builds from long-standing
strategic and economic realities – and that is the Atlantic option.

As to economic reality, Britain is already deeply enmeshed commercially with the United States and Canada. In percentage terms, Britain
trades almost twice as much with North America as do the other EU
countries as a group. At the same time, Britain's share of trade with the
EU has actually declined recently. If exports shipped on to non-EU des-
tinations through Rotterdam and other European ports are included,
together with overseas investment earnings, the EU's share of British
exports is probably about 40 per cent – which amounts to less than 10 per
cent of the United Kingdom's GDP. Conversely, the exports of a number
of countries to the EU, including those of the United States, have risen
considerably more rapidly than have Britain's in recent years, showing
that EU membership is not entirely necessary for access to the European
market. Over the last ten years, direct net investment in the United
Kingdom from the United States and Canada has been one and a half
times the corresponding figure for EU investment in Great Britain. As
well, U.K. net direct investment in North America has been more than
double its investment in the EU. These trends are continuing, impervi-
ous to EU preferences.

Now that the World Trade Organization is administering the
Uruguay Round of trade liberalization agreements, the EU's common
external tariff has fallen from 5.7 per cent to 3.6 per cent. This should
not constitute a prohibitive barrier even to a Britain that was not in the

EU, given its more bearable social costs and provided it retained control of its own currency. The fear of being frozen out of Europe by vindictive community bureaucrats is now, I believe, a complete fraud, though one would not know it to listen to the alarmist comments of many of Britain's political leaders and much of its media.

Indeed, the facts suggest that it is rather the other way around. The annual cost of Britain's adherence to the EU is nearly £10 billion in gross budgetary contributions. While almost half of this is returned in EU spending, it is spent, as former Chancellor of the Exchequer Norman Lamont has pointed out, "on things which the U.K. government would not choose to spend money on." Higher food prices in the United Kingdom because of the Common Agricultural Policy cost Britain rather more than £6 billion annually, though again about half of that is rebated directly to British farmers. The overall cost of the EU to Britain, then, is between £8 billion and £12 billion, or around 1.5 per cent of GDP. There are in addition the significant costs imposed by EU regulation, and the heavy political price of eroding sovereignty – which includes the tacit encouragement of provincial separatism, as Scottish and Welsh nationalists envision receiving the sort of direct grants enjoyed by Ireland.

Despite these costs, and the £3 billion annual trade deficit the United Kingdom runs with the EU, there are still those who deflect such unpleasantries with the noble hope that Britain will ultimately Thatcherize Europe rather than be de-Thatcherized by it. The truth is, however, that the United Kingdom could now probably assert a stronger and more positive influence on the European Union from outside than it could by going further into it. Free from its costs and interferences, Britain could export successfully into it, thus demonstrating the superior competitiveness of the so-called Anglo-Saxon model. For since the Uruguay Round, attempts by the EU to limit imports from non-members can only be sustained if they are unanimously upheld by multinational trade panels, which is very unlikely.

As a consequence of all this, it would be logical for Britain to negotiate entry into NAFTA, which will probably be renamed and which is already negotiating with the European Economic Area and European Free Trade Association, as well as with Chile. Such an expanding NAFTA would have every commercial advantage over the EU. It is based on the Anglo-American free-market model of relatively restrained taxation and social spending, which is the principal reason why, over the last fifteen years, the United States and Canada together have created a net average of two million more new jobs per year than have the countries of the European Union. NAFTA, as its name implies, is a free-trade area only. The United States will not make any significant concessions of sovereignty and does not expect other countries to do so. A trading bloc based on NAFTA and the more advanced South American countries could also expand into Eastern Europe faster than the EU. Such a bloc, after all, would not be encumbered by such impediments as the EU's Common Agricultural Policy, and its powerful urge to protect onerous French and German social costs.

There is no need to repeat here the nature of the Anglo-American special relationship, which is both broad and deep, historical and contemporary. It is enough to point out that none of the continental European countries has a particular affinity with the United States and Canada, or anything remotely comparable to Britain's dramatic modern historic intimacy with North America.

Beyond that, an even closer British association with North America could serve a broader, and very European, purpose. The British public's fear of loss of jurisdiction and socialist backsliding in a federal Europe is well-founded – and Britain, by staying outside, could be the example that might prevent the EU as a whole from smothering all its fully subscribing members with centralized Euro-socialism.

When the possibility of an Atlantic option for Britain is broached, the cry goes up in British Euro-federalist circles that the United Kingdom would be dominated by the United States. The words "fifty-first state" are often uttered derisively, even though any such association would be a loose one – and as if there were not a much greater danger of Britain being intruded upon by the Europeans. In fact, Britain's sovereignty would be in much better condition than it now is. Canada, whose distinctiveness from the northern American states is fairly tenuous apart from Quebec, has lost no additional sovereignty after entering into the free-trade agreement, even though over 40 per cent of Canada's GDP is derived from trade with the United States – more than four times the percentage of British GDP taken up by trade with the EU. More important, Canada suffers none of the jurisdictional intrusions that are routine in the British slouch to Euro-federalism.

## THE LIGHTS GO ON IN WASHINGTON

One of the reasons so few Britons think in terms of an Atlantic option is that few people in the United States or Canada encourage them to do so. True, the leaders of the opposition in Canada last year urged a NAFTA invitation for Britain, but just as the British are stuck in some unhelpful intellectual patterns, so too are many Americans.

The United States has been a supporter of an "ever closer European Union," to use the parlance of the European treaties, since the Truman administration. The initial motivation for such a policy was clear: by promoting European cooperation and integration, the United States hoped to contain the Soviet threat and avoid having to intervene a third time in a European war. If European strategic unity as represented by NATO was good, then so must be its economic – and ultimately political – unity. The American conception of European integration was thus of a piece with that of its European founders and promoters, a parallel thought natural among allies joined together in the contest with Moscow. Indeed, as that contest endured, grew more intense, and spread throughout the world in the late 1950s and 1960s, U.S. enthusiasm for European cooperation and eventually the European Common Market and Community steadily increased. With it went an urge to propel Britain into Europe, essentially to strengthen West European backbones as Cold War allies.

Over the years, the practice of America pushing Britain toward Europe continued, and it has not been abandoned since the end of the Cold War. This is partly out of habit and understandable intellectual inertia. It may be, too, that the present U.S. administration has felt, rightly, that Britain would be a force for good government in Europe. With the Continentals mired in a bureaucratically induced slog of low-growth, high-unemployment economics, it makes at least superficial sense to hope that post-Thatcherite Britain could teach them something about basic economic arithmetic, without the stigma of being importers of American capitalism. Tony Blair has hinted at this: a British Euro-capitalism.

In all of this, no argument offered by Americans or other foreigners on behalf of full British integration with Europe has had much to do with *British* national interests. And the least the U.S. government should do is stop trying to push Britain in a direction in which the British people show little inclination to go.

Happily, there is some evidence that more discerning Americans are now having second thoughts about the course Europe is pursuing. Prominent administration officials such as Deputy Treasury Secretary Larry Summers have cautioned against the dangers of bringing in Economic and Monetary Union (EMU) without accompanying structural labour market and long-term fiscal reforms. The American experience put political union ahead of economic union, and many Americans – including senior legislators and members of the current administration – have indicated their belief that trying to do things in reverse order is hazardous.

At the same time, some senior American foreign policy experts are becoming concerned about the likely influence of a centralized Europe – or of a failed attempt at a centralized Europe – on the Western Alliance and on the conduct of U.S. strategic policy. Europe's shabby and dangerous mistreatment of Turkey, the Middle East's most important country – in which the leading European powers cravenly hide behind the Greeks – is a case in point and a warning of the kind of behaviour that might characterize the new Europe. (It is, it should be noted, in stark contrast to the much more enlightened U.S. and Canadian treatment of Mexico.)

Europe could become an American problem at an even deeper level. Martin Feldstein and others have expressed concern that the attempt to manage a monetary union and the subsequent development of a political union could lead to increased conflicts both within Europe and between Europe and the United States. Henry Kissinger has suggested that the tensions inherent in the EMU gamble hold the potential for a stampede to the extremes of left and right, leading to the very instability that successive administrations have sought to prevent. Even if Europe succeeds in placing the cart of monetary union before the horse of a single labour and housing market, without sufficiently coherent political control – and there is little of that commodity currently evident – there is no reason to suppose that a united Europe would necessarily be more willing to share the burdens of global leadership.

Of course, it is conceivable that France and Germany, acting together, could rediscover a vocation for enlightened international policy-making, but on recent form it would be imprudent to count on it. Kissinger and others are surely right to say that it is much more likely that the energies of those countries would be spent emancipating themselves from the leadership of the United States, dismantling history's most successful alliance system, and possibly engaging in aggressive competition with Washington for global leadership. For no one, and certainly no American, should underestimate the extent to which Euro-federalism is inspired by a resentment of the power and success of the United States – and, as some would have it, the "Anglo-Saxons" – over the last fifty years.

The European concern to "stand up" to America has undistinguished cultural and political antecedents. It figured prominently, for example, in the writings of Werner Daitz, the head of the Third Reich's Central Research Institute for National Economic Order and Large Area Economics, and of Vichyite apologists such as Drieu La Rochelle and Francis Delaisi. Obviously, current Euro-integrationists draw no inspiration from such distasteful precedents, but these disreputable forms of anti-Americanism still lurk on the extremes of European politics and have the capacity to impinge on the centre at times of tension and crisis. The main home for such sentiments remains France, where they are espoused by both pro- and anti-European forces – and, indeed, sometimes expressed at the very top. Thus, Georges-Marc Benamou, in *Le Dernier Mitterrand*, quotes the late French president as having said in his latter years: "France does not know it, but we are at war with America. Yes, a permanent war, a vital war, an economic war, a war without death. Yes, they are very hard the Americans, they are voracious, they want undivided power over the world." And at the EU summit in November 1995 in Madrid, President Chirac, himself ostensibly a conservative, extolled the alleged victory of "European values" over the ideology of world conservatism (led by the United States). The unhelpful, not to say neurotic, French response to the pre-eminence of the United States in the world is well illustrated by recent French antics in respect of Iraq.

Such attitudes are not peculiar to France, even if they are strongest there. In Germany, even the staunchly pro-American former Chancellor Kohl stated in a speech in Louvain in 1996 that he conceived of a world of three blocs: the United States, the Far East, and the EU, and went on to urge that Europe should "assert itself" against the other two. His successors are unlikely to be friendlier or more enlightened.

And then there is Britain itself. Virtually the only political groups that speak with any enthusiasm of Euro-federalism in Britain today are the odd couple consisting of the old left and the anti-American wing of the Tories. The detritus of the old Labour Party looks to Europe to re-impose on Britain pre-Thatcher levels of social spending, taxation, and union-dominated industrial relations. The anti-American Tories are an unlikely mélange of Heathite corporatists, nostalgic imperialists, and those affecting a pseudo-aristocratic disdain for American "vulgarity." (For a recent and egregious example of the last of these, see Ian Gilmour in the *London Review of Books*, December 10, 1998. Lord Gilmour goes out of his way to express hostility to the views I expound in this essay.)

## WHAT EUROPEAN FOREIGN POLICY?

With or without Britain (but especially with it), EU foreign policy can have four possible consequences for the United States.

The first is that the EU will assume its fair share in defending liberal world order, sometimes in disagreement with the nuances of American policy, but basically acting in partnership with it. Unfortunately, this is the least likely option, not only for the ideological and political reasons outlined above, but because the European nations are cutting their defence budgets and steadily becoming less competitive arms manufacturers. For them, force is not so much an option of last resort as no option at all.

Second, EU foreign and security policy could be simply ineffectual because the decision-making process will require an approach based upon the lowest common denominator. It would be virtually impossible to achieve a consensus to do anything significant on current form.

Third, it could be ineffectual in terms of its impact on a given situation while also being obstructive of effective American responses – as in the Middle East, or in targeting weapons of mass destruction or combating rogue regimes. Thus, the EU would send the Irans, Iraqs, and Libyas of the world the message that they may continue to resist the Americans with impunity, because the more emollient and commercially minded EU will always give them a way out.

The fourth possibility is that Europe will successfully come together and form an entity – Chancellor Kohl's third bloc – that seeks gradually to challenge and diminish American influence on the Continent and elsewhere. This, certainly, is the undisguised ambition of the French.

Britain relates vitally to these four possibilities. Britain is at the centre, geographically, culturally, and politically, of an Atlantic community, whereas it is in all respects on the periphery of an exclusively or predominantly European order. Despite the British government's sincere attachment to NATO, the unintended consequence of a Britain ever more closely integrated into a European foreign and defence policy would be a Britain torn away from its natural Atlanticist vocation.

Consider, too, the implications for the United States. If a fully fledged common foreign and security policy, with majority voting, had been operating at the time of the Gulf War in 1990–91, it is certain beyond any doubt that the majority of EU nations would have voted against military action, and Britain could then not have acted in concert with the United States. Nor could Britain have bucked the inclinations of its European partners and allowed the Americans to bomb Libya from British bases in April 1986. Nor, again, could Britain have launched its own Falklands campaign.

At the start of the Yugoslav crisis in 1991, the then president of the European Council, Jacques Poos, declared, "This is the hour of Europe. If one problem can be solved by the Europeans, it is the Yugoslav problem. This is a European country and it is not up to the Americans." What ensued is notorious, but only an eventual American military and diplomatic presence secured any progress at all.

## THE POTENTIAL OF NAFTA

Unlike other EU countries, Britain has a choice. It has a common Atlantic home. If Europe realized this it would either make Euro-federalism a more comfortable prospect for Britain or, by not doing so, demonstrate conclusively just how uncomfortable Euro-federalism could be for the British. If it were to choose the first course, such shameful and punitive abuses of Britain's minority position as the overly broad and prolonged European embargo on British beef would not recur. In either case, the British government and people would be in a much better position to make an informed decision than they are now. Britain is now proceeding one unsteady step at a time, with no sense of its real destination and little serious public analysis of consequences or alternatives.

The United States is better placed than any country – even Britain itself – to halt this dismal progress. It is time Washington reassessed its view of Britain and Europe, for ultimately the issue is more important than almost anything that currently preoccupies it. If post-Thatcher Britain has been trying to "muddle through" the European question, it has at least been aware of some potential dangers of Euro-integration, and the British public has been commendably resistant to premature Euro-euphoria. There is no evidence, however, that any recent U.S. administration has thought these questions through – either with respect to the European Union itself or Britain's putative role in it. As to the latter, if Europe integrates successfully and continues to be a reliable and constructive independent ally, it will not be because Britain has tipped the intra-European scales in a sensible direction. Britain has only about 15 per cent of Europe's population and economy, and is very much the odd man out in terms of its attitudes and perspectives. Europe will or will not cohere and behave with maturity. Britain will be an influence but nothing like a determining one. Britain could, however, be decisive in assuring that an American-led bloc had a wide margin of superior strength over an integrated European rival.

Still – and contrary to widespread Euro-integrationist feeling, including the American variety – Britain will have more influence with Europe by being reasonably independent of it and not subsumed into it; by maintaining its much maligned, much envied, imprecise, but certainly special relationship with the United States and Canada. The course suggested here – continuation of British membership of Common Market; non-membership of the European political and juridical union; becoming part of the expanding NAFTA area – would give the United Kingdom greater access to markets than any other country in the world enjoys. It would be the antithesis of "little England." Britain would preserve all its options to associate more closely with Europe if it wished. The British national interest would be best served by such a course.

If, that is, it is available. That availability is up to the United States to decide. U.S. influence in Europe does not depend on its use of Britain as a Trojan horse, even if either country intended Britain to play that role. Obviously, the United States should not take any initiatives that could be construed as anti-European. But it would be appropriate, and certainly not premature, to support Canadian efforts to broaden NAFTA, and not just to the stabler countries of Latin America, the Norwegians, and the Swiss. The Poles, Czechs, Hungarians, and Turks – who, because of the structure of transfer payments in the EU (and other complexities in the case of Turkey), are going to have a very long, possibly interminable, wait for EU membership – should be brought into a renamed NAFTA as quickly as possible. All are or will be in NATO. They must be secured in the Western world, and the European Unionists, hobbled by protectionist socialism, cannot be relied upon to achieve that end.

And Britain – still one of the world's six or so most important countries after the United States – remains America's truest, most important ally. It would not be provocative to offer Britain an associate status in NAFTA. And it would certainly not serve legitimate American interests to have Britain, for lack of any alternative, either subsumed into a Europe for which the Anglo-Americans have generous but uncertain hopes – or succumb at last to Curzon's curse.

# U.S., LEAD OR
# GET OUT OF THE WAY

*National Review Online,* September 30, 2010

---

At the crossroads the Middle East is approaching – in the Iranian nuclear program, the Afghan War, the Israeli–Palestinian conflict, and the internal political evolution in Pakistan, Iraq, and Turkey – there is a confusing glimpse of what the world's most turbulent region looks like as American influence conducts an orderly retreat. All present indications are that the Obama administration is not prepared to interdict militarily the Iranian acquisition of a deliverable nuclear military capability and also lacks the political muscle or ingenuity to persuade the necessary powers of the virtues of what Secretary Clinton boldly described in more purposeful recent times as "crippling sanctions."

President Obama has muddied the waters with a lot of hopeful but rather vapid talk of nuclear disarmament, which the Russians are prepared to join in as long as it reduces American nuclear superiority, but not further, and to which no other present or imminent nuclear power will accord the slightest credence. Since not even this administration has so far succumbed to the lunacy of unilateral disarmament, and the Russians are unlikely to take this down another notch and leave themselves unnecessarily vulnerable to the antics of the Chinese, this train to nowhere has probably reached its destination already.

The effort to arm the friendly Middle Eastern countries, especially Saudi Arabia and the Gulf states and emirates, with intermediate missile defences (THAAD) is a sensible step. But to the extent that the administration thinks that it will be an adequate balm to the host countries' concerns about nuclear-warhead-equipped ayatollahs in Tehran, it is another dangerous fantasy. In one sense, the world can be grateful to Ahmadinejad and Khamenei for lifting the rock on the farce of nuclear arms control. It has been a club that anyone could join without more than gentle rifting in the club lounge, as long as they appeared to be unlikely to start pitching such weapons around indiscriminately. Despite the claims of Mao Tse-tung that China could endure a nuclear exchange and the deaths of hundreds of millions of people, the more blood-curdling noises of some of the cavalcade of disconcerting ephemeral chiefs in Islamabad, and the reactionary aberrance of the descendants of the Trekboers in apartheid Pretoria, all these countries were almost uncomplainingly allowed in. The Clinton administration's madcap sanctions against India and Pakistan illustrated the feebleness of club disapproval while making America's strategic position in South Asia completely unsustainable.

Now that a country whose leadership speaks glibly of a love of death and of its intention to obliterate Israel is thrusting into the club, to the apparent indifference of most of the neighbouring countries that have the most at risk from such a move (i.e., Russia, China, and India), all doors and windows will be open. The world will then move quickly, probably within twenty years, to a security system based on universal assured destruction. Fifty or more countries will join the nuclear club, on the understanding that a few countries will possess a semi-viable anti-missile defence and all the others will be destroyed completely if they attack another nuclear power. The Armageddon feared by the original nuclear scientific community will be at hand. And there will certainly be nuclear attacks and counterattacks, and eventually almost routine massacres of millions of people.

To forestall this fate, there is only one alternative, unless this administration has the greatest official resurrection of purpose since Neville Chamberlain abruptly gave Poland a unilateral and virtually unsolicited territorial guarantee after Hitler seized Bohemia and

Moravia in March 1939, four months after the Munich Conference had produced "peace in our time." If the United States sits like a great jelly while Iran arms up, there is only one happy ending to this chapter: the Arab powers may set aside the insane preoccupation with the red herring of Israel that has enabled them to distract the Arab masses from their chronic national failures and general misgovernment for the past sixty years and pressure the Palestinians into a sensible land-for-peace deal in exchange for Israel's knocking out the Iranian nuclear capability and returning as often as necessary to keep it down. Presumably, the Unites States will not heed the advice of the formerly sensible Zbigniew Brzezinski to shoot down Israeli planes en route to Iran (demonstrating the power of the self-destructive pandemic of the Carter administration, which has now afflicted almost everyone above the doorkeepers in that regime). This would be a regional solution, and would resolve the two biggest problems in the region (Iran and Palestine) simultaneously – like, to use a local precedent, Alexander the Great's slicing the Gordian knot.

On Afghanistan, there are now four competing arguments on the way forward. The admirable Max "Boots on the Ground" Boot wants to slog it out, defeat the Taliban, force Karzai to clean up his government to an appreciable degree, and nation-build. He quite rightly demystifies guerrilla war, pointing out that most guerrilla wars fail, and that guerrilla warriors conduct the wars they do only because they don't have the ability to conduct a main-unit war. This is a viable option if, as Boot believes to be the case, the second option doesn't work. This second option is the Henry Kissinger view that the United States should hand over the country in a series of concessions, like fried-chicken franchises, to the local groups already sponsoring them, and rely on Russia, Pakistan, India, Iran, and perhaps Uzbekistan to work out some unimaginably complicated local amalgamation of interests. The third option is that of the inimitable Joe Biden, to continue firing cruise missiles and drone-generated missiles at suspect sites, risking no American lives. This is a hare-brained idea that can be rejected on the basis of its source, without listening to the actual proposal. And fourth, a suggestion from the American left, fronted by the inevitable Bruce Ackerman, which – like everything the domestic far left has proposed in foreign policy matters in the last forty years – would humiliate America and generate chaos: cut and run.

I must profess some solidarity with the president, as quoted by Bob Woodward. Mr. Obama is right not to want to "nation-build," or to stay ten years, or to spend $1 trillion, in Afghanistan. But Kissinger's Option 2 will become feasible only as Boot's Option 1 starts to work, so Obama has to sound and be purposeful enough to start making the Boot option look plausible enough to hand off the war to the Kissinger option. This will require more finesse than anyone has shown since the Iraqi surge, but should be possible and is the best bet. I don't see how the United States can go on assisting Pakistan if the Pakistan-backed Haqqani faction of the Afghan Taliban continues to attack the Allies in Afghanistan. Either the assistance to or by Pakistan or the attacks on the Allies must stop, or the West will continue to be on both sides in the Afghan "war of necessity."

After any such denouement (but not without one, or if the United States quits Iraq overhastily), Iraq should be strong enough adequately to resist the encroachments of Iran, and the United States can withdraw to the status of a well-paid armourer (much the best domestic economic stimulus). Similarly, there is not much more to do in the Far East. The idea that China will dominate everyone in the region if the United States doesn't shore everybody up is rubbish. China is gratuitously annoying the Indians and Japanese, trespassing in Japanese waters, making irritating claims to worthless islands, meddling in Kashmir, refusing visas to Indian notables. Let them go on with it; eventually, all their neighbours, including the Russians and Vietnamese and Taiwan, will hold hands and contain them. North Korea is just a Chinese puppet state that Beijing has manipulated to annoy everyone else. Let the locals contain China, with the tangible support of the American presence in Japan and South Korea (which could be reduced) and anti-missile defences. Latin America is progressing well with minimal American involvement and the United States has wisely never tried to play a role in Africa.

Ukraine and Georgia could be divided into Russian and Western sections now. Western Europe is more than adequately strong to deal with any mischief or rambunctiousness from the Russian bear, now that it is less than half the size of its Cold War girth and shorn of the satellites. The United States was magnificent in the defeat of the Nazis, imperial Japanese, and Soviet communists, and in the inducement of China into at least state capitalism. But – apart from the facilitation of NATO expansion through Bill Clinton's bunk about a Partnership for Peace (via dismemberment of the Soviet bloc), and possibly the setting up of a post-Saddam power-sharing regime in Iraq – the United States has been completely ineffectual in the world since the original Gulf War and the end of the Cold War twenty years ago.

The United States shows no signs of being prepared to pay down its mountain of debt, and is every year forfeiting the natural respect it acquired in the 1940s and maintained to the end of the twentieth century as the world's undisputed leader. An American failure to prevent Iran from becoming a nuclear power will signal the end of American world leadership, whether Israel steps up to the task or not. The United States cannot afford to masquerade as a decisive influence where it does not have the will or judgment to assert such an influence. Unless new leadership arises in the next election to end the current-account deficit and unsustainable oil imports, reorient the country to physical production and less unproductive "services," and redesign alliances to contemporary needs and real possibilities, it should continue the orderly withdrawal already in progress. It won the Cold War, disposed of Saddam, and can retire in good order, undefeated, to a defensible perimeter. It was the indispensable country to the West, in 1917–18 and 1939–90, but it is largely dispensable now, and is providing no discernibly useful leadership at all. If it rediscovers its aptitude for successful and innovative internationalism, it can raise its level of involvement. The trend to decentralization of national influences relieves the United States of the burdens of a superpower and provides regional balances that can be influenced from Washington with relatively little exertion. On the present course, it is risking a severe humiliation, and an undignified retreat into its doghouse like a chastened puppy. The current level of official amateurism, if allowed to continue indefinitely, is going to lead to needless disaster.

# TOPPLE OUTLAW REGIMES

*National Review Online*, May 9, 2013

O nce again, Israel has demonstrated a commendable sense of self-preservation, and shown the way forward on how to deal with the world's principal current centre of violence by its example and professional military execution. It has also highlighted the torpor of much of the rest of the blowzy, sluggish world. Of course this latest massive shipment of missiles from Iran to Syria destined for Hezbollah and for delivery against the civilian population of Israel had to be intercepted. The contemptible farce that has gone on in what were, in a more pretentious but hopeful era, called the chancelleries of the world is a disgrace. The White House and the State Department, at time of writing, are still trying to pretend it didn't happen, like a thoughtful host after a guest was unable to suppress a digestive or colonic perturbation, but it is not Israel that has embarrassed itself; it is the fraternity of the silent.

The reproachful are beneath contempt. There can have been few more preposterous charades of foreign ministers standing on their presumed dignity in recent years than the deputy foreign minister of Syria solemnly announcing to the nodding and docile CNN interviewer that the Israeli action was a "declaration of war," and that Israel was assisting terrorists, including al Qaeda (as if Hezbollah, to whom Syria was shipping the missiles destroyed by Israel, were a Boy Scout jamboree). Syria has technically been at war with Israel for sixty-five years, as it has never acknowledged the right of Israel to exist as a Jewish state, as it was created by the United Nations. Syria has been identified by the United

States and other countries as a terror-exporting country for many years. It invaded and occupied much of Lebanon for decades and murdered the democratically elected leader of that country, and has been in a brutal civil war for over two years, in which over 30,000 people have been killed. The latest episode in this cycle has been the use of sarin nerve gas by the Syrian government against dissidents two weeks ago. It is not the place of a spokesman for the bloodstained Assad regime to accuse the democratic government of Israel, a society of laws and respecter of individual human rights, of lawlessness.

Syria has for many years been a witless conduit for the apparatus of terror to facilitate Iran's assault on Israel and its cultivation of the most extreme genocidal anti-Semites and pseudo-Islamic zealots. As the 89 per cent of Syrians who are not members of the governing (Shiite) Alawites have progressively abandoned the Assad reign of terror and bribery, the Syrian government's dependence on Shiite Iran has steadily increased. The ghastly wreckage of the Assad regime would implode and be trampled and destroyed and its leaders executed by their country-men in a trice if Iranian support were removed. The Syrian government exists exclusively as a tottering satrap of the demented Iranian theocracy, which apart from the lunatic reality show in Pyongyang has few rivals as the world's most uniformly reprehensible functioning government.

As the Syrian drama has unfolded, and degenerated into a struggle between the surrogates of the Iranians and the Saudis, the West has been as impotent as it was during the Spanish Civil War of the 1930s. No sane person asked for or would recommend the intervention of Western ground forces in Syria. But it has been demeaning to witness the spec-tacle of the gradual demise of official and unofficial Western deference to the Assads, from Hillary Clinton's infamous reference to Assad as "a reformer" and the pilgrimages to Damascus of Barbara Walters and the correspondent of *Vogue* magazine, to the present tongue-tied agonizing about going beyond humanitarian aid to more effective assistance. It is an understandable and a good thing that President Obama does not want to replicate the Libyan fiasco: stating solemnly that Gaddafi must go but declining to lift a finger to assist in the accomplishment of that result (until the British and French did).

The wrong criteria are being applied to these conflicts in countries that seem no longer to revel in the balmy laurels of the Arab Spring.

Regimes that have repeatedly violated international law and provoked the righteous wrath of the West and of the civilized international community generally, by traditional and conclusively applied benchmarks of national conduct, should be punished proportionately. And when the opportunity arises, they should be eliminated. The West is not, and should not be, in the business of nation-building. Gravely offensive regimes are our enemies because they have made themselves our enemies, voluntarily and deliberately. When the opportunity presents itself to get rid of such a regime at minimal cost and in accord with international law, we must take it. That is why it was a mistake for the first Bush administration to allow Saddam to survive in office after the Gulf War.

It is not the West's concern or obligation to ensure that the succeeding regime governs more gently or progressively. We aren't responsible for the governments of these countries; we are responsible for our own protection and the protection of our allies and interests, as well as for the maintenance of at least a modicum of international law. If the pattern is established of sworn and active and provokingly aggressive enemies of the West coming to swift and nasty ends, the fashion of provoking the West will miraculously go out of style. If we continue to allow ourselves to be dragged into nation-building in places where we have no mandate or national or moral interest to do so, the results will continue to be military success negated and made unacceptably costly by subsequent political failure. This can be easily distinguished from the reconstruction of postwar Europe and Japan, sophisticated countries that well knew how to operate modern economies and knew or were amenable to civilized political systems but had been smashed by war and were being subverted and intimidated by Stalinist communism and its local agents. It's also easily distinguishable from the kind of support the West gave relatively primitive countries, such as South Korea and Malaysia, as they resisted totalitarian aggression.

We should respond in scale to violations of international law, whether at our expense or not, and opportunistically move to make an example of such regimes when they so mismanage their affairs as to lose control of their own countries. When these awful governments can be eliminated easily, do it. Instead, we have helped destabilize and bring down the shah of Iran, President Mubarak of Egypt, and President Musharraf of Pakistan, who were allies, however far removed they may have been from replicating the State of Minnesota or the kingdom of Denmark in their own affairs. And we have given the ayatollahs a pass for a brutally stolen election in Iran and waffled inelegantly for years over Syria. This, of course, summarizes the contrasting errors of the George W. Bush and Obama administrations: Bush stumbled into nation-building and Obama has tried and failed to make deals with Iran and the Egyptian Muslim Brotherhood.

The policy I am proposing is not a difficult concept, and should not be difficult to enunciate, back with bipartisan support, and implement in coordination with our genuine allies (most of whom are in a state of increasing mystification about wayward American policy and the elusive current definition of the U.S. national interest).

It is also well past time that the international community agreed on criteria for designation of a failed state and on a protocol to prevent any such state from becoming a breeding ground for international terrorism. Some appropriately broad grouping of countries should agree that when a country is sufficiently ungovernable that its central government can no longer be held practically accountable for all that goes on within its borders, and there is reasonable and objectively probable cause to believe that criminal violence is likely to be exported from a lawless part of that country to another country, the international community must have a right to take preventive action to eliminate the danger at the minimum possible cost in lives and property and with the briefest infringement of that country's sovereignty. This system should have been set up and should have dealt with Pakistan's northwest frontier years ago, and simply faced down the fact of Pakistan's nuclear capacity with the honest assertion that the world was removing a threat to the government of Pakistan, not undermining that government. Where possible and practical, of course, the cooperation of the government of the failed state, or a plausible faction contending for that status, should be secured.

In the current crisis in Syria, the world should commend Israel, as Canada admirably and instantly did (despite the effort of the Arab powers to remove the International Civil Aviation Organization headquarters from Montreal), and the United States and other Western powers should assist the most respectable of the anti-Assad forces in Syria in consigning that dark era to the proverbial dustbin of history.

# THE WORLD AFTER AMERICA

*National Review Online*, March 25, 2015

The process, poorly disguised and feebly denied by the administration, of the withdrawal of the United States from the world's main overseas theatres continues. And in general, in the regions where American withdrawal has had the greatest strategic impact, the withdrawal is being managed competently by the regional powers the United States previously, and for many decades, considered it in its national interest to reinforce. In the Far East, China, still in a mighty triumph of developmental economics, though it is tapering off, has essentially adopted the foreign policy of the traditional emerging power, the slightly adolescent bravura and braggadocio of Andrew Jackson and Theodore Roosevelt, and even, though without his criminally negligent insouciance, of Kaiser Wilhelm II. Absurdly chauvinistic claims are being made about insignificant places like the Spratly Islands, and international seas and sea passages are being declared Chinese coastal waters, almost with the comical bellicosity, though not the outright buffoonery, of Mussolini claiming in the 1930s that the Mediterranean was "an Italian lake."

The U.S. Seventh Fleet still sails from Japan, but the Indians and Japanese especially are raising their naval capabilities, and there is no disposition to be more or less than respectful of China's contiguity. Despite Japan's aging population, and the failure of successive economic programs to jolt the country out of the stasis that followed the abrupt collapse of Japan's great economic challenge to the United States in the mid-1990s, it is a great economic power and is rearming. India is accelerating along the development track, out of an overcontrolled, stultified, dysfunctional economy, under a government with a clear mandate to generate swift economic growth equitably distributed. The South Koreans, Vietnamese, Filipinos, Indonesians, Thais – from all of whom China, in the powerful phases of previous dynasties, expected deference if not tribute – as well, of course, as the Australians and New Zealanders, are steadily cohering to contest China's self-assertions. In the long-hermit state of Myanmar (Burma), as in Taiwan (Nationalist China, as the Vatican still redoubtably recognizes it to be, because of Beijing's oppression of Christianity), there is studious autonomy from the People's Republic, one of the few policies on which the Burmese reformers and the heavy-handed military despotism agree.

For all its success at departing the Third World, China has been irresponsibly indulgent of rogue states, including Iran and North Korea, and appears to be somewhat outmanoeuvred by the demented nepotocracy in North Korea, which has become a quasi-nuclear power under Beijing's nose – apparently because, if China really turned the screws on North Korea, which is almost entirely dependent on the People's Republic and could be brought to heel easily (sparing the world all the fruitless negotiations with the Kim regime of the Clinton, George W. Bush, and Obama administrations), the fragile and freakish leftover from the Second World War would crumple and collapse at the feet of South Korea, almost instantly transforming a united Korea into one of the world's powers.

China has itself to blame for this conundrum, and it must minister to its steadily more complicated relations with its neighbours while its still largely command economy is forced to pitch to a domestic consumer market that is far from docile. The domestic savings rate is nearly 50 per cent, because the regime has provided only a minimal social-security safety net, and China faces the task of luring hundreds of millions of people to be consumers, to ensure continued economic growth, with political institutions that are mysterious, largely corrupt, completely unanswerable to the public, and responsive only to invisible pressures within the seething power structure of the governing

Communist Party (of a largely capitalist country). The Obama "pivot to Asia" was really just an excuse to explain withdrawal from Europe and the Middle East westward; those areas were not supposed to notice that the forces withdrawn went home and that the only expeditionary forces that made the full pivot were a few companies of Marines sent to enjoy the casino and the zoo at Darwin, Australia, which has not been under threat since a Japanese air raid in 1942, shortly after General Douglas MacArthur disembarked, announcing his inevitable return (to the Philippines).

Europe is not threatened by Russia, and the British and French possess enough nuclear force to prevent nuclear blackmail on their own. But with the weak leadership in London and Paris complementing the abdication in Washington, and German chancellor Angela Merkel hobbled by a schizoid coalition partner (the SPD, torn and waffling between Alliance and pacifist factions), there is some danger of further exposure of the erosion of the political will of the West. Germany is the greatest power in Europe and has been since Bismarck united it in 1871, but has not behaved like both a great and a responsible power since Wilhelm II dismissed Bismarck in 1890. (Wilhelm's and Hitler's Germany was a great but irresponsible power, and Stresemann's Weimar, and the Federal Republic from Adenauer to Merkel, have been responsible but diminutive, compared with the real strength of Germany.)

In the aftermath of the Soviet Union, there are three contending concepts for the future of its territories. First, there is Putin's attempted reabsorption of ethnic Russian irredentists in the former Soviet republics, as in Crimea, Donetsk, and the contested Georgian territories. Second, there is the Finlandization of the former European Soviet republics – Ukraine, Belarus, Moldova, Latvia, Lithuania, Estonia, Armenia, Azerbaijan, and Georgia – as a neutral zone subject to Russian influence but not domination, as in inter-war and postwar Finland. And the third option is a partition of those areas between people who prefer to be Russian and the rest who prefer to be in the West, preferably in the European Union and NATO, if that alliance retains any meaning (a question that has arisen from the negligence of the last two U.S. administrations). Unfortunately, there is no evidence that any person in authority in the so-called chancelleries of the West is thinking of this problem in these terms. They're just muddling along. The best course would be to give Putin a quarter of a loaf and let those ethnic Russians in the formerly affiliated states who are local majorities, and wish to remain Russian citizens, do so, and to invite all the rest into the West, as the EU stabilizes itself and Obama's successor breathes new life into NATO before the most successful alliance in history becomes a husk.

The enfeeblement of the West must be considered aberrant; these societies cannot have simply atrophied in the years since Reagan, Thatcher, Kohl, and Mitterrand, even less since Clinton, Blair, and Chirac, whose governments could at least, and did generally, act sensibly. The real objective must be to complete the demolition of czarist and Stalinist Russian imperialism while recognizing the integrity and distinction of the Russian nationality in a way that liberates those who seek liberation without humiliating Russia. And the big prize is to extend the Western world, whose eastern border was only one hundred miles beyond the Rhine when Germany was divided, to the borders of Russia, the better to assist, absolutely peacefully and by example, persuasion, and the ravages of prosperity, the Western emulators in Russia to prevail over the nativists, and to bring Russia, Eurasia, into the West on good terms and as a distinguished partner. This is the real prize, but it is totally obscured by the unfathomable mediocrity of the current cast of characters, and the danger is that Putin will exploit the feeble West and start stirring up Russians in the little Baltic states. No NATO member except Poland is going to consider such a thing, in the NATO treaty terms, as "an attack upon one is an attack upon all" call to arms. If we get through to the next U.S. presidential inauguration day without such a test, it will only be because of the munificence of the Saudis in holding oil prices down so Putin can't even afford a show of strength against the Lithuanians.

The Middle East has witnessed the most complicated withdrawal of all. Obama's response to the Israeli elections, in which he meddled shamelessly and unsuccessfully, was an outrage: spontaneous complaints from his press secretary that Netanyahu was dividing his own Jewish and Arab citizens. This is a bit rich from the spokesman for a president who has intervened prejudicially and divisively in almost every highly publicized racial incident in the United States in his time in office, accused the Republicans of waging "a war on women," and fiscally assaulted the Roman Catholic Church. And it is cheeky to address such comments to democratic Israel, where dissident Arabs are the third party in the parliament. Benjamin Netanyahu has a mandate to attack Iran's nuclear capability if he thinks it necessary to Israeli national security and would be supported by the Saudis, and tacitly by the Egyptians and the Turks. It would be better for the United States and the other five countries in the negotiations to abandon their inept meddling and let Israel get on with it, or use that prospect to extract a better agreement from Iran. And it would be better for the Saudis and Gulf states to finance the admirable Egyptian president Abdel Fattah el-Sisi in modernizing the Egyptian economy as the United States continues to sulk over the fate of the Muslim Brotherhood (of all unworthy subjects of American sympathy). The Palestinians can have their state, with a narrower West Bank and a deeper Gaza, if they recognize Israel's right to exist as a Jewish state and cease to be a launch pad for terrorist and rocket attacks on Israel. The ancient Persians, Egyptians, Turks, Jews, and Saudis will work it out in their own way and time, as long as nuclear weapons aren't in the equation, with special status for Jordan, Lebanon, and the Kurds.

American withdrawal isn't a bad idea, as long as it isn't necessarily permanent. What has been this administration's single most irritating characteristic has been retreating from the world while pretending it isn't, and claiming a completely undiminished right to advise and coerce those countries to whom it has almost ceased to be relevant. Obama has neither the will to stay nor the grace to go.

# MIDDLE EAST

## A RECIPE FOR PEACE

*National Review Online,* April 16, 2011

There is something faintly nostalgic about former U.S. national security adviser Brent Scowcroft's *Financial Times* op-ed, published Wednesday, calling for Barack Obama to "broker a new Mideast Peace." The man, the media, and the message are all, as Hillary Clinton would say, "so yesterday." It's a little like watching vintage films from the era when American leaders were first "brokering peace" in the Mideast, such as *American Graffiti* or *The Graduate.*

Brent Scowcroft, a retired air force general, was the U.S. national security adviser to President Gerald Ford, and he returned to the post under President George H.W. Bush. He is a distinguished foreign policy and strategic policy specialist but has never been considered overly original, a reputation that will not be shaken by his new suggestion.

The *Financial Times* is a justly respected newspaper, but its editorial line is always the urbane, gentlemanly, British impulse to speak softly, move in increments, generally advance the conventional wisdom; and don't stretch the imagination, catch a cold thinking outside the box, or get seriously riled up over anything short of a genuine outrage.

In this case, however, the conventional wisdom is nonsense. The counsel for President Obama to "broker peace" is on par with Pakistani president Musharraf's advice to Tony Blair to "do Palestine." The Palestinians could have peace with Israel tomorrow if they wanted it.

In any event, Barack Obama is not trusted by Israel. His chief initiative in the area to date has been to deny the existence of the agreement George W. Bush made with Ariel Sharon, whereby Israel would vacate Gaza, would dismantle some West Bank settlements, and would confine extensions of other settlements in contested areas to natural population growth. (The world's obsession with settlement abandonment as the key to peace – which Obama seems to share – is foolish: if Israel dismantled every settlement, or even turned them over for occupation by returning Palestinians, a new pretext to keep the pot boiling would be devised.)

The larger, more basic, problem is rooted in history. Amid the desperate conditions of the First World War, the British sold the same real estate twice: to the Jews to promote pro-Allied opinion in the United States and the international Jewish community, and to the Arabs to incite rebellion against the occupying Ottoman Turks. The predictable happened when both buyers tried to take possession, and there has never been any answer except to divide the diminutive space in two. This has been the subject of three wars, all of them sparked by the Arabs, and none successfully (although the intervention of Richard Nixon in the 1973 war – after he had supplied the Israelis almost with a new air force – enabled the Egyptians to claim a partial success).

Always, it is claimed that a return to the 1967 borders is the basis of peace, although those borders would leave Israel nine miles wide on its Mediterranean shore, and the West Bank and Gaza sections of Palestine separated by fifty miles. The Arabs effectively had those borders, under the control of Jordan and Egypt, in 1967. Yet they went to war and lost – events that would not normally be expected to generate reverence for the status quo ante.

The facts, which must be perfectly well-known to Brent Scowcroft, are that it is impossible to deal with the Palestinians while Hamas controls Gaza and the PLO the West Bank; that it is impossible to broker anything while the surrounding Arab powers are in turmoil; that this U.S. administration is not taken seriously by anybody in the area after the denial of the Bush-era settlements arrangement and the failure of its Iran policy; and that the solution, when the Palestinians are ready, has, as Scowcroft himself notes, largely been identified already, especially in the Taba discussions of 2001.

There will have to be some exchanges of territory, to make Israel wider between the Mediterranean and the West Bank. Scowcroft envisions a united Jerusalem serving as the capital of both countries. I don't think so; I think side-by-side Jerusalems, with the Arabs controlling their area beyond Orient House and a special arrangement and assured access to designated holy sites for all faiths throughout both countries. The Palestinian right of return would be to Palestine, and this fairy tale of one big happy Holy Land where all would be brothers, but in fact the Muslims would outnumber the Jews and expel or massacre them yet again, should finally have a silver stake driven through its heart.

A clairvoyant is not required to see that this is where it will end up. Nor is one required to see that, as Arab populations have begun to stop being distracted by the red herring of Israel and have focused on the misgovernment from which they have suffered, no Israeli flags have recently been burned nor Palestinian flags waved about by non-Palestinians.

Israel is absolutely legitimate as a Jewish state, and was so constituted by the unanimous permanent members of the United Nations Security Council, on the motion of Stalin's ambassador, seconded by Truman's. The borders have been open to legitimate debate. But when the Palestinians determine that they will no longer be used as cannon fodder, ending the indulgence that enables the leaders of the Muslim powers to misgovern, oppress, and pillage their countries, and deflect discontent by waving the bloody shirt of Palestine, the borders could be quickly established along the lines mentioned. If the Palestinians could draw the lesson of the spectacular economic growth of the West Bank – which Israel has assisted, and where Prime Minister Salam Fayyad favours peace and is the first Palestinian leader whose CV does not contain a long stint as an extremist or terrorist – and of the contrast with the collapsed economy in Gaza, which has happily served as a launch site for rockets aimed at Israeli civilians since Sharon vacated it, then peace would be imminent.

For a sensible and experienced man such as Brent Scowcroft to suggest that President Obama is in any position to broker anything in a Middle East where the Arab governments are fighting for their lives with their own people, and Hamas is still trying to kill all the Jews, is disconcerting. Even Richard Goldstone, the token anti-Israel Jew recruited by the United Nations to write a smear job on Israel's hugely provoked reprisals against Gaza, has recanted his fraudulent report.

Israel has its faults, but it is a legitimate Jewish state, and a successful society of laws and enterprise. The Palestinians have grievances, but a remedy is at hand. Israel will take half a loaf. If Palestine would also, there would be peace. But it won't happen until it is clear what Egypt, Syria, and Lebanon will look like, and whether anything will be done to curb the baleful influence of Iran in the area. If he was minded to, President Obama could do something about that, but it isn't a matter of brokerage and there is no sign of it coming.

# INTERVENE IN SYRIA

*National Review Online*, June 21, 2012

---

It pains me to take issue in any degree with my very esteemed friend Henry Kissinger, with whose foreign policy views I have almost always agreed, but I think some degree of intervention in Syria is justified. Dr. Kissinger wrote otherwise in the *Washington Post* recently and invoked the Treaty of Westphalia, which ended the Thirty Years War in 1648. I have had the opportunity to discuss his column briefly with him. As he wrote, that war may have killed as many as a third of the people of Central Europe, and "competing dynasties" did send "armies across political borders to impose religious norms." But as he well knows, there was a good deal more to it than that, and the central event was that the French leader, Cardinal Richelieu – generally reckoned the most astute statesman, with Bismarck, in the modern history of continental Europe – recruited the Lutheran Swedish king Gustavus Adolphus to carry havoc into Catholic Central Europe and specifically to atomize Germany and confound the Habsburg (Holy Roman) Empire in Vienna. Richelieu was chiefly interested in sundering Germany into as many pieces as possible in order to assure the pre-eminence of France in Western Europe.

Richelieu's cynicism shocked his contemporaries. It was he, largely, who composed the Treaty of Westphalia and left his outline to his successor, Cardinal Mazarin. Richelieu died in 1642, causing the then pope, Urban VIII, to observe that "if there is a God, the cardinal will have much to answer for; if there is not, then he was a great man." Richelieu's, and Westphalia's, argument against international intervention was generally a convenience to reinforce the fragmentation of Germany into three hundred self-governing entities, not a rigorous espousal of the sanctity of national borders. Wars continued in Europe at their traditional pace, challenging national boundaries, though not on such a general and destructive scale for 150 years. Richelieu, like subsequent European leaders from Napoleon to Metternich, Stalin, de Gaulle, and Margaret Thatcher, realized that a united Germany could dominate Western and Central Europe. The former and future British prime minister, Benjamin Disraeli, said that, quite prophetically, when Bismarck undid Richelieu's work and founded the German Empire in 1871. The truthfulness of that view is not the least important element of the current economic crisis in Europe. I don't think Westphalia really applies to Syria.

Dr. Kissinger must be correct that there should be a precise and agreed international standard for defining humanitarian outrages (and levels of collapse of failed states) that justify interventions to save the lives of large numbers of people; the world should not have tolerated the massacres of millions of innocents in Cambodia, Rwanda, and Darfur, as it did not tolerate what would have happened in the former Yugoslavia in the absence of Western intervention. It was to Senator Robert Dole's (and America's) credit when he forced President Clinton's hand with the "lift [the embargo] and strike [the Serbian aggressors from the air]" resolution in response to the unctuous European acquiescence in the ethnic cleansing of Yugoslavian Muslims. Scores of thousands of lives were undoubtedly saved. Such a standard might have to be worked out despite the opposition of China and Russia, which are engaged in ethnic cleansing of their own and object to the principle of righteous international intervention, as they could be afoul of it, however improbable it may be that any countries would attempt such a course with such formidable nations. But both of them had foreign armies on their soil in living memory.

Dr. Kissinger must also be correct that humanitarian intervention in Syria now would be impractical and mistaken unless there were enough enthusiasm for prolonged nation-building to ensure a reduction in violence, and there is no such assurance. But the argument for intervention isn't primarily humanitarian. The Assad regime, father and son, in Damascus has been extremely hostile to legitimate Western aims in the Middle East and has frequently been an active supporter of terrorism. Henry Kissinger says he is emulating Napoleon in saying that if he wanted to take Vienna, he would (and Napoleon did) do so, meaning here that if the objective is to constrain Iran's baleful influence in the Middle East, and especially on Hamas in Gaza and Hezbollah in Lebanon, action should be directed explicitly at Iran.

Here is where we slightly part company. It would be much easier to dispose of Assad and exact from whatever regime or even contest of factions that succeeded him – as a precondition of assistance – that Syria cease to be a conduit of aid to Hamas and Hezbollah than it would be to strike directly at Iran, a much larger state not now discommoded by a civil war as Syria is. On the equally authentic Napoleonic maxim of achieving a strategic goal at minimum cost and by applying adequate pressure on the most vulnerable point, getting rid of Assad could be done in a day at minimal risk to the lives of intervening forces; military assistance to the rebels and some air support would do it. Even eliminating the Iranian nuclear military threat, which I believe should be done, would be a serious aerial undertaking and might have to be repeated at intervals, and it would not necessarily affect Iranian support of terrorist activity.

There is also the much more widely held, accepted, and practised principle, which in other circumstances Henry Kissinger has strongly approved, in office and out, of replying to provocations. Syria has severely provoked the West, repeatedly and illegally and often in the most brutal manner, including attempts to blow up civilian airliners and high complicity in the assassination of the prime minister of Lebanon, as well as participation in Iran's terroristic meddling. Dr. Kissinger effectively laments that Libya has now become an arms-reshipment point for international troublemaking. But Gaddafi blew up an American airliner over Scotland, killing hundreds of people, in 1986; President Reagan almost killed him in his home with an aerial attack soon after, and if the West made a habit of killing those who had committed capital crimes against the West, there would be fewer such crimes. This is the lesson of Ariel Sharon's handling of suicide bombing in Jerusalem and Tel Aviv. There may be no shortage of such dynamite-fodder as volunteers, but when the Hamas leadership was killed in return after each such outrage, official enthusiasm for suicide bombing as an instrument of Palestinian policy quickly declined. Even bin Laden, after all his posturing as eager to die for his cause, lived and died as a coward.

It need not be an excessive concern of the West what level of humanitarian solicitude is practised by regimes that succeed those we have deposed, as long as they do not engage in genocide or repeat the provocations against the West that motivated our action against them. Barring Syrian re-enactment of the Cambodian Killing Fields, which would require international action to stop, whatever Moscow and Beijing thought of it, lifting the one finger now necessary to get rid of Assad would create a strategic improvement for the West, without a deterioration in present standards of civil government in Syria. It is not the case that any sane person seriously expects the Arab Spring to produce much democracy, and as a final principle (one that Napoleon would surely have agreed with, given his methods in times of domestic political unrest in France and elsewhere), if a hostile regime is being undermined anyway (as this one is, by the Saudis), we should be sure to be close enough to the activity to take some credit for the success of it. As it stands now, U.S. policy has earned the animosity or at least disdain of all sides and factions, as it has with its shilly-shallying and, until recently, outright appeasement of the maniacal theocracy in Iran. America must do better than this; Henry Kissinger certainly would if he were in charge.

# HOW WE GOT HERE

*National Review Online*, November 6, 2014

---

The entire kaleidoscope of countries and movements between Libya and Turkey and Pakistan and Yemen is perhaps more complicated than ever. This is an attempt to review how we got to where we are.

At the start of the Cold War, the Arab countries were almost unanimous in considering the establishment of a Jewish state in Palestine the last straw in a sequence of humiliations starting from their expulsion from France in the eighth century. After secular officers led by Colonel Gamal Abdel Nasser seized control of the Egyptian government and evicted the picturesquely dissolute King Farouk in 1952, the Soviet Union promoted Nasser's pan-Arab nationalism, especially after the United States under President Dwight D. Eisenhower pulled its promised assistance to the ambitious Aswan High Dam project, Nasser seized the Suez Canal, and the British and French pre-positioned forces in Cyprus and encouraged an Israeli invasion of Sinai. The Anglo-French, in one of the most insane enterprises in the history of either country (a vast competition), tried to assume the role of "peacekeepers" while invading Egypt to "separate the combatants" at the Suez Canal, where the Israeli army had swiftly arrived.

It was a dreadful fiasco. In 1958, after Egypt and Syria purported to merge in the United Arab Republic, Nasser's supporters staged a coup in Baghdad as Jordan and Iraq were also attempting to merge, which would have submerged the Palestinian majority in Jordan. The

putschists massacred the entire Iraqi royal family in the manner of the
Bolsheviks slaying the Romanovs, and killed the long-serving prime
minister, Nuri al-Said, as he attempted to escape disguised as a woman
(but wearing men's shoes). His corpse was dragged through the streets
behind an automobile for several days.

The smashing Israeli victory in the Six-Day War of 1967 caused
King Hussein of Jordan to hand over authority for the Palestinian cause
to Yasser Arafat's Palestine Liberation Organization, and after Nasser
died in 1970 and was replaced by Anwar Sadat, a new cleavage developed in the Arab world between those who would compromise with
Israel and those who pursued the destruction of the Jewish state. In
the Yom Kippur War of 1973, which was also, like that six years before,
unleashed by Egypt, the Egyptian army crossed the Suez Canal and
breached the Bar Lev Line, and appeared to be at Israel's throat.
President Richard Nixon effectively supplied the Israelis a new air force
and Ariel Sharon turned the tide, but Nixon and Henry Kissinger intervened to arrange a ceasefire that preserved the Egyptians' belief that
they had acquitted themselves adequately to make peace with Israel.
Eventually, in 1978, they did so, at Camp David, with the skilled medi-
ation of President Jimmy Carter. Sadat had expelled the Russians from
Egypt in 1974.

Nixon and Brezhnev were contemplating a comprehensive regional
settlement when the Watergate controversy distracted Nixon's ability to
pursue one. Thereafter, the Soviet Union did not really have sufficient
influence to be a valid co-contractant, and, in 1979, Carter was complicit in forcing out the shah of Iran, and that key country became a violently anti-Western theocracy. Nixon had been correct that the Russians
would be easier to deal with than all the countries and factions that
were going to emerge after the involuntary departure of the Russians
from the region.

Saudi Arabia was a joint venture between the House of Saud and
the leaders of the jihadist Wahhabi sect, which left the royal family
alone in exchange for a large chunk of oil revenues to finance militant Islamist teaching and infiltration and insurgent activity around the
world. Unofficial terrorism arose to surpass in violence and scope the
antics of the terrorism-supporting powers. In a pattern set by the U.S.

Marine barracks bombing in Beirut in 1983, all through the 1990s the Clinton administration underreacted to terrorist attacks, on Khobar Towers, on the U.S. embassies in Kenya and Tanzania, and on the USS *Cole* – which, along with intelligence failures, effectively produced the outrages of 9/11. Most official response to 9/11 in the Middle East, apart from Saddam Hussein's Iraq (which had been expertly evicted from Kuwait in the First Gulf War by the first President Bush and his strong team and allies in 1993), was pro-American. But much of the Arab masses were energized and enthused by the suicide attackers' massacre of (mainly) American innocents. The Americans and their allies overthrew the government of Afghanistan; drove the offending terror network, al Qaeda, and its leader, Osama bin Laden, out of Afghanistan; and eventually caught and summarily executed bin Laden in Pakistan, where much American aid was rerouted into the anti-West Haqqani Taliban in Afghanistan. The Americans and their allies were undoubtedly effective in harassing and killing al Qaeda leaders.

Starting in 2011, the so-called Arab Spring that was imagined by idealistic Westerners to be the dawn of democracy in the Arab world toppled the governments of Tunisia, Egypt, Libya, and Yemen, and generated a prolonged civil war in Syria. The most dangerous of the Arab extremist movements, Egypt's Muslim Brotherhood, was elected but so misgoverned the country that it was evicted by the army leaders it had itself installed. After the American withdrawal from Iraq, that state virtually disintegrated, and the Shiite 60 per cent majority is now under the influence of the Iranians, which was the last thing sought by the United States when it invaded and disposed of Saddam Hussein in 2003. The American pursuit of democracy caused the elevation of the terrorist organizations Hamas and Hezbollah in Gaza and Lebanon in free elections (undemocratic governments democratically elected), and Turkey elected a somewhat Islamic government in 2002, which has excoriated Israel and pandered to its former wards and dependents in the Arab world. Iran is in hot pursuit of nuclear weapons, with the result that Saudi Arabia, Turkey, and Egypt are all clamouring for the United States or even Israel to deprive Iran of its nuclear military capability. As al Qaeda was pounded by the Americans, a new Islamic militant group, Islamic State (IS), arose in the Sunni 20 per cent of Iraq; it has defeated the regular army of Iraq and invaded Syria, and has become a fourth force in the civil war in that country, against Assad, the secular Arab moderates, and the other Islamist factions. Islamic State calls for theocratic government of the Sunni Arabs, and makes little distinction in the odium in which it holds Jews, Christians, and secular or insufficiently fervent Muslims. In one of the few dividends of the ever-escalating mayhem, no one pays any attention to the Palestinians, and Israel's cordiality is being sought by former bloodthirsty enemies.

The Turkish government detests Assad so profoundly that it supports IS in Syria, instead of reoccupying the country itself, as it should; the world – including the nearly two million Syrian refugees abroad, and four million inside Syria, among whom are almost all its Christians – would welcome such an occupation of Syria. Saudi Arabia is so outraged at Russian and Iranian assistance to Assad and Hezbollah, and so irritated by the Iranian nuclear program, that it is steadily lowering the oil price (Russia and Iran cannot economically sustain an oil price below $70 per barrel). In the shambles of Iraq, the Kurds have effectively seceded from that country, with 20 per cent of Iraq's population and most of its oil, and are leading the battle on the ground against IS and replying to Turkey's hypocritical support of IS by enflaming Turkey's twenty million Kurds, who claim to have set up an autonomous zone in southeastern Turkey.

The steady decline of the oil price (assisted by increased American production and declining Chinese imports) has already forced Russia out of Ukraine and, if it does not stop the Iranian nuclear military program, Israel is standing ready for an aerial assault on the program, with broad Arab and even Turkish support. Iran is cooperating with the United States against IS, and it is feared by the Saudis and Israelis that the Obama administration will acquiesce in Iran as a nuclear threshold state, in which case the Republican leaders in Congress will try to legislate against any such understanding. The relatively quiescent International Atomic Energy Agency confirms that Iran is stonewalling inquiries it promised to assist. Because of terrorist attacks in North Sinai by the Muslim Brotherhood in some sort of collusion with IS, Egypt's military government has declared IS, which still has only about 30,000 members, "a threat to the existence of Egypt." In these circumstances, Israel is widely expected to attack Iran (with Saudi and Egyptian support), and it is also widely feared in the region that Iran will attack Saudi oil-refining and -shipping capacity to try to reinflate the world oil price. In that scenario, all the countries in the region, including Turkey and Israel, would side with the Saudis, who are trying to shift oil shipments from the Persian Gulf to the Red Sea, where they would be less easily impeded. The Middle East might then sort out its own problems somewhat, without more interference from outsiders, who have done little but muddy the waters these thirty-five years.

It must be admitted that, since the Camp David Accords in 1978 – except for President Reagan's sale of AWACS reconnaissance aircraft to Saudi Arabia in exchange for a reduced oil price to squeeze the U.S.S.R. and Iran, and the Gulf War of 1991 – foreign intervention in the Middle East has been an almost complete multinational, multi-partisan failure. Western Europe's only policy has been to be more favourable to the Arabs and less friendly to Israel than the Americans, and Russia and China have just been irresponsible and rather ineffectual mischief-makers.

Revolutionary movements always move to the left until they can't be more extreme and there is a reaction. We are there with Islamic State; and chaos always yields to the quest for order, and we can't be far from that either. The Middle East may yet struggle to the merciful end of the Obama administration without blowing up. Then either Hillary Clinton or Jeb Bush (though neither is a likely candidate for Mount Rushmore), or another contender, could still prevent or destroy the Iranian nuclear program from the air; and force Turkey to choose between expulsion from NATO and the end of EU preferences, and playing a role in calming Syria and Sunni Iraq and accepting an independent Kurdistan. The exhausted and disorganized Arab powers that haven't already done so might then be so shaken that they will finally recognize the right of Israel to coexist as a Jewish state beside a Palestine with sustainable borders. Either way, to adapt a Polish phrase, "In death there is hope."

# THE LEGITIMATE
# EGYPTIAN COUP

*National Review Online*, July 11, 2013

There is too much wringing of hands and gnashing of teeth about Egypt. Obviously bloodshed is regrettable but neither surprising in the circumstances nor likely to escalate or even continue. The Muslim Brotherhood is a vile organization; and Egypt, the West, and everyone with an interest – except the Islamist extremists and those secularists who skulk forward hiding under their piously flowing raiment – can all be grateful that the Brotherhood's plan to execute an incremental coup in Allende-like fashion, construing a 51.7 per cent mandate as a licence to sectarianize the country and translate democracy into dictatorship, has failed. Clearly, a large number of Brotherhood supporters peeled off in the one year of the spectacular failure of Mohamed Morsi's presidency. Unemployment reached stratospheric levels, and he confirmed the wildest expectations of those of us who predicted, on this site and elsewhere, that the Brotherhood would be even more economically inept than the generals had been.

At the end of the Korean War, sixty years ago, Egypt had a higher standard of living than war-ravaged South Korea. At the local manifestation of the Arab Spring two years ago, after military rule in Egypt for almost all the intervening years, by Nasser, Sadat, and Mubarak, South Korea's per capita annual income was five times that of Egypt, $30,000 to $6,000. Now, after one year of the shrill tinkering and posturing of the unprepossessing immediate past president, the ratio has expanded to more than six to one, as the Muslim Brotherhood's economic miracle generated a 17 per cent vertically descending camel ride for the eighty-four million people of Egypt. Whether it is widely touted as a cause of instability or not, this is the primary reason for Egyptian national discontent. There is absolutely no excuse for one-third of Egypt's textile industry to be shut down and for a complete absence of investment and job creation, and scores of millions of Egyptians got the message that the Brotherhood leadership were dogmatic and authoritarian wind-bags who, although they may not have had the time to develop the self-indulgent habits of the entrenched military rulers of the preceding fifty-seven years, were even less capable than the military of generating economic growth, were preoccupied with the devious and illegitimate imposition of their theocratic absolutism on a secular society, and were engaged in the unabashed rape of the democracy that elevated them. It was a swift and providential disillusionment.

The Egyptian army is the most respected institution in the country (as almost the only one that possesses any coherence or discipline), and it did enable Sadat to make an honourable peace with Israel, by crossing the Suez Canal and piercing the Bar Lev Line in the Yom Kippur War of 1973 (although President Nixon and Henry Kissinger had to intervene to prevent Ariel Sharon from forcing the surrender of the Egyptian Sinai army, an underemphasized fact in Egyptian lore). The army dented, but did not fracture, its prestige by the bungling tug-of-war it conducted with the Brotherhood for over a year following the ouster of Mubarak (who was in fact one of the better rulers in Egyptian history, which is proverbially long but not thickly forested with enlightened rulers). This time around, the army took no chances, awaited a vast public demon-stration of discontent, and gave the hapless imposter Morsi an ultima-tum. (When has a revolution produced a more implausible national redeemer? Charlie Chaplin could not have portrayed this poltroon.) The army acted almost bloodlessly with the support of a coalition of civilian interests, has installed a neutral government of technocrats, and is promising constitutional reform and new elections. It is a legiti-mate coup: a response to popular unrest, supported by the leader of the secular democrats, the principal clerical intellectual, and the leader of the long-suffering sectarian minority (the Coptic Christians).

The democratic leader, Mohamed ElBaradei (who was no prize as head of the International Atomic Energy Agency, but in the land of the pharaohs one has to take democracy wherever it can be found), is the vice-president of the interim regime, though he disapproves the recent recourse to force to disperse demonstrators. The head of the ancient Sunni Muslim university Al-Azhar, Sheikh Ahmed al-Tayeb, endorsed the coup on the night but has been sufficiently discountenanced by the army's crowd-control techniques that he has announced he is going into seclusion until the crisis is resolved. (This is an admirable response that, if emulated by most university heads in the West, would improve political discourse and could not fail to make for better academies.) The army has placed its tanks on the high ground of legitimacy, as it has entrusted the head of the constitutional court, Adly Mansour (who was chief justice for only two days before his rocketing upward mobility conveyed him to the nation's highest office), with the task of producing all-party recommendations for constitutional renewal and supervising a national referendum on proposed changes and then new elections. There is room for some wariness about the army's preparedness to leave the process completely uninfluenced, but it is scrupulously and righteously populating the ramparts of democracy and constitutionalism, and doing so with its entire arsenal, and that position is practically and morally insuperable. Charles de Gaulle demonstrated this, albeit in one of the most intellectually sophisticated and prosperous countries in the world, in 1968: determination of the course of the country by free elections, with the alternative of heavy-handed military enforcement of the conditions necessary for democracy to function, isolates lawless elements that are trying to exploit civilized discontent.

In Egypt, most of the tears now being shed for democracy are premature, and probably hypocritical anyway. The Muslim Brotherhood favoured exploitation of democracy to destroy democracy; and Salifah, the more extreme Islamist party, stupidly endorsed the army's action for the first few days because of Morsi's pallid ineffectuality, and it has now recanted. The opposition is torn between those who sullenly object to a putsch but cling to the possibilities of democratic redress, and those who are calling for a new intifada. Comparisons with Algeria are completely unfounded. That was a country where a guerrilla army fought a fierce battle with France for eight years, and although the French army effectively won the open war and severely repressed the independence fighters, the French military victory could not produce a political victory and Algeria's independence was negotiated. The emerging Algerian army was battle-hardened, but so was the civil population that nurtured them. The war had killed more than 500,000 people in a country of about nine million. Egypt has no such tradition and historically its people are gentler. The army and all militarily minded people in Egypt are arrayed with the democrats, the clergy is fragmented, and there is no tradition of a heroic struggle for independence – "the peace of the brave," de Gaulle called it.

The rule of thumb in attempted uprisings is whether the authorities will order their forces to fire live ammunition at domestic opponents, whether the orders will be carried out, and whether these measures will suffice. The new rulers in Cairo have already shown that the answer to the first two questions is affirmative, and so, almost certainly, will be the answer to the third. No serious numbers of Egyptians are going to risk their own lives to restore the Muslim Brotherhood over the sternly enforced determination of the entire military and constabulary forces to permit what they are promising will be a democratic resolution of this impasse.

Many doubt the pristine intentions of the army, but when the physical safety and liberty of people are in the balance, they will believe what they find it more convenient to believe, especially in a place where there has never been any sophisticated political culture or popular liberty. More probable than the negative Algerian scenarios being bandied about are the possibilities that Egypt will finally enjoy economically literate government; and that the most populous Arab power will lead the rest of the Arab world in setting aside the red herring of Israel that for so long has been used to distract the Arab masses from the misgovernment they have endured and will focus public attention and official energies on better government. This, as Pope Benedict XVI gently suggested at Regensburg in 2006, has been a much neglected cause in most of the Muslim world throughout these fourteen centuries of the Age of the Prophet.

# SYRIAN SLAPSTICK

*National Post*, September 7, 2013

Not since the disintegration of the Soviet Union in 1991, and prior to that the fall of France in 1940, has there been so swift an erosion of the world influence of a Great Power as we are witnessing with the United States.

The Soviet Union crumbled jurisdictionally: in 1990–1991, one country became the fifteen formerly constituent republics of that country, and except perhaps for Belarus, none of them show much disposition to return to the Russian fold into which they had been gathered, almost always by brute force, over the previous three hundred years.

The cataclysmic decline of France, of course, was the result of being overrun by Nazi Germany in 1940. And while it took until the return of de Gaulle in 1958 and the establishment of the Fifth Republic with durable governments and a serious currency, and the end of the Algerian War in 1962, and the addition of some other cubits to France's stature, the largest step in its resurrection was accomplished by the Allied armies sweeping the Germans out of France in 1944.

What we are witnessing now in the United States, by contrast, is just the backwash of inept policy-making in Washington, and nothing that could not eventually be put right.

But for this administration to redeem its credibility now would require a change of direction and method so radical it would be the national equivalent of the comeback of Lazarus: a miraculous revolution in the condition of an individual (President Barack Obama) and a comparable metamorphosis (or a comprehensive replacement) of the astonishingly implausible claque around him.

Until recently, it would have been unimaginable to conceive of John Kerry as the strongman of the National Security Council. This is the man who attended political catechism classes from the North Vietnamese to memorize and repeat their accusations against his country of war crimes in Indochina, and, *inter alia*, ran for president in 2004 asserting that while he had voted to invade Iraq in 2003, he was not implicated in that decision because he did not vote to fund the invasion once underway. (Perhaps Thomas E. Dewey would have been an upset presidential winner in 1944 if he had proclaimed his support for the D-Day landings but advocated an immediate cut-off of funds for General Eisenhower's armies of liberation.)

As has been touched upon here before, the desire to avoid America being involved in another foreign conflict is understandable. But if that is the policy, the president of the United States should not state that presidents of countries in upheaval (e.g., Bashar Assad) "must go," should not draw "red lines" and ignore them, should not devise plans to punish rogue leaders but not actually damage their war-making ability, should not promise action and send forces to carry out the action, and then have, in current parlance, a public "conversation" with himself about whether to do anything, and should not thereby abdicate his great office in all respects except the salary and perquisites.

A Senate committee has voted President Obama the authority to attack Syria. But he is the commander-in-chief. He has that authority already, and what he is doing is implicitly making the exercise of that power dependent on congressional approval. How does that square with the presidential oath, which requires of the inductee that he "faithfully execute the office" and that he "preserve, protect, and defend the Constitution"?

President Truman famously said, "The buck stops here," and he was right. The American public despises Congress, with good reason. Most of the members are venal, politically cowardly, and incompetent; the idea of those 535 log-rolling gasbags sharing the command of the U.S. Armed Forces does not bear thinking about. And if the United

States is effectively blasé about countries using chemical weapons on their people, as it apparently is about the formerly "unacceptable" development of nuclear weapons by Iran, this depressing news should be imparted to the world explicitly by the administration and not left to be surmised from the waffling of Congress.

What is more worrisome than the fact that the United States has an inadequate president is that the public still accords the incumbent a significant degree of support. If the American people, who have responded to intelligent leadership so often within living memory, have become so morally obtuse that they buy into this flim-flam, the problem is more profound than I imagined.

What America will need in 2016 is a new president who enunciates a clear policy: foreign intervention only to prevent genocide, to avenge extreme provocations, or to preserve world peace, and in accord with constitutional and international law. That policy would have cut post-Korea war-making to evicting Saddam from Kuwait and the Taliban from Afghanistan and modestly assisting the opponents of Gaddafi and Assad (as leaders who had monstrously provoked the West) and would have spared everyone the chimerical extravagance of nation-building in hopeless places. Vietnam and the second Iraq War would have been sidestepped altogether.

The Americans show no sign of wanting their country to be regarded as absurd in the world, and they are so America-centric, and so suffused with the heroic mythos of America, that they seem unable to grasp the possibility that it is.

There is a contagion that makes the condition less startling: the United Kingdom suddenly has begun to appear ridiculous too. The British replaced leaders who did not conduct wars effectively, during the Seven Years, American Revolutionary, Napoleonic, Crimean, and both world wars. But never in their history until last week have they had a prime minister who summoned Parliament to seek authority to make war and then was denied that authority. The Grand Alliance of Churchill and Roosevelt, the Special Relationship of Thatcher and Reagan, is reduced to slapstick farce.

The country that could pick up the slack and lead is Germany, but it is psychologically incapable. A third of its voters are communists, eco-extremists, or cyber-nihilists calling themselves "pirates." They are still in attrition therapy over the after-effects of Nazi and communist rule. And the European power that can't take the lead, because it is almost bankrupt, overcentralized, suffocating in pettifogging regulations and governed by idiots, is France (though it yet has the superb, often misplaced, feline confidence of a Great Power, and admittedly has been magnificent on Libya, Mali, and Syria).

Canada could play a role – but first it must acquire an aircraft carrier and the other equipment necessary to project power. For starters, we should buy one of these splendid aircraft carriers the United States is retiring because of the gridlock-fed deficit and the idiocy of sequestration, rename it HMCS *Canada*, recruit the 6,000 people necessary for the crew, partner with other countries in the aviation industry that can help provide it with the aircraft it would carry, and show the Maple Leaf flag in aid and defence missions in the world. Nearly seventy years ago, recall, we had two – admittedly much smaller – aircraft carriers despite having a population of just 11.5 million. At the least we could get a helicopter carrier.

There is real or apprehended good news in the United States. The United States is a hard-working, patriotic country with a talented workforce and a political system that can generate policy and govern and lead effectively. Unless the environmentalist extremists, who predicted that by now Manhattan would be underwater, the average temperature in Toronto in February would be 20°C, and that we would all be gasping for oxygen, find richer electoral sugar daddies than the oil industry and get political control of that country (almost impossible), the United States will be self-sufficient in energy in a few years. This will end the suicidal U.S. balance-of-payments deficit, cut the worst terrorist-supporting, oil-producing regimes in the world off at the ankles financially, and drastically reduce the federal government budget deficit.

# NO TO A NUCLEAR IRAN

*National Review Online*, February 5, 2015

---

The negotiations being conducted by the five permanent members of the United Nations Security Council (the United States, the United Kingdom, France, China, and Russia) and Germany with Iran over the Iranian nuclear program have assumed a very high importance in American domestic politics, even as the subject becomes steadily more urgent in the Middle East. The principle that the United States would not negotiate with terrorists, though it has been allowed to lapse from time to time, is being left in tatters as these discussions drag endlessly on while Iran's status as the world's leading sponsor of terrorism is intensified, as indicated by the success of the faction it sponsors in Yemen, the Houthis. (They are allied to the local al Qaeda, which claims responsibility for the *Charlie Hebdo* murders in Paris that brought on a march of two million French led by representatives of over fifty countries, including the leaders of three of the countries in the talks with Iran, and the foreign minister of one.)

It seems hard to believe, but President Jimmy Carter fired Andrew Young as the U.S. ambassador to the United Nations in 1979 for conducting clandestine negotiations with the Palestine Liberation Organization, whose almost imperishable leader, Yasser Arafat, was received by President Bill Clinton, with Israeli leaders Yitzhak Rabin and Shimon Peres (Nobel Peace Prize winners all, except Clinton, as were eventually Carter, Al Gore, and Barack Obama), in 1995, though

Arafat, despite being heavy-laden with peace laurels, had not allowed his terrorist activities to abate at all. When terrorism persists as it has, respectable countries have either to obliterate the terrorists (as the Obama administration claimed to have done, causing the reprehensible effort of the president and the then secretary of state, Hillary Clinton, to say that the murder of the U.S. ambassador in Benghazi, Libya, was the result of anger against a crank American Islamophobic video-maker); or ignore them, no matter the scale of their outrages; or negotiate with them. Whatever the failings of George W. Bush, including rather mindlessly promoting democracy in unfertile ground where it produced pro-terrorist results, as in Gaza and Lebanon and Egypt, his deeds were consistent with his words. This regime has talked the talk but stumbled and crawled from the path, and will negotiate with everyone on a no-fault, equal-opportunity basis.

The agreement being contemplated with Iran disturbs almost everyone. The ostensible outline of an agreement is to bring the number of centrifuges (which are the means of enriching uranium to nuclear-fission purposes) down from around 20,000, which is about ten times as many as are required to pursue the civilian nuclear potential that Iran claims to be its goal, to between 7,000 and 9,000 centrifuges. While it is, to say the least, discreditable that the negotiating powers are apparently content with such an arrangement (which also includes handing over a large quantity of processed material to Russia), it is to some degree comprehensible, as all of them except Germany are nuclear powers with retaliatory capacities far beyond anything Iran could conceivably aspire to; and though Germany does not have such a capability, the Iranian leadership, in the full efflorescence of its lunacy, could not possibly imagine that it could threaten Germany, much less act on a threat, without bringing down on its thickly clad heads the maximum military response of some of the other contracting powers.

Evidently, Iran's neighbours, and especially Israel – whom Iran has not ceased to threaten in the most blood-curdling terms since the day after the Shah's departure (a departure that occurred owing in large measure to the hostility of Nobel laureate Carter) in 1979 – see a militarily nuclear Iran differently. Israel sharply disagrees with the United States and the other negotiating countries about the level of nuclear capability it is safe to leave in Iranian hands. So also do Saudi Arabia, Egypt, and even Turkey, though Turkey does so very quietly given its posturing around the Middle East as co-avenger of Islam against the impudent Jewish interloper state (whose greatest ally, outside Western Europe and North America and Australia, Turkey was until the onset of the Erdoğan regime). None of them can be so abstractedly theoretical about Iran's arrival at the nuclear threshold as the five Security Council powers. Obviously, Shiite Iran is at daggers drawn with Saudi Arabia and Egypt, which are the chief Sunni powers in the great dispute and rivalry between the two major branches of Islam (to which is added the ancient Persian–Arab animosity). Iran could dangerously threaten its Sunni adversaries, including Turkey. Egypt and Saudi Arabia would feel themselves much more threatened than Israel, which, whatever the genocidal and sectarian polemics of the deranged theocrats in Tehran, possesses a very sophisticated anti-missile defence and a retaliatory capacity that could obliterate Iran. This has chiefly caused Saudi Arabia to tank the oil price and lay the rod of potential national bankruptcy on Iran, and has warmed Egypt and Saudi Arabia up to Israel as the only country that has both the ability and the will to take down Iran's nuclear capacity.

The politics of the Middle East is like a mess of eels constantly twisting and turning under the floorboards. In such an environment, for the Muslims (and Lebanese and Palestinian Christians) who can chin themselves on the existence of the Jewish state at all, Israel is an anchor of stability and a military beacon of hope. Obama has abdicated, taking Western Europe with him into the pastures of enervated lassitude to join with the Russians and Chinese in the adjoining grasslands of cynical quiescence. A valley of the weak has resulted from the endless retreat of the Obama administration, in which all attempts to disguise the withdrawal from Europe and the Middle East as a "pivot to Asia" have stopped, and from the continued Pavlovian refusal of the Germans to take up the Bismarckian torch of Europe's greatest responsible power. In these circumstances, fierce little Israel stands tall and looms almost messianically in the self-preserving thoughts of its erstwhile Saudi enemies and unenthused post-Sadat Egyptian neighbours.

The domestic American scene is roiled, and not just with the majority of Americans who do not like an unending spectacle of American weakness in the world and do not accept that it is merely, or even, the avoidance of "stupid stuff." Even before any outline of a bill has emerged, the president has promised to veto any bill that comes from Congress that threatens Iran with enhanced sanctions if it does not sign on to the prospective porous agreement. This is pre-emptive appeasement of Iran. It is unprecedented that Obama has dragooned floundering British prime minister David Cameron, who will be facing his voters in three months, into lobbying several U.S. senators in favour of the emerging nuclear agreement. Cameron has thus made himself, as the distinguished Canadian commentator George Jonas recently wrote, "Chamberlain cubed."

The president has stated that the prospective agreement with Iran, like many other intergovernmental agreements, does not require congressional ratification: an arguable case constitutionally, but in these circumstances a red flag to Congress. This pending bill is the only glance at the issue that Congress may have before the stroke is committed and Iran gets the green light to become a threshold nuclear power only about three months away from the joys of nuclear sabre-rattling. Congress has only a limited role in foreign policy (though the Democrats claimed much more in Vietnam and Central America), but it can't be shut out completely in a matter of such international security importance as the nuclear-arming of the Iranian ayatollahs. The impasse is highlighted by reciprocal breaches of normal protocol: Obama put up Cameron to lobby individual senators, which is totally improper, and Congress has invited Israeli prime minister Benjamin Netanyahu to address a joint session of Congress on March 3, two weeks before the Israeli general election, without consulting the administration. It is to this absurd and churlish depth that the conduct of the foreign policy of the world's greatest power has sunk.

This may be the last stop for the non-proliferation regime, which was never more than a club that anyone could join who would pay the scientists' and uranium miners' bills. It would be replaced by security based on retaliation and a vast increase in the number of nuclear powers. Massive retaliation kept a relative peace between the superpowers until the end of the Cold War, but the ayatollahs and those who emulate them are less worthy of confidence in their sanity and judgment than were Stalin and Mao and their heirs. (There was never the slightest question that the democratic nuclear powers – the United States, the United Kingdom, France, Israel, and even India – were interested only in deterrence.) Perhaps Winston Churchill was again prescient when he said in 1955, of the spread of nuclear arms, "Safety might be the child of terror and life the twin of annihilation." But perhaps not.

There is no longer any purchase on the disorder of events, and the Great Powers are not acting like Great Powers. The best that can be hoped is that the Senate will override Obama's veto and that the combination of Saudi oil-price reductions and the explicit, if discreet, threat of Israeli destruction of Iranian nuclear facilities from the air will patch the world through to the installation of more purposeful governments in Washington and London. (The latter could be achieved by a clear-cut Conservative victory, replacing the present coalition.)[‡‡] There are signs of hope in Paris after the *Charlie Hebdo* outrage, and German chancellor Angela Merkel might be disposed to play a stronger hand if she could regain a more determined coalition partner. It is too much to expect less mischief from the Kremlin or anything from Beijing except China's immutable, bemused disdain for everything that happens at any distance from its borders. A little leadership in the right places would go a long way.

---

[‡‡] This did occur, and David Cameron was briefly a much more purposeful prime minister without dragging the ball and chain of the Liberal Democrats around behind him. Unfortunately, he then represented a failure to extract any serious concessions from Brussels, as a triumph, lost the referendum he had pledged to call on Europe, and departed as prime minister in July 2016.

# BIBI IS RIGHT

*National Review Online*, March 10, 2015

There has always been a question whether Benjamin Netanyahu's conservative definition of Israel's security interest was an opportunistic political tactic or a matter of well-thought-out conviction that it was the necessary strategy to achieve for the Jewish state a durable security that would not be available through a more conciliatory approach. Never has that debate been conducted more vigorously than in the recent days around his address last week to the U.S. Congress, and in the lead-up to Israel's March 17 election. Netanyahu was invited by the Republican leadership only, to the disconcertion of the White House.

To all but the most rabid anti-Netanyahu faction, it was an outstanding speech in the force of its advocacy, even to those who rationally disagree with the message. Essentially, the Israeli leader told the U.S. Congress, the American public, and his own electorate that the deal being negotiated between Iran and the group of six (United States, United Kingdom, France, Germany, China, and Russia) to agree on a cap on the Iranian nuclear program that leaves that country just a few months short of a nuclear weapon would be unverifiable, would be susceptible to invalidation by a very quick, surreptitious progress to nuclear capability, and, even if scrupulously observed, would leave Iran at perfect liberty to complete its nuclear military program after ten years without infringing this or any other agreement.

Netanyahu further declared, referring to the presence in the gallery of eighty-six-year-old Holocaust survivor Elie Wiesel, that the famous expression in Jewish lore "Never again!" was now especially apt: "The days when the Jewish people remained passive in the face of genocidal enemies . . . are over. We are no longer scattered among the nations, powerless to defend ourselves. . . . For the first time in one hundred generations, we, the Jewish people, can defend ourselves. . . . I can promise you . . . : Even if Israel has to stand alone, Israel will stand."

Netanyahu has been much criticized, even by some sensible Israelis, such as former Israeli security chief Efraim Halevy, for speaking of an "existential threat" to Israel and referring to prospects of genocide and the legacy of the attempted genocide of the last century. Halevy and others allege that Iran does not, in the prevailing or foreseeable military realities, given Israel's sophisticated air defences and retaliatory power, possess such a threat and that mentioning it is an empowerment of Iran and an encouragement of the Iranians to play their hand with maximum aggressiveness.

I do not agree with this. Netanyahu has made it clear that if he retains the leadership of his country after the election, Iran's ability to inflict genocidal damage will be contested, and that if the blood-chilling Iranian sabre-rattling of recent years were to go unchallenged, that too would encourage Iranian bellicosity. But more important, Netanyahu appeared to be playing the one big card Israel holds in this game. The six powers and Iran may reach any agreement they like, but Israel has the ability, and – given the endless threats of Iranian leaders to destroy Israel – it would be difficult to deny Israel the moral right, to deliver a pre-emptive strike against Iran's nuclear weapons program. The preservation of that card and maximization of its credibility opposite Tehran requires Netanyahu to make stark references to the danger Iran poses to his people. Israel has the bunker-busting equipment that could do maximum damage to the subterranean Iranian nuclear program, and it is widely believed that Saudi Arabia, long one of Israel's most rabid opponents, has assured Israel that it could land and refuel such a mission on the way to or from Iran. This is one of the strangest turns produced in the Middle East by the stand-down of the United States as an influence in the area. It is often repeated that such a strike would cause only a temporary setback, but rarely mentioned that, if Iranian airspace can be visited once, the visit can be repeated as necessary and that each such visit would cost the already domestically unpopular theocratic regime billions of dollars to repair. Saudi Arabia has manfully played its part in constraining Iran's financial resources by cutting the world oil price approximately in half. In threatening to blast Iran's nuclear program, Netanyahu is asserting all the pressure Israel possesses, on both sides of these endless negotiations, to promote a firm agreement that actually does give some comfort to the region that Iran will not soon be a nuclear power.

His eloquent and at times rather affecting words before Congress rang much more believably as an assertion of the pre-emptive-strike option than does the desultory auto-cue comment from Washington that if agreement is not reached, "all options are on the table." Perhaps, but everyone, especially the Iranians and Israelis, expect the pre-emptive-strike option to remain there and not be enacted if it is Obama's decision. But it would be very hazardous to assume that Netanyahu is bluffing, particularly as the cheerleaders for any such action by Israel would be led by Egypt, Saudi Arabia, and Turkey, even if only discreetly and at an intergovernmental level, whatever was happening in the much-invoked, but usually irrelevant, Muslim street. Apart from other benefits to those countries, the removal of the Iranian threat would enable them to defer indefinitely their own nuclear programs, which would be their only plausible response to the arrival of Iran in the nuclear club.

Apart from reminding the world that this option was open and that the world's Jews, in the form of their state, were not now condemned to passivity, Netanyahu urged the six powers and the Obama administration to play a better game of poker. He also reminded Congress that Iran was the world's foremost promoter of terror, and of how often it had been complicit in the violent deaths of American servicemen and civilians. He naturally mentioned that, in the time that these talks had been in progress – as the six powers' position was rolled back from permanent abolition of the Iranian nuclear program to retention of it in a condition only a few months from completion, and even that only for about ten years until the removal of all restrictions – Iran had become the pre-eminent influence in Syria, Lebanon, Iraq, and now Yemen.

Netanyahu also made the generally underemphasized point that the Iranian missile program, the delivery system, is not under discussion at all. Surely no one, even in the Obama administration, imagines that these missiles will be developed and deployed for the ultimate purpose of delivering a small quantity of conventional explosives to a target in another country or continent.

He made a strong argument that the relaxation in sanctions to this date should be reversed until Iran ceases aggression against its neighbours, stops promoting international terrorism, and ceases to threaten to annihilate Israel. And he counselled that any Iranian threat to walk out of the talks be ignored: "Call their bluff; they'll be back, because they need the deal a lot more than you do. . . . If Iran wants to be treated like a normal country, let it behave like a normal country." Obama and former house speaker Nancy Pelosi complained that there was "nothing new" in the Israeli leader's remarks. But when someone is saying things that are sensible and is almost the only statesman in the world who is, changing tunes is not what is called for.

Stylistically, Netanyahu impeccably thanked and placated President Obama – though his olive branch was brusquely rejected – and his address, though very purposeful, was never bombastic; it was in fact quite elegant, including hints of Winston Churchill and Ernest Hemingway ("Some change! Some moderation!" and "a farewell to arms control"). The gravity of the Iranian threat justified his acceptance of Speaker John Boehner's invitation, which was itself justified by the administration's straight-arming of Congress by refusing to show it any agreement with Iran, and probably promoting yet another political legal harassment (in this case, of Democratic senator Robert Menendez of New Jersey, for co-sponsoring a tighter-sanctions bill against Iran). As co-chair with the Speaker, Orrin Hatch, in his capacity as president *pro tempore* of the Senate, represented a distinct rise in gravitas from the churlishly absent Joe Biden. The result of the match is Netanyahu won, Obama lost, and Boehner broke even.

The charge against Netanyahu from Halevy and many others is that he has no policy except rigidity, and that he does not believe in a Palestinian autonomous entity any more than the Palestinian leaders accept the legitimacy of Israel as a Jewish state; that, under him, there will be no serious negotiations and Israel will seek to occupy the West Bank forever. It is certainly time, if he is re-elected, for Netanyahu to address the peace process with a little more imagination. The solution has been visible at least since the famous "Moratinos non-paper" after the Taba Summit meeting in 2001, in which the West Bank would be narrowed and the Gaza Strip deepened and the two connected by a secure road to create a Palestinian entity. Israeli pre-election polls indicate that Netanyahu has gained appreciably since his speech and, despite heavy reservations about him in much of Israel, he is probably the most generally acceptable of the candidates who can be relied upon to defend Israel's security effectively. If he is returned, he really should make a serious effort to revive the Taba approach. Begin did it at Camp David and Sharon did it with Gaza, and they were reckoned to be hawks as fierce as Netanyahu until about the age Netanyahu has now attained (sixty-five). Ever since Great Britain, in 1917, in the depths of the First World War, effectively sold the same real estate at the same time to the Jews and the Arabs (who included a considerable number of Christians then), the two-state approach was the only possible solution, and if, as now seems likely, he is still in office after March 17, Benjamin Netanyahu should get on with it.

# GET USED TO
# A NUCLEAR IRAN

*National Review Online*, June 10, 2015

---

t is probably time for those of us who have strenuously opposed acqui-
escing in Iran's development of nuclear weapons to throw in the towel.
President Obama's determination to transform his and then–secretary
of state Hillary Clinton's fervent determination of yesteryear to ensure
that no such event occurred into allowing it to occur because a nuclear-
capable Iran will revolutionize the international political climate for
the better, is inexorable. Obviously, if Mr. Obama's grace of conversion
proves to be well-founded, all of us who have expressed contrary views,
often in trenchant terms, will owe him an apology. And for myself, in
that eventuality, I will apologize publicly and unreservedly. Any ability
to stop the conveyor belt of concessions to Iran, or even to slow it, has
been defeated by the ingenuity of Mr. Obama's systematic promotion of
the Iranian interest.

The Russians and Chinese, who, although they have sometimes
facilitated Iranian nuclear ambitions, presumably from an addiction to
anti-Western mischief-making, should have some concerns, as countries
with Muslim minorities, about the principal and proximate Muslim
rabble-rousing country in the world adding nuclear weapons to its arsenal. But they have been almost completely inert at the seven-power talks
that have pursued a negotiated agreement with Iran. The three Western

European powers involved, who at times were very feisty and plausible in their professed determination to do their part in preventing a nuclear-armed Iran's coming to pass, especially the French and British, have folded like a trio of three-dollar suitcases. And Mr. Obama's definition of a satisfactory outcome has evolved in less than three years from the complete abandonment of any military aspect of the Iranian nuclear program to an honour-system reliance on the Iranians, very sketchily verified, that they will not seek to join the nuclear club for ten years, though they have and will retain the unfettered ability to do so in a few months and are permitted explicitly to do so at the end of that time. Between $30 billion and $150 billion of blocked Iranian funds will be promptly released from sanctions, and almost the entire trade and financial embargo against Iran from the United Nations and most countries will be abandoned and will be practically impossible to resurrect regardless of provocations.

President Obama is treating the arrangement, in legal terms, as a presidential agreement, like those at Tehran and Yalta, which did not require any congressional approval, which may be constitutionally legitimate; and attempts to hinder its operation by the Senate require majorities that are probably unattainable. The whole effort has been further hampered by the Justice Department's coincidentally convenient indictment of the Democratic co-sponsor of a restraining bill – the former chairman of the Senate Foreign Relations Committee, Robert Menendez of New Jersey – on the customary farrago of corruption charges. Almost every aspect of the administration's effort has been shabby: the attempt to portray dissenters as warmongers, putting British prime minister David Cameron up to telephoning senators asking for their votes, staging the telefarce with the *New York Times*'s Tom Friedman that this and the pre-emptive concessions to the Castro regime constitute a portentous "doctrine" of foreign policy technique.

In about equal measure, it must be admitted that the Iranians have played their hand brilliantly; they have outmanoeuvred and discredited the traditional Great Powers and reduced them, in Nixonese, to "pitiful helpless giants." They have struck a mighty and bloodless blow for militant Islam, and their clear passage into a glide path to being a nuclear power, even if the Iranian leaders elect to take the full decade to get there, will alter the correlation of forces in the world. It will show that, after the Iraq and Afghanistan war fiascos co-authored by George W. Bush and Barack Obama, there are no remaining Great Powers in the world and even the strongest countries have no stomach for anything more than self-defence, if that. It is a cowardly, or at the very best a timid, new world.

We will all pad somnolently through the nineteen months to next inauguration day, when any of the prominent Republicans or Hillary Clinton will take the presidential oath with a presumably more precise definition of America's place in the world than the whimsical, capricious, and feckless dilettantism that has afflicted American foreign policy and accelerated the dilution of the foreign policy of its nominal allies in the last fifteen years. All that is really required, and has been required these many years, is a clear definition of the national security interests of the United States, as serious presidents or their authorized spokesmen have usefully provided from time to time – from Franklin D. Roosevelt in hemispheric matters while in Canada in 1938 and to support the war effort of the democracies in 1940 and 1941; to Harry S. Truman, George C. Marshall, and Dean Acheson, in aiding Greece and Turkey, ordering the Berlin Airlift, giving Marshall Plan assistance to Western Europe, setting up NATO, and defending South Korea (though Acheson notoriously omitted mention of this country in a seminal speech to the National Press Club in 1950); through Dwight D. Eisenhower in the Formosa Resolution, John F. Kennedy over nuclear missiles in Cuba, Lyndon Johnson on South Vietnam, Richard Nixon and Henry Kissinger in a broad redefinition to allow for improving relations with China and the U.S.S.R., and Ronald Reagan and George H.W. Bush in bringing the Cold War to a very satisfactory end.

The preoccupation of George W. Bush with democracy led to the triumph of undemocratic movements by democratic means, in Gaza, Lebanon, Egypt, and Iraq, and President Obama has attempted no definition at all of the American national security interest, returning us, in this one respect only, to the era of Calvin Coolidge. (Even Herbert Hoover managed the Stimson Doctrine of non-recognition of territorial expansion by illegitimate force, which drove Japan out of the League of Nations over its seizure of Manchuria.) Distinguished former Canadian diplomat Derek Burney recently spoke for many veterans of the Western Alliance in its prime, and spoke nothing but the truth, in saying that "hastily cobbled together coalitions under irresolute U.S. leadership are proving to be insufficient."

No reasonable foreigner can dispute the right or even the wisdom of the Americans in no longer wishing to be the world's policeman, or even the world's air-raid warden. Apart from humanitarian factors, there is no reason that Americans should care about or play any part in these frequent smash-ups of illogically conceived countries, usually patched together by European foreign ministers in the nineteenth or early twentieth century with no thought to ethnic or tribal facts on the ground. But Franklin D. Roosevelt determined, and the consensus to support his policy is almost certainly still in place, that the United States should support indigenous forces to prevent totalitarian enemies of America from securing control of Western Europe or the Far East. The European countries terribly abused the risk-sharing and burden-sharing confidence trick that enabled them to claim that the fact that they were at closer direct risk from the Soviet Union meant that the United States could pay the price of protecting them. This led to a more supine, flaccid, contemptibly impotent Western Europe today than almost anyone imagined possible, so soon after the vigorous nationalism of Charles de Gaulle and Margaret Thatcher.

The Indians, Japanese, Indonesians, Vietnamese, South Koreans, Filipinos, Thais, Australians, and New Zealanders will not need much encouragement from the United States (and surely by now don't expect much) to resist the almost Kaiser Wilhelm regional bully-boy schoolyard antics of China. As soon as his currency recovers from the hammering the Saudis gave it by tanking the oil price (when they were aiming at Iran and not Russia), Vladimir Putin will presumably expose NATO as the farce it has become by promoting the agitation of ethnic Russians in Latvia, Lithuania, and Estonia. It is unlikely that the NATO formula of "An attack upon one is an attack upon all" will be held to apply (as it did after the 9/11 attacks on New York and Washington) to those little countries that Russia has ruled for most of the last three hundred years. I am a diehard supporter of the Western Alliance concept, who always pauses on the June 6 anniversary of D-Day to recite from memory Roosevelt's brief address on that day concluding that the valour of America's sons, "pride of our nation," and its allies would produce "a peace invulnerable to the schemings of unworthy men." And I dare to hope (prayerfully) that Ukraine survives the venomous arachnoid depredations of Putin long enough for a new U.S. president to put something bracing up the backbone of the Germans. Chancellor Merkel, despite her irresolute coalition partner (the SPD), has had every opportunity to be Bismarck in drag and lead Germany back, after a lapse of 125 years, to filling responsibly the role of Europe's greatest power. She has refused military aid to Ukraine, done nothing to reduce German dependence on Russian natural gas, and failed to prevent Germany's drift toward a mindless, delusional pacifism. The eminent novelist Günter Grass, Waffen SS veteran and long-time pacifist, has died, but his confused spirit is in the ascendant.

Even in the Middle East, and even after the diplomatic triumph of the Iranian theocrats, the evaporation of outside influences is having a somewhat salutary effect on the local regimes that are still functioning throughout the borders their former colonial masters assigned them. The Iranians will presumably not rush to nuclear military capability: they would try rather to avoid a Saudi–Egyptian importuning of Israel to strike at Iran's nuclear capacity, to avoid promoting the election of a purposeful foreign policy president in the United States, to confirm the wisdom of the servile appeasement by the six major powers who were co-signatories of the Iranian nuclear agreement, and even to try to forestall a rush to nuclear arms by the Saudis, Egyptians, and Turks. (Pakistan would love to sell them the technology, but Egypt, especially, would find it an onerous expense.)

And the forces of moderation, beleaguered though they are in that region, have gained some ground. Turkey's egregious President Erdoğan has taken a good slap in the mouth from his voters: the Kurds hold the legislative balance of power, and the Kemalists and Nationalists came in almost even with Erdoğan's party in the legislative elections. His capacity to destabilize the region with his posturings from his ungainly $700-million palace should be appreciably reduced. Amnesty International, in a virtual Damascene act of conversion, has condemned Hamas, which may mean that the tired and senile leopard of the international left will be less of a nuisance on Israel's back than it has been. And, it must be said, President Obama's endorsement of the two-state solution in his interview with Al Arabiya was moderate and sensible. (Though that is what the world came to expect from U.S. presidents from Franklin Roosevelt to Bill Clinton.)

The imminent success of Iran will change the world for the worse. But stones still fall downwards, shrimps don't sing, pigs don't fly, the sun still rises each day, and a little leadership in high places would uplift the weary and slake the parched throats of a world that has been groaning for leadership.

# CELEBRITIES & FRIENDS

## A SEARCH FOR THE ABSURD

*Catholic Herald (U.K.)*, November 23, 1990

My most vivid memories of Malcolm Muggeridge, whom I knew for almost the last twenty years of his life, are of his proverbial, if usually rather acerbic, wit, of his patient and unfailing courtesy, and, right to the end, of the ironic serenity that enveloped all contemplations of his long life or of his approaching departure from it.

The singularity of his wit, as he would doubtless be happy to have it described, was based on his relentless and always successful search for the absurd, which he was confident underlay almost all human behaviour, except some spiritual activity. He used to shriek with delight at every reference he made to the alleged fact that Howard Hughes, "the wealthiest man in the world, died of malnutrition," or that Field Marshal Sir Alan Brooke was reported to have whispered of Sir Winston Churchill, at a ceremony marking the pinnacle of Churchill's wartime achievement, that he "hated more than loved" his chief.

As all of his readers would know, Malcolm was a leveller, but not of the usual envious or even cynical type. He didn't believe that the great or rich or even ostensibly virtuous were really superior to others, merely more apparently fortunate or coherently motivated. Thus, he had no difficulty bungling the prosecution of supposed Nazi collaborators in Paris after the Liberation, because he believed anyone, including himself, could be guilty of almost any offence in unkind circumstances, and jubilantly "muddied the waters" in favour of all suspects.

It was this skepticism about the conventional wisdom and complete absence of self-righteousness which led to his first great contribution to our times, the debunking of *The Guardian* of C.P. Scott and of the idolaters of Stalin.

He was perhaps the first and most effective of the unmaskers of the bleeding-heart left as when he declared, "I would rather be ruled by Stalin than by Eleanor Roosevelt," and when he produced his immortal mockery "The Character Assassination of President Richard M. Nixon by Arthur Commission Jr." His success lay in the fact that he made no particular claims for himself and started from the premise that almost all ideology and righteousness was a red herring designed to cloak and excuse acts of despotism, fraud, and wickedness. He was in some respects an anarchist, so he could denigrate without having to champion an alternative.

His favourite statesmen, "men of action" as he called them, were those with the most panache, or "mad egotism in a good cause"; e.g., de Gaulle ("*Changez vos amis!*" he said to Jacques Soustelle when Soustelle said that all his friends disapproved of the General's Algerian policy). Or those who were the most severely victimized by their sanctimonious opponents; e.g., Richard Nixon. Or those who seemed the most faithful to certain principles Malcolm respected; e.g., Ronald Reagan and the right to life. (The only occasion I know of where Malcolm showed any pride in his celebrity occurred several years ago, when an elongated American limousine with diplomatic licence plates turned up at his tiny Sussex home bearing a letter of birthday greetings from President Reagan.)

His preferred reading and favourite intellectuals were the most artistically virtuous and persevering writers; e.g., Blake, Dr. Johnson, Cardinal Newman, Tolstoy, Dostoyevsky.

When I first met him, in 1971, and interviewed him for a biography I was then writing of the long-time premier of Quebec Maurice Duplessis, whose correspondence turned up some letters from Malcolm, ecclesiastical matters were much on his mind, but he was no less humorous or ironic for that. He was, however, in that transitional state most easily apostrophised as the incumbency of St. Mugg. He was ostentatiously religious but dismissive of Rome as "interchangeable with the protestants" and of those who had trod the way to Rome such as Waugh (whom he did not like but professed to mourn as a fallen "ally in the lost battles of the future").

Knowing a little of that trajectory myself, I found that he agreed with Dostoyevsky's prediction that if the Church moved to the left it would collapse, though it seemed to me, as Wiseman was advised of the wavering Newman, that Malcolm would "come and he will come quickly." He declined to help me with a nomination I was preparing for the Nobel Peace Prize for the former archbishop of Montreal Cardinal Léger, who had retired to Cameroon to minister to lepers and other afflicted people, because he found that the cardinal (especially to judge from his brochures) was "too worldly."

It was not long after that that Malcolm successfully championed Mother Teresa for the same honour and, as he subsequently told me, decided that it didn't much matter whether he thought the Church was collapsing or not, as people had always feared or hoped that it would, as long as Christians persisted.

Above all, he was a stimulating conversationalist and an attentive and delightful host. Many there will be, and I am one of them, who will regret not having made the trip to Malcolm and the saintly Kitty at Park Cottage, Robertsbridge, more frequently these last few years. To anyone who ever made that pleasant journey, it will be deeply saddening to think of not seeing Malcolm again. The memory of him is precious and indelible.

# AN ENGLISH CANADIAN
# AND DE GAULLE

*Institut Charles de Gaulle*, November 24, 1990

This article was written at the request of and published by the Institut
Charles de Gaulle, November 24, 1990, in observation of the centenary
of the birth of General Charles de Gaulle, leader of the Free French,
founder and president of the Fifth French Republic.

---

In 1955 in Canada, in the majestic sunset of the Churchillian era, non-fiction literature was dominated by memoirs and descriptions of the activities of the eminent personalities of the late world war. The conversation of adults unfailingly returned to memories of the war. To my adolescent mind (I was born on the day of the Liberation of Paris), too much weight and self-satisfaction was attached to the recent past, however convincing the evidence it furnished of the vigour of democratic values and of the military capacities of our society.

It was in this context that I read *The Call to Honour*, the first volume of the war memoirs of General de Gaulle, with its well-known first line: "All my life I have thought of France in a certain way . . . the princess of the fables, the Madonna in the frescoes." I read this several days after having read in the Last Will and Testament of Adolf Hitler that France was "a raddled old strumpet who has never ceased to swindle and confound us and left us to foot the bill." De Gaulle's description was always more attractive and believable to me.

I followed political events as best I could starting in 1955, an era which was profoundly marked by an almost total bipolarization of the world and was dominated in the West by the political, economic, military, and popular cultural influence of the United States. The great war hero General Dwight D. Eisenhower, at once a figure of authority and kindliness as the U.S. president, governed, as Malcolm Muggeridge said at the time, "like an indulgent nanny putting America to bed." This American monolith only left a significant place in its alliance for Great Britain and its venerable chief, Winston Churchill, the most illustrious and universally admired of all the giants of the Second World War. The other countries and personalities, whatever their merits, played only secondary roles in the alphabetic alliance systems led by the United States. Their relative importance seemed to be measured in the frequency of the visits they received from Eisenhower's knowledgeable but severe secretary of state, John Foster Dulles.

I remember Churchill remarking to a journalist at the beginning of 1955 that he favoured a meeting of the Big Three (the United States, U.S.S.R., and United Kingdom, whose leaders had not met for a decade) in order to reduce tensions, and, he added, somewhat gratuitously, perhaps a meeting of the Big Four. Although I was only ten, I wondered if France, the additional country he had in mind, did not deserve a little more consideration. Could this country, so admired by de Gaulle in his internal exile, have fallen to the level of crumbled empires of the past like Spain and Turkey, or to the rank of our recent enemies, divided and unrehabilitated Germany and demilitarized and occupied Japan? (Japan seemed then to be devoted altogether to the production of paper fans and plastic flowers. Ten years later, de Gaulle described the Japanese foreign minister, when he visited him, as a "transistor salesman.")

My instinctive reaction was that it was not conceivable, nor even desirable, that the Anglo-Saxon powers would so completely dominate the non-communist world. My reasoning was that other great powers had existed since the rise of the nation state, and until relatively recently. Furthermore, to judge from the conversation of my elders, in the Second World War Germany and Japan had so threatened the Anglo-Americans that they had to seek alliance with the Russians and the Chinese. It thus seemed to me inevitable that the English-speaking countries would need allies, and not on a basis of their abject subordination of the powers then slumbering unnaturally in postwar deference to the Anglo-Saxons. This seemed to me to be true particularly because I could not then discern, any more than I do today, any American will to world political domination.

I thought that France seemed our most logical ally; in the first four decades of the century, the French army and the Royal Navy had been North America's front line against the hostile forces of Central and Eastern Europe. Of the major countries, France was the only non-Anglo-Saxon nation that had made an important contribution to the rise and development of modern democracy. France having been one of the world's great powers for four centuries, from Francis I to 1940, it seemed to me a bit premature to consign it to the proverbial dustbin of history.

To the adolescent I then was, these notions were reinforced and given some form when I discovered and read de Gaulle's memoirs, and by an interview that he gave to Muggeridge in 1955. At this point, his following in the National Assembly was only about six legislators, yet de Gaulle suavely assured Muggeridge of his return to power, inevitably and by popular demand, within a very few years. Many years later, Muggeridge told me that de Gaulle was sitting awkwardly behind a desk that was too small for him and had "bad breath." Several months later, I heard on the radio the distinguished American commentator Edward R. Murrow say that the instability of the Fourth Republic could not continue and that this could only become worse with the intensification of the war in Algeria. He said that de Gaulle waited in the wings and that if he were not successful, the communists would follow him.

I followed the fate of the last governments of the Fourth Republic with fervent and partisan interest. When the crisis came in 1958, I had no doubt of its outcome. As Bernard Ledwidge, one of de Gaulle's most admiring British biographers, wrote, "It was so right artistically, it had to be right politically also."

It was an important event for me when de Gaulle came to Canada, and particularly to Toronto, in 1960. With the exception of George VI and Elizabeth II, he was surely the first chief of state in office to visit Toronto, a city then of slight international interest which showed little sign of becoming the impressive metropolis it is today. My enthusiasm for a renewal of France in the world translated itself into an enthusiasm for French Canada also. I praised with the same ardour de Gaulle's restoration of France's historic role in the world and the emergence of Quebec from the inhibitions of ancient economic dependence and excessive traditionalism. The satisfaction that I felt in the resurrection of the French fact on both sides of the Atlantic did not flag even as it became increasingly clear that the rising confidence of the French and of French Canadians rendered no service to the Anglo-Saxons, contrary to the Anglo-French renascence of *bonne entente* that I was innocently espousing, internationally and within Canada.

Although I was only in high school, I regretted the rejection of de Gaulle's proposal for a triumvirate of senior members of NATO. And I had the same feelings when, as a university freshman, Britain moved from the Skybolt missile to the Polaris submarine, technology withheld by the Americans from France, and de Gaulle replied by vetoing Britain's application for membership in the European Common Market. Then, invoking the false pretext of nuclear non-proliferation, Canada refused to sell France uranium, which it easily procured elsewhere. And finally, I had the same uneasy feelings of disappointment when de Gaulle showed a steadily greater interest in the possibilities of an independent Quebec and the resulting dismemberment of Canada.

In 1963, conducting groups of American tourists around Paris by bus, I improvised a little spiel as we reached the end of the tour in the Place de la Concorde. I mentioned the guillotine that was there during the Reign of Terror (1793–1794) and the columned façades of State and Church facing each other from across and beyond the square in the Church of the Madeleine and the Palais Bourbon (National Assembly). I mentioned that behind the parliament loomed the dome and spire of Les Invalides, tomb of Napoleon and Marshal Foch, subtly emphasizing the role of the military in French political history. But, I assured my generally somewhat vacant listeners, de Gaulle had made Les Invalides an inoffensive symbol of the past, because unlike its principal occupant, he had put the army at the service of republican institutions, a process that, as the events of 1968 would demonstrate, still had some way to run. (I tried to rouse the interest of my patrons, who were most often from the Midwest, by inserting local angles, such as claiming, to a group from Kansas City, that we were passing on the left bank of the Seine the rooming house where their most famous fellow citizen, Harry Truman, had stayed at the end of the First World War (he had been an artillery captain), a complete fabrication. Even this did not elevate their interest or their tips, and their leader, a large man, who was one of the last to disembark from our bus, deflated me with the words, "Boy, we're Republicans, and we're none too pleased that Harry came back at all.")

On my shortwave radio, I missed none of the broadcast speeches of de Gaulle, and I followed the Algerian drama, from his magisterial "*Je vous ai compris*" ("I have understood you," said to a vast crowd at the Place du Forum in Algiers in 1958 – half of them supporters of a French Algeria and the other half in favour of an independent one – all of whom applauded) to the "*quarteron de generaux*" (cabal of four generals) speech in 1961, and through the several attempted assassinations ("My enemies don't know how to shoot"). When in 1967 he arrived at Montreal City Hall, I applauded him as the incarnation of contemporary European history. For me, de Gaulle was the veteran of Verdun who had been a prisoner of war at Ingolstadt (captured unconscious from wounds), where his cellmate was future Soviet marshal Tukhachevsky. He had participated in the repulse of the Bolsheviks from Warsaw in 1920. He had been one of the first and most persuasive advocates of air and armoured warfare in the 1930s. He had "assumed France" in the debacle of 1940, and he had been the custodian of French national hopes and traditions throughout what Churchill called "the long night of Nazi barbarism." As a political leader and figure of French literature, he had raised France and its admirers up from the depths of despair.

Naturally, I did not consider de Gaulle a liberator of French Canada. Those who cheered him had no need of liberation. The phrase "*Québec libre*" was outrageous. It was a premeditated incitement of the separation of Quebec from Canada. Québécois as I had become, I wanted him expelled at once, during the night, without even being allowed to visit the French pavilion at the Montreal World's Fair (Expo 67). Instead, after almost twenty-four hours, an official statement was made which allowed de Gaulle to cancel his scheduled trip to Ottawa. (He tried the same routine in an official visit to Ireland in 1969, where he called in a public speech at Dublin Castle for a "united Ireland." Even his weather-beaten host, the eighty-nine-year old President Éamon de Valera, a giant of Irish public life since de Gaulle was a POW, left his microphone off and the country did not respond.)

In any case, even today I do not doubt that the traditional orientation of the Canadian government toward the English-speaking peoples in the world and within Canada, as well as the Anglo-American alignment of all the Canadian leaders de Gaulle dealt with except General Vanier, fed his skepticism about Canadian federalism. He went beyond that impulse to assimilate Canada very insultingly to Rhodesia, Malaysia, Cyprus, and Nigeria; i.e., to British colonial patched-up confederations that failed, wholly or partially.

I never thought that de Gaulle's opposition to the Anglo-Saxons came from prejudice. The generous words that he addressed to Mr. Churchill when he returned to Paris on Armistice Day 1944, and the memorable toast that he made to him on that occasion, convinced me that in relations with other countries, he just put French interests above all personal considerations, a fact that he confirmed on many occasions. In his memoirs, he was generous to Roosevelt and Mackenzie King and very laudatory of Churchill. This was his comment on the defeat of Mr. Churchill in the 1945 British election: "Winston Churchill lost neither his glory nor his popularity thereby, merely the adherence he had won as guide and symbol of the nation in peril. His nature, identified with a magnificent enterprise, his countenance, etched by the fires and frosts of great events, were no longer adequate to the era of mediocrity." He wrote this although "Churchill naturally felt toward France the spirit of Pitt in his own soul."

It is not difficult to understand de Gaulle's irritation at the American flirtation with Vichy (1940–1942) and at the antagonism of the Americans over St. Pierre and Miquelon (1941), and the British in the Levant

(1942–1943). However, he was unrealistic in expecting the United States to abandon neutrality and plunge into a world war in the midst of an election campaign in 1940, and in thinking Britain would give more assistance than it did to a French government more influenced in its fighting spirit by Pétain and Baudoin than by de Gaulle and Mandel. The fall of France was not the fault of the Anglo-Saxons but of the Germans and of the French themselves. De Gaulle recognized many times, and especially in the state visits of Churchill and Eisenhower, and in his memoirs, that France owed its liberation to the British, Americans, and Canadians.

Even if his views were the natural product of a vast experience, always expressed in a style that was both concise and elegant, it appeared to me incongruous that this clever defender of romantic political ideas opposed the fundamentally romantic policy of *bonne entente*. In the last analysis, French and Anglo-Saxon interests are certainly largely compatible, within Canada as in the whole world. De Gaulle himself often emphasized this, as in his exemplary reaction to the Cuban Missile Crisis of 1962, and in leading foreign mourners at the mighty state funerals of John F. Kennedy in 1963, Sir Winston Churchill in 1965, and Dwight D. Eisenhower in 1969.

If de Gaulle had not precipitately resigned after the 1969 referendum over secondary matters of local government and university organization, apparently for obscure psychological reasons, he would have found an administration in Washington that understood and respected him. There is no doubt that it was Richard Nixon's intention to restore France to a central place in the Western Alliance. The United States had begun to withdraw from Vietnam; Nixon and Henry Kissinger had no interest in vague projects such as Kennedy's Multilateral Force, which was essentially an effort by the United States to take command of British and French nuclear forces. Nor would they have retained an exclusively close special relationship with Great Britain, and particularly not with the next British prime minister, Edward Heath, who was rather anti-American. This would have been opportune, as the general's canvass of the domestic and international left had been severely affronted by the general strikes in France and the Soviet suppression of Czechoslovakia in the spring and summer of 1968. Had he remained, de Gaulle would also have found in Pierre Trudeau a more convincing and credible interlocutor in leading a policy of conciliation between French and English Canadians, and in formulating distinct Canadian interests. He would also have learned, doubtless to his disappointment, that in Quebec bourgeois caution generally prevails over the spirit of nationalist adventure.

Despite his cavalier attitude toward the Anglo-French *bonne ententistes*, of whom I was one, my admiration for him never wavered. Apart from his exceptional and heroic qualities, what most attracted me to him, in my youth and later, was his refusal to yield, in any circumstances, to what he called "the dictates of a false discipline." It was almost impossible not to be seduced by this aspect of his personality. He tried five times to escape as a prisoner of war of the Germans in the First World War; he defied the French army high command in the 1930s that favoured a defensive military strategy; he declared by radio from Brazzaville in October 1940 that he was "the incontestable leader of France"; he organized his own parades and ceremonies to observe the anniversary of St. Joan of Arc in 1954 after the debacle at Dien Bien Phu; and on a simple but forceful injunction, he had dispersed the strikers and demonstrators of 1968. I listened with confidence on my shortwave radio as the tempest of strikes and student disorder spread in France in the spring of 1968. In that rich country, the comfortable population has the peculiar habit, from time to time, of suddenly yielding to anarchistic temptations and erecting roadblocks and hurling paving stones at the police, up to the point when, as de Gaulle realized, the people can suddenly be calmed by being made to contemplate the economic consequences of chaos. In his radio address of less than five minutes (the public television network was on strike) on May 30, 1968, this was the spectre de Gaulle raised, and he implicitly threatened the use of the heavy-handed French army in the restoration of order during the election campaign he had just announced. The spirit of disorder suddenly evaporated and the revolutionary soufflé collapsed.

On April 25 almost a year later, I listened without optimism and with some sadness to what proved to be his last address to his compatriots: "The army of those who have supported me will, in any case, hold in their hands the future of the nation." (He later wrote that of all the letters he received after his resignation, the most moving were from Lady Clementine Churchill, to whom he wrote every year on the anniversary of Sir Winston's death, and from President Richard Nixon. I happened also to be listening to my radio eighteen months later when his successor announced the death of de Gaulle in words that were unforgettable to all who heard them: "General de Gaulle is dead; France is a widow." (I found it banal and slightly undignified that de Gaulle, of all people, died of a ruptured aorta when he reached to pick up the evening television listings in his library.)

When I visited the village where he had lived and made world famous, Colombey-les-Deux-Églises, in 1975, Mme. de Gaulle had departed their home of forty years, bringing her belongings in a suitcase, to live out her days in a convent, and my opinion of de Gaulle had not changed. On his simple grave in the parish cemetery (like those of Roosevelt and Churchill, bearing only his name and the years of his birth and death), there were floral tributes from various veterans' organizations and a wreath from Mao Tse-tung. Twenty years after his death (and now, twenty-five years after that), my opinion remains essentially the same.

As custodian and voice of the French national consciousness, de Gaulle is comparable to Joan of Arc and Napoleon. While upholding the highest values of the French Revolution, he has done incomparably more than anyone else in the last two hundred years to restore the stability of French institutions so disrupted by the fall of the Bastille. He has no real rival in the history of the different French republics. He served three of them in high office: he at least perpetuated the legitimacy of the Third Republic, gave the Fourth Republic a civilized end, having predicted from the start that it would not succeed, and he was the founder and first chief of the Fifth Republic, which has already lasted longer than three of its predecessors. A more accurate comparison than with other republican leaders would be with some of the great French monarchs, such as St. Louis, Henry IV, and Louis XIV.

He was almost as great a geopolitician and strategist as Richelieu or Bismarck. The history of the nation states of continental Europe provides no other rivals to him in the political and diplomatic arts. He was the respected, if not always appreciated, peer of Churchill, Roosevelt, and Stalin. The majority of his predictions of the reorganization of Europe and the decline of the "era of rival blocs," which he opposed, proved to be prophetic with the rise of Gorbachev. The same can be said for his vision of the future of China and of Vietnam and, up to a point, in the Middle East. Even in Canada, though he misread the conservatism of the Québécois and underestimated the attractions of Canadian federalism, his championship of genuine equality for the French fact in Canada has been justified by events, even if his undiplomatic interventions were not easily excusable. But it is in France, naturally, that his legacy is most important.

De Gaulle, alone, maintained the grandeur, the permanence, and the identity of France, even as those who officially had the responsibility for doing so abdicated or were defeated. (He wrote of the last president of the Third Republic, Albert Lebrun, "As chief of state only two things were lacking: he was not a chief and there was no state.") He alone restored to France its political integrality and strength when his compatriots, demoralized and confused, determined that only he could save the French from themselves. He, more than anyone else, revived the fact of being French, everywhere in the world, from being a matter of indifference and made it a matter of pride. For this, all civilized peoples, and not just the French, owe him a great debt of gratitude. I do.

# REMEMBRANCE OF
# EMMETT CARDINAL CARTER

*National Post*, April 12, 2003

Y ou lost your brother [last year] and you're about to lose another brother." With these selfless words, Emmett Cardinal Carter began our last conversation, in his suite in the Cardinal Carter Wing of St. Michael's Hospital a few weeks before he died. He was by then terribly frail but completely sensible and of firm voice.

We conversed easily for half an hour, as we had more than a thousand times before over the last twenty-five years. He was, as always, well-informed, and we ranged over many subjects, from Iraq to our company. He had done us the unique honour of becoming a director of Argus Corporation when he retired as archbishop of Toronto and remained so to the end.

Finally there came the moment I had dreaded for years, but which I could not dodge or defer, to say goodbye. I managed the hope that I could call on him again when next in Toronto, as I always did. But I had to tell him that his friendship was one of the great joys and privileges of my life and that no one had ever had a dearer, wiser, more constant friend than he.

His sage response was very affecting. I asked him the state of his morale. "Excellent," he said. He felt no fear and had no significant regrets, was thankful for the great life he had had but already somewhat detached from it.

I asked if he was curious about what lay before him. "Yes, I am very curious. Given my occupation, it would be astonishing if it were otherwise."

When the news of his death arrived, by now so long expected but so hard to accept, I thought of our conversations of twenty years ago, often enhanced by considerable quantities of his very good claret, that led to my becoming a co-religionist of his. I told him then, under questioning, that I was satisfied that miracles sometimes occurred and that therefore, logically, any miracle could occur, even scientifically improbable ones like the virgin birth and the physical ascension of Christ. He replied that if our conversations were going to lead to a clear conclusion, I had to believe in one specific miracle.

"If the Resurrection did not occur," said the cardinal, "all Christianity is a fraud and a trumpery." Already in his seventies, he had bet his life on that proposition. He acknowledged it cheerfully, unshakeable in his faith, but making no effort to exterminate doubt.

Whether in the most informal discussion or on great public occasions, he always knew when to be flexible, when humorous, when unyielding. Even in the winter of his days, labouring under the effects of his stroke in 1980, he was never inept or inarticulate.

And he had an effortless sense of humour. When he stayed with my family and me in the opulent community of Palm Beach, Florida, I asked him on a particularly agreeable afternoon, overlooking the ocean, if this was anything like his vision of heaven. Without hesitation he replied, "If you substitute angels for helicopters, it might be an approximation."

When my associates and I were the subjects of a spurious securities investigation in 1982, I mentioned to Cardinal Carter that we had discovered illegal intercepts on our office telephones, presumably from the Crown Law Office. I wondered if the next initiative from that quarter would be a search warrant on my house, though I accepted that perhaps I was becoming paranoid, since I had done nothing wrong. My concern was that they would seize personal correspondence and records having nothing to do with what they were supposedly investigating, and leak material to the press, behaviour for which there was some precedent. The cardinal reminded me that "even paranoids have enemies," and invited me to leave anything personal I might be concerned about at his house. "I doubt that even the most zealous headline-seeker would try to search your house, but if they try that on me, we can flee together!" (No such warrant was, in fact, sought.)

Perhaps the most comical session I had with him was when he had me to dinner with the delightfully gregarious Australian novelist Morris West. As we moved determinedly into the digestifs, there began an exchange of recitations from memory of more or less apposite quotations, more theatrically rendered as their authenticity declined.

What he could not foresee, he endured. Toronto had little of the problems of other large Church jurisdictions over sex-related clerical misconduct, largely because he moved early and discreetly to screen and treat potential concerns. His dignified and successful struggle with the effects of his stroke was an inspiration to everyone, though he acknowledged he had difficulty with the pope's exhortation to "rejoice" at this providential challenge. Almost his entire address at his birthday party on turning ninety was "Old age is not for weaklings."

The agnostic or anti-clerical elements of the Toronto press alleged that he spent too much time hobnobbing with the wealthy, like Lytton Strachey's description of Cardinal Manning in *Eminent Victorians*. His working life was given over almost entirely to the disadvantaged and he vastly increased the scale of charitable and pastoral work in his archdiocese. His social life was no one's concern but his own.

And in fact his friends were very diverse. When I was in the midst of a financial crisis in 1986, I asked him, if it turned out badly, if that would affect our relations. "Of course not. The only thing I can think of that could would be if you imagined that material things are even relevant to our relations."

Cardinal Carter's favourite single literary sentence was the end of the introduction of Cardinal Newman's *The Second Spring*. It is: "We mourn for the blossoms of May because they are to wither, but we know withal that May shall have its revenge upon November, in the revolution of that solemn circle that never stops and that teaches us, in our height of hope ever to be sober, and in our depth of desolation, never to despair."

In the twenty-five years I knew him, his judgment and personality were always sober but never solemn; and never, not at his most beleaguered and not on the verge of death, did he show a trace of despair. He was intellectual but practical, spiritual but not sanctimonious or utopian, proud but never arrogant. He must have had faults, but I never detected any. He was a great man, yet the salt of the earth.

.On the day Emmett Carter died, another close friend, who had sometimes acted as legal counsel to the cardinal, sent me a message ending, "May his spirit soar and may you meet again." Those prayerful hopes were much in my thoughts at his funeral on Thursday.

# A REPLY TO TWO FRIENDS

*National Post* and *New York Sun*, December 15, 2007

For two years, I have avoided mention in this column of my legal travails, and only vary that this week, in matters already on the public record, at the request of the commissioning editor. Throughout these five challenging years, most people whom Barbara and I really considered to be friends have behaved as friends.

My late father, who died more than thirty years ago, and was a very intelligent man, if somewhat eccentric in his later years, admired William F. Buckley and Henry Kissinger more than any other living Americans. It was a particular honour, later, to have had those men as friends for more than twenty years now. They have both referred to our relations in those terms publicly many times, and Dr. Kissinger did so under oath early in these baneful proceedings. I am often asked about my current relations with them, in particular.

Bill Buckley sent the judge in our case an extremely generous and unjustifiably flattering letter about me. Given his great prestige and celebrity, it was surely useful. He also published a piece about me last Wednesday, which I saw on the *National Review* website. He confirmed that he was a friend, and that all our mutual friends were "close to unanimity of opinion that Conrad Black has nobly enhanced the human cause"; embarrassingly high praise.

However, he also wrote that he had been asked by one of my lawyers to write to the judge for me, and that this was a "painful commission. . . .

It seemed to this friend, as to quite a few others, that he [i.e., I] probably was guilty on at least one of the charges." He helpfully advised his readers that the convictions are "not quite the same thing as" what Lee Harvey Oswald did to John F. Kennedy; that I had presented an alternative defence of innocence and, even if not innocent, that what I did wasn't illegal; and that he had had to restrain himself from writing to the judge about the law and facts of the case.

For no evident reason, he also gave his bowdlerized version of why I am not, at the moment, a Canadian citizen, and concluded that "the tragedy is now complete in the matter of Conrad Black. Only he had the courage and the sweep to throw it all away. Leaving, for his friends, just terrible sadness that it should end like this."

One of the most professional journalists who covered the trial in Chicago wrote asking me if, since "WFB . . . obviously thinks the jury got it right, do you feel you are being tossed under the bus by your friend?"

No, I do not, though I am disappointed. The facts are that I asked a mutual friend to ask WFB if he would prefer not to be asked to write a character reference for me to the judge. I wanted to make it easy for him to decline. He replied that he would like to do so, and so I asked him, explaining that if, on reflection, he would rather not, I would perfectly understand. He insisted that he did wish to write the judge, and asked for guidelines, which one of my counsel sent him, asking him to avoid all discussion of the case itself. He claimed to find it a pleasing "commission." My counsel have never hinted at an alternative defence. My defence is and always has been: not guilty.

More perplexing is his assertion that my "friends," including Bill himself, thought I was probably at least partially guilty as charged. Well-disposed people who think that are likely not to be familiar with the facts and the current state of U.S. criminal procedure. Friends don't usually act like that.

Bill Buckley's late, wonderful, Canadian wife, Pat, concluded our last exchange by proclaiming that it was obvious that I was innocent. Bill Buckley and I share many philosophical and religious views. He knows my admiration for the United States. And he cannot be unaware of the gradual redefinition in recent decades of the Fifth, Sixth, and Eighth Amendment guarantees of due process, the grand jury as insurance against capricious prosecution, the prohibition against seizure of property without just compensation, speedy justice, access to counsel of choice, and reasonable bail.

He, of all people, knows, and has written countless times, that some principles transcend the convenience of those trying to defend them. He referred on Wednesday (as have some less eminent commentators) to my "raw impiety" for criticizing the prosecutors.

To question the antics of some U.S. prosecutors is not impiety. I would not expect most observers to recognize that I am fighting not just for my life and liberty but also for the benefit of certain constitutionally guaranteed rights essential to the rule of law. I did expect that from Bill Buckley, a conscientious, loyal, and intellectually fearless friend.

Knowing Henry Kissinger as well as I do, I suspected that he would behave as Richard Nixon told me he generally did when a colleague came under pressure: privately declare solidarity with both sides and separate himself, so that neither side would confuse him with the other side, until it became clear which side had won. He promised more, and I hoped for more, but Henry Kissinger is an eight-four-year-old fugitive from Nazi pogroms and has made his way famously in the world by endlessly recalibrating the balance of power and correlation of forces in all situations.

The correlation of forces between the U.S. government and me has obviously been generally unpromising, and Henry has less natural affinity for the principles involved here than Bill Buckley does. His statements, publicly and to the FBI, that I am probably guilty of something but that he "never deserts a friend," are not heroic or even accurate, but on past form not altogether a surprise either.

William Buckley wrote on Wednesday that I had claimed from the start that the charges against me "sought to vest in judicial infamy that which is in the nature of things blameless." Those "contending otherwise were obtuse and vindictive, and should be put away somewhere to prevent the toxification of the Common Law and the resources of reason on Earth." This is an endearing exaggeration. But the underlying points of my resistance are not a suitable subject of mockery from one of America's greatest champions of individual liberty.

They are both great men, in their different ways, and their friendship, no matter how idiosyncratic, would be a matter of pride to anyone, as it is to me. I am sure that they will eventually see that it is not necessary to dissemble about our relations and that I have not thrown "it all away." If our appeal is unsuccessful, they can share their "terrible sadness" with their country and aspects of its justice system.

For such men, and for the sake of happy days gone by that could yet return, I offer the other cheek, but not unilateral verbal disarmament. They need only survive and retain their faculties a while longer to see that my present embattled condition is not, as Bill wrote, "the end." I wish that for them, and all other good things.

NOTE:

Bill Buckley and Henry Kissinger are complicated personalities and our relations are complicated. I will elaborate a little on them separately.

It was about twenty-five years after I read Bill's *God and Man at Yale* in the mid-1950s, and fifteen years after his famous campaign for mayor of New York, that we met, and then happened to meet fairly often, and to frequent some shared social circles. He was always gracious and thoughtful, and his wife (from Vancouver) was uproariously amusing and spontaneous. We saw them often, and they came cruising with us on a yacht charter with another couple in 1996 in the Côte d'Azur and in Corsican waters. We are good and somewhat intimate friends.

At the onset of my legal travails, he was, as friends are, very supportive, as was his wife. But as the campaign of official leaks and donkey kicks continued, with the customary drooling amplification of the media, and the dominoes of social misanthropy fell along the great avenues of New York, as in lesser centres (such as almost everywhere in Canada), my informants apprised me now of the softening of the Buckleys' support. Bill even inflicted on our mutual friend Mark Steyn (on the subject of the charges against me) the almost unutterable platitude: "No smoke without fire." I relied on the emergence of the facts to allow the waverers the convenient luxury of an un-embarrassing revenance of fidelity. Bill, eighty, widowed by the end, and unwell, waffled across the double white line with the column to which I replied on December 15, 2007, from Palm Beach, where I stayed in our home before reporting to prison for a supposed seventy-eight-month sentence on March 3. This was my reply, which included Henry Kissinger because the FBI report of their interview with him, which they had to show me but not him, claimed that while he professed friendship for me, he believed I was guilty. (He has convincingly denied this, the FBI did nothing but lie in our case, and I will return to it.)

Bill replied to my column, which was printed in the *New York Sun* simultaneously with the *National Post*, with a very gracious public recantation, and privately that "that was quite a jolt I received from you." He continued, almost affectionately, that he was about to come to a house he had rented in Fort Lauderdale, just south of Palm Beach, and could we have dinner? Of course we did, twice, very agreeably. He published a further column, backtracking, and professing elegant solidarity. When we met, his emphysema was very evident and he was showing all his years, but was entirely sensible and conversationally lively. He volunteered that I was clearly not guilty of any illegality, and that he had underestimated the evils of the prosecution service and the malfunctioning of the U.S. criminal justice system. He also took on board, with whatever level of skepticism will never be known, that I would fight on and would be back. In the second dinner, we got on to religious matters, as he knew that the end was nigh, but was serene and felt he had done what God had created him to do and was not reluctant to depart this life for the next. A couple of weeks later, Barbara and I enjoyed his hospitality at lunch with him in the house he had rented in Fort Lauderdale, right on the ocean. In inviting us, he said that he had recommended that I be invited to be a blog-columnist on the *National Review Online*. It was a gracious gesture – I was so invited a few weeks later, and have continued in that role ever since. His rented home was a charming venue, and it was an unforgettably cordial occasion, full of amusing reminiscences and anecdotes. He walked us out, despite his infirmities, and waved jauntily as we drove away. We all knew, but did not hint, in the manner of such poignant leave-takings, that we would never meet again, at least not in this life. He died about ten days later, and I was writing my remembrance of him for the *National Post* (and reprinted elsewhere) when counsel telephoned to confirm, as I was resigned would occur, that all preliminary appeals had failed and that I was to report to prison five days later. I took up my *National Post* column as soon as I had access to email in prison.

———

My remembrance of Bill follows my column of reply, and it is followed here by my review of Bill and Pat Buckley's son Christopher's appalling quickie retrospective on his parents. This was in some ways an evil book, though I do not doubt that they had their lapses as parents, and Christopher is a pleasant and talented man and writer. My sadness at Bill's passing was not exaggerated, as these reactions often are. He was a remarkable and profoundly endearing man. But there will always remain a reservation with me about the seamless quality of his personality. He asked me to review a potboiler of his called *The Redhunter* for the *National Review*. He did not publish the review, though he offered to pay for it, because the book was being offered as an incentive to subscribe to the magazine, and he did not judge my review adequately adulatory to make it much of a circulation booster. This was in 1999, three years after we had cruised together and ten years into his tenure as a member of our advisory board, which brought him together with many prominent colleagues, including Margaret Thatcher, Valéry Giscard d'Estaing, Henry Kissinger, Gianni Agnelli, James Goldsmith, Lord (Jacob) Rothschild, and others of the same socio-economic echelon. Bill had apparently expected me to write a work of puffery about his attempted whitewash of Senator Joseph R. McCarthy: *The Redhunter*, though I did not realize it and would not have done if I had understood his purposes. When I said that I would not accept to be paid for a review that was not run, and had not realized that he was seeking mere cheerleading, which I was happy to do for him but not for McCarthy, and that he should not give it another thought, he purported to give me the *National Review*'s "Ronald Reagan Award for Conspicuous Service." It was all slightly cultish, and patronizing, though innocuous and a bit amusing.

In our long friendship, I had not much criticized his lengthy and completely unsustainable defence of McCarthy, or his outrageous endorsement of states' rights over federal civil rights laws in the Lyndon Johnson–Barry Goldwater election of 1964. They were ancient history and I liked and admired Bill and what he thought before I knew him wasn't really relevant. I wasn't much impressed by the abrupt manner in which he fired my friend John O'Sullivan as editor of the *National Review*, either; nor by his rather shabby treatment of my friend Rick

Brookhiser, but these were not matters that were any business of mine. I withheld any comment on any of this in my remembrance of him, and in my review of his son's tasteless remembrance of him, until now. I did have occasion to tell him that I thought he had unreasonably deserted Richard Nixon and fallen in with his enemies, who were Bill's political enemies also, and he was such a gentleman as to acknowledge that my biographies of Franklin D. Roosevelt and Richard Nixon had caused him to re-evaluate upwards his appreciation of both men.

But at this late date, in closing the book on the subject of Bill Buckley, I feel that I must say that while I knew him as a brilliant and entertaining and highly cultured man and a delightful companion who held the beacon of sensible conservatism in America almost alone for a whole generation until the rise of Ronald Reagan, there was also a Bill Buckley who emerged occasionally who was the continuator of the churlish and attention-seeking gadfly who disparaged all instinct to reform, didn't notice the twilight zone of the ostensibly emancipated but segregated African American, and thought it quite acceptable for a U.S. senator to accuse some of the nation's greatest soldiers and statesmen of being traitors. There was, withal, a capricious snob who prevailed upon Barbara Walters of all unlikely people to run the errand of finding out if I had had my first marriage annulled (I had) and who happily accepted our advisory fee and hobnobbed happily with the other swells yet told a random Canadian journalist that I was "star-fucking." And Bill was occasionally a ruthless and rather narcissistic man who panned his own son's novel, went to Yale for his graduation but didn't stay to see it, and thought little, as Christopher pointed out, of urinating out of the door of a moving car.

I judge people I know on what I know of them, unless they have an overarching public career that requires opinions to be based on their public records. What I knew of Bill Buckley personally was very much magnificently bonhomous and enriching. We all have our less superlative aspects, but there was something about his that, given his great talent and almost impenetrable charm, was unnervingly banal. Having got that off my chest, I will always see him as an unforgettable personality and a good friend, and it was a privilege to know him, and to close out our relations with a very personal and moving exchange of our religious views, some wonderful reminiscences, deeply moving words of appreciation, and his gracious parting gift of sponsoring me as a *National Review* writer, an honour I cherish every week, these eight years on.

I was asked to comment on the film about Bill Buckley's pyrotechnic exchange with Gore Vidal at the Democratic and Republican conventions on ABC News in 1968, and I thought the film biased in favour of Vidal, whom I also knew. Though he was cordial when I met him, we exchanged acerbities in writing and I found Gore Vidal a nauseating sociopath who revelled in his ability to repel everyone except the fawning acolytes who clung to him like parasites and made and appeared in the film about him and Bill. He was a severely maladjusted and delusional man who often wrote well, but none of whose books have lasted; an unshapely ornament of a transient and insubstantial facet of his times. Whatever my concerns about Bill Buckley, introducing the nightmarish tele-despotism of confrontational programming by pairing a twisted misanthrope with a great champion of a coherent alternative to the long-reigning political wisdom was a shabby mismatch, and parading Gore's oleaginous spear-carriers like Dick Cavett through the film to explain how Gore defeated Bill by provoking his anger when he called Bill a Nazi reminds me like a sharp electric currant of what a civilizing influence Bill Buckley was. A few people to whom Gore Vidal toadied unwaveringly, including Princess Margaret (a very amusing and outspoken woman, though not a very generous spirit), have explained Vidal's attractions plausibly. But that match with Bill Buckley was absurdly uneven: a durable and positive and stylish personality and international public intellectual; and a psychiatric hunchback whose infelicities have vanished and will not be retrieved. I include here my remembrance of him also; it is very rare that I take such pleasure in deluging the lately dead with vitriol, but Gore Vidal and I both earned the experience.

Henry Kissinger, of course, is an altogether different story, and ours is a rich and strong friendship. Our friendship did not go entirely serenely through my legal travails, but it emerged from them stronger than ever, as my relations with Bill Buckley would have, had he survived. This is not the place for a biography of Henry Kissinger. We met when he came to Toronto in 1980 to speak at a luncheon hosted jointly by *The Economist* magazine and our company, and grew steadily, through Bilderberg and Trilateral Commission conferences and elsewhere, and then socially, in New York and London. We became friends, as our wives did; he often stayed in our house when visiting London, and he and his magnificent wife, Nancy, were my witnesses with Barbara when I was inducted into the House of Lords in 2001, sponsored by Lady Thatcher and Lord (Peter) Carrington. When my legal problems arose, he began purposefully but hedged his bets, and I soon judged that the best course was to fight the case, since the charges were nonsense, and I expected to prevail, even though American prosecutors are almost always successful. He wrote a generous letter to the judge, spontaneously, as I discovered years after the event. My informants, who were numerous, said that Henry never said an unkind word about me through all the problems, unlike Bill Buckley's asinine reference to smoke and fire.

While serving my initial sentence in prison, I wrote a review of our mutual friend Alistair Horne's truncated biography of Henry and referred to my friendship with the author and the subject, though the friendship with the subject had lapsed. This prompted a resumption of correspondence by Henry, and when I was released after the U.S. Supreme Court vacation of my four convictions and lived in New York pending appeal, I encountered Henry and Nancy in the normal course of social activity in that city. He invited me to dinner in their home at Sutton Place, and I told Henry that I was honoured by our friendship and would be glad to resume it. I said that neither of us wanted to go over the painful episode that had interrupted that friendship but that I had to show him the FBI report that represented that he had reluctantly concluded that I was guilty of crimes, as charged. I said that I was forbidden to show this to him, but that I was not much concerned with such requirements of the conviction machine of the U.S. justice system. And I said that if he thought I was guilty of crimes, we would not reignite our friendship, but that if he did not, we could and I would be eager to do so. He said, "This statement is false. I said no such thing." I said I had no trouble believing that, as we had exposed the lies of the FBI many times in my trial. He said, "I don't believe you committed crimes and I never did." I said, "I believe you, and I suggest that we put the entire subject behind us and never speak of it again." He agreed, and we did.

In all of the circumstances, making allowance for the caution of a fugitive from the Nazis whose professional life has been conducted in endless measurements of the balance of power between differing contending forces, Henry Kissinger has been a great and constant friend. He visited me in prison and a week after my return from the United States came to Toronto to spend the day with Barbara and me. He is a great and a dear friend, as is his wife, and we have spoken on the telephone at some length every other week for over three years. I am still honoured to be his friend. William Buckley was not as great a man, though he was in many ways a great man, and our relations had come to the same point when we parted. Had he, too, lived into his nineties, I do not doubt that our relations would have settled at the same warm level of cordial solidarity as have mine with Henry Kissinger. I round out this note by reprinting the letter Henry Kissinger sent the chief justice of Canada, Beverley McLachlin, in her capacity as chair of the advisory board of the Order of Canada. He might as well have been addressing a cigar store Indian.

---

*July 12, 2012*[§§]

*The Right Honourable*
*Beverley McLachlin*
*Chief Justice of Canada*

*Dear Madame Chief Justice:*

---

[§§] This letter from Henry Kissinger and the following letter from the counsel of defendant Mark Kipnis to Chief Justice McLachlin, but also for consideration of the governor general and the prime minister, were completely ignored by all of them in their robotic eagerness to legitimize the mockery of justice in my American proceedings and avoid what was spuriously described as "relitigation" (which no one, and certainly not I, was requesting).

*I write to express my conviction that my friend of more than twenty years, Conrad Black, not be judged negatively in any review of his status as an Officer of the Order of Canada. I was a director of the company he chaired for a number of years. Our friendship reflected my high estimate of his moral stature and of his extraordinary contribution to the cause of freedom. My respect for him remains unaffected by the recent past. My very high regard for his integrity and character is unimpaired. Any finding by your advisory board that found otherwise would, I strongly believe, be unjust. Thank you for considering this informed and firmly held opinion.*

Yours sincerely,

Henry A. Kissinger

---

July 16, 2012

*The Right Honourable*
*Beverley McLachlin*
*Chief Justice of Canada*

*Dear Right Honourable McLachlin:*

*I write to provide my perspective on Conrad Black's prosecution in the United States. In sum, I believe Conrad Black committed no crime. In my view, he should not have been charged.*

*The remainder of this letter attempts to describe my background and knowledge of the case so you may evaluate my viewpoint and to provide the basis for the opinion articulated above.*

*I served from 1989-1999 as an Assistant United States Attorney in the Northern District of Illinois, the office that prosecuted Mr. Black. I held various supervisory positions in the Office. When I left, I was the Chief of the Criminal Division. In that role, I supervised every indictment, plea agreement, prosecution etc., undertaken by the office. I do not criticize the Office lightly. In my experience, the people in that office are of good will. As a rule, they do what they believe is right and are not motivated by politics or glory. I have respect for current U.S. Attorney Patrick Fitzgerald as well as the AUSA's directly involved in the case. But they are not infallible. In this case, they erred. This was never a criminal case.*

*How am I familiar enough with the facts of this case to opine that the case should not have been brought? I represented Mark Kipnis, the General Counsel of Hollinger International. I spent years analyzing every nuance of the facts and the law in this case. As a defense attorney am I biased in favor of Mr. Black? At first glance, I believed that an advantageous strategy for Mark was to distance himself from Mr. Black. We could tell the jury: "We do not know whether a crime was committed here. If it was, it was committed by and for Mr. Black. Mark received no benefit and did not intend to defraud anyone." As I learned the facts, it became clear to me that no crime had been committed by anyone. That was the defense we put before the jury. It was largely, but unfortunately not entirely, accepted by the jury. Mark has been exonerated. Thus, I have no further involvement in the matter. I do not represent Mr. Black. I did not view Mark and Mr. Black being on the "same side." If the evidence allowed for a defense of Mark that blamed Mr. Black for crimes, I would have put that defense forward vigorously. It did not so allow because no crime was committed. If I am biased for Mr. Black, therefore, it is only because of my strong view of his innocence after becoming intimately familiar with the facts of the case.*

*The government's case was long and complex. An explanation of its flaws would unduly tax your patience. Suffice to say, Mr. Black primarily was responsible for the growth of a media empire. He took struggling newspapers across the United States and Canada and made them into profitable ventures. He dramatically improved their quality and efficiency. My Black also has the foresight to realize that the internet was going to change media. As the market for newspapers peaked, he sold many of Hollinger's holdings. Through this astute business planning, he made hundreds of millions of dollars for Hollinger's shareholders.*

*A standard provision in the sale of a newspaper is a non-competition agreement. That is, the seller of the newspaper agrees to not compete with the new buyer of the newspaper. This helps the buyer preserve the value of the paper. It also has value. A portion of the purchase price is allocated to this non-competition agreement. No one contended this was improper.*

*When Hollinger sold its Canadian newspapers to CanWest, the purchaser of those papers insisted that Mr. Black sign a non-competition agreement. After all, he reasoned, what good is a non-competition agreement signed by Hollinger if Conrad Black is free to compete against me? The rationale for the provision becomes all the more clear when one recognizes that the manner in which Mr. Black's*

*employment with Hollinger was set up, Mr. Black
and the other executives named in the non competes
in this case were actually employed by another corporate entity, Ravelston and not by Hollinger itself.
Of course, Conrad Black was compensated for this
non-competition agreement. Because this payment was a related party payment, i.e., the amount
of money apportioned to these non-competition
agreements was decided upon by Hollinger, not the
buyer, Hollinger's audit committee had to approve
such payment. Mr. Black was not a member of the
audit committee nor did he appear before it. Rather,
Mark Kipnis presented these matters to the audit
committee. There is no question that the CanWest
non-competition payment, by far the largest made,
was presented and approved by the audit committee. The government did not assert these payments
to Mr. Black were improper in any way.*

*The government contended that the prob-
lem began with non-competition payments made
in American newspaper transactions after the
CanWest transaction. David Radler, not Conrad
Black, was in charge of the American newspaper
group over which Radler served as president and
it was David Radler who was in charge of inserting non compete agreements into the transactions
involving the American newspapers. In those transactions, Mark Kipnis used the same template for
most of the remaining transactions. He presented
these matters to the audit committee for approval.
The audit committee approved them. In public filings that Mr. Black saw and signed, the audit committee members repeatedly averred that they saw
and approved these payments. But when the glare
of public opinion was focused on the audit committee members, they suddenly claimed they did*

*not know about or approve these transactions prob-*
*ably influenced by threats from the Securities and*
*Exchange Commission which had agreed not to*
*charge them with any misconduct in exchange for*
*their testimony. The government seized upon these*
*self-serving statements and charged Mr. Black, and*
*the others, with receiving this money without autho-*
*rization. The jury did not credit this incredibly testi-*
*mony of the audit committee. They acquitted all the*
*defendants of these charges.*

*The single charge that remained against*
*Mr. Black was the smallest transaction in the case.*
*In that transaction, Mark Kipnis, because of a*
*miscommunication with Mr. Radler, did not draft*
*a non-competition agreement. Thus, the audit*
*committee did not approve that payment because*
*Mark Kipnis did not present it to them. Critically,*
*however, Mr. Black would have had no idea that*
*this was not presented to or approved by the audit*
*committee. Kipnis signed the agreements on behalf*
*of all Hollinger parties. He was responsible for*
*presenting the non-competition payments to the*
*audit committee. And the public filings contained*
*repeated representations that the audit committee*
*members had, in fact, approved these payments.*
*Thus, Mr. Black stands convicted of the smallest*
*transaction of the case based on no evidence.*

*The only other charge remaining against*
*Mr. Black was the charge of concealing docu-*
*ments in an official proceeding. Properly under-*
*stood, these charges are the most absurd charges*
*in the case. The charge was based on Mr. Black's*
*action on May 20, 2005 of moving 13 boxes contain-*
*ing personal effects from the offices at 10 Toronto*
*Street from which he was being evicted a few days*

*later. Mr. Black did not pack the boxes and was aware only that they contained personal materials accumulated over 27 years he had spent at the 10 Toronto Street office. Indeed, Mr. Vale, who was then serving as the interim president has attested that he inspected the contents of the boxes, determined that the boxes consisted of Mr. Black's personal effects, and gave Mr. Black's assistant his approval to move the boxes. Indeed by May 20, 2005 the SEC had been investigating Hollinger for several months. In connection with that investigation, over 120,000 pages of documents had already been produced to the SEC by Mr. Black's counsel. In addition, as Mr. Vale also later attested based on personal experience, various teams of lawyers had been ransacking every document in every file in the 10 Toronto Street office for months having been provided full and complete access to that office by Mr. Black and his staff. The notion that Mr. Black would, this many months after the document review at the office commenced, try to sneak out some theoretically relevant document off of the premises by moving 13 boxes in the clear light of day under the watch of security cameras he himself installed is patently absurd. Indeed, as expected, there was no evidence that a single relevant document was contained in the thirteen boxes that had not already been available to the government months earlier from some other source. Had Mr. Black wished to conceal some document from the proceedings (which he had no interest or need to have done and as the evidence has borne out that he did not do) he would not have done so in this fashion. Finally, despite the existence of a document retention order in Toronto, Mr. Black has never been accused in Canada of violating this order and is presumptively innocent of ever having done so.*

*There is no doubt in my mind that Mr. Black is completely innocent. He has spent years in jail for crimes he did not commit. I urge you not to add insult to injury.*

*If you have any questions, I would be pleased to answer them either in writing, by telephone or, if you wish, in person.*

*Sincerely,*

*Ronald S. Safer, Managing Partner*
*Schiff Hardin LLP*

# CONRAD BLACK ON WILLIAM F. BUCKLEY JR., 1925–2008

*National Post* and *New York Sun*, February 27, 2008

---

W illiam F. Buckley Jr. was one of the great personalities of the United States of the last fifty years. He was the same in private as in public: urbane, humorous, and always cordial. He was the most loyal and thoughtful of friends, punctilious, patient of the foibles of others, and completely unfazed by the ebb and flow of the fortunes of other individuals.

He was the founder and intellectual-in-residence of modern American conservatism. After the severe defeats traditional Republicans had suffered at the hands of Franklin D. Roosevelt and Harry Truman, following the onset of the Great Depression, American conservatism was a detritus of paleo-isolationists and xenophobes.

The Republican Party went for relatively liberal nominees: Thomas E. Dewey (and running mate Earl Warren) and Dwight D. Eisenhower (and running mate Richard Nixon). The conservatives began to revive with the awareness of the dangers of communism.

This movement was largely hijacked by the more demagogic zealots, most famously Senator Joseph R. McCarthy, and Bill Buckley made common cause with them, up to a point. He sought a policy of loyalty of government officials, which President Truman had called a "red herring," and was irritated at what he considered the excessive demonization of McCarthy. It particularly irked him that Eleanor Roosevelt, who had no qualms shaking hands with Stalin's prosecutor, Andrei Vyshinsky, declared that she would not shake hands with Senator McCarthy. Eventually, Buckley took his distance from McCarthy and denounced the far-right John Birch Society.

As the 1950s progressed, Buckley adopted the technique of tweaking and ridiculing the pomposity and pretentions of high-minded liberals. His books, his television program, his widely syndicated column, many debates – which he almost never lost, as much because of his verbal dexterity as the content of his remarks – and ultimately his magazine, the *National Review*, presented a rigorous but humane conservatism that steadily grew in influence.

The most famous of his debates was with Gore Vidal at, and after, the Democratic National Convention in 1968, which escalated to physical threats and in which Buckley eviscerated his opponent, verbally and in writing.

He was so articulate and civilized, a talented pianist, sailor, skier, and a worldly gentleman, who had been brought up in England and Mexico by well-to-do parents and graduated from Yale, that the New York and Ivy League liberal establishment regarded him as an irrepressible gadfly but one of them at heart.

His humanity and gentlemanliness and unfailing courtesy, as well as his wit and erudition, enabled him to take positions that affronted the liberal conventional wisdom without attracting the venomous antagonism of its leaders. His close friends included such contrary spirits as John Kenneth Galbraith, Mario Cuomo, and some of the Kennedys and Rockefellers.

His campaign for mayor of New York in 1965 against John V. Lindsay and Abraham Beame is one of the best-remembered campaigns of recent American politics. He skated rings around his opponents in all-candidates' debates and famously answered the question of what his first act would be if elected with "Demand a recount."

He won 13 per cent of the vote as a conservative and made a "victory statement" in which he assured his followers that their achievement, in winning so many votes "in the most liberal city in the world, will not go unnoticed, in Albany, in Washington, or in Moscow."

His greatest achievement was fusing conservatism and libertarianism workably, and helping the Republican Party to adopt it philosophically. From Barry Goldwater in 1964 onward, Republican leaders paid close attention to William Buckley, and many important writers and commentators graduated from the *National Review,* such as George Will.

His favourite president was Ronald Reagan, and it is regrettable that he declined Mr. Reagan's offer of the U.S. embassy in London, where he would have been a great star. Typically, he never publicly confirmed that he had received and declined the offer. He was briefly a delegate to the United Nations, under President Nixon, and wrote an amusing book about it. President Bush Sr. awarded him the Presidential Medal of Freedom, and the current president hosted a ceremony observing the fiftieth anniversary of the *National Review,* in 2005.

He wrote an astonishing number of books, most of them rather unweighty adventures of his fictional invention Blackford Oakes, of the CIA. But he also wrote substantial books on politics and theology and was one of the first champions of the flat tax, which was partially enacted by the Reagan administration, and of a more permissive policy to drug use.

He was a traditional Roman Catholic of the most tolerant and wise type, indefectible in his faith, generous in outlook, always principled but never priggish. He had many friends, millions of admirers, and almost no enemies.

He was married for fifty-seven years to Pat Taylor, of Vancouver, who died last year. They were a delightful couple, who called each other "duckie" and uttered a constant stream of witticisms. He had one of the largest vocabularies of any English-speaking person in public life but, I discovered when we and our wives took a cruise together, was hopeless at Scrabble, because he was unaccustomed to using words of eight letters or less.

This newspaper published, about two months ago, some reflections of mine on a column he had written about my legal travails. It was typical of him that he wrote me a very kind message and, at great inconvenience to himself, journeyed thirty miles to have dinner with me twice in the following couple of weeks. Though severely bothered by emphysema, arthritis, and lesser ailments, he was still a sparkling conversationalist and a discriminating gourmand.

In his address on his eightieth birthday, in November 2005, he concluded by quoting Whittaker Chambers, the reformed communist who unmasked Alger Hiss: "I'm weary, very weary." So he was these last years, but he was good-humoured, fearless, and elegant to the end. The influence of his social and political views will long survive him, and his personality will be indelibly and affectionately remembered.

# GORE VIDAL WAS A MISERABLE, HACKNEYED LUNATIC

*Huffington Post Canada*, August 7, 2012

G ore Vidal, who has died at eighty-six, was one of the most obnoxious public figures in the English-speaking world. He was predictably mourned in liberal circles where any denigration of Israel, the United States, American capitalism, the Pentagon, conservatism, conventional mores, or the accepted behaviour of the majority in the West is welcomed as liberative, insightful, or at least refreshing controversy.

In the more energetic of these precincts there was some effort to portray him as a brilliant writer who made a lasting contribution to the literature, and a piercing wit and scintillating salonnier. He was, in fact, profoundly insufferable and deeply maladjusted.

He was the apogee and caricature of a number of notorious types, fused in one ambulatory, humanoid sociopath. His best-known works, *Burr, Lincoln,* and *Myra Breckinridge* (on the basis of the first two he styled himself America's "biographer"), were rubbish; the historic novels were turgid and effectively pointless, and *Myra* was pornography of no particular merit even of that genre.

He was capable of clever and clear writing, and some of his essays were reasonably interesting and crisply turned out. But his claim to noteworthiness rested on his personality. He was the effete snob affecting charter membership in the patriciate; the poseur at intellectual populism while disdaining the masses who were the unwary and ungrateful beneficiaries of his acidulous solicitude; the nihilistic iconoclast despising all beliefs, ambitions, and attitudes commonly embraced, such as patriotism, religion, legality, most notions of family, conventional romance and sex. And most often, he was the ultimate bitchy pansexual, or more likely homosexual.

He set out with an implacable will to be obnoxious, and at this he was an overachiever. He was almost incapable of being civil, much less generous, though he cultivated a social self-assurance by cozying up to the sort of prominent women who for various reasons seek a diverting walker, like Jackie Onassis and Princess Margaret. Vidal was almost constantly and uniformly obstreperous, and attracted little of the convivial nostalgia generated by Christopher Hitchens or Norman Mailer, who were better writers, were not complete cynics, and could retain normal civilized and often spirited relationships with a variety of people.

Vidal could be relied upon to be the evocator and voice of almost every fashionable racial, sectarian, social, or political form of bigotry, an amplifier of almost any group defamation, blood libel, or imputation of conspiracy and wickedness. He was one of the most insidious and relentless anti-Semites in English-language literary circles for decades, and claimed to believe that United States public policy was dictated by self-serving Jewish crooks, starting with J.P. Morgan, who, of course, was not Jewish and had few Jewish associations. Israel was an infestation of shysters, warmongers, and murderers who stole their country and lived from the wages of oppression and racism. All American supporters of Israel were traitors.

No unfortunate event in modern American history could have failed to be a criminal conspiracy staged by those who were apparently most riled by it, while the ostensibly guilty were mere fellow victims of those in the line of fire. The attack on Pearl Harbor was well-known in advance to Roosevelt (which, as I once had the pleasure of pointing out to Vidal, leaves unexplained Roosevelt's orders, via Admiral Stark, to put torpedo nets out around anchored warships and keep constant air patrols 250 miles out from Oahu in all directions during daylight hours, orders that were not followed). President Truman ignored Japanese efforts to surrender so he could have the pleasure of dropping the atomic bombs (the Japanese rejected the request for their surrender of the Big Three at Potsdam in July 1945, which was accompanied by a warning of a new weapon of terrible destructiveness). The terrorist attacks on September 11, 2001, on the World Trade Center and the Pentagon were in fact (of course) conceived and orchestrated by the defence establishment in league with the most sinister elements of Wall Street.

Vidal obviously had no evidence for any of his deranged allegations, and carried to Goebbels-like extremes the po-faced practice of representing the absence of evidence as indicative not of any possibility that the accused was not guilty but rather of the accused parties' fiendish cleverness in hiding the evidence, since their guilt was obvious without evidence, motive, or any plausible connection to the offence. He wasn't a controversialist, he was a loopy, and at times almost psychotic, myth-maker.

Gore Vidal candidly disliked or hated almost everyone and despised almost all conventional activity and was ambivalent about the rest. He did not seek or appreciate normal civilized human relationships and would, I am confident, welcome these comments as a remembrance from me. It was his honour to be objectively loathsome and a constant generator of ulcerous abrasions and provocations, cloaked only in what he haphazardly held to be the mystique of complete cynicism and the pleasure of uniform, equal-opportunity mockery. He was so personally abrasive and unattractive, it was not energizing to hate him, but, on the basis of my mercifully slight acquaintance with him, I did despise him, though I admit his malignant vivacity of mind at times.

Where he did attain a certain distinction was in this seamless and uninterrupted insistence on being unrelievedly objectionable; a life-commitment he made and adhered to with the will and fidelity of a sacerdotal oath, which literally extended even to deliberate incontinence, to assault the olfactory as well as other senses. In his perversity he did become almost majestic, and so I salute him. And some of his written barbs were lively and will be cited for a time. But he was so hackneyed and twisted and silly and deluded, I cannot even claim to be pleased that he is dead. I suspect that he will not be missed, nor his death much lamented or even noticed by anyone. This, in his derangement, would please him too, and I do not begrudge him that pleasure; I share in it.

# RONALD REAGAN, THE ULTIMATE UPWARDLY MOBILE AMERICAN

*National Post*, February 5, 2011

---

R onald Reagan, the centenary of whose birth falls on Sunday, had perhaps, of all presidents, the most astonishingly American of lives.

Abraham Lincoln, born in a log cabin and with only a couple of years of formal schooling, was an autodidact who rose to have one of the greatest law practices in the United States, helped found the Republican Party, split the Democrats in half in the Lincoln–Douglas debates of 1858, resisted an insurgency in which nearly 750,000 people died – and which he transformed in mid-course to a war also to emancipate the slaves (for both tactical and idealistic reasons, depending on the constituency being addressed) – reunited the nation, and was assassinated at the height of his power and success, aged fifty-six.

Lincoln deserves to be an idol and probably ranks as the world's most admired, as well as America's greatest, statesman. But there isn't much about him that is typical of America, except that it was common for people to be born in poor farmhouses in the Midwest (Kentucky, in fact, despite the endless insinuations of Illinois) two hundred years ago. His life was a riveting epic of heroism, stoicism, genius and tragedy.

Anyone who reaches that great office has an interesting life. But Ronald Reagan, though he was a great president and had remarkable human qualities, was a much more typical American man than Lincoln, with an unimpoverishably happy life and sublimely happy (second) marriage, and was not a learned, much less a self-taught, professional. Nor was he a Grade B actor. In the incidentally insightful words of that insufferable poseur Gore Vidal, "He was one of the great actors of world history who had the misfortune to play in a lot of Grade B movies." His calm good humour after being shot in the chest was not acting.

Ronald Reagan was felicitous, the ultimate upwardly mobile American. He had only six jobs in a career of nearly sixty years: life-guard in Tampico, Illinois; baseball announcer in Des Moines, Iowa, California-bound in the Great Depression; film actor, including six terms as head of the Screen Actors Guild; vice-president of General Electric; governor of California; and president of the United States.

He stood in only four elections: he defeated Edmund G. "Pat" Brown (who had narrowly defeated Richard Nixon four years before) as governor in 1966 by over one million votes; defeated Jesse "Big Daddy" Unruh for the same office four years later with a plurality increased by more than 500,000; defeated incumbent President Jimmy Carter in 1980 by nearly 8.5 million votes in 1980; and defeated former vice-president Walter Mondale by over 15 million votes (carrying forty-nine states) in 1984.

After he got a good look at a 91 per cent marginal income-tax rate in his forties and became a conservative Republican, he never changed his political position. And over twenty years, America came to him. He was correct when he said, "The only welfare system we had that worked was a job"; and as president, he created eighteen million new jobs, net, while the entire European Union (except for the United Kingdom) created one million, and those in the public sector. He simplified taxes and sharply cut the rates. Claims that his job creation was mainly of "hamburger flippers" and pizza delivery drivers (honourable and necessary occupations, incidentally) were debunked by the fact that America enjoyed the greatest productivity increases in forty years.

He traded AWACS intelligence planes to Saudi Arabia in exchange for a lower oil price to deprive Russia of hard currency, ended Soviet industrial espionage by ensuring that they found and acted on plans for gas transmission that blew up a huge gas field in Siberia, worked with Pope John Paul II to destabilize communist Poland and

Sandinistan Nicaragua, and terrified the Kremlin with the prospect of a non-nuclear, entirely defensive, impenetrable anti-missile shield. The U.S.S.R. was already spending half of its GDP on defence, compared to 6 per cent in the United States, and the entire Soviet Union and international communism consequently imploded, one of the greatest and most bloodless strategic victories in the history of the nation state.

The left grudgingly called him "a great communicator" and "the Teflon president." He was a hypnotically eloquent speaker, certainly the greatest orator of U.S. presidents since Roosevelt. Despite aspersions cast on him by elitist Democrats, he hammered Bobby Kennedy and Jimmy Carter in debates, was an elegant and moving writer, and, along with FDR, he was the only U.S. president of the twentieth century to move the ideological centre of the political spectrum.

Next to Lincoln, Washington, and FDR, he was the greatest president in American history, and he got there by uniting in himself the genuine traditional wellsprings of the national character with the presentational genius of a Hollywood veteran who was "real tinsel." He led the United States to a pre-eminence no country has had since the Roman Empire and changed the world for the better; no statesman can aspire to more, and very few there have been who achieved so much, and he did it by letting America be America.

Comparisons with his successors are invidious, but he will be remembered with fondness and gratitude by all who knew him and by scores of millions who admired him.

*This column was written in observation of the centenary of the birth of Ronald Reagan.*

# WARREN BUFFETT'S POSTURE

*National Review Online*, August 18, 2011

I am far from an iconoclast, but I am getting a little weary of Warren Buffett's posturing as a social democrat. He is a brilliant investor and a pretty good aphorist, and his shtick as friendly, folksy Uncle Warren, the Sage of Omaha, though a tired routine, has been an effective one. But he is an extremely wealthy man because he is a relentlessly hardball operator. His masquerade as a public-policy expert is starting to resemble nothing so much as the antics of entertainers who try to translate their renown as vocalists or actors into political influence. But most of them are airheads, oblivious to the fact that it is incongruous to opine on the exigencies of a reformed welfare state while paying below the minimum wage to the undocumented immigrants who roll their tennis courts.

No reasonable person debates Warren Buffett's talents any more than Barbra Streisand's, but in his case, he knows what he is saying is bunk, and he should know that most of his audience is suspicious of his motives. His comments in the *New York Times* this week on why he should be taxed more are spurious, and presumably just another public-relations exercise by a mega-billionaire who sees what a shambles his friends in the administration are making and is tilting farther left to pre-empt public-relations problems. His years of padding around university campuses with Bill Gates in their corduroy trousers and Viyella shirts explaining that they weren't really interested in money were hard enough to take, but this next act, solo, as a slimmed-down Santa without beard, sleigh, or red uniform is wearing thin.

Though I consider the spirit of Commodore Vanderbilt's famous "The public be damned!" to be somewhat dated and inegalitarian, it did – like Orson Welles's statement as Charles Foster Kane (a parody of William Randolph Hearst) in *Citizen Kane* that "People will think what I tell them to think!" – at least have a ring of sincerity. As President Bush II said, in response to Buffett and others, the Treasury will deposit their cheques if they are so concerned that they want to contribute more to national revenues. They don't have to wait for the taxman, or for the legislators whom Warren (a very amiable and unpretentious man, from my slight acquaintance with him) chastises for taking only almost 18 per cent of his income. Of course, I have no standing to debate his tax rate with him, but he knows that the way to deal with the problem he identifies as paying a lower rate of tax than the people in his office and the middle class and even most wage-earners would be a wealth tax, and not a legislative fishing expedition in search of imputable income of very wealthy people less ambitious to provoke tax increases than he is.

He might stand still while the tax-swatter approached, but most of his income peers, in so far as he has any, would not. They would fly away in tax-planning terms, and what we would get is an escalation of the cat-and-mouse game of legislators and tax experts on licit avoidance. And a wealth tax, though it would be more collectible than taxes on large and unconventional incomes, would offend the American ethos of not confiscating, at least until death, the proceeds of the legitimate successes of individual American enterprise. And it would open the gates to terrible abuse. Legislators who are afraid to cut spending, pare entitlements to those who don't need them, raise the actuarial presumptions about social security sixty-seven years after its adoption and after the average life expectancy of participants has risen by over ten years, and other steps that will have to be taken, would resort to tokenistic fiscal persecution of the most affluent. Few living things, animal or vegetable, are more tenacious than a politician clinging to an envisioned panacea to justify the deferral of hard decisions. The country waited for the bust of the stimulus monstrosity, and then for the Simpson–Bowles report to be shelved, and for various futile and demeaning bipartisan jawbonings; if anyone took this Buffettism seriously, it would push things out into the next presidential term.

There are a number of incongruities in the Buffett plan. If Buffett's equity share of the taxes paid by his company, Berkshire Hathaway, were factored in, his tax rate would, I think, get to around 45 per cent. And despite his recycled exhortation not to ask what "your country can do for you," his lobby for TARP [the Troubled Asset Relief Program] and the bailout of AIG, though quite justifiable, was not disinterested, as he was a preferred shareholder, as well as a new investor, in Goldman Sachs, and the pay-through from AIG saved Goldman about $20 billion, enabling Buffett to enjoy a $3.7 billion gain on that position this year. There's nothing wrong with any of this, but designer lobbying for personal gain from official policy on that scale makes Santa look a little more versatile than a night-flying patron of the toymakers and benefactor to the tots.

Warren Buffett knows the reinsurance and many other businesses, but he seems not to realize how easily politicians yield to the temptations of demagogy. President Obama is already grumbling about the "billionaires and millionaires" and elaborating on his redistributive notions on how to "share the wealth." Anyone who owns a family home in all but the very inner cities or outer suburbs without a lot of debt on it would probably qualify for the president's description of being wealthy, and Warren Buffett made the point in his *Times* piece that most of those people are far from flush now.

More important, he knows, but did not write, that even if all his mega-billionaire comrades were soaked 50 per cent of their imputable income, it would not lower the present and projected federal annual deficits by more than one-third of 1 per cent. This prompts the question of why he is playing to the gallery like this. The top 1 per cent of American income earners – as he is perfectly aware, a number that gets us pretty far down into the ranks of run-of-the-mill millionaires – pay 38 per cent of federal personal income taxes, the following 50 per cent pay 3 per cent, and nearly half of American families pay none. Of course everyone but the very rich is worried, and most would be severely threatened if their taxes were increased.

As any experienced observer can see, the answer does not lie in chasing the very rich through the tax courts; it lies in taxes on elective transactions, including gasoline (when buying it is elective), spending reductions, entitlement reform, less government, and incentivization of savings and investment. The basic problems are that too many people (including most of those in government) are addicted to government spending, and that too many employed people don't really add any value to anything and are more of a taxation, even if they are intelligent and work hard (such as most lawyers and consultants). The best thing that could happen in patterns of employment would be if half the country's million lawyers, who bill over $1 trillion a year, donned blue overalls, bought metal lunchboxes, and went out to add actual value – make something or extract resources from the earth – and if half the silly laws and much of the access to courts for frivolous and vexatious litigation were ended.

Of course it won't happen, but for the economy to be robust again, the general addictions to public-sector spending and to the excesses of the service economy will have to be reduced. Much of it is just vocational snobbery, the common ambition to work in skyscraper offices rather than in light industry, as well as the failure to employ unskilled migrant labour in low-end manufacturing jobs and instead putting them to work in sweatshops and lettuce fields and outsourcing the manufacturing jobs abroad. At this stage, increasing supply and shrieking at the public to spend will just create more sales jobs for vendors of French and Italian luxury goods and German- and Japanese-engineered products.

Obviously, after thirty-one months in office, the administration and the congressional Democrats are hopeless in these terms, and one of the problems with the lacklustre Republican race is that none of the declared candidates has addressed real issues either. And the vacuum is unlikely to be filled by the Texas governor who jogs with a firearm in his sweat suit and had his father-in-law perform a vasectomy on him.

Warren Buffett is one of the country's most respected citizens, and has earned that status and held it for a long time. He should not be throwing raw meat to the soak-the-rich advocates, whether of the envious or arithmetically challenged variety. If he said what he really thinks, the country would listen, and it could make a positive difference. With so little leadership in the public sector, his time has come; he shouldn't squander it on nostrums like mega-billionaire taxes.

# THE REAL RUPERT MURDOCH

*Huffington Post Canada*, October 21, 2011

On October 14, 2011, the *Wall Street Journal*, in reporting on the main sentence in the Galleon insider information case, ran a series of five photographs of what were described as "corporate criminals" with their sentences attached, from Bernard Madoff (150 years) down even unto me, at six and a half years. On July 18, 2010, the same newspaper had run an extensive lead editorial, headlined "Conrad Black's Revenge," in which it recorded that the four surviving counts against me (of an original seventeen) had been unanimously vacated by the Supreme Court, the principal prosecuting statute (the much abused concept of honest services) had been struck down and rewritten, and the *Journal* graciously apologized to me for having underestimated the merits of my defence. The high court excoriated the panel of the Seventh Circuit of the Circuit Court of Appeal from which I petitioned, for, among other transgressions, the "infirmity of invented law." My cameo appearance in the *Journal*'s rogues' gallery on Friday pretended that the original sentence had never been assailed or reduced.

In the perverse American manner, the Supreme Court remanded the vacated counts back to the appellate court to assess the gravity of its own errors. This unrigorous and self-interested process produced a spurious but not unexpected resurrection of one fraud count and a finding of obstruction of justice. The fraud count involved a payment to me of $285,000. It was undisputed in the evidence that the payment had been approved by the audit committee and board of directors of the company, and the obstruction was simply nonsense, and was not pursued in the local jurisdiction (Canada) as a violation of a document retention order, and it had no monetary significance. It was accurately described by a former deputy solicitor general of the United States at the Seventh Circuit as "in forty-five years of practice the feeblest case of obstruction of justice I have seen."

It was this nonsense, maliciously retrieved to plaster a fig leaf of plausibility on a misconceived and failed prosecution (that originally sought my imprisonment for life and fines and restitution of $140 million), on the destruction of which the *Journal* had so generously congratulated me fifteen months before, that was invoked to put me in the company of Mr. Madoff and the others.

I have written elsewhere of my protracted legal travails, and the remaining entrails of them will be dealt with satisfactorily in the appropriate courts (largely, fortunately, out of the United States). What is noteworthy in this dishonest donkey kick from the *Wall Street Journal* is what it tells us about the controlling shareholder of that newspaper, the now, to return a frequently proffered favour he served on me, thoroughly disgraced, and in his own admission "humbled," Rupert Murdoch.

As I have often written before, he is probably the greatest media owner in history, and his achievements in becoming the tabloid leader in London, in cracking the egregious Luddite print unions there, in breaking the triopoly of American television networks, promoting vertical integration with television outlets and film production, and his pioneering breakthroughs in satellite television worldwide are Napoleonic in boldness of concept and skill of execution. And no one has been more vocal or consistent than I in saluting them.

I competed with Murdoch, successfully and quite cordially, in Britain for fifteen years when we had the *Telegraph* newspapers, and for a time in Australia. Our relations and those of our wives were always quite convivial. I never joined the chorus of those who objected to his newspaper cover-price cutting in London; as a capitalist I thought he had every right to cut prices if he wished. And I publicly supported him when he almost went bankrupt twenty years ago, denouncing his critics as motivated by envy.

I was naturally disappointed when, as my own legal problems arose eight years ago, his vast media organization swung into vitriolic defamatory mode, endlessly accusing me of crimes years before any were even alleged. When revelations of his own sleazy behaviour came to light in the hacking scandals in England, it also came out, confirming what I had heard from my own sources, and which I would have known from my knowledge of how his company is run and of the dark side of his nature, that Murdoch appears to have personally intervened to make reporting on my problems nastier (despite having assured me in writing that he would try to prevent excesses). My Madoffization last week almost certainly has the same exalted source.

In earlier times, whenever there had been anything even slightly unfavourable about him in any of our publications, he had called me to object, or had his British managing director call my co-chief executive at the *Telegraph*. Even as he was stoking up the media lynch mob against me, he told his latest biographer, Michael Wolff, as he told others, of his high regard for me as a publisher, as if his febrile libels and fabrications were the coincidental, spontaneous antics of autonomous underlings.

Now Murdoch's company has been stripped naked as the lawless hypocritical organization it has long been; its employees think nothing of trolling for the private conversations of the British royal family, bribing the police, meddling in criminal investigations, tampering with the cell phone of a kidnap victim, and engaging in wholesale industrial espionage.

For decades, Murdoch has smeared, lied, double-crossed his political benefactors, including Jimmy Carter, Margaret Thatcher, John Major, a long sequence of Australian leaders, and the democratic forces of Hong Kong.

When the extent of his skulduggery finally oozed out, sluggish and filthy, including the details of the British government's dotage on him, this summer, Murdoch's old possum routine didn't play as convincingly as it had in its many previous auditions, when he purported to be contrite over the shortcomings of errant employees. Bumbling into a parliamentary hearing in London, supported on each arm like a centenarian semi-cadaver, mumbling about humility, trying to represent News Corporation's board as independent when it is public corporate

America's most docile board of directors and is composed entirely of hacks, retainers, and ex-employees; scrambling and whimpering and paying millions to victims of his outrages; putting his name on a *Journal* op-ed piece about education; it's all of a piece and none of it resonates anymore. In bygone days, he somehow carried off sprawling in a black costume on a bed in a glossy magazine and ruminating about being an "ambassador to Joe Six Pack," a champion of the little guy, and a spiritual person contemplating the consolations of Catholicism. At its most histrionic, it was a passably imaginative imposture.

My admiration for his boldness and acumen and our previous twenty-five years of more than civil relations make it unpleasant, despite his unspeakable assault on me, to have to conclude that he is, in my considered belief, a psychopath. I think behind his nondescript personality lurks a repressed, destructive malice. His is, and has been proved to be, in some measure a criminal organization. This, apart from weaknesses of leadership, was always the greatest vulnerability of post-Reagan America's conservatism: its reliance on a man who would put anyone over the side and hoist any colours when the wind changed. Now that the great defamer is a tottering, cowardly supplicant and a potential candidate for criminal prosecution on at least two continents, no one should count on his continued support for more than twenty-four hours at a time.

For my part, I am already suing his company in Canada for the most artlessly libelous book since *The Protocols of the Elders of Zion*, by the defamer Tom Bower. In the extreme winter of his days, Rupert Murdoch's failing hands have dropped the mask; he is a malignant force and it would be a good thing for the world to be done with him.

*With this piece, on October 21, 2011, my war with News Corporation ended. I was almost never referred to again in its publications, and Mr. Murdoch sent out a favourable tweet after a contentious BBC interview I had in 2012. We addressed the same conference in Sydney in 2013, though a couple of days apart, and he replied to a questioner that he did not believe I had broken any laws but had been betrayed by a dishonest associate. When asked for a response, I said I took it as an olive branch from Mr. Murdoch that I was happy to receive and reciprocate.*

# PIERRE TRUDEAU WAS A DILETTANTE – BUT A SUCCESSFUL ONE

*National Post*, January 28, 2012

I regret offending my cordial acquaintance Douglas Gibson. And I salute him for coming to the defence of his authors, Max and Monique Nemni, biographers of Pierre Trudeau. I think I can set his mind at ease on some points.

Mr. Gibson reproached me in the *National Post* edition of January 18 for negatively reviewing the Nemnis' latest Trudeau volume (*Trudeau Transformed: The Shaping of a Statesman*) without reading it. But I was not reviewing the book at all, and made it clear that I was only commenting on the excerpts that had appeared in the *National Post*, and referring readers to my review of the first volume (*Young Trudeau: Son of Quebec, Father of Canada, 1919–1944*), which I did read carefully, in 2006. I detest snide, flippant, and lazy reviewers (and have encountered a few), and would go to unheard-of lengths not to be among them.

The Nemnis have had unique access to Trudeau's papers as a young man, and I do not doubt that their book is a valuable one. But however diligent their research and readable their product, like many heavily engaged biographers they seem to have a take on their subject that I believe is in some respects unsustainable. I did not criticize the

Nemnis for failure to reveal Trudeau's fascist sympathies during the war in which approximately one million Canadians volunteered to help rid the world of fascism. Rather, I criticized the Nemnis' "boys will be boys" whitewashing of attitudes, opinions, and actions of a young, educated adult, which Trudeau never specifically recanted, and only shucked for a no-more-creditable affection for international communism that survived, in a diluted form, to the end of his life.

I had many discursive conversations with Pierre Trudeau, read every edition of the magazine *Cité Libre* while he had anything to do with it, and carefully researched all public aspects of his political evolution almost up to his election to parliament in 1965 as part of the research for my book on Maurice Duplessis. Pierre Trudeau was a delightful man to have dinner with (although he would never pick up the cheque), witty and cultured, and, it need hardly be said, a formidable politician with fine natural qualities of leadership, and he was an important prime minister.

As I wrote here two weeks ago and on many previous occasions, I thought his shift of the federal–provincial rights argument to an emphasis on human rights was a tactical master stroke that left the rhetorical Quebec nationalists such as Jacques-Yvan Morin and Jacques Parizeau spluttering incoherently.

His insistence on no adjustment of federal–provincial powers and on pretending that Quebec was, in Louis St. Laurent's phrase from 1955, "a province like the others," were unreasonable; and it probably cost the federalists some support in Quebec. But these positions enabled him to revile Robert Stanfield and Joe Clark as innocents in a constitutional Babylon who would sell the store to the separatists and fumble away the country. There was some truth to this, but he could have cast a wider net for federalism.

Maintaining the federal state was the first priority of the prime minister, and Trudeau did it. We should all be grateful to him. I am. I suspect that John Turner and Brian Mulroney, who did know Quebec, could have achieved with a little honey as much as Trudeau did with vinegar alone, but they were not on offer.

These great events are for future volumes in the Nemnis' multi-part biography. Where I part company with them to date in what I have read is the dreamy characterization in the first volume of the young Trudeau as honest and true and altogether virtuous; in their presentation of Trudeau as at all times a crusader for good causes, even if somewhat misguided; and in the theory (that other reviewers have mentioned) that Trudeau was, in the period covered in the second volume, comprehensively assembling a political philosophy all through these misplaced enthusiasms for the far right and left.

As I noted in my review of the first volume and in my comments here two weeks ago, Trudeau's agitations with the Quebec Roman Catholic Church were not, as was suggested by the Nemnis, those of an ecclesiastical liberal and secularist reformer smarting under the heavy hand of an antediluvian hierarchy. They were, first, objections to Cardinal Jean-Marie-Rodrigue Villeneuve's and Archbishop Joseph Charbonneau's support of the war effort, and then to Cardinal Paul-Émile Léger's and Archbishop Maurice Roy's inadequately enthusiastic support of Quebec's already militant labour unions. Those men were all strong supporters of workers' rights but had their doubts about Quebec's labour leaders. These were doubts, in respect of such fire-breathers as Théo Gagné and Michel Chartrand, that Trudeau came to share fully and to amplify. Trudeau's patronage of the unions was the affected pose of the dilettante. (He smilingly volunteered to me in 1982 that now that he had run a government for fourteen years, he had a good deal more respect for Duplessis, who reined in Quebec's trade unions.)

Nor is there truth to the theory that Trudeau possessed any original political ideas. He was a run-of-the-mill 1960s social democrat who wanted big government, the nanny-, know-it-all state, high taxes, and the confiscation of income from those who had earned it for redistribution to those who had not in exchange for their votes (far beyond what could be justified by the acquisition of votes for federalism in Quebec, where the money transfer was also largely from the non-French to the French).

It was hard to square Trudeau's professed enthusiasm for civil rights with his friendship with Fidel Castro and other dictators who ruined their countries, such as Julius Nyerere of Tanzania, and his cold-shouldering of Soviet dissidents and other international civil rights advocates, and even the Canadian victims of the Korean airliner the Russians shot down. This was of a piece with his fawning deference to the Soviet leadership and his antagonism to Ronald Reagan, Margaret Thatcher, and even Richard Nixon, who all regarded him as little better than a communist fellow-traveller (and told me so).

His campaign to reorient the Canadian economy away from exports to the United States was authoritarian rather than based on any fiscal incentivization of competition, and was a fiasco. His pursuit of arms control was chimerical; he disarmed Canada, did nothing to reduce the country's military dependence on Washington, and produced a nonsensical plan for more conferences to agree on the unverifiable "suffocation" of defence spending.

Of course, the Nemnis' volumes on Trudeau have not yet covered his time in government, but what I have seen of their version of Trudeau's formative years as the crucible for the measured views of a mature statesman won't fly. He had no interest in a political career until the federal Liberals, desperate to take some of the Quebec Quiet Revolution thunder from the provincial government of Jean Lesage, and to put federalism's case more effectively, beseeched him and others, including Jean Marchand and Gérard Pelletier, to stand as MPs in safe districts.

His elevation to the headship of the party and government continued the grand Liberal tradition of choosing men lately drawn from outside politics (King, St. Laurent, Pearson). He took it whimsically, and much of his record was just idle dabbling, posturing, and the supreme confidence trick of saving Canada with a Charter of Rights that is revocable by each province (and has unleashed the bench on Canadian life like a swarm of hyperactive social tinkerers); and by imposing bilingual breakfast cereal boxes and television programming even in unilingual parts of the country.

It was clever enough that, as the English say, if you put a tail on it, you could call it a weasel: the rights of man and not governments, our (French-Canadian) house is all Canada, and deluges of Anglo money in Quebec in the name of social justice, gracieuseté du Canada. But it was a ruse, made more farcical by the revelation that Quebec's supreme separatist strategist, Claude Morin, was a spy for the RCMP.

The Quebec nationalists took the bait, as well as the federal transfer payments, and today Quebec is a bovine clerisy of civil servants and consultants on life support from the rich English provinces, and separation is just a romantic delusion. I think that, at heart, Trudeau was a worldly Gallican Catholic cynic who sincerely despised separatism, was bemused to find himself a national saviour, and played the role with courage, brio, and success.

I will read the Nemnis' second book. And if I have wronged the authors, I will apologize, but my comments were fair on what I clearly wrote was the subject of them. I wish the Nemnis and Douglas Gibson a full critical and commercial success in this ongoing franchise.

# SEX AND
# THE PRESIDENCY

*Huffington Post Canada*, February 28, 2012

---

The memoir of Mimi Alford, in which she details her affair as a White House intern with President John F. Kennedy, reopens an intriguing question about that president. I am one who thinks he was a talented president who would probably not have made the errors his successor did in Indochina.

President Kennedy, as Richard Nixon said at the time, did hand over Laos to "communism on the installment plan" in 1962 and confirm its status as the Ho Chi Minh Trail superhighway for the invasion of South Vietnam by the North. But having done so, and with his experience of the failings of judgment of the joint chiefs in the Bay of Pigs fiasco in 1961, he would probably have been more cautious than President Johnson was about plunging into that conflict.

President Kennedy showed superior intuition in the Cuban Missile Crisis of 1962, when he rightly suspected that U.S. intelligence did not have the whole story. Contrary to the relentlessly peddled fable of a strategic triumph achieved through a critical path of scientifically calibrated response, leading to the rubbish about the *Best and the Brightest* (who gave us Vietnam for an encore), Kennedy traded long-deployed NATO missiles in Italy and Turkey, against the wishes of those countries, for non-deployment of Soviet missiles in Cuba and threw in a promise not to invade Cuba.

This was no great victory, but unknown to the CIA, there were 40,000 Russian troops in Cuba, battlefield nuclear weapons in place which could have hit invasion landing sites, and the warheads for the intermediate-range missiles that could have reached the southeastern United States were in-country and could be installed very quickly. An invasion of Cuba would have been a much more complicated and dangerous business than the hawks in the president's inner circle who advocated it imagined. Kennedy sensed this and acted prudently.

He was internationally popular, with leaders such as Charles de Gaulle, Harold Macmillan, and Konrad Adenauer, and with the vast public, from West Berlin to Mexico City. And though he came late to the virtues of civil rights and lower taxes, and needed his successor to get these measures through, still he came, and showed the way. They were the most successful public-policy initiatives of the 1960s. He was a man for his times, cruelly removed from them. In retrospect, the four presidencies of Roosevelt, Truman, Eisenhower, and Kennedy, 1933–1963, look like something of a golden age of the presidency, like the adoptive Roman emperors of the second century: Nerva, Trajan, Hadrian, Antoninus Pius, and Marcus Aurelius.

Kennedy was a charming, interesting, and capable president. The vagaries of his sex life don't have any bearing on his historic standing as a president, but they can raise the eyebrows even of the well-disposed. Americans are by now familiar with the phenomenon of a president being sexually intimate with a teenage female intern in the White House, and JFK's peccadilloes were long ago seen in their rightful dimensions as evidence of satyriasis.

Many of the presidents have had extramarital arrangements, and some, such as Thomas Jefferson, siring seven children with his comely slave and intimate of thirty-eight years, Sally Hemings (and the author of the Declaration of Independence didn't get around to emancipating his slaves even in his will), are a good deal more controversial than JFK's antics. No one knows what goes on in someone else's marriage and it is not for others to judge. It is further to President Kennedy's credit that his paramours, allegedly including Marilyn Monroe, Angie

Dickinson, Judith Campbell Exner (whom he shared with Mafia leader Sam Giancana), and many others, were closed-mouthed adults; all the players, including Ms. Alford and Mrs. Kennedy, behaved with commendable discretion.

But for the president of the United States to take this intern around with him, to hide her from view in his car as he went to meet the British prime minister, and to be titillated by inducing her to perform oral sex on one of his aides for his own viewing pleasure in the White House swimming pool, is insalubrious and even neurotic. It is already well known that he claimed to have headaches if he went without sexual intercourse for more than a day; that he regularly worked that activity into on-job visits, as with Marlene Dietrich (after she told him she had done it with his father); and prepared for the great debates with Richard Nixon in 1960 by being serviced by paid providers rounded up by his entourage a few hours before each debate (while his diligent opponent pored through the dossiers one last time).

Though it is not optimal, I have no problem with any of this, and at an obvious, if slightly feral, level, it is impressive. But telling an intern whose principal function was pleasuring the leader of the country to give head to an aide so the president could become the chief voyeur of the nation, gives me, a JFK admirer through all the years, pause.

Again, this seems not to have affected his performance as president, and it is all of a piece with what we know of this strange marriage. (Late on election night, 1960, as the result was uncertain, Jackie drifted into the room and after watching for a couple of minutes, detachedly asked, as if inquiring whether he would be sailing the next day, "Bunny, does this mean that you're the president?")

Dwight Eisenhower's wartime companion, his driver, Kay Summersby, wrote after Ike had died that in their relations he was practically impotent, a point with which the general's son, John Eisenhower, self-interestedly took issue. There has been intense but unsatisfiable curiosity about the extent of Franklin D. Roosevelt's sexual activity with women other than Eleanor (who was relieved to be done with it) after the onset of his polio in 1921, though the medical record showing his continuing sexual capacity is unambiguous. No one will ever know, though his great love, Lucy Mercer Rutherfurd, claimed to be satisfied after he died that she was the only woman with whom he had had extramarital sex.

While the glamorous congresswoman and actress Helen Gahagan Douglas was being pilloried by Congressman Richard Nixon (after she called him "Tricky Dick") as "pink down to her underwear" (going with dexterity for the Red Scare and men's locker room votes in the same swinging stroke), she was living with Senator Lyndon Johnson (the man who would know if Nixon's charge was correct).

The takeaway message is that most of what has been known historically as "the character issue" about presidents and presidential candidates is irrelevant, unless it is a disposition to discard the Constitution and try to rule dictatorially, which no president has attempted. That was the only failing that seriously concerned the principal authors of the Constitution. The attempted impeachments of Andrew Johnson, Richard Nixon, and Bill Clinton should never have occurred, inept, neurotic, and tawdry, respectively, though the conduct objected to was.

It doesn't matter what the president's sex life is, and public concerns on the subject are rubbish. Nelson Rockefeller was almost defeated running for a third term as governor of New York in 1966 because he had had a divorce and remarried. If Monica Lewinsky had been as discreet as Ms. Alford, Mr. and Mrs. Clinton's and the nation's life would have been simpler and more serene. If Ms. Alford had gone public with JFK's antics and had the corroborative equivalent of the blue dress, she could have ruined his career. The behaviour of our leaders won't become more virtuous, but perhaps the country is becoming more worldly.

And if American public sensibilities are now less fragile on the subject of oral sex, it is a small step forward for the opponents of priggishness and hypocrisy, as most people of age enjoy it, and it is much less complicated, politically and otherwise, than the real thing.

# JEAN CHRÉTIEN: A CAPABLE CARETAKER, BUT NO STATESMAN

*National Post*, March 16, 2013

I t was a bit rich to read of Jean Chrétien patting himself on the head as a world statesman in his *Globe and Mail* interview last Wednesday. He was right to stay out of the Iraq War, but for the wrong reasons.

The Americans, British, and others were correct to dispose of Saddam Hussein, even if fear of Iraqi weapons of mass destruction was not the right reason. Saddam had ignored seventeen consecutive resolutions of the United Nations Security Council and sandbagged the nuclear inspectors while boasting in the Arab world that he had weapons that would assist in the destruction of Israel. President George W. Bush had one of his better moments (they were not frequent) when he addressed the UN General Assembly prior to the war. He told it that he wanted to prevent the United Nations from becoming another impotent talking shop like the League of Nations, which had proven unable even to produce sanctions against the serial aggressions of imperial Japan, Italy, and Nazi Germany.

This was the strongest argument for the Iraq War, and it plays exactly to Chrétien's twee nostalgia about the value and integrity of the United Nations. The second argument was to relieve the world of an overt supporter of terrorism and Iraq of a terrible tyrant who remains unlamented. Weapons of mass destruction was third, and at the time all Chrétien could give us was head-shaking tautological clichés that "proof is proof" and that in respect to Iraq's nuclear program it was lacking.

Chrétien was made to appear prescient by the insane decision of Paul Bremer and Donald Rumsfeld to disband the 400,000 men of the Iraqi army and paramilitary groups. These men marched off with their weapons and munitions as if they were going to set up quail-shooting clubs and recreational target ranges around Iraq, and not to rent themselves out as vigilantes and hired guns to the ethnic, religious, and political factions that mushroomed in the post-Saddam vacuum.

That decision must rank with failure to cut the Ho Chi Minh Trail in Vietnam and Laos and failure to detect 140,000 infiltrating Red Chinese soldiers in Korea as the greatest American military blunders since the Civil War, and neither Chrétien nor anyone else could have predicted that. In China for more than six months after the end of the Second World War, the civil authority was the Imperial Japanese Army, under the orders of General MacArthur to respect the civil population and help little old ladies across the street and prevent looting, rather than bayonet babies and rape women, as it had been doing for nearly fifteen years. Similarly, in Germany, General Eisenhower left the local police in place in 1945, on the understanding that any recourse to arbitrary force would be punishable by death. There is a well-recognized technique in the administration of occupied countries of utilizing local forces under revised orders strictly enforced. There was no reason to expect that it would not be followed after the Iraq War.

There is nothing particularly wrong with Chrétien claiming credit for a decision that proved to be correct. Napoleon said that a general's greatest quality is luck, and the same goes for politicians. Chrétien was a lucky politician and would never have held the highest political office for nearly ten years if the Conservatives had not been severely divided by the defection of the Reform Party and the Bloc Québécois. As it was, he has the dubious distinction of being the only elected incumbent prime minister in Canadian history to be jettisoned from the highest office by his own party.

He had his successes, and no federalist should forget Chrétien's heroic service as he toured around the nether regions of Quebec, from Abitibi to Roberval to the Saguenay to the Gaspé, slugging it out with the separatists in their strongholds (and in their own inflections). The Liberal leaders from the prosperous suburbs of Montreal, including Trudeau and Lalonde, were not much seen in such picturesque surroundings. His greatest legislative accomplishment was the Clarity Act (which the current leader of the opposition, Thomas Mulcair, wishes to roll back to facilitate the breakup of the country, while masquerading as the true face of federalism by appeasing Quebec's racists. This fiddle is what caused the defection of one of his MPs two weeks ago).

The Clarity Act, which requires a clear majority on a clear question for the federal government to be obliged to negotiate the secession of any province, was the least Chrétien could do after panicking in the 1995 referendum. After mishandling the campaign, he uttered a poor wail of appeal to Quebec not "to vote to break up the country." The referendum produced a paper-thin negative vote on an outrageous trick question to secede, suggesting Quebec could keep all the benefits of Confederation while exchanging embassies with the world. In the aftermath, Chrétien should have gone farther in the Clarity Act and required that if any province voted in adequate numbers to secede from Canada, any county within the seceding province that voted to remain in Canada, would remain Canadian. He legislated a half-measure. Still, it was progress.

Nor should we forget that it was under Chrétien, with Paul Martin and Ralph Goodale as his finance ministers, that the federal deficit was eliminated and replaced by steady surpluses. The achievement is not significantly diminished by the fact that it was largely accomplished by just abandoning responsibility for fields of concurrent jurisdiction to the provinces without conceding corresponding revenue sources to fund them (and the provinces largely responded by dumping the burden on the municipalities, which is why our property taxes skyrocketed). It was deficit reduction, and it has worked. Debt-hobbled provinces, including Ontario and Quebec, have themselves to blame for their fiscal weakness.

Chrétien was a pretty good caretaker, but his claim in the *Globe and Mail* interview to having been a far-sighted world statesman is hard to take seriously. He laments that Canada no longer sits on the Security Council of the United Nations and has reduced aid to Africa in favour of Latin America. He preens himself for having gone to Hugo Chávez's funeral last week, though he had not seen him since before Chávez became president of Venezuela fourteen years ago, and for having been friendly with Castro. He claims that Canada is less respected in the world than it was in his time.

This is all rubbish. As the Cold War came to its climax, the only way for Canada to have any influence at all was the way followed by Brian Mulroney: to be taken seriously by the presidents of the United States Ronald Reagan and George Bush Sr. And Mulroney was; it was a signal honour for this country that Mulroney was asked, along with Margaret Thatcher and both presidents Bush, to give a eulogy at President Reagan's state funeral. Mulroney and Thatcher had some influence with those presidents, and the realization of that fact in the world enhanced Canada's influence. This is something that Chrétien never achieved himself.

In recent years, the United States has been shamefully mismanaged, both in its huge current-account and budget deficits and by stranding almost all its major land combat units for a decade in endless, unremitting Middle Eastern wars. These conflicts have been fought well but inconclusively and with no visible improvement to the American national interest. Canada, in contrast, has been sufficiently well governed, in part by Chrétien, that there is now a potential for Canada to have some standing in the world on its own account.

What Chrétien laments was an illusion: Canada was on the Security Council because of Chrétien's appeasement of African and Latin American despotisms and of the less respectable Arab countries, including states that tolerated or incited terrorist acts and opposed the right of Israel to exist as a Jewish state. His interventions in the Middle East, as this newspaper averred, showed him to be "clueless in Gaza." Chrétien wasn't amassing influence by standing, as he did, as mute and inert as a suet pudding beside Castro as he accused the United States of "genocide"; he was merely making a fool of himself and of Canada.

He overcommitted to the United Nations, even as the corruption of the oil-for-food program in Iraq reached its murky depths, and pretended that disarmed feebleness was "soft power" and that, in Irving Layton's phrase, "the spitefulness of the weak was moral indignation."

The United Nations is a cesspool of corruption and hypocrisy, and much of its vaunted peacekeeping efforts are just primitive countries renting their armies to local factions, as in the Congo, for hard currency payments. Instead of truckling to its Mugabesque majority, as Chrétien did, making himself a patsy of contemptible regimes, or ignoring the UN, as Harper does, Canada should propose its reform as a condition of fully recommitting to the admirable organization established by the victorious Allies in 1945.

There was always more to Canadian foreign policy than grovelling to dictators and irritating the Americans, but there is no sign, even after all these years, that Chrétien understands any of this.

# MARGARET THATCHER, 1926–2013

*National Review Online*, April 9, 2013

---

The news of the death of Margaret Thatcher is not, at her age and in the condition that she has been in for some years, a great surprise or entirely sad. But in contemplation of the great career she had and the immense service she rendered the United Kingdom and the Western world, it is overwhelmingly sad. In general, Britain's greatest prime ministers have served successfully in wars with other Great Powers: William Pitt the Elder (in the Seven Years War), William Pitt the Younger (in the Napoleonic Wars), Palmerston (in the Crimean War), David Lloyd George (in the Great War), and Winston Churchill (in the Second World War). Robert Walpole, Robert Peel, John Russell, Benjamin Disraeli, William Ewart Gladstone, and the Marquess of Salisbury are also generally reckoned to be great prime ministers, either as stylish survivors, like Walpole and Salisbury, or as great reformers, and especially if their accomplishments were leavened with a tremendous wit, parliamentary legend, and literary cachet, as Disraeli's and Churchill's were.

Margaret Thatcher conducted only a secondary war (the Falklands), as Salisbury did (against the Boers), but she conducted it extremely well and to the ultimate benefit even of the enemy, as Argentinean democracy, whatever its limitations, resulted from the British rout of the Ruritanian and brutal junta that lumbered out of the Buenos Aires Officers' Club in their overbemedalled tunics to oust the nightclub singer who was the widow and successor of Juan Perón in 1976. But as a reformer, who changed the country for the better, she easily surpassed any of the others, and she served longer than any had consecutively – eleven years – since the First Reform Act in 1832 broadened the electorate and democratized the constituency system. In these two hundred years, only Gladstone, in four separate terms and a parliamentary career spanning sixty-three years, and Salisbury, scion of Britain's most exalted family (the Cecils) and chosen heir of Disraeli, in three terms, served longer than Margaret Thatcher, the daughter of a provincial grocer.

It has been a disservice to her great achievements that Margaret Thatcher has been torn down by the left, ungratefully deserted by her own party, and had her privacy violated by vulgar snobbery and snide cinematography (even if somewhat redeemed by the thespian artistry of Meryl Streep). Not too much should be read into the confused defection of the Conservative party from the legacy of the only person in 180 years who has led them to three consecutive full-term election victories. The British Conservatives leave the selection and retention of leaders to the parliamentary party, and have knifed every leader they have had since Stanley Baldwin, who took a good look at the Nazis and retired in 1937, except those who retired before they could be disembarked. Neville Chamberlain, Winston Churchill, Anthony Eden, Harold Macmillan, Edward Heath, Margaret Thatcher, and Iain Duncan Smith were pushed out, and Alec Douglas-Home, John Major, William Hague, and Michael Howard retired before that indignity could be inflicted on them. Sharper by far than a serpent's tooth is a British Conservative MP's ingratitude.

When Margaret Thatcher was narrowly elected prime minister in 1979 over James Callaghan, the United Kingdom was on daily audit from the International Monetary Fund, currency controls prevented the removal of more than a few hundred pounds from the country, top corporate and personal income-tax rates were 80 and 98 per cent, and those who had the temerity and persistence to enjoy a capital gain (which was hard to come by in Britain in that economic climate) were apt to enjoy the exaltation of soul generated by an effective tax rate of over 100 per cent. The entire economy was in the hands of an intellectually corrupt, Luddite trade-union confederation, which chose most of the delegates to any conference of the governing Labour Party, and whose shop stewards and craft-unit heads could shut down an entire industry in mid-contract for any reason, from an individual work grievance to the sour grapes generated by a poor round of darts in their local pub (on working hours).

In the year preceding the 1979 election, in what became known as "the winter of discontent," almost every industry in the country had been shut down by capricious strikes, including the airports, trains, electric power, coal mines, garbage collection, and undertaking. The captains of industry and finance in the City, the style-setters in Mayfair and the West End, the doyennes of Bloomsbury and Knightsbridge, and the denizens of the chancelleries and ministries of Belgravia and Westminster huddled in the cold and dark, dead or alive. Government-owned operations, from the steel industry to the airports, were a cesspool of inefficiency and, in the private sector, large numbers of fictitious jobs were salaried and the proceeds went as sinecures to union favourites or into a pot to be divided at the pleasure of the union bosses. It fell to Margaret Thatcher to redeem Britain from the slough of despond and lassitude in which it had been totally immersed by overindulgence of the workers' leaders in guilt over the inequalities of British life. These were brought out in vivid relief when the whole nation fought together, with egalitarian valour, through the horrors of the world wars.

The Britain whose headship Margaret Thatcher had assumed had not led a foreign military operation since the debacle at Suez in 1956, in which the British and French, by prearrangement and without consulting the United States, incited an Israeli invasion of the Sinai and then bunglingly invaded Egypt and masqueraded as peacekeepers separating the two combatants. Twenty-five years later, the Argentinians invaded the Falklands and the British forcibly ejected them. Then, as always, Margaret Thatcher did not flinch. Nor did she when the Irish terrorists blew up her hotel at Brighton, killing several of her MPs; she insisted that the conference open exactly on time the next morning and gave extemporaneously an unforgettable call to arms against the terrorists. Nor did she when, as she cleaned up the state-owned industries and disemployed hundreds of thousands of underworked beneficiaries of decades-old feather-bedding, she was reviled in huge demonstrations. She did not waffle or waver over deployment of intermediate-range nuclear missiles in Britain, Germany, Belgium, and Italy to counter the Soviet IRBMs already in place in the satellite countries. When asked whether she sought a "nuclear-free Europe," she instantly replied that she favoured "a war-free Europe."

When large chunks of her parliamentary party lost their nerve over her free-market economics – a reduction of the top personal income-tax rate to 40 per cent, elimination of all currency controls, massive privatization of industry, and right-to-work laws to remove the terror of the labour leadership – she famously told her party conference, "U-turn if you want to; the lady's not for turning." She was a rock-solid supporter of the Western Alliance and was instrumental in the balanced elimination of intermediate-range missiles in Europe and the satisfactory end of the Cold War. She is generally credited with assisting President George H.W. Bush in determining that Saddam Hussein had to be evicted from Kuwait: "George, this is no time to go wobbly." She made Britain the fourth economic power in the world, after the United States, Japan, and Germany, made her prosperous and a low-tax country, with declining public debt, improving public services, and steady trade surpluses. As she promised, she restored "Great" to Great Britain. It was, to scale, Elizabeth 1's Gloriana, without Shakespeare to publicize it, and with more than a trace of the Churchillian courage and virtue that first attracted her to a Conservative candidacy under Churchill's leadership in 1950 and 1951.

She formed her judgment of Germany when the Luftwaffe (in what must rank as one of the greatest long-term strategic blunders of the Second World War) bombed the town of Grantham, where teenage Margaret Thatcher lived. And she formed her opinion of Americans from the U.S. servicemen, black and white, whom she and her family invited home for dinner after the wartime Sunday services in her local Methodist church. She was always grateful for America's deliverance of the Old World from the evils of Nazism and communism, always supported the right of Israel to survive and flourish as a Jewish state, and never went cock-a-hoop for sanctions against what she called "the evil and repulsive" apartheid regime in South Africa, because she did not "see how we will make things better by making them worse." She was a practical person of unswerving principle.

She was a strong woman, but never a mannish one. She was an Oxford alumna (in chemistry) when they were somewhat rare, a Tory candidate for Parliament, an MP, and a female cabinet secretary when they were rare, the first woman leader of a major party in Britain, and the first woman prime minister; she assimilated this meritocratic rise, in the gritted teeth of hidebound British high-Tory traditionalism, with neither diffidence nor triumphalism. When she became the leader of the party, she entered the Carlton Club, the Conservatives' social head-quarters in St. James's Street, and when informed that ladies were not allowed in other than as guests, she replied as she brushed past the doorman, "They are now." She often worried before speeches, feared greatly for British servicemen she sent into battle, in the Falklands and Iraq, and was never flippant or blasé about the human and historic consequences of important decisions she took. She was always strong, sometimes impatient, but never arrogant. While she was sometimes overbearing with colleagues and others who could stand up for them-selves, she was always considerate of and exquisitely courteous to subor-dinates, and was beloved of the staff at Downing Street and Chequers.

Her successors have squandered most of the national economic strength and political capital she bequeathed to them. She was under-cut and stabbed more in the back than the front by her own party, for advocating in respect of Europe precisely what the great majority of the British public now believes – that European cooperation is unam-biguously good, but integration should be approached with caution by Britain, until it is not stripping institutions that have served it well for centuries in favour of well-intentioned but unfledged replacements.

Personally, it was a great honour that she (and Lord Carrington) sponsored me as a member of Their Lordships' House, and that she and the magnificent Sir Denis Thatcher came to Barbara's and my wedding party, and often to our home. When I was in London in the autumn, her advisers said that she was not reliably well enough to receive me, but they conveyed my best wishes at an appropriate moment and I cherish her warm and gracious reply. When she retired as prime minister, the party chairman, Kenneth Baker, a loyal supporter, said, "We shall not see her like again," and she said, "It's a funny old world." The following day, when she easily rebutted a no-confidence motion, the hard-left Labour MP Dennis Skinner loudly said, to great applause, "You can wipe the floor with this lot, Margaret," referring to those who would succeed her in both parties. So she could. She was a saintly woman, and one of the great leaders who has arisen in a thousand years of British history.

# PAUL DESMARAIS WAS ALWAYS A BUILDER, NEVER MERELY A SPECULATOR

*National Post*, October 9, 2013

---

Paul G. Desmarais, who has just died at eighty-six, was one of the remarkable and inspiring figures of Canadian history. This may seem an extravagant claim for such a private person, the dimensions of whose career are little appreciated publicly, especially outside Quebec, but it is nothing less than the truth.

Though his father was the leading Franco-Ontarian lawyer in Sudbury, his immense career as a financier and industrialist, spanning six decades and three continents, was self-made, uncontroversial, and an almost unbroken series of astute investments followed by the application of superior management. He was not long regarded as a mere conglomerateur and never derided as an asset-stripper. While he sometimes sold assets he bought, he was always a builder and never merely a speculator, and in Power Corporation of Canada, a bedraggled hodge-podge when he took control of it in the mid-1960s, he leaves a superb, well-balanced, and well-managed corporation strong in every field and place where it is active, with control firmly in the hands of his capable and experienced sons.

There were some disappointments, of course, as in his acquisition of 15 per cent of Canadian Pacific, after which he was blocked by an obdurate management that knew how to put the wagons in a circle to protect their own positions but fumbled the business until it disintegrated into divergent units. Paul Desmarais was by far the most successful Canadian businessman in France, and the EU generally, and was an honoured and almost legendary figure in Paris and Brussels. He was also a pioneer in commercial relations between Canada and China, starting from when he led a special exploratory business group to that country at the request of Prime Minister Pierre Trudeau in 1977. He returned often and was an esteemed emissary of this country to successive regimes in China, from the immediate aftermath of the Maoist era to the present. In his relationships, as in all things, he built methodically and imaginatively, selected goals carefully and realistically, was never overhasty, and never stayed too long with a losing proposition, rare as those were.

He was a constant and durable friend, always reliable, good-humoured, and never self-important, and though he was a subtle operator and even at times a cynical observer of the entire cavalcade of people and events, he was never devious, ungenerous, or showy. If he ever had a lapse of taste, I did not observe one in forty-seven years of cordial relations, including more than thirty years of close friendship, through all the seasons of adult life. He began with a precocious acquisition of the financially distressed public transit system of Sudbury, which he built up into the Provincial Transport Company, and when I first met him, in 1966, his office was in the old bus terminal on what was then Dorchester Boulevard (now named after René Lévesque), just west of Dominion Square in Montreal. He was completely relaxed with bus drivers and the public, milling about and buttonholing him on an endless range of pretexts. He was only thirty-nine and was already playing the political role at which he proved adept and immovable: to English Quebec, the ideal French Canadian, smart, bilingual, successful, never chippy, and the perfect advertisement for how Canada should work;

and to French Canadians, one of theirs, who was proud of his heritage and was already a great success in what was generally seen, with some reason, to be an *anglais* world. From those early days until when I last saw him, when Barbara and I spent the weekend with him and some of his family a few weeks ago, his conversation was never other than witty, insightful, lively, and in all respects a delight.

When he took control of Power Corporation, which, as the name implied, had been a holding company for hydroelectric securities but had become a rather dysfunctional congeries of interests, and moved to Place Ville Marie, a signed photograph of the then premier of Quebec, Daniel Johnson, was on his credenza. When I was next there, some months later, Johnson was dead and the signed photograph was of Pierre Trudeau. At the appropriate times, this item of decor changed over the years in detail but not in nature, to Brian Mulroney, and Jean Chrétien (and probably others, but we usually met in each other's homes or other social settings after that). He was always friendly with political leaders, including presidents of France and the United States, and many such people were associated with his company, including Helmut Schmidt, Pierre Trudeau, and Ontario premiers John Robarts and Bill Davis. He was always interested in the politicians and had some sympathy for their difficult occupation, which usually ended rather thanklessly, but there was never the least hint of an improper relationship. His success did not depend on anything but his own judgment and diligence, and he ignored the fiscal persecution and at times a climate of antagonism in separatist Quebec to maintain his unapologetic stance as a federalist and an enlightened capitalist.

He was a prodigious reader of non-fiction and a learned man; his greatest cultural interest seemed to be architecture, and here he indulged his interest with splendid houses which he largely designed, and especially one of the most magnificent homes ever built in North America, and surely the greatest treasure in this country, his palatial home and recreational complex on thousands of acres north of La Malbaie, Quebec. Here, he was the beloved employer of practically everyone in the entire area, and, as he wished, here he died, at a site that is perfection, thanks both to nature and to his own vast creation, a monument of taste, in a remote place, accessible only by invitation and not intended to impress anyone but to be agreeable to him and to those whom he cared for; *le style, c'est l'homme.*

There may not be a perfect marriage, but his, of sixty years, to Jackie, was probably as close as it gets. He was a great man, who never lost the common touch. And he was a dear friend, who will always be missed, and will never be replaced. Adieu.

# NELSON MANDELA, R.I.P.

*National Review Online*, December 12, 2013

Nelson Mandela was born into the Thembu faction of the Xhosa, the tribal equivalent of the royal family, which enabled him to receive a good education, although he was suspended from school for boycotting the food and became a lawyer only after failing three times to complete his law course at Witwatersrand. (He was the only black student, and may have been the victim of discrimination.) His noble lineage and upbringing conferred on him a stature and bearing and dignity that he never lost and that commanded the respect of all throughout his adult life.

Though the tremendous outpouring of admiration that has followed his death is certainly merited – for his generosity of spirit and immense courage throughout his imprisonment of twenty-seven years, most of it in severe conditions – the great esteem in which he is held obscures and transcends some matters of legitimate controversy.

There is no doubt that although Mandela was brought up a Methodist and was a somewhat enthusiastic Christian for a time (a Bible teacher, in fact) and that he and his image-makers have soft-pedalled his dalliance with the communists, he certainly was one for many years.

He moved to expel communists from the African National Congress in 1947, but when he joined the executive of the ANC in 1950, aged thirty-two, he was soon a Marx and Engels enthusiast, which is comprehensible for a black South African intellectual settling into the enchantments of apartheid; but his admiration of Lenin, Mao Tse-tung, and especially Stalin is a little harder to understand. His liking for Mao probably cooled a little when the People's Republic of China declined his request for arms in the mid-1950s because it judged the ANC too "immature" to be trusted with real weapons.

He led the pro-violence faction of the ANC at the start of the 1960s, contrary to the wishes of the ANC leader, Albert Luthuli; in 1961, he founded the sabotage and murder arm of the movement, called Spear of the Nation. (It was rarely effective, was frequently infiltrated by the white government's agents, and was routed by the fierce Zulus every time they clashed, which was countless times over the next thirty-five years.)

It seems that the collapse of the Soviet Union and of international communism, just as Mandela was released from prison in 1990, helped him to consider alternatives to communism, as did the antics of his wife, Winnie, whom he married in 1958, after his adultery broke up his first marriage and his wife decamped, taking the children and becoming a zealous Jehovah's Witness. Adultery played a part in the problems of his marriage to Winnie also, but that must be fairly seen in the context of a society that was traditionally not monogamous, and also in the light of some of the derring-do of the Mandela United Football Club, which Winnie, who was well to the left of her husband, led. It routinely tortured and killed people, sometimes with a device it invented: the necklace, a burning tire hung around the neck of the offender. It does not lie in the mouth of anyone who was not the victim of the evil racist regime that oppressed the black majority of South Africa to criticize Nelson Mandela for being tempted by communism, but there was a tactical aspect to his handling of the subject. He generally denied his association, and in his famous four-hour speech of 1964 at one of his many treason trials – a speech that was based on Fidel Castro's speech "History Will Forgive Me" – he denied that he was a communist, and said that he had relations with communists only because theirs were the countries that chiefly assisted racial-equality and anti-colonial movements. He concluded by saying that he was "prepared to die," and he doubtless was prepared to die, and generally did give his life, for the cause of racial equality. This is the basis of his greatness and his high place in world esteem.

He was sometimes acquitted in these trials, revealing that South Africa, like Gandhi's colonial India and Martin Luther King's southern states, could never really resort to massive repression without regard to human life, as the culture of the ruling minority, as Gandhi and King perceived, could not bear the moral implications of maximum violence (unlike totalitarian oppressors such as Hitler and Stalin). Of course the Boers, whose ancestors had trekked hundreds of miles to the north just to get out of so subversively liberal a place as the British Empire after it had abolished slavery, were much more attached to their position in South Africa than the comparative handful of British were to their status in India, or the relatively unthreatened white majority in the southern United States were to segregation. Nonetheless, the Anglo-Afrikaner ruling establishment was not prepared to dispense altogether with the prestigious pretense to due process.

It was after his 1961 acquittal that Mandela set up the cell structure of the ANC, prepared for guerrilla war (at which it had little aptitude), and toured Africa, visiting Haile Selassie of Ethiopia, Egypt's Nasser, Tunisia's Bourguiba, and Guinea's neo-communist Sékou Touré. He attended a guerrilla-war camp in Ethiopia, although he lasted only two months of a six-month course.

It was during his decades serving a life sentence, with patient, Gandhi-like endurance (though in far more severe circumstances than Gandhi ever faced), that Nelson Mandela earned the immense admiration that has poured forth on his death. In an atmosphere in which there must have been little hope, and in which his oppressors (who had operated a racist despotism for 350 years) must have seemed impregnable, there must often had been dark nights of despair. By 1985, world agitation for his release and the increasing tenuousness of the white-supremacist regime would have uplifted him; in 1985, after he had spent twenty-three years in Spartan and unhealthy confinement, the president of the country offered him a release to freedom in exchange for an unconditional renunciation of violence, and he declined, saying it was impossible to contract anything from a prison cell. In the 1970s and 1980s, he corresponded with the Anglican religious leader Desmond Tutu and with the leader of the Zulus, Mangosuthu Buthelezi. Both of them staunchly supported Mandela, Buthelezi declining autonomy for the Zulus while Mandela was confined.

This raises another question: Mandela's inability, once he was free, the president of the ANC, and the most powerful man in South Africa, to restrain the ANC from conducting a civil war against Buthelezi's Inkatha Freedom Party and its large number of tribal warriors. The Zulus won these encounters, as their ferocity is legendary (and contributed to bringing down the great government of Benjamin Disraeli by their prowess at Isandlwana in 1879). Why did Mandela, who had the authority to stop the violence, not do so? Following independence, Buthelezi, who was narrowly persuaded to participate in the country's first free elections in 1994 rather than proclaim Zululand's independence and enforce it, governed Natal and was deputy president and minister of home affairs in the Mandela government. A little more forcefulness from Mandela, who certainly possessed heroic leadership qualities, and much tribal violence and tension could have been avoided.

When Mandela finally was released in 1990, he declared that he was conducting "a purely defensive armed struggle." The white leadership had bungled away any bargaining power: if they had loosened things up years before, granted local autonomy to Zulus, Cape Coloureds, East Indians, and others, and produced a federal structure with more entrenchment of minority rights, and not sent decent people like Mandela and most of his colleagues off to prison or exile for decades, they would not have lost their entire position in South Africa and the 750,000 whites who departed the country in the balance of the 1990s. Mandela did well to placate the factions of his riven country, going to the victory of the white rugby team and setting up his Truth and Reconciliation Commission under Tutu, which ascertained the facts by granting immunity, but did not wreak vengeance. He took over a country of forty million, where twenty-three million did not have electricity, a third were illiterate, a third unemployed, and twelve million did not have clean water. Under Mandela, the ANC did provide new housing for three million, telephones for three million, electricity for two million, and education for 1.5 million more children, and better health care for all children. Once in power, he dropped his decades-long enthusiasm for wholesale economic nationalization but proved, like Lech Walesa in Poland, to be a better moral than practical leader.

Ten per cent of the population were HIV-positive at the end of his term, because, as he admitted, the government simply ignored the issue. Corruption quickly achieved stupefying proportions. A Japanese company rented the management of the South African Power Company (some years after Mandela's retirement, but the rot started with him) and sealed the deal with a publicly revealed outright bribe of $1 billion to the ANC. The former ANC deputy chairman and head of the National Union of Mineworkers, Cyril Ramaphosa, quickly became a multi-centimillionaire essentially on a straight payment of Danegeld from the Oppenheimer interests (after which there was no more talk of nationalizing anything) and the exploitation of his official position. Mandela hobnobbed with the world's most disreputable leaders, such as Gaddafi, Castro, and Arafat, condemned Israel in disconcertingly harsh terms, and accused the United States of "unspeakable atrocities." He did finally break with Robert Mugabe over that leader's ghastly Zimbabwean despotism. He was always very courteous and distinguished and possessed great natural moral dignity, but what he actually said and did after he was elected president was, on balance, slightly disappointing.

But these are cavils; he was and will always remain, in his qualities of patience and tolerance, an inspiration, and though he lived to be ninety-five, the broad African landscape yields no visible emulators of remotely comparable stature.

# ECONOMICS & THE ENVIRONMENT

## THE GREAT GREEN FRAUD

*National Post*, November 28, 2009

T ill now, I have avoided more than very limited comment on the whole global-warming carbon emissions controversy. But now that colossal spending and regulating programs impend on these issues, I must say that the Al Gore–David Suzuki conventional wisdom hysteria is an insane scam.

The basic relevant facts are that carbon emissions are not the principal factor in global warming, and despite dire contrary forecasts and ever-increasing carbon emissions in the world – especially as the economies of China and India, representing 40 per cent of the world's population, expand by 6 to 10 per cent each year – the world has not grown a millidegree warmer since the start of this millennium. And its mean temperature rose by only 1°C in the twenty-five years before that. The greenhouse effect of carbon dioxide emissions does have a gentle warming effect if it is not counteracted by unpredictable natural phenomena, but cannot be measured directly against the volume of such emissions.

The chief source of apparently informed hysteria on this subject, the Intergovernmental Panel on Climate Change (IPCC), has estimated that the mean world temperature will increase by between 1.8°C and 4°C in this century, although a tenth of that warming has already failed to occur in the last decade. But even this prediction does not remotely justify all the cant and hype that the end of the world is nigh.

Even the IPCC admits that the upper end of its forecast would, in fact, substantially increase world food production. There is no chance of achieving stated – or even (by some countries) committed – emission-reduction targets, nor any reason to believe that the attainment of these targets would accomplish anything useful other than a possible improvement in air quality. Yet the president of the United States has been promising radical progress toward an international covenant in Copenhagen next month to spend trillions of dollars in pursuit of this unattainable, undesirable target.

It would be infinitely more sensible to intensify research and invest where necessary or advisable in mitigation, adaptation, and geostrategy, such as the infusion of sulphates into the stratosphere, as happens naturally with volcanic eruptions, to reduce the intensity of the sun and provide countervailing cooling influences without thinning the ozone layer. We should keep in mind that the IPCC's worst case in its preferred (very negative) scenario is that in the next hundred years, living standards in what is now the developing or underdeveloped world will improve by only 750 per cent, instead of the 850 per cent improvement that would allegedly occur if the world's temperature remained constant, as it has in the last decade.

All responsible people want to assist the disadvantaged parts of the world and do what we reasonably can for our own descendants, but not to the point of self-impoverishment now for the sake of a marginal gain against a wildly unproved prognosis a century from now. This is the flimsiest justification imaginable for the mad slogan parroted endlessly by the eco-Zouaves, from Hollywood to the UN to Ducks Unlimited,

"Save the Planet!" as they try to force-march the world into biodegradable pastoralism.

Nor is this the grim tipping point Al Gore has made scores of millions of dollars and won a Nobel Peace Prize for decrying as the imminent apocalypse. Gore's scurrilous film *An Inconvenient Truth* is based on no original research and is a teeming rain forest of false and irrelevant claims, such as that the Pacific island country of Tuvalu is losing population because the sea level around it is rising under the relentless pressures of global warming on the polar ice caps; and the claim that, for the same reason, mosquitoes have afflicted Nairobi, Kenya, with a constant epidemic of malaria.

The inconvenience of the truth falls on Gore, not his credulous viewers, as water levels have in fact declined slightly at Tuvalu, and the country's modest population shrinkage is due to economic migrants; and malaria was much more prevalent in Nairobi a century ago, and has risen only slightly in recent years because of the ecologists' attack on the use of insecticide. The polar ice caps aren't melting at all; the ice sheets over the oceans are, but that over land is actually thickening, so water levels are not being affected.

The much-vaunted British *Stern Review* is in fact largely rubbish, devised to give the environmental baton to Tony Blair so he could wave it like a magic wand to placate the left of the British Labour Party for whom he delivered nothing else but an indiscriminate increase in public spending. It warns of a 70 per cent decline in world food production this century if its temperature forecast increases are met, relying exclusively on a study that predicts such a decline will occur to the harvest of northern Indian groundnuts only, not the world's food supply. Stern purported to forecast two hundred, three hundred, or a thousand years ahead, which is nonsense, and warns of the "deaths of hundreds of millions, social upheaval, large-scale conflicts" if $25 trillion is not spent in the next fifteen years to reduce carbon emissions by 70 per cent (and disemploy scores of millions of people).

This leads directly to the farce of the Kyoto agreement, which was supposed to be largely ratified at the Copenhagen discussions next month. Bill Clinton pledged to support this mad enterprise, as well as the monstrous racket of international trafficking in unused permissible emission balances. The U.S. Senate long ago repudiated any such adherence 95–0, in one of its few unanimous acts on a serious subject since Pearl Harbor.

Barack Obama is trying to replicate this poker game domestically in the trade part of cap-and-trade, which, as passed by the House of Representatives, will neither reduce carbon emissions nor raise government revenues but will impose a heavy burden of heating and air-conditioning cost increases on the families and employers of America. (In all of the circumstances, for the unfeasible former Canadian Liberal leader Stéphane Dion to have named his dog Kyoto could be considered cruelty to animals.)

Two of Canada's greatest and most undersung recent heroes are environmental economist Ross McKitrick and statistical mineralogist Steven McIntyre, who by their tireless research in the teeth of the entire ecological establishment, proved the former IPCC claim of drastically accelerated global warming was a fraud. These men have been prominently mentioned in the hacked emails that have just revealed the outrageous lengths the scientific propagators of the Great Green Fraud have gone to to suppress the facts.

The immensely respected former British chancellor of the exchequer Nigel Lawson had great difficulty finding a publisher for his exposé of these matters, *An Appeal to Reason: A Cool Look at Global Warming*, such is the pressure the eco-lobby can assert. He believes Green is the new Red, the anti-capitalists taking over the relatively inoffensive tandem bicycle of naturalists and turning it into a nihilistic juggernaut, the treads having been blown off their great Red Marxist tank that careened through the world for most of the last century. The eco-extremists allow the conservationists and butterfly collectors and Sierra Clubs to front their activities, just as the pacifist naïfs were often the witless dupes and "useful idiots" (in Lenin's words) of the communists.

As Lord Lawson wrote in his book, those worried about imminent environmental catastrophe, as compared, for example, to nuclear terrorism or even large meteoric collisions, "need not worry about saving this planet. They are already living on another one. . . . We appear to have entered a new age of unreason. . . . It is from this, above all, that we really need to save the planet."

# HISTORY'S GREATEST
# PONZI SCHEME

*Standpoint*, July/August 2010

V ery few of the ever-growing number of books about the recent and current world financial crisis try to identify the ultimate causes of this astounding implosion of the longest, strongest, and most widespread economic boom in history. Any such analysis by officials became impractical because it became mired in the uneven exchange of allegations between the politicians and the private financial sector. The political class locked arms from across the spectrum to blame private-sector "greed." With the exception of a few media outlets, such as the *Wall Street Journal*, this theme was taken up by the press. And this version of events has been amplified by the Obama administration's effort to claim and to execute a mandate to take the country much more sharply to the left than the public wishes or would abide. Any disposition to exchange fire with the politicians has been stifled by Attorney General Eric Holder's practice of steadily thinning the ranks of the private sector's blame-game debating team by indicting a swath of businessmen.

In fact, it was a joint government-industry effort. It could not have occurred without the legislative and regulatory coercion and monetary policy encouragement of the federal government. In the United States, despite its unabashed capitalism, the business community is politically inept. There are no Agnellis (Fiat), Dassaults (Dassault Aviation), or

Herrhausens (Deutsche Bank) to influence the government. There are many businessmen who are closely involved in industries that dominate congressional districts and largely fund the careers of these congressmen. These legislators are reliable supporters of the interests of such benefactors. Most congressmen are in what amount to rotten boroughs of about 700,000 people, seven and a half times the population of the average British parliamentary constituency. About three hundred of the congressional districts almost never change party. Once arrived at the Capitol, the congressmen form alliances with other legislators to support each other's initiatives for their local interests. This is a permutation of democracy, but is far from what the authors of the Constitution had in mind, or early admiring visitors such as de Tocqueville found.

The country largely despises the New York financial community for its intermittent reckless blundering. The only businessman with any standing in the country is Warren Buffett, who before he lost $25 billion on paper in October and November 2008 (most of which he has since recouped) had been demanding that his taxes be increased to help disadvantaged people. He has worn thin his status as America's avuncular aphorist, but has deservedly retained his prestige as an investor and as a financial epigrammatist. But he has only occasionally carried the standard for the private sector in the counter-accusations over the financial debacle.

The other great financiers skulk around like nerds or emasculated chameleons, claiming to be philanthropists and collectors and to having only a passing interest in the pursuit of lucre. Only the brave, the buccaneers, and the showmen – Ken Langone, Kirk Kerkorian, Carl Icahn, Nelson Peltz, and Donald Trump, for example – admit to being capitalists at all.

I was asked to read and comment on three books about the economic crisis: Vicky Ward's *The Devil's Casino* (about the failure of Lehman Brothers); Kate Kelly's *Street Fighters* (about the demise of Bear Stearns); and Michael Lewis's *The Big Short* (about the clever inventors of some of the more explosive financial instruments and techniques that were used to profit from it).

The first two are works of journalism based on oral recollections and contemporary media accounts, with whatever memos, text messages, and other primary material were available. No such work can comfortably be taken as authoritative, but they are diligently assembled, well-written, and portray vividly the human characters behind the impersonal drama. Lewis's book is more ambitious, as it effectively claims to identify the sorcerers who saw the opportunity, aggravated the problems, and helped to bring on the deluge, which they then exploited by a comprehensive programme of short sales. None of these books seeks to identify the larger ailments of the political and financial systems that led to these vulnerabilities. But they are all worthwhile, interesting, and engaging reads as far as they go.

They dance lightly around the regrettable fact that every part of the system failed. The U.S. government pushed the private sector into issuing trillions of dollars of bad debt. Both parties in Congress imposed the obligation on lending banks to make 25 per cent of their mortgage business commercially unjustifiable (following an upgrade of banking debt). President Bill Clinton ordered the giant government-sponsored mortgage companies (generally known as Fannie Mae and Freddie Mac) to put more than half of their huge mortgage portfolios into such investments. This was a political free lunch. Thus the Democrats took the credit for increasing family home ownership and boosting the building trade and land development industries at no cost to the taxpayer.

The financial system leapt at the opportunity presented by this massive market operation. The Securities and Exchange Commission allowed the investment banks to borrow thirty times their equity base against overvalued collateral. The requirement of quarterly adjustments of asset values to reflect market fluctuations was retained, leaving the more aggressively borrowed companies as sitting ducks to short sellers such as those Lewis wrote about.

The rating agencies approved many hundreds of billions of dollars of debt that they knew to be practically worthless. These were sold as if they came from solid issuers, with the insurance industry then picking up billions of easy dollars on swaps it must have known could blow up with any agitation.

Everyone failed. The conduct of Goldman Sachs was questionable. Its former chairman, the Treasury Secretary Henry Paulson, acted bizarrely, rushing about like a headless chicken, buying failed assets instead of preferred shares in the banks that had invested in such assets – the formula devised by the Roosevelt administration in the 1930s. He assisted in salvaging the creditors of Bear Stearns, let Lehman Brothers go to the wall, and took good care of his company's own coattails.

I used occasionally to encounter Alan Greenspan in the early 2000s, and I once asked him (during an intermission at Carnegie Hall) whether he wasn't concerned that the country had no savings. He said he was not. The public, he maintained, would do better out of rising house values than from the stingy interest rate his Federal Reserve had allowed as a return from deposit-taking institutions. My diffident reference to economic cycles brought the assurance that monetary policy would mitigate their effects. Politicians, government departments, agency heads, board chairmen, and regulators are responsible for translating the national interest into public policy and enacting and enforcing that policy. Businessmen are there to make profits and obey the law. Despite all the nauseating antics of the corporate governance charlatans, who effectively sell priggishness and collectivization of executive responsibility instead of financial performance, it is not the purpose of corporate America to divine and pursue public policy, beyond assuring that it does not affront it.

Once Congress, the administration, and the Federal Reserve had gone for broke on home ownership, when trillions of dollars of mortgage-backed debt representing almost no equity were poured out, a senior Citigroup official infamously said, "When the music is playing, everyone has to dance." That is not what one hopes to hear from the head of one of the world's greatest banks. But most businessmen are Buggins' turn intramural politicians, not auxiliary national leaders.

The banks had almost ceased to be lenders. They were distracted by and infested with financial high flyers and used their basic businesses to issue premium corporate paper, with which they bought higher-yield offerings of increasingly high risk. They merged or became one-stop financial shops, absorbing investment banks, insurance companies, and other financial service providers which had different corporate cultures.

Even the legendary banking nationalities – the Swiss, the Dutch, and the Scots – largely lost their way. The regulators, who had all the powers they needed to avoid the crisis, predictably demanded more authority as a reward for having failed so completely to use the perfectly adequate powers they already possessed.

This highlights the two fundamental problems that have created and aggravated the financial crisis. Since economics is half psychology and half Year Three maths, the crisis has demoralized America. First, no one saw the crisis coming, except the silent manipulators Lewis writes about. Second, those few professors and eccentric investors who spoke out were considered too erratic or obscure to command much prior notice.

In terrible policy failures and crises of the past, such as the mistakes of appeasement in the 1930s, there were serious people such as Winston Churchill and Charles de Gaulle who were there to lead their countries when the errors they had decried were exposed. The gigantic follies that led to the financial meltdown should have been obvious enough to arouse serious dissent, but didn't. This reveals something deeply disconcerting about the American political and business elite.

Some people detected some aspects of the approaching crisis. Even I was shrieking from the rooftops for years about the $800-billion annual U.S. current-account deficit. But again, apart from a few technical financial wizards identified in Lewis's book, almost no one predicted the tsunami of subprime mortgage defaults. I had dealt with many of the main lending banks and almost all of the leading investment banks in New York and London. I was never impressed with the service they provided or the quality of their advice. They were a cartel in New York and in London a little back-scratching society at the feet of the governor of the Bank of England.

Very few of them had any loyalty to the client. They lacked any real notion of relationship banking and just led those they advised to their habitual sources of capital, preceded by their corporate wallets. They gouged the offering price of the new debt and share issues by short-selling their clients' stock to depress the issue price, assuring a pop for their financial partners and their own trading accounts as soon as the issue came through the window.

For decades, the chief objective of the financial industry has been not to make good deals but to make many deals, take their fat fees, and to hell with the public. The regulators could have tightened some of these regulations but apparently never considered it. Greed compounded the problem, but was not its origin.

National per capita wealth is measured in gross national product divided by the population. But if Paraguay decreed that everyone in the country write a poem and sell it to someone else for $100 ten times a day for a year, Paraguay would have the fifth largest GDP in the world and per capita income of an astronomical $300,000 per year. This would be a mirage.

But so was much of the Clinton–Bush/Blair–Brown economic boom and its foreign imitators' replications. In the United States, there are now a formidable forty-eight metropolitan areas with more than one million people. All of them have clusters of skyscrapers filled with busy and talented people who don't really add value to anything. Merchant bankers promoting deals that later usually go sour; lawyers generating $1 trillion annually in legal bills, half of which should not have been run up in this insanely overlawyered country; consultants generating another $1 trillion of billings for telling well-paid executives how to do their jobs; $2.4 trillion of medical expenses, $3,000 more per capita than any other advanced country; and teeming masses of retail sales people. They don't produce much but make money move around faster and multiply transactions that add to the GDP. Yes, the learned professions, medical research, and the drug companies are indispensable, but the U.S. legal and health-care systems are hideously overexpensive, and this administration, after a few verbal throwaways, has done nothing to reduce the cost of either.

About thirty years ago, the West acted on the self-important delusion that overalls and metal lunchboxes were beneath it, and we plunged into the fool's paradise of the service economy. Some parts of that economy, such as computer programming and, up to a point, academics, are legitimate value creation, but most are not.

Even thirty years ago, sophisticated economies were manufacturing economies, balanced by natural resources, heavy industry, and professional and technical executive support of adequate depth and innovation. Resource economies were just hewers of wood and drawers of water, as natural resource importers such as Japan financed new production of everything they imported and maintained a buyers' market.

Now, with China and India, with annual economic growth rates of 6 to 10 per cent, there are steady, firm, and rising prices for almost all base and precious metals, energy, and agriculture and forest products. Manufacturing has been outsourced to developing countries, with only the most sophisticated, such as aviation, high-tech, and advanced defence production, retained. Resource-rich countries with relatively small but well-educated populations, such as Canada, Australia, and Norway, are now the most successful in the world.

When economic meltdown hit, the left, battered into a coma by Reagan and George W. Bush, rose up and proclaimed the ignominious end of Reaganomics and Thatcherism. But those leaders had left their countries in excellent condition, with current account surpluses and, in America's case, only a modest budgetary deficit. This crisis is no victory for the left.

America carried Western Europe, the Middle East, and Japan on its back for decades. It was rewarded with endless lectures on the evil of current-account deficits from those who had benefited from them. Oil imports and prices skyrocketed, French and Italian luxury goods and German – and Japanese – engineered products poured into the United States. When George Bush Sr. gave his economic message in 1992, it was to urge Americans to spend all and more than they had. This was not responsible advice.

Administrations and congresses of both parties sat as inert as suet puddings. The mighty American economy, with its highly motivated and incomparably skilled workforce, abandoned savings and investment and became helplessly addicted to perishable consumer goods, personal debt, and speculation. Millions of manufacturing jobs were outsourced. Millions of undocumented and unskilled immigrants were allowed into the country, and trillions of dollars were borrowed from China and Japan to buy outsourced manufacturing from China and Japan. None of it made any sense and the United States itself became history's greatest Ponzi scheme.

Given that, inexplicably, no one audible saw what was coming, it is not surprising that no one seems to have much idea of what to do about it. The Obama administration's Hydra-headed economic team speaks in many tongues. But it has given few hints of what alternatives will be considered to the present forecasts of a decade of trillion-dollar annual budget deficits and money-supply increases. This is a policy that will drastically erode the dollar's value. The administration is raising taxes, always an unwise action when a country is trying to shake off a recession. But it is doing so not as quickly as it is raising expenses and making imprudent concessions to Luddite labour unions. It has given most of what is left of the U.S. auto industry to the United Auto Workers, which is chiefly responsible for the industry's near-death experience.

Obama apparently bought into the fairy tale of creating millions of green jobs making windmills and solar panels. He padded around the most inane high-level conference in world history, at Copenhagen, promoting a $100-billion annual payoff to Hugo Chávez, Robert Mugabe, and other barbarous monsters for the carbon emissions that resulted from the economic growth of the advanced countries. Fortunately, the evaporation of the global-warming canards that carbon emissions had anything to do with the world's temperature eliminated this harebrained nostrum, at least for a time.

The second intractable problem is that while capitalism is the only economic system that works and is incomparably the best route to economic growth – because it is the only one that is aligned with human nature's drive for more – it will always, because of that drive, arrive at the brink of self-destruction. All the fatuous claims of Gordon Brown and Alan Greenspan to manage prudently to avoid booms and busts have been exposed as fraudulent. All the well-meaning claptrap about a social market merely slows the speed of the Gadarene rush to the brink and does nothing to change the destination.

Financiers seek profits, and as they have little sense of any broader interest will fall for almost any risk if temptation is dangled in front of them for long enough. This always leads to an economic crack-up, but governments almost never have the slightest aptitude to deal with the crisis. They have the duty to tackle it because they make and enforce laws, issue money, and control interest rates and the money supply, not because they have any talent at financial or economic management.

As we stay in the same rut, what is needed is original thinking. The only perceptible sign that someone close to the decision-making process in Washington may be thinking useful thoughts on this subject is the former chairman of the Federal Reserve Paul Volcker, who now serves as head of Obama's Economic Recovery Advisory Board. He has spoken recently about taxes on fuel and financial transactions, which would be huge revenue generators, reduce oil imports, and help prevent the re-emergence of a bloated financial industry.

There is no sign that any of the major debt-heavy economic blocs has any real disposition to pay its debt down instead of devaluing the currency in which it is denominated. But none of the major currencies is really worth anything and they are all just measured against each other. They are like mountain climbers on a bare face, connected to each other but not to anything secure. The Chinese have impressive foreign reserves, but not a word of their economic claims and statistics is corroborated or believable. By traditional standards, Australia, Canada, Norway, Singapore, and the Swiss have the world's only hard currencies.

With inflation removed from the figures, the annual rise in stock market values since 1929 is a very sober 4 per cent or so and not largely greater than productivity increases. There is no painless way to bring down the crippling debt and no apparent political will to do so. The most sensible national leaders in these terms are Germany's Angela Merkel and Canada's Stephen Harper. Yet they are not the greatest rousers of opinion since Peter the Hermit. Obama simply refuses to address the issue. His predecessor, George W. Bush, uttered the stirring tocsin, "The sucker could go down" (by which he meant the U.S. economy, not the army of voters who had twice elected him to his great office).

The greatest problem in the West is the European death wish. This anaesthetizing torpor has transformed the exaggerated hopes of a united Europe regaining its status at the centre of the world it enjoyed one hundred years ago. It is now almost incapacitated by a financial problem in Greece. The looming problems of Europe will require a political de-socialization and recovery of procreational energy or all those ancient nationalities will fade away like the North American passenger pigeon, which darkened the skies in Audubon's time but passed into extinction in Cincinnati in 1914. Europe will have to redefine itself sensibly, incentivize work and demographic renewal, stop replacing the unborn with immigrants who don't want to assimilate, and pull back from the road to extinction.

Although one who was very vocal in my reservations about Britain joining the euro, when I had some standing to make my views known in Britain, it is no pleasure to see Europe in such straits as it is now. Southern Europe appears to have signed on to a German-backed hard currency after filing a false prospectus about its own financial condition. I don't see how those countries can be revived without local devaluation that, at the least, will require two currencies – a southern and a northern euro. Continuing to throw money at the problem in such huge dollops could bring down the whole structure. It is time for the Euro-federalists to engage in an agonizing reappraisal.

Europe after the hecatomb produced by its Nazi, communist, and fascist movements was essentially liberated, revived, and coddled by the United States until the Soviet threat imploded. In the ensuing euphoria, the old continent had an intense flirtation with a continental political fantasy. And the United States has authored one of recent history's prominent ironies. It rose with unprecedented swiftness in two long lifetimes, from 1783 to 1945, from fragile colonies to the producer of half the economic product of the world, a nuclear monopoly, huge moral authority, and overwhelming military strength and popular cultural influence.

It won the greatest and most bloodless strategic victory in the history of the nation state in the Cold War, crowning half a century of inspired strategic policy. All aid short of war (1939–1941); the conduct of the Second World War in overall planning by Roosevelt and Marshall and in all theatres by Eisenhower, Nimitz, and MacArthur; and the containment of communism under nine consecutive presidents of both parties earned the United States its unprecedented primacy. Inexplicably, with all rivals laid low, the United States has spent more than fifteen years trying to spend itself richer and to drink itself sober.

Although disturbingly corrupt and gratingly commercialized, at least it remains a vital, proud, and determined country, unafraid to deploy its superb military forces for good causes. It will respond to leadership and has historically had a strong president when it had to have one, though there is no ground for optimism that he will be forthcoming from the present administration.

The revived trend to saving will free up money for investment and reduce consumption of foreign-made luxury goods. The savings rate has risen from 0 to 5 per cent, and the current-account deficit has fallen by approximately half in eighteen months, with no help from Washington. "Green" energy, entrenched oil drilling and use of natural gas, and ordinary restraint will cut America's fuel imports and create a relative oil-buyers' market. As about 95 per cent of U.S. transport is fuel-based, the country is now on both sides of the struggle with radical Islam. Saudi Arabia is a joint venture of the House of Saud and the Wahhabists, and U.S. strategic thinking will have to catch up with these ambiguities.

We should end the immediate recourse in inflationary times to automatic interest rate increases. Every 1 per cent rise in the prime rate raises the rate of inflation by 0.5 per cent until a bone-cracking recession starts the cycle over again. Governments should arm themselves with the right to impose standby tax increases and reductions that would incentivize saving and discourage inflationary spending and price and income increases. This is a more subtle instrument than raising interest rates that force the eviction of families from their homes and of workers from vulnerable businesses.

These changes would rally all the markets, if presented with some conviction and panache. They would reduce deficits while promoting sensible spending and saving.

The challenge is to harness the aggressive spirit of capitalism to produce socially desirable results, without blunting or warping the powerful motivation of self-enrichment. Just taking money from people who have earned it and giving it to people who haven't in exchange for their votes while selling a fable about social justice hasn't worked well. And awaiting the ingenuity of avarice to combine with the complacency and financial illiteracy of government to lead us from crisis to crisis won't do either.

# FACING A GLOBAL
# DEBT CRISIS

*National Review Online*, June 3, 2015

The decline in the GDP of the United States in the first quarter of this year has been officially treated as almost as much a ho-hum as the fall of Ramadi to ISIS, but at least the Federal Reserve is not relying on America's new Iranian allies to rectify the economic growth problem too. The official version of events is that a strong dollar, a severe winter, a reduced oil price and slackened activity in that industry, and a dock strike on the West Coast are to blame. These are the feeblest excuses imaginable, and if the acumen of the country's monetary managers is no more acute than their powers of improvisation in this case, the country could be in for a rougher sleigh-ride than has been foreseen.

It wasn't a severe winter, a reduction in the country's oil and fuel prices compensates for the sluggish impact on the energy sector, and none of these factors, such as they were, were unknown when official predictions were still for growth at about one-fifth of a percentage point – hardly a neck-snapping great leap forward but almost a full point above where the economy stumbled in at the end of March. This was the third time in this syncopated and feeble recovery that the U.S. economy has paused for a decline, a brief 180-degree turn, and this time it came after generating a couple of relatively peppy quarters, and as the U.S. national debt, which stood at $9 trillion seven years ago, topped out at $18 trillion.

An inundation of red ink on such a scale as to cause wise people to start building an ark could have been and was expected to produce a much faster and less vulnerable level of economic growth. There appear to be three principal messages in these results: this is not a normal turn in the economic cycle and there are more fundamental problems in the economy than there were during the Carter or Eisenhower recessions; the policies adapted for dealing with it have not been the best available; and the whole debt issue is situated in a worldwide context that is very worrisome and in some respects unprecedented.

General expectations are for a revival of consumer activity to stoke up economic growth and get the tide that lifts all boats to rise. But consumer debt is high, the middle class is squeezed, and the experiences of the last seven years have not imbued the public with a relaxed attitude to carefree spending (and if it were otherwise the consequences would be disastrous). The consumer boom of the late 1940s and the subsequent three decades replaced the nearly twenty preceding years of depression and wartime controls, and gradually became more and more a boost to the luxury-goods industries of France and Italy and the engineered-products industries of Germany and Japan than to U.S. manufacturing, which declined with the slippage of less-sophisticated manufacturing to developing markets. The increasing prosperity of all these countries benefited the United States to some extent, and created a healthier world economy – one that was more broadly based than it had been when, at the end of the Second World War, half of the world's GDP was in the United States. But to an ever-increasing degree, the United States was carrying the world on its back. This could not go on forever and it didn't.

If there were less tinkering and fewer half measures and "stimulus" boondoggles, and if those who govern would let America be America, the economy would respond quickly and effectively.

The Reagan experience of over forty million jobs being lost but about sixty million being created would be replicated, and so also might be the Reagan era's high rates of productivity increases, as, contrary to the yelps of organized labour, the new jobs were not menial jobs but largely high-tech. The United States is suffering from overreliance on service industries that generally do not add value as those who harvest agricultural products, extract natural resources, or fabricate or finish manufactured goods from components do. The United States has a large and uniquely talented and motivated workforce, and capitalism, eased and succoured by official fiscal emollients as required, will make the necessary adjustments if the economy is not straitjacketed by official pandering to apologists for aggrieved industries (even if some of them have legitimate public-policy complaints).

The debt-ridden state of almost the whole world is worrying; in the eight years since just before the 2008 problems, debt in the world has grown by $57 trillion, raising the ratio of debt to GDP in the world by 17 per cent, and the greatest national risk-taker has been China, whose debt has skyrocketed in that time from $7 trillion to $28 trillion, and represents 282 per cent of Chinese GDP, almost three times the percentage of GDP of the national debt of the United States. Half of all the Chinese loans are connected to the country's inflated real-estate sector. Shadow banking, which is unregulated and imprecisely monitored, accounts for almost half of new lending, and many local governments have borrowed beyond their capacity to carry and service their debt. China can probably manage this debt if the ratios and loan quality do not continue to deteriorate, but maintaining the country's fiscal viability and reversing the trend to ballooning debt will be a severe challenge without inducing potentially serious deflation.

Since 2008, the world has struggled to absorb the shocks of that year's crisis, radiating out from the implosion of the U.S. housing bubble, by piling on debt and vastly increasing the money supply. The consequences of that effort are that government debt, which in 2008 was smaller than corporate, household, or financial debt, has outstripped those other categories. Interest rates on government debt have been maintained at minimal rates and the United States has notoriously issued trillions of dollars of debt to the Federal Reserve rather than face the interest music of an arm's-length debt auction to free-market buyers. The world is now afflicted by a public-sector debt bubble that could rupture in any of a number of countries with instant knock-on effects.

The residual confidence in the ability of the world's central bankers and treasury officials to be successful stewards of the whole, vast, interconnected world debt structure could be very suddenly and unanswerably challenged. The stock market rise, especially where newly hatched internet companies that are not even profitable are valued at astronomical multiples of envisioned earnings – so-called unicorns, a phenomenon that has flourished in this time of artificially low interest rates – could come under severe pressure without (further) warning. Companies that are brilliant concepts but thin on cash generation, such as taxi competitor Uber ($50 billion capitalization) and social site Pinterest ($11 billion capitalization) and many others – and I do not impugn the ingenuity of their organizing principles – could be vulnerable to sharp corrective forces.

Apart from these innovative companies that have levitated beyond traditionally justifiable multiples of any value measurement, there are beleaguered companies that have established businesses that have sold themselves as opportunistic turnarounds, such as retailer J.C. Penney, whose stock price has declined in three years from $42 to $9 but whose actual financial deterioration would, by traditional criteria, have reduced the stock price almost to zero. The turnaround may be imminent, but that is based on optimistic extrapolations of trends and continued confidence in the strength of consumer demand that may be fragile.

For the United States, which, despite the remarkable rise of China, is effectively unchallenged as the world's leading economy (and almost all the oppressive conventional social wisdom of the imminent rise to pre-eminence of China has mercifully abated), the challenge is to pull the present stumbling and tentative recovery up to the standard of previous rebounds, such as that achieved by the Reagan administration's tax cuts and encouragements of economic rationalization and employment and productivity increases. U.S. economic growth over these six years of endlessly vaunted recovery has been at a rate of about 2.3 per cent, where the long-term economic performance of the country has been at an annual growth rate of about 3.4 per cent. To get this period of ostensible recovery into line with past performance and lift the burden of possible secular decline in the sustainable growth rate of the American economy, the country will have to rack up growth numbers of about 5 per cent for the next decade. The national GDP is about $2 trillion and fifteen million jobs short of that now, and each 1 per cent increase in real economic growth lowers the deficit by about $3 trillion over ten years. This is the proof of the politicians' ancient ambition to "grow" out of problems, rather than tighten belts or do other stringent and politically difficult acts that imply self-discipline and arithmetical rigour.

The way to encourage such growth and facilitate whatever adjustments are needed for the recalibration of the American economy to optimal sectoral distribution of job creation and productivity lies in the tax system, and obviously not in the *dirigiste* public-sector payroll and spending increases favoured by the quaint social-democratic time-warp notions of the Obama administration. For a reason that escapes my comprehension, the obvious and proven answers have not been attempted. These lie in cutting personal and corporate income taxes, simplifying taxes, reducing cronyist rebates and allowances, and – where revenue increases are necessary beyond what resulting growth will provide – raising consumption and transaction taxes that will affect only elective spending by relatively well-off people and corporations.

It is not beyond the wit of even the current set of administration and congressional policy-makers to alight upon a workable formula in this policy zone. The Christie and Rubio proposals, and some of the other candidates' suggestions, are a good start. But it is almost certainly beyond the ability of the present bipartisan leadership to agree on anything sensible and adopt it before another gruelling and expensive election in which the waters will be muddied by a lot of demeaning wedge issues about one or the other party's "war" against vast sections of the population. The best we can realistically hope for is that the next president and the incoming senior policy entourage will combine a little original thinking with the requirements of the moment and the new-administration honeymoon spirit to innovate and change course, as Franklin D. Roosevelt did in 1933 (though with different policies for different times), Lyndon Johnson did in 1964 with his income-tax cuts, and Ronald Reagan did in the golden window of 1981, when he cut taxes and relaunched the U.S. economy. It requires optimism to credit the Obama administration with anything more than the ability to survive to the inauguration of the succeeding regime without the economic sky falling down. And even that, as the sports announcers say, could be touch and go.

# THE GREAT CLIMATE CONFERENCE CHARADE PLAYING OUT IN PARIS

*National Post*, December 5, 2015

---

The opening of the Paris conference on climate change will be the occasion for the customary lamentations about the imminent demise of life on Earth if we do not pull up our socks as a species and reduce carbon-emission levels, and thus avoid the toasting of the world. The adduced scientific evidence does not justify any such state of alarm. Every sane and informed person in the world is concerned about pollution and demands vigilance about any clear trends of climate change and any convincing evidence that human behaviour influences the climate. Because the Copenhagen climate conference of 2009 had promised agreement on imposition of dramatic measures to reduce fossil fuel use and resulting carbon emissions, thus avoiding apprehended rises in world temperature, and broke up in acrimonious farce and recrimination, the Paris conference has been more carefully and less ambitiously prepared.

At Copenhagen, the demand arose from developing countries that the economically advanced countries had permanently impaired the underdeveloped countries and that the $100-billion compensation fund that Obama had promised to raise for the less-advanced countries was completely inadequate, mere reparations instead of a serious response to a moral debt that could only be quantified in trillions of dollars. (Obama had no takers, including his own Congress, when his Democrats controlled it, for one cent of such payments.) Obama was unable even to get an interview with the Chinese prime minister, a historic first in lack of access for a U.S. president, as the Chinese, by far the greatest carbon emitter and polluter of all countries, cheekily set themselves at the head of the G7 countries who with cupped hands and in stentorian voice demanded immense monetary compensation for the sins of the carbon emitters, also led by themselves.

The world's temperature has risen approximately 0.5°C, or almost 1°F, in thirty-five years. There has been minimal global warming for eighteen years, though carbon emissions in the world have steadily increased throughout that period. It is indisputable that the world has been warmer several times in its history than it is now, so whatever impact man may have on it, the world's temperature is evidently subject to fluctuations for other reasons. There is also legitimate disagreement about the consequences of such warming as might occur. Recent research at the University of Sussex, widely recognized for its expertise in this field, indicates that warming up to 3.5°C from where we are now would have no appreciable impact on anything, except a positive impact where increased volumes of carbon dioxide increase arable area and make crops more drought resistant. There has also been a good deal of reciprocally corroborating research in different countries by recognized experts that uniformly demonstrates that the world's temperature is much less sensitive than had long been feared to increased carbon use. Antarctic polar ice is thickening and world water levels are not rising. Apocalyptic statements of imminent consequences of not reducing carbon use have been fairly thoroughly debunked.

Not only is the evidence of the effects of increased carbon use unclear, but the economic consequences of discouragement of carbon use are very clear and very harmful to the most vulnerable countries. China and India, the two most populous countries and the first and third carbon emitters, are eagerly pursuing economic growth, which is the only method for pulling the many hundreds of millions of desperately poor people in those countries upwards out of poverty, and they are not going to change policy to accommodate the militant ecologists of the West. They don't attach the slightest credence to the alarmist comments of the more strident ecologists, other than as an excuse for demanding monetary compensation for how the economically leading countries have disadvantaged them. The International Energy Agency estimates that the underdeveloped countries as a group will emit 70 per cent of the carbon output of the world in the next fifteen years and will be responsible for all of the increase in carbon use over that time.

President Obama has called the Paris conference a "historic turning point," but it isn't, and claimed (in February) that climate change was a greater problem than terrorism. He and John Kerry (secretary of state) have several times called it the world's greatest problem. This is bunk. The pope stated that we are "at the edge of suicide." If so, it is not for climatic reasons. (The Holy See has placated the greens, but emphasized that "the Church cannot take the place of scientists and politicians.") Many in those groups are more impetuous in their assertions. And everyone seriously involved with the Paris conference knows that it is not really going to accomplish much. As Lord Ridley pointed out in the *Wall Street Journal* on November 28, the NGO spokespeople attending at Paris will scream like banshees of imminent disaster for fear of having their budgets cut, despite contrary evidence and although it is now clear that decarbonization is much more harmful to the world than increased carbon emissions.

Alternate sources of energy, such as wind and solar, are hideously more expensive and much less productive, a luxury no country can really afford, and certainly not the poorer countries. But the conference will be hamstrung. Countries will volunteer their own individual targets for reduction of carbon emissions, called Intended Nationally Determined Contributions, or INDCs. The INDC of China only predicts that such emissions will meet their peak by 2030, while, for all his militancy, President Obama's U.S. INDC will be a reduction of 26 to 28 per cent in ten years, yet the outline of hoped-for gains, which Congress will not endorse, and for years Obama will only see as a private citizen, only calls for half the volume reduction of emissions necessary to meet his pledge. The American INDC is a scam.

Even the Obama administration is demanding an involuntary international verification mechanism (much more rigorous than what it settled for in the rather more urgent matter of Iranian nuclear military development) and the elimination of the so-called firewall of separate arrangements for the developed and underdeveloped (or developing) countries. The developing countries, led by China and India, refuse, unless they are solemnly promised a $100 billion a year climate fund, as Obama imprudently pledged at Copenhagen. This remains completely out of the question and furnished the justification in advance for the developing countries to fall short of their INDC targets, which will provide the cover for the developed countries to do the same. Everyone will solemnly announce ambitious INDCs, but there will be no verification, ample excuse for non-compliance for everyone, and this charade will continue to the next portentous and verbose conference. Meanwhile, the many thousands of non-paying delegates will enjoy the delights of Paris.

Whatever Canada does is irrelevant to the world, as it is not a serious offender and only provides about 2.3 per cent of the world's economic activity and less than 1 per cent of anticipated increases in carbon emissions over the next fifteen years, in a total that there is no evidence will have any negative repercussions anyway. The new government has a very capable environment minister in Catherine McKenna, and doubtless she and Justin Trudeau will acquit themselves well, as long as they don't really imagine that much will result from the Paris meeting.

What seems to have happened is that the international far left, having been decisively routed with the collapse of the Soviet Union and of international communism, has attached itself to the environmental movement, usurped the leading positions in it from the bird-watching, butterfly-collecting, and conservation organizations, and is carrying on its anti-capitalist and anarchist crusade behind the cover of eco-Armageddonism. While this has been rather skilfully executed, many office-holders and aspirants, including Obama, have used dire environmental scenarios to distract their electorates from their own policy failures, much as Arab powers have long diluted anger at despotic misgovernment by harping on the red herring of Israel.

On the subject of such things, Steven Donziger, the much enriched champion of the Ecuadorian claimants against Chevron, whose antics I described here last week, has replied to me on his website entirely with a reference to my status as a person convicted of felonies. As readers know, I am proud to have been sent to prison for three years in the United States for crimes I would never have dreamed of committing, all of the charges of which were abandoned, rejected by jurors, or unanimously vacated by the U.S. Supreme Court, and in respect of which I received by far the largest libel settlement in Canadian history from the original sponsors of the charges. Two charges were self-servingly retrieved by a lower court panel which the high court had excoriated but remanded the vacated counts to, for "assessment of the gravity of its errors." This spurious resurrection does not disguise the fraudulence of the prosecution, and the last words to me from the trial judge were, "The court wishes you well, Mr. Black." This is a considerable contrast with the assertion by federal judge Lewis Kaplan of Donziger that he had committed a vast range of grievous crimes, including racketeering, money-laundering, perjury, obstruction of justice, and practically unlimited corrupt acts in pursuit of "an egregious fraud" in Ecuador. To be described as I was by such an accuser is a distinct honour.

# THE PERFECTLY RESPECTABLE ENVIRONMENTAL MOVEMENT HAS BEEN HIJACKED BY CLIMATE RADICALS

*National Post*, December 12, 2015

M y views of the Paris conference on the environment were published here last week and need not be revisited. But I think the phenomenon of climate change rigidity is so unusual and widespread, it is worthy of more analysis. We start from the fact that absolutely everyone is an environmentalist in the sense that the term enjoyed for many years. This was in having a concern, even if belated, for clean air and water, reforestation, preservation of species, and of all mankind being responsible stewards of the physical planet. No one today claims that lakes belong to industry, and no one, at least in the Western world, accepts the industrial smog that used to prevail in almost all industrial cities, or the untreated sewage that made most of the world's urban waterways from early in the Industrial Revolution until the last forty or fifty years a fecal ooze. In London, in the 1860s, for instance, the Thames was so foul with sewage that the windows of the Palace of Westminster had to be closed to reduce the nausea that afflicted members of Parliament and peers in their deliberations. Even with that precaution, the ghastly odour combined with the summer heat caused frequent unscheduled recesses. London was widely reckoned the greatest city in the world, though Paris, Vienna, and even New York preceded it in building comprehensive sewer systems, which did not really treat the effluent but conveyed it some distance from the nostrils of the most populous and prestigious urban areas.

The battles for cleaning up the air and water in North America, and such specific problems as acid rain, achieved very wide support and were carried, ultimately with little opposition, though the implementation was very costly to the corporate sector and municipalities, and the waste disposal picture remains far from perfect, though very much improved. On the heels of this victory, the conservation-environmental movement, which had previously confined itself to fairly notorious concerns no one could dispute, relatively quickly graduated to the higher plane of predicting the end of life on Earth due to human-generated emissions of carbon dioxide that would overheat and devastate the planet with astonishing swiftness. They went from cleaning up what everyone could see was ugly and unsanitary, to apprehended but invisible fates. The Prince of Wales, British prime minister Tony Blair, U.S. vice-president Al Gore, and many scientists and commentators, as well as the usual coterie of celebrities from the entertainment industry and the legal fraternity, and concerned figures prominent in international organizations and NGOs, caused the chorus to swell to window-rattling volume in a very short time.

An iron consensus emerged – the whole world was given the bum's rush toward a pell-mell decarbonization that, if implemented, would disemploy tens of millions of people. The end was nigh, and profoundly radical steps had to be taken at once or we were doomed, as if by inexorable collision with a giant intergalactic fireball. We all had to abandon coal, travel in carpools in electric cars, live under thatch, and move to sustainable energy, such as solar- and wind-generated power. Serious people said so, such as Prince Charles, Blair, and Gore (of course, they are not above criticism, including from me at times, but they are all sane, altruistic, and intelligent, and so are most of their prominent and ostensibly knowledgeable soulmates in this very popular cause).

My friendly and esteemed one-time debating partner, Tabatha Southey of the *Globe and Mail*, wrote in that newspaper last Saturday a column of knowledgeable guidance on "How To Recognize People

Who Don't Recognize Reality." She remarked on the change in the Associated Press style guide from "climate change deniers" to "climate change doubters," and objected that "doubters" is almost just "ponderers," and that most people she encounters who dissent from the climate change conventional wisdom "reject overwhelming scientific evidence encroaching on their world," either because they whimsically refuse to look very far into the matter or are more extreme zealots of loopy conspiracy theories imputing fantastic motives to the leading climate change advocates.

Tabatha regrets that "deniers" have been replaced, apparently to avoid confusion with Holocaust deniers, and here she is certainly correct. That is an absurd reason for banishing the word – one might just as well argue that people said to be "in denial" are Nazi sympathizers, or rabid anti-Semites. I am a doubter and a skeptic, but not exactly a denier. But I seem to fit into her category of "those who reject mainstream climate science as the pre-eminent magical thinkers of our age." This is a perfectly civil and bearable, almost a sustainable, charge, and she gives a *"Field Guide to People Who Are Really Wrong About Climate Change."* She mocks those who say that "the Earth stopped warming 15 years ago." But the problem is not just that it hasn't appreciably warmed in eighteen years, but in the sixty years prior to that it only warmed by 1°C, despite all the inflammations of the Second World War and lesser conflicts and decades of nuclear testing, stupefying increases in carbon emissions, through a vast proliferation of automobiles and decades of heavy, but in energy terms crude, economic growth in China and among many other nationalities. So global warming didn't just "stall," or even stop, it hasn't started, at least not in centuries.

The world's temperature fluctuates, but it has certainly been warmer in a number of epochs in world history than it is now. "Global warming" is an expression that once empurpled the air and debouched from the lips of all of "mainstream science's spokespeople" and their crowded echo chamber, but it silently metamorphosed into "climate change." This is a much less definitive expression, and is much more of an intellectual retreat than that of a denier to a doubter. I am, according to Tabatha, a "climate-change ostrich," but I am conscientiously trying to find any evidence that the climate is changing and that man is causing it to change, and I am not finding it. The fact that serried ranks of people are impatiently saying that the climate is changing, like Victorian elocution-school students repeating the spelling of words, does not mean that it is.

If I am an ostrich, Tabatha is hallucinatory: Where is there evidence of climate change, other than the endlessly repeated divinations of professedly clairvoyant people such as Prince Charles and Al Gore (who also told us that he invented the internet and that the Pacific island country of Tuvalu would be submerged by now – the water level there has actually declined slightly)? The "hockey stick" of sharply increasing temperatures is nonsense. Polar ice is not now melting. Kyoto cap-and-trade was an insane transfer of billions of dollars from advanced countries to the most egregious and backward despotisms. Copenhagen was an unmitigated fiasco.

Tabatha rightly decries the "climate-change loon" who sees Byzantine conspiracies everywhere, the same sort of people who believed fluoridated drinking water was a communist or Nazi conspiracy in the 1950s. Less successful, or at least harder to recognize, is the "climate-change cardinal sinner" type, who says that climate change is happening but isn't caused by humans. They are just dolts – since there is no evidence it is happening, other than long-term secular fluctuations in what has become over several millennia a familiar pattern, there is no evidence that man has anything to do with what does not, in any case, appear to be occurring. Even rarer, and I have never knowingly met one, is the "climate-change dodo," who says that climate change is happening but all species will evolve to cope with it; and the "climate-change lark," who says it's happening but there's nothing anyone can do about it so the hell with it.

I put it to Tabatha and birds of her feather that the defeated international left gravitated to the environment movement as a way of obstructing the victorious forces of the free enterprise system, gradually, instinctively, and opportunistically, not by any plan or prearrangement. They crowded onto the eco-bus and radicalized a positive and very respectable pro-Earth movement and pushed it, as waves of thought are pushed, to extremes from which they are already retreating (e.g., global warming to climate change). This may not be even be the conscious motive of many of them, though it is fairly obvious in the triumphalist Marxist revanchisme of people like Naomi Klein, celebrating by anticipation the counter-humiliation of capitalism by the alarmists of Eco-Horror Inc.

Once an intellectual fad attained such a state of permeation that it was impossible to set foot out of doors without being disparaged for unkindness to vegetables and for desecration of grass, our politicians rushed headlong to the head of the mob, overcommitted themselves to the cultish fad, rivalled each other in their trillings of virtue and shrieks of eco-vengeance. It was a perfect cycle of an apprehended event and the rousing of public opinion to meet an immense existential challenge. Horizons darkened with these absurd and noisy, bird-unfriendly windmills, and energy consumers are saddled with the preposterous costs of solar energy. There is only one fundamental problem: there is still no evidence that the world is getting warmer or that the climate is changing in any identifiable way.

I am not a climate change denier, I am an unsuccessful climate change evidence-seeker, like Jacques Cartier or Columbus peering into the distance to see a new world. And so far there is nothing there. My late friend Maurice Strong told me my Florida ocean-side home would become a natural aquarium; it hasn't. China and India would rather have economic growth and job creation than dispel the smog of Beijing and Mumbai. They are where we were in 1950, but the climate isn't changing. If it ever does, I will join Tabatha in the anti-denial thought reform counselling service, but the global warmers have already fled into the Forest Primeval.

# BOOK REVIEWS

## NORMAN PODHORETZ'S MEMOIR, *EX-FRIENDS*

*The American Spectator*, December 29, 1998

The identity of this book's author and of his subjects incites high hopes for a lively read, which are not disappointed. In his fluctuating relationship with these former friends, Norman Podhoretz traces the progress of his literary criticism (this tore it with Allen Ginsberg), his political views (goodbye to the Trillings and Lillian Hellman); and his views on Israel, Zionism, and being Jewish (exit Hannah Arendt). There were elements of all of these in the breakup with Norman Mailer, plus social and marital foibles of Mailer's as well.

The persistence of the Lillian Hellman myth is hard to understand given the notorious fraudulence of much of her autobiography, her undoubted view of the moral superiority of Stalin over Roosevelt, Truman, and Eisenhower, and her assimilation of the legal harassments of McCarthy era American leftists with the unimaginable barbarities inflicted by Stalin and his successors on millions of innocent people. "Blasphemous," Podhoretz rightly calls it.

Gnawing away inside this book, as it has in many other accounts of the same era and personalities is the question of what so many prominent and intelligent Americans thought they were doing, working so diligently to defame the United States and legitimize Soviet communism.

Liberal anti-communists like the Trillings were fairly unexceptionable. Hannah Arendt was an authentic opponent of all totalitarians until she became thoroughly addled in her later years. Allen Ginsberg and the early and middle-aged Norman Mailer were so erratic and disturbed, some compassionate allowance must be made for them. Lillian Hellman had no such excuse, but Norman Podhoretz's affectionate recollections of her are rather gallant. He described their last encounter on the sidewalk: "Hello Normie," said Ms. Hellman, "and then, with a slight shrug and a wistful smile," she sped up as Podhoretz started to slow down. That was the end.

With Hannah Arendt and even more with Norman Mailer, there is less chivalry and a little more edginess. In a debate with Hannah Arendt and Dwight Macdonald at the University of Maryland following publication of Ms. Arendt's book criticizing the Israeli seizure, trial, and execution of Adolf Eichmann (Trotsky himself once said of Dwight Macdonald, "Everyone has a right to be stupid but Comrade Macdonald abuses the privilege"), Ms. Arendt said that one of Podhoretz's remarks could only have been made by someone who had never been "in the neighbourhood of a concentration camp." The author claims out of concern for their personal relations to have suppressed the temptation to respond that growing up in America "has deprived me of the great spiritual and intellectual advantages Miss Arendt derived from living in a society that produced concentration camps, but one does the best one can." Such a riposte could have been formulated in an inoffensive but no less effective way, especially by someone of Mr. Podhoretz's agility. Thirty-five years is a long time to wait to deliver such repartee. It was Hannah Arendt who revealed to Norman Podhoretz, inadvertently, that Jews need no more justify their existence than does any other group. And he learned from her that brilliance and originality in themselves have little value as they are apt to be misapplied, as they often were in Hannah Arendt's case.

With Norman Mailer, there is a little more competitiveness than seems appropriate. His disappointment in Mailer as a writer after the great early promise of *The Naked and the Dead* is understandable and widely shared. But it is unseemly to rejoice that young critics now find Mailer passé or that Mailer spends so much time in a dinner jacket, he who for so long put on the airs of revolutionary toiler. Mailer's general political and literary views were notoriously absurd for decades, but the recitation of social abrasions between Mailer and Podhoretz, though entertaining, is unbecomingly catty in places.

The author regrets the passage of the "Family" of New York's literary elite, but he is perhaps too admiring of their cleverness, too forgiving of the damage they did, too prone to caricature "country club" rich (most businessmen may be idiots politically, but not all). He has brief words of praise for William Buckley and Henry Kissinger at the start of the book and Milton Friedman near the end. These men had an undeprived social life while they fought a lonely ideological struggle in days when Norman Podhoretz was flirting with revisionism about the origins of the Cold War and with Khrushchev's ability to reform communism.

Norman Podhoretz's early opposition to the anti-Americanism of the American left in the 1950s, and unwavering patriotism generally, even defending American philosophers from Hannah Arendt's Germanic condescensions, is admirable and is recounted unhistrionically. His desertion of the Stalinists and temporary relative toleration of post-Stalinists is fairly described (including the fact that the Trillings were to some extent right in their dispute with him). One of the best of many witty epigrams in this book belongs to Lionel Trilling, who referred to Podhoretz and Mailer's championship of the controversial psycho-philosopher Norman O. Brown as the "Norman invasion."

Podhoretz's desertion of the American left in the 1970s with other prominent neo-conservatives such as Irving Kristol, was an important intellectual development. But its impact on the election and government of President Reagan is somewhat exaggerated, as are the importance and antics generally of the little "Family" of muddled, self-important, gossip-addicted highbrows.

Some of the lamentations for the past are also excessive and give short shrift to *Commentary* magazine today in the capable hands of Neal Kozodoy, chosen by Norman Podhoretz to succeed him after Podhoretz's formidable thirty-five-year editorship.

Withal, this book is as charming and intelligent and courageous as its author. It is a fine account of his rise from Lionel Trilling's star student ("my eager hand was often in the air") to 5th and Park Avenue's virtual mascot ("Oh, so you scooted across the park in your little brown suit and your big brown shoes," Jacqueline Kennedy once greeted him) to his latter and present eminence. And it is a gripping account of the drama of one of the great figures of contemporary American letters as he "shouldered the burden of challenging the regnant leftist culture that pollutes the spiritual and cultural air we all breathe . . . with all my heart and all my soul and all my might." No sensible person finishing this very readable and entertaining little volume can fail to be grateful that he has done so.

Norman Podhoretz, *Ex-Friends* (Easton Press, 1999).

# DUTCH,
# BY EDMUND MORRIS

*The American Spectator,* October 19, 1999

---

As an acquaintance and long-standing admirer of the writing of Edmund Morris, I looked forward to this book, determined to rise above early criticism of the format which mixes fact and fiction confusingly at times. *Dutch* (Ronald Reagan's adolescent nickname) has many elegant passages, a number of interesting insights, and does reflect hundreds of interviews and comprehensive research.

Unfortunately, it is a huge disappointment and is virtually confessed to be so by the author himself. Edmund Morris sets out to explain how a president who often seemed conversationally insubstantial could be so successful, as politician and leader. He marshals Reagan's strengths: courage, eloquence, a photographic memory for certain details, fanatical determination, unshakeable optimism, patriotic fervour, clear and sound principles, tenacity, uxoriousness, physical and moral strength, immense personal charm, longevity – almost indestructibility – sure populist instincts and an enigmatic cunning the author found particularly elusive.

Reagan's shortcomings are also amply revealed: superficiality, indolence in some matters of detail, a tendency to confusion in conversation or repartee, at stark variance to his hypnotic oratorical talents, sometimes misplaced stubbornness, lack of interest in others except his wife, a cold, almost mechanical aspect central to his personality that Morris isolates, mocks, resents, but can't really fathom.

Morris lurches back and forth like a metronome between acknowledging manifestations of Reagan's greatness and admitting his own inability to explain them. He is frequently nasty and sneering, even describing Reagan at one point as "an apparent airhead," but volunteers that Reagan may simply have been uninterested in revealing much of himself or even have been skilfully practising concealment of his real motivations.

In his desperation to get at the real Reagan, Morris devises the spurious technique of claiming to have known him for over seventy years, with the result that many pages are wasted in self-indulgent fiction about a non-existent relationship. This clumsy device pops up even in Reagan's public years. Morris unctuously blames "Dutch" for driving Morris's imaginary son underground after the Berkeley disturbances in 1969, as if such an event, had it actually happened, would have been the responsibility of the governor of California. At the very end of the book, Morris claims to have been rescued by Reagan when he was a lifeguard at Lowell Park, Illinois, in 1928, many years before Morris was born (in Kenya). He did graciously but almost incongruously conclude that "the old lifeguard . . . rescued America in a time of poisonous despair and carried her 'breastward out of peril.'" I took this late inspiration as the author's metaphorical confession of how much he and all civilized people owe to Reagan and of his sorrow at his own ambivalence and ingratitude through much of this ramshackle book for which Reagan and his family and entourage gave him almost unlimited access for four years.

Such an act of contrition would not be inappropriate for the author of so uneven a work after keeping his and his subject's admirers waiting for eleven years before laying this egg. Nor is it implausible for a writer who describes how, during one of Reagan's cancer scares, he prayed fervently and lit a candle for him in a Washington church. This book is often as much a garrulous stream of the consciousness of Edmund Morris, analysand, as a biography of Ronald Reagan.

On various occasions in his narrative, the author is very respectful, as during the attempted assassination in 1981, the first meeting with

Gorbachev in 1985, the Challenger launch tragedy in 1986, the president's farewell speech in 1989, and his very affecting letter describing his struggle with Alzheimer's in 1994 ("I now begin the journey that will lead me into the sunset of my life"). Morris rightly called this handwritten swan song a "masterly piece of writing."

But each time when he seems to have reconciled his own intellectual condescensions with Reagan's undoubted human qualities, he backslides into carping, as if unable to surrender the approval of Reagan's opponents in the professoriat, the bedraggled, ulcerous, academic left whom Reagan mowed down with amiable disinterest. These elements, even now, scramble around like asphyxiated cockroaches trying to give Gorbachev the credit that largely belongs to Reagan for winning the Cold War and Bill Clinton all the kudos for the overwhelming success of Reaganomics.

Morris would have done better to shorten his book, confine himself to his laboriously collected facts, and leave the reader to make his own assessment of this extraordinary figure, since Morris can't, after fourteen years and seven hundred pages, offer a coherent one himself.

On the positive side, Reagan "beguiled" de Gaulle and de Valera, was a talented essayist at university, and to the end wrote most of his own speeches: possessed "subtlety, sweetness, clarity" of written and spoken word and was almost without vanity. This last is no small achievement for a man who was conspicuously successful at everything he did. As a lifeguard, he rescued seventy-seven people. As a radio sports announcer in Des Moines, California-bound in the Great Depression, he was, according to *Sporting News* in 1936, one of the most popular in the country. He was Hollywood's box office leading film actor in 1941 after *Kings Row, Dark Victory, Santa Fe Trail,* and *Knute Rockne, All American,* at the age of thirty. As spokesman for General Electric, his television program was an instant and constant success and he became one of America's best-known personalities and most effective public speakers. When he finally entered politics, at the age of fifty-five, he had four elections, as governor and president, and four landslide victories.

It has been an astonishing career, and Morris does record the laudations of opponents. House Speaker Tip O'Neill thought him the greatest public speaker and most popular politician he had known in his career. Gorbachev considered him an "authentic" man of "calibre" and "balance." Mitterrand admired his strength, cleverness, convictions, and success, even though he found him intellectually unimpressive. His friends, such as Margaret Thatcher, were even more positive, and Paul Nitze, who served every president from Franklin D. Roosevelt, started as a skeptic but ended regarding Reagan as "a great man." He also records the praise of such early peers as Al Jolson and Cecil B. DeMille and the friendship of Humphrey Bogart. He credits Reagan with being a sincere opponent of anti-communist Hollywood witch-hunts. He even claims Reagan unsuccessfully applied for membership in the Communist Party in 1938. He accurately describes how, literally and figuratively, he "towered over his drained little predecessor," Jimmy Carter.

But interspersed among these compliments are reservations that go well beyond fair comment. He accuses Reagan of being cold to his wife, whom he describes as "poor Nancy, the most patient wife since Cosima Wagner," but all evidence, here and elsewhere, is that he was devoted to his wife. Morris describes the pre-presidential Reagan as "so ungreat he couldn't handle power." Reagan is not even spared phrenological aspersions from his official biographer. Morris records, "I have not noticed before how low [Reagan's forehead] is, how heavy and confining the thick fine thatch above. One gets the impression that only the smoothest, most processed grain can be blown into that shallow loft, and that once it reaches capacity, it will compact and atrophy into something harder than bone." Morris describes Reagan as "courtly, beautiful, brave and blundering," and his fictional characters say scurrilous things about Reagan which the author obviously intermittently believes but oddly doesn't wish to record as his own opinion. Almost the only acerbity he avoids is any reference to the notorious movie *Bedtime for Bonzo.*

The author's ambivalence about his subject stretches from the most personal to the greatest events of his administration. Reagan the bachelor is one of Hollywood's great swordsmen in places, and an indifferent lover in others. Morris is undecided about the firing of the air controllers, the bombing of Gaddafi, Reaganomics in general, and the Reykjavik summit: though the first three were clearly successful and Reykjavik had its uses. Morris credits Reagan with having outwitted Gorbachev at the Geneva summit meeting, considered the "evil empire" speech to have been a success, but, wearing his pro-life heart on his sleeve, sanctimoniously holds Reagan responsible for 82,000 abortions under legislation he signed in California, "as against the seventy-seven [souls] he took credit for as a lifeguard."

In most respects, Morris's judgment and even elemental historical knowledge are scandalously unreliable for a serious historian. He attaches great importance to the evolution of Reagan's handwriting, is dazzled by and repeats the sequence of vehicles in Reagan's presidential motorcades, purports to believe that in the 1950s, "paranoia and concealment became the American norm"; that Reagan was both an imperialist and a pacifist; that the U.S.S.R. was not guilty of "perfidy" at the time of the Warsaw Uprising in 1944; that when Reagan visited Bitburg and Bergen-Belsen in 1985 (which Morris disapproved), Germany was "sick" and Helmut Kohl "incapacitated" (Kohl continued as federal chancellor for thirteen years). Despite his thorough research, Morris is oddly credulous toward Reagan's critics at times and subscribes to the outrageous slur that Reagan equated Nazi war dead to Holocaust victims. The president actually said that young German conscripts who died without knowing what they were fighting for or against were also victims, and that it was time to integrate Germany into Western civilization. His revulsion at Nazi atrocities began with the first U.S. Army films of liberated camps in 1945 and never wavered. Morris accurately records this and Reagan's fierce hostility throughout his life to anti-Semitism or racism of any kind.

Morris asserts that Margaret Thatcher became U.K. Conservative leader because of Keith Joseph's hubristic embrace of eugenics. (Joseph stood aside for her because he thought, accurately, that she would be a better party leader). As a jet passes overhead at a summit meeting, Morris "equated it with blood thundering through Gorbachev's birthmark." He shows a serious ignorance of U.S. election campaign funding and thought Jimmy Carter's hokey walk from his inauguration to the White House "a wonderful moment."

Morris wastes an unforgivable amount of space on himself. No reader slogs through this book to learn about Morris's career ups and downs, fictional or real, or to be told on several occasions about the author's beard.

There are also countless repetitive descriptions of Reagan's "thick, dark, Brylcreemed hair," as if the reader had no idea what Reagan looked like and needed to be reminded every five pages. Certain words, such as "splotch," "scintillant," and "querulous," are used much too often. There are also too many insertions of obscure "splotches" of poetry, doubtless designed to impress us with the author's reconditeness, but usually irrelevant. There are many sheep in the Falkland Islands, but unless an unreported cataclysm has occurred there, the islands are not "sheep-splattered."

We have to endure endless descriptions of the weather and sunlight, not just on great but on banal occasions, such as Morris's visits to Reagan's (and Louella Parsons's) hometown, Dixon, Illinois. And there are Morris's pedantic flights into foreign languages, not in search of uniquely expressive phrases: "savoir faire" and "Weltanschauungs" would be acceptable, but no such luck. We are laboured with a rhetorical "quién sabe?" and several "moments critiques," and "affrontements" and an "entrer en conversation," as if rhetorical questions, critical moments, confrontations, and conversational openings were beyond the imagination of the lumpenanglophony.

There are some fine descriptive passages, and many of the personality sketches of secondary figures are excellent, but there are too many clumsy images of Reagan as a glacier or iceberg and too many flamboyant metaphors and analogies that don't make it: "the fetid waters of memory and desire"; "I must allow these dusts of myself to sparkle in [Reagan's] waning light." This was in the introduction and Reagan's light wasn't waning, Morris's was. Quarrelling intellectuals are like "sex among iguanas." We are treated to Freudian reflections on the author's relations with his mother; there are frequent lapses into absurd stage directions for a film set, and we are told of the "Cyclopean stare of Richard Nixon." (Nixon has been called almost everything, including, by Morris, a "tormented visionary," but never, until now, a one-eyed giant.) Nixon inspired Morris to write about Theodore Roosevelt, but like most, if not all, presidents during his lifetime except Coolidge,

Franklin D. Roosevelt, and Eisenhower, Reagan had little respect for Nixon. Morris, waffling 1960s flower-person as he partly reveals himself to be, found the music at Nixon's rather uplifting funeral in 1994 (almost all America's great patriotic anthems and marches) "execrable." This is one of countless unbecoming reflections from the inhabitant of a vast glass house. In the same nostalgic leftist spirit, he portentously quotes from the discredited 1950s and 1960s fellow-traveller C. Wright Mills; why not Timothy Leary, Angela Davis, or Gus Hall?

Morris attributes Reagan's ungenerous regard for Gerald Ford to the fact that Ford wasn't elected president, though he quotes Reagan's own, more sensible explanation (that Ford was essentially ineffectual). But Morris would have us believe that he knows Reagan better than Reagan knows himself. This consideration didn't prevent Reagan from heading up the Hollywood for Truman campaign for the then unelected president in 1948. It presumably didn't colour Reagan's views of the pre-1904 unelected President Theodore Roosevelt either, Morris's chronicling of whom, up to his inauguration, led Reagan to the engagement of Morris as his own biographer.

The extreme opposite pole to Morris's prayers and offerings for Reagan are completely gratuitous bursts of ridicule of unexceptionable things, as when Reagan, a guest in the Aga Khan's house at Geneva for the 1985 meeting with Gorbachev, conscientiously fed his host's son's goldfish in one of the rooms he was using. When one of them died anyway, Reagan had his security unit scour Geneva for identical replacements and left the boy a note which Morris is pleased to describe as an explanation of "the mysteries of death and transfiguration" of goldfish.

The last years of Reagan's presidency are in an uncoordinated chapter of vignettes called "Album Leaves." Important issues and perspectives are unrecognizably compressed or passed over altogether.

This book is so idiosyncratic, and so appallingly bad in places, that it is somewhat endearing and rouses curiosity about, and perhaps even solicitude for, its overwrought author. It does shed considerable light on Reagan, shadowed though it is with Edmund Morris's wingy biases and even jealousies. But the uninformed reader would never guess Reagan's role in the end of the Cold War, or in the tremendous current prosperity of the United States. It is never really made clear that, or why, Reagan's countrymen considered him a great leader and a beloved president.

There is no reason to fear for Morris's Theodore Roosevelt project, to which he expresses great and understandable happiness to have returned, since he can probably cope with a less enigmatic president who has been dead for eighty years. Morris's interview notes and tapes will be of great help to less disturbed Reagan historians who didn't hover and fester confusedly in the Reagan White House as Morris did. But as a definitive life, *Dutch* is a ludicrous imposture. While describing rummaging through the Reagan Library, Edmund Morris declares, "The biographer lives in hope." So do we all, but the great hope invested in this book was not well-founded.

Edmund Morris, *Dutch* (Random House, 1999).

# ENDING THE VIETNAM WAR, BY HENRY A. KISSINGER

*The American Spectator*, April 2003

This book is essentially an anthology of the author's own previous writings on the subject, well-organized, well-written, and updated. While many of the passages are familiar to devotees of Henry Kissinger's previous books, this volume is a very successful resumé of the subject. The author resists the temptation to launch a full-scale assault on his most outspoken critics, confining himself to a relatively unexceptionable, elegantly worded recitation of facts, and leaving it to future, disinterested historians to judge the many protagonists in this protracted tragedy.

President Truman and President Eisenhower concluded that avoidance of a communist takeover of Indochina was vital to U.S. national security. After the descent of the Iron Curtain and the communist takeover of China, and the communist aggression in Korea, this was a reasonable position. But Eisenhower declined to intervene militarily, even after France had promised to grant independence to the constituent parts of Indochina. But he did commit the United States to the support of South Vietnam, and the avoidance of the spurious from the pan-Vietnam vote on reunification that was agreed at Geneva, a peace settlement that the United States did not sign but promised not to obstruct.

President Kennedy broadened the Eisenhower position and made it clear that he was prepared to go a good deal farther than Eisenhower had been to prevent a communist conquest of South Vietnam and Laos, which emerged as entities after the Geneva Conference in 1954. Kennedy did effectively hand Laos over as an infiltration superhighway for the North into the South with the Laos Neutrality Agreement of 1962.

It will always remain a moot point how far President Kennedy would have gone in Vietnam, had he lived. President Johnson undoubtedly felt it a legacy from his predecessor to resist the North Vietnamese. At this point, the mistakes began to accumulate, though the full, horrible price of them would only be paid much later.

President Johnson overstretched the Tonkin Gulf Resolution as a legal basis for committing 545,000 American military personnel to Vietnam. It seems to have been somewhat confected as an incident of North Vietnamese aggression. It was hypocrisy for senators and congressmen later to claim that Johnson had no authority from Congress to wage war, since Congress voted the funds for it every year. But it was not a constitutional procedure that committed Congress to the opinion of successive presidents that Vietnam was a matter of high American national interest. This made it easier for Congress to flake off from the Johnson and Nixon administrations when the going got tough.

Sending draftees to the ends of the earth to risk their lives, and in the case of 57,000 give up their lives, for a goal defined as less than victory in a war, the relevance of which to the American national interest had not been declared by Congress or comprehensibly affirmed by the president, should have been seen as extremely hazardous.

Nor, as Kissinger points out, was the war conducted very efficiently. Eisenhower gave the correct military analysis that the place to stop the North Vietnamese aggression was in Laos, where the Ho Chi Minh Trail snaked through dense jungles and permitted massive North Vietnamese infiltration of the South. General Douglas MacArthur gave President Kennedy and President Johnson the same advice.

Instead of following this advice, Kennedy placed great importance on the arrangements that had been negotiated for the neutrality of Laos, which North Vietnam contemptuously violated from the outset.

It was an act of military insanity to commit over half a million men, of whom, because of a top-heavy organization, less than 30 per cent were combat forces, trigger-pullers, to a campaign of search-and-destroy against guerrilla units in the quagmire of South Vietnam.

The entire American high command failed the country and the armed forces by implementing and tenaciously clinging to such an unpromising war plan. The country then failed the military by giving it inadequate support. Although Kissinger doesn't get into this, it was also insane to send officers and men to Vietnam for tours of different lengths; wars and enlistments, whether voluntary or not, are for the duration. The United States would not have been victorious if it had waged the world wars in this way.

The correct course, as stated by Eisenhower and MacArthur, which was finally given a half-hearted try by the South Vietnamese in 1971, was to defend the DMZ and attack directly to the west of it, across Laos, cutting the Ho Chi Minh Trail. This would leave the North Vietnamese and Viet Cong forces in the south without supplies, other than what they could ship through Cambodia, which Prince Sihanouk would have thanked the Americans for interdicting (and did when Nixon attacked the so-called sanctuaries in Cambodia in 1970). The foray into Laos in 1971 was conducted late, entrusted to the South Vietnamese, whose orders were to stop when they had taken three thousand casualties, and was a fiasco. (Nixon salvaged it by ordering a helicopter-transported ground attack on the objective, which was taken with great publicity and then secretly abandoned.)

President Johnson should have seized on the technical victory of the defeated Tet Offensive in early 1968, proclaimed Vietnamization, begun withdrawals, and imposition of the Eisenhower solution, closing the Ho Chi Minh Trail. He would have been re-elected and would have saved South Vietnam. Instead, demoralized and let down by his military and intelligence advisers, reviled by the liberal constituency for which he had done so much, he abdicated.

When Richard Nixon entered office, he had, as Kissinger writes, a choice between escalation, abandonment (since it wasn't his war), and Vietnamization. He also had an opportunity to conduct the war differently. It took many months for Nixon and Kissinger to conclude that negotiations with the North Vietnamese were useless, that after domestic American discord had hounded Johnson from office, Hanoi saw no reason to pursue anything less than American withdrawal and the complete surrender of Saigon.

Neither Nixon nor Kissinger has ever explained, in writing or in conversations with this supportive reviewer, why the incoming administration did not present the issue squarely to Congress before it could become Nixon's war. Congress should have been forced either to accept and proclaim a satisfactory result in Vietnam to be a matter of urgent national interest, as the previous presidents believed and the Democratic Congress, albeit with growing unease, had implicitly ratified. Or, alternatively, Congress, specifically its Democratic majorities, would have to accept the responsibility for the consequences of American withdrawal, which Nixon would then have effected. .

Nixon could then have stated that if the effort were approved, he would use American combat forces to prevent further infiltration of South Vietnam, attack broadly defined military targets in North Vietnam, and would Vietnamize the civil war in the South as quickly as possible. He could also have brought forward a lottery draft, as he eventually did, and could have incentivized volunteers. Domestic political bitterness would have been substantially alleviated.

Everyone has twenty-twenty hindsight. What Nixon and Kissinger did attempt was noble in purpose, frequently ingenious, and was courageously pursued. Nixon mobilized the "silent majority" of Americans, built up the strength of the South Vietnamese, responded with great force to the massive North Vietnamese offensive of April 1972. He and Kissinger negotiated what was, on its face, a reasonable peace agreement in 1973.

Kissinger is completely believable when he writes that he could not imagine that, having come this far, the United States would withhold aid from Saigon as it fended for itself and fought for its life after the Paris Peace. Nor could he see that executive authority would evaporate in the Watergate shambles. He convincingly defends himself and Nixon from the charge of having gone through four years of war to no effect and of having bought only the proverbial decent interval.

Everything that could go wrong did. Vietnam became a metaphor for national political self-hate, the supreme badge of the great liberal

death wish. Overconfident and sometimes disingenuous military briefings alienated the media, but much of the American media effectively
colluded with the nation's enemies. Nixon had always been controversial, and many failed to put the country, the health of the political system, and the institution of the presidency ahead of their dislike of the
president. Unfortunately, the president's own complexities of personality caused him to cooperate with his enemies. He ultimately made the
greatest comeback of all and crowned his astonishing career in a state
of general esteem.

The price paid by the South Vietnamese for their geographic position, the virulence of local communism, and the inconsistencies of
their great ally was horrible. This book reminds us of the treachery,
hypocrisy, or at best unfathomable naiveté, of almost all the American
opponents of the Vietnam involvement except those who only objected
that it was not strategically worth the effort. It also reminds us that the
nation's leaders, Johnson, Nixon, Ford, were, where the national interest was involved, well-intentioned, honourable, and brave men, whatever their other limitations.

Kissinger makes the point that the Vietnam effort probably saved
Indonesia from communism. When Saigon fell, the expected dominoes did not fall, but the author is probably right that it had something
to do with the Cuban involvement in Angola, the fall of the Shah, and
the Soviet invasion of Afghanistan. The fall of Vietnam led straight to
the horrifying debacle in Cambodia.

The war in Vietnam also temporarily blinded the world to the
fact, now glaringly obvious to everyone, of the overwhelming, unprecedented, power and influence of the United States. This was because,
as successive North Vietnamese leaders said, more Vietnamese were
prepared to die to unify Vietnam than were Americans to prevent it.
This need not have been the litmus test.

Geopolitically, it hasn't much mattered. The West has won the
Cold War, and most Americans who were militantly critical of their
government's Vietnam policy know that that policy, while mistaken in
many respects, was not discreditable, and that America's enemy was an
odious regime.

The greatest lesson of Vietnam is that when the cause is sensibly
explained and proper constitutional procedures are followed, most

Americans are now prepared to support the just use of force. This is a matter of much comfort in the world, despite the disconcertion of some of America's supposed allies during the Iraq War, even if it is too late for the Vietnamese. They, too, will slough off communism eventually, but only indirectly due to the great but discoordinated efforts of the United States. This is a useful, readable, and timely book.

Henry Kissinger, *Ending the Vietnam War* (Simon & Schuster, 2003).

# THE RISE OF AMERICAN DEMOCRACY: JEFFERSON TO LINCOLN, BY SEAN WILENTZ

*The American Spectator*, February 2006

This book is a prodigious feat of scholarship and organization, weaving into its narrative every political splinter group, and attempting to give appropriate weight to all the tides and currents of American sociology from the Revolution to the Civil War. No detour into labour and religious and political factionalism is too obscure to be deserving of the brief redirection of the entire narrative to include it. An endless sequence of labour and social and religious agitators – of Clodhoppers, Tertium Quids, Loco Focos, Hunkers, Barnburners, and Know-Nothings, of cameo figures from Madison Washington to Mirabeau Buonaparte Lamar to the assertive Governor Wilson Lumpkin – crowds, and generally enriches, the story. The progress of the voting franchise, by racial and property-holding criteria, is authoritatively recounted for almost all of the states.

The thoroughness of the author's research and organization of his material is exemplary. The writing, despite occasional outbursts of pedantry and a tendency to dryness that understates the farcical aspects of much of the subject, flows smoothly and is often pleasing and even stylish. It is slightly disconcerting to read of "Walter" Whitman and "David" Crockett, or that Henry Clay "coaxed" President William Henry Harrison into something "before he died" (presumably before Harrison died at least). The implications of doing so after one or both of them had died are sufficiently disturbing that the point is better not made. But these are minor cavils and this book is quite readable despite its intense detail and complexity.

It has only one serious problem: the author's relentless partisanship. He is a yellow dog Democrat who romanticizes and exalts the forebears of the present Democratic Party and denigrates their opponents with a mechanical and sometimes grating consistency.

Washington and Lincoln are too celebrated to be frontally attacked, but, not being Democrats, they are seriously diminished. Washington is passed over as an almost irrelevant figurehead as president who pre-sumably rendered some service in the Revolutionary War and had earned the respect of his countrymen. But he is presented as essentially a ceremonious constitutional monarch who indulged the alleged cupid-ity, treachery, and anti-republican tendencies of Hamilton. In fact, he suppressed the Whiskey Rebellion to preserve the government of the young republic from insurrectionists, not because he was a stooge of Hamilton's, as is implied.

"Spotty" Lincoln is presented as eloquent and cunning at times, but often devious. He apparently had almost nothing to do with found-ing the Republican Party, unjustly exploited the discomfort of the Democrats over slavery, and may not have exhausted acceptable means for avoiding the Civil War. His ultimate victory, and the salvation of the Union and Emancipation of the slaves, were mitigated by the deaths of 750,000 people in the war.

John Adams, a solid if unexciting New Englander, is portrayed as a buffoon masquerading as having martial aptitudes, a virtual counter-revolutionary, brushed aside by the virtuous Jefferson. He receives no credit for installing Jefferson over the shadowy Aaron Burr in the 1800 Electoral College vote. He and Washington and Hamilton had been upholding "a hidebound elitism." John Quincy Adams runs the author's gauntlet more successfully, but he was, after all, technically a Jeffersonian when he became president, having been Monroe's very successful secretary of state. Henry Clay is presented as a whisky-sodden schemer and poseur, wrongly seeking credit for the 1850 Compromise, which, according to Wilentz, really belonged to Douglas. Daniel Webster emerges as a bibulous and ineffectual windbag.

Jefferson, who was a slaveholder and Indian-baiter, comes through as almost without fault. "He believed that slavery was evil and that it was doomed." There is no doubt that he was concerned about the moral and practical implications of slavery, but how do we know that he thought it evil and doomed, and why did he not emancipate his slaves? Too often, Wilentz engages in unsubstantiated mind reading for the benefit of famous Democrats. Jefferson was "the only national leader in history to achieve the vast expansion of his country . . . while at the same time . . . curtailing its military." He was also the only one offered half a continent almost as a gift. Wilentz passes too swiftly and with too facile a confidence over the ambiguities created by Jefferson's ambivalence about slavery, treatment of the Indians ("merciless Indian savages," he called them in the Declaration of Independence), and attitude to the French Revolution once it degenerated into extremism.

Andrew Jackson is lionized as the champion of modern democracy in America, despite his immense services to slavery, which are glossed over, including replanting the Democratic Party on slaveholding as its strongest pillar, as well as clearing 250,000 Indians out of the South and promoting the annexation of Texas to facilitate the expansion of slavery. After Jackson's administration, the Democrats' strongest argument for votes in the North was that only they could keep the South in the Union, by not pushing it too hard over slavery. Jackson's great service to the country was his suppression of Calhoun's movement to promote the right of the states to nullify federal laws, in 1832 and 1833. The appalling treatment of the Indians is given minimal weight compared to Jackson's supposedly beneficent destruction of the Bank of the United States and his founding of the modern Democratic Party.

The author accuses the bank of having been "mismanaged," of "hastening . . . and deepening the economic crisis," and of being afflicted by "incompetence" and "larceny," but provides no evidence of this. Though changes to the status quo were necessary and justified, Jackson was clumsy and inflicted a terrible depression on the country, which swamped his chosen successor, the endearing scoundrel Martin Van Buren. Wilentz tells us that blaming Jackson for the depression of the late 1830s "now appears simplistic at best," without elaboration. Yet almost every serious historian has concluded that abolishing paper money caused an unnecessary and severe liquidity crisis. Jackson's notorious "spoils system" of replacing large numbers of civil servants in a new administration, we read, was really a desire to "ventilate and democratize the executive branch." It may have been that in part, but there is room for other interpretations, such as that it was vindictive house-cleaning and simple and corrupt patronage.

The Southern Democrats' greatest leader, and slavery's foremost apologist, John C. Calhoun, is overindulged and repackaged as a conscientious regionalist, but a unionist at heart. James Knox Polk, a capable but colourless president, is presented, implausibly, as a second Jackson, in all his democratic virtue, and the inveterate and generally spineless political trickster Martin Van Buren comes out as a man of solid principle. This was a condition he only once in fact achieved, when he ran as a third party anti-slavery candidate for president in 1848, causing the election of the Whig, Zachary Taylor. Poor Stephen A. Douglas, according to Wilentz, was the earnest compromiser Clay was not, but the ground was taken out from under him, we are told, by the crafty Lincoln. And so on.

Wilentz's partisan biases are not entirely confined to politics. He drenches the reader in details about the most obscure and evanescent religious personalities but cannot bring himself to refer to the existence of the Roman Catholic Church until page 450 (when it numbered over half a million Americans and was growing rapidly), and rarely thereafter. Orestes Brownson, who is described by his biographer Arthur Schlesinger Jr. as America's closest equivalent to Cardinal Newman, is much touted by Wilentz as a political activist. He excitedly claims that Brownson's ideas were "every bit as startling" as those of Marx and

Engels (a wild exaggeration). But when he joins the premier Christian church, where he rose to considerable influence, as the comparison with Newman implies, as far as Wilentz is concerned he walks off the edge of the earth and is not mentioned again. It is not clear whether Wilentz is papaphobic or just inexplicably distracted by cranky religious sects. Neither condition matters particularly, but the impression left by treatment of religious subjects supplements the partisan credibility problems of the political narrative.

The Whigs, who invented modern political campaigning with the picturesque Log Cabin and Hard Cider election of Harrison and Tyler in 1840, and were the source of sensible abolitionist sentiment that ultimately liberated the country from the divisive evil of slavery, are generally dismissed as an almost worthless foil to the steady progress of the Democrats toward a just and fair America. The palsied ineptitude of the (Democratic) Pierce and Buchanan administrations is soft-pedalled. Though the Republicans had a very successful launch in 1856, according to Wilentz, that party magically eructed forth out of disparate elements, and Lincoln, William H. Seward, and Thurlow Weed, Salmon P. Chase, and Simon Cameron, who are generally considered to be its founders, are given no direct credit for the birth of the Republicans.

The author recently compared (in the *New York Times Book Review*) the current Republican Party and the crumbling Whigs of the 1840s. He has clarified his views in an exchange with another reviewer in *Slate* and limited the scope of the comparison, but this puts the perspective of this book in a contemporary context. The Whigs lasted barely thirty years and only elected two indifferent presidents. The Republicans have endured 150 years and have defeated the Democrats twenty-three times in thirty-eight presidential elections, and have produced some of the nation's greatest leaders. Any comparison with the Whigs is strained.

Wilentz's admiration for the Democrats is perfectly reasonable and is an arguable view, but it is not a legitimate filter to be imposed on the interpretation of historical events by a serious historian, which he certainly is.

The discriminating reader quickly becomes alert to the author's leanings, and can compensate for them. But it is disappointing that such an important and valuable work should be so unrigorously partisan. This is also incongruous in a book that is in other respects an exemplary work of scholarship and presentation.

Sean Wilentz, *The Rise of American Democracy* (WW Norton, 2005).

# PAYBACK: DEBT AND THE SHADOW SIDE OF WEALTH, BY MARGARET ATWOOD

*Literary Review of Canada*, November 2008

Margaret Atwood's *Payback: Debt and the Shadow Side of Wealth* is a very provocative reconciliation of moral with financial indebtedness, and of the need to repay debts – especially when they have the character of penalties for previous misconduct, with severe consequences for not paying them back. She lays out a learned but never pedantic or turgid cultural history of the evolution of debt to trespass, to social thoughtlessness and selfishness. Despite the heavy moral content of her message, Ms. Atwood never ceases to be an elegant stylist with a fine sense of humour.

In these five Massey lectures, Ms. Atwood puts down the anthropological roots of a sense of fairness in matters of exchange, citing the bartering that goes on between chimpanzees and the concept of retribution for unfair trading even with subhuman but social animals in the most primitive conditions. She describes the trade-off between material and moral success, especially in early religions. Debtors and creditors, as she states several times, are "joined at the hip," and could not exist without each other. No one would lend if not reasonably confident of being repaid, and there would be no borrowers if there were no lenders.

The relationship of debt and sin naturally arises, and with it the concepts of the sale and redemption of valuables, including one's soul. We scale determinedly, with Margaret Atwood deftly leading us, the sheer heights from the familiar pawnshop to Dr. Faustus and Ebenezer Scrooge. She represents Faustus's pact with the Devil as "the first buy-now, pay-later scheme," and claims that all such transactions are the forfeiture of something valuable, one's soul or at least integrity and moral health for "a lot of glitzy but ultimately worthless, short-term junk." But are they always trades of something higher and more valu-able for something worthless? The Marlowe and Goethe versions of Faustus record the discreditable arrangements with the Devil, but they are not as reprehensible as the original disobedience to God of Adam and Eve, suborned by the same tempter, and with which sinfulness all Judeo-Christians are sullied. Cultural and social history are replete with sacrificial exchanges of, broadly speaking, one's soul, or life itself, for good or noble things, not just the redemption of scoundrels such as Sydney Carton. Dietrich Bonhoeffer, many saints, and winners of med-als for conspicuous valour in mortal combat have made pre-emptive moral first strikes against diabolical forces: the pre-redemption of what has not been pawned.

In her exploration of Faustus and Scrooge, Ms. Atwood presents them as "reverse images." Faustus makes his bargain and is ultimately called on it, in a contractual framework. Scrooge, morbidly material-istic and a grasping miser, is cautioned by his late business partner in bad dreams and emerges on Christmas morning with a new and more altruistic world view. This is interesting and diverting, but are they really reverse images, and so what if they are? Faustus was frightened of time and mortality, and had an underdeveloped or at least quite supera-ble moral sensibility. But Scrooge was fearful of poverty, consumption, kind-heartedness, and the unknown. He made no pact with anyone, but protected himself from his fears in the only way he knew. The vanity and moral cowardice of Faustus are quite distinguishable from the very different sin of avarice that afflicted Scrooge. But they both repented, sincerely – Scrooge successfully in terrestrial life, because he had made no transaction with Satan.

Somewhere in the midst of this Ms. Atwood introduces *The Merchant of Venice*. It has never been clear to me whether that drama was anti-Semitic or an exposé of the evils of anti-Semitism. I have generally thought that Shakespeare presented a Jewish caricature, then reviled anti-Semitism and wholesomely allowed all the protagonists to keep their lives. I don't believe that charging interest on debt ever passed out of fashion, or that only Jews provided credit, or that the medieval church went much beyond a largely ineffectual condemnation of usury. But I do not hold myself out as an authority on the Middle Ages, and I am not now in a place that facilitates the study of them.

Whatever their great talents, Marlowe and Dickens were not divines. Their presentations of the themes of excessive materialism and moral and physical cowardice are particularly vivid, but they are not Revelation or prophecy. In the spirit of the subject, and emboldened by Margaret Atwood's charming reminiscences of a United Church, lower-middle-class upbringing in 1930s and 1940s Toronto, I have a confession to make. I was brought up a few years later in the same city, in an episcopal but not very observant Protestantism, and apparently a somewhat more prosperous household. And I spontaneously conceived a considerable admiration for Scrooge's partner, Jacob Marley, which I have never entirely lost. To me, his is one of the great cameo roles of cultural history, like one of the strangely interrelated fathers and mothers in the *Ring Cycle*, or Orson Welles's portrayal of Louis XVIII in the film *Waterloo*. If we accept the context of pure arithmetical and unimaginative capitalism in which the fabled enterprise of Scrooge & Marley operated, then for Scrooge to protest to the chained and festooned ghost of his partner, who had admonished him to mend his ways, "You were a good man of business, Jacob," is a supreme accolade. Marley makes Scrooge seem like a hemophiliac bleeding heart, and he has always tantalized my imagination. What could he have done to have achieved such a status? Only Dickens knew.

Margaret Atwood holds that debt, and particularly the sinfulness of debt, became a "governing leitmotif of Western fiction" in the nineteenth century, citing Dickens, Zola, Flaubert, Thackeray, and Edith Wharton. Debt played a part in the works she cites, but when I read them, many years ago, I never thought that debt was the principal message of *Germinal, Madame Bovary, Vanity Fair,* or *The House of Mirth.* No doubt, as Ms. Atwood says, debt greatly expanded in the capitalist Industrial Revolution of the nineteenth century, but it had not been such a rarity before. The Reformation was partly a response to the financial and other profligacy of the Roman Catholic Church. She refers to the "occupation" of the monasteries by that very flamboyant religious leader Henry VIII, but he seized the monasteries and their contents to pay for his wars in France. He apostatized to obtain a divorce, so he could marry a woman whom he later beheaded on a false charge of adultery, for failure to produce a male heir, although the heir Anne Boleyn did produce, Elizabeth I, was the greatest monarch in British history. Having received the title Defender of the Faith, to which Ms. Atwood refers, from the pope for a paper Erasmus wrote for the king, Henry ordered his puppet parliament to continue that title for him, even though the faith had changed. It survives yet, on the British and, the last I saw, even the Canadian coinage, although a plurality of Canadians are of the faith Henry deserted and ransacked. These things are complicated, and it is hazardous to oversimplify them.

Debt was a constant problem in all ancient civilizations, especially Rome, where the currency was constantly being debased and financial ethics were very deficient. One of the original triumvirs with Caesar and Pompey, Marcus Crassus, famously operated a private-sector fire department and not only extinguished fires when prepaid to do so, but also assured a steadily growing cash flow by setting the fires prior to putting them out. The size of the money supply and of transactional activity certainly expanded with increased and more efficient commerce, but it is not clear that the social attitude to excessive debt, or the penalties for it, have changed much over the centuries.

Ms. Atwood traces the historic interchangeability of debts, trespasses, and fines, especially in various translations of the Christian Lord's Prayer. The episcopal Christian churches seem to prefer "trespasses," as matters to be forgiven, and the non-conformist Protestant churches prefer "debts." The Latin Roman liturgy *debita nostra . . . debitoribus nostris* seems to confirm debts, and the French word *amende* is a fine that, if legitimate, is also a debt. But I don't think it follows that financial debts are necessarily sins, which is why debt is ecclesiastically defined as moral as well as pecuniary. It is not and never was sinful to lend or borrow money if the purposes and terms were unexceptionable.

Even more imaginative is Ms. Atwood's effort to stigmatize "mills" and "millers" by linking the "mills of God which grind slow but grind exceeding fine" to George Eliot's *The Mill on the Floss*. Good try, Peggy, but no sale. There is no sinfulness intrinsic to an industrial mill, any more than to God's mills for sifting human conduct. Blake's infamous "dark satanic mills" are sinful because they are dark and satanic, not because they are mills. If they had avoided child labour, paid fair wages, enjoyed reasonable working hours and conditions, had scrubbers on their smokestacks, and treated their effluent thoroughly, they would still have been mills but would not have seemed diabolical even to Blake.

The next phase of this account is a lively treatment of debt collection and counter-collection techniques, from debtors' prisons and the bondage of debtors and their families to physical extortion of payment, violence both ways between debtors and creditors, acts of heavy official repression, and violent revolution by populations that consider themselves overtaxed (the famous riddles of Wat Tyler, the American and French revolutions, etc.). And then comes the payback that gives these lectures their title. As has been mentioned, everything Marlowe's Faustus did, Scrooge did in reverse, but Marlowe and Dickens lived three hundred years apart, and writers can shake up a plot in that time. Dickens was writing a Christmas story, but was he, as Margaret Atwood claims, writing of the rebirth of the Infant Jesus and of the baby Scrooge? I don't want to be weighed in the balance and found wanting in Christmas cheer and fidelity, but I find this a high hurdle. Surely Dickens's purpose was more basic and more earthbound than that: Marley liberates Scrooge from his paranoid avarice, and Scrooge finds that jollity and minor acts of charity are more fun.

Ms. Atwood treats us to a tour with the spirit of Earth Day Past, "a sententious girl, as such spirits tend to be," first to Solon's Athens and then to European society at the time of the Black Death, which she likens to a cat with a hairball. (I believe that is technically called a phytobezoar.) Are we to take this as a feline payback or redemption, perhaps for the greedy apprehension of mice? The Black Death is a virus, punishing human excess and wastefulness, and Boccaccio's *Decameron* and Albert Camus's *The Plague* are invoked. Boccaccio might make it as divine punishment, but Camus's plague was a metaphor for the Nazi occupation of France. Is Margaret Atwood adopting the Pétainist line that Nazi occupation offered the redemption of France from its inter-war sins? Surely not, but if so, what was the Liberation?

In the last section of *Payback*, Scrooge is updated to a garish, oft-married parvenu, a caricature of the vulgar, modern, nouveau riche. The tour is a delight, but again, at the risk of being a bit of a Marley, I think we have missed the nature of the real Scrooge. He was not immensely wealthy, nor was he a particularly creative or talented businessman. He was a chiseller, a miser, a cheapskate, and a misanthrope. He was too nasty to pass as a curmudgeon, but a bit more "Bah! Humbug!" and he might have made it. He clung to every farthing, but he was not a great, daring capitalist. If he had been, he would have been more confident and indulgent, and self-indulgent. Scrooge McDuck, driving his bull-dozer over his mountainous, warehoused pile of gold and silver coins, was immensely rich, but from Marlowe to Goethe and Dickens and on to Mr. McDuck is splendid but unrigorous; the cultural chain snaps.

The next spirit, a man-spirit of Earth Day Present, takes Scrooge Nouveau on to the delights and horrors of ecology and, we are told, he would remind us physically of Al Gore and the Prince of Wales. This seemed to me at first a send-up of the corn-fuelled automobile and other modern environmental excesses, but Margaret Atwood, the intrepid and knowledgeable ornithologist of Point Pelee, seems to be putting in an appearance to celebrate Scrooge Nouveau's double apo-theosis. She laments the ecological imbalance between debt and credit, between what people have taken from the world and not put back. The world's wealthiest twenty-five million people have more resources than the poorest two billion.

This is a legitimate concern, but it will not provoke a revolution as Ms. Atwood suggests. Nor is it as much the fault of the International Monetary Fund as she says, inept though that organization has often been. The poor occasionally revolt, but never successfully. Only the middle and upper classes can do that. Louis xvi had 200,000 troops and agents collecting his salt tax, but Mirabeau, Marat, Danton, and

Robespierre, much less Napoleon, were not poor and were not much concerned for the poor. Rousseau was concerned for them, but he was not a revolutionary and died before the revolution.

As for the American Revolution, it was staged and led by a few continentalist lawyers, merchants, and land owners. Washington, Jefferson, Franklin, Hamilton, and the Adamses were well-to-do, never spoke of the poor, and the Fathers of the Nation and the Champions of the Rights of Man could not quite bring themselves to emancipate their slaves in their lifetimes, although the Sage of Monticello was happy enough to procreate with them.

The best way of lifting up the world's poor is the continued adoption of market economics in China, India, and Brazil, which contain over 40 per cent of the world's population, and which have been enjoying annual economic growth rates of nearly 10 per cent, pulling scores of millions of people upward out of poverty each year. This too is a revolution of sorts, but apparently not what the author has in mind.

The Spirit of Earth Day Future is a giant cockroach that shows Scrooge the coming spoliation of the world. All is chaos and misery, reminiscent of the Black Death. Scrooge Nouveau's five wives are all peddling sexual favours in exchange for tinned sardines. Scrooge awakens and determines to fight the desolation portrayed by the Cockroach Spirit. The author then re-emerges and plays her green card, but can only give an ambivalent forecast as to which vision of the future will prevail. *Payback* is well-written, even by Margaret Atwood's very high standards, and is an etymological tour de force, although I don't really see a straight line from the Egyptian Crocodile God to the Cockroach Spirit, and the economic-terrorists have oversold the green scare. But these are minor cavils; *Payback* is a stimulating, learned, and stylish read from an eminent author writing from a heartfelt perspective.

Margaret Atwood, *Payback* (House of Anansi, 2008).

# THE UNCROWNED KING: THE SENSATIONAL RISE OF WILLIAM RANDOLPH HEARST, BY KENNETH WHYTE

*National Post*, March 27, 2009

This is one of the best biographies that has ever been written about an important media personality. Outstandingly researched, elegantly but not flamboyantly written, fair in all its chronology of Hearst's astonishing career, and in its conclusions, it is unlikely to be surpassed as an authoritative study of its subject. The author takes no psychological liberties and leaves it to the reader to judge the ultimate influence upon Hearst of his distant father, nearly forty when he was born and long absent mining and prospecting, which eventually propelled him to great wealth and the U.S. Senate; and of his doting and indulgent mother.

All his life, William Randolph Hearst had an unreasoned conviction, often outrageous but sometimes magnificent, that the rules that applied to others didn't apply to him. He travelled in Europe with his mother when other children of prosperous parents were being more formally educated. He more or less deliberately got himself thrown out of Harvard despite his parents' interventions with the head of the university on his behalf, after buying his way to social and fraternal campus prominence. He judged the academic requirements unworthy of his serious attention.

He then unselfconsciously demanded from his father control of the floundering *San Francisco Examiner*, as a matter of right after sending a few letters detailing what he thought needed to be done to transform it into a market leader. (His father had bought this lacklustre property to promote his political ambitions.) Applying for the first time the principle that A.J. Liebling eventually claimed (somewhat unjustly) in his obituary of Hearst in *The New Yorker* was his principal journalistic innovation – the sudden infusion of unprecedentedly large and precisely targeted amounts of money into the direct competition between newspapers – he did rapidly build the *Examiner*. He went on to apply essentially the same formula to the New York newspaper field in his celebrated competition with Joseph E. Pulitzer.

There were, as H.L. Mencken, most notably recognized, other innovations beyond mere extravagance directed in particular to hiring away the competition's principal stars. So suddenly did Hearst erupt in the competitive markets where he gave battle that he was like a media Napoleon, enfilading or surrounding his opponents almost before they were aware of his presence against them. Thus he hired Ambrose Bierce and many other locally prominent San Francisco writers almost before his competitors knew he was in the field, and he raided Pulitzer's executive team and many of his leading writers and editors just as abruptly.

To this point Liebling was right, but then Mencken is more accurate in crediting Hearst with going to original lengths to make his newspapers more arresting, interesting, accessible, better presented, more thorough, more opinionated and crusading, and generally more fun. Instead of reporting the news and supporting one or other political party, Hearst set out to make the news, from the local police beat to the Spanish-American War (which he did not, in fact, provoke, though he took credit for doing so). And he laid out political programs and tried to scourge politicians and political parties into the acceptance of them.

Like Napoleon and other great combat tactical innovators, he found that he could only really command effectively in one theatre at a time and that his cleverer opponents swiftly learned and used his tactics against him. Beyond San Francisco, New York, and, briefly, Chicago, and intermittently Los Angeles, he wasn't a resident publisher and either never gained or quickly lost his position of market leadership in most of the cities where he published newspapers.

When he invaded New York in the autumn of 1895, to compete with Pulitzer, Charles Dana, James G. Bennett, Whitelaw Reid, Edwin Godkin, and, the next year, Adolph S. Ochs at the *Times*, it was a bold undertaking for a thirty-two-year-old financed on handouts from his generous but exigent mother, in an arena where many had failed before him. He prevailed against a complacent, irascible, infirm and autocratic Pulitzer, but he was steadily outclassed in Chicago by the redoubtable Colonel McCormick, and, once tabloids were launched in the early 1920s, by McCormick and his cousin Joseph M. Patterson, in New York. Hearst's time as a great publisher, that is as an innovative and unsurpassable market leader, ended shortly after the First World War, as he began to be squeezed between stronger quality titles and racier tabloids. Thereafter his strength rested on the accumulated mass of his circulation in many cities around the country, coupled to the areas where his innovative genius sequentially propelled him: films, newsreels, feature services, newswires, specialist magazines such as *Good Housekeeping* and *Cosmopolitan*, and radio, in all of which and in the integration of all of which he was a pioneer, and undoubtedly, as the author of this biography discreetly incites the reader to believe, a man of some intuitive genius.

If Hearst possessed this intrepid, visionary genius of adapting or inventing and integrating media, his grasp of the principal issues of his long career as an influence on American public opinion and his judgment of the great personalities of the fifty years he spanned from the McKinley to the Truman eras, was, to say the least, very uneven. His Germanophilia was exaggerated, leading him to equate the British blockade of Germany in the First World War to German sinking of neutral ships on the high seas, and to a whitewash of Hitler despite Hearst's admirable and consistent criticism of Hitler's anti-Semitic policies. (Hearst never yielded to the temptations of anti-Semitism, detested racism and even routine, turn-of-the-century New York social snobbery, and was, it is recorded for practically the first time in this book, a promoter of Jabotinsky: "Remember Americans; This is not a Jewish problem, it is a Human problem." He was an early and unwavering supporter of a Jewish homeland, first in Africa and then in Palestine).

Hitler (a talented writer but chronically late filing his copy), Mussolini (a ponderous writer who constantly countermanded Hearst's demands that the U.S. not be urged in his columns to forgive First World War debts), Churchill, Bernard Shaw, Aldous Huxley, Kipling, H.G. Wells, Bertrand Russell, Lloyd George, Aristide Briand, Édouard Herriot, Hemingway, Dos Passos, and H. Rider Haggard were among his regular contributors. He commissioned most of America's most successful comic strips, such as *Popeye, Blondie, Buster Brown,* and *Mutt and Jeff,* and he engaged many of the country's most famous and important columnists, such as Walter Winchell, Hedda Hopper, Louella Parsons, and Damon Runyan. He invented the sob sister.

He was generally correct in his skepticism about the future of colonial empires, his railings against nineteenth-century capitalist excesses, his championship of women's suffrage, respect for workers' rights, opposition to Prohibition, programs of massive interstate public works, and his prescription for the Great Depression: a huge workfare program that presaged the New Deal. He was also prescient in his opposition to international communism and Japanese imperialism, though he encouraged paranoid hysteria on both subjects. His advocacy of defence preparedness, sensible and not overtaxed capitalism, and opposition to capital punishment were unwavering. Less fortunate was his long-standing demand for the military conquest of Mexico. And not defensible in the slightest was his insouciant financial mismanagement that almost caused his entire company to go bankrupt in the mid-1930s, when he was seventy-four. He was unflappable throughout, but there was no excuse for his having to endure such fright and humiliation. His puritanism in sexual matters, editorially and as a host in his vast houses and yachts (unshaken by the discovery of Charlie Chaplin, for one, in flagrante delicto with a woman ostensibly attached to someone else), given his own activities, as youth and adult, was bizarre.

As a builder and collector, as the author records, Hearst's tastes were excellent. Though he was fickle and ludicrously extravagant, he had a good eye as architect and decorator and almost all of his purchases were opportune, the more so because he was always in arrears in payment, often up to five years, and became so notorious a delinquent account that he frequently bought through intermediaries. His homes, especially San Simeon, were probably as close as the New World has come to the opulence of the medieval papacy and the French Bourbons, while provoking only a family financial crisis not remotely resembling a reformation or revolution.

As a judge of great personalities, Hearst was limited. Hitler, Mussolini, and, more benignly, Franklin D. Roosevelt, gulled him almost effortlessly. Every visit to Roosevelt silenced the Hearst press for at least a month, but even when the two men broke irreconcilably, Hearst accepted his quadrennial electoral setbacks good-naturedly, and Roosevelt gave Hearst some friendly advice about how to deal with his financial crisis (having previously ordered a tax audit on Hearst and his long-time companion, Marion Davies, in the hope of finding something worthy of criminal prosecution). Hearst's response to Theodore Roosevelt was unmitigated envy due to Roosevelt making more politically out of the Spanish-American War than he did. His dismissal of Woodrow Wilson as an internationalist academic was more philistinism than analysis.

Finally, Hearst has left us his personality. As the author points out, the famous film *Citizen Kane* severely defames Marion Davies, Hearst's wife, Millicent, and his mother, Phoebe Hearst. But Charles Foster Kane Hearst is an amalgam of Hearst and Orson Welles himself, and is somewhat endearing, though at best a caricature. Hearst was in some respects a spoiled child almost all his life. He assumed that creating a commotion, self-publicity, and defamation of opponents was all that was necessary to achieve the presidency of the United States; the idea that a longer or more pertinent apprenticeship might have been required never seems to have entered his mind. He ran a distant second to the nondescript Alton B. Parker for the Democratic presidential nomination in 1904. (Had he been nominated, he would have lost just about as badly to Theodore Roosevelt as Parker did.) He would have been elected governor of New York in 1906 against Charles Evans Hughes had Roosevelt not intervened heavily against him. But throughout his life Hearst, despite his grandeur, frequent brilliance, and unshakeable self-confidence, was self-indulgent and irresponsible. He never atoned for more or less condoning the assassination of President McKinley, for accusing Alfred E. Smith of poisoning New York schoolchildren with tainted milk, for representing Hitler as a reasonable man of peace despite his "irrational" antagonism to the Jews, or for his almost pathological isolationism.

William Randolph Hearst was a talented media proprietor, an epochally stylish titan, and a considerable though erratic and rarely determining influence on U.S. public policy. He was regularly outmanoeuvred by the greatest of the political leaders of his time, and though his company has flourished under his non-family successors, his influence on the United States was superficial and transitory, though perceptible throughout fifty years. His legend is deservedly great and this book readably and exactly connects the legend to the facts.

Kenneth Whyte, *The Uncrowned King* (Counterpoint, 2009).

# A BAD BOOK

*National Post*, June 13, 2009

Christopher Buckley's complicated new little book, *Losing Mum and Pup*, is more about the author than his parents. Much of it is spent trying to justify his words over his mother's corpse: "I forgive you," and his endless recitation of grievances against his father. It was my honour to know Bill and Pat Buckley well for about twenty years. I don't doubt that as parents they could have been outrageous, inattentive, and arbitrary at times, though never uncivilized. There are hints sprinkled throughout this book that there were frightful scenes, long periods of silence between each pair in this family of three and suggestions that all the disputes were the fault of one or both of the elders. For the last thirty-five years or so, Christopher responded to Pat with "a well-crafted [written] bitch-slapping," but he was always afraid of the heavy verbal artillery of his father.

There is certainly no argument about the style, originality, and genius of his parents, which are illustrated by many well-recounted vignettes. But the take-away message seems to be that the author thinks himself a writer of competitive talent to his father, with more sensible political and religious views; that he is a more honest and generous soul than his mother, and a better parent than both.

Christopher is a blancmange moderate and a run-of-the-mill agnostic who purported to find it a triumph of etymology that when awakened by New York's Cardinal Edward Egan on the telephone, offering the mighty St. Patrick's Cathedral for a memorial service for his father, he knew, though only barely, to address him as "Your Eminence."

Bill Buckley's political views were important. They were long unfashionable; McGeorge Bundy wrote the first of countless nasty reviews of him in the *New York Times* more than fifty years ago, referring to Bill's "twisted views." He endured endless opprobrium, right to the grave from the most psychotically odious of all American writers, Gore Vidal; but he advanced his opinions with eloquence, courage, wit, and trenchancy, and they influenced America.

Bill was so urbane and civilized, the genteel left became gradually convinced that he was really one of them, and was a charming gadfly. This was partly a frustrated response to their inability to defeat him in oral or written debate. And it also reflected Bill's easy friendliness with many people on the left, including J. K. Galbraith, George McGovern, John Kerry, and some of the Kennedys.

Christopher's substantial debunking of his parents includes steady disparagement of Pat as uneducated and abrasive, but clever and entertaining, and constant attempts to upstage and compete with his father. Always there is nibbling at the edges of his father's beliefs. Reagan was amiable and formidable, and "Pup" was responsible for his being president (a wild exaggeration), but Reagan was a bit vacant. Priests were often deviant, the faith was humbug, the politics campy and passé and uncaring.

When his mother fell ill, Christopher is intent on telling us, he was leaving a three-day celebration of his literary portrayal of Washington, D. C., key-noted by Tom Wolfe, and was off to Baltimore's Enoch Pratt Free Library to give an important address. Christopher deliciously recalls Marc Chagall's low opinion of his father's painting, and speculates that Bill's only visit to Lourdes in later life was to pray for the return of Christopher to the Catholic faith. He laboriously reproduces his daily text messages on hospitalized Bill's precarious condition, focusing on urinary matters, as if they were medical Psalms. The messages are moderately witty but should not have taken up nearly ten pages.

There are too many failed efforts to show off Christopher's erudition, such as his sideshow interruptus about the famous Mitford sisters. He begins with Jessica's exposé of the American undertaking industry, but focuses most on their politics, Nancy (Gaullist), Diana (Fascist), and Jessica (Marxist), without mentioning Unity (Nazi) and the surviving Debo, dowager Duchess of Devonshire (shire Tory). He imaginatively thought to sing his ailing father to sleep with a supposedly obscure Irish song, that turned out to be 'Galway Bay,' with which Bing Crosby had serenaded Americans for forty years.

And there are unspeakable transgressions of historical fact. Henry Kissinger charmed the Buckleys, but Bill never accepted his false claim that he had only had "five seconds" to decide whether to recommend that President Ford receive Aleksandr Solzhenitsyn. Christopher accepted it, but in fact, ever since, Henry has offered a more elaborate but equally implausible explanation for advising against.

Christopher would have us believe that Henry asked Bill to tell Richard Nixon during the 1968 election campaign, "If Vietnam falls [the world will see that] . . . it is fatal to be [America's] friend." Bill gave this message to John Mitchell. "The rest you know." This pseudo-worldly wink is typical of the terrible superficiality of this book. Nixon had been many times to Vietnam and had his own opinions about it. Kissinger was busy writing dovish and defeatist speeches about Vietnam for Nelson Rockefeller, who was contesting the Republican nomination with Nixon and Reagan. He was in direct contact with Mitchell already, as he was with the competing Democratic campaign of Hubert Humphrey. Neither Buckley nor Kissinger had any appreciable impact on that tumultuous campaign. And Henry did not meet Nixon at all in 1968 until after the election, and only a couple of times before.

The Buckley version of Howard Hunt, co-author of the Watergate fiasco, is also nonsense. Hunt was never, as is implied, in any physical danger because of Watergate, and he had no information whatever that could have impeached the president.

Edmund Morris's biography of Ronald Reagan was not "masterful"; it was an abomination of obscurity and misinformation, and one of the great lost opportunities of American historiohraphy.

It is not believable that Christopher Buckley declined to have Vice-president Cheney at his father's memorial service because of security considerations, or because Cardinal Egan (who was overseas) only wanted two eulogists. This was Christopher's little squeak of protest against George W. He could finally contradict his father and take a bow before his leftist friends, whose names he sprinkles through his book like Lady Bountiful dispensing her largesse.

He should have let Cheney take his own place as a eulogist; he talked about putting a jar of peanut butter and his mother's ashes in with Bill when he was buried, and imagined Pat complaining of stickiness in the coffin. He unsuitably compared himself to Mark Twain, and quotes himself to show us one more time what a blithe wit he is. And his absurdly mundane advice to people who may have to organize the obsequies of their parents is to negotiate a price with the undertaker before they die.

In the last two months of his life, Bill was for a time in Fort Lauderdale, and came twice to Palm Beach to have dinner with me. Barbara and I went to Fort Lauderdale to have lunch with him the day before he returned north. We all knew it was goodbye. He had discussed suicide with me too, at the first of these dinners, where we were alone. I referred to an article he wrote more than forty years ago about a friend who died a prolonged and excruciating death, but never abandoned the sanctity of life. Bill volunteered that after consideration, he came to the same conclusion.

I don't doubt that he and Christopher discussed suicide, nor that the *New York Times* wanted to publicize that in its obituary, but I don't believe Bill ever seriously considered it. Christopher's frequent ruminations about not wanting to be prosecuted for abetting suicide are desperately tasteless.

The chapter on sailing is beautifully written, and many of the reminiscences are touching and amusing. This is a good read, largely for unforeseen reasons, but is in many ways a bad book. There must have been many vicissitudes in that family, and I know it is terrible to lose your parents in relatively quick succession after wasting illnesses. But the time to render accounts is much later and more gently. The book has been well received by the chief subjects' ancient foes in the leftist New York establishment; I suspect because after fifty years, their opponents can finally win a debate with Bill and Pat Buckley, when they can't reply and with the complicity of their son.

Christopher Buckley, *Losing Mum and Pup* (McClelland & Stewart Ltd., 2009).

# THE PUBLISHER: HENRY LUCE AND HIS AMERICAN CENTURY, BY ALAN BRINKLEY

*The New Criterion*, March 15, 2010

This excellent study of one of America's greatest media pioneers and owners is entirely consistent with the rigour and elegance of the large body of Professor Alan Brinkley's previous work. This book is massively researched, simply written, and completely judicious. It is an excellent read. (I think disclosure practices require mention of two positive reviews Mr. Brinkley has written of books of mine.)

Where Henry R. Luce was exceptional was in his genius as a founder of magazines, where he was always successful. He was only twenty-five when he and his Hotchkiss and Yale companion, Briton Hadden, launched *Time*, the world's first news magazine, in 1923. A general news magazine summarizing a week, divided into concise pieces in distinct sections, was an astounding novelty in 1923. It was an almost instant success, and for two impecunious Ivy Leaguers in their twenties to conceive and swiftly execute such an ambitious project has few precedents in youthful media entrepreneurship prior to the internet era; perhaps Lord Northcliffe and maybe William Paley. Other candidates, such as William Randolph Hearst, Robert R. McCormick, Lord Beaverbrook, and Rupert Murdoch, had money behind them and started by fixing up existing properties, though several moved on to bold financial risk and media innovation.

Luce followed, seven years after *Time*, and after Hadden's premature death, with *Fortune*, an unprecedentedly artistically produced, specialist business magazine, which showed Luce's keen interest and generally good taste in design and photography. Despite the onset of what soon became the Great Depression, *Fortune* succeeded quite quickly and led the whole industry forward in use of higher quality paper, more imaginative photographic content, and beautifully designed Art Deco covers.

*Life* came six years later and was an instant and overwhelming success as a magazine of brilliant photography imaginatively applied to a beat as vast as the magazine's name implied. *Time* and *Life*, especially, became symbols, artifacts, and pillars of American life, to Americans and to the world, mighty and almost universal trademarks, like Cadillac, MGM, and Coca-Cola, and more than all other media titles.

Luce's fourth and last magazine launch, also a howling success, in 1954, was *Sports Illustrated*, which again applied high-quality photography to the increased time and attention a steadily more prosperous America was devoting to both spectator and participatory sports: "the wonderful world of sports." As with *Life* and *Fortune*, it frequently published work by very distinguished authors, such as William Faulkner's eccentric description of the 1955 Kentucky Derby, and John Steinbeck's long and interesting explanation of why he could not contribute to the magazine because of his interests being "too scattered and too unorthodox."

For each of these initiatives, Luce had not only a new target market, and a new magazine formula, but a profound and arrestingly expressed conceptual framework. For *Sports Illustrated*, Luce, who never had had the least interest in watching sports, and had only played tennis as a young man, wrote back to eminent advertising executive Leo Burnett when he asked the new publication's raison d'être, "We have the H-Bomb, and we have Sports Illustrated," and elaborated that while the destruction of the world loomed, people were avidly engaged in "leisure, the pursuit of happiness," which was in most cases "something to do with sport."

Luce was also exceptional among media proprietors because he combined in his own person, and relayed on to the readers, a sort of Chautauqua, earnest, principled enthusiasm, with a pursuit and promotion of literacy and even modest cultural elevation. For many years, he pre-approved virtually all content. He held the position of editor-in-chief for thirty-five years and executed it with overbearing conscientiousness.

No other prominent media owner in the English-speaking world has taken as much stylistic interest in the content of his publications, nor possessed as much competence as a writer. Hearst could write adequately, but rarely did. Beaverbrook, with great help from ghost writers, produced a number of passable but undistinguished books and often wrote purposeful but not very lapidary editorials. Luce was an inveterate and overabundant source of papers, long memos, articles, speeches, and a huge correspondence. He frequently relied on his classical education to turn his zealous sense of American manifest destiny into strong, though not overly profound, arguments.

Hadden, in particular, created a new, much-mocked style for *Time*, which Luce continued. "Backward ran sentences until reeled the mind," Wolcott Gibbs wrote in a famous hostile article on *Time* in *The New Yorker* in 1937 (returning fire on a *Time* item about *The New Yorker* two years before – it was a natural highbrow versus middlebrow running dispute).

Through most of his time, Luce had an experimental department working on new products, and every few years he effectively relaunched his magazines, to meet cultural and sociological and geopolitical changes. Thus, *Life*, after the war, became the evocator and the pictorial voice of the triumph of bourgeois, suburban, American values. Luce and Hadden and most of their writers had grown up in the shadow of H.L. Mencken, whom Hadden overtly imitated. But Luce was a Presbyterian missionary's son, born in China, and never lost his missionary fervour, though it was transposed to secular matters. He was never cynical or world-weary.

Thus, *Time* became the fountainhead of postwar anti-communism; *Life* a slick tout sheet for American popular capitalism. *Fortune* was reoriented from neutral studies of industries, design, and American progress to be the unabashed house organ for (appreciatively advertising)

American big business. And *Sports Illustrated* topped up the pursuit of popular happiness on the golf course and at the bridge table with the portrayal of the successful professional athlete as the coruscation of the American dream through evolution into a Wagnerian, if not Nietzschean, superman. No other contemporary prominent media leader had any such comprehensive notion of his editorial purposes.

Luce was also a pioneer in newsreels, where his *March of Time* played every week in 20,000 movie houses for up to half an hour before every feature, and presaged television in bringing the world to the average American in moving pictures and real voices. With martial music in the background, the stentorian voice of Westbrook Van Voorhis frog-marched the viewers through each item, all of which concluded, "Time marches on!" as the next subject came up.

Luce also took the *March of Time* to radio, where, as in the newsreels, there were fabricated dramatizations of scenes and people. (This became rarer when President Roosevelt asked that *Time* desist from attempted simulations of his distinctive inflection.) Much later in his career, Luce was also a pioneer in publishing books, from his editorial staff and contributors (including Winston Churchill, who alleviated his postwar financially straitened circumstances by unloading a lot of filler on *Life*, which Luce's editors tried to hammer into stirring Churchillian tocsins). The Time-Life Book Club, with heavy promotion in the magazines, became another large profit centre.

And while other contemporary media owners asserted their own views in their publications, none was as overtly self-righteous about doing so. Luce constantly made it clear that he required conformity with his strongly held views in what was published in his magazines. In practice, he was quite broadminded and open to new trends that he could be convinced constituted "progress." There is a hilarious description of him taking LSD under psychiatric advice at Clare's request (to try to smooth their marriage) while discussing with a visitor "the relationship between Matthew Arnold and Cardinal Newman."

He never cared about a writer's unpublished (by him) opinions, apart from those he considered to be communists or communist sympathizers. Here, Luce's performance probably possessed greater integrity than the conduct of some of his left-wing journalists, who took his generous pay packets but grumbled audible condescensions about Luce's somewhat oversimplified world view. None was more egregious than Dwight Macdonald, a capable writer and at that point only slightly reformed communist (who was once denounced personally by Leon Trotsky for air headedness). Luce's hatred of the Soviet Union, we learn, really took flight when he travelled on the Trans-Siberian Railway westwards in 1932, and his "private compartment" was shared by sweaty and malodorous peasants, including a child who was encouraged by its mother to use the small sink as a urinal.

Luce forced out Laird Goldsborough as foreign editor in the 1930s, for being anti-Semitic, pro-fascist, and ambiguous about Hitler; Theodore H. White in the 1940s, for being pessimistic about Chiang Kai-shek's chances in the Chinese civil war; and Charles Mohr in the 1960s, for doubting the airy confidence of U.S. military briefings on South Vietnam.

In many respects, Luce's views were quite admirable. He was interested in all religions, tolerant of skepticism, and he sincerely engaged in discussion of theology with renowned experts, including Reinhold Niebuhr, Paul Tillich, and John C. Murray. His own views evolved and deepened throughout his life, and seemed, according to this very thorough account, to have come to rest at disappointment in the "shallowly pietistic attitudes ... of official Protestantism"; Lecomte du Noüy's formulation that "men are Collaborators with God in charge of evolution"; and great respect for the unshakeable hostility to communism of Roman Catholics and Evangelical Christians.

Henry Luce's notions of citizenship and religion intersected in his passion for America and what he perceived to be its mission. It came to America, as Luce had fairly presciently foreseen, to lead the Christian and democratic world to victory over godless and pagan totalitarians. In support of this objective, Luce engaged in relentless propaganda, which on balance is not so hard to justify, considering the nature of Hitler, Stalin, Mao Tse-tung and Khrushchev. But he presented a whitewashed, speak- and see-no-evil picture of America that accentuated his intellectual vulnerabilities.

Mr. Brinkley very fairly presents Luce's always positive, often saccharine portrayal of America, especially in *Life*. Luce was a constant and strong supporter of civil rights (and a strenuous enemy of McCarthyism).

But he steadily de-emphasized any coverage of racial problems or political strife in the United States. *Life* had a feature called "Life Goes to a Party," which over time photographically covered an immense variety of festive occasions, from a dance hall in Harlem for underprivileged boys and girls, at "the home of happy feet," to a Ku Klux Klan rally on Stone Mountain in Georgia. The Klansmen were innocuously described as "people who sometimes behave destructively, but usually aren't up to much more than a primitive form of transvestitism." (There was a lynching of an African American every few weeks throughout the 1930s.) What Mr. Brinkley calls "*Life*'s determined amiability" was impenetrable in domestic matters.

Most psychological accounts in biographies must be read with extreme caution. Mr. Brinkley has had access to an extraordinary range of correspondence and other primary material, and this book, in addition to its other virtues, is a brilliant work of selection and organization, which enables him to enter into this murky area more sure-footedly than most biographers.

Luce combined several paradoxes in his personality. He was well-educated (Oxford after Yale), was multilingual (German and French, Greek and Latin), and he had insatiable curiosity. He was not just clever, like Hearst or Murdoch, who also attended great universities, though he was clever.

He had less of a feel for "everyman" than some other successful publishers. But his eager patriotism and fierce conviction of "America's Century" (his most famous phrase, from a landmark editorial in 1941), of its evangelizing role in the world, came from his earliest days as a missionary's son in remote China. It fitted well with the rise, throughout his lifetime, of the United States from an isolationist refuge for oppressed immigrants to bulwark, leader, and preceptor of evolved Western civilization.

In seizing and promoting this national coming-of-age, in saluting almost everything that happened, including, for a time, the New Left in the 1960s, as another manifestation of America's irrepressible creative ferment, he did become the cheerleader of Middle America, which after the Second World War, was about 80 per cent of the country. His vision of America's Century largely came true.

But Luce, though he meticulously consulted public intellectuals like Walter Lippmann and Archibald MacLeish, and was helplessly addicted to hobnobbing with the powerful, from Churchill and Eisenhower and de Gaulle to Mao Tse-tung and Chou En-lai (and in the case of the first two, assisting them financially and editorially), leapt into turbo-Americanism by instinct and upbringing, caught the wave at the crest, and made it work commercially. But it had almost nothing to do with analysis and deduction.

He was not so fortunate in his other passions, and lacked passions that would have made his life happier and longer. He did not pay much attention to China for decades after he left it, until the Sino-Japanese War in the 1930s, when a burning Sinophilia was suddenly kindled within him, compounded by a fierce determination that America must assist China into the modern world and unite with it in promoting the American way.

He was disappointed when the Second World War ended without the deployment of an American army to China to assist Chiang Kai-shek, for whom, and for Mme. Chiang, he developed an irrational and wildly inflated respect. Most of Luce's enthusiasm for the Korean and Vietnam Wars, which went well beyond the conservation of non-communist regimes in the southern parts of both countries, was fired by the hope that they would lead to direct conflict with China and the disintegration of the People's Republic. These were not well-thought-out opinions.

Intelligent arguments could be made for seeking victory in Korea and Vietnam, and were made by statesmen whom Luce admired, including Douglas MacArthur, Richard Nixon, and John Foster Dulles. But betting the ranch on the devious and ultimately incompetent Chiangs and proposing a land war in continental China, was mad.

For all Luce's cultivation of the powerful and his desirability as an ally to any American politician, he liked those who were pleasant to him, whether they paid any attention to his views or not. (They didn't.) He waffled back and forth on Roosevelt; like most people, he was overwhelmed by his personality and power when they actually met. He did not have a real problem with the New Deal, other than a general concern over the expansion of government, and he emphatically approved

Roosevelt's aid to Britain and Canada in 1940–1941. But Roosevelt didn't court him, and didn't like Luce's preachy, humourless, un-nuanced, and presumptuous manner. Patrician with a direct line to the people as he was, the president was less enthused by prim (usually Republican) Middletown, America, than Luce was. (FDR was probably closer to the view of Archibald MacLeish, who worked for him after leaving Luce, and who described *Life*'s America as "the flatulence and fat of an over-fed people whose children prepare at the milk-shake counter for coronary occlusions in middle age.")

Roosevelt did everything constitutionally possible, and more, to assist the democracies, was a brilliant war leader, and single-handedly forced recognition of China as one of the world's Great Powers in the United Nations he set up, to Luce's strong approval. Yet Luce fell head-over-heels for Wendell Willkie, Roosevelt's 1940 opponent, although Willkie campaigned on the theory that Roosevelt was leading America to war (which Luce favoured) and could never have imagined, much less passed, Roosevelt's vital Lend-Lease assistance to the democracies. Most Republicans in Congress opposed the measure in February 1941, despite Willkie's support of it. Even as Luce accused Roosevelt of "ape-like fumbling" (as he in fact manoeuvred with breathtaking agility), Luce apparently, delusionally, expected FDR to name him secretary of state. (Willkie himself fell under Roosevelt's spell and was virtually read out of the Republican Party.) Roosevelt churlishly denied Luce access to the war zones and publicly apologized to a couple of Latin American leaders for unflattering stories about them in *Time*.

Though President Truman was a staunch Cold Warrior and responded swiftly and effectively in Korea, Luce despised him as "a vulgar little Babbitt," whom he blamed for "losing China." He hated his chief foreign policy adviser, Dean Acheson, and professed to regard General George C. Marshall as "a senile dodo."

Luce worshipped Dwight D. Eisenhower, who treated him with great consideration, although Ike declined to intervene in Vietnam and followed Truman's policy of a compromise settlement in Korea. He was charmed by Kennedy and Johnson and Nixon, but only Johnson paid much attention to his policy recommendations, and then only by coincidence in Vietnam, and to his regret.

Because Luce was terribly awkward in small talk and light-hearted moments, and was so inhibited and self-absorbed, he had a very unsatisfactory married life. Alan Brinkley tastefully uses a vast cache of correspondence between Luce and his wives and paramours, to the point where he tells the reader, when appropriate, outings that led to consummation and those that didn't. One of the herniating mass of love letters in his courtship of his first wife, Lila Hotz, included the heart-wrenching romantic gambit that he could not always maintain "the calm and philosophical confidence of the idealist whose feet are planted upon the bases of the universe and whose right hand upholds the foot of the throne of God."

Relations with his second wife, the glamorous, talented, and tempestuous Clare Booth (Luce), were rarely smooth, almost never very affectionate, often competitive, and a source of intense strain to both of them for decades. Clare liked Luce's wealth and prominence, but not his stiff nature, and Harry (as he was always known) had no idea how to settle down his excitable wife. He was happy to liven up his public image with the chic wit and beauty of this exotic woman, but was constantly haunted by what he considered to be her rapacity. They each went to the brink of divorce many times, but never both in the same week, and the marriage was an intense and combative farce for most of its thirty-one years. We learn that though they were both conventionally motivated and activated sexually, and Clare wanted a child with Harry, their sex life wilted early, with each other, but not with third parties.

Luce's torrid affairs with Jean Dalrymple, Mary Bancroft, and the young Jeanne Campbell (his friend Lord Beaverbrook's granddaughter), and Clare's with General Lucian Truscott and others, were more satisfying but ended sadly in the quicksand of the Luces' enervating but ultimately indestructible marriage. It went better in their last few years, but Luce had aged prematurely. Hyper-tense, a heavy smoker, he suffered for years from heart disease and arthritis and died in 1967, at sixty-eight.

Mr. Brinkley leaves us with the inference that if Luce had lightened up a little and focused some of the misplaced (and unrequited) passion he lavished on Wendell Willkie and Chiang Kai-shek and Mme. Chiang (who turned Willkie's head also) on friendship and romance, he would, as he ultimately recognized in memos and diaries the author cites, have been much happier. He would also have been less vulnerable to *The New Yorker* and Algonquin Hotel sets' wickedly clever and wounding barbs.

Henry Robinson Luce was a brilliant publisher and editor, a very intelligent man, but not, as he claimed to his first wife (Clare would not have put up with it), the most intelligent man in the world. (Einstein, he explained, was a "specialist.") He was a sincere patriot and Christian, an honest and capable businessman, and a strange phenomenon. And this account of his remarkable life and career is an outstanding biography.

Alan Brinkley, *The Publisher* (Alfred A. Knopf, 2010).

# THEODORE ROOSEVELT'S HISTORY OF THE UNITED STATES: HIS OWN WORDS, SELECTED AND ARRANGED BY DANIEL RUDDY

*The American Spectator*, June 17, 2010

This is a very diligent and scholarly pastiche of Theodore Roosevelt's voluminous historical reflections, put together with such skill and evident grasp of the material that it often seems it could have been composed as a single volume by the author. As anyone even slightly familiar with TR would expect, the text tends to be epigrammatic, and is carried through dozens of two- to six-page sub-chapters on historic personalities and events by Roosevelt's invective-laden, gloriously emphatic, and usually acerbic opinions about everyone.

The ranks of those he admires are thin, distinguished, and in a few cases surprising. He goes to ingenious lengths to find new heights from which to praise George Washington, though he acknowledges that he was "not a genius," and was a capable but not consummately brilliant military commander. Rather, Roosevelt's praise of the first president's integrity, courage, and judgment are expressed in even greater superlatives than is conventional. The author's intellectual snobbery does not come into play on this subject, and Washington's astute land acquisitions in the West, which made him one of America's wealthier men, and were not at all improper but drew on knowledge acquired in his military capacities, are not mentioned, though such factors are sometimes a terrible bugbear with TR in judging others.

Roosevelt's admiration for Abraham Lincoln is almost as great as his admiration for Washington and is based on the usual grounds for Lincoln's generally recognized, irresistible, claims to greatness. Almost to his own surprise, TR admires Lincoln's gradual loss of personal animus, so that after 1858 he almost never attacked an opponent personally. It is one of Lincoln's many distinctions that he always seemed pained rather than angered by betrayals, reversals, and the failings of others, but it is slightly surprising that TR admires that.

Andrew Jackson comes out quite well as a capable general and a fierce president who crushed secessionism for thirty years by his rough treatment of the South Carolina nullifiers and his threat to hang his vice-president (John C. Calhoun). Roosevelt also admired the revocation of the charter of the Bank of the United States, even though it led first to deflation and then to inflation and a horrible economic depression. He ignored Jackson's championship of slavery and his severe mistreatment of the Indians (whom Roosevelt strenuously disdained).

Beyond that, among the presidents, the unlikely fourth-place finisher is Zachary Taylor, because of his support of the Clay-Webster compromisers. (He even defends Taylor for putting down mats on the floors of the White House so he could spit on them without having to look for cuspidors.) Even more surprising than Taylor is the next nominee to the pantheon, Chester A. Arthur, whom TR considered "very good." He is followed by Grover Cleveland, who gets good marks as an honest, pleasant man, though overinfluenced by corporate interests. There is a gentlemanly nod to the Adamses, and to U.S. Grant as a general and autobiographer. After that, Roosevelt lays about him with a broadax and makes a hecatomb of his other predecessors and two subsequent presidents.

His premier victim is Thomas Jefferson, whose "influence upon the United States as a whole was very distinctly evil." The Declaration of Independence is not mentioned, and Jefferson is reviled as someone who did not really believe in the central government; who fathered nullification and therefore secessionism; was "the most incapable executive that ever filled the president's chair"; was a coward opposite the provocations that led to the War of 1812; and was "the underhanded but malignantly bitter leader of the anti-national forces" against Washington. He does credit Jefferson with being a sincere democrat and for exploring the West, but his opinion of the third president is extreme, relentless, and not entirely rational.

His strictures are often hilarious, and his description of Jefferson and Madison trying to deal with Napoleon and Talleyrand is an example: "These two timid, well-meaning statesmen . . . now found themselves pitted against the greatest warrior and lawgiver and one of the greatest diplomats of modern times . . . whose sodden lack of conscience was but heightened by the contrast of their brilliant genius and force of character – two men who were unable to so much as appreciate that there was shame in the practice of venality, dishonesty, mendacity, cruelty, and treachery." There is some truth to all that, but Jefferson, Madison, and their minister in Paris and fellow Virginian and next president, James Monroe, did make the Louisiana Purchase at a very advantageous price. TR discounts this because America was bound to get it. In fact, Britain could have got it, and protected it, as it protected Canada.

Lesser presidents are attacked with almost more ferocity than their status justified. To call Tyler "mediocre, is unwarranted flattery. He is a man of monumental littleness." Franklin Pierce, in the words of Thomas Hart Benton, whom TR admired, was a man of "undaunted mendacity, moral callosity, and mental obliquity," who, said TR, "had the will but lacked the courage, to be a traitor."

Benjamin Harrison, whom he served in the Civil Service Commission, was "a genial little runt, a cold-blooded narrow-minded, prejudiced, obstinate, timid, old, psalm-singing little, grey, Indianapolis toad." William McKinley, to whom he owed his elevation to national office, "had the backbone of a chocolate éclair." His comments on nonpresidential politicians were equally declarative. Alexander Hamilton and John Marshall were great men; Henry Clay "excellent"; Benton was a favourite; Franklin was important but inconstant; John Jay diligent and pure; John Hay interesting but naive; Winfield Scott a good soldier but "flatulent"; and William Jennings Bryan "a professional yodeler, a human trombone" and a Judas goat for radical revolution.

His opinions of people who weren't American politicians were no less amusing. Rudyard Kipling was a "bright, nervous, voluble, underbred little fellow" but "an entertaining genius." Tolstoy was "a sexual degenerate . . . a diseased mind." The founder of the British Labour Party, Keir Hardie, was "an un-hung traitor," George Bernard Shaw "a blue-rumped ape," and Winston Churchill "a dreadful cad" (an outrageous charge).

TR's assault on Woodrow Wilson is the fiercest of all. He concedes Wilson's intelligence: "Wilson is a wonderful dialectician, with a remarkable command of language." But he used his talents entirely for "cowardly infamy. . . . His soul is rotten through and through." Again, these comments are not rational. Roosevelt claimed that The Hague Convention required that the United States go to war over the German invasion of Belgium (it didn't) and that the sinking of the *Lusitania* required a U.S. declaration of war on Germany (it didn't; Germany abandoned unrestricted submarine warfare for two years.)

When Wilson did take the country to war, TR congratulated him in an address worthy of Lincoln and asked to take a regiment to war as he had in Cuba. This is not recounted in this book, but Wilson said Roosevelt had the irresistible charm of an adventurous boy, but didn't want a fifty-nine-year-old former president in indifferent health (he died the next year) going into the inferno of the Western Front. He cautioned TR that this wasn't a Boy's Own Annual "splendid little war" like Cuba.

That TR tired of Wilson's humbug about being "too proud to fight" is understandable, but he should have appreciated that he led a united country into war, that he was a prophet as the first person to inspire the masses of the world with a vision of enduring peace, and that he was an extremely effective war president who mobilized and sent into battle in France huge forces with astonishing speed and decisive effect. Wilson was no Madison (of whom TR was even more contemptuous than he was of Jefferson, because of Madison's unseemly flight from Washington before the British burned down the White House).

Theodore Roosevelt's energy, brilliance, historical insights, high ethics, and strength of character are all vividly here. But there are problems. He wanted to go to war with Britain in 1895 over the border between

Venezuela and British Guiana. "This country needs a war. I don't care whether our sea coast cities are bombarded or not. We would take Canada." This was a mad enterprise. The United States would not have won a war with the British Empire if it was fully engaged; Canada would have been defended, and the inhabitants of Atlantic coast cities might have become quite bored with being shelled by the insuperable Royal Navy. (Roosevelt felt Canadians were inferior, as mere colonists, even though Canada had been an independent country for thirty years by this time.) It was only three years later that Roosevelt moved to a profound Anglophilia that never deserted him thereafter, because Britain had given moral support to the United States in the Spanish-American War.

With all his informed and immoderate opinions, it is hard to imagine how TR was a capable president, but he was, in a time of peace when the United States was unchallenged in its hemisphere and not overly active outside it. And he did have extraordinary insights at times: "If Russia chooses to resist the growth of liberalism . . . she will sometime experience a red terror which will make the French Revolution pale."

As to Japan, "Sooner or later they will try to bolster up their power by another war . . . we have what they want most: the Philippines . . . our heel of Achilles. . . . [Now] combatants endeavour to strike a crippling blow before the actual declaration of war. I have urged as strongly as I know how the immediate building of impregnable fortifications to protect Pearl Harbor."

Theodore Roosevelt was a brilliant, erratic, and partly mad figure, and extremely interesting for all that, as this book very clearly and readably portrays.

Daniel Ruddy, *Theodore Roosevelt's History of the United States* (Smithsonian, 2010).

# WINSTON'S WAR:
# CHURCHILL, 1940–1945,
# BY MAX HASTINGS

*National Review,* Summer 2010

---

This is an interesting and important book by a very capable historian. (Max Hastings and I worked quite cordially together for a number of years in the 1990s at the *Daily Telegraph* in London but have had no contact for some years.) *Winston's War* does not bring, nor pretend to bring, a great deal that is new to the well-known story of Churchill's war leadership. But it offers an insight into his foibles, his attitudes and attachments to people, and the humane, decent, and tender aspects of his intimate nature that only the most omnivorous Churchillian reader would not find very revealing.

The book also makes clear the evolution that has taken place in the received historical view of its subject. The vindicated prophet and galvanizer of the Finest Hour of 1940–1941 remains, and always will. But the evocator and voice in the wilderness of the new resistance against Soviet communism has yielded to the humanitarian eccentric and polymath, who proves more admirable and loveable than infallible and underheeded.

This evolution is tangled in the British people's learned and popular conceptions of their country's modern history, and especially its complicated relations with the United States. There has been a long-running tug-of-war between Churchill and Roosevelt historians about the comparative merits of the two as policy-makers. Churchill opened up a tremendous lead in this race, because he survived Roosevelt by twenty years, carried out his own promise to write the history himself (for which he was awarded the Nobel Prize for literature), and engaged in ambitious revisionism.

It suited the whole constellation of the U.S. government's postwar enemies to heap abuse on Roosevelt for having been swindled by Stalin into handing over Eastern Europe to be trampled by Stalin's Red Army. Disgruntled British imperialists, grumpy about the inexorable and not always suavely gracious rise of America, rallied around the view of historian Arthur Bryant that Roosevelt was a sap, out of his depth with Stalin, and envious of Churchill. (This was a little hard to take from Bryant, who several months after the outbreak of the Second World War published *Unfinished Victory*, admiringly referring to Hitler's coming triumph, traceable in part to the Führer's "Cromwellian qualities.") The Euro SocDems who wished to appease Russia and give equivocation a chance in the Cold War – the Willy Brandts and Pierre Trudeaus and even, for a time, Denis Healey – claimed that Roosevelt lowered and legitimized the Iron Curtain. De Gaulle and his followers took up the same cry, to show that only they, and not the Anglo-Saxons, could defend Western Europe. And, most damaging, the bedraggled Flat Earth Society of the U.S. Republican right – at the worst, Joseph R. McCarthy (who accused Truman, Marshall, and Eisenhower of being commies too) – defamed Roosevelt as a Stalin dupe.

Churchill avoided any direct criticism of FDR, but mischievously poured gasoline on the fire with the woeful tale of the world caught between a physically and mentally decrepit Roosevelt and a completely inexperienced Truman. For good measure, he produced, after the Tehran Conference, what Hastings calls "one of his great sallies, no less pleasing for its misplaced self-belief": he said that he was the "little English donkey" between "the Russian bear and the American buffalo" but was "the only one who knew the right way home." (This presaged Harold Macmillan's comment, fifteen years later, that Anglo–American relations were like those between the Greek and Roman empires.) The best line of the Tehran Conference was actually Churchill's "The truth deserves a bodyguard of lies." In this case, he certainly gave it one.

Roosevelt had cautioned Churchill at Tehran about improving social services, moving India and other parts of the Empire to self-governing Commonwealth status, dismantling part of the class system, and taking the lead in organizing Western Europe, to give the public the confidence that they had been fighting for reform and their own betterment and not just against Nazis and for an Empire. It was all good advice from an invincible democratic politician.

There was never one word of truth to the Yalta myth: that conference guaranteed independence and democracy for Eastern Europe. It was Churchill who signed away Hungary, Romania, and Bulgaria to Stalin in Moscow in December 1944, calling "the naughty piece of paper" a "temporary arrangement," as if he did not know who he was dealing with. Max Hastings describes this as an act of desperation. Perhaps it was, but why did he do it?

Hastings does recount Churchill's opposition to the cross-Channel invasion of France, his terror that it would be a failure, but he leaves out the conviction of the chief of the general staff, Alan Brooke, that Stalin supported it only because he thought it would be a failure, like Gallipoli, Narvik, Dunkirk, Greece, Crete, and Dieppe. And he omits the lengths Roosevelt went to, staying in the Soviet legation in Tehran (where he knew his suite was bugged) to pre-arrange Stalin's support of the French landings, rather than Churchill's proposed mad dash up the Adriatic.

Churchill loved conferences, affecting a military uniform, and clearly enjoyed them a good deal more than Roosevelt and Stalin did. (They were not parliamentarians, and were not much accustomed to conferring or debating.) And with Roosevelt he will always remain the co-author of the astounding achievement of leaving it to Russia, between 1941 and 1945, to take, among the Big Three, 90 per cent of the casualties of war and end up with a temporary and squalid squattership in Poland and the Balkans, while FDR and WSC brought Germany, Italy, and Japan into, and France back into, the West as democratic and soon prosperous allies. These are impregnable historic accomplishments.

If the Churchillians had clung to the Yalta myth, his reputation would have started to unravel. Max Hastings has laid down the real bridge for Churchill to hold – his inspiring leadership in the early years of the war – and builds his further standing on his splendid personality rather than on false disparagements of others.

Of course, Churchill has long been admired as a wit, and rivalled in that among British prime ministers only by Disraeli, and as a magnanimous winner and gracious loser throughout his life. ("If the people want Clem Attlee, let them have him. That's why we fought and won the war." The corresponding statement from Roosevelt, after his unheard-of fourth presidential victory, about his opponent, Thomas E. Dewey, was, "I still say he's a son of a bitch.") Churchill had a readier sense of humour than Roosevelt, Stalin, and de Gaulle, and an irresistible sense of fun. This book gives much evidence of that.

When he was very tired and discouraged in 1944, when the conduct of the war was really in the hands of his allies, he told his wife, the magnificent Clementine, how exhausted and fed up he was. She replied cheerfully, "Don't be; think of how Hitler and Mussolini are feeling." He instantly replied, "No, Mussolini has had the pleasure of executing his son-in-law." His mood quickly responded to this self-help.

There are a few gaps in Hastings's book. Market Garden, Montgomery's play for the Western Front breakthrough that ended with the bridge too far and left the Canadian Army squatting on Dutch rooftops after German flooding, is not mentioned. Americans generally blame Market Garden for the German ability to launch the Battle of the Ardennes. The European Advisory Commission (EAC) is also not mentioned. The EAC set the German occupation zones, and the British voted with the Russians to put Berlin in the Russian zone, because they could thus get a larger occupation zone than their divisional strength warranted. Roosevelt didn't want the zones demarcated, because he correctly foresaw that once Eisenhower's armies crossed the Rhine, the Germans would collapse in the west but fight to the last cartridge against the Russians.

But this book is only incidentally intended to be about such things. It is really a close-up look at a great man and statesman. Churchill was fallible, after all, but he was a humane and artistic romantic and adventurer, the stylish and amiable repository of the virtues of a civilizing Empire. His greatness remains as the mighty single-combat warrior of the early war, whose personal courage, as Stalin said at his sixty-ninth birthday celebration during the Tehran Conference, had changed the world; as the original co-captain of the winning side in the war, and in the Cold War; and as the most human, compelling, and diverse of the great twentieth-century national leaders.

Max Hastings is uniquely qualified for the task he has undertaken: a quick-starting, energetic former war correspondent and editor, and an accomplished military historian who writes with unembellished force, precision, and a wonderfully detached appreciation of the humorous (such as an American officer's phobia about anyone with "a red moustache, a swagger stick, and a British accent"). He brings to the study of Churchill the man, husband, father, friend, and employer the sensitivity of a powerful man who has also lived intensely in all those roles. This is an excellent and timely portrait of an always fascinating character, by a thorough and often elegant writer.

Max Hastings, *Winston's War* (Alfred A. Knopf, 2010).

# A JOURNEY: MY POLITICAL LIFE, BY TONY BLAIR

*The New Criterion*, December 2010

---

This is an amiable memoir, from a very amiable politician. Everyone is "a nice guy." Almost no one, no opponent, no leader of any other country except Saddam Hussein, is not "a nice guy," and like a children's prize day, almost everyone gets a superlative. Lee Kuan Yew was the smartest, Bill Clinton politically the cleverest, George W. Bush the most principled, Nicolas Sarkozy the most energetic, Paul Keating the most entertaining (undoubtedly true, even over apparent runners-up Silvio Berlusconi and Deputy Prime Minister John Prescott – strong contenders certainly). Ariel Sharon was the toughest; with that strange British weakness for scatology, Blair pronounced Sharon "someone who could make the shit go back up the bull's bottom." Condoleezza Rice is, perhaps, the most decent.

His selections and prize-givings are fair, from my limited acquaintance with most of the recipients. Politicians do tend to be affable or they don't win elections, and Tony Blair is a very gracious and companionable, as well as a successful, politician. Apart from Margaret Thatcher, he is the only British prime minister to win three consecutive full terms since the expansion of the electorate in the First Reform Act of 1832, the only leader in the history of the Labour Party to be consecutively re-elected to full terms at all, and one of the very few

British party leaders never defeated in a general election, personally or as leader. But it is a little like reading or speaking with Donald Trump: everyone and everything is great.

Those people whom he has occasion to describe other than with perfunctory awards for their particular characteristic of expertise are generally limned out with insight and often originality. Non-political, or at least non-partisan, personalities, such as Princess Diana and Queen Elizabeth, are sketched perceptively, and the elements of leadership challenges, such as the fraught week between Diana's tragic death and the affecting state funeral (in which the author played a decisive and constructive role), are well described. Tony Blair is undoubtedly a very positive and generous-hearted man, an authentic and thoughtfully religious man, in a field crowded with devil-take-the-hindmost cynics at home and smash-and-grab scoundrels abroad. It is much to his credit that he preserved his meliorist views – his genuine affection for most people, his respect for and the respect of his peers – managed to stand for principles that were often unpopular, and made his way so successfully in such a hazardous occupation.

From time to time, Tony Blair's almost impenetrably bonhomous carapace reveals a tiny aperture through which emanate less saintly reflections. He loses patience with the editor-in-chief of the *Daily Mail*, Paul Dacre, a saturnine and capricious manipulator, but never with the even more sinister and ruthless Rupert Murdoch, presumably because Murdoch can still be helpful to Blair as a still-young ex-premier. (He is, even now, only fifty-seven.) Murdoch dumped him, as he has deserted all political leaders who were ever helpful to him, except for Ronald Reagan, but Blair was leaving office anyway and chose to overlook it. Blair's contempt for the so-called working press, especially the BBC, shines through his roseate benignity, and he is certainly entitled to that. He is a little absent-minded about the occasions when he asked us (I was then the chairman of the *Telegraph* newspapers) to help the government with Northern Ireland and with Iraq, and I know I was not the only Conservative national newspaper publisher who did so.

There are also cameo appearances of ego and even, astoundingly in such a spotlessly virtuous narrative, of deviousness. Of his unsuccessful campaign for the presidency of Europe (a misnamed trapeze act of a job with uncertain powers that was awarded instead to a cipher), he wrote, "I was a big figure, not someone easy to have around if you were worried about your share of the limelight." The implication is he would overshadow the national leaders in Europe, including the president of France and the chancellor of Germany. Despite Blair's and others' unceasing efforts to confederate Europe, the powers of the nominal president of the European Union are limited and fluid, and, like fluid, run quickly downhill in any test with the principal national leaders.

Blair walks us in meticulous detail through the long minuet he conducted with Gordon Brown for the Labour Party leadership and control of the government following the death of John Smith in 1994. Blair outmanoeuvred Brown for the leadership, and a nebulous understanding emerged that he would hand over to Brown after two terms – nebulous because, like most verbal commitments to hand over a great office, or anything of value, it was subject to re- or misinterpretation. No one not privy to every element of these intricate discussions can know exactly what happened, and Blair and Brown, the only people who meet that criterion, clearly do not agree about it. Blair believes that he had to be elected to a third term to protect "New Labour" and its reforms from Brown's tendencies to backslide into "Old Labour," the union-dominated, tax-and-spend socialism that made the Conservatives the natural party of government between the fall of the last Liberal prime minister, David Lloyd George, in 1922, and the emergence of Blair's confection of New Labour in 1997. (In the seventy-five years between those dates, the Conservatives governed for forty-six years, and also dominated coalitions for nine years, against twenty years of Labour rule.) Blair clearly rewrote the rules to run for a third term, continued to improvise on them as he served half that term, and handed Brown a thoroughly discredited regime when he stepped down in 2007.

Blair's explanation for his struggles, as one who states, doubtless with perfect justification, that he could intuit the mindset of contemporary middle Britain, was that he gauged public opinion correctly but did not agree with it. This is the traditional challenge of the leader, and the litmus test for great leadership: to lead opinion to a more enlightened perspective. Thatcher led opinion away from the socialist basket case the previous Labour regime of Harold Wilson and Jim Callaghan had left when she sent them packing in 1979 for an eighteen-year Conservative tenure of government. Roosevelt led American opinion to all aid short of war for Britain and Canada in 1940–1941; Truman led it out of isolationism to support the Marshall Plan and NATO. Ronald Reagan led them into monetarism, supply-side economics, and the Strategic Defense Initiative.

Blair recognized that British public opinion was unconvinced on Iraq and that it blamed Israel for the attack on Hezbollah in Lebanon in 2006. In his explication of these matters (and he is now the European Union's representative in the Middle East), he shows his finest quality, courageous and righteous defence of principle, but also one of his worrisome traits – a naive difficulty in grasping the less constructive aspects of national interest. He makes a very strong case that Saddam Hussein had to be deposed: the international case of Saddam's violation of seventeen United Nation's Security Council resolutions and violation of the Gulf War ceasefire terms, as well as his barbarous despotism. And he forcefully makes the point that Hezbollah is a terrorist organization and that, ghastly though the consequences of war for innocent civilians are, Israel had the right to require the abatement of terrorist cross-border raids and rocket attacks.

Blair was effective leading on the first issue and has testified impressively on the Iraq War and the absence of a WMD discovery in post-Saddam Iraq, but he did not try to lead opinion on the Israeli incursion into Lebanon in 2006, even though the major Arab powers, especially Egypt and Saudi Arabia, overtly supported it. He purports to believe that the Palestinians would make peace tomorrow if they were sure that Israel would allow them to be really independent, and that the Israelis would agree to Palestinian independence simultaneously, if convinced that the Palestinians would really accept the permanence of a Jewish state. And he seemed to take seriously former Pakistani president Musharraf's assertion that it would be much easier to deal with al Qaeda and the Taliban if Blair and Bush would just "do Palestine," as if that were a simple matter. Palestine has been sustained and aggravated as a problem for sixty years by the Arab powers because it is the hair shirt of Arab failure and thirteen centuries of Arab retreat and because it conveniently distracts the Arab masses from the tyranny and misgovernment inflicted on virtually all Arab citizens, except, to a degree, those that live in Israel.

Blair also purports to believe that we just have to stay the course in Iraq and Afghanistan and conciliate the Palestinians and Israelis. While his defence of the invasion of Iraq and removal of Saddam are cogent, he seems not to understand why it went so horribly wrong between the invasion in 2003 and the surge in 2006. Next to the failure to sever the Ho Chi Minh Trail in Vietnam and the failure of military intelligence to detect and warn MacArthur and Truman that there were 140,000 Red Chinese troops across the Yalu in North Korea in early 1950, the greatest military blunder in American history was the disbanding of the 400,000 members of the Iraqi army and police, dismissed into unemployment but allowed to retain their weapons and munitions. What could "the admirable and committed" Bremer and Rumsfeld have imagined – that they would all become target-shooting or game-hunting enthusiasts, instead of, as happened, hired factions in a civil war? According to Tony Blair, this policy was "open to dispute." It does not do to write, as he does, that the Iraqi army melted away – it was officially abolished. Much of it could have been rallied to a post-Saddam regime, and at least kept out of the ensuing bloodbath of which it became the chief cause and executant, if it had been handled like the German and Japanese forces after the Second World War. (The Japanese army, under American orders and with drastically changed rules of engagement, kept order in much of China for six months after their surrender.)

The same inexplicably simplistic perspective (for such an agile politician) pops up elsewhere. Thus, Britain must have integration with Europe and retention of the Special Relationship – not to say, in Churchillian terms, Grand Alliance – with the United States. After ten years of government, he had not moved the needle on British public opinion over Europe, and he never grasped that you cannot engage in this sort of strategic bigamy: the perpetuation of an alliance of two great sovereign Ships of State (Longfellow's verse famously sent by Roosevelt to Churchill in 1941 and read over the airwaves by Churchill) while plunging into total Euro-immersion.

He dismisses as nonsense the Thatcherite view of Europe, although the European Union, except for Britain, has not really created a new private-sector job in ten years, and the southern countries clearly sold the Europeans a false prospectus on joining the Euro, expecting Germany and France to pay for it. Yet he congratulates himself on the French defeat of the integrationist Treaty of Lisbon, as it enabled his government to escape its own promise of a plebiscite and subscribe by mere adherence, jammed through Parliament by government whips in the teeth of a hostile public opinion.

The point, as he must know better than anyone, given that he is the undisputed British heavyweight political champion of post-Thatcher Britain, is that the public do not want to go back to pre-Thatcher industrial relations, and Blair spared them that; do not want to go back to pre-Thatcher taxing and spending, and Blair and Brown crept up on it like Birnam Wood on Dunsinane; and do not want their relations with the United States, the key to Britain's influence and even survival in the last sixty years, subsumed into a Continental diplomacy dominated by the Wilhelmstrasse and the Quai d'Orsay. He fails even to try to explain why Europe, which would drag Britain backwards in all these areas, should be embraced so wholeheartedly by an electorate that he completely failed, after ten years of half-hearted effort, to persuade of its virtues.

Blair identifies the effort of the French, Germans, and Russians to form an alternate pole of influence to the Anglo-Americans before the start of the Iraq War, yet blames America for not developing a relationship of perfect trust with Russia and advises it to avoid the same mistake with China. Of course, he is too astute and worldly not to realize that Great Powers become friendly with each other by aligning their interests together, not by cooing at each other like New Labour doves in London's famous squares. He does not, as far as I could detect, mention the Commonwealth once, despite the fact that the combined GDP of just the United Kingdom, India, Canada, Australia, and Singapore would be the third largest in the world, after the United States and the European Union, and larger than China's and Japan's combined.

This leads us to this memoir's greatest problem: Tony Blair is pretty clear in his view, which he implies is almost unquestionable, that he was an important and successful prime minister. But he wasn't especially successful. He promoted the Labour Party from an occasional contrapuntal appeasement of the need for a change in governing party in a democracy, to a respectable alternate government, but it didn't work and ended in shambles. He says it is inevitable that leaders are unpopular after ten years, but he's incorrect – it isn't inevitable. If Thatcher had finessed it at all, she would have been fine for a fourth straight Conservative term, which John Major took instead. If health and the Constitution had allowed, Dwight D. Eisenhower, Ronald Reagan, and even Bill Clinton would have been alright for a third term, as FDR was.

Blair claimed to me when he was opposition leader that he would be more "radical" than Thatcher with health care, that a Labour Party leader was needed to apply the rod to the backs of the nurses' and teachers' unions, "as a Republican U.S. president had to go to China and a Likud leader of Israel had to make a deal with Egypt." In this book, he claims to have achieved "radical" change in the National Health Service, education, pensions, and crime prevention. This is bunk. The Health Service, with billions more thrown at it, remains Europe's largest and most inefficient employer (after the disappearance of the Red Army); education is still mired in the Luddite time-and-motion obtuseness and the philistinism of the teachers' unions; and pensions are no longer adequately funded. Blair did not get around to any of this until more than seven years into his mandate, and then only in half measures. His unctuous distinction between New Labour and Brown's Old Labour was largely a blend of self-serving artifice and outright delusion.

Tony Blair claims to have been a "radical" reformer (in the British sense of profound, not the American usage of extreme). In furtherance of this argument, he spends several pages on the changing of weekly Prime Minister's Questions (in Parliament) from two fifteen-minute sessions to one of thirty minutes, and a page on expanding the G8 conference to a G13 (and now on its way to a G20), as if more conferences between government leaders were any sort of reform. They bore and irritate almost everyone, including the participants, the taxpayers who foot the bill, and the world. He has bought wholly into the most horrifying climate change horror scenario, even though global warming has been by only 1°C in the last thirty-five years, despite more than a doubling of carbon emissions. He proclaims his rival Gordon Brown to have been a great chancellor, but Brown only followed Paul Keating's advice: "Take it off them any way you please," but if you raise income taxes, "they'll rip your f***ing guts out." (Brown and Blair did take it in every other way, and in the end "they" ripped Labour's guts out anyway.) Next to Alan Greenspan's and Robert Rubin's, Gordon Brown's reputation has been shredded by the recession more thoroughly than any other economically prominent person's, ahead of lions of the private sector such as Sandy Weill and Jack Welch.

Tony Blair limped out of office, claiming he had lost popularity because he didn't explain Iraq and Lebanon (which had no direct British involvement) thoroughly and because of the remorseless effluxion of time, then artfully handed Gordon Brown, who squandered the pristine condition of Britain's finances left by Thatcher, a grenade with the pin pulled. His government was a disguised, long-fuse disaster, yet another Labour Party disaster. And though his foreign policy was Alliance-based and commendable, so too were Attlee's and Harold Wilson's.

There is a jolly foreword to the American edition enunciating the greatness of America, a cheerleading effort presumably prompted by the U.S. publisher. The author's admiration of America, for its idealism, meritocratic democracy, and scale, are sincere and nicely formulated. What Blair seems not to realize is that the United States emerged from the greatest, most bloodless strategic victory in the history of the nation state at the end of the Cold War and has for twenty years, under the presidents he knew and extols (Clinton, Bush, and Obama), made the greatest mess of domestic and foreign policy since the 1920s, if not the prelude to the Civil War. Outsourcing tens of millions of jobs while admitting fifteen million unauthorized, unskilled aliens, carrying the European and Japanese luxury-goods and engineered-products industries on their backs while gorging themselves on Muslim and Venezuelan oil, and issuing trillions of dollars of worthless real-estate-backed debt has made for an insane and aberrantly self-destructive public-policy prescription. Unfortunately, Tony Blair was part of it, albeit a small part, a mere second, but he seems to have missed the action, like one of Caesar's bodyguards on the Ides of March. With all this said, A Journey is less self-serving and mendacious than most political memoirs, and is as engaging a read as anyone who has had occasion personally to appreciate the thoughtfulness, decency, and effervescence of its author, as I have, would expect.

Tony Blair, A Journey (Knopf Canada, 2011).

# THE JONAS VARIATIONS: A LITERARY SEANCE, BY GEORGE JONAS

*National Post*, December 10, 2011

My distinguished fellow columnist in these pages, and my wife Barbara's former husband, George Jonas has become a dear friend over the past twenty years, and a source of generous encouragement and inexhaustible wise counsel. He has several times written here supportively in the lengthy legal travails inflicted upon me by the U.S. prosecutocracy and its Canadian quislings, which are now dragging toward their weary, banal end. It is somewhat shaming that I have not found the occasion to write anything about George until now.

Providentially, his publisher last week sent me, in the U.S. federal prison where I am confined, a copy of George's latest book, *The Jonas Variations: A Literary Seance*, a random series of poems in eight languages other than English that George has translated or adapted or otherwise radically reconfigured while retaining the integrity of the original. George is originally Hungarian and also is fluent in German, and is, of course, one of Canada's most distinguished poets and prose writers and commentators, an astounding feat for someone writing in his third language.

He arrived in Canada in 1956, a fugitive from the Soviet suppression of the Hungarian uprising, having, as a nine-year-old, narrowly survived the pogroms and anti-Semitic liquidations of the Nazis and their local partisans. When he married Barbara, the Toronto rabbi, in a premarital interview, questioned the depth of George's Jewish convictions; he assuaged his concerns by responding that he had been "a good enough Jew for Hitler." He also famously replied, when some friends put on some authentic Hungarian gypsy music for him, that he had fled Hungary, secondarily to escape communism and primarily so as not to hear any more Hungarian gypsy music.

His latest book is a work of genius. Of the languages from which he translates and adapts poems, I am qualified to judge only those from French, but many others are obviously hugely imaginative and, however close their connection to the original, are brilliant in English, as in George's conjuration of a poem by the proto-fascist adventurer Gabriele D'Annunzio to the late journalist Oriana Fallaci's philippics against the Arab intrusion in Europe. "One woman only, in white, a chic crusader, / makes a last stand for the western realm / in Rizzoli's Mall between Duomo and La Scala / against a tide from the Gulf States to Ghana, / wielding a quill-shaped cudgel . . . good luck, Oriana!"

There are frequent nugget-sized Georgeisms: "The spine is a divining rod for poetry." (His may be.) On the "dangers of a Viennese flophouse inmate like young Hitler" reading in Nietzsche of "Superman," the "master race," the "Will to Power," the "slave morality," a "dead God," and Zarathustra's "whip," and being able to act on it all: "Presumably, that was why, after the Tree of Knowledge, God considered it wiser to shut down operations in the Garden of Eden."

I had known that Hitler derived all the little that he knew of America from reading Karl May's pulp Western novels, and that May himself had never been in America; but not that May had spent much of his life, including the years of his literary production, in prison, "writing juvenilia tailor-made for nine-year-olds like" the then-child George Jonas. (For obvious reasons, I also endorse using one's time in prison to write for publication.)

Of Germany's renowned Jewish poet Heinrich Heine, who remarked in the 1830s that Germans "begin by burning books and will end up by burning people," George Jonas writes that "few observations have proved more prophetic." Kurt Weill defined himself as a "communist first and a musician second," but "his music proved to have a longer shelf life than his politics. He was addicted to the same type of ugly round spectacles as the playwright Bertolt Brecht. There was a time when all Marxist intellectuals seemed to wear hideous glasses for extreme myopia. My father thought they went well with their ideologies."

As in any conversation with George, there are many aphorisms. Of (obscure) Sapphic medieval French poet Louise Labé, "all we know [is] that she had been handed from one French rope-maker about thirty to forty years older than herself (her father), to another (her husband), which may be enough to turn any young woman into a lesbian."

"Some writers loom larger than their works; some remain smaller. Virginia Woolf would be an example of the first; Jeno Heltai is an example of the second." From the book of Jonas (the Old Testament prophet, no relation to the author): "Those who stand mute are accomplices to evil." So they are. "Death entitles people to keep some things to themselves." Of the Swiss poet Carl Spitteler: "intelligent, visionary, sardonic, versatile, mythopoeic, and largely unread . . . it is easier to be compared to Homer and Milton than to find an audience." "When children are too young to read about sex, they don't. It bores them. When they're interested, they're not too young."

Many of his descriptions of his subject poets are in themselves memorable. The Prince of Poets, Paul Verlaine, had a "magnificent spirit" that was "encased in the body and central nervous system of a disease-ridden, dysfunctional, alcoholic, bisexual, lecher." His young intimate Arthur Rimbaud (whom Verlaine shot), probably an even greater poet, had "a stormy, absinthe-drenched, scandal-ridden, wild and brilliant career as a poet," between the ages of fifteen and nineteen.

Benvenuto Cellini was a "Renaissance Man in his virtues and in his vices . . . in art, music, and literature, as much as in braggadocio, manslaughter, and child molestation." François Villon, the "exceptionally gifted lyricist and balladeer, [and] by his own credible admission, also a thief and a killer . . . disappears from history January 5, 1463, the date of the commutation of his death sentence by hanging to a new term of banishment." Who knew?

There is much about the tragic fate of many of these poets. Hugo von Hofmannsthal died of a stroke two days after his son's suicide. Gyula Juhász often attempted suicide, finally successfully, and never recovered from the nervous breakdown he suffered when he was

awarded Hungary's most prestigious prize for poetry three years consecutively. Georg Trakl committed suicide at twenty-seven. Attila József lay
down in front of an oncoming train at thirty-two. And Miklós Radnóti
was executed by Nazi militia at thirty-five, an event rendered poetically
by the author, who narrowly escaped the same fate himself.

The only one of these poets George knew, and thanks to him I
knew him also, was the great George Faludy, who died in 2006, aged
nearly ninety-six. His memoir of flight from the Nazis and imprisonment by the Russians, *My Happy Days in Hell*, has inspired me in my
own (assuredly relatively gentle) imprisonment. My one lengthy and
hilarious dinner with him was in Budapest about fifteen years ago, and
his sparkling conversation conformed entirely with his confession to
the Soviets in Hungary of having been a spy for the CIA, directed by
their super-agents "Walt Whitman and Edgar A. Poe." Though he was
a public hero and virtually the national poet of Hungary, he was yet
ignored by, as George Jonas writes, "the tin-eared eunuchs of the literary establishment." This is the perfect description of such impudent
claques everywhere (it is hard not to think of the infestation of trivial
philistines in Canada's very own *Quill & Quire*).

George Faludy lived for twenty-two years in Toronto, and George
Jonas, Barbara, and I went to a little naming ceremony after him of a
parkette by the mayor of Toronto in 2006, about a month after he died.
It was attended also by his widow (sixty-four years younger than he).

There is a cameo role for Canada in this book, as Rainer Maria
Rilke inspired Hugh MacLennan's *Two Solitudes*. And George writes,
for Dezső Kosztolányi, from his imagination to be sure, a postcard
poem from Ottawa, of all places.

All this is just a teaser for the poems, the meat of this fine volume.
My favourites are from Goethe, Kürenberger, de Musset, Laforgue,
Juhász, Baudelaire, Storm, and Jammes, all with the author's variations,
but the competition is fierce.

This delightful book has reminded me how much I have missed
my dinners with George, and how much I look forward to resuming
them. George, 8 p.m., May 7, 2012, at the Toronto restaurant of your
choice. Congratulations and please keep as well as you can.

George Jonas, *The Jonas Variations* (Cormorant Books, 2011).

# THE PATRIARCH: THE REMARKABLE LIFE AND TURBULENT TIMES OF JOSEPH P. KENNEDY, BY DAVID NASAW

*The National Interest*, November/December 2012

---

*The Patriarch* is a thorough and balanced biography that illuminates American public policy from the time of Herbert Hoover to the brief era dominated by the subject's sons. David Nasaw, an accomplished writer, explores all of the controversial high points of Joseph Kennedy's career meticulously, and the record is usefully set straight in many places. For the most part, the narrative is absorbing.

It is well-known that Kennedy's father and father-in-law were prominent Irish Boston figures. It is less widely known that his father, Patrick J. Kennedy, a prosperous financier, gave him an upbringing similar to what upper-middle-class Protestant East Coast families generally provided, including Boston Latin School and Harvard. Joseph Kennedy made no bones of the fact that he did not see it as his role to fight "for the British" during the First World War, although he seems to have been too pugnacious a character to have believed that the United States should accept passively the German submarine sinkings of American merchant ships on the high seas. He was no pacifist, as he amply demonstrated after Pearl Harbor, and was certainly not a coward. But Kennedy used political connections to obtain a draft-exempt position in the ship-building industry after America's entry into the Great War.

After the war, Kennedy joined a Boston merchant bank, Hayden Stone, and largely fulfilled his early ambition of cracking the Boston Brahmin financial establishment. Previously, he had been head of the Columbia Trust Bank, where his father was a director and substantial shareholder. He took this company over as almost a private bank for his stock and investment plunging at Hayden Stone. Kennedy proved a preternaturally agile investor and was almost always successful in generating gains, yet not always with complete probity. Though well established at Hayden Stone, Kennedy saw that he would never be entirely accepted. As the Roaring Twenties began in earnest on Wall Street and across the land, he shifted his sights to the immensely larger New York financial market.

Kennedy soon saw that motion pictures were a growth industry, chronically mismanaged by fly-by-night impresarios who knew nothing of administrative economies, whatever their talents at cinematic artistry and marketing. It also was a glamorous industry. He set out to achieve fame and fortune and accomplished no less. He began with film distribution in New England but quickly moved on to industry-wide arrangements and production. "Joseph P. Kennedy Presents" became a familiar tag on film credits, and Kennedy helped amalgamate several film houses in the manner of new industries that consolidate swiftly.

Nasaw estimates that Kennedy quintupled his net worth between 1926 and 1929 – to perhaps $30 million in today's money. Using his own trust company to make loans to himself (a bold but perfectly legal move), Kennedy bought a growing number of movie theatres and soon took control of the Film Booking Offices of America, Keith-Albee-Orpheum, Pathé Films, and First National Corporation. He also conducted extensive negotiations with David Sarnoff of the Radio Corporation of America. Then he withdrew from them profitably as they consolidated into Radio Keith Orpheum (RKO).

Despite his ostentatious Roman Catholicism, Kennedy was proud of his extensive sex life and his many attractive companions – including, over decades, legions of assistants, secretaries, masseuses, and even young female golf caddies. But in Hollywood, he was able to fish greedily in the pool of starlets and aspirants to stardom. Here Nasaw strays into the swirling waters of surmise and mind reading. He assumes Kennedy's Catholicism actually enabled him to commit such egregious serial infidelities against the mother of his nine children. Nasaw asserts his theory through the memoirs of Gloria Swanson, one of the greatest and sexiest stars of the 1930s, with whom Kennedy had a torrid affair, notorious in Hollywood but studiously ignored by his wife, Rose, who professed not to notice. Nasaw does effectively debunk, by barely referring to it, the Swanson allegation that Boston's Cardinal William O'Connell,¶¶ a notoriously imperious and abrasive man, attempted to order Swanson to desist from the relationship.

Swanson broke rather angrily with Kennedy and accused him of exploiting her financially. But before that, Kennedy combined his romantic and industrial ambitions in setting himself up as Swanson's producer and financial adviser. He cast her as the lead in a new film by Hollywood's most temperamental director, Erich von Stroheim, a "self-destructive madman." It was shut down mid-shoot after more than $1 million had been wasted on it. Kennedy then cast Swanson in the 1929 film *The Trespasser*, which premiered in Europe very successfully. Afterward, Joe and Rose Kennedy joined Gloria and members of both families on the return ocean passage to New York. Kennedy lavished copious attention on Swanson while Rose, expecting their ninth child (Edward), stayed above it all.

Kennedy flourished in the Depression. He was a pessimist except on the question of his own ability to succeed, and he recognized that America's prosperity in the late 1920s was uneven and that the stock market was overbought. He sold shares and assets and was largely liquid and nearly debt free when the crash came.

David Nasaw does usefully debunk two Kennedy financial legends: one was that he had made a great financial score on the Yellow Cab

---

¶¶ It was a notorious story in our family that Cardinal O'Connell has been rude to my mother in 1935 when she was waiting for her aunt in front of the Boston Museum of Fine Arts, dressed very properly. O'Connell took her to be a woman of disreputable purpose and an unfortunate scene occurred. It is a pleasure, after these eighty years, to have occasion to describe him as the irascible and obnoxious man he apparently was.

Company and the original Hertz rent-a-car business. He did moderately well, but John Hertz declined his offer to invest heavily in the car-rental venture. Nasaw also disposes of the malicious canard that Kennedy was a bootlegger during Prohibition. But like many others Kennedy foresaw the end of the Prohibition folly, which effectively delivered one of the country's greatest industries into the hands of organized crime. He secured large stocks of premium scotch and exclusive importing arrangements, founded Somerset Importers, and collected huge profits. Kennedy also led a syndicate that included Walter Chrysler, the automobile manufacturer, and the investment banks Lehman Brothers and Kuhn, Loeb & Co. Together they bought large quantities of stock in Libbey Owens-Ford, an auto-glass manufacturer, and wash-traded huge volumes of stock among themselves while promoting the outright fraud that their company was related to Owens-Illinois, which made glass bottles and presumably would profit from repeal of Prohibition. It was brazen and cynical, but these "pump and dump" activities didn't include the filing of written misrepresentations. Hence, it wasn't illegal.

Kennedy's departure from Pathé Films after it ran into trouble was a case study in the use of insider information. Kennedy arranged the takeout of his own stock in the company, which flattened the interest of uninformed minority shareholders. Then he short sold the stock as the company collapsed into the hands of Kennedy's buyer, RKO. When he appeared at the subsequent shareholders' meeting, according to the *New York Times*, "heavily armed private detectives were unable to preserve order," although they did prevent physical violence. Kennedy was greeted with epithets but remained relatively unfazed. He short sold other stocks, but he also bought, as long-term investments, shares and other assets that he believed had been sold down to the point of being underpriced in the panic and distress. According to Nasaw, Kennedy's net worth rose steadily through the Depression, even as deflation flattened values.

Like most Boston Irish, Kennedy was a Democrat, but he did not support New York's Irish Catholic governor Alfred E. Smith when he ran for president in 1928 against Republican Herbert Hoover. Kennedy viewed Smith as a clownish Irish pol, rather like four-term Boston mayor James Michael Curley (once elected from a jail cell). This was an unjust rap on Smith. True, he had a broad Lower East Side accent and left school at age ten, but he was a reform governor and scrupulously honest. Kennedy identified with the educated and modern engineer and businessman Hoover, who had distinguished himself distributing aid in war-ravaged Europe and engineering big projects in China. But Kennedy became concerned during the Depression that the economic and social problems of America were so serious that the United States could blow up in social discord. He had respected Franklin D. Roosevelt from a distance in the First World War, noting that he was completely without religious prejudice as he led the pro-Smith faction in the Democratic Party at the 1924 and 1928 conventions. Kennedy saw a necessity for some radical adjustments to avoid complete catastrophe, while Hoover offered nothing but reinforcement of failure.

In this, Kennedy showed far more prescience than most businessmen, who harrumphed and quavered in their clubs, quoting the Bible, Mother Hubbard, and Dickens about the immutability of the economic cycle. The Roosevelt–Kennedy relationship was strange. Kennedy had the Midas touch but was completely inept politically; Roosevelt, an unsuccessful financial dabbler, was the all-time heavyweight champion of electoral politics in the democratic world. Writes Nasaw, "What is remarkable about their relationship is how adept Roosevelt was at getting from Kennedy what he needed and how regularly he would resist giving much back." This was part of Roosevelt's genius and ultimately extended even to Churchill and Stalin. Kennedy never understood it.

Throughout his thirteen-year career as presidential candidate and president, Roosevelt needed only two things from Kennedy – to help persuade publisher and media owner William Randolph Hearst to abandon the spoiling candidacy of House Speaker John Nance Garner of Texas at the 1932 Democratic convention; and to soothe the Irish Americans while FDR gave all aid "short of war" to Britain as he ran for a third term in 1940.

Roosevelt had succeeded Smith as governor of New York and supplanted him as the leading Democratic candidate for the presidency after Smith's 1928 defeat. The Democrats required a two-thirds convention majority to nominate a presidential candidate, and Hearst, by promoting the Garner candidacy, denied Roosevelt that majority.

Hearst was a militant isolationist who generally preferred the Germans to the British. Because he suspected Roosevelt (with some reason) of being an internationalist, he fluffed up the Garner candidacy, although Garner himself had no interest in the nomination. Roosevelt inched toward the two-thirds majority he needed through the third ballot, but his famous campaign managers, Louis McHenry Howe and James A. Farley, had no more delegates to bring over.

Kennedy had struck up a cordial relationship with Hearst in his Hollywood days and succeeded in getting through his switchboard at San Simeon. He persuaded Hearst to release Garner from the spoiling campaign in exchange for Garner getting the vice-presidential slot. Garner got the vice-presidency, which he later described as "not worth a bucket of warm piss." Thus was Roosevelt nominated in a political climate that almost guaranteed his election, given the magnitude of the Depression.

Kennedy's public career, though it had its moments, was a crushing disappointment, only ameliorated in his old age by the rise of his sons. On the first of Roosevelt's railway campaign trips, Kennedy's bonhomous talents as raconteur and his political largesse made him popular with some of Roosevelt's entourage, while his insidious, swashbuckling self-promotion raised hackles with others. Roosevelt won by over seven million votes, and he didn't need Kennedy to pad his majority.

Kennedy possessed administrative talents, as he had shown in the film industry and would demonstrate again soon. His gamecock aggressiveness and tendency to feel exploited or underrecognized served him well at trading, where he kept his eyes open and his guard up. But he lacked the self-confidence of a great leader. Roosevelt was an American aristocrat who spoke French and German, the cousin and nephew-in-law of a beloved president, connected to the Astors, Belmonts, and Vanderbilts. As he said of the polio that afflicted him in his young adulthood, "If you spent two years in bed trying to wiggle your toe, after that anything would seem easy."

Roosevelt's intuition of the tides and currents of popular opinion were as demiurgic as, and much more complicated than, Kennedy's shrewdness as an investor. He had the confidence of the well-born and much-loved only child, amplified by having overcome his terrible affliction and having achieved immense political popularity. He was an enigma. As one of his vice-presidents, Henry Wallace, said, "No one knows him." His sometime assistant secretary of treasury and of state, Dean Acheson, said Roosevelt ruled like a monarch – not a bourgeois British monarch but a Bourbon – by a combination of divine right, natural aptitude, and popular will. "He called everyone by his first name and made no distinction between the secretary of state and the stable boy." His successor, Harry Truman, said of FDR, "He was the coldest man I ever met. He didn't give a damn personally for me or you or anyone else. . . . But he was a great President."

Joe Kennedy was not equipped to deal with such a man – charming to everyone but revealing to no one. In the administration's early days, Kennedy fumed to Roosevelt's entourage about not being offered a job, then sent the president obsequious messages suggesting his inauguration "seemed like another resurrection," as he put it in one letter. Roosevelt, on the other hand, read Kennedy exactly – a rich man who thought his commercial acumen could be transposed into other fields, convinced he could buy anything and anyone (starting with the president's avaricious son James). It was the meeting of a guileless, hypersensitive, ethnic outsider and striver with an unfathomably enigmatic, overpowering national ruler and political magician. Kennedy never realized what and whom he was dealing with; Roosevelt knew precisely whom he was manipulating.

Finally, the call came in the summer of 1934. Roosevelt found himself less concerned about the feckless Republicans than about the rabble-rousing splinter groups led by Louisiana boss Huey P. Long, radio priest Charles E. Coughlin, and the retirees' pied piper, Francis Townsend. Thus, he created the U.S. Securities and Exchange Commission (SEC) to round up the millions who were convinced that shady stock market practices, false prospectuses, and crooked trading had brought on the Depression. He viewed Kennedy as someone who knew all the financial tricks but was an unambiguous capitalist and no apologist of the pre-crash ancient regime. It was an astute appointment. As Roosevelt disarmingly explained to an incredulous reporter: "Set a thief to catch a thief."

Nasaw exaggerates the crisis in financial markets at the time of Kennedy's installation. Of the approximately seventeen million unemployed at the time of Roosevelt's inauguration, about five million had been re-hired by the private sector and seven million put to work in the New Deal workfare programs that built what would today be called infrastructure (Lincoln Tunnel, Triborough Bridge, Chicago waterfront, Tennessee Valley Authority) and conservation projects. The rest were at least receiving direct unemployment compensation, and the stock market had risen by more than 100 per cent from its early 1933 low. Kennedy's task wasn't really, as Nasaw writes, to restore confidence in investors, though there was an aspect of that; it was to satisfy people that the markets functioned honestly and that the administration was not hostile to business.

It is a moot point whether the United States would have been better off without the monster the SEC has become, meddling and indicting in all directions and terrorizing the liver out of people throughout the economic system. But Kennedy staffed the commission with able people, ran it fairly and efficiently, and gave it a good launch. He retired in autumn 1935, and everyone agreed he had acquitted himself with distinction. He also entertained lavishly in Washington, previewing Hollywood movies after dinner. The president himself often enjoyed and reciprocated his hospitality. In early 1937, Roosevelt gave Kennedy the chairmanship of the derelict Maritime Commission, saddled with protectionism, uncontrollable employment costs, and a history of regulatory zeal. Kennedy studied the situation, then prepared an excellent report on what should be done to fix the U.S. merchant shipping industry. Thus did he master another difficult assignment. Now he was ready for the real payoff, earned for his enthusiastic backing of the New Deal in a business community that generally felt threatened by it.

Roosevelt fully understood Kennedy's mercurial personality and his delusions of aptitude for higher office. Some in his entourage blanched at the thought of rewarding Kennedy, but Roosevelt argued that sending him to London as ambassador would get him out of the way and dampen his unceasing manoeuvring and backbiting. Besides, it would be a refreshing change of pace for the staid Court of St. James, which exasperated Roosevelt with its tendency to appease Hitler, as reflected in the diplomacy of prime ministers Ramsay MacDonald, Stanley Baldwin, and Neville Chamberlain.

But Roosevelt underestimated the extent to which Kennedy would tuck himself in with the Chamberlain coterie and become a witless dupe of the appeasers and indirectly of Hitler. It was one of the most catastrophic appointments in U.S. diplomatic history (rivalled by his almost simultaneous nomination of the Stalin bootlicker Joseph E. Davies to Moscow). Roosevelt got more than he bargained for when he sent Joe Kennedy to London in March 1938.

The pugnacious Irishman arrived just before the German Anschluss of Austria, and he fell in at once with the British government's appeasement policy. Kennedy made himself the spokesman for the most absurd notions: German economic conditions required expansion; only an enlargement of American trade could avert war; Chamberlain's desertion of Czechoslovakia was "a masterpiece."

Kennedy told the incoming German ambassador, Herbert von Dirksen, as he had told his predecessor, Joachim von Ribbentrop, that he understood completely Germany's concern with Jews and that Jewish influence in the media was responsible for Germany's hostile press in America. According to Dirksen's diplomatic cables, Kennedy said Hitler's "ideas in the social and economic field which were responsible for such extraordinary achievements in Germany, would be a determining influence on the economic development of the United States." Kennedy soon was sending cables to Washington predicting America would have to enact fascist economic controls; far from considering Roosevelt too economically interventionist, he was soon predicting American corporatism. He had no more economic moorings than he had any notion of geopolitical reality. He became preoccupied with the danger of war to the safety of his sons. He sent a weekly newsletter to various prominent Americans, including Walter Lippmann, William Randolph Hearst, columnist Drew Pearson, his paid mouthpiece Arthur Krock, and various isolationist journalists and senators, in which he poured out his pre-emptive grovellings to Hitler. Nasaw records, "It was apparent now, six months into his tenure, that Joseph P. Kennedy was unfit to serve as ambassador."

Kennedy was like a hyperactive child, never content to let events take their course. When Chamberlain and his foreign minister, Lord Halifax, decided to take a harder line, Kennedy briefly got in step. He invited the Lindberghs, who were living in Germany, to London and commissioned a report from Charles Lindbergh on the effects of war. Lindbergh produced a hair-raising forecast of utter aerial devastation of Britain. At a dinner at the Astors' splendid Cliveden estate attended by Chamberlain, Kennedy read a letter from Germany from his son Joseph. When he finished, wrote fascist sympathizer Anne Morrow Lindbergh, Kennedy looked "like a small boy, pleased and shy . . . like an Irish terrier wagging his tail." When Chamberlain and Halifax veered back to appeasement as the Czech crisis reached its climax, Roosevelt had to veto Kennedy's request that one of the prime minister's defeatist addresses be broadcast directly to the United States.

Only a few weeks after the Munich summit meeting between Chamberlain and Hitler, a Polish Jew in France murdered an official of the German embassy in Paris. Hitler and his spokesmen unleashed the horrible pogrom of Kristallnacht (the night of the broken glass), in which scores of Jews were murdered, thousands were imprisoned, and hundreds of synagogues were burned. Roosevelt, who had called for the "quarantine" of the world's dictators a year before, pulled the U.S. ambassador to Germany, and Hitler withdrew his from Washington just before he was expelled.

As Hitler propelled Europe toward war, Kennedy torqued himself up to lurid political fantasies: the United States would have to adopt a fascist economic model. He badgered Arthur Krock to get the Senate Foreign Relations Committee to call him as a witness, as he considered himself an expert on European affairs. After Hitler seized Prague and all Bohemia in March 1939, Chamberlain and Halifax abandoned appeasement and unilaterally guaranteed they would defend Poland, but Kennedy took the failed policy to new depths. He proposed to the British and American governments that Hitler be offered cash incentives not to attack his next target, Poland.

He explained to Lippmann in June 1939 that the Royal Navy was "valueless" because the German air force could sink it, after effortlessly brushing aside the Royal Air Force. When the Nazi–Soviet pact was concluded, Kennedy begged Roosevelt to urge Poland to negotiate with Hitler, as if that could have accomplished anything. He was clearly in a delusional state.

Fortunately, Roosevelt paid no attention to any of it. He had known from the beginning that it would come to war with Hitler, that Germany was too strong for France, that appeasement would almost certainly fail, and that civilization could only be saved by the United States, preferably after Germany was immersed in the morass of Russia, with Japan in the morass of China.

Kennedy was now a virtual mental case. On September 30, 1939, he wrote the president three letters saying that Britain could not be saved and wasn't worth saving, and that it had only gone to war to save its colonies (which Germany didn't want). Neither the moral nor strategic implications of the war were remotely comprehensible to him. Roosevelt had a raving fascist sympathizer in his embassy in London. But he was secretly planning to break a tradition as old as the Republic and run for a third term, and so he had to keep Kennedy in place and out of the domestic debate. Roosevelt couldn't deal with Chamberlain, so he spoke with the British ambassador, first Ronald Lindsay and then Lord Lothian, and struck up direct communications with the returned head of the navy, Winston Churchill, whom he had not liked when they met in the First World War but now embraced as someone who would carry the fight to Hitler. (His initial message to Churchill purported to thank him for a hitherto unacknowledged book Churchill had sent him – seven years before.) Kennedy, in what Roosevelt described as "typical asinine Joe Kennedy letters," urged that America fight in its own backyard. Roosevelt understood it was better to stop the enemy, using the forces of other countries, on the far sides of the Atlantic and Pacific.

On May 20, 1940, with Churchill (a warmonger and a drunkard, in Kennedy's view) now prime minister and with Germany slicing through France, Kennedy wrote Rose, "My God how right I've been in my predictions." Of course, it all turned, and he soon resented the prowess of the Royal Air Force and Churchill's eloquence, seeing them as somehow increasing the likelihood of U.S. involvement in war. He was at this point, as Nasaw rightly summarizes, "exhausted, lonely, frightened, bitter, and self-pitying." He claimed to believe that if he had been allowed to meet Hitler, he could have worked it out. Kennedy's private plan was to take over Canada, Mexico, and Central America militarily and impose a fascist dictatorship in the United States, though he shared this brainwave only with himself in his private notes.

Roosevelt played a supremely deft hand, resupplying the British Army by executive authority after the Dunkirk evacuation, selling his policy of all aid short of war, insisting the best way to stay out of war was to keep the British and Canadians in it, engineering a bogus draft of himself for a third term as president, lending Britain fifty destroyers and instituting the first peacetime conscription in American history. Nasaw presents this gripping drama well, though there are a few irritating lapses, such as the references to Sir Alexander Cadogan as a lord and the resuscitation of the hackneyed myth that Hitler deliberately allowed the escape at Dunkirk by holding back two armoured divisions. As the Blitz opened in September 1940, Kennedy bet one of his officials that "Hitler will be in Buckingham Palace in two weeks."

Kennedy was desperate to leave his post and spent much of his rime in the British countryside, out of harm's way. He was now despised by the British for wailing that Britain was finished and that Roosevelt was insane and incompetent. He let it be known to friends in the administration that he had written an inside account of Roosevelt's dealings with the British government, for release if he were not back in America before the election – an act of gross insubordination, as well as a falsehood, as he didn't know the full inside story. He believed the presence of the Labour Party in Churchill's coalition showed that socialism, and therefore Nazism, was "budding up so fast that these fellows don't recognize it."

Kennedy finally returned to America, arriving just a few days before the election. Roosevelt cleverly invited Joe and Rose to the White House without any press involvement. When they met, the president adhered to his practice of ignoring the vast accumulation of Kennedy's insolences and disloyalties and told him that all his problems were due to the "officious" people in the State Department, whom he would clean our as soon as the election was over. There is some dispute about what was said next; only Roosevelt, Joe and Rose Kennedy, Senator James Byrnes and the president's assistant, Missy LeHand, were present. But there seems little doubt that Roosevelt warned, obliquely or explicitly, that Kennedy's sons would have no future in the Democratic Party if Kennedy defected at this point. Kennedy gave a speech for Roosevelt three nights later and paid for it himself. Though not effusive, it was an unambiguous endorsement. Roosevelt was re-elected comfortably enough, whereupon Kennedy went public with his crusade against the war and his assertion that Britain was washed up. He even gave a three-hour anti-Semitic harangue to a largely Jewish movie-industry audience in Hollywood. He retired as ambassador and did not return to England until after the war. If he had just behaved like a normal diplomat, with any idea of the moral forces at issue in the war and the real strategic balance, he could have served through the war, gained great distinction, and possibly have even been the vice-presidential candidate in 1944 or 1948.

He didn't break openly with Roosevelt personally, but he wasn't relevant anymore, and Roosevelt paid no attention to him. As Nasaw accurately states, he had never been able to accept the reality that being an "insider" meant sacrificing something to the team. His sense of his own wisdom and unique talents was so overblown that he truly believed he could stake out an independent position for himself and still remain a trusted and vital part of the Roosevelt team.

After Pearl Harbor, Kennedy grandly telegrammed Roosevelt, "I'm yours to command." Roosevelt ignored him. Kennedy, believing Roosevelt had provoked Hitler into war, now made a specialty of being abrasive and obnoxious to the great office-holders he met. Kennedy's latest crusade, which began shortly after the war, was against any attempt to combat communism in Europe. He was as faithful a dupe to Stalin as he had been to Hider, and he fatuously debated with Truman and Eisenhower as he had tried unsuccessfully to do with Roosevelt. He had no notion of or respect for the greatness of any of them, or of Churchill, only a chippy sense of his own right to know better.

Nasaw gives him too much credit for starting a "great debate" over postwar involvement in Europe and East Asia. It wasn't much of a debate, and Kennedy didn't contribute much to it. He never grasped that

Hitler was incompatible with Western civilization, that a rampant Nazi Germany was a mortal threat to the United States, and that Roosevelt had made the United States the supreme power in the world while Stalin took over 90 per cent of the casualties in fighting Hitler. America's pre-war rivals – Germany, Britain, Japan, France, and Italy – were all docile American allies now, and functioning democracies.

Kennedy retained his genius for profit and invested intelligently, including in America's largest building after the Pentagon, the Merchandise Mart in Chicago. It must be said that his most endearing characteristic was his devotion to his children. He was always accessible and concerned, never overly stern or too busy for them. Nasaw believably explains that Kennedy acted reasonably in ordering a lobotomy for his mentally handicapped daughter Rosemary in 1942. When it failed, he was horribly upset, and even more so by the deaths of his eldest son, Joe Jr., heroically in a 1944 bombing mission, and his universally liked daughter Kathleen, in an air accident in 1948. He made prodigious efforts to assist his surviving sons in their political careers, getting John F. Kennedy's books "edited," published, and excerpted, financially assisting James Curley back into city hall to open up for Jack the congressional district that had once been held by Rose's father, and contributing tangibly to the effort to keep Joseph R. McCarthy out of Massachusetts when JFK ran for the Senate there in 1952. He had been egregiously tolerant of McCarthy, a red-baiting grandstander who sought to attach the communist label to Roosevelt, Truman, Eisenhower, and General George C. Marshall – four of America's greatest statesmen. The third Kennedy son, Bobby, was McCarthy's assistant committee counsel for six months.

He contributed generously to his son's presidential campaign and was a member of the strategy committee. But he did nothing to indicate that JFK was not his own man. The author suggests John Kennedy shared some of his father's reservations about overreaching for the defence of Europe, but he soon got over those. This book is not a history of that campaign, but it does pass rather swiftly over the extent of Nixon's potential grievances. There is little doubt that Illinois – won by Kennedy by less than nine thousand votes out of nearly five million cast, with many ballots missing – was stolen; nor that Nixon won the popular vote, if the votes in Alabama had been allotted fairly between Kennedy and the splinter southern Democrat, Senator Harry Byrd. The many other very close states, including Texas, are not referred to specifically, and the election was really a toss-up. Nixon had a right to contest it, and he deserves credit for not forcing the issue.

Joseph Kennedy, turbulent soul that he was, felt that too few Roman Catholics had voted for his son in 1960 and too many Protestants had voted against him because of his religion. Yet he was rightly jubilant at being father of a U.S. president.

In 1962, Kennedy suffered a stroke that left him half paralyzed, wheelchair-bound, and unable to speak. He became a prisoner in his own body, much as his daughter Rosemary was. His thoughts on the assassination of his son can only be imagined, and the similar fate that befell Robert Kennedy nearly five years later finished the father, who died on November 18, 1969, aged eighty-one.

Next to his love of his children, his most admirable quality was his appreciation of classical music. He was a congenial companion and a fine-looking, nattily dressed man. But he excelled only at financial speculation and administration. Apart from his talents as a sire and parental provider and motivator, he was an improbable person to earn the title of this book. And his family, as Marlene Dietrich's daughter said, all had "smiles that never ended." They scarcely seem to merit the crazed idolatry they have received. But, thanks to the patriarch, they were numerous, tremendously ambitious, wealthy, and led eventful lives. It was really only a dynasty for the decade of the 1960s, a glamorous and tragic meteor of a family that fleetingly brightened the sky of America and then passed on. They were not brilliant exactly, but they were attractive and energetic and remarkable, though only JFK and his wife, Jacqueline, would qualify as classy. But the thought of what the Kennedys were and might have become lingers yet, and will for a long time.

David Nasaw, *The Patriarch* (Penguin Press, 2012).

# NAPOLEON: A LIFE,
# BY ANDREW ROBERTS

*The New Criterion*, November 2014

The distinguished historian Andrew Roberts has written his greatest book to date and made an important contribution to the vast Napoleonic literature. His *Napoleon: A Life* is a monument of research and organization, adheres to the author's well-established high stylistic standard, and reaches a new summit of thorough and balanced treatment of probably the most gigantic personality in the history of the world (barring those widely regarded as partially divine). Every significant or interesting aspect of Napoleon's life is dealt with: the general, the administrator and reformer, the lawgiver, academician and intellectual, the promoter of science, the ardent womanizer and lover, public-relations genius, politician, and creator of an immense mystique that has not slipped or become outdated these two centuries. And his career is examined from all angles, including his administration's financial record and fiscal and social consequences, his intricate diplomatic history, and even, at many stages, alternative and comparative steps to those he took.

Napoleon was probably the most prominent personality in the world from shortly after he took over the tattered and demoralized ragamuffin Army of Italy in 1796 until his death in 1821, after six years of exile following Waterloo. And few people have remotely approached him in celebrity: Alexander the Great, Julius Caesar, Lincoln, and a few twentieth-century statesmen, evil and benign (Hitler, Stalin, Mao Tse-tung, Churchill, Roosevelt), but it remains to be seen if they will have the same staying power. It need hardly be said that Napoleon remains a figure of intense controversy and that biographical treatment of him by respectable authors runs the gamut from hagiography to demonization. Hard though it is to believe, there are significant quantities of new correspondence and documents that have recently emerged and which give this book (whose British title is *Napoleon the Great*) an advantage on sources over any previous life of Napoleon. There is also here a relentless and entirely successful effort by the author to address each point and trait of controversy fairly and present the arguments and give his reasoned and persuasive judgment of each issue.

To refresh the memory of the casual Napoleonic reader: with an unpaid, half-equipped rag-tag of stragglers and conscripts, he effectively bundled the Austrian Empire out of Italy and moved on to take over Egypt and part of what is now Israel. But with his fleet demolished by Nelson, he returned to France and led a *coup d'état*, outwitting many other factions and elder politicians and revolutionaries to become master of France at the age of thirty, initially as First Consul, and then for eleven years, including a ten-month exile in Elba, Emperor ("of the French Republic" at first, and then less discordantly "of the French"). He fought sixty major battles, won at least fifty-four and drew several, and was frequently victorious against heavy odds, in unpromising conditions, and often by recourse to audacious and often brilliant tactics. He revolutionized almost every aspect of land war: training, rapid deployment, logistics, coordination of infantry, cavalry, and artillery, and the scope of operations. The Duke of Wellington reckoned his presence opposite added the equivalent of 40,000 good soldiers to the forces of any other contemporary commander (and remarked that Napoleon's death made him the world's foremost commanding general).

As a ruler, at one point he was effectively governing almost all of Europe, from the gates of Cadiz to Moscow, and from Copenhagen to Naples, and he did so with astonishing energy and thoroughness. He promulgated the Civil Code, which he has partly written, and which was widely emulated (including in Louisiana and Quebec); brought in the metric system; abolished the tenacious vestiges of feudalism; promoted science, education, libraries, museums, and art galleries in France and elsewhere; and generally suppressed official anti-Semitism. Though he largely squandered the exaltation of soul of the egalitarian Republic, he buried for all time the worst offences of the *ancien régime* and ran a distinguished meritocracy that cleared away the worst abuses of the class system in France and much of Europe.

Andrew Roberts deals with the usual leading charges against Napoleon very judiciously, from the massacre of 3,000 Turkish prisoners at Jaffa (a shabby business with some extenuating circumstances) to the murder of the Duc d'Enghien (a drumhead execution but following on egregious royalist provocations and plots against Napoleon and his family), and including the familiar accusation that he was a warmonger, a man with no human qualities, hubristic (a word that here, as in some other works of this author, is slightly overused), and that he was a monster who was indifferent to casualties and without any empathy or concern for anyone. In all of the circumstances, Napoleon was much more sinned against than sinning, was inexplicably forgiving of ceaseless treachery from Talleyrand, the egregious foreign minister; the equally infamous police minister, Joseph Fouché; most of his own family; a number of his own marshals; and a large number of people who owed him much but betrayed him shamelessly. Of particular value is Andrew Roberts's severe debunking of the widely held British historical view that Napoleon was essentially the precursor to Hitler, that the many hundreds of thousands of people killed in the Revolutionary and Napoleonic Wars were practically as explicitly murdered by Napoleon as the victims of the death camps of the Third Reich were by Hitler. Part of this theory is that Napoleon almost alone was responsible for the breakdown in the Peace of Amiens in 1803 and for the continuance of war through seven successive coalitions bankrolled by Great Britain.

These are the views of familiar historians such as Alistair Horne, Max Hastings, and Paul Johnson, and it reflects the British propaganda of the time and the judgments of contemporary British leaders, including Wellington, who, though he conceded that Napoleon was the world's greatest general, thought him in other respects a thug and a "bully."

Wellington took no account of Napoleon's status as an intellectual much admired by Goethe and a respected member of the French Academy, a statesman, an overpowering and almost always charming personality, and as a man who loved his wives and children and was astoundingly forgiving of subordinates and most enemies. Napoleon was always philosophical, famously remarking, early in the retreat from Moscow, that "from the sublime to the ridiculous is a single step." He was beguilingly charming, even on the trip to St. Helena, was unshakeably physically courageous and fearless in mortal combat, and was an infallibly eloquent orator and often writer. Roberts debunks the theory that he had a "Napoleon complex," as he was of average height; shows that he was generally courteous and popular with those who were subordinate to him; and that the collapse of the Peace of Amiens was at least as much the fault of the British government as of the French.

British contemporary opinion was that Napoleon was a monster, and this became a traditional view legitimized by most British historians (though with conspicuous exceptions such as A.G. Macdonell and David G. Chandler). Napoleon was treated with provoking insolence and disingenuousness by a number of European statesmen, especially the long-serving Austrian foreign minister and chancellor Klemens von Metternich, "the coachman of Europe." His monarchic contemporaries – the mad "Farmer George III" and dissolute Prince Regent, the deranged czars Paul and Alexander, and the mediocre sovereigns in Vienna and Berlin – were not his peers. The only foreign statesmen of stature were Pitt and Fox and Castlereagh; Metternich; the papal foreign minister Ercole Cardinal Consalvi; and Washington and Jefferson.

If, instead of setting up the Empire and inflicting on occupied Europe his generally rather incompetent and avaricious siblings as national kings, Napoleon had created the second Republic with renewable seven- to ten-year terms for himself as president, he would have kept much of the *esprit* of the Revolution and led a much stronger state. The entire French political tradition had been Richelieu's absolute centralized monarchy and Colbert's state-directed economy, which in the hands of less talented successors deteriorated into the inefficacy and disaffection that became the Revolution and ultimately the Terror, before slackening into the unfathomable corruption of the Directory.

By these standards, Napoleon was a comparative liberal, and it will never be known whether the constitutional monarchy and free press that he established in the Hundred Days of his restoration would have lasted if the Waterloo campaign had gone differently.

While his performance as commander and statesman was almost flawless from 1796 to 1806, where Napoleon did disappoint was in compounding his lack of understanding of naval affairs with his unshakeable conviction that he could win an economic war with Great Britain and could endlessly force his continental blockade of Britain on all Europe from Portugal to Russia. Britain was undoubtedly inconvenienced by the Continental System (which purported to bar British goods and services from Europe), but its navy could secure from Latin America most of what Europe had supplied Britain and could induce smuggling all over Europe, and while British exports fell sharply, the home market could pick up much of the slack. Britain was strained by Napoleon's counter-embargo but not near cracking, and in the end the Continental bar on trade with Britain could not be rigorously imposed, particularly on Russia and Spain. The attempt to do so alienated all Europe, including much of France.

Once Napoleon swaddled himself in the monarchist largesse of the Empire, dumped the popular Josephine to marry a Hapsburg and get an heir, and was drawn into endless quagmires at both ends of Europe, in Spain and Russia, he steadily lost his ability always to defeat his enemies as they learned from his ten years of successful war-making and reconstructed their armies along modern lines. He also misjudged the French themselves, whom he imagined capable of conducting a brutal guerrilla war like that fought by the Spanish and by the Russians, which culminated in the burning of Moscow by its inhabitants. The French grew so tired of war, taxation, and conscription and casualties that they greeted the invading allies in 1814 as liberators. And the strain of fighting seven wars against coalitions while administering most of Europe with his unbounded curiosity and energy resulted in a reduction of the brilliance of Napoleon's generalship. He was still inspired in crossing the Berezina out of Russia and in the frontier campaign of 1813–1814, but Leipzig was misconceived and the Waterloo campaign was thoroughly bungled. He could have salvaged an expanded France and the guardianship of much of Germany and Italy after the Russian debacle, and could still have kept his throne, though over a shrinking France as his enemies closed in in 1813, but he was always too late in taking stale-dated peace offers and did not understand the extreme animus of Metternich, Czar Alexander, Pope Pius VII (whom he had imprisoned for four years), and the Prussians, though he was never in any doubt about the objectives of the British.

All of this is presented in well-paced narrative by Andrew Roberts, with exactly the right balance of sufficient detail to avoid superficiality, but never so much to cause this always-gripping epic to flag. There are asides to note Josephine's sexual prowess (including the mysterious "zig-zag") and the cameo roles played by Napoleon's more than twenty mistresses, and a great many other piquant and often humorous but apposite vignettes. Apart from the life of its central character, an endless procession of adventurers, charlatans, psychopaths, and crooks is described, as well as many heroes among a rich cast of the ignoble and the tragic as well as the virtuous. The pictures and maps are excellent, and the story, supported by a formidable and exhaustive 4,000 footnotes, surges along at the speed achieved by the Emperor in his "seven league boots," right to the last of what Chateaubriand (an opponent) called "the mightiest breath of life that ever animated human clay." Napoleon was one of the greatest military commanders and rulers in history, a dazzling personality at which the world still marvels. "He built an empire, handed down laws for the ages, perfected the art of leadership, and joined the ancients" (in the pantheon of giants), wrote Andrew Roberts in justifying the original title, *Napoleon the Great*. The book was aptly named and so worthy of its subject that it too will be regarded as great, in a very crowded field.

Andrew Roberts, *Napoleon* (Viking, 2014).

# STALIN: VOLUME I, PARADOXES OF POWER, 1878–1928, BY STEPHEN KOTKIN

*The New Criterion*, May 2015

*Stalin* is a formidably documented, densely detailed book of 739 pages that gets the reader from Stalin's birth in 1878 up to 1928, just six years into his thirty-one-year tenure as general secretary of the Communist Party of Russia and then the Soviet Union. Two more volumes are promised, which makes the author, Stephen Kotkin, a candidate for the status of the Robert Caro of English-language Russian political biographies. It is a laborious read, because of detail and a slightly cavalier approach by Mr. Kotkin to avoiding even elemental simplifications in presenting Stalin's tortuous, completely devious nature and the unrelievedly treacherous atmosphere of a revolutionary life, when dodging and agitating no less than when exercising practically unlimited power. But these are small cavils with a work that is very hard to put down, very convincing in the rigour and fairness of its judgments, and brilliant at conveying the vast sweep of the events of the late Romanov era, the Great War, the 1917 Russian Revolutions, and the febrile plotting and backstabbing that led to apparently natural but premature deaths (Lenin, Sverdlov, Frunze, and Dzierzinski) or violent deaths of almost all the players except Stalin and a few of his most assiduous disciples (Molotov,

Kaganovich, Mikoyan, Voroshilov, and Kalinin). It was a deadly game every day for at least the last three decades of this volume; one false step was often a mortal error, and a false step could only become so because of a subsequent capricious, sadistic, completely unforeseeable change of course by Stalin. And though Stalin played a brilliant hand at his terrible game of terror, conspiracy, revolution, war, and maximum-risk policies generally, he came close to disaster many times. His survival in absolute power until his natural death at a full age (seventy-four) – despite the deadly stakes and compromised health since his peasant youth and countless Siberian penal confinements – confers on him the status of one of the giants, and one of the monsters, of world history.

Because of his Georgian accent, his lack of a strong voice due to pulmonary and other health problems in his youth and young manhood, and his furtive nature, Stalin perfected techniques of self-promotion based on his strong suits: guile, thoroughness, cynicism, acute insight into the foibles and weaknesses of others, complete absence of human attachments, immense charm, and quiet and quickly formulated persuasiveness that didn't play well with huge audiences but won him almost every round at Politburo and Central Committee meetings. Though Lenin and Leon Trotsky (Stalin's great rival until he deposed, expelled, and ultimately assassinated him) were hypnotic public speakers, Lenin, despite being a brilliant and decisive strategist, was slightly disorganized, and his physical stamina gave way completely at the age of fifty-one; Trotsky had no political judgment and was an indifferent administrator. These facts have often been written before, but, apart from Simon Sebag Montefiore in his volumes on how Stalin manoeuvred in the Kremlin inner circle, no one has assimilated the vast quantity of material released in the post-communist era as Kotkin has, and no one has applied it, as he has, to the full range of Stalin's activities from his earliest days. The volumes covering the most important decades, in national and world terms, of Stalin's career as the Soviet Union's absolute ruler promise to be a major contribution to the Stalin literature. (So prodigious is the detail that it emerges that Stalin's chef at his country dacha outside Moscow was Vladimir Putin's grandfather.) Stylistically, it is a bit laboured in places, and there are scores of sentences that begin "True," without having stated what it was whose exception was about to be announced. There is also overfrequent recourse to the slightly twee "Be that as it may," but, for this reader at least, these punctuations became almost endearing and somehow made it all seem more Russian.

Despite its scholastic rigour and thoroughness, this account necessarily leaves us wondering at Stalin's motives, between complete cynicism and ruthless pursuit and retention of absolute power, and Marxist convictions. Kotkin believes that Stalin was a convinced Marxist and only varied from that conviction for tactical reasons in face of necessity for his own survival. That may be correct, and I have no standing to take issue with such a knowledgeable authority, but I don't think it is clear that Stalin really was an unflinching Marxist, especially as he was an unlimited cynic, a very well-read and well-informed – and in all respects extremely intelligent and perceptive – man, and Marxism was clearly, by the latter years covered in this book, nonsense as a political and economic system. I hesitantly suggest that Stalin swaddled himself in Marxist orthodoxy more often to wrong-foot his opponents and exploit the confected and amplified sacred reverence for Lenin and Marx as a method of faulting and destroying rivals than because he thought it was the best course – or even cared whether it was – as long as mistakes did not compromise his hold on power and the Soviet Union's place in the world.

This volume ends as Stalin completes his rout of Trotsky, Kamenev, and Zinoviev and prepares to evict Rykov, Tomsky, and Bukharin; that is to say, all who had been his colleagues in the Politburo when Lenin, who had been severely invalided for three years, died in 1924. Trotsky, Kamenev, and Zinoviev tormented Stalin with the "Testament" of Lenin (so dubbed by Trotsky), which was probably forged by Lenin's wife, Krupskaya. In the purported "Testament," Lenin sought Stalin's removal as party general secretary, alleging Stalin's "rudeness" as well as his lust for power – both legitimate complaints. Stalin countered with claims of fraud, reminders that Kamenev and Zinoviev had opposed the October Revolution, and that all had opposed the New Economic Policy (NEP) in 1921, which saved the Revolution by proclaiming "socialism in one country" and accepting private, rather than collective, agriculture. Stalin staged several resignations as general secretary, in the assurance that the Politburo and Central Committee majorities would reject them.

In the next volume, we will read (doubtless in implacable detail) of the execution or outright murder (Trotsky) or suicide (Tomsky) of all of these old comrades. And it ends as Stalin, who had smeared Trotsky for opposing Lenin's NEP deferral of collectivization of agriculture, prepares to collectivize agriculture by force, with disastrous results. These included the deaths of five to seven million people from hunger and exposure imposed on them by the regime, as well as outright massacres of recalcitrant farmers, chronic hunger inflicted on forty million people, and the loss of millions of tons of grain and the majority of the entire Soviet population of livestock, sheep, horses, pigs, and goats. What he liquidated his rivals for proposing, he effected himself as soon as he had won that deadly contest. Kotkin thinks Stalin followed the correct course of dogmatic Marxism-Leninism as soon as he was able politically to do so. I am not so sure that there wasn't an element of showing that his power was so absolute that he could murder millions of innocents in a dubious cause, and was so free of the constraints that bound everyone else except the most absolute autocrats in Russia's tumultuous history, precisely by adopting the policy of those whom he had judicially murdered for advocating just that policy. How better to impart the lesson of his absolute dictatorship?

One of the many strengths of this account is the way it conveys the relentlessly murderous atmosphere. Those who schemed against the Romanovs were taking their lives in their hands every day; the leaders of the Revolution were constantly being accused of "treason" (Lenin's preferred formulation for dogmatic or policy differences), of being "anti-party," "counter-revolutionary," or agents of the bourgeois and capitalist imperialists. The penalty for all these offences, which were constantly being bandied about, was death. Once his agricultural collectivization program was cranked up, Stalin promulgated police powers to execute people pre-emptively and without trial if the local leaders of the secret police judged individuals capable of infractions.

Another strength is the clarity the author brings to the engineering of Stalin's totalitarianism. He was a successful commissar of nationalities in the early years of the Revolution and installed loyalists in many of the fringes of the country. Once installed as general secretary, Stalin directly controlled the media and the secret police: he wrote a great deal in the press and read everything from the ubiquitous police. Where the Communist Party dominated the cadres of the state and the armed forces, the secret police (OGPU, forerunner of the NKVD and KGB) infiltrated the party and monitored everyone; they reported directly to Stalin on all aspects of local opinion and official performance throughout the country. Almost any perceived deviation from Marxist-Leninist orthodoxy (or past deviation from Lenin's instructions, even if the deviations had not really occurred, or if they had and Lenin was not much concerned with them) was grounds for the stages of one's fall, and there were thousands who replicated this sequence: dismissal from office, removal from committees, expulsion as a party member, indictment for treason, torture until fraudulent public confessions were made to spare one's family and get it over with, execution, and finally suppression from photographs, official history, and living memory. And the desire to placate and impress Stalin was so great and self-interested that there were always volunteers to lead the indictment of others, allowing Stalin to play the reluctant and equable father of the nation above this distressing fray and to indulge the next wave of accusers, as they, on a nod from the general secretary (Stalin was also the premier for his last twenty-two years), accused the previous accusers and sent them, too, to receive a bullet in their heads in the basement of the Lubyanka (OGPU headquarters). Successive police ministers, on being toppled, charged, tortured, and executed, handed on to their successors the spent bullets "K" and "Z" that were discharged into the heads of Kamenev and Zinoviev. A capricious totalitarian cultivated a culture of mortal roulette and sudden, terrible destruction.

Kotkin's first volume vividly recreates the surreal and paranoiac ambiance of the early and middle revolutionary government. Not only were all dissenters tarred with the brush of being monarchist revanchists, imperialist capitalist tools, or crooks (or some or all of these), but the Bolshevik government sought sophisticated machinery, agricultural equipment, motor vehicles, and machine tools from the West, and proposed to pay for them on credit secured by access to Russian markets and receipt of Russian grain and oil. But, without much recognition of the incongruity of it, all the while the Russian government was trying to foment worker revolt in these countries. Stalin gave cash and propaganda assistance to the miners and other participants in the British General Strike of 1926; constantly, if ineffectually, promoted the American Communist Party; encouraged extreme labour activity in France; and actively and directly promoted unsuccessful armed uprisings in Germany and China. This was a new but unsuccessful application on a grand scale of Lenin's famous dictum that "the capitalists are so stupid, they will sell us the rope we hang them with." Kotkin well makes the point that the Great Depression saved the Soviet Union. The West was suddenly desperate for sales of industrial goods and, ending its principled boycott of the Bolshevik state, sold all the industrial machinery it could to the U.S.S.R., whatever its revolutionary agitations, on the easiest terms. This greatly facilitated the modernization of the physical plant of Soviet heavy industry and contributed importantly to that country's survival of the Second World War, as we will see in the next volume. Britain restored diplomatic relations with the Kremlin, broken after the 1926 General Strike; Germany sent back an ambassador after a lapse of several years; and even the United States exchanged ambassadors with the Kremlin in 1933, though little practical good came of it until international relations heated up six years later. The Great Depression was not seen as the lucky break for the Soviet Union that it was, but rather as the confirmation of the death spiral of capitalism and the legitimization of everything Lenin and Stalin had done, even though Russia's economic progress through the 1920s had lagged far beyond that of all other major powers, including Japan and Mussolini's Italy.

Kotkin's summary of the subject of this somewhat turgid but magisterial work is

> *Closed and gregarious, vindictive and solicitous, Stalin shatters any attempt to confine him within binaries. He was a despot who, when he wanted to be, was utterly charming. He was an ideologue who was flexibly pragmatic. He fastened obsessively on slights yet he was a precocious geostrategic thinker – unique among Bolsheviks – who was, however, prone to egregious strategic blunders. Stalin was a ruler both astute and blinkered, diligent and self-defeating, cynical and*

*true-believing. The cold calculation and the flights of absurd delusion were products of a single mind. He was shrewd enough to see right through people, but not enough to escape a litany of nonsensical beliefs. Above all, he became ever more steeped in conspiracies. But Stalin's hyper-suspiciousness . . . closely mirrored the Bolshevik Revolution's in-built structural paranoia, the predicament of a Communist regime in an overwhelmingly capitalist world, surrounded by, penetrated by, enemies, [as] the Bolsheviks unwittingly yet relentlessly reproduced the pathologies and predations of the old regime. . . . He was a leader; he made history, rearranging the entire socio-economic landscape of one-sixth of the earth. Right through mass rebellion, mass starvation, cannibalism, the destruction of the country's livestock, and unprecedented political destabilization, Stalin did not flinch. Feints in the form of tactical retreats notwithstanding, he would keep going even when warned to his face in the inner regime that a catastrophe was unfolding. . . . This required extraordinary maneuvering, brow-beating, and violence on his part. It also required deep conviction that it had to be done. Stalin was uncommonly skillful in building an awesome personal dictatorship, but also a bungler, getting fascism wrong, stumbling in foreign policy. But he had will. . . . History, for better and for worse, is made by those who never give up.*

This is, on balance, a very good book and I am looking forward to its sequels.

Stephen Kotkin, *Stalin: Volume I* (Penguin Press, 2014).

# THE HITLER OF HISTORY, BY JOHN LUKACS

*Sunday Telegraph*, January 2000

---

With this dense, formidably researched, but very readable volume, John Lukacs enhances his well-earned reputation as one of the most original contemporary historians of Europe. Even avid students of the Third Reich are apt to learn some unsuspected fact of Hitler's character, or at least some interesting reflection from his voluminous writings and recorded conversations.

Most readers would not have been aware that Hitler's father lived in the building where Napoleon's second Empress, Marie-Louise, exchanged her Austrian for her French entourage on her way to her marriage. Some will be reassured to know that Hitler did not really complain that Churchill "could cruise for weeks around the world in a white silk blouse and a floppy sombrero." It was surprising to read that he had said to Speer, "Perhaps I am not a pious churchgoer. . . . But deep inside I am still a devout believer. . . . Whoever fights bravely and does not capitulate . . . will not be abandoned by the Almighty but receive the blessing of Providence." And it was astonishing to me to read that Eva Braun's sister claimed that Hitler and his mistress had prayed together before committing suicide.

Few would have known that Hitler learned about the American West and was much interested in cowboy history from reading the works of Karl May, or that he had had the cigarette airbrushed out of Stalin's hand in the official German photograph of the signing of the Nazi–Soviet Pact: "The signing of a pact between two great nations is a solemn act; one does not do that with a cigarette between one's fingers."

Some of Hitler's trenchant remarks are almost refreshing. "I am not a dictator and will never be one . . . any popinjay can rule as a dictator." Or, "Why should I nationalize the industries? I will nationalize the people." I had forgotten that he referred to the British appeasers as "my Hugenbergs" (after the industrialist who had generously contributed to Hitler's rise in the unfounded hope of influencing him), and that he had told Speer that highways would be his Parthenon.

Mr. Lukacs offers a kindly opinion of Hitler's little-read poems: "Of course, Hitler was no Rupert Brooke, but the poems are not laughable." Among the decisive elements in Joseph Goebbels's adherence to Hitler was Hitler's assertion to him in 1926: "God's most beautiful gift bestowed on us is the hate of our enemies, whom we in turn hate from the bottom of our hearts."

Mr. Lukacs has a considerable storehouse of apposite phrases from a wide variety of sources. Pascal tells us that "opinion is the queen of the world." Napoleon, we are reminded, remarked that "there are two human occupations where an amateur is often better than a professional: prostitution . . . and War."

The author, too, has considerable aphoristic talents: "Generalizations, like brooms, should sweep and not stand in a corner"; and "Religion is not pure either, because of the inevitable human alloy; but then without that alloy faith, like gold, is unusable." Better still, "Many professional historians, bombinating in their airless circles, tend to ignore or dismiss Churchill the historian."

*The Hitler of History* is not a biography; it is a discussion of a full range of conventional historical treatments of Hitler, from the David Irving whitewash, rigorously exposed here, to the theory of Hitler the diabolical or satanic, which the author also opposes as unjust and overly convenient. However, Mr. Lukacs points out that, according to St. John of the Apocalypse, Hitler possesses a number of agreed-upon characteristics of the Antichrist.

We read of his greater development in Munich, with his witnessing of the "ridiculous and sordid episode of the Munich Soviet Republic with its Jewish and European intellectuals, et al," than in Vienna. In that city, though, he "recognized . . . that life is but a continuous bitter struggle between the weak and the strong . . . and that life is not ruled by the principles of humanity but by victory and defeat."

John Lukacs does better than anyone else I have read at explaining the phenomenon of Hitler, the nature and limits of his genius, and the very high and continuing interest in him. Hitler's claim to genius is in his ability, unlike, we read here, the characters of Dostoyevsky, to translate his thoughts into generalized ideas and then to have those ideas change the world, at least for a time. He was not, as Pius XII rather belatedly claimed, a "satanic apparition," a metaphysical notion that tends to acquit people of their moral responsibilities. Mr. Lukacs affirms that Hitler was undoubtedly profoundly evil, but in La Rochefoucauld's category of those "who would be less dangerous if they had not something good about them." He was one of the group Jacob Burckhardt had predicted would arise of "terrible simplifiers." He briefly produced such a state of national serenity that German birth rates and marriage rates shot up and crime rates shrivelled. Jails were empty and judges idle.

Hitler possessed none of the nobility his admirers claimed for him, nor the ridiculous aspect Chaplin and sometimes even Churchill tried to attach to him. His artistic interest, and at times temperament, were not an affectation. Mr. Lukacs credits him with significant architectural aptitudes and rightly points out his talent to attract and impress certain notable writers, including Jules Romains, André Gide, Wyndham Lewis, and Ezra Pound. The author also rightly makes the point that Hitler, not his colleagues or his party, was overwhelmingly popular, and that his popularity began to rise before the onset of the Great Depression.

By careful analysis, Hitler is portrayed as much more of a nationalist than a racist, though he was extreme in both respects, an upholder of defined *kultur* and an enemy of civilization. And in his disdain for the bourgeoisie, the aristocracy, and the capitalists, he was a somewhat authentic socialist, though he always dismissed Marxism, with considerable accuracy, as unsustainable nonsense. His anti-communism was, however, a tactical pandering to the Slavophobia and the fear of Bolshevism of susceptible constituents or neighbouring countries.

We learn that Hitler was not as optimistic as his generals about Germany's ability to defeat the U.S.S.R. and enigmatically described Russia, on the eve of his invasion of it, as like "a ship in *The Flying Dutchman*."

The explanation here for his decision to invade – that if he were successful, Churchill and Roosevelt or their successors would eventually have to concede their inability to dislodge Hitler from control of Central Europe and make peace – is reasonably convincing.

Where Mr. Lukacs slips somewhat is in his attempted explanation of Hitler's declaration of war on the United States after Pearl Harbor, because he "could hardly betray his Japanese ally by welching on the principal item in their alliance." Since Hitler's only interest in Japan was its potential for discomforting Stalin, which it didn't do, why couldn't he? A statesman of Roosevelt's agility and strategic insight would presumably have found some pretext for plunging into war with Germany, but Hitler could have made it difficult for him. Hitler could probably have held Britain and Russia off indefinitely, but once he was at war with the United States as well, Churchill and de Gaulle immediately saw, he was doomed. And Lukacs also goes a little lightly over Hitler's explanation to the German public that war with the United States was brought about by the Jewish entourage of Roosevelt. This was as foolish tactically as it was substantively, and the author underemphasizes the degree to which Hitler was, by this time, at least intermittently, a raving lunatic.

Mr. Lukacs concedes the impossibility of discerning the sources of Hitler's genocidal hatred of Jews and of his propensity to hate generally, and graciously spares the reader excessive psychoanalytical speculation.

Lukacs rightly credits Hitler with inspiring and almost demiurgic powers of will, and debunks the notion that he had an exclusively apocalyptic view of Germany's future. A little more challenging is the notion that Hitler offered the reasoned critique of the July 20 plotters that they had no idea of what to do after they had killed him and that reports of the barbarity of his vengeance are exaggerated. (Realistically or not, from Rommel and Canaris down, they intended to surrender in the west and make peace in the east and shut down the death camps.)

In his brilliant survey of the range of German historical treatment of Hitler, the author is perhaps a little too indulgent of those who credit Hitler with unintended decolonization, particularly the creation of Israel and the rise of pallid despots like Perón.

And perhaps the demarcation of the line between Hitler's legitimate continuation of Bismarck and respectable German nationalism and his evil perversion of them could have been more clear.

Withal this is a masterly, absorbing, and succinct study that pulls together an immense volume of conflicting historical interpretation and offers important insights into current German intellectual trends. On balance, it is persuasive, somewhat reassuring, and very necessary.

*Yale University Press (U.K.), threatened by a lawsuit from David Irving, Holocaust denier (or at least of Hitler's responsibility for the Holocaust), declined to publish Lukacs's book in the United Kingdom until I gave them an indemnity for any costs of a lawsuit, as long as it was rigorously contested. There was no lawsuit, or any grounds for any.*

John Lukacs, *The Hitler of History* (Alfred A. Knopf, 1998).

# *KISSINGER,*
# BY NIALL FERGUSON

*The New Criterion*, November 2015

There is no doubt that Niall Ferguson's *Kissinger* is a brilliant book by an outstanding historian about a great and durably interesting statesman, who is also a distinguished historian and gifted strategic thinker. Niall Ferguson has produced the first volume of a commissioned work that is intended by the subject and the author to be definitive. The author has done the necessary to establish his impartiality and has made very extensive use of the immense archives that Henry Kissinger has opened to him. And the author has gone to admirable lengths (even by his always meticulous professional standards) to read very widely in background areas relevant to Henry Kissinger's Jewish and German origins and has interviewed in depth a great many of the subject's acquaintances in the forty-four formative years before he ascended to great offices of state.

There have been a number of other talented secretaries of state, including James Monroe, John Quincy Adams, Daniel Webster, William H. Seward, John Hay, Henry L. Stimson, General Marshall, Dean Acheson, George Shultz, and James Baker. And there have been many extremely prominent Americans whose careers included, but did not reach their peak of success in, that office, including Thomas Jefferson, James Madison, Henry Clay, John C. Calhoun, James G. Blaine,

William Jennings Bryan, Charles Evans Hughes, Colin Powell, and Hillary Clinton. But none of them have attracted as much or as intense an interest for their strategic precepts, historical and strategic writings, or foreign policy execution as Henry Kissinger.

I have the distinction of having been a good friend of the subject for more than thirty years (and a cordial acquaintance of the author for almost as long), and I have read and even written a good deal about Henry Kissinger and reviewed most of his career with him, though not very systematically. But it was a revelation to read how astonishingly quickly and almost effortlessly he brushed aside the handicap of his status as an immigrant with very limited means and no natural entrée to the higher echelons of American society. He turned each step of his career into a startling and original upward movement and success. From the Jewish community of two thousand in the rather nondescript Bavarian city of Fürth, his family departed Germany (after lengthy formal processing, including by the Gestapo) shortly before the infamous pogroms of Kristallnacht in 1938, and, after a stopover with relatives in England, arrived in comfort in New York on the elegant and popular liner *Île de France* in September 1938. An American cousin of Mrs. Kissinger had promised that they would not burden the country financially. His parents resided thereafter, to the ends of their long lives, in a modest apartment on the Upper West Side of Manhattan, and Henry worked in a shaving brush factory on Fifteenth Street while attending a local school. He went to City College and then was drafted into the U.S. Army in 1942. After quite rigorous training in South Carolina and Louisiana and a stint studying engineering in Pennsylvania under an armed forces education advancement program, he was assigned to the 84th "Railsplitters" infantry division and shipped back to Europe and into combat in Germany, starting in November 1944.

He has never made the least attempt to dramatize either his memories of the first five years of the Third Reich, which his parents, unlike many relatives, presciently departed just in time, nor his distinguished service in action, for which he was quickly promoted from private to staff sergeant, and from which he naturally joined the U.S. occupation denazification program as a member of the army Intelligence Corps. At the age of twenty-two, he was effectively the military governor of

Bensheim, a pleasant Hessian town of about 20,000, and was very effective, but judicious, in identifying and removing Nazi officials without offending the proverbial reasonable German. He has always denied that he was particularly traumatized by the Nazi terror that drove his family from their homeland, or that he was overly emotionally reflective about his swift return as an official in the army of the avenging occupying power to which they had fled just six years before.

From the earliest postwar days, he saw the emerging complexities of German public opinion and the subtleties of navigating among the far left in Germany, the numerous former Nazi sympathizers, those who would seek German reunification and neutrality or even "Finlandization" opposite the U.S.S.R., and those who could be rallied as the vanguard of a new and respectable German federal democracy to the Western Allies and as a barrier to Russian advances to the West. (The zones of occupation got the Russians in one place to a hundred miles from the Rhine. These were agreed by the European Advisory Commission, where the British voted with the Russians, as Roosevelt didn't want a demarcation of occupation zones, believing, correctly, that once the Western Allies had crossed the Rhine, they would move very quickly, as the Germans would fight fiercely in the east but surrender quickly in the west to put their defeated country in the hands of its more civilized enemies. Ferguson seems to buy into parts of the Yalta myth and imagines that these zones were agreed to at that conference.) Kissinger had read and even seen enough European history to know that Germany was the strongest power in Europe and that that was why Richelieu had sought its fragmentation in the Thirty Years War (posthumously successfully at Westphalia) and why Napoleon and Metternich had continued that policy through and after the Napoleonic Wars.

Kissinger gained entry into Harvard under Roosevelt's GI Bill of Rights. His graduate thesis was an astonishingly recondite philosophical treatise titled *The Meaning of History*, nearly 100,000 words, that summarized the apposite thoughts of dozens of great cultural figures, from Homer to Sartre and Bertrand Russell. His doctoral thesis in 1954 was the basis of his extraordinarily perceptive and successful book *A World Restored: Metternich, Castlereagh and the Problems of Peace, 1812–1822*, about the political reconstruction of Europe after the French

Revolutionary and Napoleonic Wars. He started a successor volume, on Bismarck, which he has not completed. In writing about Metternich, he described the ingenuity and tenacity deployed to keep the ramshackle and polyglot fraud of the Austrian Empire going, while keeping Germany divided; as for Bismarck, Kissinger saluted the achievement of the creation of the German Empire, though recognizing its flaw: it could only prevent the coalescence of the principal powers surrounding it – France, Russia, and Great Britain – if the quality of Bismarck's statesmanship could be continued by his successors. This was impossible, and the result was the catastrophic hecatombs provoked by the hyperactive and neurotic, childlike Emperor Wilhelm II and the sometimes brilliant but psychotic and wicked Adolf Hitler. From the first days after the Second World War, Kissinger was considering how Western Europe could be stabilized in alliance with the United States, Russia kept out of Western Europe, and the majority of Germans persuaded to keep their nerve and stay in the West, though divided, and resist the call of disarmed, neutral reunification. He was an early critic of George Kennan's concept of "containment" of international communism as insufficiently purposeful.

Henry Kissinger graduated tenuously onto the Harvard faculty with a Rockefeller Foundation grant that enabled him to be a research fellow. With his customary energy, he set up an annual international affairs seminar and a thoughtful magazine, *Confluence*, and attracted a great range of distinguished participants and contributors. Even eminent people who declined his invitations, from Albert Camus to Richard Nixon, were interesting correspondents who became aware of this young academic who was only in his early thirties when Camus died and Nixon was cranking up to run for president for the first time. He became an associate professor and was practically the first person of any intellectual seriousness – despite the presence in the serried ranks of the Democratic Party of people knowledgeable about foreign policy (including the defeated presidential nominee Adlai Stevenson and Kissinger's Harvard friend Arthur Schlesinger) – to suggest real alternatives to the Eisenhower–Dulles defence posture of reduced ground forces after Korea, enhanced nuclear forces ("more bang for the buck"), and "brinkmanship," with its accompanying threat of "massive retaliation" – i.e., nuclear response – for almost any Soviet or Chinese provocation. Though Eisenhower started the de-escalation of the Cold War with "Atoms for Peace" and Open Skies (reciprocal permitted aerial reconnaissance), he was so averse to involvement in enervating conventional wars around the perimeter of superpower areas of influence, such as Korea, that he spent the 1950s threatening the major communist powers with utter destruction, as the United States retained a large lead in deliverable hydrogen bombs and warheads.

Kissinger's *Nuclear Weapons and Foreign Policy*, published in 1957, became instantly famous and widely discussed. The president gave it to his rather belligerent secretary of state, John Foster Dulles, with the commendation that the author could be right. This was again an astonishing position of influence for a thirty-three-year-old Jewish German immigrant. Kissinger's suggestion was that there be an intermediate stage between inadequate conventional response to the overlarge Red Army and a full nuclear assault. This was the use of short-range tactical nuclear weapons that would restrain the blast area, not compel maximum counterstrikes, and would also compensate for Soviet conventional superiority in Central Europe (and potentially opposite the Asian communists). There were critics who claimed that it would inevitably lead to maximum nuclear exchanges, and there was much agitation in German political, intellectual, and media circles, with which Kissinger quickly developed and retained his familiarity, that the superpowers meant to settle any disputes by killing all the Germans and a few neighbours, but not significant numbers of each other. And it was becoming more difficult to make the point in either part of Germany that German division and vulnerability were the consequences of profound German strategic and moral misjudgments in the recent past.

It is hard to recall it now, but in the late 1950s it was widely believed that the U.S.S.R. was gaining economically on the United States, that the decolonized world would tend naturally to side with the communist powers over the West, and that a "missile gap" was developing in the Soviets' favour over the United States. These beliefs were reinforced by the Sputnik launch and the contemporaneous failure of the first attempted U.S. satellite launch. (There was no excuse for Eisenhower, one of the world's most authoritative militarists, to tolerate the currency of this myth, as he had certainly maintained American deterrent strength, as was revealed eventually by his successor, John F. Kennedy, after he had exploited the "missile gap" politically.) When Vice-President Richard Nixon lost very narrowly, and in fact questionably, to Kennedy, the president-elect ransacked Harvard, of which he was an alumnus, to fill his administration. Kissinger had by this time become a paid adviser, though he retained substantial independence, to the governor of New York, Nelson Rockefeller. McGeorge Bundy, Kissinger's former department head and cordial colleague, retained him on Kennedy's behalf as an adviser on European and strategic matters generally, but he was kept at a distance by Bundy. It all reminded Kissinger of the academic politics he was trying to escape. Kissinger did not believe that Kennedy's response to the building of the Berlin Wall ("the anti-fascist defence barrier," as the Russians called it) was adequate, and he shared the concerns of the West German chancellor, Konrad Adenauer, that the new administration would not do anything serious to preserve the dream of German unification, and of the French president, Charles de Gaulle, that the Americans were not serious about defending Western Europe at all, a view de Gaulle promoted to enhance French influence in Europe.

These sentiments were aggravated by the Cuban Missile Crisis, which Kennedy successfully represented as a triumph by withholding the fact that the United States pledged to withdraw already-deployed U.S. missiles in Turkey and Italy, as well as giving a pledge not to invade Cuba, both strategic retreats for the West. Kissinger agreed with de Gaulle that Kennedy should have been stronger in both instances, and he was in some agreement with de Gaulle's proposal for a senior tier of the United States, France, and Britain in NATO, though he thought Germany and a rotating fifth member would have to be added. Kissinger also agreed with de Gaulle (whom he did not meet for another decade) that the Kennedy proposal for a Multilateral or Atlantic Nuclear Force, accompanied by endless demands from Washington for increased European conventional forces, was bound to drive France, and possibly Germany as well, toward the Russians, since it was really just an effort to put Anglo-French nuclear forces under American command through NATO. Kissinger made his views known very ingeniously through an endless series of imaginative and persuasive articles in learned journals and op-ed pieces, through his German and French intellectual and military contacts, and through speeches by Rockefeller, who was vying for the leadership of the out-of-office Republicans with Nixon and Senator Barry Goldwater.

It was another milestone for Kissinger, still in his thirties, to have become such a renowned strategic authority. As the Kennedy and succeeding Johnson administrations descended further into Vietnam, Kissinger visited there three times and became an early authority on the failings of American policy. He saw that the war was not properly supported by Congress or the public and was undertaken without real allies except South Korea. He also realized that the Pentagon had no idea how to conduct a guerrilla war and that not only was there no plan to cut off supplies and reinforcements from the North, there had in fact been none since the Laos Neutrality Agreement of 1962, which turned much of that country into what became known as the Ho Chi Minh Trail. Kissinger, like Nixon, had opposed the Laos giveaway. Kissinger also headed an astounding semi-private-sector peace negotiation, via two prominent French communists, with Ho Chi Minh personally. Kissinger clung to these fruitless negotiations long after it should have been clear that Hanoi was not dealing in good faith. Ho was in fact just trying to lull the Americans prior to the massive Tet Offensive in early 1968.

Ferguson goes to great lengths to debunk the theory that Kissinger had anything to do with an attempt by the Nixon campaign to arouse Saigon's hostility to a Johnson peace initiative. The Nixon archives confirm the same message: both men are victims of a smear campaign, especially the fabrications of two of the most scurrilous myth-makers of recent times, Seymour Hersh and Christopher Hitchens. Lyndon Johnson was trying to throw the election to his vice-president, Hubert Humphrey, with a spurious claim of a peace breakthrough. In tactical terms, the battle between Nixon and Johnson (on behalf of Humphrey) was one of the most egregiously cynical in American history – Nixon had been cheated by the Kennedys in 1960 and was determined that it would not happen again. Kissinger's hard-earned expertise and perspective on Vietnam helped bring him, at the age of forty-four, Nixon's invitation to be National Security Adviser after the narrow Republican election victory in 1968.

Niall Ferguson describes this remarkable progress in a readable, businesslike manner, with heavy but not laborious reliance on original primary material backed by his own wide cultural insight. But there are a few tenuous premises in Ferguson's portrayal of Kissinger as an idealist prior to holding high office and a realist thereafter, as the author tries to square the circle of Kissinger's opinions from academic appreciation of statesmen such as Metternich and Bismarck to his own principles of Western democratic values, somewhat suspiciously meshed, it is implied, with rather vague invocations of Kant, Goethe, and other pillars of traditional German education. Ferguson implies that, as this volume ends, Kissinger was on the verge of making a Faustian bargain that mortgaged principle to power in ways that alienated some of his loyalists and, it can be inferred, may compromise Kissinger's coming achievements. It is certainly true that the contrast is startling between Henry Kissinger's meteoric rise from 1945 to 1968 and the fact that since he left office in 1977 with President Gerald Ford (who is misrepresented in a photo cutline as having been nominated vice-president with Nixon in 1968), Kissinger has rarely been seriously utilized by the succeeding seven presidents. Jimmy Carter was a moralistic naïf, and Ronald Reagan thought Nixon and Kissinger made too many concessions, in Vietnam, arms control, and even the Panama Canal, and (he told me) he had reservations about Kissinger's loyalty to Nixon in office. Kissinger and Nixon were chess players; Ronald Reagan would be a poker player. All were right for their times and all were successful, and they, with Margaret Thatcher, John Paul II, Helmut Kohl, and a few others, won the Cold War. But the Clinton and George W. Bush secretaries of state were inadequate, despite Colin Powell's distinction elsewhere, and Henry Kissinger was still in his prime and would certainly have spared George W. some terrible mistakes. The implication is that he foreshortened his career and compromised himself by his deviousness, and adopted a Bismarckian-Gaullist view for short-term gain, but this is conjecture, a teaser, as this book ends just before the Nixon administration was inaugurated. The complexities of the Nixon–Kissinger relationship are only subtly intimated; the volume ends in Wagnerian mists of foreboding.

There are also a few factual soft points in the ramp-up to volume II. Ferguson not only buys into the fiction that Roosevelt was duped by Stalin (almost a universal misconception among British historians), but also the myth that Nixon was a bad man. Nixon was temperamental, awkward, cynical, and somewhat maladjusted, but he was a courageous, brilliant, and very successful president. He was sandbagged by his enemies, with whom, inexplicably for such a survivor, he almost cooperated in his mishandling of the absurd Watergate affair. Ferguson gives him no credit for quelling the left and attributes the turn of the chaotic tide of the 1960s to mysterious forces of history, as in de Gaulle's astounding rout of the general strike and the *événements* of 1968. Ferguson acknowledges that we don't know if Johnson's stand in Vietnam, mismanaged and ill-considered though it was, helped prevent a communist takeover in Indonesia in 1966, a point that Nixon often made.

Ferguson does think that Vietnam was always a lost cause, but it only was as Johnson conducted it. The Tet Offensive was one of the great victories of U.S. military history, but Johnson had been let down by his commanders and threw in the towel. If instead he had declared impending victory, given the "Silent Majority" speech that Nixon gave in November 1969, announced the Vietnamization of the war and the beginning of irreversible American troop withdrawals, suspended draft calls, followed Eisenhower and MacArthur's advice to cut the Ho Chi Minh Trail by extending the DMZ across Laos, invaded the Cambodian sanctuaries and mined Haiphong Harbour as Nixon later successfully did, he would have been re-elected and the Saigon government would have won within the borders of South Vietnam. Hanoi could not have taken the aerial pounding indefinitely if Johnson had stopped the on-again, off-again attempt to trade bombing pauses for reduced infiltration. As it was, the South defeated the North Vietnamese and Viet Cong in April 1972 in their next big offensive, with no ground assistance, though heavy air support, from the United States. The Vietnam tragedy had many chapters to run and only ended when the Democrats, who had plunged into the war and then deserted Johnson, bloodlessly destroyed Nixon and delivered all Indochina to the Vietnamese communists and the Khmer Rouge.

Some of Niall Ferguson's dramatic allusions (*Waiting for Godot*, *The Mousetrap*, and Aristophanes's *Peace*, including Trygaeus's flight to Mount Olympus on the giant dung beetle), like some of his historical assumptions, are a stretch. But this is a formidable work of scholarship and a riveting lead-up to the extended climax of a great world drama and of the career of a great and unique statesman. The reader gets to its end with regret and with anticipation for the sequel.

Niall Ferguson, *Kissinger* (Penguin Publishing Group, 2015).

# SECTION 9

# MEDIA

The statement below was published in October 1996 in all fifty-nine
of our Canadian daily newspapers, English and French (out of a total
of 105 in the country), in response to a CBC Television news report that
my associates and I were planning to use these newspapers to stampede
Canadians toward arch-conservative public-policy options and annexation to the United States. (Canada was, effectively, federally, a one-
party Liberal state at the time, as the Bloc Québécois, Reform Party,
Progressive Conservatives, and New Democrats divided more or less
equally between them the 60 per cent of the electorate the government
did not have, assuring a large and apparently durable Liberal majority.)

R eaders of this and affiliated newspapers, particularly in the Southam
chain, can be certain that, contrary to the fear that the CBC tried
to incite on Monday and Tuesday of last week, my influence will not
transform these newspapers into propagators of extreme right-wing and
annexationist views.

I declined to cooperate with CBC's *National* background news
program because I was privately and accurately informed that it was
preparing a smear job. I was advised the producers had the same inspiration as frivolous litigants whose action is now pending (and which I
am looking forward to rebutting) that alleges that I constitute, almost
unto myself, a menace to freedom of expression in this country.

The fabricated and orchestrated concern is that I am so extremely
conservative in my views, so overbearing in my methods, and so commercially avaricious, that I will cause our newspapers to come precipitately down market as they assault the readers with extreme opinions.

My associates and I have never held such opinions. Nor have the daily newspapers we have owned in Canada for twenty-seven years ever advocated such a course. No editors of ours have ever retired because of interference from my associates or me.

In thirty years in this industry we have built up one of the largest and highest quality newspaper companies in the world, that has brought some credit to Canada internationally. This has not occurred by recourse to the formula invoked by the CBC.

Our objective is to produce high-quality newspapers at an acceptable level of profit. The Southam company was not, in general, doing this, which is why most circulations were crumbling and a century of retained earnings had evaporated when we bought effective control of it earlier this year after most other Canadian newspaper owners had largely or wholly departed the industry.

Unlike our febrile adversaries in the CBC and the dreary procession of tired and authoritarian leftists trotted through their program, we see no contradiction between quality and profitability.

Unlike them and the agitating special-interest groups with whom they are holding hands (at the unconsulted taxpayers' great expense), we seek no more than a fair hearing for a range of intelligible news, and the clearest possible distinction between reporting and comment.

(I pledge that if I am ever personally associated with so crude and unprofessional an assault on a question of public interest as the CBC's treatment of me last week, I will retire.)

The prospect of the varying of the virtual monopoly the soft left has had on central outlets of information in Canada has presumably motivated them to this fantastic imputation of a conspiracy to a *coup de presse*.

My associates and I have a long track record in this country. We have had our share of controversy but we have never departed the mainstream of Canadian opinion and our names and views do not frighten reasonable people. I suggest that of greater concern is the factional hijacking of the state-owned national television service so that reputable citizens may be arraigned before a televised kangaroo court over their implied lack of patriotism and of socialist ideological fervour.

It is not our sense of moderation and dedication to the best interests of this country that should inspire public vigilance. It is the antics of those whose definition of freedom of expression is the muzzling, intimidation, or defamation of all those who do not share their views.

C.M. Black

October 23, 1996

# PETER NEWMAN

*National Post*, September 6, 2005

I would not normally respond to a critic in a book like this, but
Newman's defamation of my wife and me was so monstrous,
especially to Barbara, it stirred my sense of gallantry. I ignore other
authors who have libeled us, Tom Bower, who is not much known in
Canada, and Bruce Livesey, who is not a very significant writer.

---

Forty-five years ago Peter Newman was an industrious and interesting Ottawa parliamentary journalist. A few years later, he wrote
his first commercially successful book, *Renegade in Power*, about
John Diefenbaker. It was a good read, but it was gossip and deformed
perceptions of Mr. Diefenbaker for decades. His following book,
*Distemper of Our Times*, about Mr. Pearson, established the author's
bipartisan, equal-opportunity love for malicious gossip. In a country
where historical writing had largely been in the hands of rigorous
scholars but turgid writers, such as Donald Creighton (biographer of
Sir John A. Macdonald), Newman seemed to make Canadian contemporary history interesting to Canadians.

The problem with this perception was that what he wrote was not
history. Having written books myself about two of the most famous
U.S. presidents, requiring years of research and over 3,000 footnotes
from serious sources, I can recognize research and its absence. As
the subject of one of his books, I know Newman's technique. He
interviews many people, has researchers scan the media, and uses

every catchy or amusing phrase, regardless of believability, and presents them in a light and sequence that makes his usually destructive case. He then quarrels with his researchers and helpers, who denounce his lack of rigour. In reading hundreds of books and thousands of articles about Franklin D. Roosevelt and Richard Nixon, I encountered scores of examples of this sort of work, more and less accurate, more and less entertainingly written, than Newman's work. But none of them were written by people who garnered their country's highest civilian honour, or were generally taken seriously as writers. Kitty Kelley has yet to win the Presidential Medal of Freedom for her biographies of Frank Sinatra, Elizabeth Taylor, Jacqueline Kennedy Onassis, and others, as well-researched and written as most of Newman's work.

His Canadian establishment books (including the one about me) put on the airs of serious sociology dressed up in lively descriptive writing; but they were really just unsubstantiated gossip and obsequious interviews conducted by a credulous author. Again, Canadians were pleased to read about other Canadians in lively books. But they were reading novels and would have done better to read seriously talented fiction writers like Mordecai Richler, Robertson Davies, or Margaret Atwood. Peter Newman does little work and is not an honest writer.

Thirty years ago, the late Jerry Goodis, a kindly and talented man, wrote of Newman's love for exaggeration, mentioning his reference to then former finance and justice minister John Turner's table at Winston's restaurant as "the Colombey-les-Deux-Églises of Canada." (This was the village in Champagne made famous by General de Gaulle's house, where he patiently waited twelve years for the Fourth Republic to flounder to an end.) If John Turner's banquette at Winston's was Canada's Colombey, why not also Chartwell, Mount Vernon, Monticello, Hyde Park, Corsica, and somewhere across the Rubicon? Or did those banquettes belong to other Canadian politicians? Goodis told me that Newman had never spoken to him after he wrote about that and others of his absurdities.

In his history of the Hudson's Bay Company, Newman wrote that he had seen a frying pan in the upper branches of a tree in Northern Canada that must have been left by an early employee of that company.

The elements in Northern Canada do not leave frying pans in upper branches of trees undisturbed for two hundred years. And trees don't grow that way. Branches remain where they are, the trunk rises and new branches grow above the earlier ones. This was pure invention, for no purpose – a fable. His entire vast written product is littered with such fabrications. He has hacked for so long, he endlessly repeats previous lines as if they were eternally witty. Stockwell Day must be the fifth politician he has called "the best seventeenth-century mind in Ottawa," or some such.

In his autobiography he recounts being strafed by the German air force at Biarritz. I have often been in Biarritz and know some permanent residents. I commissioned some research with the local newspaper and the official history of the city. There is no record of the German air force being active over Biarritz in 1940, and it wasn't a rational military target. Given the author, I am prepared to fear the worst.

In that book, and in his promotion of it, Newman claimed an intimate knowledge of my wife's and my sex lives, with each other and elsewhere. He knows nothing of these subjects; the passages are frequently defamatory. Only a qualified psychotherapist could say what would possess an author who takes himself seriously to write such drivel. His principal comment on my current legal travails has been to regale Canadian television viewers with predictions that I will spend many years being sexually assaulted in U.S. correctional institutions. I think not, but I will leave that one also to the psychotherapists.

When he published his book of unauthorized recordings of twenty-year-old conversations with Brian Mulroney, he timed the publication to coincide with the former prime minister's hospitalization with a serious illness. Mulroney recovered and sued. Newman's publisher (Random House) fired him, and his libel lawyer resigned, for not telling them the truth. He paid all Mulroney's legal costs out of his revenue from the book and contracted not to write about him again. When he reviewed Mulroney's book for *Maclean's*, he had to hand over his entire $5,000 fee to Mulroney as a penalty.

It is well-known that for some years there has been a lack of rapport between Jean Chrétien and me. I have not read his book, and if there are references to me in it, I doubt if they are complimentary or even accurate. But Newman reviewed this book for the *Globe and Mail* so acidulously that its publisher, the gracious and equable Louise Dennys, took a paid advertisement in that newspaper debunking Newman's review.

Newman confers credit on Chrétien for the Clarity Act, which contributed importantly to the resolution of Canada's greatest problem in the preceding thirty years, Quebec separatism. Yet he fails to comment on Chrétien's forty-year battle against the separatists, not from a safe constituency as a parachuted notable, like Pierre Trudeau, but in the trenches of Saint-Maurice. He dismisses Chrétien's ten years as prime minister as a "baleful interregnum" between Mulroney and Stephen Harper.

"Banal" perhaps, but the primary meanings of "baleful" are evil or calamitous or extremely sad. Chrétien's time wasn't baleful and wasn't an interregnum. Newman is often reckless with words, as he is with the truth. In the same review, he assimilates Liberal leadership changes to papal elections. Popes die in office; no Canadian federal Liberal leader has since Laurier. While at large in Roman Church matters, he confuses the Immaculate Conception with the Virgin Birth. In one of his favourite shuffles, he doubtless considers them to be "essentially" the same thing. As is so often the case, he knows nothing about it, and neither is relevant to reviewing a book about Jean Chrétien.

Now seventy-eight, shambling about in his ridiculous sailor's cap, bilious, oily, and at least verbally incontinent, Newman is pitiful, but not at all sympathetic. His repulsiveness may be mitigated by senescence as well as neurosis, if not dementia, but he has become unrelievedly tiresome. Canada and Canadian letters and journalism would benefit from his subsidence. To adapt from the British humour magazine *Private Eye* (about Harold Wilson), "All things bright and beautiful, / All creatures great and small, / Myth-maker Newman has double-crossed them all."

# ANN COULTER,
# JOHN MOORE, AND ME

*National Post*, March 21, 2009

I don't know, and have never heard, left-wing Toronto-based radio host John Moore, who wrote dismissively of Ann Coulter in the *National Post* on March 11. I am told that he has advised his homeward-bound radio listeners that I verged on – or actually committed – crimes for years prior to the persecution I am enduring. He thus goes one better than the Red Queen, who only wanted the sentence and the verdict ahead of the evidence; Mr. Moore prefers them in the absence even of a charge, illustrative of the sort of hypocrisy that conservative author Ann Coulter rightly imputes to a certain strain of liberals.

For now, I will put aside Mr. Moore's comments about me – having been defamed by many more formidable slanderers in the last six years – and turn my attention to Ms. Coulter, a cordial sometime neighbour of mine in Palm Beach, a friend in fact.

We disagree on many political subjects, often in hilariously animated exchanges, and she is a delightful and memorable personality. She is a well-educated lawyer, who clerked for a distinguished judge, has kept her university-era and other old friends, and is much preoccupied these days taking care of her unwell mother.

In his March 11 *Post* article, Mr. Moore wrote of Ms. Coulter with a sanctimony as broad and flat as the Canadian Prairies: "One wondered if even she took herself seriously," in reference to her latest book, *Guilty: Liberal "Victims" and Their Assault on America.*

I can report that she doesn't, particularly, and never did. She is a rational conservative, slightly to the right of Ronald Reagan, and a practising, middle-of-the-road Christian. This puts her within, albeit on the right side of, the American mainstream, a position that perhaps corresponds with Mr. Moore's idea of the Middle Ages.

As she is in a highly competitive business (conservative commentary in a generally conservative country), she has developed some successful promotional techniques. She is the *ne plus ultra* of pulverizing and scandalizing the soft left, implying revisionism about Senator Joseph R. McCarthy and Darwinian evolution, though she believes in due process and is not a creationist. She stakes out a number of positions on other current and philosophical issues which provoke the holders of the conventional liberal wisdom to react like wounded animals, but she really differs only marginally from standard, respectable conservative views on most subjects.

Through her career as a commentator, she has had pies thrown at her while the invited speaker at public occasions, has had glasses of wine poured over her head at supposedly civilized social gatherings, and has endured all manner of boorish outrages from people too obtuse and impenetrably earnest to realize what a grand and successful send-up and put-on much of her career has been.

With her long blond hair, micro-dresses that may incite the prurient to hope for an occasional fleeting glimpse of her underwear, and photographs on her book jackets of her in leather dresses, arms akimbo, like a stern but voluptuous school mistress, she is not, as Mr. Moore wrote, "faux glam." She is eccentric, alluring, and slightly outrageous, with a hint of being a bit gamey.

There are teeming masses of outspoken conservative commentators, but Ann Coulter doesn't fade into their ranks. She has more presence than any, an almost Eleanor Roosevelt matrician accent (a pleasant acoustical contrast with blowhards such as Bill O'Reilly), is wittier than almost all, and is the Rocky Marciano undefeated champion at causing cuckoo birds to debouch violently from the priggish, belligerent minds of liberal Eagle Scouts like John Moore.

She lives well, is an international celebrity, a star among her peers; and to judge from his March 11 article, Mr. Moore is a perfect foil for her. He refers to the "spectacular flame-out of the American right" in the last year; former congressman Tom DeLay is "disgraced"; "Web sites and talk shows . . . inflicted fourteen years of divisive and incompetent rule on America (if you count House majorities)"; the Republican Party is "lobotomized"; and we have reached the nirvana of what Mr. Moore portentously calls "the new age of Obama."

At his end of the kindergarten teeter-totter, Mr. Moore's purposeful little feet are triumphantly on the ground, and Ann and Rush and George W. are in the air, "flailing their limbs" like Kafka's giant bug.

What planet does Mr. Moore live on? U.S. conservatives didn't perish after the rout of Barry Goldwater (1964), nor the Democratic left after the massacre of George McGovern (1972). Ann Coulter was not an uncritical admirer of George W., and publicly preferred Hillary Clinton to John McCain.

Both sides come to bat; a very few politicians make a real difference, and apart from when great principles are at stake, politics is a game – more important and spectacular, especially the way it is played in the United States, than other sports admittedly, but not the sort of morality play that justifies Mr. Moore's epochal platitudes.

Barack Obama defeated the septuagenarian McCain's blunderbuss campaign by only about 6 per cent, following an unpopular Republican president and in the midst of the worst recession in seventy years. What "new age of Obama" is Mr. Moore thinking of: the hecatomb of the Obama designees for high office who didn't get to the ethical finish line; or the attempted cancellation of union elections by secret ballot; or the re-enactment in the AIG bonus fiasco of disturbed children trying to put up a pup tent in the dark? For that matter, did Ann and Rush really win all those elections for the Republicans, and were the last fourteen years in the United States really a public-policy desert? And what was the twice-chosen Bill Clinton – a resident subject of a top-level research project on satyriasis that Ann and Rush thought it would be fun to have in the White House for eight years?

Moreover, why does Mr. Moore conclude that a charge laid by a notoriously partisan Texas prosecutor manages to "disgrace" his target

(Tom DeLay)? I know something about U.S. justice and that is not how it works.

Ann Coulter gets a little carried away at times, but at least she knows how her country functions; she has had to beat off legal persecution as well as liberal food-warriors, and the debauched lurchings of countless zealots of all shadings. She isn't demure, but she has built a good and entertaining business for herself, while selling nearly two million books.

John Moore, to the slight extent I am aware of him, is that stock Canadian figure – the envious voyeur of real personalities. And what has he ever done that was noteworthy, apart from coming last in a 2006 episode of the television quiz show *Jeopardy!* (and emerging with negative winnings)? Isn't he the quintessence of what Canada should be outgrowing: a humourless windbag, the head boy of a righteousness school where everything is as it seems, all things and people are good or bad and political changes are the dawn of paradise or the onset of a new dark age?

People should be judged by their peers, but in the media, as in courts, they rarely are. Ann Coulter will be scandalizing ponderous oafs such as Mr. Moore long after tired, day's-end Toronto motorists have tuned him out.

*John Moore and I have since become quite cordial; while we are frequently opposed on public-policy matters, he is a civilized and convivial man. Acidulous public exchanges often yield such positive results, one of the dividends of public controversy. Former congressman DeLay was completely vindicated.*

# SQUANDERING
# WHAT'S LEFT OF
# THEIR CREDIBILITY

*National Post*, April 10, 2010

---

During the debate over Ann Coulter's recent trip to Canada, there was much commentary about how strident conservatives have developed such large followings in the United States. To many Canadians and Americans, the prominence of Rush Limbaugh and the others is taken as evidence that the United States is becoming a society of extremists, racists, and heartless reactionaries.

That is not, as I wrote last week, a fair description of Ms. Coulter; nor of the other prominent conservatives on the American airwaves – even that tedious Fox News blowhard Bill O'Reilly, the relentlessly partisan Sean Hannity, or Michael Savage, a quasi-learned eccentric whom the British have insanely banned as an undesirable (not that he has the slightest wish to go there).

The large gorilla lurching around the room is that all these people are in successful revolt against the traditional U.S. mainstream national media. Apart from Henry Ford's popularization of the automobile, it has been the most successful American revolution since Paul Revere's ride.

The average American talk-radio devotee or Ann Coulter admirer would probably not articulate in detail the reasons for his disaffection with the traditional media, beyond imputing to them a few attitudes deemed to be unpatriotic, overindulgent of the welfare-dependent and of antagonistic foreigners, and scornful of civic, religious, and cultural traditions embraced by the majority of Americans.

Forty years ago, there were William F. Buckley, an amiable, brilliant, patrician gadfly, personally friendly with the liberal elites, and Paul Harvey, a Chicago traditionalist only slightly to the right of the mainstream of the country. There were a few others, but nothing like the sharply dissentient figures who now evoke and express the anger and disillusionment of tens of millions of otherwise mainly reasonable Americans.

Three contemporary events triggered this schism: Vietnam, Watergate, and the press's self-commendation for its handling of both of them.

In the case of Vietnam, Richard Nixon believed that the South Vietnamese army's victory in the fierce struggles of April and May 1972, with no U.S. ground support but very heavy air support, indicated that a non-communist regime in Saigon might survive if the United States was prepared to enforce the peace agreement with air power in the event of violations. Although the Senate ratified the agreement, it quickly assured that there would be no further significant support of South Vietnam, with the encouragement of the national media. Of course we will never know, but there is a chance that Nixon was correct and that the Saigon government might have survived the fifteen years until international communism collapsed and American air interdiction became insuperably accurate, if the U.S. simply had honoured its pledges, ratified by the Senate, to Saigon.

As Vietnam was being progressively abandoned, Nixon was driven from office over the nonsensical Watergate affair. There were improprieties, and Nixon's handling of the incident was incomprehensibly and uncharacteristically inept. But his presidency had been one of the most successful in the country's history; it is not at all clear that he had committed any illegalities; the actual counts of impeachment were bunk; the extent of the president's national security prerogative has never been constitutionally established; and driving him from office when more proportionate measures were available was not justified.

For their key role in these humiliations, the national media proclaimed themselves the saviours of American democracy, and for decades almost all journalists professed to be investigative journalists, which usually meant malicious myth-makers who were the enemies of almost anyone who was actually trying to accomplish anything. It was unutterably irritating, and millions of Americans knew intuitively that they had been disserved.

Instead of screaming epithets, looking down their professional noses and trying to quarantine and marginalize Rush Limbaugh and his fellow travellers, the traditional media of 2010 should try to regain the public's trust. They could do this. There is certainly plenty to take issue with in what Rush and the rest put in their shop windows every day.

But most of these venerable media outlets have continued to adhere to the techniques that alienated so many of their readers and viewers. In the controversy over abuse of minors by Roman Catholic clergy, the *New York Times*, on March 25, produced a story accusing the present pope of preventing any disciplining of a Wisconsin priest who apparently molested a large number of deaf boys between 1962 and 1974. The *Times* asserted that the clergyman was "never tried or disciplined," and that the effort to do so "came to a sudden halt when he appealed" for leniency to then Cardinal Ratzinger.

In fact, the misconduct led to an absolute prohibition on the priest celebrating any sacraments in public or having any unsupervised access to minors or involvement in education. The Holy See published a direct rebuttal of almost unprecedented force and promptness the next day.

Cardinal Ratzinger changed the procedure in such cases from trials to an administrative process, reopened cases, and imposed accountability throughout the Church and has met with groups of victims. His conduct has been reformist and well within the area of a man doing his best to deal with a very difficult problem, essentially of determining where the Church's belief in the recoverability of human souls from sinful misconduct gives way to the obligation to hand over criminal cases to secular authorities. The Church has made many mistakes, apart from these horrible incidents themselves, and the pope may have made mistakes, but he was doing his best in a very difficult position and there was no hint of the media-imputed official unconcern, or dishonesty.

But for the *New York Times* – the almost unapologetic employer of Walter Duranty, Stalin's most useful idiot in the Western media, a newspaper now surviving financially on a loan shark's lifeline from the less than impeccable Mexican businessman Carlos Slim – for an instant it was like looking for and excitedly producing the Watergate "smoking gun." They reflexively and maliciously threw muck at the pope and elicited a withering rebuke within a few hours. In setting out to destroy the moral authority of the world's premier religious leader, they did savage violence to what was left of their own.

This is the sort of abuse of the public's trust that keeps tens of millions of Americans listening to Rush Limbaugh and Ann Coulter, in addition to their own talents. Earnest Canadian critics of these pundits are attacking a consequence, a symptom, and not so bad a symptom, of what is a very serious problem.

# A HOUSE THAT
# MURDOCH BOUGHT

*War at the Wall Street Journal: Inside the Struggle to Control an American Business Empire, **by Sarah Ellison**; Morning Miracle: Inside the Washington Post, **by David Kindred**; The Kingdom and the Power: Behind the Scenes at the New York Times, **by Gay Talese***

*The National Interest*, November/December 2010

---

These three books are all of the genre of unabashed fascination with broadsheets, written in the implicit and fervently held belief that prominent American newspapers and what happens inside them – the infighting, the breaking of stories, and the principal personalities behind these activities – are vital and interesting. Unfortunately, I don't agree. Having been the controlling shareholder of several of the world's best or best-known newspapers (the London *Daily Telegraph* and *Sunday Telegraph*, *The Spectator*, *The Sydney Morning Herald*, Melbourne's *The Age*, *The Australian Financial Review*, the *National Post* of Canada, the *Jerusalem Post*, the *Chicago Sun-Times*, and scores of others), I can attest that they are really only interesting to those directly concerned with their daily machinations. These books all dote on the minutiae of the three great American newspapers they describe, respectively, the *Wall Street Journal*, the *Washington Post*, and the *New York Times*.

I have known the principal recent players at the head of those three daily print media, including the last two Sulzbergers (Arthur Ochs Sr. and Jr.) to publish the *Times*, as well as Sydney Gruson, a foreign editor turned executive-board member, John Oakes, once of the editorial page, executive editor from 1977 to 1986 Abe Rosenthal, and some additional prominent Timesmen; Rupert Murdoch and his sidekicks at the *Journal*, the group there before Murdoch, led by Peter Kann, the CEO of Dow Jones & Company, as well as his wife, one-time publisher Karen Elliott House; and Kay and Don Graham of the *Washington Post* – former publisher and current CEO, respectively – along with Ben Bradlee, now a vice-president-at-large. There is not one that I disliked, nor any whose intelligence wasn't or isn't evident, but few of them were unusually interesting people to know, have dinner with, or talk to.

Murdoch, because he is probably the most successful media owner in history (so international, innovative, and daring), and has, when he can be loosened up to part with them, a considerable store of astute and mordant aperçus, should be a bottomless storehouse of interest. But he is generally not overly forthcoming, rather monosyllabic, an enigma whose banter is nondescript bourgeois filler delivered in a mid-Pacific accent. His idea of humour is pretty coarse, in the Australian manner, without being very original, or very funny.

Murdoch has no discernible attachments to anyone or anything except the formidable company he has built. His periodic foraging trips for media attention (the oddly hoped-for story where he's made to seem human) usually lead to hilarious fiascos, such as the journalist Michael Wolff's effort at comradely biography combined with sophomoric mind reading, a sort of Charlie Rose approach in *The Man Who Owns the News*: phrases like "Rupert and I thought . . ." abound. Of course no one could possibly have the least interest in what – or if – Wolff thinks, and Wolff couldn't have had any idea what was on Rupert's mind, because Rupert never lets anyone know what he's thinking. Murdoch's centenarian mother was "okay" (about as affectionate as it gets with Rupert); no business associate lasts long, except perhaps Michael Milken as an exotic financial guru, and economist Irwin Stelzer as a random and chatty ersatz muse. Save for Ronald Reagan, Murdoch turned on every politician he ever supported in every country where he has operated; he discarded every loyal lieutenant, two wives, and countless friendly acquaintances, as if he were changing his socks. Murdoch is a great white shark, who mumbles and furrows his brow compulsively, asks questions and listens, and occasionally breaks loose and has pictures taken of himself dressed in groovy black, pushing a baby stroller through Greenwich Village, or has stories written about his supposedly popish-leaning religiosity, published as humanizing touches, much like his orange-dyed hair, in the Sumner Redstone style.

Certainly Murdoch is interesting as a phenomenon, if not as a person, a man who is airtight in his ruthlessness, unlimited in his ambition, with the iron nerves to have bet the company again and again. And although he has had some narrow escapes, he always emerges in fighting form. That story is fascinating, but he has the self-confidence never to try to impress people, is monotonous as a public speaker and unfathomable as a personality in regular conversation. Someone who could grasp and present the scope of Murdoch's talents and ambitions could produce an interesting book, but it would have to be done by acute observation and intuition, and from a bit of altitude, because it is impossible to get anything but a banal smoke screen with occasional ripples of humour out of the man himself. I have long thought that his social philosophy was contained in his cartoon show *The Simpsons*: all politicians and public officials are crooks, and the masses are a vast lumpen proletariat of deluded and exploitable blowhards. Almost all studies of Murdoch, including the reflections on him in Sarah Ellison's book *War at the Wall Street Journal* on his takeover of the paper, where she was a reporter, are mosquito explorations around his shins, which is all he cares to reveal.

Kay Graham, on the other hand, was a very gracious and unpretentious woman. She never tried to disguise that she was the ugly duckling of the *Washington Post's* controlling Meyer family (with her financier, government-official, and publisher father, Eugene, and her intellectual, "harpy," political activist mother, Agnes), only grabbing real control of the paper when her husband abruptly committed suicide – like, as former *Post* journalist David Kindred aptly writes in *Morning Miracle*, Edwin Arlington Robinson's Richard Cory (the rich gentleman who, despite his privilege, takes his own life) – short-circuiting his plans to divorce Kay and replace her with his paramour. And she only became a famous publisher because of the Watergate affair. This was an event of vast importance to the country generally and to the national media, but unfortunately I part company radically from Mr. Kindred's retailing of it as a triumph of the free press.

Graham was an exceedingly honest and generous-minded person, as is her son Don, but that is not to say that they have been epochally interesting or original people either. Ben Bradlee is a noisy macho man, a live wire at a dinner party, indeed pretty entertaining even at a quiet lunch, but he was an energetic and fearless producer of news stories, not a memorable intellectual, or even a very thoughtful champion of the newspaper. It was fun to impeach a president; I suppose it was if you didn't consider the consequences or the iniquity of it.

Former *Times* journalist Gay Talese's study of his then employer, *The Kingdom and the Power*, is a real period piece, a classic like the film *Easy Rider*, and like *Easy Rider*, it is now difficult to see why it ever was a classic. "You do your own thing in your own time. You should be proud," said Peter Fonda to some Latino farmer, conferring the approbation of the age on this generic worthy. The self-importance of the early Sulzbergers is captured clearly, and the leading personalities of the paper in the last fifty years are described accurately, but far too idolatrously. Except for Sydney Gruson, who was a Jewish, Irish, Canadian leprechaun with a startlingly good sense of humour, especially when he was married to Flora Lewis, who spent time at both the *Times* and the *Post*. They slugged it out verbally – Don Rickles and Joan Rivers going at it – but they weren't endlessly interesting either. Abe Rosenthal, shabbily treated by the current Arthur Sulzberger at the end of a distinguished career, was an amiable journeyman, far from the foreign- and public-policy expert he fancied himself to be. Then-journalist James "Scotty" Reston was an opinionated, neat little bantam rooster, whose 1942 book, *Prelude to Victory*, was an exercise in hortatory boosterism, as if he felt that the oratorical efforts of Roosevelt and Churchill were insufficient to rouse the English-speaking peoples to their stern tasks. Various of the other leading Timesmen – managing editor Clifton Daniel, Turner Catledge, the paper's vice-president at the end of his career, and others – were of the Burberry-wearing, clichéd, Second World War correspondent type, of whom Edward R. Murrow was probably the greatest exemplar: affecting a worldliness that vastly exceeded their comprehension of what they were chronicling, as is usually the case with journalists; men who became legends to themselves a bit prematurely. When I first feared that the group had suffered acutely from wartime Londonitis was when Walter Cronkite, another of them, accompanied President Nixon to China in 1972 and declared with great solemnity at the end of the first day of the visit that it was blessed with "a Hitler moon." An arcane elaboration followed that must have caused many viewers to think that Walter had been jet-lagged into insensibility. This was apparently a good moon for the night bombing of Germany in the mid-1940s. The fact was that the war years were the good years to all of them. It was an exciting time, it was history, they had huge audiences and readerships and were wooed with passion by their British hosts, especially the man-starved and, in any case, pretty sexually accessible women of and around the British upper classes. At times, Mr. Churchill's daughter and daughter-in-law were having torrid affairs with Murrow, Lend-Lease administrator Averell Harriman, and the U.S. ambassador, John G. Winant. As I wrote in my biography of Roosevelt, "Mr. Churchill [was] an indulgent father and a full-service ally." No one doubts who were the good guys between Churchillian Britain and Nazi Germany, and these people reported it well, but rather than dashing cavaliers womanizing in humanity's interests in male-denuded wartime Britain, they were self-important pawns of their hosts and forerunners of the naive American droves of tourists in Europe in the 1950s and 1960s – John Gunther and *Time* magazine readers, armed to the teeth with Arthur Frommer's *Europe on 5 Dollars a Day*. For the rest of their long and very media-exposed lives, they always seemed to derive some legitimacy, grandeur, and professional and patriotic pedigree from the fact that they rode the baggage train of General Eisenhower's armies through liberated Europe. I never doubted that it was all newsworthy, an utterly virtuous and brave cause, that it was fun and adventuresome, and that they all performed professionally very capably, but there was always to me something irksome about the airs of the veteran, of the all-knowing witness to diluvian events that these fortunate and physically unthreatened men took upon themselves. This emerges in Talese's book, but in grovelling adherence and respect, not agnosticism, much less dissent.

This is the problem with so much of this writing: it aggrandizes the downright uninteresting power brokers of a dying genre that – most damningly – is slowly collapsing under the weight of its own substandards. Talese opens with an astonishing double-narcissism-mirror trick: the *Times* gives large play to a story that President John F. Kennedy regretted that the paper did not give more attention to an intelligence piece they had published which accurately predicted the sort of Cuban-exile amphibious action that was about to take place at the Bay of Pigs. Its own managing editor, Clifton Daniel, said JFK believed that if the *New York Times* had played the story more strongly, the administration might have abandoned the operation. As retold by the *Times*, the president lamented that the patriotic faction of the paper, which wanted to play down its advance scoop for national security reasons, prevailed over those who wanted to magnify a great reporting coup. The *Times* was to protect the administration from itself and cause the president to change military and strategic policy. This has to be the supreme coruscation of the collective institutional megalomania of an overmighty press. Talese and Daniel have performed a great service in revealing this orgy of self-importance, though not the service they probably expected. It is not unlimitedly flattering to JFK either.

In a jerky to-and-fro, pitching forward and back, Talese takes almost a hundred pages of flashbacks to get us through a twenty-minute prelude to one of Daniel's daily editorial conferences. There are ten pages on the selection of a new Washington bureau chief. No one today could imagine that any of this really matters very much. The *Times* has recommended the losing candidate in seven of the eleven presidential elections since the book was originally published, in 1966. Former *Times* political columnist Tom Wicker reported on the weekend before Richard Nixon's inauguration in 1969 that he might well blow up the world. (He tried to expiate his pathological hostility with a rather favourable biography of Nixon twenty-two years later.) Then-columnist

Reston pronounced Reagan a failure as president in 1984 and predicted he would give up and go back to California like Gene Autry, singing, "Back in the Saddle Again" (rather than be re-elected by forty-nine states and a fifteen-million-vote plurality as he was).

Nothing in this book prepares the reader for the *Times* to write off the $1 billion it invested in the *Boston Globe*, or for the paper to go on life support with a usurious bond issue to Carlos Slim, the Mexican telco king, who is the apogee of the red-in-fang-and-claw corporate buccaneer about whom the *Times* is usually keenly censorious. These are more malleable principles than Talese conditions us to expect. Walter Duranty, the drooling Stalin apologist, and his like-minded successor Harold Denny in the Moscow bureau during the 1930s, are glossed over in two neutral sentences, and the fact that the interminable Arthur Krock, Washington bureau chief for twenty-one years, was in the pay of Joseph Kennedy for much of that time is omitted altogether.

Ms. Ellison describes a frequent occurrence in the newspaper industry, as a long-time enterprise-controlling family splits over the publication's future, supporting this or that manager. In the case of Dow Jones, publisher of the *Wall Street Journal*, the case is one of a keenly interested elder generation of relatives who feel proprietary about the newspaper and the resentful cousins and in-laws who criticize the company's performance and grumble about low dividends. A wealthy outsider arrives (Murdoch), exploiting the split and buying the property. And then there's the fact that Murdoch soon wrote off his $5-billion investment. The grumbling relatives put the conquering lion of tabloid newspapers, television, and film over the barrel even more expensively than had Walter Annenberg when he sold Murdoch *TV Guide* for at least $2 billion more than it was worth. This was the real news, in addition to the fact that for the first time in his long career, Murdoch actually has bought a quality title and raised the quality of it. He added a sports section, an inserted magazine, and made the stories less ashen and more accessible, with no diminution of quality. Perhaps one of the rare examples of news as NEWS.

The same moral-journalist-as-overhyped-pseudo-celebrity-with-little-real-talent is seen over and over again – including at the *Washington*

*Post*. With commendable candour, Mr. Kindred declares himself in his first sentence "a hopeless romantic about newspapers." He is certainly entitled to that, but from my more than forty years in the business, in six countries as an owner and scores of others as publisher-traveller (doing my miniature *New York Times* role of calling on local heads of government and foreign ministers), I am long cured of any such romance. I think that most journalists, like most people, are pleasant enough to meet, but few can write properly, few report thoroughly, many are frustrated at being chroniclers rather than the persons whose deeds and words are reported. As a group, they often claim to be a craft, if not a learned profession, but generally act like an industrial trade union. Mr. Kindred thinks they have great loyalty to the proprietors. Perhaps where there is no competition, this is the case. In Washington, D.C., there is concern for position, pay, and prerogatives that masquerades as loyalty to the status quo. But where there is rivalry, like in London, as the late Lord Rothermere, erstwhile chairman of Associated Newspapers (the *Daily Mail*, the *Mail on Sunday,* and the *Evening Standard*), said to me over dinner, after poaching one of my editors, "They are actors, and we own the theatres. They perform on our stages but don't give a damn about us, and will go elsewhere tomorrow for an extra farthing a week."

Kindred subscribes to the triumphalist school of Bob Woodward evangelism, and thinks that Woodward and Carl Bernstein were the precursors of the great, crusading, truth-seeking reporting that, with Watergate, brought on a golden era of investigative journalism. He does not mention Woodward's book *Veil*, where the author simply invented a hospital-deathbed interview with former CIA director William Casey, nor the wild exaggerations of the Watergate literature that claimed Woodward and Bernstein feared for their physical safety while reporting the crisis. There is some mention of Deep Throat (Mark Felt) but none of the fact that although Nixon suspected Felt was the informant, he insisted on being called as a witness when Felt was charged by the Carter administration with criminally violating the privacy of the Weather Underground urban terrorist organization, as Nixon considered Felt's actions justified by legitimate national security concerns. Nixon was jostled on his way into the court, heckled inside it, and gave extensive exculpatory testimony. His offer of personal financial aid to the defendants was declined, but his strong recommendation to Reagan to pardon Felt and his co-accused, which was followed, went unacknowledged by the beneficiaries – as did Nixon's gift to them of Champagne when they were absolved. Kindred mentions none of this.

He concludes by celebrating that the *Washington Post* "will survive" because of Washingtonpost.com. As a former subscriber to the *Post*, I can attest that their related website is a relatively vigorous effort to keep abreast of other media, but it remains essentially an attempt to attract people into the printed newspaper and to keep the vast overhead of printing and physical distribution viable. The *Post* should survive, but that is not assured by anything we have seen up to now.*** Kindred buys into the theory that newspapers are necessary to expose abuses by police and prosecutors. The fact is that the local and national media have been severely complicit in the shredding of most protections of individual rights, civil liberties, and due process in the Bill of Rights. While the media slept or applauded, the grand jury has become a rubber stamp for prosecutors, and the Fifth, Sixth, and Eighth Amendment guaranties against uncompensated property seizure, and of due process, access to counsel, an impartial jury, prompt justice, and reasonable bail, have been eviscerated. The media have said practically nothing while the United States has pursued an insane and hypocritical War on Drugs, emptied the mental asylums into the prisons, and incarcerated between six to twelve times as many people per capita as Australia, Canada, France, Germany, Japan and the United Kingdom, comparable prosperous and sophisticated democracies. In these areas, the media, national and local, have pandered to public fear of violent crime and have incited the mindless paranoia of the nation and the reactionary authoritarianism of people – like television host Nancy Grace demanding the pre-emptive imprisonment of a great swath of suspects. Mr. Kindred is clearly a sincere idealist, but he seems to have the utmost difficulty recognizing how inadequate the press has been in warning of

---

*** The eventual sale of the *Washington Post* to Jeff Bezos, founder of Amazon, for $250 million, less than 10 per cent of its ostensible value ten years before, undermines David Kindred's optimistic scenario, though it is survival of a kind.

visibly approaching economic and societal dangers. He is so steeped in
the rites of his occupation that he thinks eating in a public place with a
Pulitzer Prize winner is, as he reveals, almost a process of canonization
for the laureate's prandial companion.

These books are fairly accurate accounts of what they describe, but
they constitute a thousand pages of overblown prose about people who
don't deserve the attention, and institutions that are very fallible sacred
cows. The *Times* and *Post* books are essentially snapshots of a moment
in the lives of those properties, where the *Journal* book at least describes
a takeover, albeit a friendly one. But they are exercises in journalistic
narcissism, to the point that the mundane is exalted, the twitches and
ticks of the media leadership are thought implicitly to be newsworthy
and interesting, and the whole function is implied to be in safe hands
and running smoothly, serving the nation and the world conscientiously.
None of that is true.

The media are threatened not only by technological changes but
also by the public's disillusionment with them as a reliable source of
news. In fact, it does go back to Kay Graham and the Watergate affair,
because it was those decades ago that the press began to celebrate itself
while slowly losing the faith of its leadership until there was little left but
angry partisan personalities squawking from rooftops. The *Washington
Post* book's blind and mute acceptance of the Watergate myth makes
the deficiencies of the media's own self-image abundantly clear. The
media's treatment of Vietnam and Watergate was irresponsible, because
a war was needlessly lost and millions of people murdered in Vietnam
and Cambodia and a president unjustly chased from office – no matter, the media riotously continues to celebrate these events as its finest
modern hours.

The *Washington Post* and *New York Times*, in particular, enjoyed a
reverent trust that is such an important part of the Talese and Kindred
books. Their influence, as opposed to their efficacy, as a source of ordinary information and advertising, suffered an almost mortal wound in
public esteem, as did almost all those that urged the desertion of South
Vietnam and led the lynch mob against Richard Nixon, published
the Pentagon Papers, and then, after the destruction of the Nixon
presidency and the defeat of the United States in Vietnam, showered

themselves with awards and claimed credit for the salvation of constitutional democracy.

The myth-making only ended with the Nixon character assassination (in which, it must be said, he effectively and inexplicably participated himself by his mismanagement of the problem). That was preceded by a whitewashing of John F. Kennedy, naturally assisted by the horrible nature of his death and the great dignity with which his wife and family bore the tragedy.

The happy and unthinking foot soldiers of the lore, such as David Kindred, repeat like boot-camp marchers the mantra of the *Washington Post*'s triumph in destroying one of the most successful presidencies in the country's history.

The quality of news reporting has deteriorated steadily for decades. Walter Lippmann really was an icon for whose opinion people waited before deciding how to vote. Scores of millions watched Walter Cronkite administer his friendly moustache (a little like Vichy chief of state Marshal Pétain's for the French, though his was white), with his country-doctor bedside manner of imparting the news, and appreciated the crisp authority with which fellow newscasters Chet Huntley, David Brinkley, Howard K. Smith, Frank Reynolds, and E.P. Morgan acquitted the same task. Now we have pretty female and male talking heads describing freakish but supposedly heartwarming human-interest divertissements and earnestly giving family medical alerts. At the height of the controversy over the proposed downtown mosque in Manhattan, the admirable Diane Sawyer opened with an item about an assault on a Muslim New York taxi driver. This isn't national news at all, and the function of telling the real news has been largely wrenched from the hands that formerly held it.

A large part of the country does not trust the industry now, and the news-delivering credibility of the old media has sharply declined, whether the Kool-Aid-drinking devotees of Washingtonpost.com see it or not.

The news media can regain credibility if they cease to make exaggerated claims of virtue and increasingly focus on quality and fairness of reporting. The tabloidization of network newscasts and the intrusion into comment of strident vulgarizers and ideologues will diminish if the national media moderate their relentless elitist liberalism. Their from-on-high perch, a poor condition in and of itself, creates a reaction that divides the market and popular opinion along stark ideological lines, shrinking the traditional centre. It coarsens and envenoms public discussion, and it will not cease until the public sickens of it and cultural warriors rediscover the virtues of civility. The *New York Times* and the *Washington Post* should mend their ways, not least their endless claims to the status of national redeemers. But they are not traitors and should not be branded as un-American by their accusers.

As print media evolve into a twenty-four-hour product, edited to suit the preferences of individual subscribers, those who play it down the centre, where the majority of Americans always are, and behave professionally, will prevail. Costs will be transferred to the subscriber and reduced to an internet signal as readers print out their own individualized newspapers on more sophisticated home printers than we have now. Exclusive writers who will draw many readers, joined by editing and rewrite teams, will build out under the familiar and respected trademarks of great broadsheets. Somewhere along these lines lies the future.

The romantic nostalgia and hushed reverence of the authors reviewed above will become steadily less relevant to what will be a fierce struggle for survival, though all three of those great titles should be among the living, especially the *Wall Street Journal*, if a man of the seventy-nine-year-old Murdoch's cunning and determination can hang on usefully for another decade.

# THE CRONKITE SYNDROME

*Cronkite,* by Douglas Brinkley

*National Review Online,* July 18, 2012

D ouglas Brinkley's biography of Walter Cronkite tells you all any
sane person would want to know about the subject, and tells it flu-
ently and with rigorous attachment to sources.

It also tells a greater tale, of the ideological and policy uniformity of
the U.S. national media in the sixty-five years following the Second World
War, and of the unselfconscious solidarity of the liberal media-academic
complex, serenely oblivious to the alternative interpretations of their antics
in the Vietnam War and the Watergate affair. There is not the slightest
consideration, in the mind of the author or his subject, that Vietnam
could have been won; that, the war having been started by the Kennedy–
Johnson Democrats, there was any plausible alternative, morally or in
policy terms, to ensuring the swiftest possible defeat of the United States
and a communist takeover of Indochina. Nor, in 667 pages of text, is a
syllable of consideration invested in the possibility that hounding Nixon
from office and tearing the administration apart was anything but an act
of courageous professional munificence and national purification.

Those seeking to discover the wellsprings of the public rage against
the national media that has been the fertile ground from which have
grown Fox News, Rush Limbaugh, Ann Coulter, Hannity, Beck, and
the entire Tea Party, scores of millions of people shaking their fists at

the liberal journalistic-academic and Hollywood and Wall Street establishment, need look no farther than this book.

Walter Cronkite was a personally decent and convivial man, who literally couldn't kill a fly, was kind to his children, generally helpful to juniors, authentically curious about the news, and, in his time, an energetic reporter. And he had humanitarian qualities not widely shared among his soulmates; he credited Richard Nixon with a dignified exit and approved President Ford's pardon of him. The source of his prominence, though Brinkley does not exactly write this, was serendipitous luck: he had the reassuring voice of a country doctor on his house calls, and a moustache that was mature and comforting, not raffish and worrisome like Errol Flynn's or Clark Gable's, much less absurd, like Hitler's. His vast cult of Middle American unaffected worldliness was a scam: he influenced the colour and sequence of stories with his liberal biases, carefully disguised behind his earnest, homely mask.

Further, and I knew him slightly and can attest to this, the dirty little secret about Walter was that he was not intelligent outside his craft. I rented a house near him on Martha's Vineyard one summer and encountered him on the Manhattan circuit a number of times. He could not have been more pleasant and was neither vain nor haughty, but he didn't actually know much about most of what he reported. This was surprising, given his 1950s television program *You Are There*, recreating great historic moments. I remember one of his records of famous speeches and news items from the recorded age in which he explained that after the Munich Conference's abandonment and carve-up of Czechoslovakia, Poland and Hungary seized chunks of the stricken country "as a buffer against Germany." When I knew him well enough, I asked Walter about this, since his explanation was historical and geographic nonsense, and he was puzzled, but surmised he was accommodating Polish-American and Cold War opinion.

When he accompanied President Nixon to China in 1972, he reminisced with fellow correspondents at the end of one of the days that the visit clearly enjoyed "what we called in the war, a Hitler moon." I thought at first that he had flipped. He explained that this meant good light for bombing German targets in 1942–1945, but it still seemed a pretty strange metaphor for a diplomatic visit.

He was, with Edward R. Murrow, Eric Sevareid, Theodore H. White, and others, one of those who implicitly claimed a worldly insight and even a dashing and adventurous past for having seen war as a correspondent and some of the great capitals of the Old World in the extreme winter of combat. Cronkite got closer than most to the action, and liked to wear a military correspondent's uniform. He was a good reporter, but he was only a reporter, until his transmogrification into an allegory of credibility as a newsreader. Throughout his journalistic career he was an avid partisan, though on air he generally made a respectable effort to disguise it. But in his summit days as the CBS News anchorman, he was also a CBS radio opinion-commentator. As Brinkley accommodatingly puts it, "The horror of Nixon's continuation of the Vietnam War obliged Cronkite to become a left-leaning CBS radio editorializer."

Brinkley approvingly remarks that Cronkite used such dissimulations as "It is believed by some people" to attack Nixon, and that Cronkite said, "The fun part of it was taunting Nixon." Cronkite "also attacked the Nixon administration with some regularity for abandoning the poor, race-baiting, and violating the U.S. Constitution." He didn't report that Nixon spared the country the nightmare of court-ordered busing of children around metropolitan areas for school integration; that Nixon, through private-sector district and regional agreements, ended school segregation throughout the country; or that levels of poverty and the crime rate declined appreciably under his administration.

Of course, Cronkite was perfectly entitled to his opinions, and even to express them, as long as they were billed as comment and not just reporting; but, though he was fairly professional, that was not always the case. He owed much to his exposure as a correspondent in General Eisenhower's armies, and his greatest journalistic success was his return with Eisenhower to Normandy twenty years after D-Day; but he objected to Ike's running for president, because he was just "trying to exploit his status as a war hero." So had George Washington, Andrew Jackson, Theodore Roosevelt, and seven other presidents. Cronkite had every right to support Adlai Stevenson but no grounds to consider that a general was ineligible to run for president.

Cronkite was regularly considered as a potential candidate by the Democrats. Robert Kennedy asked him to run for the U.S. Senate from

New York, and he was urged, even on bumper stickers, on George McGovern as a vice-presidential candidate in 1972. Brinkley helpfully volunteers, "What Cronkite most admired about McGovern, why he would have at least considered running on the Democratic ticket, was his conviction that Nixon's mad B-52 strikes against Hanoi and Haiphong, which were killing tens of thousands of North Vietnamese civilians, were reprehensible." They didn't kill large numbers of civilians, and helped end the war. When "Cronkite suspected that the Nixon administration was trying to build support for its latest commitment to the South Vietnamese army," he, ex–war correspondent though he was, ignored the fact that that is what one normally does with allies, and that Nixon completely extracted the United States from the war initiated and largely lost by Walter's Democratic friends, and the South Vietnamese army defeated the communists, with U.S. air support, in April 1972.

Brinkley tells us that "Walter Cronkite forfeited electoral politics to protect the integrity of American journalism." It is mind reading to surmise his motives, though premonitions that McGovern was going to run the most disastrous and incompetent campaign in U.S. history may have figured in them. Given his position, he should not have allowed his name to be bandied about as a political candidate. By his endless subtle attacks on the U.S. effort to salvage a non-communist South Vietnam, Cronkite contributed importantly to the destruction of the integrity of American journalism.

I have been through all this in other columns and places, but the South Vietnamese, with periodically renewed U.S. air support, could have won, after the departure of American land forces, and Cronkite's demand for a negotiated peace after the 1968 Tet Offensive, which he knew to be a call for surrender as Hanoi wouldn't negotiate anything else at that time, misread what happened on the ground in Vietnam, helped sink his friend Lyndon Johnson, and filled Cronkite with a hubristic attachment to defeat in Vietnam that he never reviewed in the light of later positive changes in the course of the war.

Almost all of Watergate is a fraud, with the possible exception of Nixon's (probably unprovable) motives in authorizing payment of legal fees and family expenses for some of the defendants. The whole

Cronkite–Brinkley thesis that "Nixon [was] the anti-hero [and] worked on the dark side of politics" was a monstrous defamation of a capable, though sometimes neurotic, president, and an almost mortal wound to America as a political society. Until liberal America comes to grips with what it did in Vietnam and Watergate, or at least abandons its affectation of moral certitude and exaltation about them, there will be no workable political consensus in America. And barring another Reagan miracle (the avoidance of which was the main reason Brinkley's mentor, Stephen Ambrose, recanted his phobia about Nixon in his verbose three-volume biography of Nixon and lamented the move to impeach him), there will continue to be failed presidents and venal Congresses (of both parties).

Douglas Brinkley was once commissioned to review a book of mine and reviewed me instead, and I will not do the same to him. Readers should be aware that he is as much of a Democratic hack as Cronkite. He is also notoriously discourteous, a contributing editor of the vulgar lowbrow glossy *Vanity Fair,* and one of the chief propagators of the myth of John Kerry as an enlightened war hero altogether imaginable as president. But he is an adequate writer and competent researcher. There's nothing wrong with being a Democrat, but relentless partisanship isn't history. This is an informative life of Walter Cronkite, but more importantly, a demonstration of the size and vigour of the virulent liberal aneurysm that still threatens the American political bloodstream.

*With respect to my* National Review Online *piece posted earlier today, "The Cronkite Syndrome," the following comment was subsequently posted.*

*A Personal Note – July 18, 2012*

*Douglas Brinkley, author of the recent biography of Walter Cronkite, telephoned me to complain that I had wrongly stated in my column this week that he had reviewed my book about Franklin D. Roosevelt. He said that he "loved" my book and had never reviewed a book of mine. I said that I would write an apology at*

*once and ask that it be posted at once, and would find*
*out for his interest and mine who did write the objec-*
*tionable review (in the Los Angeles Times), more of*
*me than of my book, that I had mistakenly assigned to*
*him. I googled appropriately and found a quite obnox-*
*ious review of my book (a joint review of my book and*
*Jon Meacham's interesting book about the relation-*
*ship between Roosevelt and Churchill) from the Los*
*Angeles Times of April 11, 2004. The review is as I*
*described it and is represented as the work of Douglas*
*Brinkley and no one else. If Mr. Brinkley did not write*
*the review, he should require a correction from the L.A.*
*Times, the real writer should be identified, and I will*
*then apologize to Mr. Brinkley. In the meantime, I*
*thank Mr. Brinkley for his kind verbal reflection on my*
*Roosevelt book, so sharply at variance with the review*
*that bears his name.*

And the follow-up.

Douglas Brinkley called back and we sorted out our differences very cordially. He did write the review I mentioned, but I perfectly understand
how he could have forgotten. The matter is now closed.

# THE *TORONTO STAR*'S IDEOLOGICAL SHAKEDOWN OPERATION

*National Post*, December 21, 2013

It is time to infuse Christmas cheer and year-end goodwill into my relations with the disgraced *Toronto Star*. Columnist Rosie DiManno's Monday reply to my column last Saturday was based mainly on unexceptionable quotes from me – so in a sense, I wrote much of her article. I agree with her that Barbara (my wife) and Barbara's former husband (and my dear friend), George Jonas, are certainly better writers than I am. My only objections to what DiManno wrote are that Barbara has not had "five" husbands, that she has never had cosmetic surgery, and that my "remainder-bin biographies of dead people" (most biographies are of dead people) have sold a quarter-million copies and now command high prices on Amazon.

My recollection of our meeting thirteen years ago is different, also.

I recall that she threatened to jump off Christie Blatchford's roof if I didn't hire her, and I said that "that would be an overreaction." And when someone else said she wanted to show if she could fly, I said, "So jump." But it doesn't much matter, and is no basis on which to embitter relations for thirteen years. (My clearer memory of that party is of another female journalist who offered me sexual intercourse in exchange for an interview, an offer I declined with thanks and a commendation for her enterprise.)

Since my television interview with Toronto mayor Rob Ford two weeks ago, Mr. Ford has backpedalled about the controversial claims he then made about *Toronto Star* reporter Daniel Dale's 2012 visit to the periphery of Mr. Ford's property. (During our interview, Mr. Ford had said, "He's taking pictures of little kids. I don't want to say that word, but you start thinking, What's this guy all about?")

Mr. Ford admitted he was only repeating what his neighbour told him he had seen Mr. Dale doing. (This aspect of Mr. Ford's account was the subject of the follow-up questions that DiManno and CBC Radio host Carol Off and other members of the *Star* claque have falsely claimed I did not ask.) Mr. Dale is avenged. The mayor is chastened for his factual liberties and reminded of the virtues of the truth and of moderation in all things. I got a good story. Moreover, I am – as I told the CBC I would be if the mayor's account proved inaccurate, despite my repeated questions – "disappointed" (to quote the chief of police of Toronto on a related subject).

Mr. Dale was traduced, but he was not defamed, by Mr. Ford's comments; and no one said anything about pedophilia except the *Star* and its allies. Ford's cascade of apologies has brought all those who have opined on this subject to the same place.

In another aspect of the Ford controversy, a number of people have angrily sent me copies of a letter that the disgraceful John Honderich – the chair of the board of Torstar Corporation (the *Star*'s owner) and a former *Star* publisher – assumedly approved for distribution to seventy prominent Torontonians, urging them to agitate for the mayor's removal in midterm, and taking them to task as moral outcasts of the community for not joining in the full Christmas revelry of the *Star*'s attempted putsch.

Of course, Honderich has a perfect right to send letters to whomever he chooses – either directly or by means of using *Star* reporter Marco Oved as his sock puppet (as he presumably has done in this case, since it was sent with, and in furtherance of, Honderich's own published editorial). He even has the right to strain the credulity and indulgence of addressees with the sophomoric tocsin "The *Star* is reaching out . . .

This is for the historical record . . . To be clear, we are asking specifically for your views on the mayor's political record, his behaviour and if he remains fit for office. We will be publishing the names and responses of all we contact. If you do not wish to respond, we appreciate if you would tell us why. If we receive no response, we will publish that also." But it is disgraceful behaviour, and Honderich and the *Star* owe an apology to all those whom they attempted to intimidate.

This letter-writing campaign was the sequel to Honderich's editorial comment on December 5 (copies of which were helpfully included with the seventy letters, so as to make clear whose clout, and whose threats, were behind the outreach campaign). In that column, he declared, "So where are Toronto's business, cultural, academic, and moral leaders when it comes to the Rob Ford saga? . . . The silence has been deafening. Where are the well-reasoned op-ed pieces in newspapers? Where are the full-page ads from concerned thought leaders?"

Of course, those slackers! Why aren't they shoring up the *Star*'s collapsing revenues when it is trying to short-circuit the legal process and dump a mayor in the middle of his mandate with no due process or legal formalities – what has become of those tightwad shirker-advertisers?

Honderich continued, "Where are the petitions or outraged interviews? Only one-time Ford ally Denzil Minnan-Wong [a city councillor] showed real leadership in heading the motion to have Ford stripped of his powers." No, he showed rank opportunism in trying to put himself forward as unelected mayor after seconding Honderich's attempted midterm coup.

"And what of the city's top bankers?" he asked. Has Honderich taken complete leave of his senses? Are the country's big banks to wade into this squalid municipal fracas? This is pretty wingy, not unlike Rosie threatening, under the influence of a joint, to jump off the roof of Christie Blatchford's house fifteen years ago if I didn't raid her away from Honderich.

The attack by the mayor's brother on police chief Bill Blair, Honderich wrote, "was downright vicious. . . . And certainly this newspaper has never been so successfully villainized as was done by the Fords on their weekly radio show. For us, there has been a price to pay."

No, I think not: no martyrdom for the *Star* here. And it has been constantly villainized, with good reason, for over a century. For all its inanities, the *Star* can weather the grumpiness of the Ford brothers. In trying to usurp the role of police, courts, and the provincial Parliament to assist in its own effort to depose an elected mayor and replace him with the unfeasible Olivia Chow (whom the *Star* never ceases to trumpet), the newspaper has presumed to chastise civic leaders in every field for not joining in with their corporate egomania.

Of course, the mayor's conduct has been outrageous and unacceptable, and it has not offended the *Star* alone. But the *Star* does not make and break mayors. The people choose mayors, and apart from the voters, only the courts and, in extreme cases, the provincial legislature have the right to deselect them. We will see if the mayor's confessions of wrongdoing and apologies and promises of abstemiousness are sincere. If they are, he deserves the respect due someone who kicks a dangerous and bad habit. In any case, barring new and terribly egregious acts, the voters will decide, not the disgraced posturers and power-seekers of the *Star*.

Honderich concluded his article, "Just imagine if the mayor of New York, Chicago, or Boston had acted like Rob Ford. Can you ever envision the leaders of those cities remaining so silent?" Not since a *Star* reporter misstated the number of graven presidential images on Mount Rushmore in an article about me twenty-one years ago have I felt such an irresistible urge to refresh the *Star's* official memory of a few historic facts.

One of New York's greatest and most popular mayors, James J. Walker, remained in office without a peep from civic leaders until 1932, when then New York governor Franklin D. Roosevelt forced his retirement, and he left the country and did not return for two years until assured that then President Roosevelt would not prosecute him for embezzlement and tax evasion, which he could have done. Boston's James Michael Curley was imprisoned in his fourth term as mayor after being convicted of racketeering, amid a resigned civic quietism (and was pardoned by President Truman). The Democratic Party of Chicago has been in office in Cook County, Illinois, uninterruptedly for eighty-four years, and the Cermak–Kelly–Nash–Arvin–Daley machine has systematically removed to its own profit everything except the copper roofs of the city's churches for its own enrichment, and all manner of local officials have been convicted, as have legions of Chicago judges and other office-holders; and the leaders of all three cities have rarely uttered a pathetic little DiManno-ish squeak of objection. Yet even the righteous Daniel Dale effectively admitted that Rob Ford has saved the city $638 million over four years and is financially unblemished.

A more apt question from Honderich would be what the civic leaders of those cities would have done if they had ever received, on behalf of the chairman of a local third-rate newspaper, such a barefaced attempt at ideological blackmail as Honderich authorized on this occasion, and which severely irritated those who sent it on to me.

It won't fly – any of it. The mayor has been administratively competent but a behavioural embarrassment. The *Star's* attempted coup was a failure, and the hare-brained effort to dragoon civic leaders, bankers, and advertisers into the plot backfired. Rosie's column of reply to me on Monday was so feeble, I take it as an olive branch in the last gasp of the *Star's* failed attempt to purge the city's elected mayor without any due process. I offer some resolutions for 2014.

May the mayor keep on the wagon, stay away from crack, and keep his facts straight. May the *Star* stop trying to be Toronto's nasty nanny. Rosie should keep (all) her feet on the ground, but not by jumping off the roof. I accept her incoherent peace offering and I will not reinitiate hostilities. Merry Christmas to everyone, and baronial seasonal wishes upon the *Star* and all its Pharisees, that they may be shrived, and that grace may be restored to them.

*John Honderich and I have since restored our formerly cordial relations and substantially agree on many public issues, and we both like newspapers. Rob Ford finished his term as mayor without further incident but died prematurely and was widely mourned.*

# TIP OF THE ICEBERG

*National Review Online*, February 11, 2015

N BC anchor Brian Williams, who, after ten years of what Mao Tse-tung condemned as "putting on the airs of the veteran," is in limbo after being exposed as a fraudulent poseur as a war correspondent under fire in Iraq. But this is tokenism, scapegoating; many prominent news commentators are in the entertainment business, as are most politicians, and there is a strong tradition among them of egocentric fabrication. It is implausible, and even bizarre, for the higher-ups at NBC News to become so unctuous about Williams when the whole industry is infested with myth-makers and tendentious partisans who, in their daily reporting, can often be assumed to be taking liberties with the truth whenever you see their lips move.

They take after the politicians about whom they report. The last Democratic presidential candidate who was not caught flat-footed in untruths was the ill-starred trivia question Michael Dukakis (1988). Bill Clinton famously got to the edge of perjury with "It depends upon what the meaning of the word *is* is," and, though an effective president in many ways, was even more of a charming dissembler than most successful politicians. Al Gore claimed to have invented the internet, and much of what he alleged in his environmental film *An Inconvenient Truth*, which made him a Nobel laureate and helped him on his way to becoming a centimillionaire, was a fiction, starting with the imminent disappearance beneath the waves of the island country of Tuvalu, because of melting polar ice. John Kerry, the 2004 nominee, was caught red-handed inventing his status as a hero of the Vietnam swift boats, and the incumbent president's liberties with the facts are too notorious to be recited here. A fine example was last week's speech at the National Prayer Breakfast, where he twice invoked the name of Jesus Christ in pejorative contexts that he would not replicate for the Prophet, and effectively equated Islamic terrorism (not that he is capable yet of putting those words consecutively, or of admitting that there is such a thing) to the Crusades, the Inquisition, slavery, and segregation.

The presumptive 2016 Democratic nominee, Hillary Clinton, was let off very lightly by the media for her barefaced assertion that, as wife of the president, she had had to dodge sniper fire at Sarajevo airport during the Bosnian War. When the news film was produced of her arrival on a placid day with a festively costumed band and curtsying little girls presenting bouquets, she blamed her "misrecollection" on the mischievous distortions of jet lag. Not even so feeble an excuse as that was offered when she told an audience in New Zealand that she was particularly pleased to be there because her parents were so impressed by the conquest of Mount Everest by New Zealander Sir Edmund Hillary that they named her after Sir Edmund. Unfortunately, Sir Edmund scaled the highest mountain in the world to its peak in 1953, almost six years after Mrs. Clinton was christened Hillary (1947).

This is not to suggest that Republicans are always pillars of veracity, but they have more often tended to embarrassing candour or sincere confusion, as in Mitt Romney's lamentation of the 47 per cent of Americans who receive benefits from the government, or John McCain's response to the 2008 financial crisis, which ranged, in that fraught week, from soothingly quoting Herbert Hoover, to rage against greed (an attitude imputed exclusively to the private sector), to demanding the dismissal of the chairman of the SEC and his replacement by, of all bad brainwaves, Andrew Cuomo, to suspending his campaign, such as it was, saying nothing at a White House crisis session, and supporting a Republican economic reignition plan that was rejected by Congress. All in all, George W. Bush's stirring admonition that "the sucker" (i.e., the U.S. economy, not the electorate, though they were for these purposes one and the same) "could go down" was more coherent.

Most often in living memory, Republican presidents have been in the Eisenhower tradition of mangled syntax; it was deliberate obfuscation with Ike, but not with Gerald Ford and the Bushes.

There lingers in public memory a benign nostalgia that previous newsreaders and anchors were people of immense integrity and insight. The most frequent beneficiary of this veneration is Walter Cronkite, who was a very agreeable man who had a reassuring manner. But Walter was only a reporter; he didn't know much history or geography, and his attempts to explain political phenomena were generally banal or simply mistaken. It didn't matter, Walter just made it up (as mentioned in the review of his biography earlier in this section).

His greatest moment as a conscientious journalist is generally taken to be his assertion in Saigon, after the Tet Offensive in 1968, when he returned to his hotel in his Second World War war-correspondent's full kit, including an army helmet, and declared that the United States was losing the Vietnam War. In fact, it had just won one of the great victories in U.S. military history. If President Johnson had had the military instinct of a good commander-in-chief, as Lincoln and Wilson and Franklin D. Roosevelt did, he would have given a speech proclaiming victory and incorporating most of what was in Richard Nixon's Silent Majority speech of twenty-one months later, would have begun withdrawals, and would have been re-elected. Instead, as all the world knows, he folded, and was chased from the White House by Ho Chi Minh, as his theatre commander, General William Westmoreland – who had ignored the advice of Douglas MacArthur and Dwight D. Eisenhower to cut the Ho Chi Minh Trail – asked Johnson for a completely unfeasible further 200,000 draftees. As Nixon demonstrated, contrary to Cronkite's portentous asseveration, the war was still salvageable with a change of commander and strategy.

Walter Cronkite didn't deliberately lie, as Brian Williams and many of these politicians have, but the whole group of prominent American Second World War foreign correspondents – Cronkite, Edward R. Murrow, Eric Sevareid, Theodore White – pretended to a more sophisticated geopolitical worldliness than they possessed as they introduced isolationist America to the world in a hazardously simplistic fashion. Cronkite was energetic, and was present at many events, especially

Anwar Sadat's trip to Jerusalem, but his opinions were never based on anything more than good, old-fashioned, Norman Rockwell American altruism. Ed Murrow's sepulchral smoke-wearied voice did wonders for British war propaganda as he narrated the Blitz from London in 1940. The weightier comments at CBS News were generally left to Eric Sevareid, who claimed to be the heir and protégé of Murrow and Walter Lippmann, the most famous of the pundits. But none of them look very prescient in retrospect. Lippmann thought FDR a lightweight when he was running as a candidate for the White House, then urged him to institute a virtual fascist dictatorship to fight the Depression; never really understood his war policy, though he was an early appreciator of the need to get Charles de Gaulle on board; and he opposed retention of U.S. forces in Europe after the Second World War. Sevareid's departure comments from CBS in 1977 were among the most pompous utterances ever telecast in the United States.

Almost the entire media apparatus was complicit in what amounted to the bloodless assassination of Richard Nixon, albeit that he effectively cooperated with it by bungling the Watergate affair. But that does not excuse the collective self-canonization of the Nixonicides, who confected and transmitted the myth that Nixon assaulted the Constitution, even threatened their physical safety, and was, in all American presidential history, uniquely morally unqualified to be president. There is no real evidence that he committed crimes and there never was any, and there is no doubt that his one full term was one of the most successful in the country's history, which is why he was re-elected by eighteen million votes. And there is particularly no justification for the media's complacent and hypocritical quiescence in the subsequent lies of the chief Watergate assassin, Bob Woodward, which have been detailed elsewhere in this section.

By all means, send Brian Williams packing, but do not imagine that that will preserve or retrieve one jot of the self-shredded credibility of the U.S national media. They went from utter credulity in Vietnam to complete defeatism, crucified the president who got seriously into the war, and then crucified the president who saved the war, and helped deliver Indochina to the North Vietnamese communists and Khmer Rouge, who killed millions in the postwar massacres.

They tried to assimilate Nicaragua and El Salvador to Vietnam; denied at every turn that Reagan's defence build-up and anti-missile defence would produce any progress in arms control or the Cold War; never had the faintest hint that forcing the U.S financial industry into trillions of dollars of undersecured mortgages could lead to trouble; and have conducted a stentorian hallelujah chorus for the most incompetent president since James Buchanan (Obama). Of course, there have been many good newspeople, but the network newscasts are now just social-interest pap and they don't resonate with the country. They betrayed their viewers and listeners, and not with harmless piffle like Williams's invented derring-do; and that is why they have been displaced by social media and by independent commentators like Rush Limbaugh, Laura Ingraham, and Ann Coulter.

What is called for is what has been missing: repentance and integrity. Apart from basic freedoms, the principal criteria of a flourishing democracy are the rule of law and a free and responsible press. Inexplicably, in the United States, both have failed – not completely, to be sure, but both get failing grades. Fortunately, the country itself is overwhelmingly strong and can survive almost anything. It undoubtedly possesses the genius of renewal, and this is probably already under way. But firing Brian Williams is like the wife of the bankrupt socialite (Lionel Barrymore) in the 1933 film *Dinner at Eight* promising to fire the florist.

# RELIGION

## WHY I BECAME
## A ROMAN CATHOLIC

*National Post*, September 29, 2009

My religious upbringing in Toronto was casually Protestant. My family was divided between atheism and agnosticism, and I followed rather unthinkingly and inactively in those paths into my twenties.

When I moved to Quebec in 1966, I was astounded by the omnipresence there of Roman Catholicism. In researching my book about Maurice Duplessis, I steeped myself in the relations of Church and state in traditional Quebec, and interviewed many prominent clergymen. I had had the usual English-Canadian view that the Church had allied itself with reactionary political elements to slow the progress of Quebec and keep it in superstitious retardation.

There certainly had been reactionary, and even racist and quasi-fascist, elements in the Quebec clergy, but they never predominated.

My research revealed that only the Church had sustained the French language in Quebec, the demographic survival of French Canadians, and the prevalence of literacy, provision of health care, and even most capital formation for nearly two centuries after the Battle of the Plains of Abraham in 1759.

Of course, Quebec had been a priest-ridden society, with a great deal of meddlesome, priggish excess, but with all the secularization that has occurred in Quebec, relatively few problems of deviant behaviour have been unearthed or even alleged.

In Quebec as in France, those who persist in the practice of the faith are not the oldest, poorest, or most desperate, though those are there, but a very random group, including elegant young women, evidently successful men, bright students, unselfconscious, curious, and assured. The spiritual edifice of the Church functions obliviously to market share, and there is a common strain of intelligent and hopeful faith, regardless of fashion, age, or economics. Whether in packed and mighty cathedrals like St. Peter's or St. Patrick's (New York), a simple wooden building like the Indian church in Sept-Îles, Quebec, in primitive religious structures in Cameroon, at fashionable resorts like Biarritz, Saint-Jean-Cap-Ferrat, Portofino, or even Palm Beach ("The Lord is my shepherd, even in Palm Beach," as a guest homilist proclaimed some years ago), or in the improvised chapel in my prison as I write, there is a discernible, but almost inexpressible, denominator that unites communicants. I am still impressed by the purposeful spring in the step of people approaching a Catholic Church as the hour of a service peals.

It may be that I was startled to discover this because I was so accustomed from my early years to think of Protestantism, except for the evangelicals, as conditional and tentative, protesting, after all, against the worldliness of Rome. When I first went to Rome, in 1963, I had just read a description of John Updike's, in The New Yorker, of his first visit to St. Peter's, in which he was astounded by the grandeur of the basilica, by its size, solidity, magnificence, architectural genius and collections of high art, that he felt compelled to add his name to thousands of others written in the graffiti in the wall of the curved stairway to the cupola, forty-four storeys above the ground (in a building constructed continuously between the fifteenth and eighteenth centuries). I dimly and roughly remembered Byron's words "Worthiest of God, the holy and the true. . . . Majesty, power, glory, strength, and beauty, all are aisled in this eternal ark of worship undefiled."

It was hard not to see what he meant. The sense of indulgent receptivity of this incomparable building was somehow emphasized by its ostentatious affordability of indifference to those who would come as skeptics or antagonists. My visits to Lourdes and Fatima in the ensuing couple of years revealed concepts of mass faith in the miraculous, scientifically attested to, that were also amazing to a former spiritually slumbering Protestant, and difficult to ignore or discount.

Undoubtedly a formative occasion was my visit to Paul-Émile Cardinal Léger, the very respected former archbishop of Montreal, at his mission and hospital at Yaoundé in the Cameroons, in the summer of 1971. His extraordinary elegance of thought and clarity of expression, and the simplicity of his existence, in contrast to his previous opulence in Montreal (he bought my aunt's house), made a deep impression. I became a vice-president of his foundation and continued in that role for over a decade. Cardinal Léger was one of the most impressive men I have known.

By the time I left Quebec in 1974 and returned to Toronto, I was satisfied that there were spiritual forces in the world, and that it was possible, occasionally and unpredictably, to gain something enlightening and even inspiriting from them. I had lost faith in the non-existence of God, and began to pray in 1970. By 1974, I was praying at the end of each day, developing my own groping formulations of worship.

I read a good deal of the most admired arguments in support of God's existence, especially Aquinas and Newman. When Gerald Emmett Carter became the archbishop of Toronto in 1979, I quickly became an acquaintance, then a friend, and eventually an intimate. He never pressed his religious views or attempted to proselytize. I frequently stopped at his house, in Rosedale, on my way uptown from my office, and we discussed a good many subjects, sometimes ecclesiastical ones, usually over some of his very good claret. These were tumultuous years in my commercial and, at times, personal life also. His counsel was only given when requested and was always wise.

From the early 1970s to the mid-1980s, I approached Rome at a snail's pace, latterly under the gentle and patient instruction of my eminent friend. Having concluded that God existed, I could not seriously entertain the thought of not trying to be in contact with Him. And since I believed in general and prayed to and worshipped Him, it was not long before I wished to do so in some framework, to benefit from accumulated wisdom and traditions and from a community of faith.

It was not especially challenging, given my light Protestant upbringing, to stay in the Christian tradition. From all accounts, Christ appeared to be a divinely inspired person, in traditional parlance, a divine. There was no reason to doubt that he told St. Peter to found a church. I had never much doubted that, whatever its "inanities, fatuities, and compromises" (a quote from Cardinal Léger), the Catholic Church was the premier Christian church.

As a nominal Anglican, I had always had some problems with Henry VIII as a religious leader. The Anglicans, moreover, have never really decided whether they are Protestant or Catholic, only that they "don't Pope," though even that wavers from time to time. Luther, though formidable and righteous, was less appealing to me than both the worldly Romans, tinged with rascality though they were, and the leading papist zealots of the Counter-Reformation.

The serious followers of Calvin, Dr. Knox, and Wesley were, to me, too puritanical, but also too barricaded into ethnic and cultural fastnesses, too much the antithesis of universalism and of the often flawed, yet grand, Roman effort to reconcile the spiritual and the material without corrupting the first and squandering the second. Fanatics are very tiresome, and usually enjoy the fate of Haman in the book of Esther; of Savonarola, Robespierre, Trotsky, Goebbels, and Guevara.

Islam was out of the question; too anti-Western, too identified with the thirteenth-century decline and contemporary belligerency of the Arabs, and the Quran is alarmingly violent, even compared to the Old Testament. Judaism, though close theologically, is more tribal and philosophical than spiritual. And it was the spiritual bait that I sought, that converted me from atheism, that I premeditatedly swallowed, and that prompted me to agitate the line and be reeled in by the Fisher of Souls. I thought it more likely that the 80 per cent of the early Jews who became Christians, starting with Christ, had correctly identified the Messiah than that the proverbially "stiff-necked" rump of continuing Jewry are right still, ostensibly, to be waiting for Him.

It need hardly be said that the Jews are the chosen people of the Old Testament, that they have made a huge contribution to civilization, and that they have been horribly persecuted. But being Jewish today, apart from the orthodox, is more of an exclusive society, and a tradition of oppression and survival, than an accessible faith. The Eastern religions, to the very slight degree that I have studied them, are philosophical guides to living, not frameworks for the existence and purpose of man. In terms of real religious affiliation for me, it was Rome or nothing.

In the spring of 1986, my dear friend, as he had become, Cardinal Carter asked me my religious beliefs. I recited my plodding baby steps on the ladder: there were spiritual aspects to life that were not mere superstition and that constituted or at least evidenced God; that Christ was divinely inspired, had told St. Peter to found a church, and that the legitimate continuator of that church was Roman Catholicism. I desired to be in communion with God, and accepted that the surest means of doing so, though not sure, and not the only one, was as a communicant in the Roman Catholic Church. I believed that miracles occurred, though I couldn't attest to particular ones, that given the wonders of creation and of the infinite, and the imperfections of man, we all properly belonged, frequently, on our knees before an effigy of the Creator or His professed and acclaimed son, and that sincere and concentrated worship could be enlightening. I also, like Chesterton and countless millions of others, wished some method of being "rid of my sins," as I agree with Newman that "our conscience is God speaking within us." I had been availing myself of a dispensation Cardinal Carter had given me to take the Roman Catholic sacraments for five years.

The cardinal replied that I was "at the door," but that the one point I had to embrace if I wished to enter, and without which, all Christianity, he boldly asserted, "is a fraud and a trumpery," was the Resurrection of Christ. If I believed that, I was eligible; if I did not, I wasn't. What he was asking was not unreasonable, and I reflected on it for a few minutes and concluded that since, as defined, I believed in God and in miracles, I could at least suppress doubt sufficiently to meet his criterion. I considered it a little longer to be sure that I wasn't allowing momentum, contemplative fatigue, or my great regard for him to push me over the finish line.

After a silence of perhaps five minutes, I said that I thought I could clear that hurdle. He asked me if I wished to be received. I did, and was, in the chapel in his home a few days later, on June 18, 1986. I have taken the sacraments at least once a week since 1982, and have confessed when I feel sinful. This is not an overly frequent sensation, but when it occurs I can again agree with Cardinal Newman that our consciences are "powerful, peremptory, unargumentative, irrational, minatory and definitive." The strain of trying to ignore or restrain an aroused conscience can be intolerable. Confession and repentance, if sincere, are easier, and more successful.

Though there are many moments of skepticism as matters arise, and the dark nights of the soul that seem to assail almost everyone visit me too, I have never had anything remotely resembling a lapse, nor a sense of forsakenness, even when I was unjustly indicted, convicted, and imprisoned, in a country I formerly much admired. Cardinal Carter and Cardinal Ambrozic consecrated a chapel in my house in 1996 and I use it every day when I am there. My religion is reinforcing, intellectually stimulating, and altogether enjoyable.

# PUSHING THROUGH
# IMPURE WATERS

*National Post*, March 27, 2010

---

The molestation allegations against the Roman Catholic Church not only have horrified all reasonable people, but have been seized upon by the Church's enemies to flay it to perdition. Though it is distressing, I cannot blame them for that. The facts are grim and are compounded by the excruciating reluctance of ecclesiastical authorities to do the obvious and the necessary to put such a scandal behind them.

The Roman Catholic Church flourishes as an organization (as opposed to a faith) only because it is a dictatorship. Once elevated, the pope can speak with the authority of nearly two thousand years, a fairly clear succession of about 270 predecessors, and the canonical jurisdiction to interpret all texts and traditions and impose his will on the clergy. Those who disagree are free to dissent within the Church, lapse or apostacize (as Martin Luther and Henry VIII). In congregational churches, the authorities can be revoked, and can proliferate and fragment, as in Islam, where every mullah is relatively autonomous. In other episcopal churches (Eastern Orthodox, Anglican-Episcopalian, Lutheran), schisms may occur. But the ark of the "one, holy, Catholic and Apostolic Church" of Rome moves on, "timeless and immutable." It will move through and beyond the present squalid controversy, like a great ship pushing through narrow contaminated waters until the last, sordid details from the furthest corner of the Catholic world have been churned up and have assaulted the senses of the just. This is as it should be.

In the vast honeycomb of the Roman Catholic Church, there are 1.2 billion nominal adherents, of whom probably 800 or 900 million consider themselves to be communicants, roughly as many as in all of Islam. After every conceivable enticement has been dangled in front of every possible retroactive complainant to reach into the mists of personal antiquity and produce a grievance, thousands have done so. Many have been frauds, such as the scurrilous allegations that scarred the last • years of the late archbishop of Chicago, Joseph Cardinal Bernardin, before the accuser recanted and repented.

But there have certainly been many thousands of legitimate abuses, perhaps a few scores of thousands, among the many hundreds of thousands of clergy and many hundreds of millions of people entrusted to them at some point. It is the nature of the world that it could scarcely be otherwise. Nor was it otherwise in secular schools or schools associated with other denominations. The lore of Britain's most illustrious schools is full of deviant and sadistic abuse. Winston Churchill, when first lord of the admiralty, spoke of the Royal Navy's traditions of "rum, sodomy, and the lash." Those of us who went through the roughly comparable private schools of Canada remember such conduct there. And these were not underpaid celibate papists reeking of peat, potatoes, and whiskey in the austere, monastic fastness of Ireland, whose very barrenness invites strange thoughts.

What is noteworthy in this torrent of alleged and, in many cases, undoubted abuse in secretive Catholic institutions is not that these ghastly incidents occurred but the unevenness of their occurrence and the clumsiness of the high official responses, and some of the antics of the Church's ancient foes.

Distinguished archbishops such as Paul-Émile Cardinal Léger of Montreal and Emmett Cardinal Carter of Toronto acted preveniently, doing everything possible to separate the most susceptible clergy from temptation, and lest their relevant vows be severely tested. A great archdiocese is an immense administrative challenge and responsibility. Not all occupants of those posts could be inspired choices, and some were not.

These derelictions that have come to light are shameful, disgusting, and outrageous, but they are not especially surprising. All of the modern popes and curial cardinals, and surely most of the bishops, must have had some general awareness of these acts. I suppose it is understandable, but not so easily excusable, that they were not immediately uplifted, as the rest of us are supposed to be, by the possibilities of confession, repentance, and the shriven joy of mending one's ways.

The failure of the popes to order an audit of these matters throughout the Church, to impose a remedial regime, to punish and reward, atone and make restitution pre-emptively of the inevitable arrival of secular law enforcers, busloads of incentivized and spontaneous litigants (many after mnemonic feats of precise, distant recollection), and the teeming assault squads of the media, was unpardonable. It was that worst of acts, both immoral and mistaken.

Only those intimately aware of how the Holy See operates and well-acquainted with the personalities involved could hazard an explanation of why it all went so horribly wrong. The most likely explanation is the dismal, commonplace combination of fear, wilful ignorance, misplaced hopefulness, and arrogance of office. That usually assures that the very last nauseating sinfulnesses will, excruciatingly, emerge.

They will, and should, ooze out, if they are not volunteered in a more orthodox and dignified procedure. Those of us who believe that the Roman Catholic Church is the principal continuer of the church that Christ allegedly asked St. Peter to found are appalled, though not altogether surprised, at its human failings. And we, or at least I, believe that even more than those organizations with a less exalted mission, the Roman Catholic Church must nobly endure, as it so often sternly prescribes, the redemptive mortification its failings sometimes impel.

These frightful dramas not only help cleanse the Church and restore its accessibility to believers. They have the incidental, tactical advantage of inciting the Church's legion enemies. Thus, when the shambling controversialist Christopher Hitchens, a somewhat entertaining and talented provocateur, and even occasionally a useful one (as in his anti-terrorist derring-do), goes forth to war, the mood lightens. In these pages, he last week jumped unticketed aboard the rhetorical bus of Hannah Arendt and wrote, of this immensely scholarly, cultured, conscientious, exquisitely courteous pope, that "Ratzinger himself may be banal, but his whole career has the stench of evil."

We know that the crisis is passing. Prairial is giving way to Thermidor. The mad overreach of the cafe revolutionaries has forfeited their audience. The bourgeoisie is tired of throwing paving stones at the authorities and have lost the energy to topple the mute bronze and stone effigies of great, or at least famous, men. It is time to execute the executioners and then disassemble the guillotines. Terror is become frivolity when Hitchens is wearing its cockade.

In his perplexed belligerency, Hitchens had already set upon Mother Teresa as a crook and a hypocrite. He reminds me of the young Mussolini shouting to his followers, "There is no God! If there is, may he strike me down now! You have five minutes. . . . Time's up, God!" I have often wondered if Il Duce thought of that bravura as, bearded and hiding in a German army uniform among real Wehrmacht evacuees in an open truck, he tried to flee Italy at the end of the war – before he was apprehended and quietly led off the truck, remaining perfectly docile while briefly detained and summarily executed, and was then displayed, hanging upside down over a Milan gas station, his corpse desecrated by the Italian masses who had screamed their adulation of him for twenty years before.

Everyone's time will be up, but not the human spirit's; nor that of its greatest ecclesiastical trustee *per omnia saecula saeculorum*.

# GLOBAL PERSECUTION
# OF CHRISTIANS

*National Review Online*, February 9, 2012

Perhaps the gravest underpublicized atrocity in the world is the persecution of Christians. A comprehensive Pew Forum study last year found that Christians are persecuted in 131 countries containing 70 per cent of the world's population, out of 198 countries in the world (if Palestine, Taiwan, South Sudan, and the Vatican are included). Best estimates are that about 200 million Christians are in communities where they are persecuted. There is not the slightest question of the scale and barbarity of this persecution, and a little of it is adequately publicized. But this highlights the second half of the atrocity: the passivity and blasé indifference of most of the West's media and governments.

It is not generally appreciated that over 100,000 Christians a year are murdered because of their faith. Because Christianity is, by a wide margin, the world's largest religion, the leading religion in the traditionally most advanced areas of the world, and, despite its many fissures, the best organized, largely because of the relatively tight and authoritarian structure of the Roman Catholic Church, the West is not accustomed to thinking of Christians as a minority, much less a persecuted one.

The ratings of offending countries always put North Korea as the worst, followed by Iran, Afghanistan, Saudi Arabia, Somalia, the Maldives, Yemen, Iraq, Uzbekistan, Laos, Pakistan, Sudan, and, farther back but still prominently odious, Libya, Syria, Oman, Egypt, Kuwait, the Palestinian Authority, Vietnam, Cuba, and China. While there is no shortage of incidents in India, where there is serious religious friction between Hindus, Muslims, and Sikhs as well, most offending countries are Islamic or communist.

The reluctance of the leading predominantly Christian countries to speak out against these outrages is remarkable. Many of the delinquent countries are ostensible allies, such as Afghanistan, Saudi Arabia, Iraq, Pakistan, Oman, Egypt, and Kuwait. Obviously, some countries (Afghanistan, Iraq, Somalia, etc.) are in too chaotic a condition to be expected to maintain religious liberties, but Saudi Arabia is a tightly controlled state that in many respects cooperates closely with the United States. It is a joint government of the royal House of Saud with the leadership of the extremist Wahhabi Islamist sect, and while the Saudi government is a functioning ally, especially against any extension of Iranian influence among Shiites in Sunni-led countries such as Bahrain, Saudi Arabia also pays for 95 per cent of externally financed Islamist institutions across the Muslim world. And these are overwhelmingly fundamentalist and virulently hostile to the West and to all non-Islamic religions. Official Saudi media regularly condemn and incite violence against Christians and Jews.

The recent Muslim attacks on Egypt's Christian Copts caused the military to intervene against the Christians, killing dozens of them, which action the military government then blamed on the "inexperience" of the soldiers involved. (Unlimited experience is not required to foretell the consequences of firing automatic weapons and rifles at unarmed demonstrators at point-blank range.)

Many of the outrages are perpetrated by groups the West is conditioned to thinking of as minorities, especially Muslims in general. But the response of the Western secular leaders to these monstrous events has been achingly slow. British prime minister David Cameron did recently promise that there would be no British aid to countries that mistreated religious minorities. But it has become almost a cliché for shabby leaders of underdeveloped countries to attack Christian minorities. Zimbabwe under the infamous Robert Mugabe is one of the latest regimes routinely to attack Christian institutions because of Roman

Catholic, Anglican, and Evangelical criticism of the violence and corruption of his governing ZANU party. South Sudan was the scene of perhaps the vilest and most widespread abuse, as the Muslim Sudanese government killed approximately a million South Sudanese Christians and animists over the last decade or so. (Unfortunately, tribalism in South Sudan, the world's youngest country, has partly replaced the oppression of the Muslim north.) The Palestinians, despite their generations-old and very effective portrayal of themselves as a dispossessed and brutally abused minority, discriminate scandalously against Christians, even though the local Roman Catholic authority for many years, Michel Sabbah, was obsequiously deferential to the terrorist Arafat regime. And the anti-Christian violence in Nigeria has flared up dangerously, though in that country the Christians are almost as numerous as, and more prosperous than, the Muslims, and the frictions are largely on tribal, geographic, and economic as well as sectarian lines.

In general, secular oppression strengthens the Christian churches, a lesson the Chinese are already starting to learn, to their embarrassment. They admit to 80 million Christians in China, though the real number is probably about 120 million, or almost 10 per cent of the country's population. There are about 30 million people combined in the Protestant front organization and the Chinese Catholic Patriotic Association, the state-dominated Catholic "Church" that John Paul II and Benedict XVI have refused to acknowledge (causing the Vatican to continue, with commendable unconcern for diplomatic fashion, to recognize Taiwan as China). This official framework conforms exactly to Napoleon's famous dictum that "of course, the people must have their religion and of course, the state must control it." But as many as 90 million Chinese are in "house churches," semi-secret Christian, mainly Roman Catholic, congregations that evade the overlordship of the communist state and are growing rapidly.

In the twentieth century, the number of Roman Catholics in Africa grew from 1.9 million to 130 million, an advance of over 6,700 per cent (and most of the 1.9 million who started the century were French North Africans). In 1900, one-quarter of the world's Roman Catholics were in the southern hemisphere. If present trends continue, the corresponding total will be three-quarters in 2050.

In the end, the effort to stamp out spirituality, exalt materialism, and reduce religious structures to mere appendages of discredited pagan and atheistic governments that commit the ancient Roman heresy of elevating the incumbent rulers to the status of presumptive deities is bound to fail. Man is not perfectible; men are not gods; and spiritual forces exist. Even horrible crises like the sexual-abuse scandals in the Roman Catholic Church are matters of defective and sinning personnel, not invalidations of the Ark of eternal truths, which is why Roman Catholic Church attendance and recruitment have not been much affected by it.

However great the suffering and oppression inflicted on Christians by godless regimes, the effort won't succeed. Where the problem is religions persecuting other religions, as in the mistreatment of other sects in Islamic countries, the more frequent outcome is the flight of the oppressed, as the Jews and most of the Middle Eastern Christians have shown.

This raises again the troubling indulgence of the persecution of Christianity by the West. It is an Achilles' heel of Western tolerance that it causes the West to hesitate to complain of the conduct of communities regarded in the West as underdogs, even when they are oppressing Christians. Christianity is, after all, the beneficiary of 1,700 years of establishment and dominant market share and the author of no mean sequence of abuses itself, from the Crusades to the Inquisition to Victorian humbug.

That, unfortunately, is not a full explanation of this inattentive lassitude. The shameful truth is that most Western media are atheistic and consider Christianity fundamentally no better than the Muslims who attack and kill Christians and desecrate the moral and religious foundations of the West.

The diverting but insubstantial gadfly Christopher Hitchens was more widely mourned in the Western media than any Christian victim of the Muslims or communists in recent memory. The atheism of most of the Western media and academia has made the West vulnerable to the outrageous allegations of the Muslims that the West is an anthill of infidels. And it has left our political leaders relatively indifferent to Islamic and communist oppression of Christians, as their electorates are underinformed of these atrocities by the media and don't require a robust official response to them. This encourages the Islamists and communists to believe that they may continue to impress their follow-ers and gratify their own ideological and intellectual inferiorities by beating up the local hostages of the brand leader with impunity.

The West must resolve to defend human rights whenever it is not wholly impractical to do so, at least with splendid tongue lashings such as the Holy See regularly administers in these matters. And, where pos-sible, Western society and its governments must insist on adequate pub-licity of these atrocities and appropriate punishment of them.

More generally, we, the whole West, are going to have to come to grips, eventually, with the Enlightenment. A quest for knowledge is not a war with faith; spirituality is not usually an infelicitous amalgam of superstition and philistinism; and moral relativism, taken outside mid-field, leads inexorably both to heresy and to secular wickedness, which are often identical. The failure to grasp this intellectual and philo-sophical nettle for 250 years rests heavily upon us today, and can only become more onerous.

# YES, THE CHRISTIAN WEST

*National Review Online*, July 31, 2013

One of the many problems that arise from the cross-currents in the Middle East and the activities of radical Islamists is that the Western response is almost entirely confined to concerns about terrorism, and, to a degree, to the need to prop up the less odious regimes against the more barbarous and aggressive. These are certainly desirable lines of defence, but they leave some large fields of combat vacant. Militant Islamists endlessly denounce the West as degenerate, morally decrepit, godless, and a vast zone that is bankrupt in terms of the human spirit. Because so much of the secular leadership of the West, and so many of its institutions, are agnostic, and the state religion of the West is, in effect, atheism, we discard in advance one of the strongest cards the West possesses in this contest with deranged and aberrant Islam. Judeo-Christians were the pioneering monotheists, the Jews about 3,500 years ahead of the Christians, and the Christians 600 years ahead of the Muslims.

There are about as many practising Roman Catholics in the world as there are practitioners of Islam, and that is not counting Protestant and Orthodox Christian churches, in which there are hundreds of millions more practising Christians. This is not just a question of market share: the development of Christian theology and religious philosophy and connected art, ramifying into painting, sculpture, and literature, vastly surpasses that of Islam or of any other religion, much less that of any secular creeds that would affect to shoulder the vast body of Judeo-Christian thought and creativity aside. Because our governments, with few exceptions, are so infested – stuffed, in fact – with agnostics, they are complicit in the Islamic campaign to represent the West as a completely corrupted materialist society with no connection to or belief in any spiritual concepts or any moral imperatives. All is relativism and there is nothing that is right or wrong, and even a terrorist attack that massacres the innocent is the expression of frustrations that inevitably are a response to some provocation or shortcoming of the West, and even as we deter or even punish terrorist acts we must contritely mend our ways and pull up our moral socks.

Broadly speaking, in the interests of liberating themselves from any review by ecclesiastical leaders and facilitating the materialization of all values by pitching almost all political questions as matters of pecuniary redistribution, our governments make it easier for the critics of the West to denounce us as a society of no beliefs, in which everything can be bought. While there is no known reason to believe that this bulked heavily in the minds of President Obama and his advisers when they unleashed the spurious and outrageous campaign to impose upon the Roman Catholic Church the obligation of ensuring payment for the contraceptives (as well as sterilizations and inducement of miscarriages) of students and employees of Church-related organizations and institutions, that was an across-the-board win for the enemies of the West. The government of the most powerful Western country went to war against the premier Christian Church and the leadership of the largest religious denomination in the United States. It was Obama's own little Bismarckian *Kulturkampf*, which dismisses religious convictions as part of a partisan "war on women" and promotes and makes believable to the uninformed (who are a majority of the world's Muslims) a version of Western society that is profoundly irreligious.

This reinforces the Islamists' argument that they are without religious rivals, that they alone are aligned with God and are defending godliness against the "corruption on earth" that that murderous lunatic swaddled in violent religiosity, the Ayatollah Khomeini, was always imputing to his opponents. And Islamist fanaticism is also fostered by the ghastly quietism with which Western governments appease the

Islamists and ignore the endless outrages committed against Christians, even more than Jews, in the world. Nothing could better encourage the sense that the West is cowardly, decadent, and heretical than the feeble acquiescence of all of the West except the Vatican in Islamist persecution of Christians in the Middle East. A century ago, Christians still made up 30 per cent of the population of the Middle East, but that number is only about 3 per cent today. In only two years since the toppling of Egypt's President Mubarak, some Egyptian Christians have been publicly crucified, a Coptic church was burned down with no intervention from the new Muslim Brotherhood regime, hundreds of Christian women have been brutally assaulted, and over 100,000 Copts have fled Egypt.

Prior to the overthrow of Saddam Hussein, whom it is difficult to conceive of as a force for religious liberality, there were as many as 1.4 million Christians in Iraq. In recent years, seventy churches have been attacked, nearly a thousand Christians have been murdered, and the Christian population is down to fewer than 200,000. Iraqi Catholic archbishop Bashar Warda says, "We need to bear the cross, but it is becoming heavy." Before the beginning of the present violence in Syria, there were 80,000 Christians in the city of Homs; none remain. About 300,000 Syrian Christians have fled, an inordinate number of the country's refugees, while Western governments, particularly that of the United States, have waffled and prevaricated.

Muammar Gaddafi is even harder to imagine as a champion of religious toleration than was Saddam Hussein, but there were about 100,000 Christians in Libya when the armed struggle to get rid of him began. The Roman Catholic bishop of Benghazi had 10,000 people in his diocese two years ago; now only a few hundred remain. Readers will recall that it was here that the U.S. ambassador and three other officials were murdered in the American consulate, and to maintain the fiction that it wasn't a terrorist incident but rather a spontaneous mass response to the anti-Islamist video of a religious kook in California, Secretary of State Hillary Clinton came on television to assure the Muslim world that the United States had the utmost respect for Islam. It would be hard to imagine anything more skillfully conceived to incite contempt for the United States and the West as a whole, and to inflame Muslim religious chauvinism, than that pathetic and falsely motivated address.

Iran's Assyrian Christian population has fallen from 100,000 in the late 1970s to 15,000 today. The only remaining Christian minister in Pakistan was assassinated in 2011. Over 200,000 Christians have fled the violence in Mali, and even in Lebanon, traditionally a half-Christian country, where to preserve that myth no census has been taken since 1932 and the real Christian share of the population is about a third, there is a steady decline. In 2009, Pope Benedict counselled his Middle Eastern co-religionists in an open-air address at Amman attended by about 40,000 people to persevere, to join with the moderates of other faiths, but to "bear witness against the desecration of women." Israel has never persecuted Christians, although that has not prevented the Palestinian Christian leadership from often being shameless lickspittles of Arafat and his collaborators and successors, but since 1946 the population of Jerusalem has changed from 30,000 Christians, 31,000 Muslims, and 97,000 Jews to 14,000 Christians, 230,000 Muslims, and 460,000 Jews, prompting fears that Jerusalem will become a "Christian Disneyland" where Christians visit but do not reside.

Pope Benedict understood the Islamist threat and often referred to it in moderate and reasonable terms (though that did not prevent many Muslims from imagining that they could silence him by assimilating him to the Danish cartoonist – still, today, under threat of his life – who caricatured the Prophet). The Roman Catholic Church, though it took an unconscionably long time to do so, has finally grasped the nature of the threat against it from Islam, but most Western governments are still appeasing the source of that threat, and the government of the United States, for its own discreditable purposes, is conducting its own, comparatively gentle war on Christianity, instead of embracing it, with all respect for secularism, ecumenism, and non-belief, as the greatest ally it has in its attempt to tame and defang aggressive Islam. Giovanni Cardinal Lajolo said on behalf of the Holy See in 2006: "Islamist countries demand religious rights for their citizens who migrate to other countries, but ignore this principle for non-Muslim immigrants in their own lands." This hypocrisy should be forcibly discouraged.

Stalin infamously asked, "How many divisions has the pope?" The answer was, more than Stalin thought, and more than Stalin's heirs. It is strategic folly, and a betrayal of the nature of our civilization and its history, for American and other Western leaders to attempt to defend against Muslim extremism while conducting an excruciating charade to pretend that the West is un-Christian. Fortunately, that is not true, and the Islamists should know it.

# MAKING SENSE OF
# POPE FRANCIS

*National Review Online*, October 23, 2013

A few weeks ago, there was a brief flurry of mindless enthusiasm in *The Guardian*, one of the Western world's most pathologically biased atheist, socialistic, and anti-American newspapers, over the notion that Pope Francis was abandoning the traditional battlements of Roman Catholicism and fleeing into the theological tall grass, after his interview in August with the editor of the Jesuit publication *La Civiltà Cattolica*. If such a thing happened, *The Guardian* would, as its premature ululations of self-satisfaction indicated, not even commend the Holy See on adopting a more contemporary view, but would gloat and prance and preen as only the British middlebrow left can, because its regular announcements every year or so for most of the last century that the Roman Catholic Church was finally crashing to earth like a gigantic bumblebee were coming true. In such circumstances, *The Guardian* might even, because it understands by osmosis that to many this is the British way, have doffed its flat wool cap with a few condescending words of appreciation of Cardinal Newman, Evelyn Waugh, and one or two other elegant Catholic writers, befuddled stooges of unscientific superstition though they were.

Few scenarios could be more improbable than that *The Guardian* would have got such a story right, and the aroma of a journalistic rat was especially pungent because of the source of this breathlessly imparted aperçu, which seemed to have escaped other sections of the media, even those almost as unwaveringly antagonistic to Rome as *The Guardian*. There were no columns by the giggly twins of the *New York Times*, Maureen Dowd and Gail Collins, reciting for their readers, like rosaries, recollections of their exposure to medieval mental torment in their Catholic youth, nor specials from CNN's Anderson Cooper (or even the inimitable Wolf Blitzer, the hirsute would-be Victor Hugo lookalike from Buffalo) on the decline and fall of the Roman Church.

If the most militantly outspoken of the Church's critics had understood what Pope Francis was saying, they would be less (self-)satisfied. He said that the "Church is the home of all, not a small chapel that can hold only a small group of selected people . . . a nest protecting our mediocrity. The Church needs most . . . the ability to heal wounds . . . nearness, proximity." It is "sometimes locked up in small things, in small-minded rules . . . [and must be] merciful, and take responsibility for the people, like the Good Samaritan. . . . If a homosexual person is of good will and is in search of God, I am no one to judge. . . . When God looks at a gay person, does he endorse the existence of this person with love, or reject and condemn this person? We must always consider the person, the mystery of the human being. God accompanies persons, and we must accompany them, with mercy."

"We cannot insist only on issues related to abortion, gay marriage, and the use of contraceptive methods," he said. The precepts of "the Church are not all equivalent," and we "cannot be obsessed with the transmission of a disjointed multitude of doctrines to be imposed insistently." *The Guardian*, since the decline of its aggressively secular social-Christian views a century ago, has essentially held that Christianity and all religion is bunk (other, perhaps, than those strains of it that became especially vigorous in their condemnation of Christian pre-eminence). And what its glib writers chose to see in Pope Francis's comments and to float as a trial balloon over the *partibus infidelium* of its readership was a papal white flag – a preliminary to surrender, and to the admission that there were no faithful left and that Roman Catholicism was an antiquarian emporium of humbug and hypocrisy where an inordinate number of homosexuals and aged celibates invoked pious flim-flam to misdirect the sexual mores of the thin ranks of the remaining credulous few. The jig was up, the cassock lifted, and there was nothing underneath it.

This interpretation did not hold water or air, and shrivelled, like most *Guardian* opinions on most subjects, and dropped almost silently into the dustbin of opinionated British leftist nonsense, a vessel that has been overflowing since W.E. Gladstone was a backbencher.

What the pope was really saying was that the Roman Catholic Church must not allow its critics to continue to portray it successfully and falsely as obsessed with the vagaries of people's sex lives, and as fanatically and principally preoccupied with such matters; that it must be clear that all human life is sacred, that all people are souls to be cared for and respected, and that it is a reasonable surmise that any plausible characterization of God would not be a deity who approved the creation of life that was condemned to be irredeemably evil from the start and would not be deserving of any consideration. At the same time, the Church must be seen by all, despite these efforts to smear it as a neurotic gaggle of prurient scolds and hypocrites, as really in the business of caring for and about everybody. This is not a new interpretation: it is a new counterattack on those who have said or implied that Roman Catholicism was incompatible with anything except the personal life of eunuchs, and eunuchs who kept their hands to themselves.

Shortly after Francis's election, it was possible to believe that the cardinals had put the wagons in a circle and chosen a pontiff as bulletproof and squeaky clean on questions of molestation in his archdiocese, material self-indulgence, and collusion with reprehensible secular governments as it was humanly possible to be, to conduct a final desperate defence of Catholic tradition in all sex-related matters. But it now appears that what really happened was that the cardinals chose a man more motivated and able than his recent predecessors to make the point that a counsel of perfection in these matters does not exclude any sincere person from the Church, and that such matters are less important than the faith itself and its application in a positive, merciful spirit of Christian tolerance and generosity. It is little wonder that the Western world's atheistic media, after suspending their premature triumphal joy, puzzled out the plain, simple meaning of Francis's words and realized that the pope was not surrendering; he was giving them notice, with exquisite courtesy, that they would be debunked in their effort to sustain their relentless defamation of Catholicism as a ghastly medieval moral torture chamber run by geriatric charlatans.

The disbelief of atheists is understandable and consistent, but their pre-emptive defamation of the world's principal religious institution on false allegations of fetishistic bigotry is not.

# THE SHABBY, SHALLOW WORLD OF THE MILITANT ATHEIST

*National Post*, March 21, 2015

Having spent a very enjoyable two hours in conversation with Dr. John Lennox, professor of mathematics at Oxford University and one of the most rational and persuasive advocates of a Christian theistic view of the world, it has come back to me what a shabby level of mockery and sophistical evasion many of the militant atheists are reduced to, in comparison even with the famous skeptics of earlier times. People like Bernard Shaw, Bertrand Russell, and Sigmund Freud wrote and spoke well, and were more able than is rigorously admissible now to cloak themselves in the inexorable march of science and reason. Their witty if gratuitous disparagements of Christianity were much more effective than the coarse blunderbuss of my late quasi-friendly and frequent adversary Christopher Hitchens.

I met Dr. Lennox in the context of my televised conversations for the Vision TV program *The Zoomer*, and I naturally looked at a number of the many debates Dr. Lennox has had around Britain and the United States with prominent militant atheists, including Richard Dawkins, Peter Singer, and the inevitable Hitchens. Dr. Lennox is one of the world's most eminent mathematicians and he is on the side of those men of science and reason such as Sir Isaac Newton, whose reaction to discoveries of the intellectual and natural wonders of the universe is to be more convinced than they had been before of the existence of a divine intelligence that had created such an intricate and complex mechanism as the universe we are steadily coming to know better.

The current militant atheists: those well-known and learned professionals who not only strongly dispute the existence of God but are hyperactive on the international speaking and debating circuits evangelizing random audiences not only to the non-existence of God – hardly a novel contention nor one any of them puts forth with much originality – but also to the evil and destructiveness of religion itself. Richard Dawkins has often said that "the very idea that we get a moral compass from religion is horrible."

Yet neither he nor his fellow vocal atheistic militants, such as Singer, Stephen Hawking, Jonathan Glover, and Richard Rorty, all formidable academics, can dispute that without some notion of a divine intelligence and its influence on the culture of the world through the various religions (though the principal religions are not interchangeably benign or influential), there would be no serious ethical conceptions. Communities untouched by religious influences have been unalloyed barbarism, whatever the ethical shortcomings of some of those who carried the evangelizing mission among them. Without God, "good" and "evil" are just pallid formulations of like and dislike. As Professor Lennox reminded me, Dostoyevsky, scarcely a naive and superstitiously credulous adherent to ecclesiastical flim-flam, said, "without God, everything is permissible."

This is a large part of the core of the atheist problem, and it is complicated by the vulnerabilities of some of its peppier advocates. Singer sees nothing wrong with bestiality and considers the life of a human child to be less valuable than that of a pig or chimpanzee. It is rather frivolous to raise Hitchens in this company; he was a dissolute controversialist who was a fine writer in his prime, had some enjoyable human qualities and fought to a brave death from cancer, but was a nihilistic gadfly who spent himself prematurely in an unceasing frenzy to *épater les bourgeois*. He entertained, until he became unbearably repetitive, but no one with an IQ in triple figures was shocked by him.

Dawkins almost raves about the extremes that "faith" can drive people to, but was struck dumb like Zachariah in the temple when Lennox pointed out, in a very lengthy debate at the University of Alabama in 2009, that atheism is a faith – clearly one that Dawkins holds and tries to propagate with considerable fervour. In general, something a person believes and can't prove is supported by some measure of faith.

The articulate spokesmen for God's existence accept that they cannot prove their case, though Aquinas, Cardinal Newman, and others make a good balance of probabilities argument (accepting a broad definition of God as a higher creative intelligence). The atheists purport to disprove the theistic case, but they have never got past their inability to dispute that spiritual forces and perceptions exist or that unexplained developments that are in fact miraculous sometimes occur, and they are reduced to imputing falsely to believers the view that anything they can't explain is in the "gap": God's secret work. Of course no serious person espouses anything of the kind and much more frequent is the swift recourse of atheistic scientists to the worm-eaten chestnut that there is a finite amount of knowledge in the world and that every day the lights of pioneering science are leading us closer to a plenitude of knowledge.

In fact, that is not our experience: all great scientific discoveries demonstrate man's genius, but also reveal that the extent of the unknown was greater than had been realized. Freud's discovery that man could not control his subconscious; the discovery of the potential of the atom including for human self-destruction; Galileo, Copernicus, and Kepler's discovery independently of one another that the world revolved around the sun; all expanded the vastness of the unknown still to be explored.

Nor can the atheists ever grapple plausibly with the limits of anything, or with the infinite. They rail against "creation" – but something was created somehow at some point to get us all started. They claim evolution debunks Christianity (though all educated Christians, including Darwin, acknowledge evolution) – but evolution began somewhere. When taxed with the extent of the universe and what is beyond it, most atheists now immerse themselves in diaphanous piffle about a multiverse – but the possible existence of other universes has nothing to do with whether God exists.

There is also in this glorification of the apostolic and enlightening role of science more than a trace of a schismatic priesthood: the ecclesiastics won't lead the world to its meaning but the scientists will. Apart from replicating the worst traits of the dogmatic theologians, it reminds us of the tendency of people to fill an official absence of God with the elevation of man in His place. This was the practice of leading pre-Christian Romans, eventually elevating themselves to the status of gods and compelling public celebration of it. This trait was evident in Robespierre's celebration of "The Supreme Being," whose agent he claimed to be, in the communist pursuit of "the new man" at a cost of the lives of tens of millions of innocents, and in the pagan festivals exalting Adolf Hitler staged by Joseph Goebbels and Albert Speer.

The two sides of this argument are asymmetrical. The atheists can sow doubt well, and spruce up their arguments with Hitchensesque flourishes such as the physical mockery of some prominent clergymen and the disparagement of the religious leadership credentials of Henry VIII and Borgia popes and some of the bouffant-coiffed, mellifluous, and light-fingered televangelists. They rant against the evils of superstition and can still render a fairly stirring paean to the illimitable liberty and potential of the human mind.

Religious practice can certainly be targeted as a pursuit of the hopeful, the faith-based, and the uncertain. But they badly overreach when they attack the intellectual underpinnings of Judeo-Christianity, from the ancient Judaic scholars and the Apostles to Augustine to Aquinas to Newman; deny the existence of any spiritual phenomena at all; debunk the good works and cultural creativity and conservation of the major religions; and deny that the general religious message of trying conscientiously to distinguish right from wrong as a matter of duty and social desirability is the supreme criterion of civilization. The theists defend their basic position fairly easily and only get into heavy weather when they overinvest in the literal truth of all the scriptures – though the evidence for veracity of the New Testament is stronger than the skeptics admit, including of Christ's citations of God himself: "And God said . . ."

It is in the nature of the world that we don't know, but the decline of Christianity is much more of a delusion than God is and even more wishful, and the serious defenders of a divine intelligence such as the delightful John Lennox almost always win the argument, as he did with Dawkins and the rest. There is a long way between these two poles, and agnosticism is a much more rigorous position than the belligerence of the proselytizing atheists, but that is not a stance that stirs serious people to militancy. They have been weighed in the balance and found wanting.

# A REPLY TO MY ATHEIST CRITICS – THEY PROTEST TOO MUCH

*National Post*, March 28, 2015

Not since I have written about cats and dogs has a column of mine in this newspaper stirred such a voluminous and highly charged response as my reflections here last week on John Lennox's success in debates, as a scientific Christian, with the most articulate and learned atheists on the anti-God debating circuit. These exchanges have become almost an itinerant counter-ministry of the media and academia throughout the Western world.

Most messages I have received have been favourable, but the tenor of the unfavourable messages the newspaper and I have received is so generally vitriolic, and often abusive and bigoted, that they incite my return to the subject. Obviously, if I had any problem with people taking exception to what I write, I wouldn't write for publication, and as I have probably been more severely and lengthily defamed than anyone in Canada since Louis Riel (where the calumniators often had truth as a partial defence), I am not bothered by it. None of the abuse was noteworthy and there were only three cyber-assailants who were so unrelievedly uncivil that I asked my IT adviser to ensure that I never received anything from their addresses again.

To refresh memories, I referred last week to the hyperactive atheist zealots who, in Richard Dawkins's words, declare that "the very idea that we get a moral compass from religion is horrible." I wrote that societies uninfluenced by serious considerations of a divine intelligence do not have as advanced and institutionalized notions of ethics, equity, and impartial justice as those that have been; that the atheist militants generally refuse to admit atheism, too, is a faith; that they can't really dispute the existence of spiritual forces in the world, other than by consigning them to the hitherto unknown, or the conjurations of hysterics, the delusional, and charlatans.

I wrote that the atheist advocates still sidle up to the shopworn theory that science will lead us all to a state of total knowledge and self-knowledge and that the theists are in fearful flight from the oncoming juggernaut of knowledge; and that many atheists claim that evolution puts all God theories on the skids. I referred only summarily to the usual and generally rather overworked operatics of the atheists in mocking religious practices and prominent individual clergy and in sprinkling acidulous reflections on the entire history of Christianity, in particular.

The forces of history are claimed to be rolling inexorably toward the 100 per cent triumph of righteous reason and science and the disappearance of all traces of religiosity and theology, apparently after an intellectual assault equivalent to the U.S. Marines' final destruction of the defenders of Iwo Jima by incineration from flame-throwers. Because of the shortcomings of all these lines of attack, I recorded that the most capable and learned advocates of the existence of a divine intelligence in the universe generally prevailed in these debates, although neither side could prove its case. I did not write anything of my own religious beliefs.

Of course, I expected to arouse a hornet's nest among the atheist determinists who always seem personally affronted and threatened by any suggestion that a sane and passably intelligent person could believe one scintilla of any theory that conceded that religious faith and belief are logically defensible. In the letters section of the *National Post*, I was accused of being addicted to a fantasy that "there is a juju in the sky who created our universe," and that all atheists "lack moral and ethical principles." I was taxed with misrepresenting Charles Darwin as a

Christian: he was at times in his life, and to a full age, like many people whose religious views evolve.

I was accused of using the absurd conduct and claims of some atheists as proof of God's existence, and was subjected by direct correspondents to the unutterably irritating sophistry that as Christians are claiming the existence of God, they have to prove it, and that therefore atheists win the argument automatically, because God's existence cannot be objectively and demonstrably proved. I did write that the advocates of God's existence (and mentioned Thomas Aquinas and Cardinal Newman, as well as Professor Lennox) made a better argument for the balance of probabilities on their side than the atheists did on theirs. All three sources were rather cavalierly dismissed by some readers, who clearly (and to say the least) are not their peers. All the other charges against me that I have listed were derived entirely from the disturbed imaginations of my more febrile atheist readers.

The important part of this exchange is the light it sheds on the contemporary atheist mind and the state of our society, where such belligerent enemies of important traditions in our civilization have arisen and seized control of almost all the media and academia. It became overwhelmingly fashionable in the last fifty years to debunk religiosity as stupid, irrelevant, and wilfully ignorant. The particular bugbear was to portray the principal denomination, the Roman Catholic Church, as a coterie of septuagenarian celibates and closet queens scolding the world about their sex lives, as that institution staggered on creaking limbs and with failing sight to its long-appointed extinction, a hollow primitive fraud and retardant to the march of knowledge. These are familiar and even understandable opinions, but it is not easily understandable how people holding them got a stranglehold on the commanding heights of information and education.

The pertinent facts are that spiritual forces are abroad in the world and have widely been identified, even in such statements as Bismarck, whom Pope Pius IX described as "Attila in a helmet," saying that "All a statesman can do is listen for God's footfall and touch the hem of his garment as He passes." Darwin referred to "the Creator" in the second edition of *On the Origin of Species*; Einstein, Napoleon, Shakespeare, and Lincoln all believed in God, and most people believe that there is something beyond the material world we all know. It is not just or reasonable for the atheists endlessly to impute to the believing majority the motives of mass ignorance, the desperate striving of failed lives, the humdrum obtuseness of the bourgeoisie, or the pursuit of psychological security by the avariciously prosperous. Atheists cannot know, as they have not experienced, the expanded intuition that Richelieu, otherwise one of the greatest cynics in the history of Europe, and countless others have found in sincere religious meditation.

The Judeo-Christian message of conscientious behaviour has had an immense impact on Western civilization, and approximately 95 per cent of the clergy of the Christian churches are decent people doing their best. The services of the Catholic Church in particular in conserving civilization through the Dark Ages, producing the Renaissance, and imparting literacy and pastoral and medical care to countless millions of the underprivileged for many centuries, vastly outweigh the damage done by religious intolerance and hypocrisy. We are all sinners and none of us gods. I have always believed that with religion, as with sex, people should inform themselves and decide their own preferences and precepts, be discreet about them, and respect the practices of others unless they are sociopathic or insane. That is what I do as a Christian and also as a former atheist and agnostic, familiar with their attractions also.

The atheists' domination of our centres of learning and information is a great vulnerability in the West: it creates acute resentment and dissent among the more religiously tolerant majority, separates learning and information from the greatest pillar of our civilization's historic development, invites contempt from violently sectarian societies, especially Islamists, and is repugnant to the entire concept of freedom of thought and expression that our universities and free press are supposed to be defending. This is why people like John Lennox, who flatten the marquee atheist tribunes at every encounter, perform such a valuable service. And it must also have something to do with the reaction, like that of roaring and wounded animals, of a distinct minority of my correspondents last week. If God were dead, they would not still be trying, very unconvincingly, to kill Him.

# ATHEISTS RENOUNCE AND ABSTAIN FROM RELIGIONS – THEY DON'T REFORM THEM·

*National Post*, May 16, 2015

I had the pleasure this week of meeting Ayaan Hirsi Ali at a most convivial social occasion, having just read her latest book, *Heretic*. Most readers will be aware that she fled an arranged marriage as a very young Somalian Muslim woman and abandoned her faith, going first to Germany and then to the Netherlands. She began her new life as a factory cleaning lady and rose to be a Dutch member of parliament and a prominent activist for the victims of militant Islam. She is now a fellow at the John F. Kennedy School of Government at Harvard University and the wife of eminent Anglo-American historian Niall Ferguson, and is an elegant, charming and courageous woman.

She states that Islam is "incompatible with modernity," and summarizes that it primarily requires unlimited faith in the existence and sacred authority of God, Allah, and Muhammad his prophet; prayer five times a day; daytime fasting for the whole ninth month of Ramadan; the practice of charity, and, if possible, at least one pilgrimage to Mecca in one's lifetime. Only the first of these is seriously problematical (as opposed to personally inconvenient).

Hirsi Ali's five requirements for reform are revisions of Muhammad's semi-divine and infallible status and literalist reading of the Quran, particularly those allegedly revealed to the Prophet at the launch of his most radical phase in Medina, in the last ten years of his life; the de-emphasis of life after death over the present life; the abandonment of the draconian sharia law derived from the Quran; an end to empowering individuals to enforce that law arbitrarily; and an end to the frequent and capricious recourse to jihad, holy war.

The author's summaries of problems and solutions is plausible, but if her suggestions were enacted, Islam would become just a Golden Rule fellowship; her authority to recommend anything so radical, moreover, suffers for her being not just an apostate but an atheist. This, as I gently suggested to her, is where her heartfelt argument becomes tenuous. Atheists renounce and abstain from religions; they don't reform them.

Her call for a Reformation is easy to misunderstand, as the Christian Reformation was anything but atheistic. It was a peculiar alliance between zealots like Luther, Knox, and Calvin (who were almost as fervent as the Islamists Ms. Hirsi Ali dislikes most), and charlatans like Henry VIII (whom, given her feminist views, she could not seriously admire). The Sunni–Shiite split was dynastic, and not doctrinal like Christian schisms.

Muhammad started out as Jesus Christ spent his whole life, as a preacher, and said that he was a continuator of Abraham, Moses, and Christ himself. He had been only moderately successful at this vocation when, aged fifty-two, he was driven out of Mecca to Medina, transmogrified into a warrior, unlike those he claimed to emulate, and became a great and often very ruthless conqueror.

Allegedly, God Himself dictated the text of the Quran to Muhammad, via that well-travelled messenger the saint and archangel Gabriel. Though this is widely disputed by Islamic scholars not under immediate threat of execution or torture for heresy, it does constitute a sharp contrast with the origins of the Bible. The Quran was propagated as Islam spread, unlike the Bible, which was only gradually composed over centuries following the death of Christ.

While no knowledgeable person would dispute that Christianity has been invoked as an excuse for a good deal of unjustifiable militarism, it is comparatively tolerant and has very rarely claimed the right to extort adherence under pain of death, which is unfortunately rather commonplace in the history and current practices of Islam. As a result of its allegedly divine authorship, the Quran has stressed omnipotence over free will, the moral value of martyrdom, and a vast and ferocious definition of God's will. The author reverts to her experience in the Netherlands to explain that the tendency of the Muslim immigrants to that country to litter and not to dispose properly of garbage, when criticized by the host nationality, was ascribed (with doubtful theological authority) to God's will. Christians pray for God's guidance or intercession; Muslims recite God's alleged words as written in the Quran.

Hirsi Ali says that she is an optimist, essentially because so many of militant Islam's practices are so odious, and because, despite the professed fidelity of most Muslim populations, there are scientifically canvassed majorities in all major Muslim countries that are concerned about Muslim extremism. She does not believe that militant Islam will be sustainable, as she puts it, in the "absence of reason," with its belief that there is no real distinction between secular and canon law, its requirement for endless combat and the death penalty for people of other views, and its reliance on the recruitment of martyrs to acts of terror by fantastically explicit Quranic descriptions of heaven. ("There will be two gardens containing all kinds of trees and delights . . . these places are built of emeralds and jewels. . . . On each bed [there will be] a girl having sweet black eyes. . . . Each believer will be given such strength in the morning as he can cohabitate with them.")

She must be right that ultimately it will be hard to sell what sounds like an upscale bordello advertisement as the word of God. Her conferral on Muhammad of the status of "greatest lawgiver of all time" only holds where Quranic law supersedes all other law, and this departs from the criteria by which that honour has historically been contested by such legislators as Hammurabi, Justinian, Napoleon, and James Madison.

She is skeptical that Islamic regimes will be able to go on maintaining authority with religious police, public executions (with executioners as talkative media personalities), and honour killings conducted in enforcement of family traditions even in liberal non-Muslim countries. She is right, too, that the West is being both unjust and unwise in not responding more strongly to the massacre and lesser harassment of Christians by Muslims (as well as communists) in many countries, and that the tendency of Western liberals to indulge Islamist extremists as wholly unrepresentative has the opposite effect to the one intended. But her perspective is not regard for Christianity but a desire to mobilize the great, if sleepy, power of the traditionally Christian West against those who made her youth miserable and have tormented her ever since.

I think she asks a lot when she calls for Muslim reformers to be accorded the same renown in the West as Alexander Solzhenitsyn or Voltaire – who were, broadly, Westerners calling for reform of the West. For obvious reasons in her own harrowing experience, she exaggerates the threat of Islam to the West. Very few Muslim countries have objectively been successful, and they are not a menace on the scale of Hitler or Stalin, cunning totalitarians at the head of great, militarily powerful, more or less Western nations. Islamist terrorists are a horrible nuisance, but they aren't capable of destroying our civilization and have accomplished almost nothing since the 9/11 (2001) attacks except a few random bombings and shootings. It is not the West that will reform Islam, except in so far as Muslims yield to the temptations of our supposedly decadent mores and folkways, depicted to the Muslim masses on ubiquitous modern media.

But these are relatively minor cavils. She is a remarkable personality and this is an interesting and readable book.

# PERSONAL & GENERAL

This was my statement on giving up Canadian citizenship, an act that was much misunderstood, which I promised at the outset to reverse, and which was caused by Jean Chrétien giving false advice to the Queen, which he and her advisers knew to be false, and by the refusal of the Canadian courts to defend my right as a Canadian citizen not to be discriminated against because I was, like many others, and in my case on the advice of the Chrétien government, a dual citizen. As I wrote, I still expect to resume dual citizenship in the normal course and would have done so by now but for the legal onslaught against me in the United States, assisted by Canadian quislings.

The Court of Appeal of Ontario has sustained the Prime Minister of Canada's notion of dual citizenship. This notion entitles him to diminish the civil rights of a citizen of a foreign country by virtue of the fact that that individual also happens to be a Canadian. The Queen, as chief of state of both countries in this case, understandably cannot choose between the conflicting advice of the British and Canadian prime ministers. I am thus now the only adult, sane, solvent, unincarcerated citizen of the United Kingdom ineligible to receive an honour in that country.

Unfortunately neither the Trial nor Appeal Courts in Ontario referred to my status as a U.K. citizen, one of the principal elements of my legal case, nor did the Court of Appeal judgment deal with the essence of the argument my counsel presented. It made no reference to the undisputed fact that the Canadian government had approved the application of the British government in respect of the honour it wished to confer on me in Britain, prior to the questionably motivated intervention of the Canadian Prime Minister. None of this inspires optimism about the prospects of pursuing the legal option in Canada.

In the circumstances, I am forced to choose between the two nationalities I hold. For a wide range of reasons, citizenship of Canada is not now for me competitive with that of the United Kingdom and the European Union. I moved to renounce my Canadian citizenship several months ago when the Ontario Court of Appeal entered its sixth month of deliberation on a point of law, rather than fact or merits. The adjudication of these matters, if any court in Canada would hear them, would take many more years, with appeals. After eight months the court has largely ignored even the legal point and immunized the Prime Minister from judicial review. I hope that, given the length he has gone to to force this choice upon me, the Prime Minister will not now contest my right to take this logical final step and that we will both be spared the indignity of my litigating to do so.

Having opposed for thirty years precisely the public policies that have caused scores of thousands of educated and talented Canadians to abandon their country every year, it is at least consistent that I should join this dispersal. I will retain a home and office in Canada and my position at the *National Post*, which will continue to advocate thoughtful alternatives to the long-standing course of Canadian public policy. Personally, after fulfilling a couple of pre-arranged speaking engagements, when I am no longer a Canadian citizen I do not expect to have any further public comment on Canadian affairs.

I take this step with regret but without rancor and will undo it when circumstances are more favourable. My hopes for Canada will always be as positive and ambitious as they were in the decades when I was proud to be a Canadian citizen and resident. In somewhat comparable circumstances nearly forty years ago, Roy Thomson said, "Irrespective of legal formality, I will always be a Canadian." So will I.

Conrad M. Black
New York
May 18, 2001

# I AM NOT AFRAID

*National Post*, March 10, 2007

This is the last of these columns I shall write before I have to defend myself against the unfounded charges that have stalked and shadowed me these several years. The trial of the facts that approaches has been amply publicized, but I hope I may be permitted a few reflections now.

When the life that I had worked more than thirty years to build, as a serious, reasonably respected newspaper publisher, was suddenly assaulted with extreme violence on every side more than three years ago, my wife and I returned to Canada, seeking a legally and financially defensible perimeter.

Apart from those who knew us well, there were cries of joy that I might be a corporate wrongdoer, and an almost Times Square New Year's countdown to my anticipated conviction.

Other than receiving news of a well-advanced terminal illness, an experience of which we have unfortunately had some experience in our family, I can hardly imagine a more startling change of life and prospect, since I had done nothing illegal. The principle of the presumption of innocence was largely ignored by the press and regulators.

Friends offered financial assistance, as my income suddenly almost dried up, yet my expenses, especially related to self-defence, multiplied. I managed to refinance myself, but was no less grateful for their offers. A legal team was assembled.

It was always obvious that the lies agreed upon by parties in interest with the complicity of parts of the press would likely become a criminal prosecution. Our companies, which had been built almost from nothing into billions of dollars of tangible value (not creatively accounted vapour), were, in the manner of these times and jurisdictions, transformed into platforms from which we were tormented.

As the largest shareholder, I was made to pay for my own persecution. The immobilizations or seizures of assets, defamatory leaks to the press, and never-ending harassments, continued, year after year (precious years at this stage in life). Eventually, I was, and am, posting bond of almost US$40 million, which is some kind of a record high. But I was able to stabilize finances, return to writing (with great thanks to the editors of this newspaper); the novelty of our discomfort abated, and life and the war of attrition ground on. Finally, our enemies would have to prove the innocent guilty, not just to the malicious and the envious, but in a court of justice.

There was great irony, whose piquancy was never lost on me, that I, who have been denounced in the parliaments of the United Kingdom and Canada for excessive pro-Americanism, should be so savagely attacked by the U.S. prosecution system. Frustratingly, I could not seriously reply to the wild allegations, shovelled out by the usurper regimes in our companies or in garish prosecution press conferences, about our claimed excesses, as counsel urged that all response must be held for trial. Such is the unevenness of the system. I had to rely on the innate decency of most people to wait until the other side was heard and require that a presumption of guilt had at least to be substantiated.

From there it was a fairly short step to the Big Battle, which required even those elements of the media that had danced on Barbara's and my supposed graves like Transylvanians heaping garlic on the resting place of Count Dracula to acknowledge my resuscitation. Big Battles cannot be conducted with corpses. As I know the facts and believe in the fairness of twelve randomly selected Americans, I am confident of the outcome.

It has been a splendid time to be in Canada. A united Conservative Party, for which I and many others fought, has produced a federal two-party system for the first time in a hundred years in Canada. The huge economic growth of China and India has enabled Canada to keep its generous social benefits and reduce taxes to a point where the brain drain to the United States should now dry up. Richard Bradshaw and Jack Diamond, who are from far countries, have built a fine national opera house where the performances are of outstanding quality. The percentage of Canada's GDP that is exports to the United States has declined from 44 per cent to about 35 per cent. Quebec separatism, a spectre that hobbled the country for decades, has died. Canada has become one of the ten or twelve most important countries of the 198 in the world. Those of us brought up to believe that Canada's foreign policy was to tug at the trouser leg of the Americans and British must realize that it is unnecessary and undignified to continue do so.

For the first time in decades, not having a large executive job, I have been able to appreciate and comment on national affairs. I left this country when the courts upheld the right of the then prime minister (Jean Chrétien) to create a subcategory of one in a foreign country (the United Kingdom), ineligible to receive an honour in that country for services deemed to have been performed in that country, because Chrétien did not approve of coverage (in this newspaper) of his government's financial conduct (coverage that has since been vindicated). I said I would be back (though I anticipated a less controversial return). I was also, for commercial reasons, departing the newspaper business (but had not foreseen such a perturbed exit strategy). The years have been full of surprises.

Barbara and I go now to try these issues at the bar of Abraham Lincoln and Clarence Darrow, in the city that I have long regarded as the great, brave heart of America. We have survived the "shock and awe" campaign of intimidation, defamation, and asset seizures. We built a great company that our accusers have destroyed to their own profit, as they have been sumptuously paid to obliterate over $1 billion of shareholder market value. We acted lawfully and are not afraid.

Despite its legal vagaries, the United States remains the indispensable country of Western civilization of the last century, a society of laws in a largely lawless world, and a country overwhelmingly composed of decent people.

I have no bitterness to those who have opposed me in this country, apart from a few outright thieves, who know who they are. To my wife,

children, family (including my ex-wife), friends, in this and other countries, colleagues, fellow parishioners, and the thousands of email and
postal correspondents who have inspirited me through these challenges, my gratitude is beyond my ability to express here.

In Toronto, we are cat and dog owners, and Barbara has just received
a little Hungarian puli from Alberta, an adorable but dignified little
proof to its older companions that life goes on. We will be back before it
is much bigger.

I will write here when I can; justice will prevail, and Barbara and
I will celebrate with our friends, never more easily identified than in
these challenging days. When nightmares pass, all things are possible.
I have never been happier to be Canadian.

*The fact is I had no confidence in American justice, but although
American prosecutors win over 99 per cent of their cases, 97 per cent are
without trial, because of the abuse of the plea-bargain system. None of my
co-defendants was going to crack, we would tear the cooperating witness
to pieces, and prosecutors only win about 80 per cent of the cases that are
tried. I knew how weak the prosecutors' case was, so I still believed we had
a good chance.*

*The open-heart surgery Eddie Greenspan had undergone reduced
his effectiveness as my chief counsel, and he did not always manage his
diabetes. Eddie had not brushed up on American procedure and was very
vulnerable to prosecution interventions. When he prepared properly, he
tore down their witnesses very effectively. On other occasions he was sluggish and ineffective.*

*The American lawyer he had engaged, Eddie Genson, had a sort of
Vaudeville Act that amused and distracted the jury, but they both lacked
the stamina for a four-month trial and were so used to guilty clients in
squalid cases, they never really understood the case. Even with all these
problems and heavy odds, we would certainly have won or mistried all
counts at the outset if the jurors had followed the judge's instructions not
to trade verdicts in order to get a unanimous verdict (90 per cent not guilty).*

# TUTOR HAS HIS REWARD

*National Post*, November 14, 2009

M y arrangement with my gracious temporary hosts includes the understanding that while I write a great deal for publication in many places in several countries, I do not describe what happens here, other than in the sketchiest terms. I depart slightly, but inoffensively, from that understanding to record some experiences I have had as a tutor in English to high-school-leaving candidates here.

There are approximately 1,800 residents in this institution, the low-security facility in the federal prison at Coleman, Florida, where I reside pending the U.S. Supreme Court's disposition of the 15 per cent or so of the charges made against me four years ago that survived the trial.

They comprise a rich and varied canvas of personalities and experiences, from misbegotten innocents almost saintly in their naive and stoical endurance of injustice, to egregious but usually engaging scoundrels, to invariably courtly and wryly entertaining alleged pillars of organized crime. I find almost all people interesting, and have had absolutely no difficulties with anyone here, residents or the regime.

The education department offers various courses in trades and skills, from plumbing and engineering to computer operation and conventional typing, and residents who cannot establish that they matriculated from secondary school are conscripted into attempting to do so. They tend to be a very disparate and rather undermotivated group.

It was my good fortune that some of the managers of the library here were aware of books I had written and convinced the education superior that I should do something in that area and not wait to be dragooned into tending dandelions in the compound or emptying recycling bins and the like. Everyone here "works," but the tasks, though not the pay scales, sometimes remind me of the infamous pre-Thatcher Spanish practices of Fleet Street, where absentees or fictitious people were paid for performing non-existent jobs.

There were enough teachers, almost all of them inmates, but it was thought that I might be able to assist in specialized work with a few candidates for the English diploma. (This was in addition to an evening course I was giving in U.S. history in one of the residential units.)

I was given a table and a chair at the back of the Vocational Training pavilion, where, for a few weeks, my reading of newspapers and other material was sporadically interrupted by improbable scholars wending their downcast way toward me on a forced march: I was the last resort before they were effectively declared inaccessible to higher education.

I hadn't liked teachers when I was at school, except for a few that I remember with gratitude, and as I generally prepared myself for examinations, I was never much convinced of their importance beyond elementary education. The last thing I wanted was more intimate contact with them.

In fact, my greatest moment of enthusiasm for the government of Quebec, and there haven't been many in the last forty-five years, was when Premier Daniel Johnson (Senior) – for whom I occasionally wrote speeches that he rarely used – in 1967 broke a French-language teachers' strike on the Island of Montreal. He did this by threatening to decertify the teachers' union, arrest its executives, impound its assets, and place a Quebec provincial policeman in every classroom while he and the vice-premier, Jean-Jacques Bertrand, delivered the lectures by closed-circuit television to the students and the teachers' salaries were rebated to the taxpayers of Quebec.

To my regret at the time, as a rural newspaper editor, the teachers caved and Quebec was denied this most promising experiment in progressive education.

As an observer, and later as an employer and as a parent, I have been dismayed by the deterioration of the state education system in a number of jurisdictions in several countries.

None of this prepared me in the slightest for the cynicism, skepticism, and defeatism I encountered when, well past retirement age and in the most unpromising circumstances, I, involuntarily and with no professional formation, launched my pedagogical career with unpromising and, to say the least, chronically unenthused charges.

I began with relaxed conversation, to put them at their ease, make the point that I wasn't part of the regime but rather was a victim of it as they were; that I wasn't trying to force them to do anything but offered an opportunity if they wanted to make something out of their time here, and in doing so to get the better of their tormentors. This preliminary discussion gave me a sense of how great the cultural hurdles were going to be, and usually, though not always, they were fairly daunting.

Rousseau was correct that one-on-one is the most effective way to teach. I did the obvious things, which are not possible with a full class, of adapting humorous examples from their own lives for sentence structure and the meaning of words, to make them easier to remember, and of assigning essay subjects tailored to their own interests.

One gambit that never failed, though it often generated reams of salacity, was "Describe the sexiest woman you have ever seen."

I devised tactical essay-writing techniques for special needs, urging spelling- and grammar-challenged candidates to memorize twenty polysyllabic words for timely insertion and commending Hemingway's "The Snows of Kilimanjaro" as illustrative of the virtues of short, simple sentences.

I found myself becoming an impassioned champion of the thirty-two-year-old small-time drug dealer who had six children with five women, none of them attached by the bourgeois relic of matrimony; and of the charming and elegant young man who had one child and an ex-wife but wasn't aware of the spelling of his son's name. It was impossible not to like the world-weary Cuban ex-CIA operative, the Puerto Rican fisherman from Key West who was illiterate when he began with me, and the *Sopranos*-like former bill collector of one of the New York

Mafia families. (He sat next to me at a religious service one day and whispered the question of how much could be got for the candelabra – a joke.)

My little domain grew to four tables and ten chairs, and two other tutors for other subjects, a former teacher and commodities trader from Arkansas, and an atomic submarine torpedoman and graduate of the U.S. Navy nuclear propulsion course, from Tennessee. Our tables became a sort of Hot Stove Lounge, with colourful reminiscences interspersed with novel study techniques on all the subjects being tested, but with a good, almost constant esprit around the tables.

The Bureau of Prisons holds these high school matriculation examinations every month or two, so I have had about one hundred students. Almost all have graduated, though some needed two or even three tries.

We tutors have been largely responsible for almost doubling the number of graduates annually from this facility. I would not meet the usual definition of a socialist, and many of my students acted unwisely and unscrupulously to get where they are. But many are victims of legal and social injustice, inadequately provided for by the public assistance system, and overprosecuted and vengefully sentenced. The greater competitiveness of the world makes the failures of American education, social services, and justice unaffordable, as well as repulsive.

In tens of millions of undervalued human lives, as in the consumption of energy and the addiction to consumer debt, the United States pays a heavy price for an ethos afflicted by wantonness, waste, and official human indifference. In other advanced countries, the custodial system is dedicated to the sort of work that has almost accidentally flourished here.

It has been my good fortune to be well-received in some learned and distinguished places, and I am always grateful for considered applause, but never more so than when complimented by my students on receipt of my advanced tutor's certificate at our graduating ceremony here a couple of months ago.

It is unjust that I am here at all, and I hope not to be here much longer, but I have rarely been more delighted than when formerly surly and sluggish students embrace me when they learn they have graduated, as they hasten to telephone or email their families. This unbidden sojourn has given me a taste of the rewards of teaching. It pains me to verge on platitudes, but life's rewards do sometimes come in strange ways and unexpected places.

*I was able to assist several of my old students in enrolling in university by correspondence, and two graduated after release, finishing their courses in person, and I have kept in touch with many. Without exception, they have flourished on release and remain good friends.*

# THE TRUTH ABOUT CATS AND DOGS

*National Post*, March 13, 2010

The ancient struggle between dog lovers and cat lovers traditionally has favoured the canines, at least in the English-speaking world. Dogs were the manly animals, guarded the hearth, herded the sheep, helped at the hunt and shoot, retrieved the newspaper, and were usually gentle with children.

Cats cannot really be put to any domestic use, except apprehension of mice and rats. They are often affectionate, but are not very demonstrative companions. But they require almost no attention, don't need help or advice going to the bathroom, rarely mind being left outside, because even pampered housecats can usually catch their own dinner, and they are magnificent physical machines. The feline faction has gained ground in recent years, because of the profusion of working couples who could not leave a dog indoors all day.

My purpose here is to de-escalate, even slightly, the friction between the vast opposing armies of feline and canine admirers. This reflects my own circumstances, as my wife, Barbara, has become, in my brief and untoward absence, a caricature of a dog-lover, setting out from our homes in Toronto and Palm Beach kitted out like a British girls' public school games-mistress with a variety of leashes, whistles, timepieces, enticements, and fecal-disposal apparatus. She defiantly sends me, a traditional cat-fancier, photographs portraying her as an apparent fugitive from an Agatha Christie movie who has turned walking the dogs into exotic simulations of an all-weather, open-ended, search and rescue mission.

In general, I find dogs are perhaps often more loveable than cats, but cats are more impressive. Dogs can have a sense of humour; their loyalty and eagerness to please can be very affecting. They often bond to their owner in a way that is total adherence. And they have almost human qualities. They wag their tails in happiness, whine and cry in sadness, are embarrassed when they try and fail, as in chasing a squirrel, and are contrite when they make a mess. They are almost guileless and only a heart of stone does not find a good-natured dog very endearing.

The pleasure of cats is in their confident bearing, their elegance. Even when startled, their responses are so agile, they are not even momentarily awkward. Almost everything a cat does is graceful, down to, but not quite including, the most mundane acts. Even tomcats, unkempt and with tangles in their fur, have a certain inseparable dignity, like a feline John Malkovich. Cats can jump up to a crowded mantelpiece and walk along it without disturbing the most fragile curio, and move on, almost silently. All but the most feral cats scrupulously manage their own hygiene, and even when they clean their paws and claws, they are graceful; the only creatures that make fastidiousness interesting to watch. Some dogs, whatever their virtues, are silly or ungainly, but cats are neither. I have always thought that to like or even understand the French, you should like cats: the intelligence, confidence, elegance, self-absorption, and cynicism.

I have generally always had an aversion to the time-consuming aspects of being a pet owner. I first developed a deep admiration for cats when, as a twelve-year-old at my parents' cottage, I was entrusted with keeping the interior of the boat house shipshape, including the boats. The chief problem was bird droppings. My older brother's efforts with a large-bore shotgun displaced nests, scattered feathers, and put out a window, which effectively aggravated the problem. Even the sparrows, who aren't particularly tactically astute, realized that my brother was pursuing a Pyrrhic course and didn't budge.

I borrowed the neighbour's domestic, long-haired, grey cat. After three days, the birds had fled for their lives and did not return. I watched some of this. At no point was the cat agitated, embarrassed, triumphalist;

he did not waste a unit of energy and made no effort to frighten the birds by being threatening. It was an astoundingly professional, natural, and efficient performance. He caught two birds, and it was clear that he would catch them all if they didn't leave. I have never since considered "pussycat" a pejorative description.

At our home in Toronto, there is an extensive property tapering off into a ravine, and we often have foxes around the house. It has been interesting to see them interact with the cats. They are about equally clever and devious and fascinating to watch. Usually the foxes become exasperated and chase the cats, with evidently unplayful intentions. The cats run up the trees and preen themselves with insolent nonchalance. Sometimes, when we put the dogs and cats out together, they formed a unitary home team and the cats bait the foxes, who pursue the cats but quickly retreat when facing the heavier canine units. It's a bloodless preliminary round of nature's regime of fang and claw.

Cats are always the worthy miniatures of lions and tigers. They slink and stalk, rest vigilantly, and sleep easily, like their huge and fierce relatives. Their habit of psychopathically killing birds and chipmunks even when they are not hungry is unattractive, but is the nature of the beast. Watching the prides of lions hunt on the Discovery Channel reveals, writ large, the cunning instincts of even the suburban domestic housecat. They intuitively enfilade and surround, and try to surprise their little prey. Before you dog owners become too sanctimonious, canines chase almost anything that moves, including, if the dogs are large enough, cats, but are not so often successful at it.

My bona fides as a feline supporter should now have been established, but I must admit that Barbara is winning our tug-of-war. She likes cats but loves dogs, and her dogs are splendid and good-natured, though they would be dangerous to any assailant of her. As others take care of them, it is challenging not to fall for them and I miss them. I am now an equal-opportunity liker of individual cats and dogs, though I still find cats a more interesting species. They are, after all, generally more intelligent. I have never seen a stupid cat.

A friend of mine in England who was a brilliant zoologist and owned two private zoos, including magnificent groups of tigers and lions, and often went into the tiger cages himself (although he lost three keepers to them over the years), told me that the intelligence of the great cats was clear in their relative inactivity. They only did what was necessary to eat, and apart from that were sedentary, dormant, or sexually occupied. No creature bothers them except armed men. And they never have trouble eating adequately, though in the severest droughts, lions sometimes take extreme and undignified measures, such as climbing trees and stealing from the leopard's larder, driving the occupant farther up the tree.

These domestic quadrupeds enlist the fierce devotion of almost everyone. Even monsters such as Hitler and Goebbels loved their dogs. So did Mackenzie King, John Diefenbaker, and Lester Pearson. Richelieu, Salisbury, and famously T.S. Eliot, loved their cats. The multi-faceted Mr. Churchill liked both.

We had two well-loved dogs die recently. It was very upsetting, even though I had not seen them in over a year. When my greatest of cats, Sidney the Siamese genius, died twenty years ago, I did something of which I would never have thought myself capable. He was the cleverest, friendliest, and most elegant cat I have known. We had a game of trying to confine him to the basement, but within five minutes he would casually reappear, like Houdini, once via a dumb waiter. The long-term score in this match was 30-something for Sidney, and for the bumbling humans, o, but he was a sportsmanlike champion. He was even patient with our young children, except when my son, then three, "patted his whiskers," and even then his response was measured.

When he died, I had him buried in our garden, under a small marble slab, bearing the lines, from Arnold, "Composed and bland, / Imperious and grand, / As Tiberius might have sat, / Had Tiberius been a cat."

More like Augustus, Hadrian, or Constantine, I think, but these are the hopeful biases of a proud owner. We get very attached to our dogs and cats, but they do tend to bring out the best qualities in us.

*My wife, who is a much more experienced columnist than I am, told me reactions to dog and cat columns vastly exceeded even those about abortion and the death penalty. She was right as usual.*

# MY PRISON EDUCATION

*National Post*, July 31, 2010

---

I n my twenty-eight months as a guest of the U.S. government, I often wondered how my time in that role would end. I never expected that I would have to serve the whole term, though I was, and am, psychologically prepared to do so, now that I have learned more of the fallibility of American justice, which does convict many people, who, like me, would never dream of committing a crime in a thousand years.

Most evenings as a captive, I telephoned my wife, Barbara, at between 11 and 11:30 p.m., just before the telephones were shut down for the day. I did so on Monday, July 19. Her opening gambit was, "What have you heard?" and I dimly replied, "Nothing special."

"You haven't heard?"

Thus did I learn, as the emails had been down in the entire compound for five days, that my appeal bond application had been granted. Half an hour later, when I was in bed using my night light to do a crossword puzzle, two fellow residents approached, a few minutes apart, to say that they had heard of it on the BBC World Service.

Tuesday was a day of feverish to-ing and fro-ing, as bond was discussed and arranged, and terms debated, and the local personnel of the Bureau of Prisons strove to keep up with the paperwork as my status inched, line by line, on their computer screens, toward the gate.

As a matter of principle, I refused to pack up anything until I was assured of actually leaving. To pack up belongings and then have to unpack them would have been insufferably demeaning. I made only very cautious replies to inquiries about leaving: "Soon, I hope."

The court appearance to fix terms was in Chicago on the morning of Wednesday, July 21, where I was represented, with his customary agility, by my outstanding counsel, Miguel Estrada.

By prearrangement, I called my wife at shortly after 11 a.m. Again, she began, "What have you heard?" "Nothing," was my dynamic response, which surprised her, as there were already extended television accounts of the Chicago proceedings. "You leave today. Bail of two million dollars has been posted [by my dear and generous friend Roger Hertog]. A car is coming to collect you at about three. I'll see you tonight."

Barbara was in Toronto and it was our eighteenth wedding anniversary. She couldn't make her reservation on Air Canada: she could see on television the driver she had arranged to pick me up marooned outside the gates of the prison complex. He had no authorization to prove he was ordered for me and not simply a ruse of the press. Faxes flew back and forth delaying her departure.

Finally, the only way to get to Palm Beach that night, just before midnight, which she was able to do, was to charter from a well-wisher at a knock-down rate (basically the cost of aviation fuel) a sluggish medevac plane without a washroom.

In the Coleman low-security compound, there are 1,800 residents, and it is a little universe terminally addicted to gossip about the custodial system and especially the goings-on of the group confined there. By this time, there were large numbers of journalists and photographers clustered at the gate of the Coleman complex and ongoing television coverage watched with some bemusement by my fellow residents in the television rooms of the residential units.

A steady stream of well-wishers from all factions of the compound came to say goodbye as I put my books and papers and a few clothes items into cardboard boxes. (The only article of clothing that I took that was not among the few things I had bought myself was the nondescript brown shirt bequeathed to me when he left by the don of one of the famous New York gang families.)

The Mafiosi, the Colombian drug dealers (including a senator, with whom I had a special greeting as a fellow member of a parliamentary upper house), the American drug dealers, high and low, black, white, and Hispanic; the alleged swindlers, hackers, pornographers, credit card fraudsters, bank robbers, and even an accomplished airplane thief; the rehabilitated and unregenerate, the innocent and the guilty, and in almost all cases the grossly oversentenced, streamed in steadily for hours to make their farewells.

Most goodbyes were brief and jovial, some were emotional, and a few were quite heart-rending. Many of the nearly 150 students that my very able fellow tutors and I had helped to graduate from high school came by, some of them now enrolled in university by cyber-correspondence.

Veterans of even twenty years in the federal prison system could not recall anyone being bailed in mid-sentence like this, and particularly not on the heels of a unanimous Supreme Court decision.

I was overwhelmingly enthused to leave, especially in these circumstances, after the U.S. Supreme Court's rewriting of the open-ended statute that had been used against me, a catchment, as the chief justice of the United States said at our hearing, for anyone a prosecutor takes against.

It had been an interesting experience, from which I developed a much greater practical knowledge than I had ever had before of those who had drawn a short straw from the system; of the realities of street level American race relations; of the pathology of incorrigible criminals; and of the wasted opportunities for the reintegration of many of these people into society. I saw at close range the failure of the U.S. War on Drugs, with absurd sentences (including twenty years for marijuana offences, although 42 per cent of Americans have used marijuana and it is the greatest cash crop in California). A trillion dollars have been spent, a million easily replaceable small fry are in prison, and the targeted substances are more available and of better quality than ever, while producing countries such as Colombia and Mexico are in a state of civil war.

I had seen at close range the injustice of sentences one hundred times more severe for crack cocaine than for powder cocaine, a straight act of discrimination against African Americans, that even the first black president and attorney general have only ameliorated with tepid support for a measure, still being debated, to reduce the disparity of sentence from 100 to 1 to 18 to 1.

And I had heard the vehement allegations of many fellow residents of the fraudulence of the public defender system, where court-appointed lawyers, it is universally and plausibly alleged, are more often than not stooges of the prosecutors. They are paid for the number of clients they represent rather than for their level of success, and they do usually plead their clients to prison. They provide a thin veneer for the fable of the poor citizen's day in court to receive impartial justice through due process.

And I had the opportunity to see why the United States has six to twelve times as many incarcerated people as other prosperous democracies (Australia, Canada, France, Germany, Japan, and the United Kingdom), and how the prison industry grew and successfully sought more prisoners, longer sentences, and maximal possibilities of probation violations and a swift return to custody.

Before I got into the maw of the U.S. legal system, I did not realize the country has forty-eight million people with a criminal record (most for relatively trivial offences,) or that prosecutors won more than 99 per cent of their cases. There, at Coleman, I had seen the courage of self-help, the pathos of broken men, the drawn faces of the hopeless, the glazed expression of the heavily medicated (90 per cent of Americans judged to require confinement for psychiatric reasons are in the prison system), and the nonchalance of those who find prison a comfortable welfare system compared to the skid row that was their former milieu. America's 2.4 million prisoners, and millions more awaiting trial or on supervised release, are an ostracized, voiceless legion of the walking dead; they are no one's constituency.

Of course, I was glad, jubilant, to leave (though a return is not an impossible result of the pending rehearing), but also grateful for many of the relationships I had formed; enlightened by my observation of American justice on the other side of the wall; and happy to have got on well in an environment very foreign to any I had known before.

My departure was processed quite cordially and the personnel even conducted us to a back exit, through a padlocked gate far from the media, and shook hands and waved as I slipped the bondage of the U.S. government. It had been twenty-eight months and eighteen days since I arrived. The send-off was more congenial than the reception, and the ride back to Palm Beach was on the same roads over the same flat, scrubby landscape of strip malls and bungalows as the approach. It seemed more verdant and welcoming on the way back. The drive was contemplative and uneventful.

I was delighted to be back in my home, which the prosecutors had tried to seize for years. For the first time since I was last there, I enjoyed pristine quiet, free of loudspeakers, screamed argument, and the snoring of a hundred men. I had a glass of wine, and waited for Barbara, to celebrate the happiest of all wedding anniversaries.

# FOND MEMORIES OF
# THE ROAD HOME

*National Post*, December 20, 2010

---

Among my most agreeable Christmas time remembrances are coming home by car from university, as an undergraduate (from Carleton University in Ottawa), a graduate student (from Laval University in Quebec City), and a post-graduate student (from McGill University in Montreal). I always gave lifts home to a number of friends, so there were frequent stops as we progressed from our university homes toward and into Toronto, where my family lived. This jovial annual ceremony unfolded, with a couple of breaks, between 1962 and 1972. It was always very close to Christmas, and followed a strenuous time of cramming for examinations, celebrating when possible, and conducting a generally successful goal-line academic stand in the examination halls. All of those cities had deeper snow and generally colder temperatures than Toronto, and we started out more warmly clad than would be necessary at the final destination. Laws governing drinking in cars were more relaxed, especially in Quebec. I never drank while driving, but my passengers were a little more festive, and my car was always full of people who considered that their holidays had already begun.

I had rather large Chevrolet, Oldsmobile, and Buick sedans through those years that could hold as many as seven people, adequately comfortably by collegiate standards. As there were stops to disembark people at intervals along the routes, there were warm and often extended farewells and holiday greetings, including sometimes the parting of the romantically involved. I participated in this rite a couple of times, and it generally led to an uplifting pause for secluded, shared reflection. On the long drive from Quebec City, where I was a law student, to Toronto, there were apt to be stops at places such as Trois-Rivières or the Eastern Townships, as well as two or more drop-offs in greater Montreal, and a final stop in Cornwall or Kingston before the disgorgements in Toronto. It was in these activities that I came particularly to appreciate the hospitality of French Canadians. Without exception, I would be welcomed into the homes of my friends and wholeheartedly offered every conviviality.

I remember once stopping in Knowlton, Quebec, a significant detour from the direct route, and briefly joining a fierce poker game. Several times, my continuing passengers and I were not allowed to move on without sharing in a delicious meal, usually with some, though never an excess of, wine, mulled or otherwise. On the last leg of the trip, the last 150 miles or so into Toronto, the number of people in the car had thinned out quite a bit, as, especially in the case of Laval (a French-language university dating from the eighteenth century), almost all the students were from somewhere in Quebec. We often encountered other homecoming students – easily discerned by their age, appearance, and the nature of their hand-held chattels – hitchhiking and picked them up. They usually entered quite effortlessly into the itinerant spirit of the car.

The ambiance throughout these trips, which could easily be stretched out, when from Quebec City to Toronto, to nine or ten hours with all the stops and diversions, was overwhelmingly cheerful and witty. Everyone's talents as a raconteur always seemed to reach their highest (and sometimes most ribald) point, and there was, on these occasions, a complete lapse in any sense of competitiveness or misgivings in the merry-making, as all had something to celebrate and – in that way never quite to be replicated in post-university years – much to look forward to. The sense of having scraped through another term, the anticipation of home, the warm collegiality of university friendship, the unique comradeship of having taken higher level university examinations together, all joined with the general Christmas spirit to create a delightful atmosphere that always returns happily to memory every year at this time. This happens even in, as is now the case, a place so far removed in time, clime, and circumstances as Palm Beach, Florida, where Santa's sleigh has always had a credibility gap coming through our palm, orange, banana, and avocado trees.

Just this little retrospective brings back to me rich memories of fellowship in hopeful and relatively carefree days. Thoughts go back to long-lost friends, some no longer living, some unheard of for decades, but all remembered fondly, summed up in that evocative and stirring omnibus toast "to absent friends." And there was a tradition, when I finally returned to my parents' house, where, though I have modified and enlarged it, I still live when in Canada, and to which I shall return when the Babylonian Captivity inflicted on me by the vagaries of American justice ends. My father, a night owl not well-known for his passionate attachment to temperance, bade me sit, reversed our usual roles, and prepared and handed me a mahogany-coloured bird bath of a glass of Scottish whisky. These are simple but dear memories; that they cannot be re-enacted takes nothing from their rich, imperishable, bittersweet serenity. A Merry Christmas to all, especially absent friends and family.

# TO BARBARA, "MY PERFECT VALENTINE"

*National Post*, February 12, 2011

Public Valentine greetings are a depth of questionable taste I have never before plumbed. But as this is the first Valentine's Day in eight years I have not spent either in or apprehending my unjust residence in an American prison for offences I would not have dreamed in a thousand years of committing, I am throwing caution to the gentle breezes of Palm Beach, as they rustle the majestic royal palms. It will be twenty years this fall that I "set out my stall," as Barbara and I have agreed to call my marriage proposal (since she did not, because of my complicated syntax and word choice, recognize at first that that was what it was). And it will be nineteen years this summer that we have been married. There have been no serious strains between us in all that time, and I feel the same or even greater romantic magnetism now as in that whirlwind courtship of such pleasant memory.

As Barbara is an opera enthusiast, I used to tell her that ours was a great love story, Eloise and Abelard, Romeo and Juliet, Tristan and Isolde, with a happier ending, on the "lived happily ever after" model. It has and has not been that, but the best is still to come. I have been persecuted, and Barbara was under no obligation to share fully in the life-enhancing and undoubtedly character-building experience of sharing that fate with me completely. But she has, and no one can know, and it is beyond my power adequately to express here, what her constancy has meant to me.

For more than four years before I was sent to prison, she toiled with me against the heavy odds generated by the legal and media onslaught. She endured an avalanche of abuse directed at her (although she wasn't accused of anything) as extravagant, flakey, apt to bolt, domineering, and what Kafka called "nameless crimes." For the next twenty-nine months, she led a lonely life in Florida, in a climate that aggravated her medical problems. And once or twice every week, she got up at 3 a.m. to drive over four hours to see me, endure the inanities and indignities whose infliction is the raison d'être of the personnel of the Bureau of Prisons, to sit with me in a crowded and noisy room under the envious and probably deviant gaze of officials dedicated to harassing visitors and assuring the absence of tactile indications of any intimacy. And then she drove four hours back to rattle around with her canine comrades in our underoccupied house.

On these visits, which it need hardly be emphasized were the highlight of every week for me, she went to great trouble to dress up, a real novelty in those surroundings (without transgressing any of the authorities' absurd and capricious dress codes that were sadistically invoked as a pretext to send visitors away), and to be cheerful and informative, and never to betray a hint of fatigue or discomfort. Every visit was a supreme triumph of the human spirit and her benign and indomitable will over infirmity and the relentless forces of discouragement. So great was the strength of her personality and determination not to yield to harsh circumstances that even some of the most sociopathic correctional officers became rather amiable and asked me between visits when she would be back. She comforted other visitors, and helped some in different ways, and worked prodigies for my legal battle, including interviewing and recommending counsel for our successful appeal to the Supreme Court of the United States, which is the reason that I write this from my home and not from a prison.

When I was a guest of the great and complacent American people, I would prevail upon a couple of my artistic fellow residents to produce Valentine and other cards, often with humorous depictions of Barbara's splendid dogs, and other appropriate animals, including Valentine bears and Easter bunnies. Residents were entitled to three hundred minutes of telephone use per month (apart from special and confidential legal conferences, of which I had a great many), which, as Barbara and I did not telephone on visiting days, left us about twelve minutes per night, as I handled almost everything else by email. She had a mobile telephone that was always with her, of which only I had the number, and it is my mobile phone now, a valiant little machine, a bit dated in its simplicity. By such threads do time-tested, well-suited relationships survive the hammer blows of the justice system, dedicated as it is, despite endless humbug to the contrary, to destroy the lives of all in its maw.

Just before my four-month trial began in Chicago in 2007 (which disposed of 90 per cent of the allegations against me), I published a biography of Richard Nixon I had written, in part, as a diversion from the legal tensions. The dedication is: "To Barbara, through good and bad times, she has been magnificent. No man could ask more and few could have received so much. She is beyond praise and criticism."

That was nothing but the truth then, though not the whole truth, and it was before the worst came. What happened next, the trial, the interregnum, the Babylonian Captivity, called forth transports of heroism and devotion. To do justice to them would strain the descriptive capacity of superlatives.

It is better now, and the prospects are brightening. We are almost at the "ever after" part at last. I never doubted that those awful days would pass, but they would not have passed so soon, nor been even as endurable as they were, without my perfect Valentine, who will always have all my love.

# THE STATEMENT CONRAD BLACK DELIVERED TO JUDGE AMY ST. EVE AT HIS RESENTENCING HEARING IN CHICAGO ON FRIDAY

*National Post*, June 25, 2011

---

On the occasion corresponding to this four years ago, the fact that the counts that had survived the trial were under appeal spoke for itself, and I didn't think it appropriate to say much more. As we are now back, one last time, in your court, at the weary end of this very long and fiercely contested proceeding, there are a few things that I think should be said.

The prosecutors have never ceased to accuse me of being defiant of the law, of disrespecting the courts, and of being an antagonistic critic of the American justice system. Nothing could be further from the truth. I have obeyed every order of this and other courts, every requirement of the United States Probation Office, in this and other cities, and while I was its guest, every rule and regulation of the BOP, no matter how authoritarian. I have been and remain completely and unwaveringly submissive to legal authority, yours in particular.

What I have done is exercise my absolute right to legal self-defence, a right guaranteed to everyone who is drawn into the court system of this and every other civilized country. All my adult life I have been a member of the moderate section of what is commonly called the law-and-order community, and I shall remain in it, whatever sentence you impose on me today. I always keep a firewall between my own travails and my perception of public-policy issues; otherwise I would retain no credibility as a commentator.

Your Honour, many years ago, when I was a student and licensee in law in Quebec, I read a large number of cases from British and French courts, including the principle established by the eminent British jurist Lord Denning that "parties coming to court must be prepared to practise what they are asking the court to approve." The prosecutors have never ceased in this case to advocate respect for the law, and to accuse me of lacking it.

But since that is an unfounded complaint, the real source of their irritation must be that as chief defendant, I have led the destruction of most of their case, and have successfully protested my innocence of charges of which I have, in fact, been found not to have been guilty. I understand their disconcertion that of the seventeen counts they originally threatened or actually launched against me, all were either not proceeded with, abandoned, rejected by the jurors, or vacated by a unanimous Supreme Court of the United States. But the problem is not my lawlessness; it is the weakness of their case. I have done nothing but uphold and respect the rule of law and the system of justice, in which my faith has never flagged.

This entire prosecution and a number of civil suits as well, were based on the report of the special committee of the board of Hollinger International, directed by its counsel, Richard Breeden, and published in September 2004. That report accused me of having led a "$500-million corporate kleptocracy." The non-competition payments almost entirely legitimized in this case were described as "thefts." And the authors of the report promised to lead the company back to unheard-of levels of profitability. They did, but not in the direction indicated. I launched the largest libel suit in Canadian history against Breeden and the others responsible for writing and publishing this infamous report.

My libel suit, and several other lawsuits around this case, are being settled, including a sizeable payment to me on the libel claim. This is the ultimate collapse of the Breeden special committee report, whatever other interpretation the defendants in the case may, consistent with their notions of accuracy throughout these proceedings, seek to place on it.

The authors of the report were not prepared to defend it where they would not have an immunity for perjury as most of the government witnesses did here. Nor were they prepared to defend their self-directed largesse of $300 million as they drove the company into bankruptcy, taking down $2 billion of shareholder value with it.

Over 80 per cent of that value belonged to ordinary people throughout the United States and Canada, the type of people Mr. Cramer spoke about at the opening of the trial when he likened us to masked and violent bank robbers who stole depositors' money at gunpoint, because we had supposedly rifled the shareholders' family college funds. And Breeden's original action of January 2004, containing the false charge that I had threatened the special committee, repeated just last month by the government in its pre-sentence filings on May 27, has also been abandoned.

Mark Twain famously said that "a lie gets halfway round the world before the truth gets its trousers on." It is very late in this case, Your Honour, but the truth has almost caught up with the original allegations.

I have at times expressed concern about the ethics of some of the prosecutors in this case, Your Honour, but never of the role of prosecutors, or of the necessity to convict criminals and protect society. But I must emphasize that I consider that the prosecutors, too, are victims. If they had not believed Breeden's lies, now effectively abandoned in the face of my libel suit, the U.S. attorney would surely not have launched such a fantastic assault on us.

And I can assure the assistant U.S. attorney that I did not say on Canadian television that I was like the person checking his own expense account. I said that for the appellate panel that had been excoriated by Madam Justice Ginsburg on behalf of a unanimous Supreme Court, when assigned the task of assessing the gravity of its own errors, to resurrect these two counts after a gymnastic distortion, suppression and fabrication of evidence, was like someone reviewing his own expense account.

Your Honour, these are, in any case, very threadbare counts. Is it really conceivable to you that if I were inexplicably seized with the ambition to embezzle $285,000, I would have it ratified by a committee and then, after what the minutes of the meeting described as "extensive discussion," by the whole board? I would have to have been mad.

And obstruction: It is clear from the evidence that I had nothing to do with selecting or packing the contents of the boxes, had no knowledge of any SEC interest in them after complying with five of its subpoenas, and after being assured by Mrs. Maida that it did not violate the Canadian document retention order, and checking with the acting president of the company, whose letter you have, I helped to carry out the boxes under the gaze of security cameras that I had installed. When these boxes arrived here, they were very full, so if I had taken anything out of them, why would I not have put them at any time over many weeks in my pockets or a briefcase? Your Honour, again, to remove documents improperly in this way, I would have had to be barking, raving mad, and insanity is almost the only failing of which the prosecutors have not accused me.

I would like to express here my gratitude to you, Your Honour, for sending me to a prison with email access, where I was able to stay in touch with supporters and with readers of my newspaper and magazine columns. And I must also express my gratitude to the originally small but distinguished and often intellectually brave group of friends, but also of total strangers, who never believed I was guilty, when that was a less fashionable position than it has become. Their numbers grew to be an army that now includes many people in every American state and Canadian province, and region of the United Kingdom, and people in many other countries.

And my gratitude to the many friends I made, inmates and correctional personnel, at the Coleman low-security prison, whom I shall not forget, is beyond my ability to express today.

I am of the tradition that tends not to speak publicly of personal matters, but Your Honour, I hope it is acceptable to you if I vary that practice slightly, and briefly, in concluding today. As you would know, or could surmise from many letters that have been sent to you by qualified people, and as is mentioned in the pre-sentencing submissions, I believe in the confession and repentance of misconduct and in the punishment of crime. I don't believe in false or opportunistic confessions.

It is not the case, as has been endlessly alleged by the prosecutors, that I have no remorse. I regret that my skepticism about corporate governance zealotry, though it was objectively correct and has been demonstrated to have been so in the destruction of these companies, became so identified with the companies themselves that the shareholders all suffered from it.

I regret that I was too trusting of the honesty of one associate and the thoroughness of some others, and the buck has stopped with me. I repent those and other tactical errors and mistakes of attitude, Your Honour, and I do not resent paying for those errors, because it is right, and in any case inevitable, that people should pay for their mistakes.

I concluded many years ago in my brief stint as a candidate psychoanalyst that it is practically impossible to repress conscientious remorse. And I concluded some years later in reading some of the works of the recently beatified Cardinal Newman, that our consciences are a divine impulse speaking within us, as Newman wrote, "powerful, peremptory, and definitive." My conscience functions like that of other people, and I respond to it, if not precisely as my accusers would wish. But they are prosecutors, not custodians of the consciences of those whom they accuse.

Your Honour, please do not doubt that even though I don't much speak of it, my family and I have suffered deeply from the onslaught of these eight years. I agree with the late pope who said "Life is cruciform." All people suffer. It is a stern message, but need not be a grim one. We rarely know why we suffer, and only those who have faith even believe there is a reason. No one can plausibly explain in moral terms a natural disaster, or a personal tragedy. I see life as a privilege and almost all challenges as opportunities, and have always tried to take success like a gentleman, and disappointment like a man.

Whatever the reason my family and I have had to endure this ordeal, for our purposes today, in these personal questions, I only ask that you take into account the messages you have received about collateral medical problems in my family. I do not worry about myself, and I will not speak further in open court of the worries I do have for my family. But I most earnestly request, Your Honour, as someone who has shown and expressed family sensibilities several times in this case, that they too be taken into account in your sentence.

And I believe that even if a reasonable person still concludes that I am guilty of these two surviving, resurrected, counts, tortuously arrived at and threadbare though their evidentiary basis now is, that the same reasonable person would conclude that I have been adequately punished. I only ask you to recall the criterion you eloquently invoked near the end of the trial that the justice system not be brought into disrepute by an unjust sentence.

I conclude by quoting parts of a famous poem by Kipling, with which I'm sure many in the court are familiar, and which I had known too, but not as well as I knew it after it was sent to me by well-wishers from every continent except Antarctica. And to the extent I was able, I tried to keep in mind throughout these difficult years, what Kipling wrote, which was, in part and as memory serves:

> *If you can keep your head while all about you are losing theirs and blaming it on you, If you can trust your own counsel though all men doubt you, but make allowance for their doubting too; If you wait but are not tired of waiting, Are lied about, but don't deal in lies, If some men hate you but you don't stoop to hating, And don't look too good or talk too wise; If you can talk but don't make words your master, Can think but don't make thoughts your aim; If you can meet with triumph and disaster, But treat both those imposters just the same.*

And I address this directly to the prosecutors and some of the media:

> *If you can bear to hear the truths you've spoken, Twisted by knaves to make a trap for fools, And see the work you gave your life to broken, And stoop to fix it up with worn-out tools.*

*If you can make a pile of all your winnings, And risk it on a turn of pitch and toss, And lose and start again at your beginning, And never say a word about your loss.*

And Kipling goes on to say that the reader will then be a man. Your Honour, when I first appeared in your court six years ago and you asked me my age, it was sixty-one. If I'm not a man now, I never will be.

I never ask for mercy and seek no one's sympathy. I would never, as was once needlessly feared in this court, be a fugitive from justice in this country, only a seeker of it. It is now too late to ask for justice. But with undimmed respect for this country, this court, and if I may say so, for you personally, I do ask you now to avoid injustice, which it is now in your gift alone to do. I apologize for the length of my remarks, and thank you, for hearing me out, Your Honour.

*These remarks, though carefully considered, were delivered* ex tempore. *Judge St. Eve sharply reduced the sentence, warmly commended me on my success as a prisoner, and concluded: "The court wishes you well, Mr. Black."*

# I KNOW EXACTLY WHAT
# TO EXPECT UPON
# MY RETURN TO PRISON

*National Post*, September 3, 2011

---

Though I suspect many readers are as bored with the subject as I am, I yield to the commissioning editor's request for some reflections on returning to prison. Having spent twenty-nine months in a federal prison already, I know what to expect; I have seen the immediate future, and it doesn't work very well; but it is survivable. Like any trip of any duration, it requires a lot of wrapping up of pending matters. Packing is not a problem, since I am not allowed to bring anything in except eyeglasses and a small religious object. As soon as I kiss my wife goodbye, I will be meticulously strip-searched and my clothes sent back to her in a parcel as I join the sartorial style-setters of the residents of the Bureau of Prisons. I am planning a fierce pursuit of fitness and weight loss, building upon the partial success of my previous sojourn with the same congenial hosts, which has been interrupted by my last four months of rather sumptuous dining in New York.

Hoping that authors still receive some indulgence for crassness as they hustle their books, I do invite anyone with any residual interest in these matters to look at my book about it, which will be published this week, A *Matter of Principle* (McClelland & Stewart). I have been pre-recording a good deal of promotional interviews for it in New York, for Canada and the United States, these past two weeks. I must confess to having made a mistake in yielding to the publisher's urgings to talk to a writer for *Vanity Fair*, a slick but vulgar glossy that usually decapitates its subjects. By the standards of that magazine, it was fairly civil and made a number of the points I wanted to make. But about half of it was snide and I was mocked for being talkative, when all I did was answer the writer's questions. It is the first time, in much and long experience with the media, that I have been raked over the coals on those grounds. Having agreed to be interviewed, it would have been eccentric to reply with nothing but a variant of John Foster Dulles's immortal response to a press question: "No comment, and that's off the record."

Perhaps it will do something for book sales, but I doubt it. I don't commit crimes, but I frequently make mistakes, and this foray into the U.S. media jungle was one of them. I will not reply to the piece here, or anywhere else, other than a few points. I wish to salve concerns that have been expressed on the internet that I indicated what my current economic net worth is. I did not, other than that it had appreciably diminished in the last eight years. And, though it only speaks to the author's thoroughness and doesn't indicate any malice, I certainly did not say that the chapel at my home in Toronto consecrated by Cardinal Carter and Cardinal Ambrozic dates to when I was two years old. At that time, my family lived in Forest Hill (Toronto), my parents were, as they remained, rather sketchily practising Protestants, and they would have been astounded, though not disconcerted, to think that fifty years later a Roman Catholic place of worship would be built at their future home. This only reflects the ease with which the author, surprisingly for a reputable business non-fiction author, engaged in pure, inexplicable, invention.

I also resent the underestimation of aspects of my formal education; I was expelled from two private schools, but also quit a third, I suspect, a forenoon before being expelled from it too. I not only failed first year at law school, as was accurately reported, but very nicely managed the more astounding feat of failing my freshman undergraduate year, but did recover to earn both those degrees and a third (despite a minor dust-up over my thesis at the Senate of McGill University, where I was nobly assisted by my former school master, Senator Laurier LaPierre).

And Barbara is once again the victim in *Vanity Fair* of completely false imputations of addiction to private jet travel, and the total fiction that she dragged me into a turbo-social life. To the extent we had any such life, it was my fault and responsibility. My distinguished maternal grandfather, after whom I am named because I was born on his birthday, said in the early phase of my school problems, "For some people, experience is a slow teacher." In my case, it is probably more accurate that I am a slow learner, but I have now learned to stay away from some kinds of journalists.

My only fear for the next seven months is the sadness of being separated from Barbara, although I am also resigned to tedium. I am not returning to custody like one of Santa's toy-making happy elves singing "*hi-ho*," but one does what one must; "Ours not to reason why," and so forth. I will be editing my next book, *Flight of the Eagle: The Strategic History of the United States*, and preparing for the demolition of the spurious civil claims that remain in Canada, plus whatever job I am assigned, and will do what I can to make the time pass quickly.

There will be an email, though not an internet, connection, so I should be able to continue this and other columns I write, unless the authorities decline to renew my previous arrangements. It is much to the credit of the Bureau of Prisons that it permitted me to file columns when I was last their guest (by agreement, I did not write about the prison I was in and contributed what I was paid to our family's charitable foundation). I would not rule out that officialdom is shirty about the disintegration of its case and what it might possibly construe as my failure to be adequately chastened by being sent, and sent back, to prison.

If my confinement does anything to encourage any of the other victims of this awful system, it is, as I suggested at the end of my *National Post* column last week, an honour. And I continue to believe, as I quoted Henry D. Thoreau in this space when I first reported to prison in March 2008, that "under a government which imprisons unjustly, the true place for a just man is also in prison." I don't have much choice, as I would never consider fleeing, but in that one sense,

I belong there and am happy to return. I do expect I will come back to the United States eventually, but will look forward to meeting my American friends when they come to Canada or Britain.

As I have often said, the United States has certainly not ceased to be a great country just because it has persecuted me; it hasn't ceased to be a great country at all. Though I go to a place where the avoidance of complete cynicism is a challenge, I will try to make the most of it, and accept my fate focused on the better life beyond the gate and on the encouragement of many kind souls. My plan is to divide the number of days I have to serve by the number of pounds I hope to lose, keep in mind the range of sticks and carrots with which my superhumanly fat-averse wife will reward performance, and downsize myself toward liberty in increments. I will try to gain from the experience, and again fervently thank all those who have been supportive in these prolonged travails. I will be back in the spring, and to a quieter life than I have known for a long time. Next year in Toronto and London.

# REMEMBERING MY OLDER BROTHER, MONTE

*National Post,* October 22, 2011

My brother, Monte (George Montegu Black III), died nearly ten years ago, but arises constantly in my thoughts and dreams, always pleasantly and true to life. There were just the two of us in our family, and he was four years older, not a great gap among adults but a huge difference between children.

It was among the greatest good fortunes I have had that my brother, unlike other older brothers in families we knew, never abused his superior strength or even his worldlier gift for repartee. I knew other boys whose older brothers were terrible bullies, and so understood from earliest days the extent of my good luck.

I tried to repay his generosity with purposeful solidarity in the one-sided debates that arise between children and their parents in any family, and a strong bond developed between us that never weakened, even though we rarely lived in the same place after he went away to school when I was ten. After that, schools, universities, and careers kept us generally in different cities, apart from holidays, until I returned to Toronto from Quebec in 1974, when I was thirty.

That we were generally in different cities did not mean that we did not stay in touch or have some shared economic interests, often cross-investments in the most hilariously implausible enterprises; and often put forth, at least on his part, in sales pitches of tremendously colourful sales-manship. "The road to recovery is paved with" whatever he was pushing at the time. "Intriguing" prospects kept appearing, such as the "Wipe-o-matic automobile headlamp," regrettably some decades ahead of its time.

Despite the vagaries of speculation, we progressed, and although I was mainly active in the community-newspaper business, we became more closely involved together in the financial industry in gradually more serious activities. We worked hard, and we played pretty hard too (he had a young family and I was a bachelor), and we got on.

We reached a higher level of corporate involvement when we bought our late father's shares in what was known as the Argus group in 1976. Our parents died just ten days apart in July of that year, one from a long battle with cancer, and the second suddenly from an accident. At the end of that difficult day, I went to my brother's house, he poured me a glass of mahogany-coloured Scottish whisky, of which we were both sizeable consumers at the time, and, grasping the occasion with-out losing his imperishable sense of humour, he sipped thoughtfully and said reflectively, "Holy Jesus! We're orphans."

We had a most amicable division of assets in 1986, as he became a venture capitalist, a field for which he had considerable aptitude, as he was a visionary in some areas and less conservative financially than I was. I focused on the international newspaper business. We were no longer in the same offices, but the rapport of thirty-five years adapted again, without strain. We were certainly very different personalities. He liked country music, detective stories, and raunchy movies, and used to refer to me as "one of these humanists" because I rarely read fiction and wrote about history.

But in all seasons of life, through a difficult divorce, some financial pressures (which he successfully surmounted), and other travails, he remained bonhomous, indomitable, and always able to reduce almost anything to a quip. These were never flippant or escapist, and always retained the implicit determination that almost anything could be overcome, without alarm or despair or a loss of proportion, or even of the absurdity of a great deal of life itself.

In his youth, my brother was one of the greatest natural athletes I have known (an area where I, unfortunately, was rather shortchanged). Though this talent gave some ground, over years, to his later penchant to be a gourmand and a tastevin, it never led him to vanity or conceit. Always popular, and generally more sociable than I was, he was never a cad or even inconstant, or ever an ungenerous friend or less than a gentleman.

Impatient with and contemptuous of sharpers, he didn't have the fixity of purpose to bother much with excessive lawyering and political manoeuvring. He didn't stay long where he wasn't enjoying himself, and generally he did enjoy himself.

This was the cruel irony of his early death, yet he managed even this unjust fate with his unfailing flair and even good humour. He was diagnosed with inoperable esophageal cancer in February 2001, and a variety of non-surgical treatments were prescribed. He took an active and informed interest in the pursuit of exotica (he was a knowledgeable investor in cutting edge pharmacology), and even advised, detachedly, on procedures that did not require a general anesthetic, as they were in progress. He was very happy in his second marriage and they received friends jovially at his home until late in the illness. Though he spoke of having been dealt "the queen of spades" and was under no illusions about where the tale would end, he went to literally superhuman lengths to avoid the maudlin, the mawkish, the gloomy, or anything remotely related to self-pity.

Even faced with the supreme test, he never moved his philosophical compass. He was not an atheist, but doubted that there was a God he could propitiate, but was confident that he had lived a decent and honourable life. He would not change his theological tune, or the volume or cadence of it, even as the supreme possible audition approached.

This stage of life, as all who have been through it with a loved one know, can be conversationally oppressive. But with Monte, witty discussion of current affairs never dragged, yet there was never the feeling that his medical condition was the unmentioned 900-pound gorilla in the room.

Our last words were in his hospital room, two days before he died, on January 10, 2002, aged sixty-one and five months. His first wife was in the same hospital, just two doors away, and died a day ahead of him. They had never really reconciled, but there was some commingling of those conducting the vigils. Between my brother and me there was no need for farewells or memorials; we exchanged amusing reminiscences and compliments, and when his concentration started to give way under the heady medication, I quietly withdrew, hoping that it might still not be the end. There was not, as there never had been in fifty-five years, anything to bridge, paper over, apologize for, or even seriously regret between us.

That seamless solidarity persists, as revenances of his bons mots of long ago occur, churned up by similar events or personalities, and as he comes into my dreams, always revealing again the jaunty realism of his nature. It is consoling to see how porous is the finality of death, after all.

His funeral at Grace Church in Toronto, where he had been married, and from which our parents had been buried twenty-six years before, was very heavily attended, attesting to his great popularity. Asked by my sister-in-law to speak, I kept it good-humoured; and in deference to his great talents as a sportsman in his early years, when I had known him best, I quoted from Housman's "To an Athlete Dying Young," ending, "Today, the road all runners come, / Shoulder-high we bring you home, / And set you at your threshold down, / townsmen still, of a stiller town." Snow was lightly falling and there was a good deal of snow on the ground, a piper played as we left the church, and light departed as we were at the graveside. The reception at our house afterward was a warm occasion of renewed relationships, many after a lapse of decades, a conviviality completely appropriate to the man whom we all mourned.

The last words of my remembrance of him at the church were that "It was and will always remain a privilege to be his brother." That was nothing but the truth then and has not diminished since.

# MY BATTLES WITH CHRISTOPHER HITCHENS

*National Post*, December 24, 2011

As Christmas remains a religious occasion, a few thoughts from that perspective commend themselves.

This newspaper seems to have been plunged into mourning for Christopher Hitchens, perhaps best known for his belligerent atheism. I must say that I had a few fierce written exchanges with Christopher over the years, mainly in Britain's *Spectator* magazine, but not on religious matters. In our polemical battles, which were entertainingly acidulous and ungentlemanly on both sides, the arguments he made were so unmitigatedly fatuous, he always seemed to me rather silly, more a pest than even a gadfly, much less a sage or wit.

Our first pyrotechnic outburst came when President Reagan had just endured a cancer operation and was about to meet Mikhail Gorbachev. Christopher wrote that Reagan should resign the presidency and not embarrass the West by having to interrupt the summit meeting every fifteen minutes to go to the lavatory. It was, as I wrote, an utterly tasteless (and inaccurate) prediction (and not without its ironies, given its author's subsequent medical history). Christopher retreated ungraciously, especially after the Reagan–Gorbachev meeting was universally seen as a success. However, when Ronald Reagan died, in 2004, widely hailed as a popular and outstanding president, Christopher carped after him as "an idiot."

The last real dust-up we had was over his "book" about Henry Kissinger's supposed role in the overthrow of Chilean president Allende in 1973. (To those of us who write properly researched and referenced non-fiction books, it is a little hard to take 80,000 ill-tempered words thundered incoherently out in unsubstantiated accusations as more than sophomoric pamphleteering.) Hitchens dismissed the complete absence of any supporting evidence for his thesis as merely illustrating the fiendish cleverness of the accused. I argued in my *Spectator* review that made for an unconvincing case (little imagining how disagreeably familiar I would personally become with the technique).

I would have participated in the recent Munk Debate in Toronto between Christopher and Tony Blair about religion if I had been able to leave the United States, but I listened to it carefully. Christopher repeated his usual well-tried disparagements, with some spontaneous witticisms, as Blair's very flaccid comments warranted, and certainly won easily on the night. Blair failed to attack any of atheism's vulnerabilities, and was surprisingly inept for a talented forensic debater and genuinely committed Christian.

If pushed, atheists always fall back on the shortcomings of individual clergy and a variant of Bertrand Russell's vacuous old fable that there is a finite amount of knowledge in the world and every day man is a step closer to possessing all of it. I have no problem with atheists generally, but their arguments are rubbish when they go beyond general skepticism, and the only atheists who aren't somewhat disturbed are those who don't much think about it and are serenely uninterested in otherworldly thoughts.

Christopher's claim that Mother Teresa was "a bitch" and a "fanatic" had no basis at all. And his rages against Pope Benedict were founded on the pope's teenage conscription into a non-political German antiaircraft battery, which never fired a shot and from which he deserted at the first opportunity, and his supposed facilitation of Boston's Cardinal Law's flight from justice. (Law returned to the United States for eighteen months and answered all the grand jury's questions, but Christopher was never much interested in the facts of a case.)

I'm sorry he died, and if my friends David Frum and Jonathan Kay grieve for Christopher, I'll take their word for it. (My wife, Barbara, had a very convivial talk with him at the Frums' house last year despite all the fire we have exchanged and I was grateful to him for speaking well of some of my books.) But I never saw why the norms of civilized behaviour and comment should be waived for him, and cannot say I will really miss him (any more than I think he is now missing me).

I have it on good authority that Christopher Hitchens was disappointed that the child-molestation scandal, appalling though it was, did not bring the Roman Catholic Church crashing to earth like the Zeppelin *Hindenburg* at Lakehurst, New Jersey, in 1937. People of that mindset are always particularly infuriated, century after century, at the stubborn failure of the Roman Catholic Church simply to fold its wings and fall to the ground. In their desperation, they even rejoice at perceived setbacks to Rome by what they consider to be lesser sectarian antagonists. (The recent acquisition of the Reverend Robert Schuller's Crystal Cathedral, designed by Philip Johnson and familiar to scores of millions of Sunday television viewers of the *Hour of Power*, by the Roman Catholic diocese of Orange, California, for $51 million should remind even the most blinkered materialists not to underestimate the strength of invisible means of support.)

This pope has responded effectively to the sexual-abuse crisis, and there has been no discernible reduction in general church attendance or recruitment. The most important, and perhaps least recognized relevant fact is that more than 95 per cent of the Roman Catholic clergy are dedicated people who have sacrificed a great deal to lead a Christian life and have educated and otherwise cared for hundreds of millions of people with exemplary devotion and self-discipline. At this time of year, especially, those millions of humanity's benefactors should be remembered.

My current and thankfully soon to be departed surroundings incite me to constant gratitude that Pope Benedict is almost the only prominent person in the world who regularly expresses solicitude for the many millions of imprisoned people in the world (an inordinate number in the United States). And I am prompted to cite a Christmas excerpt from Pope John Paul II's 2000 message on the subject, which is frequently invoked by his successor: "Public authorities who deprive human beings of their personal freedom . . . must realize that they are not masters of the prisoners' time. In the same way, those who are in detention must not live as if their time in prison had been taken from them completely; it needs to be lived to the full. . . . In many countries' prisons, life is very precarious, not to say altogether unworthy of human beings. . . . In some cases, detention seems to create more problems than it solves. This must prompt rethinking with a view to some kind of reform. . . . Such a process is based on growth in the sense of responsibility. None of this should be considered utopian."

Both popes have elsewhere inveighed against the imperfections of the prosecution services and the evils of false convictions. I am in a relatively endurable prison, but even Christopher Hitchens, if he had suffered such a fate as mine, rather than the much harsher one that has felled him, would be less dismissive of the leaders of Christianity.

A Merry Christmas to all, including Christopher, wherever you are.

Since the death of Christopher Hitchens has moved me to such verbosity, I'll add something about the death a few days later, of the great Václav Havel (but not about the unspeakable Kim Jong Il). The Czechs were the only people that fell behind the Iron Curtain that were not specifically disposed of in the Churchill–Stalin spheres of influence agreement of October 1944, nor specifically promised democratic government in the Yalta Agreements of January 1945 (though all occupied territories were in Yalta's Declaration on Liberated Europe). No memoirist, not Truman, Churchill, Eisenhower, Marshall (through his official biographer), or Brooke, shed any light on why the Red Army was allowed to take Bohemia and Moravia. Detachments of the U.S. Army reached Prague, but withdrew. If they had not, Václav Havel would never have had the consciousness-raising experience of being sent to prison, and would probably have led his people twenty years earlier, had he sought that honour.

*This piece was filed, with the following letter to my* National Post *editor, just before I left prison for the last time, while my status in Canada was still being debated, in May 2012.*

Dear Jonathan,

This is a world exclusive by anticipation. If things don't turn out as I expect, we will have to pull it, and I will write for the next week instead of taking the first of two weeks' holiday. I must swear you to secrecy, as there is surprising interest in this last step, and I mustn't comment on my official reception in Canada before it happens. This may be a bit long, but if you want it cut, or otherwise changed, let me know please by midday Thursday, because after that the machine may be cut off. If all else fails, please give a colour-coded edit to Joan, and I will check it with her by 'phone on Friday before I have left Miami. I'm looking forward to seeing you.

Best,

Conrad

# FREE AT LAST

*National Post*, May 5, 2012

N o one who has not been unjustly accused and incarcerated can
know with what pleasure and relief he would depart the jurisdiction that has tormented him, having been unable to do so for five years,
and returns to his home of sixty years. This was my experience yesterday.

Throughout those five years, I had rarely spent more than a few
waking minutes without that revenant thought of passing inwardly
through the gates of my home again. Given the endless harassments of
the last nine years, I had a tentative, darting, thought that at the end, it
would all go smoothly at last. It did.

The capacity and disposition of the U.S. Bureau of Prisons to
irritate those in its maw must now be, along with advanced military
hardware, the principal official manifestation of the fabled American
exceptionalism, and release from its grip must be one of the most frequent versions of the current American Dream. But the BOP sent me on
my way very cordially.

I had been a day short of eight months at the low-security federal prison in Miami. It has quite a pleasant layout, surrounding a
pond frequented by ducks, gulls, coots, and turtles, and the architecture of a junior college. I had got on well, with no abrasive moments
with anyone. The personnel of the regime were a job lot ranging from
Neanderthalean stupidity honed by quicksilver impulses to aggression,
to very decent and effective people. The residents spanned a wider

range, from a few nasty arsonists and others with violent, now-distant pasts, through low-life swindlers, the small fry of the phony Drug War, to people given horrifying sentences for sitting in their own homes downloading child pornography, but not creating or distributing it, to some quite interesting people of varied commercial background. All had their stories, real or fictionalized, and most were interesting in their way.

There were a few very gracious and cultivated former narcotics eminences from Puerto Rico and Florida, but many more Central American peasants who had been paid what was for them a princely sum to drive drug-laden boats or vehicles to pre-arranged drug busts, gaining financial security for their families from the arrangers, who received sentence reductions for their false tipoffs, and commendations for the arresting officers. They would spend five to seven years in the relatively commodious surroundings of a low-security federal prison, and live more comfortably ever after.

This is one of the many spontaneous flourishes of the American system (though the incidence of this sort of thing has declined in recent years). About 10 per cent of the people in our prison, like me, are completely innocent of the charges that brought us there. About 20 per cent are mentally impaired, pharmacological zombies who prior to 1975 would have been in mental treatment centres and would be better off there. About 20 per cent were voyeuristic but not physical sex offenders, who don't belong in such a place either. Very few of the rest would be of any possible danger to anyone, and imprisoning them, as opposed to community service and treatment where appropriate, is nonsense. Almost all of these men have been grossly oversentenced by the standards of any other civilized country, in deference to the multi-partisan hysteria about law and order (a cause current imprisonment policy does not advance), and to the requirements of the bloated public- and private-sector American prison industry. This is not the place to develop this theme, but I fervently hope that Canada goes no farther in emulation of the appalling shambles of American penal policy.

I had taught a course in U.S. history to quite knowledgeable fellow residents, using the draft of my next book, a strategic history of the United States, as the text. It was neither the tutorial challenge nor the pleasure of helping those most in need of a helping hand that I had had at my former prison, but the sessions were lively and interesting, and this was a smaller prison with generally more educated inmates closer to the end of their sentences. And my stay was brief; just what had been thought necessary to put a fig leaf of plausibility on the spurious and tattered prosecution of my co-defendants and me after the last vestiges of it had been unanimously vacated by the U.S. Supreme Court.

It wasn't a violent or disorderly place; my legal battles had been widely followed and appreciated among the inmates, and the Bureau faithfully upheld my arrangements at my former prison of accepting my column-writing for this and other publications. Many of the personnel of the regime generously complimented me on some of my U.S. political commentaries in the *National Review Online* and the *Huffington Post*. I have managed to get well-organized for my financial relaunch. As prison goes, this was as good as it gets in the prisoner-unfriendly U.S.A., but not so good as to obscure the fact that I should never have been prosecuted, nor that I was desperately ambitious to leave and put it all behind me. Heavily supported by counsel, as one must be in the United States for the safe performance of almost any act less mundane than the preoccupations of the lavatory, I went from the prison to the Immigration and Customs Enforcement authorities. They were perfectly agreeable and soon took on board that my desire to leave their country vastly exceeded their mechanical ambition to ensure that I did so.

Yesterday, of all days, the joys of survival were irrepressible. On the airplane from Miami to Toronto, Barbara and I were able for the first time in nine years to plan and muse almost unconditionally, and without any Damoclean menace, lurking, imminent, and yet unknowable. It is an inexpressible feeling, but it doesn't, between Barbara and me, and my sons and daughter and a few other intimates, need any expression.

It had been a very difficult time; we dealt with it as best we could, and it was ending as well as it could, given the very uneven correlation of forces between the U.S. government and its Canadian quislings, and me. There is a little legal mopping up to be done, but not heavy duty combat compared to the last nine years, and a final appeal to sanity in the American juridical system to be made. Finally, comes now the reckoning with those who obscenely enriched themselves while destroying our Canadian companies, under court protection, all in the name of the innocent stakeholders they impoverished. I look forward to it.

Canadian immigration officials could not have been more courteous. Suspense had flourished in some circles over what sort of welcome I might receive in Canada. It was never appropriate of me to comment on it, but I was never aware of any serious suggestion that I not be allowed to set foot in the country, which is all I was seeking. I will sort the rest out later, as any other temporary resident would.

I had come down our long driveway thousands of times, and returning from many more exotic places than Miami, but never after such a protracted and daunting challenge. Barbara had planted some new trees in the orchard and spruced up the house a bit, and for the last several months she had been sending me snapshots of different rooms and of the grounds. It was very reassuring to go from room to room and see my books and displayed historic documents and ship models exactly as I had placed, left, and remembered them. With a little recreation, we will be ready for normal life again at last. I have replied to every individual supportive contact, but my gratitude to the very large number of those who have encouraged us is beyond my ability to record here.

I will do some things differently and will look forward to a quieter, but not uneventful, life. My long minuet with the Canadian media can peacefully subside; it had its lively moments. Apart from a final update of my book about these travails, I have nothing more to write or say (or unsay) about them, and am focused altogether on new projects that need not be disclosed. Apart from what modest attention I may attract as a writer, I yield my small share of the spotlight's attention to others, with my very best wishes.

*The foregoing column, including alternative endings, was composed in the United States, as the author's conditions of return to Canada did not initially permit him to work for a Canadian employer.*

# HONOURS DO NOT MAKE A MAN, ANY MORE THAN THE WITHDRAWAL OF HONOURS UNMAKES ONE

*National Post*, February 3, 2014

In response to the many good wishes I have received over my departure from the Order and Privy Council of Canada, I will, as I always do, reply to everyone who has contacted me by email – but their numbers are such that it will take a while, and I ask for patience. I take it as an omen that for the first time, at any stage of this long and relentless persecution, I have not received a single negative message.

Two important issues emerge from this controversy. It had been obvious for two years that the honours and awards staff that administers these matters were rabid in their ambition to remove me, and I publicly referred to their ambitions in this regard as "orgasmic." I learned long ago that honours do not make a man, any more than the withdrawal of honours unmakes one. It was obvious that no Canadian court would have even been seized of such spurious charges as I faced in the United States, and certainly no guilty verdicts would have been returned, and even the American system effectively pitched all the counts. But the grinding of the notorious Chicago court system managed to circumvent the U.S. Supreme Court by spuriously retrieving two absurd convictions the high court had vacated.

From their very first abrupt and officious communication, it was clear that the honours bureaucrats had deemed me to be a convicted criminal who merited not even the most basic courtesies or due process regarding my Order of Canada status. I quickly realized that these prancing figurines in the governor general's entourage who manipulate this honours system did not wish to be confused by the facts and were scandalized by the notion that anyone might seek a hearing on this matter, though the statute establishing the Order provides for one.

After the Canadian courts decided that they could not impose a hearing, I wrote the following letter to the governor general of Canada, David Johnston, on December 18:

> *Your Excellency:*
>
> *Your heraldic officials have successfully litigated to prevent a hearing on the matter of my status as an Officer of the Order of Canada. I am reliably advised that it is the practice of the Advisory Board of that Order to approve the recommendations of staff. Their adamant opposition to a hearing on this matter, which the Order's rules would permit, together with the tone of their correspondence, make their bias perfectly plain.*
>
> *Though it seems futile to repeat what has been made evident in previous letters to your staff, I cannot dismiss this calumny without a final summing up. Perhaps it is inevitable that given a little power and no accountability, some officials will be unable to resist the excitement of using it arbitrarily and spitefully. There is nothing before those officials that could give legitimate cause for denying my status had they seriously examined the matter. All counts against me were abandoned, rejected by jurors, or unanimously vacated by the U.S. Supreme*

*Court. That two counts were revived against me only speaks to the flaw in the U.S. Justice system which allows a lower court judge whose reasoning has been excoriated by the high court to resurrect two of the minor counts vacated in order to save a fig leaf of credibility for a failed prosecution and vitiated judgment. None of this could have happened in the courts of this country.*

*I won the largest defamation settlement in Canadian history ($5 million) from the sponsors of the prosecution. In all of the circumstances, I decline to continue in a process that I consider to be unjust in respect of an honour, the retention of which, as matters have evolved, appears to rest largely in the hands of unaccountable officials of inflexible views, in an ex parte proceeding. I will not seek to appeal to the Supreme Court of Canada; will not activate the efforts a number of friends in each echelon of the Order of Canada have offered to press on my behalf with the advisory board; and will not communicate further with the Herald Chancellor.*

*I enclose a copy of my book, which covers the events that gave rise to this issue (not one aspect of which has been disputed), and copies of the letters sent to the Chief Justice of Canada in her capacity as chairperson of the Advisory Board of the Order of Canada by the principal trial defence counsel, Mr. Safer, and by my former corporate colleague Dr. Henry A. Kissinger, should you wish to consider the matter if and when it gets to you. If my surmise of the process is correct and you receive a recommendation that my continuation as an Officer of the Order of Canada is not appropriate, and you accept that recommendation, I would be grateful if you would take this letter as my retirement as an Officer of the Order of Canada. If you decline to have any suspensive aspect to the issue, please accept this letter as my resignation as an Officer of the Order of Canada effective on your receipt of this letter.*

*As we have known each other for many years, I hope you will pardon my adding that it is not the least disappointment I have suffered in my persecution by the U.S. prosecutors to discover that my native country, in matters of its highest civil decoration, follows the vagaries of the U.S. justice system with such undeserved deference, drastic though its variance indisputably is in this case with any procedure or practice that would occur or be in the least acceptable in this country. It has been a painful episode and I hope it is not an unjustified liberty for me to ask you to close it as you see fit as decorously as possible.*

*With personal best wishes and compliments of the season to you,*

*Yours sincerely,*

*Conrad Black*

Whether I continued to hold these distinctions was not significant, but the process of Canada demeaning itself by robotic conformity to injustices inflicted in the United States (or any foreign country) on the holders of Canadian honours without any real review is a matter of some general interest. If Canada's highest honours can be stripped away from someone because of processes that would not be acceptable in Canada, and thus validated in Canada without any due process or by qualified people – only by gnomish and nasty officials clinging like limpets to their own prejudices and piously declining to "relitigate" – the consequences reflect poorly on Canadian sovereignty and maturity as a country.

I do not believe that Canadians, if they thought about it, would accept that the unknowable, and in this case meticulously documented, caprices and irregularities of a foreign justice system at great variance with their own should be able to determine without any due process or accountability the status of holders of Canadian honours, and especially not in a Molièresque parlour-room farce conducted by a poltroon styled as a herald chancellor.

That brings up the other point that is significant: as readers can see from the letter reproduced above, I in fact resigned, but gave David Johnston the opportunity to do the right thing – not accept the advice to withdraw my honours, which he was free to do – if he wished. I correctly predicted that the bobble-headed worthies of the official snobocracy called the Advisory Board of the Order of Canada would nod the herald chancellor's sanctimonious misinformation on to Johnston.

(I am confident none of them could give any explanation of my ostensible conviction except the malicious fantasies of the libel defendants who originally uttered them and whom I relieved of $5 million.) And I expected that Johnston would be resistless against the tug of the strings attaching his articulating joints to the hands of the hovering officials.

The Federal Court of Appeal had declined to require the hearing that may be requested, on the very grounds of the governor general's right to decline the recommendation he received from the Advisory Board. I had said I would retire if denied a hearing, and I did so, but in deference to the court and the governor general, I thought I should leave open the option for him to decline the juggernaut of rubber stamps the herald chancellor would solicit and propel into his lap. As I wrote in my letter to him, I tried to wind the matter down, by forgoing an appeal or any lobbying by my supporters in the Order, and I invoked decades of casual but cordial acquaintance to ask Johnston to do what he thought best, but do it decorously.

The herald chancellor himself called my counsel on the late afternoon of Friday afternoon, January 31, to be sure that he had my email address; to be sure, that is, that they expelled me before I confirmed my resignation (though I did not believe there was any need to confirm it). Government House issued a statement that was, in fact, false, as I had already resigned; presumably to inflict as much irritation and affected consequentiality as possible. (The Privy Council issue, of which I had no notice whatever, was at least consistent, and was so insultingly communicated by Johnston's own email, and in the name of the prime minister, it was almost piquant.)

The second issue raised is whether Canadians really want these functions exercised in this secretive, tortuous, dishonest way by such churlish people. My history of Canada will be published later this year. The subtitle is "Rise to Greatness," and it is often a gripping and prideful tale, but I am afraid the country's institutions and the people who operate them have not entirely kept pace with what Canadians as a people have accomplished.

This incident will pass quickly and Canadians will sort the process out. I am moving on; this has been an annoying sideshow, but I have won 99 per cent of the battles and, as I told the trial judge, always try to take success like a gentleman and disappointment like a man. Though I would not accept these honours if they were offered under this regime again, I will try to behave in a way that will cause fair-minded people to think I have earned them. And, not that too much weight should be attached to these either, I am content with the honours I already have from countries less obedient to the perversities of a half-demented, much-criticized Chicago judge than Canada is.

For my opponents, no further argument on this subject from me will be useful, and for my friends, I trust none is necessary. Perhaps the most eloquent of the very large number of messages I have received was the one signed "Tim": "F—k 'em." Good thought, Tim, whoever you are, but my contempt for them is so profound and complete that I don't think they deserve even that sensation.

# ON THE
# ONTARIO SECURITIES
# COMMISSION

*National Post*, March 7, 2015

---

The Ontario Securities Commission's recent decision to ban my service as an officer or director of a company in its jurisdiction, a ban I had imposed on myself for the last twelve years and undertook to continue, is a thoroughly contemptible effort to bury in righteous ordure its own shameful history in the controversies where I was long embroiled.

It sandbagged my final effort in 2005 to salvage the Hollinger group from court-supported saprophytes with a proposal to privatize the Canadian Hollinger at a good historic price, and a litigation trust should any shareholder want to sue us. A media frenzy instantly arose when there were allegations in 2003 of the improper payment of non-compete fees to my associates and me in newspaper asset sales made as we exited that business in contemplation of internet competition. Our independent local bench and regulators slavishly bought the media line.

I had welcomed a special committee to examine the company and made a so-called restructuring agreement with the counsel of the special committee (Richard Breeden, former head of the Securities and Exchange Commission). Breeden and the others immediately violated all its terms and caused the company my associates and I built to sue us for over us$1 billion. I negotiated the sale of the group to British interests, but Breeden was able to intervene to stop it in Delaware, where our American company was incorporated. A special committee (Breeden) report was published that accused us of conducting a "$500-million corporate kleptocracy" and many other inflammatory charges. We counter-sued, and I sued Breeden and the co-authors for libel. In the report, Breeden and the others promised unheard-of levels of profitability for our companies. They delivered, but not quite as foreseen.

The staff of the osc strongly supported us in public hearings on our privatization plan and the minority shareholders voted 87 per cent in favour of it. Breeden was milking our American company, which would have come back under our control, for $1 million a week, and he "lectured" the osc (as he said to the *Globe and Mail*) that it must stop our privatization.

In Canada, the compulsive, twitching fit of copycat, me-too, branch-plant emulations of the sordid American justice system had already begun. Canadian judges established fawning protégés and cronies in rich sinecures in our companies, from which we were barred from exercising any influence, and they took another immense lawsuit against us. Court-protected bloodsuckers and charlatans took $100,000 a month in directors' fees each, the highest in the known world, as they rifled through the treasury of the prosperous company we had left behind, and bought luxury condos and speculated with their windfall incomes, the gift of Canada's judges and regulators. A "restructuring officer" took over $800,000 a year for many years to restructure up his own lifestyle.

In obedient submission to Breeden, the osc crumpled like rag dolls, launched yet another large lawsuit against us, on top of those of the sec, Breeden, et al., and the usurpatory regime at the Canadian Hollinger. The osc dutifully killed our offer. The companies all cascaded into bankruptcy under the avarice and incompetence of the officially supported replacements of those who had built the companies. Thus did the osc, guardian of the stakeholders' interest, vaporize $300 million of shareholder value in the Canadian company and nearly $2 billion in the U.S. company. It never can be said to have had clean hands in this matter after that, and its holy self-righteousness now is a monstrous irony.

Breeden's report brought the much-sought criminal indictment in Chicago a few months after the rejection of our privatization attempt, in my case seventeen fantastic counts (racketeering, money-laundering, etc.). In the scandalous operation of the U.S. plea-bargain system, the testimony of a "cooperating witness" with immunity from perjury charges (whom the prosecutors eventually accused of perjury, as if anyone else had extorted and rewarded it) helped produce four convictions against me. I was sent to prison, ultimately for three years and two months. I found it quite interesting, got on well with everyone, and as a tutor I was able to help over one hundred inmates matriculate from secondary school. As I told the London *Daily Mail*, in the compound of my prison there was a "more interesting and intelligent group than the management committee of the Toronto Club."

The U.S. Supreme Court unanimously vacated the four convictions, but in the perversity of the American system remanded back to the lower courts it had excoriated the assessment of "the gravity of their errors." The era had already begun of trying to keep a fig leaf of seriousness for this failed prosecution, an impulse that made its final appearance at the OSC last week. Two counts were spuriously retrieved: the receipt of $285,000 that was approved by directors and published in the company's public filings, but incompletely documented by the company secretary in what the trial judge concluded was a clerical error; and the removal of boxes from my office which did not contain any material the SEC did not already have, were not selected or packed by me, were not covered by document retention orders, and which we carried out under security cameras I had had installed to be sure that I could not be accused of covert activity – all with the approval of the acting president of the company and the representative of the court-appointed inspector. I completed my much-reduced sentence.

All of the lawsuits against me collapsed. Breeden's lawsuit for over $1 billion and my counter-suit were settled for $6 million, net, to me; the Canadian litigation committee's lawsuit was settled for $5 million, a fraction of what its authors received for claiming to have a serious case for nine years. The SEC lawsuit was settled for $4 million, because I was stuck with the Delaware decision and, as in the litigation committee's suit, I could not have recovered enough of my legal expenses to reduce the net cost below the settlement amount even if I won in court. I admitted no liability. The U.S. tax issue was resolved for less than 3 per cent of the original much-publicized claim.

My libel suit, greeted at first as a matter of hilarity, was settled for $5 million to me, by far the largest such payment in Canadian history, after Breeden and the others had gone all the way to the Supreme Court of Canada to try to prevent it being heard in this country. None of them could face examination under oath. On all of this litigation combined, I netted a slight gain (though legal costs were considerable). The libel settlement was effectively the death of the allegations, as the special committee report was the source of the farrago of civil and criminal actions, but the media lynch mob of the early years rarely mentions that outcome.

The OSC claim was abandoned too, except the nonsense of the ban I had already voluntarily conceded. I disputed that the U.S. proceedings conferred that right on them. The U.S. actions would never have got off the ground in Canada or any other juridically serious country. I had an unblemished compliance record for thirty years as one of the most active people in Canadian financial markets. To paraphrase Groucho Marx, I would not now be associated with a company that reported to a regulator that has performed so contemptibly as the OSC has in this matter. This episode shows again that Canada must not allow the OSC to become a national regulator.

With both the Order of Canada, from which I was removed last year in a misleading press release from the governor general (as I had already retired from it in a letter to him because I regarded the whole review process as a kangaroo court), and at the OSC last week, I was accused of seeking to "relitigate," when all I sought was a summary hearing by Canadian criteria, not a retrial of facts at all. In both places there was an irresistible urge to prostrate Canada before this fraudulent American miscarriage, apparently from an infelicitous combination of national timidity, offended *amour-propre* at the failure of the onslaught against me, and personal animus (which is only requited by me toward a few individuals).

As I wrote in my recent history of Canada, this country has a more distinguished history than most of its people realize, and a brilliant future, if it can purge the reflex to the false comity of subservience. We must have civilized relations with the United States, but that does not mean government by frightened, priggish servitors of even America's least salubrious foibles. (And no sane American is asking for that.)

Given the evil nature of the American system and the odds against me there (a 99.5 per cent conviction rate), together with the fact that Breeden had torqued the rabid Chicago prosecutors up to demanding life imprisonment and the complete impoverishment of my family and myself, it has worked out well, despite these irritating local after-tremors. All fair-minded people knowledgeable of the case, in both countries, are aware that I broke no laws. Now it is over.

# ADDRESS TO THE CATHOLIC LAWYERS' ASSOCIATION

Osgoode Hall, October 2013

---

Your Eminence, Madam Chief Justice,

I think we live in a time when some of our principal occupations are fundamentally dissatisfied with their place in society. Businessmen resent that they do not have the academic prestige of a learned profession and they have expended billions of dollars of their companies' and in some cases their own money to propagate the fiction that business is an academic subject. It isn't. Business is an intuition supplemented by experience, and one of the most frightening statistics in the United States today, along with the $17-trillion national debt and the $700-billion current-account deficit, is the fact that there are 440,000 business school students in the United States. This means that probably $200 billion a year is spent to enable professors who have rarely administered anything or made any appreciable amount of money to teach essentially esoteric subjects to aspiring business people in vastly ornate monuments to the egos of captains of industry. Business ethics classes should consist, not of an elaborate course consuming a year but of a one-minute admonition to be sure to observe the governing statutes and regulations.

It is a notorious fact that worries everyone that our societies in the West have vastly increased our commitment of resources to elementary and secondary and undergraduate education, and yet standards of education of basic language use and simple mathematics and general knowledge are inferior to where they were when I was a school student, more than fifty years ago. And to compound the problem, and doubtless an important part of it, the teachers, an ancient and vital occupation, which normally would qualify as a learned profession, often behave like an irresponsible industrial union. They fail as a group to offer any defence of their deteriorated level of service to society, and sometimes even sanctimoniously strike in the middle of the school year. They do this contrary to contractual undertakings, while inundating the media with pious assertions of their devotion to the welfare of the students and their fervent desire not to blackmail the parents of the students.

There is nothing that is more important to a modern society of responsible citizenship and ordered liberty than a free press. And the media frequently join in collective associations that purport to have some professional standing but have no such criteria for membership or defined professional standards. All literate adults, and certainly everyone in this room, are familiar with the sloppiness, the malice, the unaccountability, of almost all of the media, and the indifference and Olympian posturings that await any aggrieved party who tries to set the record straight.

The claims to professional standing are even more cavalierly flouted by journalists than by teachers, and they routinely claim a rich lode of benefits while crying like endangered banshees if any editor, publisher, or program director calls them to account for sloppy mis-statements of facts or biased summaries of even simple matters.

I recently had a sharpish exchange with a furtive organization calling itself the Canadian Association of Journalists, which claimed an unlimited right to circulate monstrous libels without any obligation to publish a response or correct, much less apologize for, them. The so-called working press, though in my experience they are far from being martyrs to the work ethic, demand that employers grant them entire liberty to inflict whatever they wish on the public, and that anything less than complete liberty is a compromise of freedom of the press and the public's right to know. It is like saying that management must take no interest in the quality of consumer goods, soft drink executives should have no right to comment on the taste of their beverages, and automobile executives should have no right to take an interest in the appearance, comfort, and performance of their cars. Everyone recognizes the absolute need of a free press, and attempts to regulate it, such as those now being undertaken in the United Kingdom, will fail, deservedly. But what we have is a fundamentally unsatisfactory arrangement of the media having immense power inadequately incentivized to use it responsibly, a condition that disserves society and affects standards of public information.

I have referred to these other important occupations in order to dissipate in advance any suspicion you might otherwise have that I am singling out the law for unrepresentative criticism. I am a law graduate, from Laval University. I enjoyed my time there and had the benefit and the challenge of learning the language as well as the law, but never intended to practise and did not attempt the bar course. I was already engaged in the newspaper business and was, I think, perhaps the only person in history who was the publisher of a daily commercially successful newspaper while also a law student. In the intervening years, I have engaged a very large number of lawyers, including many of the best-known and most capable lawyers in this country, the United States, the United Kingdom, and Australia. While I did not wish to practice, essentially because I did not wish to work for others but rather for myself and for my own account, I care for the law, and despite what I am saying about the legal and other professions, I think that society functions well, given that it is run by people.

With that said, precisely the motive that caused me not to practise law I think afflicts many people who do: they resent the client, and specifically resent the fact that though the law is one of the premier learned professions, it exacts its income from clients who, for the most part, lawyers do not regard as their intellectual peers. Simply stated, a great many lawyers extract their livelihood purporting to follow instructions from people they do not intellectually respect. I must emphasize that I have never felt myself the victim of such condescensions, and of course I am aware that many clients are tiresome, ignorant, demanding, and generally annoying people. But the law is not only a learned profession, it is also a service industry.

Other occupations have comparable frustrations. The professor of business and of other subjects can never get completely away from Shaw's famous dictum that "he who can does, and he who can't teaches." Even when I was an elementary school student, I thought some of those who exercised such control as teachers did in those days were people who could not make it in the real world, and so chose to become figures of authority in this quasi-Lilliput. Having employed many thousands of journalists over many decades, I have thought almost from the outset that a very large number of them are fundamentally frustrated and offended that they spend their lives reporting on the sayings and doings of others and no one is much interested in what they think. A junior reporter with a byline, if not closely edited, and they rarely are, has greater power than that journalist is usually qualified to exercise, and the results are notorious and, as I have said, practically unappealable.

Fortunately, there are inspiringly competent and dedicated people in every field, obviously including the law. But other occupations do not swaddle themselves in their institutional indispensability – the law is, as we all know, the ultimate authority. It is what we must do and what is enforced and for those who do not wish to be outlaws or active revolutionaries, it is inescapable, however poorly composed or mistakenly or unjustly imposed. It clothes itself always in the raiment of the distinguishing hallmark of civilization. The blindfolded lady holding the scales of justice, the truisms we were all brought up with about one's day in court and all of us being equal before the law, of what is legitimate and not just what is necessary, and what is morally right and socially best, and has to be obeyed, this is what distinguishes civilized human society from barbarism, lower orders of animals, and the jungle. All occupations have or affect a group pride, but none other, not even the doctors or the most fervent of the clergy, Your Eminence, takes unto itself this holy mission of legitimacy, civilization, and moral authority, of indispensability to human society, supported by the authority of the state.

And other occupations are not paid for dealing with what their profession itself creates. Lawyers make laws, argue the laws, and judge the application of the laws. Doctors normally treat accidents or spontaneous medical occurrences; teachers provide a certain level of familiarity with given subjects. Clergy and architects are normally approached by choice; so even are business school professors. But lawyers are inescapable and are at every stage of the legal process.

Many of you know as well as I do how poorly the system often really works. There are too many laws and regulations, and they are spewed out in unmanageable quantities every year. No person would claim that your colleagues in legislatures and regulatory bodies are deliberately creating work for the profession, but I have never seen anything quite as predictable as the eagerness of the courts and taxing masters to ensure that lawyers' bills are paid, no matter how exorbitant, and, within reason, no matter how professionally poor the service. I speak – and I would not say this if it were not already publicly disclosed – as, I hope, the only person in the room who has personally paid legal bills in excess of $30 million. I have had the full range of quality of professional service, from superb to abominable, but I had to pay full rate for all of it. Precisely the pecuniary preoccupations that you have laboured your business clients with to the point of inciting a collective inferiority complex is now the chief distinguishing activity of a very large number of lawyers. These law firms are businesses, and not always very well run businesses. You know, most of you, better than I do, how often unsustainable guaranties are made to graduating lawyers, and excessive investments are often made in office luxuries and swank addresses. As for the impartial bench, with respect, Heather, in my experience, they are often, as my friend George Jonas put it, merely the zeitgeist in robes.

I hope you will pardon me a few illustrative reflections on my own recent legal travails. I will not comment on the merits, a subject where I believe my views are well-known. Court-sponsored professionals, in Canada and the United States, hijacked corporations in complete contravention of the presumption of innocence, which proved in our case to be a well-founded presumption. They drained and squandered $2 billion of shareholders' equity, bringing financial hardship to tens of thousands of homes in every part of Canada and the United States, while siphoning off as a reward for this unfortunate commercial miracle they engineered $450 million for themselves. All counts against me were abandoned, rejected by jurors, or unanimously vacated by the U.S. Supreme Court. Yet I could not get any traction until the U.S. High Court remanded the vacated counts back to a lower court it had excoriated for, *inter alia*, "The infirmity of invented law," to assess the gravity of its own errors. It self-servingly retrieved two counts. No other serious jurisdiction in the world except the United States would have tolerated this procedure. The Supreme Court of Canada unanimously upheld the lower courts and required my accusers to face my libel suit in Canada. My accusers settled my libel claim for $5 million, 250 per cent higher than the largest previous libel settlement or award in Canadian history.

What litigation of mine remains before the local courts is just a mopping-up operation against, as I have publicly described them, the "charlatans and bloodsuckers" still arguing their right to rifle through the pittance that remains of the prosperous company they destroyed. The Ontario Securities Commission doomed the company by declining to allow our privatization bid in 2005 at the behest of my chief libel defendant. This makes the piffle of its present harassments doubly irritating, but if I must deal with the osc, I will do that at the osc.

In the United States, the legal profession has been fully complicit in the destruction of elemental individual rights. The U.S. Bill of Rights, which is the basis of that country's claim to being a font of human liberty and individual freedom, in the Fifth, Sixth, and Eighth Amendments to the Constitution, promises due process, no seizure of property without due compensation, the grand jury as an assurance against capricious prosecution, an impartial jury, access to counsel, prompt justice, and reasonable bail. I received none of that. I posted $38 million in bail, was denied counsel of choice by an illegal asset freeze in an *ex parte* proceeding based on what was proved to be a false affidavit from the FBI, and was hounded for almost a decade even though there was practically no case. The pyrotechnics of the U.S. attorney, following the rubber-stamp approval of the in-camera charges before the Grand Jury, thoroughly poisoned the rather limited minds of the jury pool. It isn't a system of justice at all; the United States operates a conveyor belt to its bloated and corrupt prison system. The United States has 5 per cent of the world's population, 25 per cent of its incarcerated people, and

50 per cent of its trained lawyers, who consume about 10 per cent of its gross national product. Prosecutors in the United States win 99.5 per cent of their cases, 97 per cent without a trial, compared to 61 per cent in Canada and barely 50 per cent in the United Kingdom. There are forty-eight million Americans with a criminal record and even deducting the twenty-year-old drunk driving and disorderly conduct convictions, which still prevent such people from being admitted as visitors to Canada, over 15 per cent of adult American males are designated felons. This is a scandalous state of affairs; many lawyers are concerned, but where is the professional outrage and where was the Supreme Court when the Bill of Rights was put to the shredder?

Like most of you, I believe in the confession and repentance of misconduct and the punishment of crime, but in a proportionate and, if possible and merited, a merciful way as conducive as possible to salvaging the accused for useful life in society. That is not the American way, where the prison system is designed to destroy permanently those consigned to it. In the largely private-sector prison system, and for the vast and politically hyperactive correctional officers' unions, organizations to promote the welfare of a million unskilled workers who person the prisons, prisoners are the commodity and there is an insatiable demand for more of them. The role of the judge is usurped by mandatory minimums, and the great majority of the judges are ex-prosecutors and have never freed themselves of that bias. And the plea-bargain system is just usually the terrorization of witnesses into producing inculpatory perjury in exchange for an immunity, including to prosecution for perjury. It is with great disquiet that I see any aspects of the American justice system being imported into this country.

So this is not just a screed, please allow me a few well-intended suggestions. We must have a serious effort to consolidate statutes and avoid the endless proliferation of them: over 4,000 new laws and regulations a year in the United States carrying heavy sanctions. There should be a standing committee consolidating and simplifying this welter of mousetraps and booby traps for the unsuspecting. The corporate governance rules must be reformed and complainants must not be allowed to ransack corporations for their own profit as they are transformed into platforms to persecute those who created the value in them. This is what happened in our case. Bankruptcy laws are now largely just a racket for those who operate them under court protection, and they desperately need to be radically changed. Prosecutors must not have an absolute immunity as the Thompson case gave them in the United States when it was confirmed that prosecutors had deliberately suppressed exculpatory evidence for a man who sat on death row for fourteen years. Prosecutors must be free to do their jobs but not to terrorize society.

Prison for non-violent criminals is nonsense; it makes things worse. Non-violent people should contribute the equivalent number of years of designated work at prisoner pay scales and food-stamp diet and live in equivalent conditions to assisted housing during their sentences, with not more than weekly relief from that regime. Obviously, violent criminals must continue to be segregated from society. The plea bargain must be severely policed to avoid abuses, and drugs should be legalized; the War on Drugs is a colossal failure and large sections of government have been suborned by the illegal drug industry. Hard drug users should be compelled to take treatment. I regret to say that there are too many lawyers and their work does not contain enough added value. The legal industry grows, as if on steroids, and it is in part a taxation on all those who do productive work that does raise value. Legal invoices haven't skyrocketed on the basis of supply and demand; they have been juiced upwards by a cartel. Most lawyers, most of the time, are not worth ten times the hourly rate of a good plumber or carpenter. The founders of our modern common law jurisdictions never intended for these societies to be as litigious as they are, to become prosecutocracies or carceral states, or for the law to be more of an industry than a profession.

I am a person of some means and assured access to the media. Less fortunate people are ground to powder, after the legal system and the media have crucified them. The public defender and legal-aid systems are completely inadequate, and very few people can go very far in this legal system without running out of money. My distinguished former counsel Brendan Sullivan, Edward Bennett Williams's successor as chairman of Williams & Connolly, famously said that "the American lawyer is not a potted plant." No, but he is fed like one, and Brendan certainly knew how to crank out the invoices. We as a society are going to have to do better for the unwary and the disadvantaged with legal problems.

The law often is famously an ass, but the profession is running a risk of turning it into a spavined ass. Do not imagine that lawyers are a beloved segment of our society. And some of us can endure obloquy more philosophically than, I suspect, the Law Society of Upper Canada could, as the outrageous persecution of Joe Groia indicates.

I have had a difficult time, but I have survived. Not having made any reference to Thomas More, at the weary end of these remarks, I will cite Cardinal Newman. "Blessings of friendship to my door, unasked, unhoped, came. They came and they went. They came to my great joy, they went to my great sorrow. He who gave took away." But I am in rebuild mode now, and human nature being what it is, there were many pleasant surprises too, and my ability to attract attention to my persecution assured a steadily growing army of supporters, and, of course, as fortunes have returned, so have some absentee friends of yesteryear.

I am often asked how I sustained my morale through those challenging times, and I conclude with this thought, from the introduction to Newman's *The Second Spring*, given at Oscott when the Roman Catholic Church was re-established on a diocesan basis in Britain after a lapse of three hundred years after the apostasy of that great religious leader King Henry VIII. My dear and always lamented friend Emmett Cardinal Carter asked me to render it at his ninetieth birthday, where I imagine some of you were present.

The future Cardinal Newman said,

> We have familiar experience of the order, the constancy, the perpetual renovation of the material world which surrounds us. Frail and transitory as are its elements, restless and migratory as is every part of it, never ceasing as are its changes, still it abides. It is bound together by a law of permanence, it is set up in unity, and though it is ever dying, it is ever coming to life again, dissolution does but give birth to new modes of organization and every death is the parent of a hundred lives. Each hour, as it comes, is a testimony, how fleeting, yet how secure, how certain, is the great whole. It is like an image on the waters, ever the same though the waters

*ever flow, change upon change; each change cries out
to the next like the alternate seraphim in praise and in
glory of their maker. The sun sinks to rise again; the day
is swallowed up in the gloom of the night, to be born
of it as fresh as if it had never been quenched. Spring
passes into summer, and through summer and autumn
into winter, the more surely by its ultimate return to triumph over that grave toward which it resolutely hastens
from its first hour. We mourn for the blossoms of May
because they are to wither, but we know that May shall
have its revenge upon November, in the revolution of
that solemn circle that never stops and that teaches us
in our height of hope ever to be sober, and in our depth
of desolation never to despair.*

Thank you

# INDEX

Bezos, Jeff, 598
Biden, Joe, 297
*Big Short, The* (Lewis),
434–35, 437
bilingualism/biculturalism:
and Charter, 59–60;
federal promotion,
14, 58–59; history,
116; Quebec laws, 15,
17–18, 64
Bill C-51 (Anti-Terrorism
Act, 2015), 87–90, 132
bin Laden, Osama, 110–12,
316, 319
Black, Conrad: Catholic
Lawyers' Association
speech, 718–27;
charges against,
and trials, 396–97,
659–62; friendship
with Thatcher, 418;
induction into House
of Lords, 372; libel
suit and settlement,
453, 685, 709, 711, 714,
715–16, 723; *Matter of
Principle,* 691; mixed
support from Buckley,
364–66, 367–68;
mixed support from
Kissinger, 364, 366,
367–68, 372, 373–74;
Newman's defamation,
580; prison release
(2012), 703, 705–6;
prison release on
bail, 672–76; prison
return, 690–93;
renouncement of
Canadian citizenship,
657–58; resentencing
statement, 683–89;
resignation from
Order of Canada,
707–12, 716; Southam
newspapers, 575–77;

travels home from
university, 677–79;
tutoring role in prison,
663–67, 671, 674,
704–5
Black, George Montegu
"Monte," 694–97
black people (U.S.): civil
rights under Johnson,
178; drug charges,
172–73, 674–75
Blair, Bill, 610
Blair, Tony: debate with
Hitchens on religion,
699; on Diana's death,
245; environmental
issues, 431, 455; and
European Union, 279,
281, 284, 288; memoir,
520–27
Bloc Québécois, 16, 63, 410
Boehner, John, 338
Boot, Max, 297–98
Bouchard, Lucien, 276
Bower, Tom, 399
Bradlee, Ben, 199–200, 202,
203, 591, 593
Breeden, Richard, 684–85,
713–17
Brennan, William, 191–92
Bre-X, 79–80
Brezhnev, Leonid, 318
Brinkley, Alan, 500–509
Brinkley, David, 600
Brinkley, Douglas, 602–7
Britain: against German
reunification, 241–42;
economic options,
284–85, 442; economic
ties with North
America, 280, 285–87,
293–94; and European
Union, 279–80,
281–82, 286, 292, 293;
and France, 353;
incarcerations, 675;

and Iranian nuclear
program, 330, 335, 341;
and Middle East, 317;
monarchy, 243–47;
nuclear power, 306;
sells same land to Jews
and Arabs, 119, 310, 339;
status in world, 278–79,
285, 294, 328, 351
Brown, Edmund G. "Pat," 389
Bruno, Joseph, 230
Buckley, Christopher, 369,
370, 496–99
Buckley, Pat, 365, 367, 369,
383, 496–99
Buckley, William F.:
character and
personality, 369–70,
372, 381–82, 384;
death, 368, 497, 499;
friendship with Black,
364–68, 370–71, 373;
life and work, 381–84;
son's biography, 369,
496–99; and Vidal,
371, 382
Buffett, Warren, 391–95, 434
Burney, Derek, 343
Burr, Aaron, 185–86
Bush, George H.W.:
economy and
industry, 182, 439;
failures, 302–3; foreign
policy, 271; German
reunification, 242;
Gulf War, 319; respect
for Mulroney, 412
Bush, George W.: 9/11,
263; criticisms, 162;
economic policies,
183, 441; failures, 342,
614–15; foreign policy,
112, 271–72, 331, 409;
Middle East, 310
Buthelezi, Mangosuthu,
426–27